FREDERICK DOUGLASS

ALSO BY PHILIP S. FONER

FREDERICK DOUGLASS

a biography by

Philip S. Foner

THE CITADEL PRESS
NEW YORK

B
D f

Second paperbound edition, February 1969
Published by Citadel Press, Inc.
222 Park Avenue South, New York, N.Y. 10003
Copyright 1950, © 1964 by International Publishers Co., Inc.
Manufactured in the United States of America

PREFACE

In February, 1817, a Negro child was born in Maryland who was destined to become one of the nation's most distinguished citizens. Born a slave, he lifted himself up from bondage by his own efforts, taught himself to read and write, developed a great talent as lecturer, editor, and organizer, became a noted figure in American life, and gained world-wide recognition as the foremost spokesman for his oppressed people and courageous champion of many other progressive causes of his time.

The name of this man is Frederick Douglass. It should be a famous name in American history—placed beside the names of Jefferson and Lincoln. Yet only recently has it been rescued from the oblivion to which it was assigned by our historiography.

James Ford Rhodes' *History of the United States* devotes seven volumes to the period 1850-1870. Yet Rhodes leaves even the careful student with the impression that Douglass was just another of the many minor figures with which this exhaustive work is filled. John B. McMaster treats Douglass even more casually in the ten volumes of his *History of the People of the United States,* referring to him only once, briefly, and then not even taking the trouble to spell his name correctly. Edward Channing's six volumes had little room for mention and none for interpretation of Douglass' role. Professor Dwight L. Dumond of the University of Michigan, in his book, *The Anti-Slavery Origins of the Civil War,* finds space to present obscure white Abolitionists like Augustus Wattles and Calvin Waterbury, but Douglass is not so much as mentioned.

It was, in part, to remedy this deplorable situation in American historiography that I undertook in 1944 to collect and prepare for publication the writings and speeches of Frederick Douglass. These were published, beginning in 1950, under the title *The Life and Writings of Frederick Douglass,* in four volumes. Each volume was introduced by an extensive study of the man and his times covering the period of the specific volume.

Since the appearance of these volumes, Douglass' stature has been increasingly noted by historians and by Negro publications, climaxed in

the September, 1963, issue of *Ebony,* the widest circulating Negro magazine. In this issue, commemorating the hundredth anniversary of the
Emancipation Proclamation, a portrait of Frederick Douglass dominates
the entire front cover. Its presence is explained in the following paragraph:

"Frederick Douglass, father of the protest movement, is a worthy subject
to grace the cover of any publication commemorating the centennial of the
Emancipation Proclamation. Born a slave, he escaped to freedom while still
young and devoted a long and fruitful life to the winning of freedom for all
Negroes. A fervent integrationist, he was the first of the 'freedom riders'
and 'sit-inners.' He felt that true freedom could not come for him until all
Negroes were free and equal."

In providing a biography of Frederick Douglass to accompany the four
volumes of his writings and speeches, I had planned from the beginning
that it would appear some day as a separate volume. I believe that the
present is a most appropriate time for its appearance, a time when the
struggle for full freedom and equality for the Negro people is more
intense and widespread than at any time since the days of Reconstruction.
The life and principles of Frederick Douglass are both an inspiration and
a guide for the successful conclusion of this struggle.

In quoting from Douglass' writings and speeches, I have tried to
present his words as they appeared in their original form. However, I have
deemed it advisable to change the lower-case spelling of the word Negro
to the upper-case spelling. The latter has become fairly general during the
past generation as the result of continued pressure from the Negro people
and their supporters, who justifiably pointed out that while other nation-
alities were honored with a capital letter, Negro continued to be spelled
with a small n. Toward the end of his career, Douglass began to use the
upper-case spelling in his writings. It was the judgment of the writer that
the upper-case spelling of the word Negro should be used throughout
the volume.

Occasionally, too, the reader will come upon words in Douglass'
speeches and writings which are correctly considered scurrilous and part
of the parlance of the adherents of "white supremacy." In using them,
Douglass made it clear that he was doing so only to indicate the contempt
expressed by the pro-slavery apologists for the Negro people. These words
have not been fully spelled out in this volume. By presenting the words
in this form the writer believes that he best expresses the deepest indignation of all decent people at the slanderous attacks on the Negro people
revealed in these epithets.

In the preparation of this study I have had the generous assistance and cooperation of the following: the libraries and personnel of the American Antiquarian Society, American Philosophical Library, the Frederick Douglass Memorial Association, Henry E. Huntington Library, the Historical Society of Pennsylvania, the Library Company of Philadelphia, The Library of Congress, The National Archives, New York Historical Society, Ohio State Archeological and Historical Society, Rutherford B. Hayes Memorial Association, The Schomburg Collection, New York, and the Wisconsin State Historical Society; the libraries of Fisk University, Harvard University, Moorland Foundation of Howard University, New York University, Oberlin College, Syracuse University, University of Rochester, and Yale University; the public libraries of Boston, New York City, and Rochester. I also wish to thank the late Dr. Carter G. Woodson, the late Mr. Arthur B. Spingarn, and Henry P. Slaughter for making available to me writings and speeches of Frederick Douglass in their personal collections.

PHILIP S. FONER

Croton-on-Hudson
December, 1963

Contents

PART FOUR RECONSTRUCTION AND AFTER

Let me give you a word of the philosophy of reform. The whole history of the progress of human liberty shows that all concessions yet made to her august claims, have been born of earnest struggle. The conflict has been exciting, agitating, all-absorbing, and for the time being, putting all other tumults to silence. It must do this or it does nothing. If there is no struggle there is no progress. Those who profess to favor freedom and yet deprecate agitation, are men who want crops without plowing up the ground, they want rain without thunder and lightning. They want the ocean without the awful roar of its many waters.

This struggle may be a moral one, or it may be a physical one, and it may be both moral and physical, but it must be a struggle. Power concedes nothing without a demand. It never did and it never will. Find out just what any people will quietly submit to and you have found out the exact measure of injustice and wrong which will be imposed upon them, and these will continue till they are resisted with either words or blows, or with both. The limits of tyrants are prescribed by the endurance of those whom they oppress. In the light of these ideas, Negroes will be hunted at the North, and held and flogged at the South so long as they submit to those devilish outrages, and make no resistance, either moral or physical. . . .

WEST INDIA EMANCIPATION SPEECH, AUGUST, 1857

Here is a part of the platform of principles upon which it seems to me every loyal man should take his stand at this hour:

First: That this war, which we are compelled to wage against slave-holding Rebels and traitors, at untold cost of blood and treasure, shall be, and of right ought to be, an Abolition War.

Secondly: That we, the loyal people of the North and of the whole country, while determined to make this a short and final war, will offer no peace, accept no peace, consent to no peace, which shall not be to all intents and purposes an Abolition peace.

Thirdly: That we regard the whole colored population of the country, in the loyal as well as in the disloyal States, as our countrymen—valuable in peace as laborers, valuable in war as soldiers—entitled to all the rights, protection, and opportunities for achieving distinction enjoyed by any other class of our countrymen.

Fourthly: Believing that the white race has nothing to fear from fair competition with the black race, and that the freedom and elevation of one race are not to be purchased or in any manner rightfully subserved by the disfranchisement of another, we shall favor immediate and unconditional emancipation in all the States, invest the black man everywhere with the right to vote and to be voted for, and remove all discriminations against his rights on account of his color, whether as a citizen or as a soldier.

ADDRESS DELIVERED IN COOPER INSTITUTE, NEW YORK, FEBRUARY 13, 1864

What Abraham Lincoln said in respect of the United States is as true of the colored people as of the relation of those States. They can not remain half slave and half free. You must give them all or take from them all. Until this half-and-half condition is ended, there will be just ground of complaint. You will have an aggrieved class, and this discussion will go on. Until the public schools shall cease to be caste schools in every part of this country, this discussion will go on. Until the colored man's pathway to the American ballot box, North and South, shall be as smooth and as safe as the same is for the white citizen, this discussion will go on. Until the colored man's right to practice at the bar of our courts, and sit upon juries, shall be the universal law and practice of the land, this discussion will go on. Until the courts of the country shall grant the colored man a fair trial and a just verdict, this discussion will go on. Until color shall cease to be a bar to equal participation in offices and honors of the country, this discussion will go on. Until the trades-unions and the workshops of the country shall cease to proscribe the colored man and prevent his children from learning useful trades, this discussion will go on. Until the American people shall make character, and not color, the criterion of respectability, the discussion will go on.

SPEECH ON THE OCCASION OF THE TWENTY-FIRST ANNIVERSARY OF
EMANCIPATION IN THE DISTRICT OF COLUMBIA, APRIL, 1883

From Slavery to Freedom

Once when Frederick Douglass was asked exactly when and where he was born, he replied: "I cannot answer; don't know my age. Slaves have no family records."[1] All any biographer of Douglass can say is that the man who was christened Frederick Augustus Washington Bailey and later became world famous as Frederick Douglass was born in February, 1817, somewhere in Tuckahoe, Talbot County, on the eastern shore of Maryland, the son of an unknown white father and Harriet Bailey, a slave.

Douglass never knew his father[2] and his knowledge of a mother who worked on a plantation twelve miles distant was "very scanty."[3] He had seen her four or five times, perhaps, up to the age of seven when the shadowy relationship was terminated by death. In his later life he recalled one of her rare, unexpected visits. She had walked the twelve miles after a long day's work and had brought him a large ginger cake. "I dropped off to sleep and waked in the morning to find my mother gone," he recollected. "I do not remember ever seeing her again. Death soon ended the little communication that had existed between us, and with it, I believe, a life—judging from her weary, sad, downcast countenance and mute demeanor—full of heartfelt sorrow."[4]

Douglass spent much of his early childhood in and around the slave cabin of his grandparents, Isaac (a free Negro) and Betsey Bailey. "Grandmamma Betty" was a warm-hearted person who spent her time making nets for catching shad and herring, planting seedling potatoes for nearby farmers, and nursing the children of her five daughters.[5]

When Douglass was seven years old, he was taken from his birthplace to the home of his master, Captain Aaron Anthony, on the banks of the river Wye. Captain Anthony owned three farms in Tuckahoe and about thirty slaves, but most of his time was spent in managing the twenty or thirty farms and the thousand slaves of Colonel Edward Lloyd. On the plantation Douglass lived like other slave children: brought in the cows in the evening, kept the chickens out of the garden, swept the front yard, ran errands, and did other simple chores.

It was here that Douglass first discovered the true face of slavery and the humiliations that went with it. Soon after his arrival at the plantation his Aunt Esther was given a brutal flogging. The seven-year-old Negro child was not to forget the tormented screams of the woman as each of the forty lashes with a heavy cowskin drew fresh blood. Later, he saw a cousin of his stagger wearily into the plantation, bare-footed, her neck and shoulders mutilated, open gashes on her head and her face streaming with blood. This was the work of a drunken overseer; the girl had dragged herself twelve miles to beg protection from her master. The young boy learned fast when he heard the master order the girl to go back to her torturer. She deserved "every bit of it," he shouted. And if she wasn't quick about leaving he would "take off the rest of the skin himself."

Life at the big house opened young Douglass' eyes. He compared the food-laden tables with the meager diet of the slave, and the fine clothes of the master and mistress with the slave's tattered wardrobe. The yearly wardrobe of a male slave consisted of two shirts and two pairs of trousers to be worn whatever the weather. These great contrasts remained with Douglass; they helped to create in him a burning hatred of the slave system.

His own experiences at the Lloyd plantation fed fuel to this hatred. He was yet to learn what it meant to be whipped with a cowhide, but he grew familiar with hunger and cold. Whatever the season he walked about almost naked, wearing only a coarse tow linen shirt which barely reached his knees. On cold nights he slept with his head and shoulders in a sack, but the frost bit into his feet breaking the skin open and forming deep gashes. He ate coarse boiled corn-meal—when he could edge his way to the trough on the kitchen floor where the mush was placed, and push aside the children scrambling for their portion. To add to his troubles, Aunt Katy, the cook, did not like him, and delighted in making him go without food. Several times a day he would follow the waiting girl to get the crumbs from the table cloth and the small bones flung out for the dogs and cats. He often fought with old Nep the dog for the crumbs which fell from the kitchen table.

It was only the kindness of Lucretia Auld, his master's daughter and wife of Captain Thomas Auld, which saved him from starvation. He would sing under her window, and it pleased her to reward him with a slice of bread and butter. It was also from Miss Lucretia that Douglass "received the first kindness that I ever experienced from one of a complexion different from my own."[6] He had been in a fight with another slave boy, receiving a heavy blow which left a scar on his face. He had come home screaming with pain. Lucretia Auld called him into the parlor, bound up his head, gave him a biscuit, and told him to go out to play with the other children. This simple act remained a bright memory in the bleak life of a slave child.

But such acts of kindness could not stop the constant pangs of hunger, nor make his coarse linen shirt seem any warmer on frosty days. Fortunately for young Douglass, another factor was at work. Slave labor in Maryland agriculture had ceased to be profitable. Consequently after 1820 it was common to farm slaves out to townspeople where they could be employed as house-servants and mechanics. This happened to Frederick Bailey.

In the spring of 1825 the eight-year-old slave was overjoyed to learn that he was being sent to Baltimore to live with Hugh Auld, a relative of the Anthony's. "Going to live at Baltimore laid the foundation, and opened the gateway, to all my subsequent prosperity," was the way Douglass put it.[7] This was to be the first of the many turning points in his eventful life.

For seven years Douglass worked for Hugh Auld, first as a household servant and later as an unskilled laborer in his shipyard. During the period he experienced comforts such as he had never known before. Yet he was seldom allowed to forget that he was a slave. Hearing his new mistress, Sophia Auld, read the Bible, a burning desire to learn to read consumed him. In response to his plea, his mistress taught him the alphabet and how to spell words of three or four letters. But the lessons ended the moment her husband learned of the boy's progress. In Douglass' presence, Hugh Auld forbade further instruction, shouting that "learning would *spoil* the best n——r in the world." Once a slave knew how to read there would be no keeping him![8]

These words only inspired the boy with a greater determination to learn. His former teacher was now the chief obstacle; as if to atone for her error, she kept constant vigilance over him, snatching any book or newspaper she saw in his hand, and making sure he could obtain no reading matter. But by various ingenious devices Douglass continued his education. He turned to school boys in the streets in out-of-the-way places where he could not be seen, and converted them into teachers. Out of his pocket would come the leaves of books he had raked "from the mud and filth of the gutter," a copy of his Webster's spelling book, and a slice of bread to pay for the lessons. While his tutors munched the bread, he talked to them about slavery. "Have not I as good a right to be free as you have?" he would ask the urchins. He was comforted by their sympathy and by their confidence that something would yet happen to make him free.[9]

With the first fifty cents he earned by blacking boots he bought the popular school book, *The Columbian Orator*.[10] This book deepened his hatred of slavery, and as he read and memorized the speeches of Chatham, Sheridan, and Fox in behalf of human rights, he began to understand his position. He was a victim of oppression, and if these great men were right, it was wrong that he or any man should be doomed to slavery. As he walked about the streets repeating to himself the words of Sheridan and Chatham, he kept asking himself: "Why am I a slave? Why are some people slaves, and others masters? Was there ever a time when this was not so? How did the relation commence?" He found no satisfactory answer to these questions, but when he heard his master and his friends denounce the Abolitionists, he resolved to discover who and what they were. Finally, in the columns of the *Baltimore American* he found a report that a vast number of petitions had been submitted to Congress, praying for the abolition of the internal slave trade. From that day, probably some time in February, 1833, "there was hope."

The thought of escaping from slavery frequently occurred to him. Two Irishmen whom he had met on the wharf advised him to run away to the North where he would be free. But he hesitated. He was still too young, and he wished to learn to write so that he himself could fill out the necessary pass.

While working in the shipyards he mastered the essentials of writing. During the slack periods he would copy the letters that made up the names of the ships; then using the streets as his school, his playmates as teachers, and the fences as his copybooks and blackboards, he learned to write. In later life in responding to a request for his autograph, he said: "Though my penmanship is not too fine it will do pretty well for one who learned to write on a board fence."[11]

In Baltimore Douglass enjoyed a life he never dreamed was possible when he was a slave on the plantation. He was much better fed and clothed, freely moved about the city, and was never whipped. Yet he could not escape the sufferings of slave life. He made the acquaintance of two slave girls who lived directly opposite the Aulds on Philpot Street. They were constantly being whipped by their sadistic mistress, and the head, neck and shoulders of the fourteen-year-old Mary were "literally cut to pieces." He watched with a heavy heart as the girl fought with the pigs for the garbage thrown into the street.

As he sat on Kennard's wharf, at the foot of Philpot Street, he saw men and women chained together being placed on board ships bound for New Orleans. He was profoundly moved by their piteous cries and their heavy footsteps as they moved from the slave pens to the vessels. Forty years later in a speech in Baltimore, he recalled this tragic sight and declared: "I then resolved that whatever power I had should be devoted to the freeing of my race."[12]

The comparative freedom of life in Baltimore was brought to an abrupt end as a result of Captain Anthony's death. The change of ownership placed Douglass in the possession of Thomas Auld, Anthony's son-in-law, a cruel, tight-fisted master who lived at St. Michaels, some thirty miles from Baltimore. The slave who returned to plantation life after seven years spent in the city was bound to get into difficulty with his new master. From books Douglass had learned of all the evils of slavery, and his hatred of the institution was deepened by the rigors of the plantation system after the comparative freedom of life in the city. He made no effort to hide his dissatisfaction with the meager diet provided by the kitchen at St. Michaels, and he infuriated Mr. and Mrs. Auld by his refusal to call his owner "Master" instead of "Captain."

When Douglass began to teach a Sunday School class for colored children, Master Auld decided that he had better take steps to provide his young slave with proper conditioning. Consequently, on the following Sunday, men armed with sticks and stones invaded the school, disrupted the class, and warned the teacher "to watch out." Douglass seemed determined to be another Nat Turner, said Master Auld, and if he did not mend his ways he would most certainly "get as many balls into him" as had the Negro slave rebel of 1831. Actually, Turner was hanged, but despite the inaccuracy, the warning indicated that trouble lay ahead.

Auld was not satisfied with merely a warning. Determined to crush young Douglass' spirit, he hired him out to Edward Covey, a professional slavebreaker. From January to August, 1834, the young slave was overworked, flogged daily, and was almost starved to death. After six months of such treatment, he was indeed "broken in body, soul and spirit." There seemed nothing left but either to kill Covey and then commit suicide or to fight back. Steeled by desperation and a combination of hope and fear, the youth found the courage to turn on his tormentor one day and soundly thrashed the Negro-breaker. The result was that Covey abandoned the whip and ignored Douglass for the four remaining months of hire. The slave never forgot the episode:

"This battle with Mr. Covey was the turning-point in my career. I was a changed being after that fight. I was nothing before, I was a man now . . . with a renewed determination to be a free man. . . . The gratification afforded by the triumph was a full compensation for whatever else might follow, even death itself. . . . I now resolved that, however long I might remain a slave in form, the day had passed forever when I could be a slave in fact. . . ."

Following his release, Douglass worked for two years on the plantation of a neighboring slaveowner, William Friedland. Conditions were a good deal better here; he had a kind master, enough food, was not overworked, and was even able to conduct a secret Sunday School for forty slaves. But kindness, food, and a few leisure hours were not enough. When he was at Covey's, beaten every day, he was concerned only with self-preservation. Now he began to think of freedom; the very privileges he enjoyed made him desire it the more. "If a slave has a bad master," he once explained, "his ambition is to get a better; when he gets a better, he aspires to have the best; and when he gets the best, he aspires to be his own master."[13]

Early in 1836 Douglass decided to escape. Together with other slaves, he planned to seize a canoe, paddle down the Chesapeake, and follow the North Star to freedom. But one of the men disclosed the plan before the fugitives could get away. As the leader of the group and originator of the conspiracy, Douglass was put in chains in the Talbot county jail. He expected to be sold to the slave traders and shipped to New Orleans, but his master balked when the idea was proposed by the planters in the neighborhood. Instead, Auld, hoping to subdue Douglass' insubordination by kindness, sent him back to Baltimore with a promise of freedom when he reached twenty-five—provided, of course, that he behaved himself.

For the next two years, from the summer of 1836 to the summer of 1838, Douglass worked in the Baltimore shipyards, first as an apprentice, then as a skilled caulker. During the first eight months of apprenticeship he came to know, through bitter experience, "the conflict of slavery with the interests of the white mechanics and laborers of the South." Forced to compete with slaves, the white workers found it impossible to get decent wages. Consequently they sought to keep slaves out of the trades, and demanded the ousting of all Negro artisans, free as well as slave.

When such a drive got under way at the shipyards of William Gardner on Fell's Point where Douglass was apprenticed, he became the victim of the campaign. Douglass was attacked many times. At one time, he fought his attackers so violently that it required four white apprentices, armed with bricks and heavy hand spikes, to finally lay him low. He was long to remember with bitterness how fifty white mechanics stood about during this brutal attack, some crying, "kill him—kill him—kill the d—d n——r, knock his brains out—he struck a white person." Much later in his life he came to understand that the southern white worker was almost as much the victim of the slave system as was the Negro.[14]

From Gardner's shipyards Douglass was transferred to a yard of which Hugh Auld was foreman. Here he rapidly became an expert caulker. Within a year, he was earning a dollar and a half a day, the highest wages paid caulkers in Baltimore. At first every penny of his earnings went to his master, but in May, 1838, he was able to persuade Auld to let him work for himself and in return would turn over a weekly payment of three dollars. Douglass bought his own tools and clothes, went about bargaining for his own employment, and every Saturday night handed over three dollars to his master.

In the evenings, after a day's work in the shipyard, Douglass extended his education. He met free Negroes who were well versed in literature, geography, and arithmetic, and he sought to learn from them. As a slave he was not able to join any of the forty benevolent institutions established by the free Negroes of Baltimore, but he was permitted to become a member of the East Baltimore Improvement Society as a special concession.[15] Here he took a prominent part in debates and here, too, he met Anna Murray, who afterward became his wife. Anna was one of twelve children of Bambarra and Mary Murray, slaves, and the first of their five children born in freedom, escaping by one month the fate of her older brothers and sisters born in slavery. At the age of eighteen she had left her parents' home in Denton, Maryland, and had gone to work as housekeeper for a well-to-do family in Baltimore. In the little circle of the East Baltimore Improvement Society she associated with free Negroes, but she was drawn to the slave, Frederick Bailey. They fell in love and planned to marry.

The meeting with Anna Murray intensified Douglass' desire for freedom. It was no longer a desire for himself alone. Freedom, now, would enable him to marry the woman he loved, not as a chattel but as a man.

Anna shared his feelings, encouraged him to escape and gave him her nine years' savings.

A dispute with Auld in the summer of 1838 hastened the day of escape. One Saturday evening, Douglass failed to turn over the three dollars to Hugh Auld and went instead with some friends to a camp meeting about twelve miles from Baltimore. Returning the next evening he was met with a furious outburst: "Now you scoundrel! You have done for yourself," Auld said. "You shall hire your time no longer. The next thing I shall hear of, will be your running away. Bring home your tools and your clothes, at once. I'll teach you how to go off in this way."[16]

In retaliation Douglass did not work the next week and on Saturday night there was no money to turn over. A violent quarrel followed which almost ended in blows. Douglass decided that the time had come for him to escape to the North. To allay Auld's suspicions he worked for a few weeks. On Saturday nights, he turned over his earnings to Auld who became so amiable that he returned twenty-five cents of it to Douglass, advising him to make good use of the money.

On Monday, September 3, 1838, Douglass bade farewell to Baltimore and slavery.

To effect his escape Douglass used a method familiar in southern seaport communities. He had had frequent contacts with free Negro sailors in the shipyards and had found them sympathetic to the plight of the slaves. From a sea-faring friend named Stanley who was his height, he borrowed a sailor's suit and a sailor's "protection," a paper listing the physical features of its owner who, as a free American sailor, could move about the country. (The suit was later returned to its owner by mail.) Douglass hopped the last car while a friend, Isaac Rhodes, threw his bundle into the moving train as it left the Baltimore station for Philadelphia. In this way he avoided buying a ticket which would have subjected him to the close scrutiny of the ticket agent who was bound to check the description on the "protection."

Fortunately, the conductor on the train was satisfied with the "protection." Nor did he pursue the matter further when Douglass replied, on being asked for the "free papers" which all free Negroes were required by Maryland law to produce on demand, that his "only pass was an American Eagle." Having passed the conductor's inspection, Douglass' chief worries seemed over, but at Wilmington his heart almost stopped beating. He ran into Frederick Stein, for whom he had once worked, and on a train bound south from Philadelphia, he caught sight of Captain

McGowan of Baltimore whom he knew intimately. But he was so perfectly disguised that neither of the men recognized him.

In the late afternoon of September 3, Douglass arrived in Philadelphia, where he "lived more in one day than in a year of . . . slave life." The next day he was in New York City.[17]

Douglass' joy vanished rapidly as he walked the streets of the metropolis which the Abolitionists referred to as "the prolongation of the South," where "ten thousand cords of interests are linked with the Southern Slaveholder."[18] He was lonely and afraid. In New York City a fugitive slave was no safer than in Baltimore. And in the midst of the crisis of 1837, there were few opportunities for a free Negro to earn a livelihood. In desperation, Douglass finally revealed his plight to a passing sailor who introduced him to David Ruggles, the Negro secretary of the New York Vigilance Committee.[19]

For several days Douglass remained hidden in Ruggles' home and it was at this time that Anna Murray came North and joined him. On September 15, twelve days after his escape, they were married by the Rev. James W. C. Pennington, who had fled from a Maryland master ten years previously. Two days later they were on their way to New Bedford, Massachusetts, where Ruggles believed Douglass' skill as a caulker would secure him a livelihood. In his pocket the fugitive had his marriage certificate, a five-dollar bill which Ruggles had pressed upon him as the couple departed, and a letter of introduction to a Mr. Shaw in Newport whom they were to approach for funds if they did not have enough to carry them to New Bedford.

They arrived in Newport without funds to continue their trip by coach to New Bedford, but pushed ahead none the less, anxious to get to a place of safety. Their baggage, seized as security by the driver, was redeemed by Mr. and Mrs. Nathan Johnson, the family to whom they had been sent. The newlyweds felt at home immediately with this prosperous Negro family, who took great pains to make them forget their first experiences in the North. It was Johnson, moreover, who gave the name "Douglass" to his guest. In New York Frederick had dropped his two middle names, and changed Bailey to Johnson. As there were a great number of New Bedford Negroes with that name, his benefactor, who had just finished reading Sir Walter Scott's *Lady of the Lake,* suggested the name by which he was soon to be known on both sides of the Atlantic.

With Johnson's encouragement Douglass began his search for work as a free man. His first day's job was loading oil on a sloop bound for

New York, and dirty and back-breaking as it was, he went at it with a pleasure he had never experienced before. No master waited at the end of the day to rob him of his wages. Whatever he earned would be his own. The next day he sought work as a caulker—and made an important discovery. No one would hire him because white caulkers refused to work with Negroes. Forced to accept the fact that prejudice against Negroes was not confined to the South, he put aside his caulking clothes, borrowed a wood-horse and saw from Mr. Johnson and went in search of whatever work would come his way. There was no question of how hard, how dirty, and how menial it might be. For the next three years he sawed wood, shoveled coal, swept chimneys, rolled oil casks, drove a coach, carried the hod, waited on tables. His hands became hard. His earnings averaged only a dollar a day, but the family's scanty income was supplemented by Anna's earnings as a domestic servant. Her cheerful spirit, her thrift and economy helped immeasurably during those early days in New Bedford. The pillows, bed linen, dishes, knives, forks, and spoons, a trunk of clothing and furnishings which Anna had brought from Baltimore made their two rooms on Elm Street overlooking Buzzards Bay a comfortable home. While he worked with saw, buck, and axe, Anna was at the washboard adding her share to the daily earnings. Even after her children came (Rosetta was born in June, 1839, and Lewis sixteen months later), she worked as a domestic whenever she could spare time from her household duties.

The day-to-day task of eking out an existence for a growing family did not afford Douglass many opportunities to satisfy his longing for education. But he applied the same ingenuity that had stood him in good stead as a slave. "Hard work, night and day, over a furnace hot enough to keep metal running like water was more favorable to action than thought," he wrote later, "yet here I often nailed a newspaper to the post near my bellows and read while I was performing the up and down motion of the heavy beam by which the bellows were inflated and discharged."[20]

Soon after they had settled down in their new home, Douglass began to make himself a part of the Negro community of New Bedford. Having been class leader and choir member of the Sharp Street Methodist Church in Baltimore, he sought to renew his religious contacts. He joined a local Methodist church, but remained there only a short time. He discovered that Negroes were second-class communicants, sitting in a special section of the church. In disgust he walked out of the church, never to return. He tried other churches in New Bedford with the same result, and finally joined a small sect of his own people, the Zion Methodists, where he soon became a leading member of the congregation and a local preacher.[21]

Before he had left Baltimore Douglass had already heard of the Abolitionists and of their work to end slavery. He had received help from them en route to New Bedford, but actually he knew very little of their activities. Four months after he had come to New England there came into his hands a copy of William Lloyd Garrison's *Liberator*. So deeply was he moved by the paper that despite his poverty he became a regular subscriber. Every week he read the journal avidly, studying its principles and philosophy. "The paper became my meat and my drink," he wrote six years later. "My soul was set all on fire. Its sympathy for my brethren in bonds—its scathing denunciations of slaveholders—its faithful exposures of slavery—and its powerful attacks upon the upholders of the institution—sent a thrill of joy through my soul, such as I had never felt before!"[22]

Douglass was not satisfied to sit at home and thrill to the paper. He began to attend the Abolitionist meetings held by the Negro people of New Bedford. The first printed reference to Frederick Douglass appeared in the *Liberator* of March 29, 1839. It reported an anti-colonization meeting of the Negro citizens of New Bedford at the Christian Church on March 12, at which Douglass was one of the speakers in favor of resolutions condemning slavery, commending Garrison "as deserving of our support and confidence," and denouncing the African colonization movement in the following terms:

"That we are *American citizens,* born with natural, inherent and just rights; and that the inordinate and intolerable scheme of the American Colonization Society shall never entice or drive *us* from our native soil."

Douglass became more and more involved in the Abolitionist activities of the New Bedford Negroes. Every fortnight he attended a social meeting at the home of John Baily to discuss anti-slavery principles and events. A white Abolitionist who attended these sessions observed that in the discussions "the colored people acquire the habit of thinking and speaking; a circumstance which may, in a great measure, account for the self-possession of their manners, and the propriety and fluency of their language." Among these New Bedford Abolitionists Douglass was gradually assuming a position of leadership. On June 30, 1841, he was chair-

man at a meeting called to censure the Maryland Colonization Society
for "threatening to remove the free colored people out of that state by
coercion." The Negroes urged their brethren in Maryland to resist intimidation and condemned an attack on David Ruggles who had been
roughly handled for combating segregation on the steamboat operating
between New Bedford and Nantucket.[23]

On August 9, 1841, Douglass attended the annual meeting of the
Bristol Anti-Slavery Society, held in New Bedford. Here in old Liberty
Hall, a large, dilapidated building, with doors off their hinges, windows
broken by stones thrown to break up Abolition proceedings, Douglass
first heard William Lloyd Garrison. It was a red-letter day in the life of
the young Negro, barely twenty-four years of age and but three years removed from slavery, because on that day, he saw in the editor of the
Liberator the mission for his own life. "It may have been due to my having been a slave," he wrote toward the end of his life, "and my intense
hatred of slavery, but no face and form ever impressed me with such
sentiments as did those of William Lloyd Garrison." Douglass himself
entered into the discussion and made a distinct impression upon the
Abolitionist leader who reported to his paper that at the meeting were
"several talented young men from New Bedford, one of them formerly a
slave whose addresses were listened to by large and attentive audiences
with deep interest."[24]

The following day, Douglass took his first vacation. With Garrison
and forty other Abolitionists, white and Negro, he attended a convention
at Nantucket. The trip was not without incident. Captain Phinney of
the steamboat *Telegraph* refused to leave the dock until the Negro passengers aboard agreed to occupy separate quarters. Some of the delegates
left, but, after a long delay, a compromise was worked out. All of the
delegates went to the upper deck which was set aside for their use. During the sixty-mile voyage, the delegates, with Francis Jackson presiding,
held an anti-slavery meeting on deck to protest the segregation practices
of the steamship company.[25]

The next morning, August 12, at the convention in Athenaeum Hall,
Douglass was called upon to speak by William C. Coffin, a New Bedford
Abolitionist. Douglass, trembling and ill at ease, came forward to the
platform and spoke with deep sincerity of his own life as a slave. Greatly
stirred, Garrison followed with an exciting address using Douglass' remarks as his text. He asked the audience, "Have we been listening to a
thing, a piece of property, or to a man?" "A man! A man!" came from

five hundred voices. Then he asked if they would ever allow Douglass to be carried back to slavery and received a thunderous "No!" in reply. "Will you succor and protect him as a brother man—a resident of the old Bay State?" was the next question. "Yes!" shouted the audience with such vehemence that "the walls and roof of the Athenaeum seemed to shudder."

That evening Douglass spoke again, and, as in the morning, the group was moved by his eloquence. In his report of the convention, the *Anti-Slavery Standard* correspondent devoted special attention to the Negro delegate from New Bedford:

"One, recently from the house of bondage, spoke with great power. Flinty hearts were pierced, and cold ones melted by his eloquence. Our best pleaders for the slave held their breath for fear of interrupting him. Mr. Garrison said his speech would have done honor to Patrick Henry. It seemed almost miraculous how he had been prepared to tell his story with so much power. In the evening, which was to be the last meeting, he was again called forward, and listened to by a multitude with mingled emotions of admiration, pity and honor. . . .

"Then Garrison arose, and burst forth into a more eloquent strain than I had ever heard before. He eulogized, as he deserved, the fugitive who had just spoken and anathematized the system that could crush to the earth such men."[26]

Before the convention adjourned, John A. Collins, general agent of the Massachusetts Anti-Slavery Society, urged Douglass to become an active lecturer for the organization.[27] Douglass was reluctant to accept, doubting his own ability, but finally agreed to work for the society for three months. He was to travel with Stephen S. Foster, and, in addition to lecturing, was to get subscriptions for the *Liberator* and the *Anti-Slavery Standard*. His salary was to be four hundred and fifty dollars a year.

Douglass returned to New Bedford convinced that his usefulness as an Abolitionist agent would not last beyond the three month period. Events were rapidly to show how seriously he had underrated himself, and to prove that this was but the launching of a great career.

The Garrisonians and Abolition

For ten years after his Nantucket speech Douglass was part of a small but steadily growing army of men and women who constituted the Garrisonian wing of the anti-slavery movement. Around William Lloyd Garrison, the leader of this army, the fires of controversy still rage. A new school of historians has arisen who contend that the Garrisonian influence in the Abolitionist movement was relatively negligible and argue that by his intemperate and violent language Garrison actually did more to retard than advance the anti-slavery cause. Many historians, northern as well as southern, have long contended that the Garrisonians really brought on the Civil War by vilifying the slaveholders.

Although the recent studies revealing that the anti-slavery impulse came as much out of the West as out of New England have thrown valuable light on a hitherto neglected phase of the Abolitionist crusade,[1] the fact remains that the work of Garrison and his associates must still loom large in any analysis of the forces responsible for emancipation. Whatever his shortcomings, Garrison was the most indomitable figure among Abolition forces. He possessed to a marvelous degree an undivided devotion to the struggle, the supremacy of a single purpose, the stern stuff out of which a fighter for unpopular causes must be made. His uncompromising stand against slavery struck home with such force that it riveted the attention of all men on this cause.

Many Americans had written and spoken against slavery long before Garrison's day. Anti-slavery sentiment in America had its origins coincident with the introduction of slavery in the colonial period, and was greatly advanced by the literature produced just before and during the Revolutionary War. In his famous pamphlet published in Boston in 1764, *The Rights of the British Colonies Asserted and Proved,* James Otis denounced the institution of slavery and affirmed the Negro's inalienable right to freedom. Nathaniel Appleton of Cambridge, Massachusetts, writing in 1767, placed himself squarely for abolition at any cost because of man's "natural right to be free." Eight years later Thomas Paine published an essay, "African Slavery in America," in which he denounced slavery as no less immoral than "murder, robbery, lewdness and barbarity," and called upon Americans to "discontinue and renounce it, with grief and abhorrence." Thomas Jefferson, who had urged the Assembly in Virginia to emancipate the slaves in the colony as early as 1769, in the first draft of the Declaration of Independence, labeled the slave trade "a cruel war against human nature itself, violating its most sacred rights of life and liberty."

In his *Autobiography*, Jefferson relates what happened to this passage from the original draft of the Declaration of Independence:

"The Clause . . . reprobating the enslaving of the inhabitants of Africa was struck out in complaisance to South Carolina and Georgia, who had never attempted to restrain the importation of slaves, and who on the contrary still wished to continue it. Our Northern brethren also I believe felt a little tender under these censures; for tho their people have very few slaves themselves yet they had been pretty considerable carriers of them to others."

Anti-slavery literature emphasized the inconsistency between slavery and the Declaration of Independence. Thus a correspondent who signed himself "Free Negro" asked: "Do the rights of nature cease to be such, when a Negro is to enjoy them? Or does patriotism in the heart of an African, rankle with treason?"

Under the impact of this revolutionary spirit, Negroes themselves, led by Absalom Jones, Prince Hall, and William Cuffee, became involved in the struggle; they protested the payment of taxes to a government denying them the rights of citizens; and they demanded freedom as a reward for fighting in defense of their country. Negroes also organized resistance to the slave trade and, in New England, even petitioned state legislatures for emancipation.[2]

These early protests against American slavery yielded rich rewards. By 1808 the African slave trade was abolished, slaves were freed in Vermont, New Hampshire, Massachusetts, and Ohio, and gradual emancipation was provided for in Rhode Island, Pennsylvania, New Jersey, New York, and Connecticut. Although slave labor in these states had already decreased in importance as an economic factor and was being replaced by free labor, these early anti-slavery activities hastened the day of freedom.

Beginning with the Pennsylvania Abolition Society in 1775, anti-slavery organizations spread throughout the North and the South. Until 1829, members of state and local bodies met in national meetings of the American Convention of Delegates from Abolition Societies.[3] But these meetings accomplished little of significance. Emancipation was still the ultimate goal, but the American Convention made no hard and fast rule as to how or when it could be secured. "The best method is still a question," it reported in 1821. "We cannot expect a speedy accomplishment of that event."[4]

There was always a small group of forthright and militant Abolitionists scattered through the Convention, but they were seldom heard and never countenanced by the conservatives who talked of gradual emancipation but did nothing to advance any program which might antagonize the vested interests. The reasons are fairly obvious. With the growth of the textile industry in England and New England, the invention of the cotton gin, and the expansion of the plantation system into the fertile land of the southwest, anti-slavery sentiment in the South gradually receded. By the late 1820's slavery represented a property interest amounting to billions of dollars, covering the whole plantation system and numerous northern industrial and commercial activities that rested upon servile labor. Small wonder so many anti-slavery men hesitated to antagonize this powerful economic and political alliance and could only give pious expressions in favor of gradual emancipation.

Whatever potential power there was in the American Convention of Delegates from Abolition Societies was dissipated by the rise of a new organization, the American Society for Colonizing the Free People of Colour of the United States. This organization disguised the issues and split the forces of the anti-slavery groups both in the North and South.

Formally organized on December 28, 1816, in the Hall of the House of Representatives in Washington, it was the culmination of colonizing efforts dating from the Revolutionary era. Prior to 1815, almost all colonization plans had called for the removal of Negroes, free or slave, all eventually to be emancipated. But the new society, dominated by southerners—the president and eight of the thirteen vice-presidents were from the South—was not only anti-Negro but pro-slavery. Such leaders as Andrew Jackson, Henry Clay, and Bushrod Washington gave the society great prestige but unfortunately many anti-slavery men, including even some who later became militant Abolitionists, threw their support to the new organization, believing they would find in the society the best answer to their problems.

Although by 1833, there were 97 local colonization societies in the North and 136 in the South, from 1820, the national society had been able to colonize only 2,885 Negro people. After the first enthusiasm, the society began to lose strength mainly because free Negroes opposed the plan; they refused to be uprooted, opposed being moved out of the country en masse, leaving hundreds of thousands of their people in slavery. The Negroes understood that the leaders of the Colonization Society were not interested in freeing slaves but in shipping troublesome Negroes out of the country, thereby strengthening their control over those who remained in bondage.[5]

In 1817, less than a month after the founding of the American Colonization Society, the free Negro people of Richmond and Philadelphia declared their opposition to any plan of deportation in the guise of repatriation. Other meetings followed in northern and border state centers. The delegates to the National Convention of the People of Color in Philadelphia in 1831 incorporated in their *Conventional Address* the declaration:

"The Convention . . . would respectfully suggest to that august body [the American Colonization Society] . . . that, in our humble opinion, . . . they are pursuing the direct road to perpetuate slavery, with all its unchristian-like concomitants, in this boasted land of freedom; and, as citizens and men whose best blood is sapped to gain popularity for that institution, we would, in the most feeling manner, beg of them to desist; or if we must be sacrificed to their philanthropy, we would rather die at home. . . ."[6]

Therefore, during the years when many white anti-slavery men were growing more cautious, the cause did not lack for militant fighters. The Negro people battled both slavery and the colonization movement and spoke out sharply on these issues. While the National Convention of the Delegates from Abolition Societies was offering a program which breathed gently upon the southern slaveholders and their northern allies, the Negro conventions came out boldly for human freedom. In 1827, *Freedom's Journal,* the first periodical published by Negroes in the United States, raised the demand for immediate emancipation of the slaves and conducted a brilliant campaign against the Colonizationists. Two years later, David Walker, the Boston agent for *Freedom's Journal,* issued his revolutionary *Appeal . . . to the Coloured Citizens of the world, but in particular, and very expressly to those of the United States* which was as advanced a call for the overthrow of slavery as anything to come from the Abolitionists in the next few decades.

Beginning with 1830 the anti-slavery crusade burst forth with a new intensity and within a few years was to establish itself as one of the most profound revolutionary movements in the world's history. The Negro slave rebellion in Virginia led by Nat Turner in September, 1831, was a portent of the sharply accelerating conflict between pro- and anti-slavery forces. On October 21, 1831, James Forten, the militant Philadelphia Negro reformer, wrote jubilantly that the Turner rebellion would strengthen the anti-slavery cause by "bringing the evils of slavery more prominently before the public. . . . Indeed we live in stiring [sic] times, and every day brings news of some fresh effort for liberty, either at home or abroad—onward, onward, is indeed the watchword."[7]

These were indeed stirring times. A new society was developing west of the Alleghenies, putting its mark on the social and political life of the entire country. A young labor movement was rising in the East, protesting the hardships of a rapidly expanding industrial system. Ecclesiastical revolts and religious revivals were asserting man's innate goodness and capacity for self-improvement, expressing this conviction in an interest in the weak and helpless—temperance reform, prison reform, and, logically, in the condition of the slave. It was an "age of great movements" which showed a "power to exalt a people," said William Ellery Channing, the New England liberal. "It was an era of sympathy with the suffering, and of devotion to the progress of the whole human race." This new anti-slavery movement was part of this great stirring, this upheaval, this effort to re-establish American democracy upon the principles of the Declaration of Independence. It was part of a great democratic and humanitarian impulse, for Abolitionism sprang up in a rich soil that gave us at the same time public education, woman's rights, peace, temperance, and utopian socialist movements.[8]

The leaders of the new anti-slavery movement had a great many differences of opinion on numerous matters—political action, "the woman question," non-resistance, disunion, the nature of the Constitution—but there was one idea which the majority held in common, and that was the inefficacy of "gradualism." They took their stand on immediate emancipation to save the nation from the sin of slave-holding. There was no time to waste. The eyes of the entire world were on them. It was their duty not only to themselves but to the slaveholder and to mankind the world over to save their brothers and sisters in bondage.

As we have shown, William Lloyd Garrison can scarcely be called a pioneer in the anti-slavery movement. Nor was he the first to raise the demand for the "immediate and complete emancipation" of the slaves. But it is to his credit that he was the first to build an organized movement capable of conducting a struggle to achieve this goal.

On Saturday, January 1, 1831, in Boston, Garrison issued the first number of the *Liberator,* through which for the next thirty-odd years he was to preach the gospel of the abolition of slavery. The first number contained an address to the public which sounded the keynote of Garrison's career. He announced his determination to attack the system of slavery until "every chain be broken, and every bondman set free." He repudiated every plan for gradual emancipation and proclaimed the duty of immediate and unconditional liberation of the slaves. Then announcing his program for the future, he boldly wrote:

"I will be as harsh as truth and as uncompromising as justice. . . . I will not equivocate—I will not excuse—I will not retreat a single inch— and I will be heard."[9]

To put into operation machinery with which to fight for his principles, Garrison organized the New England Anti-Slavery Society in 1832, and, in the following year, in Philadelphia, rallied the remnants of the local and national societies under a new organization known as the American Anti-Slavery Society. Soon after Garrison joined hands with George Thompson, Daniel O'Connell, Thomas Clarkson, and other Abolitionists in the British Isles, arousing international attention to the new movement.

The American Anti-Slavery Society rapidly attracted as active participants such men and women as Wendell Phillips, Arthur and Lewis Tappan, John Greenleaf Whittier, Maria Weston Chapman, Stephen S. Foster, Theodore D. Weld, Elijah P. Lovejoy, Gerrit Smith, Theodore Parker, Lucretia Mott, the Grimke sisters, and other well known people. Negroes shared in the leadership of the organization from its very inception. Several Negroes were delegates at the founding convention; three Negroes were among the sixty-two signers of the Declaration of Sentiments, and the Board of Managers included James G. Barbadoes of Massachusetts, Peter Williams of New York, Robert Purvis, James McCrummell, John B. Vashon and Abraham D. Shadd of Pennsylvania.[10]

The American Anti-Slavery Society was launched at a most critical period in the struggle over slavery. Cotton was king, and every southern institution, the schools, churches, and economic agencies which had criticized slavery before the invention of the cotton gin now paid homage to the new monarch whose throne rested on the labor of four million enslaved human beings. Economics books were rewritten to sing the great advantages of slave labor over free labor. The inferiority of the Negro was "proved" *a priori*. The Southerners devised the "Positive Good" theory which declared that slave labor was essential to the development and progress of the nation; that the Negro was destined, by all evidence, to be kept in a subordinate position; that slavery lifted a whole race of heathens to a Christian status; and that the institution improved the white people because it afforded leisure time for the development of culture and the arts. The ruling class was determined to permit no compromise between its economic interests and the pleas of humanitarians. The southern states prohibited manumission unless provision was made for the removal of the Negroes from the state. The status of slavery and the slave was summarized by the Supreme Court of North Carolina in 1829:

"The end [of slavery] is the profit of the master, his security, and the public safety. The subject is one doomed in his own person and his posterity to live without knowledge and without the capacity to make any thing his own, and to toil that another may reap the fruits. . . . The power of the master must be absolute to render the submission of the slave perfect. In the actual condition of things it must be so. There is no remedy. This discipline belongs to the state of slavery. . . ."[11]

Not without cause did the British Abolitionist, Charles Stuart, say: "Truly, your country, in all its leading outward features, is making itself a spectacle equally disgusting and ridiculous to all independent and manly intelligence. Applauding liberty, yet keeping slaves! Calling the slave trade piracy if practiced in Africa, but ready to wade through blood to honor and sustain it in America! Boasting of freedom, yet grasping tenaciously its gross idolatry of a white and its atrocious abhorrence of a colored skin."[12]

It was at this point, in the 'thirties, that the Abolitionists launched their campaign to capture the minds of the people and turn them against the system of oppression that was fastening the shackles of slavery even more securely upon the Negro people.

In the forceful Declaration of Sentiments adopted by the American Society at its founding convention, the delegates pledged:

"We shall organize anti-slavery societies, if possible, in every city, town, and village in our land.

"We shall send forth agents to lift up the voice of remonstrance, of warning, of entreaty and rebuke.

"We shall circulate unsparingly and extensively anti-slavery tracts and periodicals."[13]

The struggle to carry out this pledge was waged with a fervor, persistence and skill rarely matched in our history. The handful of Abolitionists worked out a thoroughgoing propaganda; circulated petitions by the thousands which they showered on Congress and state legislatures; appeared before legislative committees; sent out traveling agents; slipped printed handkerchiefs bearing anti-slavery slogans into bales designed for Southern markets, and mailed pictures depicting the cruelties of slavery. At the same time they did not neglect the free Negro people. Above all, they held anti-slavery meetings in every conceivable place, from a stable loft to a church. There was a round of annual meetings—meetings of the New York, the Massachusetts, the New England, the Western (Ohio), and the American Anti-Slavery Societies. Then there was the annual anti-slavery celebration of West India Emancipation on August 1st. There were anti-slavery bazaars, anti-slavery soirees, and anti-slavery festivals. Resolutions were passed, ardent speeches made and hymns were sung. Typical was the following stirring song written by Garrison:

> *I am an Abolitionist,*
> *I glory in the name*
> *Though now by Slavery's minions hissed*
> *And covered o'er with shame:*
> *It is a spell of light and power*
> *The watchword of the free:*
> *Who spurns it in the trial-hour,*
> *A craven soul is he!*[14]

The central features of Abolitionist agitation were the lecturers or "traveling agents"; the printing of newspapers and periodicals; the publication of books, leaflets (broadsides), and cartoons.

The system of "agents," who traveled from town to town explaining the principles of Abolitionism and forming local societies, was developed to a very high point by Theodore Weld, a master at all forms of agitation, and Elizur Wright, organizational genius of the American Society. Agents had to be of good moral character, sincere, fully steeped in the subject, financially trustworthy, and, as Wright wrote to Weld about one candidate: "Has he the *'vis Vividu,'* the galvanism that can reanimate the dead as well as the steadfastness that can withstand the onset of the living?" Meeting these qualifications, which might be investigated for a month or more, an agent would then begin his travels, "mobbed out of the big cities and pelted out of the little ones," jolting over primitive roads in hard coaches from day to day, speaking in barns, churches, taverns, schools, and private parlors—on the town common or in the nearest forest when nothing else could be had.

Since services rendered the slaves were freewill offerings, it followed that all able to do so should work without compensation. Others—those "who had no extrinsic means of livelihood"—were allowed "what they consider absolutely indispensable to a bare subsistence." The salaries were $8 a week if unmarried and those who had a wife and family at home received $600 a year and traveling expenses. The "Instructions to Agents" further adjured them to remember that "silver and gold are the Lord's" and to be frugal in their expenses. By way of implementing this advice, Elizur Wright scanned each agent's monthly expense and work reports with a stern, economical eye.[15]

These work reports convey in the simplest, most dramatic way the sincerity, courage, and self-sacrificing devotion of the anti-slavery agents. These traveling lecturers made every possible sacrifice and frequently went hungry. A mobbing was an every-day occurrence. James Russell Lowell's poem described Stephen S. Foster thus:

> Hard by, as calm as summer even,
> Smiles the reviled and pelted Stephen;
> Who studied mineralogy
> Not with soft book upon the knee,
> But learned the properties of stones,
> By contact sharp of flesh and bones.

The peak of achievement of the work of traveling agents came in 1836-37. Some seventy were selected, then summoned to a convention in New York City, to which about forty came. There Theodore Weld, as "the central luminary," held forth for a fortnight at the three daily sessions. Garrison wrote:

"The questions discussed were manifold—such as, what is slavery? What is immediate emancipation? Why don't you go to the South? The slaves, if emancipated, would overrun the North. The consequences of emancipation to the South. Hebrew servitude. Compensation. Colonization. Prejudice. Treatment and condition of our free colored population. Gradualism, etc., etc. All the prominent objections to our cause were ingeniously presented, and as conclusively shown to be futile."

Weld's prodigious efforts, added to a program of speaking from five to fifteen times in a single town, night after night, finished his speaking days forever. He lost his voice; and only long afterwards was he able to speak even in conversation without pain. He turned his talents, however, to writing at which he was equally a master.[16]

From its beginning, the American Society stressed the importance of publishing and distributing newspapers. Without reaching very large circulations, the Abolitionist papers multiplied in number and influence. In 1834 the *Liberator* had a weekly circulation of 2,300, and 75 per cent of its readers were Negro people. The weekly *Emancipator*, published by the New York Anti-Slavery Society, reached a circulation of 3,800 copies. There were 14 Abolitionist periodicals published in 1839, and 26 weeklies in 1843. By then the columns of many other newspapers had been opened to Abolitionist ideas and writers.

It required unremitting attention and sacrifice on the part of Abolitionist leaders and supporters to maintain their press. Selling at an average of two dollars a year, the anti-slavery weeklies operated at a loss. Financial campaigns were constantly undertaken, special appeals were made through the paper's columns, and agents had to remind audiences that a chief cause of the financial difficulties stemmed from the failure of subscribers to pay up their subscriptions. Most often the appeals would be heeded. Money would come in, sometimes generous contributions from wealthy donors like Gerrit Smith, a Peterboro, New York, landowner with varied reform interests, sometimes handsome legacies or a young lady's bracelet. Large contributions, however, were not too frequent, and most often the anti-slavery movement had to depend upon the receipt of letters such as the following from the West Boxford Female Anti-Slavery Society containing $2 and the statement:

"We are a feeble band of small means but what we have we wish to appropriate to the best advantage. . . . 'The Cause' is one dear to our hearts, and it will be a source of the highest gratification to do anything for its advancement."[17]

One of the great contributions made by women to the Abolition movement was the accumulation of funds necessary to carry on the anti-slavery work. The Annual Anti-Slavery Fair, sponsored by the Female Anti-Slavery Societies, became a vital source of funds for the cause. The Fair was usually held the week before Christmas so that people could buy Christmas gifts and at the same time contribute to a cause dear to their conscience. All through the year female societies and sewing circles sewed and knitted. European friends made annual contributions of money and articles. In 1841 Mrs. Maria Weston Chapman who organized the Boston Fair for a period of twenty years, wrote to Lydia M. Child: "Petersburg, Paris, Geneva, Rome, London, Glasgow, all

Ireland, the lovely city of the Cape, and the Haitian city of Santiago
are all contributors." Friendly merchants made donations or sold articles
at wholesale prices to the ladies. In 1840 among the articles offered at the
Boston Fair was "jewelry of friends who had renounced it for their
own wearing for the sake of the cause" with the hope that the new
wearers would learn to renounce it in the future!

Most of the Anti-Slavery Societies were poor; the largest income
received for a single year by the American Society was $47,111.74; the
Massachusetts Society collected approximately $6,000 annually and most
state societies received only $3,000. Yet, despite their lack of funds,
the Abolitionists carried "the word" into every nook and cranny of
American life. They kept the community astir; they made people think
and talk. The philosophy and the method of this unprecedented campaign for educating the American people were perfectly summed up by
Wendell Phillips in the statement:

"Our aim is to alter public opinion. Did we live in a market, our talk
should be of dollars and cents, and we would seek to prove only that slavery
was an unprofitable investment. Were the nation one great, pure church,
we would sit down and reason of 'righteousness, temperance, and judgment
to come.' Had slavery fortified itself in a college, we would load our cannons
with cold facts, and wing our arrows with arguments. But we happen to
live in the world,—the world made up of thought and impulse, or self-
conceit and self-interest, of weak men and wicked. To conquer, we must
reach all."

As the campaign to "reach all" got under way, the ranks of the
Abolitionists steadily increased. In 1834, there were 60 auxiliary societies;
in May, 1835, there were 200; in May, 1836, there were 527. The number
climbed to 1,000 in July, 1837; by 1838 it had jumped to 1,350 and in
1840 there were over 2,000 societies with a membership of 200,000.[18]

The rapid growth of Abolitionist sentiment during the 1830's was
not merely the result of effective propaganda. Many Americans were
seeing clearly that there was an identity of struggle for Negro freedom
and for freedom for all people, and that the democratic rights of all
people were threatened by the same power which kept millions of slaves
in chains. There was a growing conviction among many people that
to preserve their own civil and political liberties they had to support the
struggle for the democratic rights of the Abolitionists to fight slavery.

This issue was crystallized by the struggle over the right of petition.
For some years anti-slavery petitions were few in number. On Decem-

ber 12, 1831, John Quincy Adams, who was to lead the petition fight, presented fifteen petitions, which were referred to committees who reported against granting their plea. It was not until 1835 that petitions again reached Congress in sufficient volume to provoke discussion. With the beginning of 1836, however, they became headlines in the news. In the Senate, Calhoun introduced a motion against their reception which, after many weeks of debate, was defeated. A similar measure in the House provoked a debate lasting several weeks. Finally, the whole question of reception was referred to a special committee, at the head of which was Pinckney of South Carolina, which recommended that "all petitions relating to the subject of slavery or the abolition of slavery, shall, without being either printed or referred, be laid upon the table, and no further action whatever shall be had thereon." When the vote was taken, John Quincy Adams rose, and, instead of voting, pronounced the measure "a direct violation of the Constitution of the United States, the rules of this House, and the rights of my constituents."[19]

This was the famous "Pinckney gag," which, in various forms, was repeated each session until 1840, when it was made a standing rule of the House. Many Americans, however, who objected to Abolitionism, leaped to the defense of any group to petition Congress for whatever cause.

Step by step Abolitionism became identified with civil liberty. During the campaign in Congress to deprive the Abolitionists of the right of petition, the Philadelphia Trades' Union observed that the petitions of the Abolitionists and those of the trade unions in behalf of the ten-hour day received the same treatment. William Leggett, acting editor of the *New York Evening Post* and a spokesman for the labor movement during the Jacksonian era, attacked the government's interference with the mail privileges of the anti-slavery journals, and warned the workers that their journals would be next. When the Mayor of Philadelphia prevented Frances Wright, the courageous woman reformer, from lecturing in that city on the subject of slavery, the *National Laborer,* organ of the Philadelphia Trades' Union, the city central labor body, stated:

"The people need not be surprised at this, when they remember that it is the same Mayor who demanded the enormous bail of $2,500 for the appearance of the Schuylkill laborers to answer the charge of riot, who were afterwards discharged because there was no crime found against them."[20]

The increase in Abolitionist sentiment continued after 1840 as the aggressions of the slavocracy mounted. But the American Anti-Slavery Society did not reflect this increase. In 1840 the Society had reached its peak. The split in the organization between the Garrisonians and other Abolitionists stopped further growth.

The opponents of slavery were by no means solidly united in creed or strategy. One school insisted that the only proper and effectual instrument for the extermination of slavery was moral suasion; another maintained that moral suasion had to be buttressed by political action; and still another believed in direct, militant action and called for resistance in a physical sense.

Garrison and his followers were adherents of the first school of thought. They pledged major emphasis on the thesis that the way to get rid of slavery was to establish "in the hearts of men a deep and wide-spreading conviction of *the brotherhood of the human race;* that God hath indeed made of one blood all nations of men for to dwell on all the face of the earth"; that fighting evil with evil was to be condemned; that the slave should be urged not to resist his torturer with carnal weapons, for that was sin; that spiritual, not material means were the only moral way to achieve good. The warfare was to be no wild crusade, but a holy war, a sacred strife, waged not with earthly fire, "but with weapons fresh from the armory of God . . . Prayer . . . Faith . . . and the word of God!" Said Wendell Phillips: "Those who cling to moral effort are the true champions in the fight . . . We are working *with God,* and the times and the seasons are in His hands."[21]

Yet the Garrisonians never fell asleep at their moral weapons. The movement was always kept in vigorous operation. In spite of this, it became clear to many Abolitionists that moral suasion would not by itself free the slaves. The controversy over the right of petition encouraged many of them to seek abolition by political action and if necessary, even to form an independent political movement.

At first Garrison was favorable toward using the ballot-box against slavery. In an *Address to the Abolitionists of Massachusetts,* he wrote:

"Do not stay away from the polls. Go and scatter your votes. This is the true way to make yourselves felt. Every scattering vote you cast counts against the candidate of the parties; and you will serve as an effectual admonition to them, to nominate the next time, men whom you can conscientiously support."

But he opposed the formation of a political party by the Abolitionists on the grounds that it would be dangerous, if not fatal to the cause. He argued in this way:

"If we were a political party, the struggle for places of power and emolument would render our motives suspect, even if it did not prove too strong a temptation to our integrity. If we were a distinct party, every member of it must vote for its candidates, however he might disagree with them on other points of public policy. Experience seems to show that under a free government, there cannot be at one time, more than two powerful political parties."[22]

And very soon Garrison even retreated from his early endorsement of political action. He studied the Constitution and concluded that in giving "solemn guarantees" to slavery, it was "a covenant with death, and an agreement with hell." He cited the clause which legalized the slave trade for a period of twenty years; that which allowed the slave masters to swell their representation in Congress, and the clause which pledged the military power of the United States to put down servile rebellion and to enforce the fugitive slave law. These constituted a trinity of evil, and branded the Constitution a compact of fatal compromise. These provisions, moreover, expressed the exact purpose of its authors. Consistent Abolitionism was impossible under the Constitution. Slavery was intrenched in the fundamental law of the nation; consequently, anyone who would defend and uphold the Constitution, as was implicit in the act of voting and holding office, partook of the guilt of the slaveholders. As one of the Garrisonians put it: "The Abolitionists cannot conscientiously support or swear to support the Constitution. They cannot thus support God and mammon."

From denouncing the Constitution, Garrison moved next to denouncing the "blood-soaked" American Union, and, as early as 1832, led the Come-Outers (those who advocated leaving the Union). "There is much declamation about the sacredness of the compact which was formed between the free and slave States in the adoption of the Constitution," he write in the *Liberator* of December 29, 1832. "A sacred compact, forsooth! We pronounce it the most bloody and heaven-daring arrangement ever made by men for the continuance and protection of a system of the most atrocious villainy ever exhibited upon the earth . . ." Adopting as his watchword, "No Union with slaveholders," Garrison openly advocated the dissolution of the Union as the only means of freeing the slaves.

The Garrisonians fulminated against the churches as vigorously as they did against the state. They called "the church and clergy of the United States as a whole . . . a great *Brotherhood of Thieves,* inasmuch as they countenance the highest kind of theft, *i.e.,* man-stealing." Phillips remarked: "If I die before emancipation, write this for my epitaph. 'Here lies Wendell Phillips, infidel to a church that defended human slavery— traitor to a government that was only an organized conspiracy against the rights of men.'" Garrison not only denounced the churches as forming "the bulwark of American Slavery," but he repudiated the divine inspiration of the Scriptures. It was harmful, he argued, to refer to the Bible as the Holy Book, inasmuch as nobody knew who had written it or when it had been written. A staunch Anti-Sabbatarian, he held as superstition the setting aside of the first day of the week for religious purposes, attributing the practice to the machinations of the "priestcraft" for selfish ends.[23]

When to such beliefs was added Garrison's insistence that women should participate equally with men in the leadership of the anti-slavery societies, not a few Abolitionists were shocked. The "woman question" became a pivotal factor in the anti-slavery movement and a major issue in the conflict between Garrison and his opponents in the American Anti-Slavery Society. On May 7, 1839, the American Society at its annual convention voted, 180 to 140, to allow all *persons* present to be seated as members. One hundred and twenty members went on record as protesting the decision, stating that the right of women to speak, vote, and hold office was against the recognized rules of propriety, was a breach of faith against those who joined the society believing it to be an organization of men, that at the organizing convention the women did not sign the Declaration of Sentiments nor enroll as members, and that this was a step to enlist the anti-slavery movement in a cause foreign to its purpose.

Those in favor of women's participation, led by Garrison, stated that the constitution of the American Anti-Slavery Society made no distinction between men and women, but said, "All persons who consent to the principles" were to be admitted. The Executive Committee published a statement declaring that the action of the convention was not to be construed as committing the society to the principles of women's equality with men in public affairs; it became evident that there was a serious cleavage in the organization.[24]

The conflict reached its climax at the meeting of the American Society in 1840. Garrison's opponents, led by the Tappan brothers, attempted to capture the national society, to reverse the action allowing women to serve on committees with men, and to oust Garrison from a position of power. As every Abolitionist present was to have a vote, Garrison chartered a steamer at Providence to take a boatload of his followers to New York to save the society from falling into the hands of his opponents. A rallying cry went out through the *Liberator*. The response was prompt: over four hundred delegates were prepared to "preserve the integrity of the anti-slavery movement." Persons of all ages, color, and conditions, from veterans to new recruits, poured into the steamer. They filled the berths and floors in the cabins, and over-flowed on the deck.

When the group arrived at the convention, they made "clean work of everything with crushing unanimity," to use Garrison's words. On a test vote Abby Kelley was nominated to the Business Committee by a vote of 557 to 451. Lucretia Mott, Lydia Maria Child, and Maria Weston Chapman were put on the executive committee. Some of the opposition delegates were so exasperated by the result that they left the meeting.

Garrison's opponents insisted that Abolition must be divorced from no-government, non-resistance, theological heterodoxy, and equality of the sexes. Garrison's doctrines, they claimed, weakened "the staff of accomplishment." Accordingly, Lewis Tappan, after the adoption of the resolution admitting women to membership, urged its opponents to meet in the lecture room under the church to organize a new society. All the ministers present accepted the invitation as did many others, and the American and Foreign Anti-Slavery Society was speedily organized.[25]

The new society recognized the "rightfulness of government," urged political action as a duty and declared that the admission of women to take part in its proceedings was an innovation "repugnant to the con-stitution of the society," "a firebrand in anti-slavery meetings, and con-trary to the usages of the civilized world." Its program naturally drew within the organization the more conservative and prudent members of the old society, those who "could not swallow Garrison." But it also attracted those who disagreed with Garrison's presentation of the Constitution as a pro-slavery document and who believed firmly in the value of anti-slavery political action.

The American and Foreign Anti-Slavery Society never became a powerful organization, and expired after a feeble existence of thirteen years. Most of its members identified themselves with the Liberty Party.

They claimed that the Constitution had been misinterpreted, the text blameless, that it was, to the contrary, an Abolitionist document. Basing themselves on an anti-slavery constitutional interpretation the "New Orgs," as they were called, contributed to the growth of political Abolitionism.

Disgusted by the split in the movement and unwilling to join either organization, groups of anti-slavery men floundered about after 1840. Gerrit Smith expressed the viewpoint of the no-organization Abolitionists in a letter to Theodore D. Weld on July 11, 1840:

"Like yourself, I can go neither with the Old nor New Anti-slavery Organization *at the present*. I am sick, heart sick, of the quarrels of abolitionists between themselves, and I apprehend that for *the present* at least, these organizations will be the occasion of keeping up and aggravating these quarrels. Could we all be in one Organization, and meet in it with fraternal harmony, then anti-slavery organization would be as dear to my heart as it ever was, and then it would be greatly and gloriously effective, as it once was."[26]

The schism affected the American Anti-Slavery Society to a considerable extent, the annual income dropping immediately from $47,000 to $7,000 and not rising above $12,000 until 1856. The number of local societies and the total membership immediately decreased and was never fully recovered. As a result the Garrisonians banded themselves more tightly together and, in defiance of their opponents, reaffirmed their purpose to maintain their program without modification. Once again they announced their intention to conduct a moral war against slavery, and avowed their confidence in conscience, reason, and discussion as the surest means with which to pull down the strongholds of oppression. Once more they denounced the "sectarian organizations called churches" to be "combinations of thieves, robbers, adulterers, pirates and murderers."[27] They branded the Constitution a pro-slavery document, and proclaimed as their slogan: "A Repeal of the Union between Northern Liberty and Southern Slavery is essential to the abolition of the one and the preservation of the other." On October 1, 1844, Garrison summed up his creed in a letter to Henry C. Wright:

"Politically, the American Anti-Slavery Society has 'passed the Rubicon,' in regard to this blood-cemented Union; and on its banner is inscribed the motto, 'No Union with Slaveholders.' No step has yet been taken in our cause, so trying to those who profess to be abolitionists, or that is destined to make such a commotion in Church and State. It will alienate many from our ranks, but their defection will be our gain. 'The battle is the Lord's,' not man's, and victory will be achieved not by numerical superiority—not by physical might or power—but by the Spirit of Truth, and the omnipotence of Love."[28]

Whatever the Garrisonians were guilty of, however impractical Garrison may have been concerning political and social processes, he and his followers, Negro and white, must be credited with rousing America's conscience to the extent that Abolition, a relatively unimportant issue in 1830, became by the 'fifties the all-important question which had to be faced by every man and woman.

Anti-Slavery Agent

Douglass joined the ranks of the Abolitionists at a time when his services were sorely needed. The slaveowners had succeeded in formulating a defense of slavery which was extremely disconcerting to the Abolitionists. They emphasized its divine origin and sanction, and argued that slavery was especially beneficial to the Negro, that the condition of the slave in the South was far better than that of the northern and the English factory worker. They argued that the vast majority of the northern anti-slavery agitators had never seen slavery as it really existed and consequently did not know what they were talking about.[1]

In support of their "peculiar institution" the slaveholders and their sympathizers let loose a flood of propaganda. They painted a most beautiful picture of slavery as "it really existed." There was so little work for the slaves to do, went these lyrical outbursts, that there were "few who cannot perform them by midday or within an hour or two afterwards"; they were "always provided with clothing and all necessary, though plain food"; their clothing consisted of "winter and summer suits, the former, a jacket, waist coat, and overalls of Welsh plains and the latter, osnaburg homespun or other substitutes. They have shoes, hats, and handkerchiefs and other little articles, such as tobacco, pipes, rum, etc." Furthermore, the slaves even possessed "most of the civil freedom of the white man," and enjoyed a measure of security entirely foreign to the workers in northern factories who could be dismissed at a moment's notice and who, during periods of unemployment, were left to starve in their miserable hovels.[2] Maryland was held up as the symbol of justice to the slave. One pamphleteer argued:

"Maryland enjoys what I deem the proud eminence of being of all the states, the first in friendliness toward the African. This state may be adduced as an example of the mixture of the two races without amalgmation and with least oppression."[3]

A number of Abolitionists had already exposed the lies of the pro-slavery propagandists. By citing evidence from southern newspapers in his masterly tract, *Slavery As It Is, the Testimony of a Thousand Witnesses,* Theodore Weld had demonstrated that slaves were "overworked, under-fed, have insufficient sleep, live in miserable huts, generally without floors, and with a single apartment in which both sexes are herded promiscuously; that their clothing serves neither the purposes of comfort nor common decency; that barbarous cruelty is inflicted upon them. . . ."[4]

Still the Abolitionists needed something concrete and irrefutable to offer to the very persuasive arguments coming from the South. Obviously the need could best be filled by the Negro himself. Who else could refute so effectively the testimony of those who upheld slavery and argued that the slaves actually benefited from their bondage? Small wonder that after 1840 the number of Negroes employed as Abolitionist agents "grew in leaps and bounds." As John A. Collins pointed out in a letter to Garrison early in 1842:

". . . The public have itching ears to hear a colored man speak, and particularly *a slave*. Multitudes will flock to hear one of this class speak. . . . It would be a good policy to employ a number of colored agents, if suitable ones can be found."[5]

When Garrison and his associates heard Douglass in Nantucket they recognized that here was a man who embodied all the qualities their cause needed. Here was a man, a slave for twenty-one years, who could bring to the lecture platform first-hand knowledge of the institution. What a contrast to the rosy picture painted by the pro-slavery propagandists was the ugly story of slavery as Douglass had seen and experienced it! Masters were not kind; slaves were not cared for morally and spiritually; hours of labor were not reasonable; slaves were not happy and contented; slavery was not beneficial to the Negro. Moreover, the terrible experiences Douglass cited had occurred in a state in which slavery practices were said to be comparatively mild! His story revealed how rotten was the moral fiber from which slavery was spun. What hypocrisy to speak of the religious beliefs of the slaveholder when a master could "come through" with his religion and immediately afterward gather a mob from his own white congregation to disperse a Sunday school conducted by a slave! How could the slaveholder claim God's sanction to a system which permitted Covey, the "slavebreaker," to lock up a young woman with a hired male slave for breeding purposes! Douglass recounted the wild joy of the Negro-breaker and his wife when the young woman gave birth to twins. There was no legal marriage for the slave; slave-breeding was the chief source of wealth in some of the southern states; the "best blood" of the Virginia whites could be found in the slave-markets of New Orleans; mulattoes were, for the most part, sold as mistresses for planters. The entire account was told with an absence of personal animus, for Douglass aimed his darts at no man. His target was always the *slave system* which robbed master and slave alike of the dignity of human beings. He insistently pointed out that the abuses of slavery were necessary to the maintenance of the system.

When Douglass told his story to the public, he spoke with unquestionable authority, a late "graduate from the 'peculiar institution' with his diploma written on his back," as John A. Collins used to say in introducing him. That his words carried conviction is evidenced by the amazing response to his lectures from the outset of his work as an agent for the Massachusetts Anti-Slavery Society.

During his first three months as a lecturer, Douglass traveled usually with John A. Collins, but at county-wide meetings they would be joined by Garrison, Pillsbury, Foster, Abby Kelley, and other leaders of the movement. Yet the presence of these veterans did not detract from the attention received by the new recruit. At Abington, Douglass' appearance "gave a fresh impulse to anti-slavery." A crowded audience at Georgetown listened enraptured, and, at a convention of the Worcester North Division Society, during the first week in October, 1841, a resolution was adopted welcoming him and extending to him "the right hand of fellowship." On hearing him at a convention of the Plymouth Society on November 4, the editor of the *Hingham Patriot* was reminded of Spartacus, the Gladiator.

"He is very fluent in the use of language," he wrote, " choice and appropriate language, too; and talks as well, for all we could see, as men who have spent all their lives over books. He is forcible, keen and very sarcastic; and considering the poor advantages he must have had as a slave, he is certainly a remarkable man." A similar report was sent from Rhode Island the following month by N. P. Rogers, editor of the Concord *Herald of Freedom*. Describing a meeting in Franklin Hall, Providence, Rogers wrote:

"The fugitive Douglass was up when we entered. This is an extraordinary man. He was cut out for a hero. In a rising for Liberty he would have been a Toussaint or a Hamilton. He has the 'heart to conceive, the head to contrive, and the hand to execute.' A commanding person over six feet, we should say, in height, and of most manly proportions. His head would strike a phrenologist amid a sea of them in Exeter Hall, and his voice would ring like a trumpet in the field. Let the South congratulate herself that he is a fugitive. It would not have been safe for her if he had remained about the plantation a year or two longer. . . . As a speaker he has few equals. It is not declamation—but oratory, power of debate. He has wit, arguments, sarcasm, pathos—all that first rate men show in their master efforts. His voice is highly melodious and rich, and his enunciation quite elegant, and yet he has been but two or three years out of the house of bondage."[6]

Douglass had journeyed to Rhode Island together with Rogers, Garrison, Pillsbury, Collins, Foster, and Abby Kelley in an effort to defeat the adoption of a state constitution restricting the suffrage to white persons. At first the Abolitionists had participated actively in the struggle led by Thomas Wilson Dorr for a wider extension of the limited franchise. (By 1841 Rhode Island was the only northern state which had not adopted white manhood suffrage.) But when the "People's Party" denied the suffrage to free Negroes in the new constitution which they submitted to the vote of the people, the anti-slavery men felt betrayed, and the Rhode Island Anti-Slavery Executive Committee issued a circular calling on all Abolitionists "to make a combined and vigorous effort against the proposed constitution." The Abolitionists held a series of enthusiastic meetings at which nearly a thousand dollars was raised to fight the proposed constitution. Several of these gatherings, addressed by Douglass, Foster, and Miss Kelley, were broken up by mobs opposed to "n——r voting," but the Abolitionists persisted and continued to denounce the "white" clause. Douglass made such a deep impression at the annual convention of the Rhode Island State Anti-Slavery Society that he was appointed on a committee "to go before the Suffrage convention to meet in this city next week, and protest in the name of the Abolitionists of this State, against the insertion of the word 'white' in the new constitution."[7]

From the beginning of his career as a lecturer, Douglass moved beyond the narrow limits prescribed for him by the Garrisonians. He had been hired to tell the story of his slave experiences, and in his first public addresses he discussed nothing else. But within two months, he was discussing the "progress of the cause." At the Hingham Anti-Slavery Convention, early in November, he launched into a discussion of the superiority of moral suasion over political action in the battle against slavery, and called for the dissolution of the American Union. He denounced the pledge of the North to return fugitives as "the bulwark of slavery" since it discouraged slaves "from making any attempts to gain their freedom," and he concluded that "he is no true Abolitionist who does not go against this Union."

There was nothing original in these remarks. Douglass was simply saying what Garrison and his colleagues had said many times. Yet they reveal that he was already widening his range on the platform. As early as mid-December, 1841, in a speech before the Plymouth County Anti-Slavery Society, Douglass struck the central theme of his career as an Abolitionist—the twin battle against slavery in the South and prejudice in the North. He denounced slavery, but reminded his audience that in Massachusetts he had been dragged out of railroad cars after paying his full fare; that in New Bedford he could not find work as a caulker, and in the same city he had seen Negroes discriminated against even in church.

"You degrade us [he cried bitterly] and then ask why we are degraded— you shut our mouths, and then ask why we don't speak—you close your colleges and seminaries against us, and then ask why we don't know more."[8]

Here was no mere copy of other Abolitionist lecturers. Here was a spokesman for his people who experienced their degradation every day of his life, and who could express in vivid, burning language the pent-up indignation of the American Negro.

Douglass may have contributed little that was original in his early anti-slavery speeches, but he did give the movement a newness of life that could not have been obtained otherwise. The speeches of most of the Garrisonians were by now pretty well set into a pattern, and everyone knew more or less what they would say. Each speech contained a fervent appeal for the slave, a denunciation of the slave system and of the church and politicians supporting it, a condemnation of the Constitution as a pro-slavery document, and a cry for separation from the South. Douglass utilized this formula in his speeches, but he also brought variety and freshness. He could denounce slavery and the slaveholders as bitterly as the other Garrisonians could, and his invectives were no less piercing. But he also injected into his speeches a sense of humor. He could thrill his listeners with an account of his battle with Covey, at the same time getting them to burst into laughter as he described the expression on the Negro-breaker's face as he went down in the filth of the cowpen. He could bring shouts of glee from the audience as he portrayed his master,

Mr. Auld, first being converted, the tears rolling down his cheeks as he worshipped God, then the same Mr. Auld, on the same day, dispersing a group of slaves who were assembled to worship the same God.

His fine sense of humor and mimicry was a keen weapon, and he used it devastatingly. At Faneuil Hall, the Cradle of Liberty, he enlivened a meeting one evening with "a very funny imitation of the way in which slaveholding clergymen would exhort their servants to obey their masters." He delivered this remarkable piece of mimicry time and again to the delight of his audiences and to the embarrassment of the southern clergy. In a canting tone of voice he would begin:

"They the ministers would take a text—say this:—'Do unto others as you would have others do unto you.' And this is how they would apply it. They would explain it to mean, 'slaveholders, do unto *slaveholders* what you would have them do unto you:' and then looking impudently up the slave's gallery . . . looking high up to the poor colored drivers and the rest, and spreading his hands gracefully abroad, he says (mimicking), 'And you too, my friends, have souls of infinite value—souls that will *labor diligently* to make your calling and election sure. Oh, receive into your souls these words of the holy apostle—Servants, be obedient to your masters.' (Shouts of laughter and applause.)

" 'Oh! if you wish to be happy in time, happy in eternity, you must be obedient to your masters; their interest is yours. God made one portion of men to do the working, and another to do the thinking; how good God is! Now you have no trouble or anxiety; but ah! you can't imagine how perplexing it is to your masters and mistresses to have so much thinking to do in your behalf! You cannot appreciate your blessings; you know not how happy a thing it is for you, that you were born of that portion of the human family which has the working, instead of the thinking to do! Oh! how grateful and obedient you ought to be to your masters! How beautiful are the arrangements of Providence! Look at your hard, horny hands—see how nicely they are adapted to the labor you have to perform! Look at our delicate fingers, so exactly fitted for our station, and see how manifest it is that God deigned us to be his thinkers, and you the workers—oh! the wisdom of God.' "

This sermon was usually followed by a parody on the "Heavenly Union," a hymn sung weekly in the churches of the South. The hymn itself ran as follows:

> *Come, saints and sinners, hear me tell*
> *The wonders of Emanuel.*
> *Who saved me from a burning hell*

> *And taught my soul with Him to dwell*
> *And gave me heavenly union.*

> *When Jesus from His throne on high*
> *Beheld my soul in ruin lie.*
> *He looked on me with pitying eye*
> *And said to me as he passed by,*
> *"With God you have no union."*

To Douglass it seemed that the very use of this hymn in worship, while the church sanctioned slavery, constituted extreme irony. Hence, he composed a travesty on the hymn, parts of which went:

> *Come, saints and sinners, hear me tell*
> *How pious priests whip Jack and Nell,*
> *And women buy, and children sell,*
> *And preach all sinners down to hell,*
> *And sing of heavenly union.*

> *They'll bleat and bray and do like goats*
> *Gorge down black sheep, and strain at motes,*
> *Array their backs in fine black coats,*
> *Then seize their n——rs by their throats*
> *And choke for heavenly union.*

> *They'll raise tobacco, corn and rye,*
> *And drive and thieve and steal and lie,*
> *And lay up treasure in the sky,*
> *By making switch and cowskin fly*
> *In hope of heavenly union.*[9]

As reports from people who had heard Douglass poured into the *Liberator* and the *Anti-Slavery Standard*, the Massachusetts Abolitionists realized that they had gained an invaluable asset to the cause. In his annual report to the Society, John A. Collins bestowed lavish praise upon the young orator who had traveled with him to "upwards of sixty towns and villages" on a tour covering 3,500 miles.

"His descriptions of slavery," he wrote, "are most graphic, and his arguments so lucid, and occasionally so spiced with pleasantry, and sometimes with a little satire, that his addresses, though long, are seldom tedious, but are listened to with the most profound respect. He is capable of performing a vast amount of good for his oppressed race."[10]

Douglass responded eagerly to the invitation to continue as a lecturing agent for the Massachusetts Society.[11] The winter and spring of 1842 found him again stumping through eastern and central Massachusetts in company with Garrison, Samuel J. May, Charles Lenox Remond, and the Hutchinsons, "the minessingers of American freedom," a musically self-trained family who sang anti-slavery songs. Everywhere his speeches aroused enthusiasm. By his talks, said the *Herald of Freedom,* Douglass had "already made color not only honorable, but enviable." On May 25, 1842, a newspaperman, not especially friendly to Abolition, heard Douglass speak at the Gordon Street Chapel in Boston and came away with "a sentiment of respect for his talent, his good sense, and his zeal in a cause. . . ."

"We have seldom heard a better speech before a popular assembly," he wrote in the *Boston Courier* of May 26, 1842, "better, we mean, as to the language and the manner. Many of the speakers who followed him, and of a lighter complexion, men, who boasted that they were ministers, and who had, doubtless the advantage of education, which the man of color could never have enjoyed, might well be desirous of emulating the appropriateness of his elocution and gesticulation, and the grammatical accuracy of his sentences."

Writing to Garrison from Northbridge, a veteran Abolitionist observed:

"It has been my fortune to hear a great many anti-slavery lecturers, and many distinguished speakers on other subjects; but it has rarely been my lot to listen to one whose power over me was greater than Douglass, and not over *me* only, but over all who heard him."[12]

But the life of a Negro anti-slavery agent was not all applause and praise. Douglass was forced to face the most humiliating discrimination in hotels, steamboats and railway cars. He resolved soon after he began his work as a lecturer to protest politely but firmly against segregation in public places and on common carriers. Consequently he was frequently handled roughly. Usually when a conductor asked him to leave and sit in the Jim-Crow car, he would ask: "If you will give me any good reason why I should leave this car, I'll go willingly; but without such reason, I do not feel at liberty to leave." The conductor invariably replied by calling in assistants and together they would drag the resisting Negro into the car set aside for the Negro people along with several seats he managed to hold onto. Invariably, too, Douglass was left bruised and with his clothes torn.

In many communities hoodlums attacked anti-slavery speakers and disrupted their meetings. Douglass was always the first to be singled out. In the middle of his speech he was often forced to leave the building followed by a mob howling, "get the n——r!" "kill the damn n——r!" Frequently, the meeting was held out-of-doors as it was impossible in many communities to find a hall or church that would permit a Negro to use its facilities. In Concord, New Hampshire, one Sunday afternoon, Douglass stood on a street-corner and collected an audience by appealing to the sympathies of the church-goers. In Grafton, Massachusetts, he wrote and distributed a leaflet announcing: "Frederick Douglass, a fugitive slave, will lecture on Grafton Common this evening at 8 o'clock. All who wish to hear the workings of Slavery from one of its own recipients are invited to attend." Because the leaflets were distributed late in the afternoon, Douglass feared that the citizens would think the meeting was planned for the following night. So he got a bell and made the rounds announcing his own meeting.

"The shoemaker left his bench," wrote a citizen of Grafton, "the mother her domestic avocations, to listen to the sound of the bell and the voice of the fugitive bondman, who announced himself as the speaker of the evening. At the hour appointed a multitude assembled, and Frederic[k] drove into their midst, and in his anti-slavery chaise he addressed an attentive audience for more than an hour."[13]

Douglass drew courage to brave all sorts of difficulties for the cause by the sympathy of a number of his white Abolitionist friends who would never allow him to suffer discrimination alone. Once on hearing that Douglass was compelled to ride in a filthy Jim-Crow box-car, Wendell Phillips stepped to his friend's side in the presence of a group of cultivated spectators and walked with him straight into the miserable car, saying: "Douglass, if you cannot ride with me, I can ride with you." Men like Phillips would go hungry rather than eat in a dining-room from which Douglass was excluded.

From the middle of August until the end of October, 1842, Douglass was employed by the American Anti-Slavery Society. He spent these months with Collins and Abby Kelley touring western New York. On August 30, he spoke for the first time in Rochester where he was to spend twenty years of his life. He was deeply impressed by the cordial and progressive community and the warm reception he received at the home of Isaac and Amy Post, two locally prominent Abolitionists. The pleasant memory of his first visit to Rochester greatly influenced Douglass in the choice of the city for the publication of his weekly paper, *The North Star,* in the fall of 1847.[14]

On his return from western New York Douglass was hurled into the struggle around the Latimer case. George Latimer, a fugitive slave, had fled to Boston from Norfolk, Virginia, in October, 1842. He was arrested without a warrant and thrown into a Boston jail solely on a warrant order to the jailer of Suffolk County from James B. Gray who claimed to be his owner. Friends rallied to the slave's side and demanded a trial by jury. When Chief Justice Shaw denied the demand and refused to grant a writ of habeas corpus, the movement to save Latimer gained tremendous momentum.

Boston was wild with excitement. Placards were distributed and handbills posted throughout the city denouncing the outrage, and summoning the citizens to a meeting in Faneuil Hall "For the Rescue of Liberty!" "Agitate! Agitate!" cried the *Liberator* of November 11, 1842. "Latimer *shall go free! . . .* Be vigilant, firm, uncompromising, friends of freedom! friends of God!" Whittier sent a clarion call from Massachusetts to Virginia:

> *No slave hunt in our borders,*
> *   no pirate on our strand!*
> *No fetters in the Bay State,*
> *   no slave upon our land!*

In the first public letter he ever wrote, dated Lynn, November 8, 1842, Douglass informed Garrison that in New Bedford Remond and he had spoken day and night during the first week of November in behalf of "our outraged brother" who had been "hunted down like a wild beast and ferociously dragged through the streets of Boston." All the meetings had been characterized "by that deep and solemn feeling which the importance of the cause, when properly set forth, is always calculated to awaken."[15]

In mid-November Latimer was purchased from Gray for four hundred dollars, and then set free. Around this event, the Abolitionists organized a series of celebrations with Latimer as the central figure. Douglass, a prominent speaker at the celebrations, was moved by Latimer's freedom to unusual brilliance.[16] The reporter for the *Salem Register* could not forget Douglass' address at the festivities in his city:

"The most wonderful performance of the evening was the address of Frederick Douglass himself a slave only four years ago! His remarks and his manner created the most indescribable sensations in the minds of those unaccustomed to hear *freemen* of color speak in public, much more to regard *a slave* as capable of such an effort. He was a living, speaking, *startling* proof of the folly, absurdity and inconsistency (to say nothing worse) of slavery. Fluent, graceful, eloquent, shrewd, sarcastic, he was without making any allowance, a fine specimen of an orator. He seemed to move the audience at his will, and they at times would hang upon his lips with staring eyes and open mouths, as eager to catch every word, as any 'sea of upturned faces' that ever rolled at the feet of Everett or Webster, to revel in their classic eloquence. Douglass possesses great powers of humor, which he indulged freely on Monday evening in giving some of the neatest and severest home thrusts at the 'peculiar institution' of which he professed to be a *graduate,* which it was ever our fortune to hear."[17]

In 1843, Douglass was occupied with the Hundred Conventions through which the Garrisonians hoped to build a strong movement in the western states. At the tenth annual meeting of the American Anti-Slavery Society, a proposal to hold a series of conventions in the West had been discussed, but the meeting adjourned before action could be taken. When the New England Society met in May, 1842, the matter received prominent attention, and, Douglass, a member of the Executive Committee, had urged the adoption of the proposal. The motion was promptly carried.[18]

Douglass, Remond, George Bradburn, John A. Collins, Jacob Ferris, William A. White of Watertown and Sidney B. Gay, editor of the *Anti-Slavery Standard,* were selected as speakers to tour the West. The agents, divided into two groups, were to move singly or in pairs to various towns in a county, and occasionally unite and exchange services. When a county had been thoroughly canvassed, the agents were to assemble for a gigantic meeting before going on to the next county. The tour was scheduled to last six months.

Douglass and Remond left in July and held their first meetings in Vermont where they met with unreceptive audiences. At Middlebury, students of the Congregationalist College placarded the town with posters describing Douglass as an escaped convict from the state prison. From Vermont they went to Syracuse where, owing to the opposition of the leaders of the Liberty Party, they were unable to secure a church or hall for their meeting. Undaunted, Douglass held his first meeting in a park and was gratified to see his audience grow from five persons to five hundred. During the following two days they addressed their audience in an abandoned church.[19]

But the question of a meeting place was the least of the difficulties Douglass faced in Syracuse. John A. Collins had become an enthusiastic disciple of Fourierism, the program of utopian socialism expounded in the United States by Albert Brisbane, Horace Greeley and George Ripley. In 1843, it was gaining numerous adherents. When Collins arrived in Syracuse, he set out to make converts for his new cause. At the anti-slavery meetings, he argued that the Abolitionist movement was "a mere dabbling with effects," that if slavery were abolished and private property allowed to exist, it would simply be abolition in form and not in fact, and that the universal reform movement would "do more for the Slave than the anti-slavery movement."

Douglass and Remond objected to Collins' tactics of organizing an anti-slavery meeting. After discoursing at length on the limitations of Abolition, Collins would invite the audience to attend a utopian socialist meeting to be held immediately after in the same hall. They criticized the preaching of Fourierism to an audience which had come to hear about the evils of slavery, and accused Collins of using the anti-slavery platform to convert the participants to utopian socialism. Douglass made it clear that Collins had a perfect right to advocate the abolition of all property rights and the establishment of a new social system; he even had the right to advocate anti-slavery and universal reform at the same time. But he decidely had no right to serve as an agent of the Anti-Slavery Society and attack Abolitionism as useless. Douglass felt strongly about this, confiding to Maria Weston Chapman of the Massachusetts Society that if the Board of Managers sanctioned Collins' conduct he would be compelled "to write them resigning my agency in carrying out the one hundred conventions plan." But Collins resigned as general agent of the Massachusetts Society, and Douglass continued his tour.[20]

It is important again to emphasize that while Douglass was not a utopian socialist, he sympathized with Collins' desire to establish a more "equalitarian society" in which all exploitation of man by man would be abolished. But like those who correctly criticized Socialists for claiming that the struggle for Negro rights was unimportant since with the abolition of capitalism all oppression would end, Douglass condemned Collins for considering the anti-slavery movement as unimportant. It is significant that Collins resigned as an anti-slavery agent because he was convinced that nothing could be accomplished through the Abolitionist movement.

From Syracuse Douglass went to Rochester and then to Buffalo where he attended the sessions of the National Convention of Colored Men. Then, with William A. White, they pushed on to Indiana, well aware that among the inhabitants were many former southerners who had not left behind their hatred of Abolitionism. Their fears were justified. Douglass had experienced rough handling many times since his first tour as an anti-slavery agent, but these were mild compared to what he met with in Pendleton, Indiana.

Douglass and White sensed trouble as soon as they entered Pendleton on September 15. Some of the townspeople were enraged because Dr. Fussell, a prominent local physician, had invited the ex-slave to be his house guest. Only because the meeting was cancelled by rain was violence avoided the first night. The following day the meeting in the woods had barely started when a mob of rowdies, armed with pistols, clubs, stones, and eggs, broke into the gathering and began howling, screeching, and hurling brickbats. Douglass was about to get away when he was told that White had been attacked and knocked down. He quickly decided that more than "moral suasion" was needed to handle this situation. As White wrote in a report to the *Liberator*:

"Frederick Douglass who, at the time, was safe among the friends, not seeing me, thought I was knocked down, and seizing a club, rushed into the crowd. His weapon was immediately snatched from him. . . . [He] fled for his life, and ten or more of the mob followed, crying, 'kill the n——r, kill the damn n——r.' . . . The leader of the mob soon overtook him, and knocked him down and struck him once with his club, and was raising it the second time to level a blow which must have been fatal had it fallen, but I, by dint of hard running, came up in time to throw myself upon him, and stop him in his murderous purpose. . . ."

Douglass, nursed by Mrs. Fussell, was able to speak at a meeting the next day. But he never forgot the experience. Three years later he wrote to White that it still "haunted his dreams." He had gone "to bed thinking about Pendleton."[21]

After Pendleton, the rest of the trip eastward was almost routine. Everywhere they went the people wanted to hear Douglass. "All along in this State," George Bradburn wrote from Ohio, "as elsewhere, our friends complain of being made to lie to the people, in announcing Douglass for our meetings." The agents concluded their tour at Philadelphia where they joined in the celebration of the tenth anniversary of the formation of the American Anti-Slavery Society.

The Board of Managers of the Massachusetts Anti-Slavery Society hailed the Hundred Conventions as a "magnificent movement." "We doubt," they declared, "whether there has ever been in the history of the cause, so great an amount of wholesale agitation produced at so small an expense or accomplished in so short a time." Although less than $450 had been collected by the agents during their tour, the society at its annual convention in January, 1844, voted to sponsor a series of one hundred conventions within the Bay State. Douglass, White, and Pillsbury were chosen to cover the territory and in the winter months of 1844 they traveled through the central counties of Massachusetts.[22]

Once again the agents met with a favorable response. At Concord, New Hampshire, "the house was crowded with the best of our people—no clergy—and but few of the bigots who are past hearing." Douglass, wrote the reporter for the *Herald of Freedom,* "made a masterly and most impressive speech":

"It was not what you could describe as oratory or eloquence. It was sterner, darker, deeper than these. It was the volcanic outbreak of human nature, long pent up in slavery and at last bursting its imprisonment. It was the storm of insurrection; and I could not but think, as he stalked to and fro on the platform, roused up like the Numidian lion, how that terrible voice of his would ring through the pine glades of the South, in the day of her visitation, calling the insurgents to battle, and striking terror to the hearts of the dismayed and despairing mastery. He reminded me of Toussaint among the plantations of Haiti. There was a great oratory in his speech, but more of dignity and earnestness than what we call eloquence. He was not up as a speaker, performing. He was an insurgent slave, taking hold on the right of speech, and charging on his tyrants the bondage of his race. One of our editors ventured to cross his path by a rash remark. He better have run upon a lion. It was fearful, but magnificent, to see how magnanimously and lion-like the royal fellow tore him to pieces, and left his untouched fragments scattered around him.

" . . . He is a surprising lecturer. I would not praise him, or describe him; but he is a colored man, a slave, of the race who can't take care of themselves—our inferiors, and therefore to be kept in slavery—an abolitionist, and therefore to be despised. . . . He is one of the most impressive and majestic speakers I have ever heard. The close of his address Sunday was unrivalled. I have heard the leading anti-slavery speakers, as well as the pro-slavery orators, and the great advocates at the bar; and I have never seen a man leave the platform, or close a speech, with more real dignity, and eloquent majesty. . . ."[23]

Pleased though they were with Douglass' effectiveness on the platform, his associates were becoming convinced that his development had been too rapid. As early as 1841 Stephen S. Foster had warned Douglass, "People won't believe that you were ever a slave, Frederick, if you keep on in this way." Collins had added, "Better have a little of the plantation speech than not; it is not best that you seem too learned." But Douglass refused to be stereotyped and stunted, and despite repeated exhortations to "give us the facts, we will take care of the philosophy," he refused to confine himself to repeating the story of his life over and over again.

"I could not always follow the injunction," he wrote later, "for I was now reading and thinking. New views of the subject were being presented to my mind. It did not entirely satisfy me to narrate wrongs; I felt like denouncing them. . . . Besides I was growing and needed room."[24]

The conflict on this issue was inevitable. Many middle and upper-class white Abolitionists could not see the former Negro slave as anything but an exhibit. The white anti-slavery leaders would be the main actors; the Negroes would be the extras or only part of the stage props. Some white Abolitionists were sorry to see Douglass' rapid development as a brilliant thinker and orator. Instead of being proud that this former Negro slave had been able in such a short time to equal and even surpass many of the white spokesmen against slavery, they were worried by it and even resented it.

Yet Douglass was soon to discover that the fears of his advisers were not entirely groundless. He began to hear and read statements expressing doubt as to his ever having seen slavery.

"Many persons in the audience," wrote a Philadelphia correspondent in the *Liberator* of August 30, 1844, "seemed unable to credit the statements which he gave of himself, and could not believe that he was actually a slave. How a man, only six years out of bondage, and who had never gone to school a day in his life, could speak with such eloquence—with such precision of language and power of thought—they were utterly at a loss to devise."

Douglass was aware that if such reports continued, they would be fatal to his effectiveness as an Abolitionist agent. So he resolved to throw caution to the winds and write the story of his life. During the winter months of 1844-1845 he was busily engaged in setting down an account of his slave experiences. His *Narrative of the Life of Frederick Douglass,* a small volume of 125 pages selling for fifty cents, with introductions by Garrison and Phillips, came off the press in May, 1845. The book immediately became a fast seller, was translated into French and German, and, by January, 1848, when eleven thousand copies had been published in this country, it had gone through nine editions in England. One of a long series of autobiographies of fugitive slaves, it was by far the most effective. "Considered merely as a narrative," went a review in the *New York Tribune,* "we never read one more simple, true, coherent and warm with genuine feeling. It is an excellent piece of writing, and on that score to be prized as a specimen of the powers of the black race, which prejudice persists in disputing." The reviewer for the *Lynn Pioneer* considered that "the book, as a whole, judged as a mere work of art, would widen the fame of Bunyan or Defoe. It is the most thrilling work which the American press ever issued—*and the most important.* If it does not open the eyes of this people, they must be petrified into eternal sleep."[25]

" . . . I have many times heard the author vividly portray the evils of slavery [a woman reader wrote to Garrison]. I have often heard him recount with deep feeling the endless wrongs they are made to endure—but, oh! never before have I been brought so completely in sympathy with the slave—never before have I so fully realized the doctrine of our blessed Savior, 'Whatsoever ye do unto the least one of these, ye do it unto me.' . . . May his narrative incite us to renewed diligence in our labors for the slave! May the author become a mighty instrument to the pulling down of the strongholds of iniquity, and to the establishing of righteousness in our land!"

The *Narrative* was immediately popular in England and Ireland; newspaper notices lauded "its native eloquence." It furnished evidence that "the argument, if it can be so termed, which would uphold slavery on the ground of the slaves' natural inferiority, has no foundation as regards such a man as the writer, and therefore totally fails in its general application." One editor spoke of Douglass as "a fugitive slave, who, as but yesterday, escaped from a bondage that doomed him to ignorance and degradation, now stands up and rebukes oppression with a dignity and a fervor scarcely less glowing than that which Paul addressed to Agrippa."[26]

At the meeting of the New England Society in Boston on May 27, 1845, a resolution was adopted which "joyfully" welcomed "to our ranks the new anti-slavery lecturer, the *Narrative of the Life of Frederick Douglass,*" and commended it to all "who believe the slaves of the South to be either well treated, or happy, or ignorant of their right to freedom, or in need of preparation to make them fit for freedom." Ironically enough, when Wendell Phillips, who proposed the resolution, had first read Douglass' manuscript, he had advised the author to burn it before it went to press, fearing that since the book unmistakably divulged his identity and that of his master, he would no longer be safe in the United States. Douglass refused to heed his friend's advice, but he recognized the basis for his fears. This knowledge that his life and liberty were now in jeopardy hastened his determination to go abroad, a desire that had been growing in his mind for several months.[27] Another and probably a stronger reason for his decision to visit Europe was expressed by James N. Buffum, one of Douglass' closest friends, in a letter to Gerrit Smith on June 21, 1845:

"I write to inform you that our friend and co-labourer Frederick Douglass has concluded to visit Europe this season, to lay before the people of that country the claim of the Slave. He has come to this conclusion after a time of deliberation and consultation, with many of our wisest and best friends. He will go out as a representative from the prison-house of bondage and not as the representative of any sect or party. He will stand up before that people as one who has experienced the withering and blighting influence of Slavery upon his own Soul. His friends are confident that he will be of great service to the cause, in exciting a deeper hatred in the breasts of the English people of American Slavery, and thereby creating a warmer sympathy for our cause. When they shall see before them a man so noble and eloquent as Frederick, and learn from his own lips, that he is only seven years out of bondage; that he has now the marks of the whip upon his back, which he will carry with him until the day of his death, that he has near and dear relatives that are now pining in bondage; they will realize to a considerable extent, the horrors of the American Slave trade; the effect cannot be otherwise than good.

"In years past, the friends of the slave in this country have been cheered and encouraged by the contributions and words of sympathy which have come to them from across the waters, from the philanthropists of Europe. To express to them our deep appreciation of their benevolent labours, to encourage them to continue their friendly assistance, will be among the objects of Frederick's mission."[28]

Douglass' reluctance to leave his family which now included two more baby boys, Frederick, Junior, and Charles Remond,[29] was assuaged by the knowledge that the proceeds from the sale of the *Narrative* would go to his wife, thus substituting for his earnings on the lecture platform.[30] With a purse of $250 raised by Abolitionist friends and $350 saved from the sale of his autobiography, with letters from Phillips and Maria W. Chapman to sympathizers in England,[31] Douglass prepared to sail for Liverpool.

When Douglass left the United States he was already being hailed as the rising star among the Negro people. Wendell Phillips spoke for all the Garrisonians when he wrote to Elizabeth Pease of London: "If you ever see him, Remember that *in my opinion*, you see the most remarkable and by far the ablest colored man we have ever had here."[32] Douglass was even known to many Negroes in the South. An editor of the Philadelphia *Elevator,* a Negro paper, disclosed that when he went to Maryland, he had been visited "by at least a dozen colored persons, some of them slaves, and others freemen, who had heard that we knew Frederick at the North, and who wished to hear news of their old friend. They knew him by his assumed name as well as by his real name and related to us many interesting incidents about their former companion."[33]

"Be yourself," Phillips told Douglass as he was departing for England. "Be yourself, and you will succeed." Not even Phillips, however, dreamed that the success would reach such heights. His European visit gave Douglass an international reputation. He returned to the States a world figure, a mighty power for freedom.

A Chattel Becomes a Man

On August 16, 1845, accompanied by the Hutchinsons and James N. Buffum, Douglass sailed for Liverpool on the Cunard steamer *Cambria.* Buffum's efforts to get first-class passage for Douglass had failed for what was politely referred to as "complexional reasons," and Douglass was forced to travel steerage. Every morning during the eleven-day trip, however, he joined his colleagues on the promenade deck, mingled with the passengers, and sold copies of the *Narrative.* The captain of the steamer was disposed to be friendly to his Negro passenger and ignored the protests of southerners on board. But the night before the *Cambria* docked at Liverpool, the explosion came. Douglass, at the invitation of the captain, was lecturing on American slavery. He was constantly interrupted by catcalls, and as soon as he finished a sentence several slaveholders would yell out, "That's a lie!" When he offered to present documentary proof, they rushed at him with clenched fists. The captain knocked down one man and quieted the others by threatening to put them in irons.[1]

The cordial reception in Liverpool made it easier for Douglass to push out of his mind the bad experience on board ship. Three days after landing, Douglass and Buffum, parting company with the Hutchinsons, left for Dublin. Douglass stayed at the home of Richard D. Webb, the local agent of the *Anti-Slavery Standard,* and arranged with his host for the printing of two thousand copies of the *Narrative* for which he would not have to pay until the whole edition was sold.[2]

In Dublin, Douglass was amazed by the response to his anti-slavery work. "Our success here," he wrote to Garrison on September 16, "is even greater than I had anticipated. We have held four glorious anti-slavery meetings—two in Royal Exchange, and two in the Friends' meeting-house —all crowded to overflowing."

From the beginning of his stay in Europe, Douglass became involved in many reform movements. First he resisted this tendency, believing that he should reserve all of his efforts for the anti-slavery cause. But he soon became convinced that it was impossible to divide the struggle against oppression into separate compartments. On February 26, 1846 he explained his decision to Garrison:

" . . . though I am more closely connected and identified with one class of outraged, oppressed and enslaved people, I cannot allow myself to be insensible to the wrongs and sufferings of any part of the great family of man. I am not only an American slave, but a man, and as such, am bound to use my powers for the welfare of the whole human brotherhood."[3]

Douglass endorsed the temperance crusade sponsored by Father Theobald Mathew and spoke out for the repeal of the Act of Union which almost a half-century before had abolished the Irish Parliament. The very day of his arrival in Dublin, he spoke at a temperance gathering, and later delivered several temperance addresses in the city. In late September he spoke at a huge repeal meeting at Convention Hall where he shared honors with Daniel O'Connell, the Irish liberator. Douglass sat enthralled by O'Connell's oratory and his courageous message. O'Connell announced that he was not ashamed of being assailed for attacking American slavery and proclaimed that wherever slavery existed he was "the enemy of the system or the institution."[4]

After five happy weeks in Dublin, Douglass left for Cork. Here he was no less successful. He spoke at eleven public meetings, addressing overflow audiences on each occasion, the "suffering poor," as the *Cork Examiner* put it, "thronging to listen to exposures of the American slave system by one who has in his own person suffered under its iniquities." As in Dublin, he spoke on temperance as well as anti-slavery. He even took the temperance pledge from Father Mathew, observing that he was "the fifth of the last five of Father Mathew's 5,487,495 temperance children."[5]

Leaving Cork with the hearty good wishes of a large circle of friends, Douglass went to Belfast, then to Liverpool and Birmingham. In Birmingham he spoke to an audience of seven thousand at the annual meeting of the Birmingham Temperance Society. He then returned to Belfast on December 19 for another lecture. "I had expected a good deal from Mr. Douglass," wrote a correspondent of the *London Inquirer* from Belfast, "from what I had seen of him in public prints; but high as were my expectations, they were more than realized. He is, in truth, a wonderful man. . . . Who could listen to his heart-rending description of the horrors of slavery, and not heartily hate the institution." At a public breakfast in his honor, presided over by a member of Parliament, Douglass was presented with a fine edition of the Bible by the Belfast Auxiliary of the British and Foreign Anti-Slavery Society.

The four months Douglass spent in Ireland were the happiest he had ever known in his life. The complete lack of anti-Negro prejudice, the open door everywhere made him cry out for joy.

"The warm and generous cooperation extended to me by the friends of my despised race," he wrote to Garrison from Belfast on January 1, 1846, "the prompt and liberal manner with which the press has rendered me its aid—the glorious enthusiasm with which thousands have flocked to hear the cruel wrongs of my down-trodden and long enslaved countrymen portrayed—the deep sympathy of the slave, and the strong abhorrence of the slaveholder, everywhere evinced—the cordiality with which members and ministers of various religious bodies, and of various shades of religious opinion, have embraced me and lent me their aid—the kind hospitality constantly proffered to me by persons of the highest rank in society—the spirit of freedom that seems to animate all with whom I come in contact—and the entire absence of everything that looked like prejudice against me, on account of the color of my skin—contrasting so strongly with my long and bitter experience in the United States, that I look with wonder and amazement on the transition."[6]

After more than fifty lectures in Ireland, Douglass went to Scotland which he found "in a blaze of anti-slavery agitation." Here he and Buffum, who had rejoined him, became involved in the exciting battle to compel the Free Church of Scotland to return contributions made by American slaveholders. The Free Church (an organization based on the right of congregations to control the appointment of their own ministers) had sent a deputation to the United States in 1844 to form an alliance with churches in this country and to solicit funds to build Free Churches and pay Free ministers in Scotland. An outburst of indignation arose from American Abolitionists when the delegation announced its intention of visiting the southern states, but, ignoring these protests, the delegates raised £3,000 from slaveholders, entering into an alliance with southern churches. They justified their action by denouncing the Abolitionists as belonging to the tradition of "the infidels and anarchists of the French Revolution," asserting that the slaveholders were "entitled to be regarded as respectable, useful, honoured Christians, living under the power of the truth, labouring faithfully, and serving God in the Gospel of His Son." Most members of the Free Church in Scotland were not impressed either by the diatribe against the American Abolitionists or by the eulogy of the slaveholders, and a loud cry arose that the money collected in the South was tainted and should be returned. Douglass added his voice to this demand, speaking in halls decorated with posters proclaiming the slogan of the day—"*Send Back the Money.*" "We shall continue to deal our blows upon them—crying out disgorge—disgorge—disgorge your horrid plunder," he wrote to Francis Jackson from Dundee, "and to this the great mass of the people here have cried Amen, Amen."[7]

Douglass toured Scotland during the spring of 1846. The most memorable part of the trip was his visit to Ayr, the birthplace of Robert Burns. An "enthusiastic admirer" of the Scottish poet, Douglass was happy to see the cottage where Burns was born and where so many of his favorite poems had been written. He cherished for a long time his meeting with Burns's sister, Mrs. Geggs. "I have ever esteemed Robert Burns," he wrote after the visit, ". . . but never could I have had the opinion of the man or his genius, which I now entertain, without my present knowledge of the country, to which he belonged—the times in which he lived, and the broad Scotch tongue in which he wrote."[8]

Douglass' happiness in Scotland was marred by an incident which was to have an important bearing on his relations with his Abolitionist friends at home. Maria Weston Chapman, leader of the Boston Female Anti-Slavery Society and editor of its gift-book, the *Liberty Bell,* had written to Richard D. Webb warning the Irish Abolitionist to keep an eye on Douglass and Buffum lest they be won over by the anti-Garrisonian wing of the English anti-slavery movement. Mrs. Chapman, it seemed, was not too concerned about Buffum who was wealthy, but was worried lest Douglass "might be bought up by the London committee." Douglass, when shown the letter, was furious at the lack of faith in his integrity and sent a sharp rebuke to Mrs. Chapman assuring her that he was still a Garrisonian, but pointing out in clear and decisive language that he would not tolerate any efforts to supervise and control his activities. "If you wish to drive me from the Anti-Slavery Society," he wrote, "put me under overseership and the work is done. Set some one to watch over me for evil and let them be so simple minded as to inform me of their office, and the last blow is struck."[9]

That Douglass was capable of thinking for himself on major issues confronting the anti-slavery movement and was prepared to challenge the Abolitionist leaders when he believed they were wrong is illustrated by two incidents which occurred about this time. When Richard D. Webb objected to the inclusion of letters of endorsement from clergymen in the English edition of the *Narrative,* the Negro shot back:

"You ought to have thought of your prejudice against priests sooner. If clergymen read my *Narrative* and approve of it, my prejudice against their office would be but a poor reason, for rejecting the benefit of such approval. The enclosed is from Mr. Nelson the Presbyterian Minister. I wish both it and that of Dr. Drew to be inserted in the second edition. To leave them out because they are ministers would be to show oneself as much and more sectarian than themselves. It would be virtually forbidding their casting out devils because they follow not us. The spirit of bigotry and sectarianism may exist, and be as deeply rooted in those who condemn sects, as those who adhere to them."[10]

While in Edinburgh, Douglass was invited by George Thompson, a leading English Abolitionist, to speak at a mammoth public meeting to be arranged in London under the auspices of the British and Foreign Anti-Slavery Society, which six years before had broken away from the Garrisonians. Well aware that his friends in America would look with disfavor upon his presence at the meeting, Douglass believed that it was his duty to "speak in any meeting where freedom of speech is allowed and where I may do any thing toward exposing the bloody system of slavery." Hence, he accepted the invitation, making it clear that his presence did not signify an endorsement of the doctrines of the organization.[11]

On his arrival in London, Douglass learned that a crowded schedule had been planned for him. "Frederick has crammed a year's sensations into the last five days," wrote George Thompson on May 23. "On Monday he poured forth at the Anti-Slavery Meeting. On Tuesday at the Peace Meeting. On Wednesday at the Complete Suffrage Meeting. On Thursday at the Temperance Meeting, and last night he had an audience of 2,500 to hear him for nearly three hours. . . ."[12] At the final meeting held at Finsbury Chapel in his honor, "with the edifice crowded to suffocation," Douglass delivered a devastating attack on American slavery. Out of his own personal experience, he presented one picture after another showing the horrors of the slave system. To the charge that American affairs should not be discussed in other countries, he replied that slavery in America was not America's problem alone, but the problem of mankind; that slavery was so monstrous a sin that no single nation by itself could achieve its removal. Since America lacked the moral stamina to remove this blight on her free institutions, he called on the people of Britain to assist in the struggle. He concluded on the following note:

"To tear off the mask from this abominable system, to expose it to the light of heaven, aye, to the heat of the sun, that it may burn and wither it out of existence, is my object in coming to this country. I want the slaveholder surrounded, as by a wall of anti-slavery fire, so that he may see the condemnation of himself and his system glaring down in letters of light. . . . I would have condemnation blaze down upon him in every direction, till, stunned and overwhelmed with shame and confusion, he is compelled to let go the grasp he holds upon the persons of his victims, and restore them to their long-lost rights."[13]

At the conclusion of the address, Thompson arose and referred to a conversation in which Douglass spoke of how he missed his wife and children. Thompson proposed a subscription to bring Douglass' family to England. Fifty pounds were contributed while he was talking and thirty more at the end of his appeal. Thompson was certain that "an ample sum" would be raised "to bring them over and make them comfortable while they are among us."[14]

In the summer of 1846 Douglass was happy to have William Lloyd Garrison with him in England. The Abolitionist leader had been invited by the Glasgow Emancipation Society in the belief that his influence would be decisive in the campaign to compel the Free Church to return the gift to the southern clergy. On July 31 Garrison arrived at Liverpool and a few days later he and Douglass began a journey from one part of England to the other—reorganizing the enemies of slavery in Britain and denouncing the slaveholders and their apologists in America. On August 4, they attended the opening session of the World Temperance Convention held at Covent Garden Theater in London. Neither was an official delegate, but they were "politely furnished . . . with a ticket" admitting them as members of the convention.

Before the convention adjourned, Douglass had stirred up a hornet's nest with a speech attacking the official American temperance movement. He was sorry that he could not join the American delegates in lauding the progress of the cause in their country while there were three million American slaves beyond the pale of the American Temperance Society and four hundred thousand free Negroes almost as completely excluded as the slaves. He reminded the audience that on August 1, 1842, members of a temperance society in Philadelphia, composed solely of Negroes, had been assaulted by a ruthless mob, beaten and dispersed when they attempted to augment their ranks by parading through the streets. One of their churches was burned and their temperance hall destroyed. Worried by the heated emotions these remarks were arousing, the chairman whispered to Douglass that his speaking time had expired. With shouts from the audience urging him "go on! go on!" Douglass continued for a few minutes, but refrained from further reference to anything "that particularly related to the colored people of America."

The American delegates were furious. Reverend Kirk, a Boston clergyman, charged that Douglass had given a false picture of the temperance societies in the United States. Reverend Samuel Hanson Cox of Brooklyn, New York delivered a broadside against Douglass in a long, angry letter to the *New York Evangelist*. He branded him as a "colored Abolition agitator, and ultraist," charging him with "ruining almost everything [at the convention] that had preceded him." He accused him of lugging into a temperance convention an anti-slavery discussion and said he had "been well paid for the abomination." To top it all, he claimed that Douglass was trying to arouse a war spirit in England and America.

Douglass' reply to Reverend Cox was extremely effective and resulted in making friends for himself and the Abolition cause in England and in his own country. He emphasized that the motive for the attack was to ruin his influence in Britain. He pleaded guilty to the charge of being an Abolitionist, an ultraist, and expressed pride in his connection with the struggle to overthrow slavery. Furthermore, he denied the impropriety of discussing slavery in the temperance meeting and the statement that his speech had ruined all that had preceded him. He denied receiving pay for the speech he had made, but declared he had as much right to receive pay for speaking as Reverend Cox for preaching. In one of his brilliant sallies of sarcasm aimed at Dr. Cox, he said:

"And is slavery only an 'imputed evil'? Now, suppose I had lugged in anti-slavery (which I deny)—you profess to be an Abolitionist. You, therefore, ought to have been the last man in the world to have found fault with me, on that account. Your great love of liberty, and sympathy for the downtrodden slave ought to have led you to 'pardon something for the spirit of Liberty,' especially in one who had the scars of the slave-driver's whip on his back, and who, at this moment, has four sisters and one brother in slavery. But, Sir, you are not an Abolitionist, and you only assumed to be one during your recent tour in this country, that you might *sham* your way through this land, and the more effectually stab and blast the character of the real friends of emancipation. Who ever heard of a true Abolitionist speaking of slavery as an 'imputed evil,' or complaining of being 'wounded or injured' by an allusion to it—and that, too, because that allusion was in opposition to the infernal system? You took no offence when the Rev. Mr. Kirk assumed the Christian name and character for slaveholders in the World's Temperance Convention. You were not 'wounded or injured,'—it was not a 'perversion, an abuse, an iniquity against the law of reciprocal righteousness.' You have no indignation to pour out upon him. Oh, no! But when a *fugitive slave* merely alluded to slavery as obstructing the moral and social improvement of my race, you were 'wounded and injured,' and rendered indignant! This, sir, tells the whole story of your abolitionism, and stamps your pretensions to abolition as brazen hypocrisy or self-deception."[15]

Douglass' conflict with Reverend Cox revealed to a wide public on both sides of the Atlantic that in the North as well as the South there was an indifferent, if not pro-slavery, element among the clergy who did not want the evils of slavery exposed to the intelligence of the world. It also showed how deeply the pro-slavery forces feared the influence of the brilliant fugitive slave and how eagerly they sought to silence him.

Pro-slavery journals in the United States went to ridiculous lengths in their demands that the British refuse Douglass a platform, even arguing that the Negro orator was embarrassing the three million Negro people held in slavery. "The slaves," said one journal, "would be very indignant at the conduct of their representative in England could they be made acquainted with his tantrums." There was scarcely a Negro "on a South Carolina rice plantation, or in a Louisiana sugar house, but what, amid all his degradation, would scorn the acts of Frederick Douglass. The man is lowering, in the eyes of English courtesy and intelligence, the character of our slave population."[16]

To the charge that he was a menace to his native land because he was "running amuck in greedy-eared Britain against America, its people, its institutions, and even against its peace," Douglass had a ready answer. At one time, he declared, America and the American people were regarded in Europe as "the best friends and truest representatives" of the sacred cause of freedom. But the growth of slavery had created the very opposite attitude toward the United States. A person truly devoted to the interests of America and its people would seek to restore the United States to its former position as the symbol of freedom. "I am earnestly and anxiously laboring to wipe off this foul blot from the otherwise fair fame of the

American people," he wrote to Horace Greeley from Glasgow on April 15, 1846, "that they may accomplish in behalf of human freedom that which their exalted position among the nations of the earth amply fits them to do."[17]

Within a week after the Temperance Convention, Garrison formed an "Anti-Slavery League for all England," its main function being to co-operate with the American Anti-Slavery Society. At the League's first public meeting, held on August 17 at the Crown and Anchor Tavern, Henry C. Wright opened with a speech that was a "scorcher." Douglass followed, "making one of his very best efforts." "I never saw an audience more delighted," Garrison wrote to his wife. The five and a half hour meeting closed with a speech by Henry Vincent, a Chartist leader. Garrison felt encouraged by the proceedings which he described as "a real, old-fashioned, old-organized American anti-slavery meeting (such, as I am quite certain, as was never before held in *England*)."[18]

Late in August, the American Abolitionists held a meeting at Bristol. Although there was an admission charge, they spoke to an overflowing audience. The presence of the mayor of the city gave the proceedings a stiff, formal tone which took the "warmth" out of Garrison and caused Douglass to "labor under embarassment." Still the Negro made "one of his very best speeches which produced a powerful effect." From Bristol Douglass and his mentor went to Exeter and then back to London where they spent a Sunday afternoon "rolling balls on the greensward" with a Unitarian minister.[19]

Towards the end of September the visiting reformers became involved in another battle. The preceding year, a group, composed mainly of Methodists and Free Church adherents, had formed an International Evangelical Alliance. In August, 1846, at its first big meeting, the Alliance began consideration of the question of excluding slaveholders from membership. But a committee, headed by Reverend Cox, introduced a report which skillfully avoided the main question, and the Conference accepted this report with a sigh of relief.

Thus, no action was taken on slaveholder membership. But the London Abolitionists were not so easily satisfied, and, viewing the Alliance's action as an approval of slavery, called a public demonstration of protest for September 14. Garrison and Douglass were invited to share the platform with George Thompson. Hisses from Alliance sympathizers in the audience greeted Garrison when he opened the meeting, with the only effect that his speech was "less consecutive than it otherwise would have been." He was followed by Thompson who proposed a series of resolutions condemning the Alliance. Douglass brought the meeting to a close with an address which was "warmly applauded."

Following the anti-Alliance demonstration, Douglass left for northern England and Scotland. On September 25 he spoke at Sunderland in Durham County with Mayor Robert Brown in the chair. The reporter for the Durham County *Herald* was lavish with his praise. "We have rarely listened to an orator so gifted by nature," he wrote, "and never to a man who more thoroughly threw his whole heart into the work in which he is engaged." The orator journeyed to Glasgow, Paisley, Edinburgh, and Dundee as an agent of the Scottish Anti-Slavery Society, and returned to Liverpool on October 10 to meet Garrison. There by a pleasant coincidence while having breakfast one morning he happened to see a former slave associate of his in Baltimore. It was a happy reunion, and for several hours the two friends sat discussing their former life in the South and comparing notes on their experiences since their escape from bondage.[20]

Early in November Garrison sailed for America. Douglass' thoughts, too, had been turning homeward. Although England offered a permanent home for himself and his family, free from all the hardships incident to life for a Negro in America, Douglass refused to stay. There was too much to be done at home; he was anxious to get into the struggle being led by the Abolitionists against the Mexican War and to do what he could to defeat the forces who were "calling upon the free citizens ....to leave their homes families and friends to go and fight the plundering battles of Slave holding Texas." In one of his most eloquent utterances he told a London audience:

"Since I have been in this land I have had every inducement to stop here. . . . I should have settled down here in a different position to what I should have been placed in the United States. But, sir, I prefer living a life of activity in the service of my brethren. I choose rather to go home; to return to America. I glory in the conflict, that I may hereafter exult in the victory. I know that victory is certain. I go, turning my back upon the ease, comfort, and respectability which I might maintain even here, ignorant as I am. Still, I will go back, for the sake of my brethren. I go to suffer with them; to toil with them; to endure insult with them; to undergo outrage with them; to lift up my voice in their behalf; to speak and write in their vindication; and struggle in their ranks for that emancipation which shall yet be achieved by the power of truth and of principle for that oppressed people."[21]

Douglass was fully aware that his former master was biding his time and awaiting his return to begin proceedings to have him restored to slavery. In July he had written to his old friend White for advice: "William do you think it would be safe for me to come home this fall? Would master Hugh stand much chance in Mass.? Think he could take me from the old Bay State? The old fellow is evidently anxious to get hold of me." Despite this concern over his safety Douglass was determined to return home and wrote his wife to expect him on November 20. Only the insistence of Garrison and Thompson that he stay abroad at least six months longer led him to alter his plans.[22]

When Douglass finally did return to America in the spring of 1847, he came home a free man. Late in 1846, his English friends, led by Ellen and Anna Richardson of Newcastle, had raised $710.96 to purchase his emancipation from Hugh Auld to whom his brother Thomas had transferred ownership. What a day in the life of Frederick Douglass when the bill of sale was handed over to him by his benefactors![23]

Douglass' joy was somewhat diminished by the storm of criticism the news of his freedom aroused among groups of Abolitionists in the United States. They charged that the purchase was a recognition of the "right to traffic in human beings." It was also "impolitic and inexpedient" because by the ransom Douglass had "lost much of that moral power which he possessed, as the representative of the three millions of his countrymen in chains, taking, as he did, his life in his hands, appearing, wherever he appeared, with all the liabilities which the law laid upon him to be returned to stripes, torture and death." Garrison, who had "gladly contributed" his "mite" to the purchase fund was deluged with indignant letters accusing him of having violated a cardinal principle of the anti-slavery creed. Justifying the negotiation, he reminded his critics that although he had always contended that the demand of the slaveholder for compensation "was an unjust one," he had never maintained that it was wrong "to ransom one held in cruel bondage." "We deny," Garrison editorialized, "that purchasing the freedom of a slave is necessarily an implied acknowledgment of the master's right to property in human beings."[24]

The heated controversy raged for more than three months in the columns of the *Liberator* and other anti-slavery journals. In a reply to Henry C. Wright who had urged him to repudiate the transaction, Douglass stressed the practical importance of the purchase, called Wright's attention to the fact that as a fugitive slave he could be seized by his master and returned to slavery the moment he set foot in the United States, and assured him that his changed status would not weaken the bonds that connected him with the slaves. "I shall be Frederick Douglass still," he concluded his masterly defense, "once a slave still. I shall neither be made to forget nor cease to feel the wrongs of my enslaved fellow-countrymen. My knowledge of slavery will be the same and my hatred of it will be the same."[25]

Douglass' last months abroad were so crammed with lecture engagements that in one month, he spoke almost every night. By March the pace was beginning to tell, and some of his addresses lacked their usual forceful delivery. An observer at Warrington noted that he appeared "to be suffering from great debility owing to the large amount of fatigue he has lately endured." Nevertheless he continued to score success after success and to convert large audiences to the cause.

Late in March Douglass prepared for his departure. In London, on March 30, his friends tendered him a public farewell attended by 1,400 persons "of great respectability." Deeply moved, the honored guest spoke regretfully of leaving the country in which he had been treated "with utmost kindness, with the utmost deference, with the utmost attention." He had known these last nineteen months "what it was for the first time in my life to enjoy freedom." The oppressed Negro people would know how England felt about slavery, and that it "would give them patience under their sorrows, and hope of a future emancipation." He would always remember the "sea of upturned faces" at the farewell meeting, for it would be "daguerreotyped upon my heart."[26]

A few days later Douglass left for Liverpool. Here he was brought back to the realities of the life that faced him in his native land. In London he had purchased a ticket for passage on the *Cambria*, but on reaching Liverpool he was informed by the Cunard agent that he could not sail unless he agreed to relinquish the berth he had ordered. These measures, he was assured, were merely precautionary. Douglass had caused a commotion on his previous passage, and the company was seeking to prevent a repetition of the disturbance.

Douglass was furious, but anxious to return home, he yielded. In a letter to the London *Times,* he laid the facts before the British public, confident that it would "pronounce a just verdict on such proceedings." His confidence was more than justified. The British press promptly condemned the agent's action in editorials carrying the headings: "A British Bow to an American Prejudice," "Pro-Slavery Persecution in England,"

"Shameful Violation of the Rights of Man," "Disgraceful Prejudice Against a Man of Color," "England Made Ashamed," "American Intolerance in the Port of Liverpool," "Disgraceful Conduct Toward Frederick Douglass, The Liberated Slave." "We call upon the whole nation," cried *Howitt's Journal,* "to resent this disgrace to the English name! . . . to demand of Government to take up the matter, and to insist on the Line of Packet Company making a public apology for this surrender of the honour of the British nation." The apology came sooner than the *Journal* had expected. In a public letter to the editor of the *Times,* S. Cunard expressed his regrets and guaranteed that "nothing of the kind will *again take place in the steamships with which I am connected.*" Even then the incident was not too quickly forgotten in England, and Elizabeth Pease was confident that the exclusion of Douglass "will do more . . . to help the anti-slavery cause than all the lectures which F. D. has delivered on this side of the Atlantic—powerful and convincing as they have been."[27]

In his enforced privacy during the sixteen-day voyage across the Atlantic, Douglass had ample opportunity to reflect on the exciting experiences of the previous twenty months. They were happy memories. His experiences on stage-coaches, railroads, steamboats, and in taverns, hotels, and other public places had not been marred by a single instance of discrimination. He had made many warm friends and acquired a host of admirers. He had come to know many of the most distinguished men in Britain—Clarkson, Lovett, Richard Cobden, John Bright, Benjamin Disraeli, Robert Peel, Daniel O'Connell, Lord Brougham, George Thompson. He had left behind in England thousands of people who were now more than ever convinced that "a system which can doom such men as Douglass to the whip and fetter" must be destroyed. And his visit was to play an important part in increasing the sentiment in Britain toward the achievement of that goal.

He had left America a slave, he was returning a free man. He had come to England almost unknown, he was now famous. In his own country his prestige had increased. "He will be warmly welcomed by the Abolitionists," wrote Garrison upon learning that Douglass had sailed, "and, doubtless, more kindly regarded by people generally, in consequence of the generous and honorable reception given him in Great Britain." Small wonder Douglass rejoiced:

"What a contrast is my *present* with my former condition? Then a slave, now a free man; then degraded, now respected; then ignorant, despised, neglected, unknown, and unfriended, my name unheard of beyond the narrow limits of a republican slave plantation; now, my friends and benefactors, people of *both* hemispheres, to heaven the praise belongs!"[28]

Douglass returned home grown to his full stature, with a spirit fearless and daring, with a deeper hatred of slavery and discrimination, with an unyielding determination to assert his "equal right as a man and a brother,"[29] a living symbol of what millions of Negro people in the United States could contribute to civilization once their chains of bondage were broken.

Founding "The North Star"

Douglass had barely settled down after his arrival from abroad when a series of welcome-home gatherings took place. Late in April, a reception was held in the Lyceum Hall in Lynn, his home town, and numerous speeches congratulated him on the success of his "philanthropic mission." He responded with a sketch of his travels and adventures abroad, but told the audience that he had not yet "got his sea-legs off" so could not go deeply into the significance of his experiences in Europe. Ten days later, on May 3, the Negro people of Boston, assisted by their white friends, held their public welcome. They were followed by the Negro people of New York City who gathered in the Zion's Church to voice their joy at Douglass' success. On May 25 his friends in New Bedford extended their welcome, particularly praising Douglass for his decision to leave "the valuable and social inducements held out to him by the people of Great Britain, for the purpose of returning to America, to again identify himself with the suffering slave, and with those who are laboring against great obstacles to procure his liberation. . . ."[1]

At the meetings of the American Anti-Slavery Society in New York during the second week of May, Douglass was officially welcomed by his leading co-workers. On this occasion he made his first important address since his return, and startled even the most avid Garrisonians with the fervor of his remarks. He out-Garrisoned the Garrisonians as he launched into a bitter attack upon his native land in which "three millions of my brethren, some of them my own kindred, my own brothers, my own sisters, . . . are now clanking the chains of Slavery upon the plains of the South. . . ." Replying to Garrison who had referred to the Negro orator's "love and attachment" to America, Douglass declared amidst cheers and hisses:

"I cannot have any love for this country, as such, or for its Constitution. I desire to see its overthrow as speedily as possible, and its Constitution shivered in a thousand fragments, rather than this foul curse should continue to remain as now."

The remainder of the address was much calmer, as he brilliantly justified his criticism of American institutions abroad, and his role at the World's Temperance Convention. The full text of the speech, as it appeared in the *New York Tribune,* was reprinted as a pamphlet by a group of Baltimore slaveholders who pointed to it as proof of the dangers inherent in the Abolitionist movement.[2] But most readers of the *Tribune* agreed with John Greenleaf Whittier that it was "a notable refutation of the charge of the natural inferiority urged against the colored man."[3]

Once the celebrations welcoming his homecoming were over, Douglass turned his attention to the launching of an anti-slavery paper. During his last months abroad a number of his English friends had offered to supply him with an annual income sufficient to enable him to be free from worry and "to devote his whole life and energies to the Anti-Slavery Cause." Douglass had rejected the offer because it would be fatal to his effectiveness in the struggle against slavery to be separated "from mutual hardships in a common cause." Instead, he suggested that he would be happy to receive a printing press, enabling him to establish a weekly newspaper under the editorial management of Negroes. For such a paper, if run efficiently, "would be a *telling* fact against the American doctrine of natural inferiority, and the inveterate prejudice which so universally prevails in this country against the colored race." His friends eagerly seized upon the suggestion and raised a testimonial fund which rapidly exceeded two thousand dollars.[4]

On his return to the United States, Mary Howitt, one of his closest English friends, wrote Douglass asking him whether he was still interested in publishing his paper. He replied promptly:

"You speak of the printing press, and ask shall I like to have it? I answer, yes, yes! The very best instrumentalities are not too good for the cause; I should feel it quite improper to express myself thus, if the proposed present were merely an expression of personal consideration. I look upon it as an aid to a great cause, and I cannot but accept the best gifts which may be offered to it. . . . I hope to be able to do a good work in behalf of my race with it."[5]

The history of Negro journalism in the United States before 1847 was not one to inspire much confidence in Douglass' project. *Freedom's Journal,* the first American Negro newspaper, died a few months after its appearance in the spring of 1827. In January, 1837, the second Negro newspaper, *The Weekly Advocate,* edited by Rev. Samuel Cornish, came into being in New York City. In March of the same year, it was renamed *The Colored American* and ran until 1841, during which time it was edited successively by Cornish, Dr. James McCune Smith of New York City, a graduate of medicine of the University of Glasgow, Scotland, and Rev. Charles B. Ray. In August, 1838, David Ruggles published *The Mirror of Liberty* in New York, first a quarterly and then a monthly magazine devoted to the welfare of the free Negro. Publication ended in September, 1841.

With the 1840's came a substantial increase in the number of Negro publications. In Albany, New York, in 1842, Stephen Myers edited *The Elevator. The National Watchman,* with which William G. Allen was associated, was circulated from Troy, New York, beginning in the latter part of 1842 and lasting until 1847. *The Clarion* was published by the Rev. Henry Highland Garnet in Troy, but was short-lived. *The People's Press* was edited in New York City by Thomas Hamilton during 1843. In the same year, Martin Robinson Delany edited *The Mystery* in Pittsburgh. *The Ram's Horn,* edited in New York City by William Hodges, was published in January of 1847 and died in June of the following year.[6]

That these papers lacked stability is hardly surprising. The circulation was usually small, the subscription list confined for the most part to the city in which the journal was published. The Negro papers faced great difficulties: there were few Negro merchants and professional men who bought advertising; the Negro people were too poor to make substantial contributions to requests for funds and not many white people were interested in Negro Abolitionist journals. Thus the publications constantly needed financial assistance. Consequently, nearly all of the journals expired after a valiant battle to exist.

But this did not discourage Douglass. He did not doubt his ability to make a good editor. The literary quality of his letters from abroad had aroused considerable amazement among leading newspaper men. Horace Greeley of the *New York Tribune* wrote that in one of Douglass' letters to Garrison there were passages "which, for genuine eloquence, would do honor to any writer of the English language, however eloquent." Thurlow Weed, editor of the *Albany Evening Journal,* corroborated Greeley's judgment of the letter, commenting that it gave Douglass "rank among the most gifted and eloquent men of the age."[7]

Confident that the money to launch his project was available, Douglass broached the plan to his New England associates. He was dismayed to learn that they did not share his enthusiasm. Phillips was convinced that a newspaper would ruin him "pecuniarily" in three years.[8] Garrison argued that the paper was not needed since several journals published and edited by Negroes were already in existence; that it would fail for want of support ("The land is full of the wreck of such experiments"); that editorial work would interfere with Douglass' work as a lecturer, and that he was better fitted to speak than to write. "We have no doubt," he summarized, "that Mr. Douglass would display much editorial ability, but the experiment remains to be made. Of one thing we and his friends are certain: as a lecturer, his power over a public assembly is very high. ... With such powers of oratory, and so few lecturers in the field where so many are needed, it seems to us as clear as the noon-day sun, that it would be no gain, but rather a loss, to the anti-slavery cause, to have him withdrawn to any considerable extent from the work of popular agitation, by assuming the cares, drudgery and perplexities of a publishing life. It is quite impracticable to combine the editor with the lecturer, without either causing the paper to be more or less neglected, or the sphere of lecturing to be seriously circumscribed."[9]

Douglass could have replied (as did some Abolitionists critical of Garrison's reasoning) that the editor of the *Liberator* seemed to be capable of combining lecturing and editorial duties. But he was unwilling to offend Garrison, who more than any other man was responsible for his success, and so he temporarily abandoned his plan. Publicly he based his decision on the four journals, which, under the exclusive editorship of Negroes, had come into existence since the entire idea of publishing a paper had taken root in his mind. His British friends assured Douglass that when he considered it advisable to launch his newspaper, the capital would be available.[10]

Resuming the lecture platform, Douglass took his place with the Abolitionists as in former days. In August he made preparations to assist Garrison "in carrying the torch of conscience into dark places of the West." The western tour grew out of an invitation extended to Garrison early in the year by the Western Anti-Slavery Society to address its annual convention at New Lynn, Ohio. When Garrison announced his acceptance, he was deluged with requests from anti-slavery societies in New York and Pennsylvania to visit them on the trip.

The tour started smoothly enough. At Norristown, where the Eastern

Pennsylvania Anti-Slavery Society was celebrating its tenth anniversary, Garrison, Sidney B. Gay, Robert Purvis and Lucretia Mott were enthusiastically received, but Douglass was "the 'lion' of the occasion." A day later a public meeting was held in honor of Garrison and Douglass by the Negro people of Philadelphia. The Negro Abolitionist held the audience "spell-bound for more than two hours."[11]

But these were deceptive signs. On a train bound for Harrisburg, Douglass was ordered out of the car by one of the passengers, a local lawyer, and dragged out of his seat when he refused to leave. The incident was but a prologue to the reception which faced the Abolitionists in the state capital. A large and attentive audience gathered in the Harrisburg courthouse, listened quietly to Garrison's speech. But when Douglass began to speak, the storm broke. Cries of "Out with the damned n——r!" began as the mob took possession. They set off firecrackers, threw cayenne pepper all over the place, and hurled stones, garbage, and rotten eggs at the speaker. The mob was still at it when Garrison arose and calmly announced that if this was a specimen of Harrisburg hospitality and "love of liberty" the visitors were quite happy to depart.

The experience did not dampen the ardor of the two men. Nor did the strenuous trip across the Alleghenies. Many times Garrison was deeply angered because Douglass was not permitted to sit at the table and, for two days and nights, "scarcely tasted a morsel of food." The greeting at Pittsburgh, where a committee of twenty white and Negro friends, "with a colored band of music," received them at the station cheered them. Douglass and Garrison, now joined by Stephen Foster who had consented to make the trip "though with much inconvenience to his domestic arrangements," held five crowded and enthusiastic meetings in two days. Garrison assured his wife that "he had seen nothing like it on this side of the Atlantic." The fact that two meetings in New Brighton had to be held in the upper room of a flour store because the churches had refused to open their doors to the Abolitionists did not diminish his enthusiasm.[12]

August 18 saw the travelers at an anti-slavery meeting at New Lyme, in northeastern Ohio, held in a huge tent with an audience of four thousand. Although many of the western Abolitionists had repudiated the Garrisonians and followed the Weld-Tappan group, Garrison's influence was still strong in the Western Reserve which, according to the Cleveland *Plain Dealer,* was "the favorite stumping ground of the fanatical disunionists of the East" where they were always "sure to gather a crowd to listen to their ravings." People came from far distant communities to see the leader of the American Anti-Slavery Society and his famous Negro companion, one Negro farmer riding three hundred miles on horseback to be present.[13]

After Benjamin S. Jones, editor of the powerful *Anti-Slavery Bugle* of Salem, Ohio, had opened the convention, a choir sang a poetical welcome to the honored guests. The verses to Douglass went:

> *And our hearts are made glad by the presence of one*
> *Who was chattelized, beaten, and sold in our land;*
> *Who is guilty of naught, save that Africa's sun*
> *Pressed his ancestor's brow with too heavy a hand.*
>
> *He can tell of the woes that have gnawed at his heart;*
> *Of the lash that has left its deep scar on his back;*
> *How the tenderest ties are torn rudely apart,*
> *And the soul and body both doomed to the rack.*[14]

The visiting Abolitionists were deeply moved by the New Lyme meetings. "Enthusiasm . . . is unequalled," wrote Garrison. "Opposition to our holy cause seems stunned." Never had he attended a convention where such fervor for the movement was displayed. They had made a "host of friends," and when the convention adjourned, they were kept "busily engaged for some time in shaking hands and bidding farewell."

Six days later, the Abolitionists were at Oberlin, having attended meetings in four towns en route. On August 27, they began a series of lectures which were well attended. Later Asa Mahan, president of Oberlin College, the great anti-slavery center, entertained Garrison and Douglass at dinner. The visitors were impressed by the courtesy displayed toward them and by the Oberlin hospitality. They welcomed the opportunity to rest in a congenial atmosphere, for the trip had proved to be more arduous than they had anticipated. They had spoken every day since entering Ohio, and, to keep the appointments arranged for them by Samuel Brooks, the agent of the Western Anti-Slavery Society, they had been compelled to travel to towns thirty to forty miles apart. Speeches delivered in tents, in drafty halls, and in the open air with rain pouring down in torrents, were detrimental to good health, and Douglass, troubled by tonsilitis, had been forced to cancel several of his scheduled addresses.

"Our friends here have so multiplied the meetings," Garrison complained on one occasion, "that not an hour is left us for rest. They are unmerciful to

us, and how we are to fulfill all the engagements made, without utterly breaking down, I do not know. Douglass is not able to speak at any length without becoming very hoarse, and, in some cases, losing the ability to make himself heard."[15]

Following their Oberlin visit, the Abolitionists passed through Rich-
field, Medina, Massilon, and Leesburg on their way to Salem, addressing
enthusiastic audiences in every town. Five thousand sympathizers welcomed them in Salem at what the *Anti-Slavery Bugle* called "the largest
anti-slavery gathering ever convened in the county." A week later at
Cleveland they found that the local *Plain Dealer* had prepared the city
for their arrival with the announcement that the "menagerie is coming,"
and had slyly suggested that the visitors be given the same treatment they
had received at Harrisburg. Successful meetings, however, were held, and,
on the second day, Garrison told the audience that neither he nor Douglass had met with any violence since coming to Ohio. Douglass assured
the gathering that he had found "nothing mean, narrow, or churlish about
a true Buckeye." Discussing the two speakers, the Cleveland *True
Democrat* observed:

"Mr. Garrison is a pleasant, clear, forcible, and logical speaker. He car-
ries his point by real sledge-hammer argument. Douglass is more eloquent.
He moves upon the passions of his audience and handles with a master's skill
the weapons of the orator."[16]

The meetings at Cleveland were the last which Garrison and Douglass attended as friends. The pace had begun to tell on the older man,
and before the Cleveland trip had ended, Garrison collapsed. He had
spoken at an open-air meeting in a drizzling cold rain and had been
chilled to the bone. When he returned to his rooms, feverish and exhausted, he was placed under a doctor's care. Douglass insisted on
remaining with his friend but Garrison urged him to continue and
carry out their scheduled engagements.

Worried and depressed, Douglass left for Buffalo. A week later he
was disturbed to learn that Garrison's condition was critical. He kept
reproaching himself "for leaving at all." Half-heartedly he went through
his talks in Buffalo, Rochester, and Syracuse, but his mind was troubled.
On October 8, 1847, Samuel J. May wrote to Garrison:

"Frederick Douglass was very much trouble[d] that he did not get any
tidings from you when he reached Syracuse on the 24th. of September. He
left you reluctantly, yet thinking that you would follow in a day or two; and

as he did not get any word from you at Waterloo, nor at Auburn, he was almost sure he should meet you at my house. His countenance fell, and his heart failed him, when he found me likewise in sad suspense about you. Not until he arrived at West Winfield did he get any relief, and then through the *Liberator* of the 23d."[17]

May's description of Douglass' concern does not seem to have made any impression upon Garrison. Writing to his wife five weeks after Douglass' departure, the Abolitionist expressed surprise that his recent co-worker had "not written a single line to me, or to anyone else in this place, inquiring after my health, since he left me on a bed of illness."[18]

It was not Douglass' supposed indifference which was alone responsible for Garrison's annoyance. It was aggravated by Douglass' conviction that his original plan to publish an anti-slavery weekly had been correct. The hateful discrimination Douglass had encountered early on the western tour had convinced him of this. "I had not decided against the publication of a paper one month," he wrote to an English friend on November 1, "before I became satisfied that I had made a mistake and each subsequent month's experience has confirmed me in the conviction." Now more than ever he believed that the example of a journal excellently managed and edited by a Negro "would be a powerful evidence that the Negro was too much of a man to be held a chattel."[19]

Garrison was considerably vexed by Douglass' decision to go forward with his plans in spite of the objections of his colleagues. He complained to his wife that Douglass had "never opened to me his lips on the subject, nor asked my advice in any particular whatever! Such conduct grieves me to the heart. His conduct about the paper has been impulsive, inconsiderate, and inconsistent with his decision in Boston. . . ." Douglass' insistence that he had revealed his plan to Garrison before he was taken ill in Cleveland did not help matters. Garrison had "no recollection whatever of it."[20]

Undeterred by Garrison's attitude, Douglass went forward with his project. With $2,174 forwarded by his English friends he bought "an excellent press, and nearly the necessary printing materials," and was happy to learn from expert printers that they were the best that could be obtained in the United States. Where to publish was the next problem. The site had to be removed from that of the *Liberator* and the *Anti-Slavery Standard*. Originally he had thought of publishing in Cleveland, but the following announcement in the *Ram's Horn* of November 1, 1847, revealed that he had finally decided to operate from Rochester:[21]

"PROSPECTUS FOR AN ANTI-SLAVERY PAPER TO BE ENTITLED—*THE NORTH STAR.*

"Frederick Douglass proposes to publish in Rochester, New York, a weekly anti-slavery paper with the above title. The object of *The North Star* will be to attack slavery in all its forms and aspects; advocate Universal Emancipation; exact the standard of public morality; promote the moral and intellectual improvement of the colored people; and to hasten the day of freedom to our three million enslaved fellow-countrymen.

"The paper will be printed on a double medium sheet, at $2.00 per annum, paid in advance, and $2.50 if payment be delayed over six months. . . ."[22]

Rochester offered vast potentialities for an anti-slavery publication. "Perhaps in no other communities of the north," writes a historian of the city, "was there a more intense feeling of hostility to slavery and of indignation over the wrongs inflicted upon the Negro." Most of the Abolitionists in Rochester, due to the work of Myron Holley, were not Garrisonians, but there was a tolerance and receptiveness toward anti-slavery men of all shades of opinion. Furthermore, Rochester boasted an active female Anti-Slavery Society which had been organized in 1835 and with which were associated some of the outstanding women of the country—Elizabeth Cady Stanton, Susan B. Anthony, Amy Post, Sally Holley, Sojourner Truth, and Mrs. Samuel D. Porter.[23] An anti-slavery journal would receive the support of the Female Anti-Slavery Society in building circulation and in meeting operating expenses. Douglass knew from his first visit to Rochester that the homes of many citizens would be open to him and that here he and his family could build lasting friendships.

Toward the close of 1847 Douglass moved to Rochester to prepare the first issue of his paper.

" . . . I shall enter on my duties with a full sense of my accountability to God, the slave, and to the dear friends who had aided me in the undertaking," he wrote as he prepared to depart from Lynn. "In the publication of the paper, I shall be under no party or society, but shall advocate the slave's cause in that way which in my judgment, will be best suited to the advancement of the cause."[24]

Editor and Publisher

On Friday, December 3, 1847, a new era in Negro journalism in the United States was inaugurated. The first issue of *The North Star* came off the press, its masthead proclaiming the slogan: "Right is of no Sex— Truth is of no Color—God is the Father of us all, and we are all Brethren." The role of the paper was that of a "terror to evil doers," and while it would be "mainly Anti-Slavery," its columns would be "freely opened to the candid and decorous discussion of all measures and topics of a moral and humane character, which may serve to enlighten, improve and elevate mankind. . . ." A report of the National Convention of Colored People held at Troy early in October, and a long letter by Douglass to Henry Clay commenting on the Kentuckian's speech in behalf of colonization, were the main features of the first number. The first page stated that the subscription rates were two dollars a year, *"always in advance,"* and that advertisements not exceeding ten lines would be carried three times for one dollar.

The editors were Douglass and Martin R. Delany who had just resigned the editorship of the Pittsburgh *Mystery,* a Negro paper. William C. Nell, a self-taught Negro and a devoted Garrisonian, was listed as publisher. The printing office was located at 25 Buffalo Street, in the Talman Building, opposite Reynolds Arcade. It was a simple room. Douglass' desk was in one corner; cases of type and the printing press occupied the rest of the space. Two white apprentices, William A. Atkinson and William Oliver, and Douglass' children assisted in setting the type, locking the forms, folding, wrapping and mailing the paper. Although Douglass had his own press, the paper itself was printed in the shop of the *Rochester Democrat.*[1]

On the whole, reaction to the first issue was favorable. Samuel J. May spoke of his "delight" in reading the paper, Garrison praised it, and Edmund Quincy observed in the *Liberator* that its "literary and mechanical execution would do honor to any paper new or old, anti-slavery or pro-slavery, in the country." In England, *Howitt's Journal* augmented the chorus of approval with the remark: *"The North Star* may rank with any American paper, for ability and interest; it is full of buoyancy and variety. . . ."[2]

Not all joined in welcoming the new arrival. The *New York Herald* urged the people of Rochester to throw Douglass' printing press into the lake and exile the editor to Canada. The *Albany Dispatch* was a bit more subtle. It merely warned the citizens of Rochester that the presence of a paper published by "the n——r pet of the British Abolitionists" would be a "serious detriment" to the community, and suggested that they "buy him off." Undoubtedly there were those in Rochester who approved of these suggestions, but they were a distinct minority. The Rochester *Daily Advertiser* observed that the mechanical appearance of the first issue was "exceedingly neat," that the leading article indicated "a high order of talent," and that the editor was "a man of much more than ordinary share of intellect."

More important was the welcome extended the paper and its staff by the printers' association of Rochester. In January 1848 the publishers and printers' union of the city invited Douglass and Nell to an anniversary celebration of Benjamin Franklin's birthday. When the hotel refused to allow the Negroes to enter the dining room the guests sharply protested and the manager was compelled to rescind the order. At the dinner, in response to a toast in his honor, Douglass said: "Gentlemen of the Rochester Press—promoters of knowledge, lovers of liberty, foes of ignorance, despisers of prejudice—may you continue to give the world noble examples by a free and intelligent union of *black* and *white*."[3]

In the first issue Douglass made a solemn pledge to his readers that "*The North Star* shall live." He kept his promise, but it was only by the most heroic effort. Due to the generosity of his friends abroad, Douglass started his paper debt-free, but he had to depend upon subscriptions to meet publication expenses which, in 1848, amounted to sixty dollars a week. A mailing list of seven hundred was not enough to keep the paper solvent, and, on January 12, 1848, Douglass complained to Delany who was on a subscription tour: "Subscribers come in slowly, and I am doing all I can by lectures and letters to keep our heads above the water." A week later he wrote: "The work is up hill just now, but I hope there is a good time coming." Three months later the situation had become so critical that on April 28, 1848, Douglass was compelled to mortgage his home to keep the paper alive. On May 5, 1848, *The North Star* contained an urgent appeal to its friends and readers "for immediate pecuniary aid." "We have exerted ourselves to obtain subscribers, and have succeeded to an encouraging extent; but it is impossible in our circumstances, commencing as we did with but a small number of subscribers, to obtain a sufficient number to float unencumbered from week to week." This was but the first of a series of appeals that were to accompany the existence of Douglass' paper.[4]

"Things have not turned out at all as I expected," Douglass wrote ruefully four months after launching *The North Star*. His paper had received little support from the Boston Abolitionists, partly because it had been started against their advice and partly because it did not denounce all Abolitionists who were not Garrisonians. On the other hand, the political Abolitionists had withheld their support because they regarded the weekly as too strongly tainted with Garrisonianism. In short, all groups of the Abolitionist movement felt only "a negative interest" in Douglass' paper. What was most grievous to the editor was the response of the Negro people. Douglass explained this to his own satisfaction by attributing the indifference "to the long night of ignorance which has overshadowed and subdued their spirit,"[5] but he could not hide his bitterness over the fact that in May, 1848, *The North Star* had five white subscribers to every Negro. "Tell them," he editorialized later, "that a well conducted press in the hands of colored men is essential to the progress and elevation of the colored man, and they will regard you as one merely seeking a living at public expense, 'to get along without work.' "[6]

That the paper survived the first difficult year was due mainly to Douglass' own tireless work and the assistance of a few devoted friends. Originally it had been planned that Douglass remain in Rochester and edit the paper while Delany traveled about getting subscribers. But this went by the board almost immediately. Month after month in all kinds of weather, Douglass would depart on lecture tours to raise funds, supplying his readers with a detailed account of his experiences. A typical letter from the editor went:

"The scanty editorial matter which I have sent to the paper for the past two weeks, has been written on the wing, and in the midst of pressing engagements. You will sympathize with me when I tell you that I find it necessary to go abroad in person to secure the number of subscribers requisite to the support of our paper. This ought not to be, and would not be the case if suitable agents could be obtained, who would enforce the claims of the paper upon the public, and secure subscribers and subscriptions for it. But these we have not, and in consequence find it necessary to go forth myself. I regret this only on one account, and that is, it deprives me of the time and means of making the paper what I desire and what it ought to be."[7]

During this first year, Douglass spent about six months out in the field, raising funds through lectures and subscriptions. He had mortgaged his home, was "heavily in debt," and the paper itself was over two hundred dollars in debt. But he did have the satisfaction of having completed the first volume. "It has lived through one year," he wrote joyfully on December 22, 1848, "has made its appearance regularly—has not missed a single Friday morning since the day of its first publication—those who subscribed at its commencement have not lost their money by the *'going down'* of the paper." A few weeks later Douglass' spirit soared when he learned that at an anti-slavery fair held by the Negro women of Philadelphia one hundred dollars had been raised for *The North Star*. It was not so much the money itself as the knowledge of "the esteem in which *The North Star* is held by those who feel the crushing weight of American oppression." "We believe," Douglass wrote joyfully, "it was the first fair ever held in this country by colored ladies, to sustain a press under the sole management of persons of their own complexion. We take it as an evidence that, whatever others may think of the expediency of establishing such a paper as we have tried to make the *North Star,* the oppressed themselves feel the value of it."[8]

Women had much to do with the continued existence of Douglass' weekly. Indeed, were it not for Julia Griffiths the paper on many occasions would have been forced to suspend publication. Miss Griffiths, a daughter of a close friend of Wilberforce, the British Abolitionist, had met Douglass at Newcastle-on-Tyne during his tour abroad and they had become fast friends at once. She had raised funds to help launch his paper and had furnished him with a "valuable collection of books, pamphlets, tracts and pictures." Learning, in the spring of 1848, that *The North Star* was faring poorly, she wound up her affairs in England and with her sister came to Rochester to assist in putting the journal on its feet. "She came to my relief," Douglass wrote years later, "when my paper had nearly absorbed my means, and I was heavily in debt, and when I had mortgaged my house to raise money to meet current expenses; and in a single year, by her energetic and effective management, enabled me to extend the circulation of my paper from 2,000 to 4,000 copies." In a single year, too, Miss Griffiths "paid off a debt of between seven and eight hundred dollars."[9]

An indefatigable worker, with good business sense, Julia Griffiths moved into Douglass' home soon after her arrival and devoted herself exclusively to managing his paper. She took charge of the finances of *The North Star* in the summer of 1848, and, separating Douglass' personal finances from those of the paper, enabled him to pay off the mortgage on his home by March 18, 1853. She organized numerous projects to raise funds, sponsoring fairs, mailing innumerable personal appeals for financial aid, and building a strong movement among the women Abolitionists in Rochester. Gradually the financial strain was eased. By May 1, 1851, when the paper enjoyed a circulation well over 4,000, the situation had improved so that Douglass was able to report to Gerrit Smith: "The 'North Star' sustains itself, and partly sustains my large family. It has just reached a living point. Hitherto the struggle of its life has been to live. Now it more than lives."[10]

In the summer of 1851 *The North Star* amalgamated with the *Liberty Party Paper,* a weekly journal edited and published by John Thomas in Syracuse. This paper had fewer than seven hundred subscribers and was in great financial distress. The merger resulted from a suggestion by Gerrit Smith, the financial backer of Thomas' paper. Douglass was to become the editor of the new publication, Thomas the assistant editor, and Julia Griffiths the business manager. A new printing office and a good press would result in a "good looking paper . . . free from all typographical, grammatical, orthographical, and rhetorical errors and blunders." Smith advanced two hundred dollars for the purchase of the press and type and promised to provide a monthly donation toward the paper's upkeep.

After considerable bickering with John Thomas over the salary of the assistant editor and the location of the paper, the merger became an accomplished fact. "God grant that the fruit of our union may prove a blessing to the slave, and to suffering man everywhere and of every grade," Douglass wrote to Smith on June 18, 1851. Twelve days later, the first issue of the new weekly, now named *Frederick Douglass' Paper,* appeared. Its motto, proposed by Smith, was "All Rights For All."[11]

Essentially the weekly was a continuation of *The North Star.* However, one notes the absence of the usual "F.D." at the bottom of Douglass' articles. For three years these initials had adorned every issue of *The North Star* as proof to doubters that "an uneducated fugitive slave could write the English language with such propriety and correctness. . . ." But now Douglass was assuming "in full the right and dignity of an *Editor*—a Mr. Editor if you please."[12]

With Smith contributing to its support, the paper was able for two years to meet its expenses. But after 1853 it again ran into difficulties. "Money! Money!! Money!!" Douglass appealed to delinquent subscribers on April 8, 1853. ". . . We greatly need your assistance, just now. The expence of publishing a paper like ours is very great—and depending, as it does, almost wholly upon its *subscription* list, it can only be sustained and its Editor left unembarrassed by *prompt payment* on the part of *subscribers.*" The situation grew worse. By June, 1855, when Douglass instituted the policy of advanced subscription payments, the journal was fifteen hundred dollars in debt, and almost double that amount was due from delinquent subscribers.[13]

That the debt was not even greater was due again to the tireless efforts of Julia Griffiths. "In referring to those who have assisted us in keeping up the paper during the year," Douglass wrote later in 1854, "and for the past three years, we are indebted to none more than to that ever active and zealous friend of the slave, Miss Julia Griffiths." A year before this emphatic tribute was delivered, Miss Griffiths had launched a plan to raise one thousand dollars, in ten-dollar gifts, toward a sustaining fund for the paper. By January, 1854, she had collected four hundred and twenty dollars. Among the forty-two donors were Smith, Sumner, Chase, Greeley, Seward, William Jay, Henry Ward Beecher, Arthur and Lewis Tappan, Horace Mann, Cassius M. Clay, as well as several prominent Negroes. William Johnson, one of the Negro contributors, also published an appeal to his people urging them to support the drive for funds:

" . . . If there is any one thing more than another, that we need in a public way as a fixture, it is that of a newspaper, conducted and published by a colored man, through which our views and sentiments may be known as a people; and since God has raised up as a man in the person of Frederick Douglass, who has demonstrated to the world that he has the ability to vindicate the rights of man, with equal force, either on the platform as an orator, or as an editor of a newspaper, it becomes the duty of every colored man and woman to sustain Frederick Douglass and his paper."[14]

With the assistance of the Rochester Ladies' Anti-Slavery Society, of which she was secretary, Miss Griffiths in 1853 published a gift-book, *Autographs for Freedom,* to aid Douglass' paper. Several hundred gift-books had been issued in this country before the Civil War, and the anti-slavery cause alone had produced five before *Autographs for Freedom* made its appearance. The new feature of Miss Griffiths' volume was the autograph which followed the author's essays, letters, and speeches. Like the other anti-slavery gift-books, it was designed to be sold at Abolitionist fairs and bazaars, though Douglass also offered the volume to subscribers as a means of extending the circulation of his journal.[15]

Commenting on the English edition of *Autographs for Freedom,* the

British Banner observed: "The book is deeply interesting, and as presenting the aggregate of liberal sentiments from cultivated and enlightened minds, possesses a peculiar value." Among the "cultivated and enlightened" contributors were Negro leaders such as J. McCune Smith, George B. Vashon, William G. Allen, Charles L. Reason, James M. Whitfield, William Wells Brown, J. M. Langston and Douglass himself; public figures such as William H. Seward, Horace Greeley, Gerrit Smith, Horace Mann, and Joshua R. Giddings; preachers and philosophers such as Theodore Parker, Ralph Waldo Emerson, and Henry Ward Beecher; and women reformers such as Harriet Beecher Stowe, Antoinette Brown, Caroline M. Kirkland, Catherine M. Sedgwick, and Jane Swisshelm. Most of the contributions were brief—frequently a page in length—and few were outstanding for their literary merit. But the volumes did contain some previously unpublished work by prominent writers, and some of the contributions by the Negro authors rank high in the literature of the anti-slavery movement.[16] The 1853 issue featured a little-known work of fiction by Frederick Douglass entitled *The Heroic Slave,* a short story about Madison Washington, who led the famous uprising in 1841 on the *Creole,* a ship engaged in the domestic slave trade.

The proceeds from the two issues of *Autographs for Freedom* did not solve Douglass' multiplying financial problems. With her usual ingenuity, Miss Griffiths hit upon the plan of returning to England to raise funds. Armed with letters vouching for the merit of Douglass' journal, she arrived in her native land during the spring of 1857. Lewis Tappan's letter praised Douglass "as a man deserving entire confidence. . . . His paper is well conducted." Charles Sumner's testimonial was brief: "I have a high opinion of Frederick Douglass and his efforts. His paper is doing a very good work." Speaking for the Negro people, James McCune Smith wrote:

"The friends of slavery, driven from argument to argument, finally point to the Blacks, and exclaim in triumph. 'See them! Are they benefiting by freedom?' So long as we can point to Frederick Douglass, and his paper, we have a triumphant reply to that question; they both stand full in clear living light, and prove more than a volume of statistics of our relative freedom from vice, crime, and poverty."[17]

Miss Griffiths was well received by the British Abolition societies. Douglass was still remembered by the English public and his paper had quite a few subscribers. In 1855 *The Anti-Slavery Reporter,* organ of the

British and Foreign Anti-Slavery Society, had urged English reformers to subscribe to Douglass' weekly.

"It is the only newspaper in America," the *Reporter* pointed out, "owned by a coloured man, who has been himself a fugitive slave; and its own intrinsic merit, as well as the interest of the Abolition cause generally, require that, above every other anti-slavery journal, it should be sustained."[18]

How much Miss Griffiths raised for the paper is difficult to determine. We do know she organized at least fourteen Ladies' Associations which pledged to aid the journal with annual donations from between five and twenty pounds. The number of English subscribers was also increased, but this did not help financially, since the added cost of postage absorbed any gain from foreign subscriptions. To meet this problem, Douglass in June, 1858, issued an edition of *Douglass' Monthly,* for circulation in the British Isles only. By excluding advertisements and items of purely local interest he was able to decrease the size of the journal so that it could be mailed overseas profitably.[19]

Meanwhile, the struggle to keep the weekly afloat in the United States continued. With debts steadily mounting it became more and more difficult to issue the paper and in 1859 the weekly came out in a reduced size. Yet even this emergency measure was of little avail. During the first six months of 1860 the paper was "running behind its income at the rate of $25 to $30 per week," and by July the receipts had fallen "nearly to nothing" while the weekly expenses were forty-five and fifty dollars. There was no alternative but to suspend its publication. With a heavy heart Douglass announced his decision to Smith on July 2, 1860:

"You may well believe that after nearly thirteen years of effort to put the paper on a permanent basis and make it an established anti-slavery instrumentality, that I am now very sorry to give up the struggle. There is no escape and I submit. I shall hereafter only publish my monthly paper."[20]

For three years longer Douglass continued to issue the *Monthly.* Although the magazine did not exert the influence of a weekly paper, Douglass made it a powerful weapon in the battle against slavery during the most critical years of the Civil War.

Despite the trying circumstances under which he was compelled to publish his journal, his busy life as a lecturer and participant in the anti-slavery movement, Douglass' paper was so interesting and instructive that it won praise from readers at home and abroad. Only when one recalls that Douglass had never had a day's schooling when he launched his paper, had had "no regular or sound rules of grammar," and had done little reading, does the magnitude of this accomplishment become clear. He owed much to Julia Griffiths who taught him the rules of grammar and spelling, and used her blue-pencil mercilessly to perfect his writing.[21] But essentially the paper was the product of Douglass' own thinking and planning. After June 29, 1848, when the joint editorship with Martin R. Delany was dissolved, the journal was under Douglass' exclusive control. It was due primarily to his own unusual powers that he was able to supply to the anti-slavery movement the only paper other than the *Liberator* and the *Anti-Slavery Standard* which survived over a number of years.

In format and typography Douglass' paper was not very different from the other anti-slavery weeklies. Like the *Liberator,* the *Anti-Slavery Standard,* the *Anti-Slavery Bugle,* and the *Pennsylvania Freeman,* it consisted of four pages of seven columns each. The first page usually featured the full text of anti-slavery speeches in Congress or at Abolitionist conventions. Foreign reports also rated a front-page position as did reports of local, statewide, and national anti-slavery meetings. The second page was filled with editorial matter which sometimes poured over onto the next page. When Douglas was ill or too busy with lectures to write his usual editorials the page was taken over by John Thomas, Julia Griffiths, James McCune Smith, William J. Watkins, and others.[22] The third and fourth pages were generally devoted to clips from other sources, a procedure common among all ante-bellum journals, poetry, instalments of novels running serially, book reviews or "literary notices" as they were elegantly called, announcements of anti-slavery tracts, advertisements of all kinds of pills, "all sorts of horse medicines" and ointments, and the letters of the paper's regular contributors.[23]

The poems bearing such titles as "The Fugitive Wife, "The Time to Die," "Wrong Not the Laboring Poor," and "Where the Spirit of the Lord is, there is Liberty," made up for their deficiencies in literary style by their spirited devotion to the cause. Since Douglass also printed many of Whittier's anti-slavery poems, his readers did not lack for good verse.

An outstanding feature was the letters from the paper's contributors, all of whom were Negroes. J. McCune Smith's weekly letter from New York signed "Communipaw," and William J. Wilson's report from Brooklyn under the pseudonym of "Ethiope" would do credit to any paper for their literary qualities and brilliant reportage. Samuel Ringgold Ward's letters from Canada, Amos Gerry Beman's from New Haven, Loguen's from Syracuse, George T. Downing's and H. O. Wagoner's from Chicago were written in a vigorous prose style and were replete with important information on developments in their communities. To ignore these articles is to overlook a significant source of information on life among the free Negroes of the United States and Canada during the ante-bellum period.

However, it was Douglass' writings which carried the paper. He brought to his newspaper writing a remarkable feeling for words, a gift for vivid phrases, a sensitiveness to language forms and a wonderful sense of humor. But he was aware of his limitations—"To those whose lives have been mainly spent in the classic shades of long-established institutions of learning (as ours have not)"[24]—and he continually sought to overcome them. He avidly read the books, pamphlets, and tracts donated by his friends, and his pursuit of knowledge was unending. "I am this summer endeavouring to make myself a little more familiar with history," he wrote to Gerrit Smith after a lecture tour. "My ignorance of the past has long been a trouble with me."[25] The results of such studies could be seen in the columns of his paper. Keen and mature observations on national and international issues written in a virile and sonorous style featured each number. Soon contemporary journals were concluding that as an editor, Douglass was even more effective than as a speaker, and this despite the fact that he was widely recognized as one of the outstanding orators of his day. A century later, Douglass' editorials retain the same vigor and freshness, the same mature and penetrating analysis that evoked such enthusiastic approval from his readers and journalistic colleagues.

Douglass set high standards for himself and his contributors. Typographical and grammatical errors angered him and he insisted on careful writing. He was determined to prove that a paper edited by a former slave compared favorably with the best-edited weeklies of the period; and he succeeded so admirably that Negroes felt a sense of pride in the paper. White reformers pointed to it constantly as a perfect refutation of the charge of inferiority of the Negro people and an answer to the question whether fugitive slaves who came North "do or do not necessarily become thieves or paupers." *The Rising Sun,* a contemporary Negro journal, voiced the sentiments of the vast majority of the free Negro population of the North when it declared: "Frederick Douglass' ability as an editor and publisher has done more for the freedom and elevation of his race than all his platform appearances."[26]

Douglass looked upon his decision to establish a paper as one of the most important acts of his life. His editorial experiences contributed immeasurably to his own development and "intellectual expansion." The very necessity to speak out week after week on every important issue of the day compelled him to analyze events carefully and to reach conclusions based upon his own thinking. He had to study for himself, make his own decisions, and shoulder all responsibilities. As he stated in his autobiography, his work as editor caused him to read and to think and to express himself in clear and concise language. It ended his period of apprenticeship under Garrison and Phillips and made him self-reliant. These were the busiest years in his life and it was of this period that he spoke when he said: "If at any time I have said or written that which is worth remembering or repeating, I must have said such things between the years 1848-1860."[27]

No less important was the fact that as newspaper editor Douglass was brought into closer contact with the Negro people and their problems. From the day that he made his first Abolitionist speech in Nantucket until the time that he founded *The North Star* he had moved almost exclusively among white Abolitionists and only occasionally had he discussed issues confronting the Negro people other than the abolition of slavery. Now he began to build a closer relationship with other Negro leaders and with the Negro people themselves, to examine the whole range of Negro problems, and to pry into every facet of discrimination. Barely eight months after the paper had started, James McCune Smith commented:

"You will be surprised to hear me say," he wrote to Gerrit Smith, "that only since his Editorial career has he seen to become a colored man! I have read his paper very carefully and find phase after phase develop itself as regularly as in one newly born among us. The Church question, the school question, separate institutions, are questions that he enters upon and argues about as our weary but active young men thought about and argued about years ago, when we had Literary Societies. . . ."[28]

Douglass' paper was a symbol, to the Negro people, of what could be done in the way of self-improvement and achievement, to the white people, of the wealth of talent and ability that would be contributed to the national culture if the Negro were free. Every achievement of the Negro people was reported in the journal, and talented Negroes were encouraged to use their abilities to "vindicate us at the bar of public opinion from the oft-repeated assertion that genius may not flourish under a sable brow." In August, 1850, Douglass wrote proudly:

"It is not the least among the good offices of the *North Star* that it searches out and brings to the light of day those of our despised people whose manly characters serve to reflect credit upon themselves and all with whom they are identified."[29]

Throughout its career Douglass' paper carried suggestions for the betterment of the position of the Negro people, materially and otherwise. The editor minced no words in criticizing free Negroes who were indifferent to the anti-slavery cause, voted for slaveholders, and belonged to proslavery churches. "Every one of us should be ashamed to consider himself free while his brother is a slave," Douglass declared. To leave the struggle against slavery to the white people was to concede that the Negroes did not wish to be free, as well as to rob freedom of its value. "For our part," he proclaimed, "we despise a freedom and equality obtained for us by others, and for which we have been unwilling to labor." He called upon Negro leaders who had left the United States for a life free of prejudice in Europe to return home, join the anti-slavery crusade, and "work faithfully in the cause of our elevation—our emancipation from every species of servitude." He knew from experience that it was "very *pleasant* to be where one can inhale a pure atmosphere," but he reminded Negroes abroad that the battle to break the chains of the slaves must receive the first consideration.[30]

In editorials Douglass continually stressed that the free Negro and the slave were chained together and must rise and fall together. He deplored the indifference to education of some free Negroes as tending to keep the slaves in chains by perpetuating slanders against the Negro people. "To strengthen prejudice against the *free*," he argued, "is to rivet the fetter more firmly on the slave population. Only show that the free colored man is low, worthless, and degraded, and a warrant for enslaving him is readily acknowledged." The free Negro must not resign himself to a position of inferiority in American society. Both for his own sake and for the sake of his brother in chains, he must allow no feeling of fright or disillusionment to stand in the way of his self-improvement. The strongest argument for emancipation was a Negro proving by endeavor and achievement that he was as good as the white man. The white man and the Negro were equals, and the white man was superior only when he outstripped the Negro in improving himself; the Negro was inferior only when he proved himself incapable of accomplishing what his white brother had accomplished. It must no longer be white lawyer and Negro wood-sawyer, white editor and Negro street-cleaner, white intelligent and

Negro ignorant, "but we must take our stand side by side with our fellow countrymen, in all the trades, arts, professions, and callings of the day."[31]

Douglass' severest editorials were reserved for Negroes who accepted discrimination instead of fighting for their equal rights. When Miss Elizabeth Greenfield, "the Black Swan," sang at concerts at which the Negro people were excluded, Douglass lashed out at her for betraying her people.[32] When Samuel Ringgold Ward lectured in the Second Presbyterian Church in Philadelphia despite that fact that the notice for the meeting announced that "the lower Saloon will be appropriated exclusively to our white fellow citizens," Douglass issued a special supplement to *The North Star* denouncing his friend's "shameful concession to the spirit of slavery and prejudice. . . ." He wrote bitterly:

"What use will the revilers and slanderers of our people make of this concession? Why this, and none else than this: that we are sensible of our own inferiority; that we are conscious of our own unfitness for the society of white people; that it is quite proper we should be separated from them in the house of prayer; that the two varieties of the same family ought not to be allowed to occupy an equal footing; that the lower and commodious part of the church —the house of *worship*—*should be reserved* for white people *exclusively,* and that colored people should be separated and sent up stairs—colonized."

He closed the supplement on a prophetic note:

"The colored people of this city and country have had enough of this playing fast and loose, and the time has come, unless I mistake the signs of the times, when they will demand of those who stand forth as their advocates, an inflexible adhesion to the principle of equal and impartial freedom."[33]

It was Douglass' firm conviction that a Negro leader should take issue with every case encountered of prejudice against color. The readers of his paper knew that the editor applied this principle, for they regularly came upon lengthy accounts describing Douglass' battles against segregation. The following report in *Frederick Douglass' Paper* of an encounter between the editor and a hotel clerk in Cleveland is typical:

"At the ringing of the morning bell for breakfast, I made my way to the table, supposing myself included in the call; but I was scarcely seated, when there stepped up to me a young man, apparently much agitated, saying: 'Sir, you must leave this table.' 'And why,' said I, 'must I leave this table?'

" 'I want no controversy with you. You must leave this table.'

"I replied, that I had regularly enrolled myself as a boarder in that house; I expected to pay the same charges imposed upon others; and I came to the table in obedience to the call of the bell; and if I left the table I must know the reason. 'We will serve you in your room. It is against our rules.' 'You should have informed me of *your rules* earlier. Where are your rules? Let me see them.' 'I don't want any altercation with you. You must leave this table.' 'But have I not deported myself as a gentleman? What have I done? Is there any gentleman who objects to my being seated here?' (There was silence round the table.) 'Come, sir, come, sir, you must leave this table at once.' 'Well, sir, I cannot leave it unless you will give me a better reason than you have done for my removal.' 'Well, I'll give you a reason if you'll leave the table and go to another room.' 'That, sir, I will not do. You have invidiously selected me out of all this company, to be dragged from this table, and have thereby reflected upon me as a man and a gentleman; and the reason for this treatment shall be as public as the insult you have offered.'

"At these remarks, my carrot-headed assailant left me, *as he said,* to get help to remove me from the table. Meanwhile I called upon one of the servants (who appeared to wait upon me with alacrity) to help me to a cup of coffee, and assisting myself to some of the good things before me, I quietly and thankfully partook of my morning meal without further annoyance."[84]

The frequent appearance of such reports in Douglass' paper gave courage to large sections of the Negro population in the North and made them more determined to combat segregation wherever they met it.

Douglass' vigorous denunciation of colonization is an outstanding example of the contribution he made as an editor to clarifying problems confronting the Negro people. For some time after 1835, colonization agitation was unable to get much of a hearing in the North, as it came to be considered, to paraphrase Cornish and Garrison, merely an effort to strengthen the props of slave institutions. In the late 1840's, however, Henry Clay and the various compromise groups around him renewed the colonization program in the hope that it might lessen the tensions growing in the country over the slavery question. When Douglass founded *The North Star,* colonization agitation was again in full swing. Immediately he dedicated the journal to the battle against the colonizationists.

After reading a speech by Clay on the colonization question, Douglass set out to answer him in a long discussion printed in *The North Star* for January 28, 1848. Clay's attempt to revive the Colonization Society, he claimed, was a most dangerous threat to every Negro in America, for it might easily unsettle his plans for self-improvement "by teaching him to feel that this is not his home," dishearten and subdue his enterprise by causing him to feel that all effort at self-elevation was in vain, "that neither knowledge, temperance, patience, faith, nor virtue, can avail him anything in this land." In one paragraph, he demolished Clay's speech:

"It is an insult, an insolent and tyrannical assumption on the part of Mr. Clay, or anyone else, to tell us, or any part of the Colored people of this country, that he wishes us to go anywhere. We are at home here; and our staying here is evidence that we wish to stay here; and to tell us that he wishes us to go is an insult, which, if offered to Mr. Clay instead of the despised blacks, would subject the perpetrator of the insult to the indignation of the community. Our right to stay here is as good as that of Mr. Clay, or any man-stealer in this land; and God helping us, we will maintain this right before all the world."

With the publication in *The North Star* of Douglass' answer to Henry Clay, the most effective opponent of the colonization movement made his appearance on the scene. In editorial after editorial Douglass hammered away at the theme that colonization was the "twin sister of slavery"; that the United States was the native land of the Negro; that "he, of any one has a right to the soil of this continent" having for more than two hundred years "toiled over the soil of America, under a burning sun and a driver's lash—ploughing, planting, reaping, that white men might loll in ease," and having "fought and bled for this country"; that "his attachment to the place of his birth is stronger than iron," and that those who advised the Negro to emigrate were "his worst and most deadly enemies."[35]

Douglass also advanced the concept of Negro nationhood as an argument against colonization. Individuals could and might emigrate, he conceded, but nations never. And the Negro people in the United States, he maintained, "are becoming a nation in a nation which disowns them, and for weal or for woe this nation is united."[36]

The capstone of Douglass' argument and his most useful contribution to the discussion of colonization was his claim that Negroes and whites could live and work together as equals; that prejudice against color was not invincible; that it was already giving way "and must give way"; that it was an inevitable by-product of slavery and would be overcome as soon as the Negro people were given the same opportunities as their white brothers. The free Negroes, he declared, were making rapid advances in this direction, and were being retarded by the colonizationists who strengthened prejudice against the Negro people by declaring that it was inevitable and God-ordained because of "the natural inferiority of the colored race." It was the duty of the Negro people to defeat the vicious campaign which sought to prove that they were a blight upon American civilization, to "help free their brethren, rather than leave them in chains, to go and civilize Africa." We are Americans, cried Douglass, and we want to live in America on equal terms with all other Americans. "Brethren," he appealed, "stay where you are, so long as you can stay. Stay here and worthily discharge the duties of honest men, and of good citizens."[37]

Douglass' paper also combated the doctrines of white chauvinism which provided the slaveowners with ideological weapons "proving" the "inherent supremacy" of white people, and therefore their right to be masters, and the "inherent inferiority" of Negro people, and therefore their duty to be slaves. Especially did Douglass lash out against the so-called ethnologists, anthropologists, sociologists, and historians who offered alleged proof of the "natural inferiority" of the Negro and the necessity of his filling the God-ordained role of slave to the white man. He pointed out that the ideology of "white supremacy" was as necessary to the system of chattel slavery as the slave trader, the lash, and the bloodhound, and demonstrated that the fostering of a belief in the innate inferiority of the Negro people was part of slavocracy's complex system of control. Douglass called on every Abolitionist to develop the sharpest struggle to expose the propaganda from colleges, pulpits, politicians, and press which constantly drummed out the concept of the inferiority of an entire people.[38]

Douglass himself contributed considerably to the exposure of these pseudo-scientific theories. On August 4, 1854, his paper carried the entire text of his speech at Western Reserve College. Entitled *The Claims of the Negro Ethnologically Considered,* Douglass' address demolished the theories of a number of ethnologists and anthropologists who had prostituted their science in the interests of slavery by proclaiming that the Negro was not a man. After expressing his gratitude that he who had never had a day's schooling in his life had been called to speak in the halls of a university, Douglass demonstrated that the Negro was a man and that he had a common origin with all other men. This he proved by arguments in which, as the *Ohio Observer* remarked, "he exhibited considerable knowledge and research."[39]

So wide was the interest aroused by the publication of this Address in *Frederick Douglass' Paper* that it became necessary to reprint it as a pamphlet. Distributed throughout the North and West and even in Europe, it became a powerful weapon to combat the presumed "subhumanity of Negroes" dictum of the pro-slavery ethnologists and anthropologists.

"It is one of the marvels of the age," commented the *National Era* when the Address first appeared in Douglass' paper, "that a fugitive from slavery, reared to manhood under all the weight of its depressing influences, should be the author of this able and learned Address. This fact alone is the best refutation of the atheistical fanatics, who would exclude the Negro from the pale of manhood."[40]

Douglass' paper was both a powerful tribune in the anti-slavery movement and the outstanding organ of leadership for the free Negro people of the North. It clarified basic issues confronting the Negro people; it gave them courage to carry on against innumerable obstacles, and it coordinated the struggle against slavery and for full equality. The following resolution, introduced by Dr. James McCune Smith and unanimously adopted in 1854 by the New York Literary and Productive Union, composed of Negroes, voiced the sentiments of the Negro people in the United States:

"Resolved, That we recognize in *Frederick Douglass' Paper,* the organ of the enslaved and down-trodden throughout this land—an instrument, which proves beyond gainsaying, the practicability, the safety, and the glory of Emancipation, and of *Self-Emancipation.*"[41]

In the next period we shall see how Frederick Douglass used this "organ of the enslaved and down-trodden throughout this land" in developing political parties devoted to the cause of Abolition and in changing a pro-slavery United States into an anti-slavery one.

The Universal Reformer

When Frederick Douglass wrote to Garrison in 1846 that he could not allow himself "to be insensible to the wrongs and sufferings of any part of the great family of man," he struck a theme which he was to carry out during the rest of his life. Six months after the founding of *The North Star,* he announced in the journal:

"Standing as we do upon the watch-tower of human freedom, we can not be deterred from an expression of our approbation of any movement, however humble, to improve and elevate the character of any members of the human family."[1]

The editorial columns of Douglass' paper are replete with such expressions of approbation. Douglass spoke favorably of the temperance cause, although he was critical of the fact that many of the organized societies were cool to Negro membership.[2] He called himself a Chartist, and announced that he was "even in favor of more radical [re]forms than they have yet proposed." He hailed the movement to abolish "the bloody and inhuman practice of flogging in the Navy."

"Of course," he editorialized, "we hate the whole naval system, and would sign a petition to have it utterly blotted out of existence . . . and if we cannot abolish the navy, let us do what we can to abolish the barbarous inhumanity of subjecting the soft flesh of man to the cursed and bloody scourge."[3]

Douglass enthusiastically supported the universal peace movement sponsored by Elihu Burritt which enlisted workingmen in the crusade to outlaw war. He endorsed the land reform movement, declaring that "the welfare of the world demands the abrogation of monopolies." "What justice is there," he asked, "in the general Government giving away, as it does, the millions upon millions of acres of public lands, to aid soulless railroad corporations to get rich?" He was convinced that through the distribution of free land to the people, many of the evils of society could be abolished. "Multiply the free homes of the people," he argued, "let each man have around him the blessed influence of family and home, and the rampant vice and rowdyism of our country will disappear."[4]

Douglass' paper featured many calls for the abolition of capital punishment, and offered prayers that the day would come when "throughout the Union and throughout the world, this barbarity will be forever cancelled."[5] But Douglass did not confine himself to pious utterances in behalf of the cause. In the fall of 1858 he took part in a pioneer effort in which he suffered bitter discrimination but showed his moral courage. That year he joined Susan B. Anthony, Isaac and Amy Post, Samuel D. Porter, and others in an effort to prevent the execution of one, Ira Stout, who was about to be hanged for murder. Douglass drew up a call for a mass meeting which Susan B. Anthony circulated.

"The undersigned, citizens of Rochester, and others, believing Capital Punishment to be unfriendly to the progress of civilization, hostile to a true religion, repulsive to the best instincts of humanity, and deprecating the effects of executions on the public mind, do respectfully invite a general attendance of the public at a meeting to be held at City Hall, Thursday Evening, October 7th, at 7 o'clock, with a view of securing, in the case of Ira Stout, condemned to be hung for the crime of murder, commutation of the sentence of death to imprisonment for life."

A counter handbill was immediately distributed by the more conservative citizens of Rochester calling upon the public to assemble in the City Hall and "rescue the meeting from the hands of the fanatics and save the city from the disgrace of being supposed in favor of the abolition of the gallows." Fully aware that trouble was brewing, the adherents of the abolition of capital punishment went ahead with their plans, and Douglass prepared a set of resolutions to be read to the meeting for approval.[6]

When the person designated to serve as chairman failed to make an appearance at the meeting, Douglass was chosen to replace him. "We all felt that a man of *power* must be obtained for chairman," explained one of the sponsors of the gathering, "or the meeting was lost. Such a man is Frederick Douglass; he yielded his own feelings to serve, in this most trying hour, the cause of humanity." A storm of hisses greeted Douglass when he mounted the platform. The mob yelled: "Put in a white man!" "Down with the n——r!" "Whitewash him!" Douglass lashed into the crowd.

"Seldom," wrote an observer, "have we heard such earnest eloquence as fell from the lips of Mr. Douglass, as he stood before the maddening crowd,

and defended the right of Free Speech. Insulted almost beyond parallel, and
. . . beyond endurance, not once did he forget the dignity of his position or the
responsibility of the office with which he was invested. Much of his speech,
so happily did he use his rich and powerful voice, was distinctly heard above
the terrible noise of the mob."

Douglass read his resolutions denouncing capital punishment and
asking Governor King to commute Ira Stout's punishment to imprisonment for life. But it was impossible to act on them. Yells, groans, hisses,
stamping of feet, whistling, and vile epithets greeted the reading. When
some of the rowdies attempted to attack Douglass, the mayor came to
the platform and asked the chairman to adjourn the meeting. Douglass,
with his daughter upon his arm and his sons by his side, left the hall,
"surrounded by a gang of ruffians, heaping all measure of sayings upon
him, for the simple and only reason that 'he wore a skin not colored
like their own.' "[7]

Next to Abolition and the battle for equal rights for the Negro
people, the cause closest to Douglass' heart was woman's rights. In the
anti-slavery agitation women took an active and significant part, and
no one knew better than Douglass how deeply the Negro people were
indebted to the tireless efforts of the women's anti-slavery societies. In
reports from communities he was visiting, Douglass regularly devoted
space in his paper to descriptions of the work of the anti-slavery women.
He constantly stressed the unique contribution of the annual fairs conducted by these women.

"In bringing together persons who stand aloof from anti-slavery meetings," he wrote, "attracting attention to the subject of slavery, acquainting the
community with our mode of operating upon public opinion, removing the
green-eyed monster—prejudice against color, and demonstrating the industry,
taste, skill and disinterestedness of those engaged in the anti-slavery movement, the Anti-Slavery Fairs thus held are pre-eminently successful."[8]

For the women themselves who organized the fairs he had only the
highest words of praise:

"We never feel more ashamed of our humble efforts in the cause of
emancipation [he wrote in The North Star of January 8, 1848], than when we
contrast them with the silent, unobserved, and unapplauded efforts of those
through whose constant and persevering endeavors this annual exhibition is
given to the American public. Anti-slavery authors and orators may be said
to receive compensation for what they do, in the applause which must, sooner
or later, redound to them; but not so with the thousands whose works of use

and beauty adorn this fair. It is for them to work, unnoticed and unknown, and sometimes unenquired for; and many of them unable to see the good that results from their efforts."

While Douglass believed that the anti-slavery movement was doing much "for the elevation and improvement of women," he understood fully the need for an independent, organized movement to achieve equal rights for women. On July 14, 1848, *The North Star,* which featured the slogan, "Right is of no sex," carried an historic announcement:

"A Convention to discuss the Social, Civil and Religious Condition and Rights of Women, will be held in the Wesleyan Chapel at Seneca Falls, New York, on Wednesday and Thursday, the 19th and 20th of July instant.

"During the first day, the meetings will be exclusively for women, which all are earnestly invited to attend. The public generally are invited to be present on the second day, when Lucretia Mott, of Philadelphia, and others, both ladies and gentlemen, will address the Convention."

Thirty-five women and thirty-two men, courageous enough to run the risk of being branded "hermaphrodites" and "Aunt Nancy Men," responded to the call for the world's first organized gathering for woman's rights. Douglass was the only man to play a prominent part in the proceedings.

A "Declaration of Sentiments" adopted by the convention proclaimed: "The history of mankind is a history of repeated injuries and usurpations on the part of man toward woman, having in direct object the establishment of an absolute tyranny over her." Sixteen facts were "submitted to a candid world" by way of proof, after which the Declaration demanded that women "have immediate admission to all the rights and privileges which belong to them as citizens of the United States." Eleven resolutions were then introduced which made such demands as the right of women to personal and religious freedom, the right to vote and to be elected to public office, to testify in courts, equality in marriage and the right to their own children, the right to own property and to claim their own wages; the right to education and equality in trades and professions.[9]

The only resolution that aroused controversy and was not unanimously adopted was the ninth, asserting that it was "the duty of the women of this country to secure to themselves their sacred right to the elective franchise." Many of the delegates, even Lucretia Mott, felt that the demand for the right to vote was too advanced for the times and would only heap ridicule on the entire movement. But Elizabeth Cady

Stanton who had introduced the proposal was determined to press the issue, and looked about the Convention for an ally. "I knew Frederick, from personal experience, was just the man for the work," she told an audience of suffragists years later. Hurrying to Douglass' side, Mrs. Stanton read the resolution and asked him to speak on the question. Douglass promptly arose, and addressed the delegates. He argued convincingly that political equality was essential for the complete liberation of women. The resolution was adopted by a small majority.[10]

In 1888, a few years before his death, Douglass recalled his role at the Seneca Falls Convention, and told the International Council of Women:

"There are few facts in my humble history to which I look back with more satisfaction than to the fact, recorded in the history of the Woman Suffrage movement, that I was sufficiently enlightened at the early day, when only a few years from slavery, to support your resolution for woman suffrage. I have done very little in this world in which to glory, except this one act— and I certainly glory in that. When I ran away from slavery, it was for myself; when I advocated emancipation, it was for my people; but when I stood up for the rights of woman, self was out of the question, and I found a little nobility in the act."[11]

In *The North Star* of July 28, 1848, Douglass praised the action taken by the Seneca Falls Convention, announced his support of the "grand movement for attaining the civil, social, political, and religious rights of women," and bade the women engaged in the crusade his "humble Godspeed." Two weeks later, on August 2, he attended a series of meetings in Rochester to ratify the program of the Seneca Falls Convention. Again he was called upon to argue the merits of the suffrage resolution, and, "in a long, argumentative and eloquent plea," convinced many delegates who were hesitant about demanding the ballot. Not only was the proposal adopted, but the women of Rochester, persuaded by Douglass' arguments, voted to petition the state legislature to grant them the ballot and dedicated themselves to continue the appeal year after year until it was granted. Douglass hailed their stand, declaring "that the only true basis of right was the capacity of individuals."[12]

At the anti-slavery meeting held in Boston in 1850 an invitation was extended from the speaker's desk to all those who were interested in a plan for a National Woman's Rights Convention to meet in the ante-room. Nine women responded and entered the dank and dingy room. From this little meeting came the plans which resulted in a call signed by many prominent men and women for the first National Woman's Rights Convention to meet in Brinley Hall, Worcester, on October 23, 1850.

Douglass was in Massachusetts at this time, organizing opposition to the Fugitive Slave Act. He read the call for a national convention to consider "the question of Woman's Rights, Duties and Relations," and arranged his schedule so that he could be in Worcester on October 23. The attendance at the convention was large, representatives from nine states being present. Douglass, Garrison, Wendell Phillips, S. S. Foster, and Sojourner Truth were a few of the many Abolitionists who served as delegates. The motto of the convention, "Equality before the law without distinction of sex or color," was evidence of their influence.

The convention voted to petition the legislature of eight states to grant the ballot to women. A national committee was appointed to achieve this goal as well as to seek the repeal of property laws discriminating against women, and the opening to women of all government and professional positions. Wendell Phillips was made treasurer of the committee.

Over in England the *Westminster Review* in an elaborate article by Mrs. John Stuart Mill noted the Worcester convention and endorsed the proceedings. But in America the newspapers pelted it with abuse. It was "the Hen Convention," and its members "ismizers of the rankest stamp." "Woman's office," shrieked the New York *Mirror,* "are those of wife, mother, daughter, sister, friend—Good God, can they not be content with these?"[13]

In spite of this cheap ridicule the woman's movement gained momentum. Douglass continued to lend it his active support. Few indeed were the woman's rights conventions held during the 'fifties at which Douglass was not a featured speaker and whose proceedings were not fully reported in his paper. Susan B. Anthony even advised Gerrit Smith to look in Douglass' weekly for regular notices of woman's rights gatherings. Invariably the notice would be accompanied by an editorial comment hailing the meeting and expressing the editor's hope that the proceedings "will have a powerful effect upon the public mind." In 1853 when Douglass was thinking of changing the name of his paper, he rejected the proposed title, *The Brotherhood,* because it "implied the exclusion of the sisterhood."[14]

Douglass was a prominent figure at several conventions which pioneered in condemning discrimination because of sex. He was the presiding officer at the national convention of Colored Freemen at Cleveland in 1848 when a resolution was passed affirming a belief in the equality of the sexes and inviting the women present to participate in the proceedings. Two months later, at Philadelphia, Douglass was one of the organizers of a convention of Negro people at which a similar invitation was extended to women, white as well as Negro. Lucretia Mott decided to accept the liberal invitation:

"We are now in the midst of a convention of the colored people of this city," she wrote to Elizabeth Cady Stanton. "Douglass & Delany—Remond & Garnet are here—all taking an active part—and as they include women & *white* women too, I can do no less, with the interest I feel in the cause of the slave, as well as of woman, than be present & take a little part—So yesterday, in a pouring rain, Sarah Pugh & self, walked down there & expect to do the same today."[15]

At the Colored National Convention at Rochester in July, 1853, Douglass, chairman of the Committee on Declaration of Sentiments, wrote to Gerrit Smith: "We had one Lady Delegate—Mrs. Jeffrey of Geneva—strange to say we had good sense to make no *fuss* about it."[16]

Douglass was a member of the executive committee of the Radical Abolitionists which met in Worcester in 1860 to consider the feasibility of establishing a political party on strict anti-slavery grounds. The gathering invited women to participate in the proceedings, an invitation which marked the first effort made "to organize a political party upon a basis of absolute justice and perfect equality."[17] The stand was in keeping with Douglass' role as a reformer. To the powerful appeal he had made for freedom from chattel slavery, he had added the demand for the broadest liberty for all people.

Douglass and the Negro Convention Movement

Although Douglass' best work in the battle against slavery and prejudice was done on the platform and in his newspaper, he made notable contributions in the organized movement of the Negro people, especially as a leading figure in the ante-bellum Negro conventions. Here he joined forces with other Negroes in public life to protest, petition, and carry into operation a program of, by and for the Negro people of the United States.

The Negro convention movement started long before Douglass became actively involved in the anti-slavery struggle. Beginning with 1817, the year of Douglass' birth, local and state-wide meetings of Negro people were held in many northern communities in protest against the American Colonization Society. The agitation increased during the 1820's when the Colonization Society purchased Liberia and began its propaganda campaign throughout the nation. Through this agitation, thousands of American Negroes for the first time felt a sense of communication with groups from other sections of the nation. It was inevitable that this development would lead to a realization among the Negro people that their ultimate victory lay in an integrated program representing a national viewpoint.

Events during the late 1820's hastened the movement for a national organization of the Negro people. In 1829, the Ohio courts declared that the Black Laws adopted in that state in 1804-1807 were still constitutional. These laws restricted the freedom of Negro people and demanded of each a $500 bond for good behavior. Unwilling to wait for officials to enforce the decisions, groups of white citizens in the southern part of the state took matters into their own hands and gave notice that the Negro people either post the bond within a limited time or get out of the state. When the Negroes disregarded these warnings or were slow to act, mobs fell upon them, on one occasion killing a number and destroying the property of the others. Overnight, Negro communities in Ohio were emptied as the Negro people fled into Canada, into western Pennsylvania, or into other states in the Great Lakes region.[1]

Fearing that legislators and mobsters in the East would follow the pattern set by Ohio, Negro leaders decided to plan concerted action on a nation-wide scale to stem the tide of repression. A circular issued by five Negro leaders in Philadelphia called for a convention of Negro delegates from the several states "to meet on the 20th Day of September, 1830, to devise plans and means for the establishment of a colony in upper Canada, under the patronage of the General Convention. . . ." Forty delegates met under President Richard Allen of Philadelphia,[2] organizer and first bishop of the African Methodist Episcopal Church, and concurred upon a proposal to buy extensive Canadian land with a view to establishing a colony of free Negroes. But their most significant achievement was the recommendation of formation of a parent society, to be called the National Negro Convention, with auxiliaries in different towns and cities.

In the six years following 1830, the National Negro Convention met annually and adopted programs for the security and elevation of the Negro people.[3] In addition, the convention founded a series of organizations, known as the Phoenix Societies, in the urban areas of the North.

Under the direction of Rev. Christopher Rush, Rev. Theodore S. Wright, and Rev. Peter Williams, Jr., these local societies made proposals to improve the moral welfare of the Negroes, and to instruct them in literature and mechanical arts.

A series of dissensions which had been brewing since 1831 split the National Convention after its 1836 meeting. Some of the delegates were convinced that Canadian colonization was still the most urgent business at hand. Others felt that it was necessary to concentrate upon building a better social order in the United States. Some were beginning to support political action while others clung to the Garrisonian doctrine of moral suasion. One group doubted the efficacy of associating with any set of white Abolitionists and advocated restricting the convention to Negro membership. Another, convinced of the inability to achieve equality for Negroes in existing institutions, favored continuing the establishment of separate schools and churches for the Negro people. The latter was opposed by a group of Pennsylvania Negroes under the influence of the wealthy Robert Purvis, William Whipper, and James Forten, Sr., who refused to recognize any special needs and problems of the Negro people requiring separate organizations, and called for their immediate and complete integration into American life.

In 1836, the Pennsylvania-dominated American Moral Reform Society, organized a year before to extend the work of the Phoenix Societies, withdrew from the National Convention, set up its own constitution and published its official organ, *The National Reformer,* edited by William Whipper. Meeting annually from 1836 through the early 1840's, the society endorsed the platform of Garrisonianism, and proclaimed that the Negro people attend only those schools and churches open to both races. The Garrisonians through the *National Anti-Slavery Standard* and the *Liberator* supported this point of view.

Opposition to the Moral Reformists grew as it became clear to many of the 500,000 free Negroes in the United States that the white people were not anxious to share their institutions with Negroes. In 1840 a demand arose for the holding of a new National Negro Convention and so Committees of Correspondence and local and regional bodies were established. In September, 1840, the National Reformed Convention of the Colored People met in New Haven, under the leadership of David Ruggles. The delegates emphasized two points in their proceedings: the importance of Negro initiative in "extricating themselves from the tyrant's yoke," and the degrading influence of slavery upon the free Negro population. Through the efforts of Ruggles, William C. Nell, Rev. Pennington, and John B. Vashon, the American Reform Board of Disfranchised Commissioners was organized and met in New York City in 1841.[4]

Although the American Moral Reform Society and the Reformed Convention were shortlived, the state conventions and local auxiliary societies progressed rapidly during the 1830's and early 1840's despite the unfortunate factionalism in the national movement. Innumerable Negro organizations sprang up throughout New England and the Middle States. Societies of free Negroes appeared in the great western centers of Detroit, Chicago, and Cincinnati. State conventions were held annually in the western states of Ohio, Illinois, Michigan, Indiana, and in the border state of Maryland.[5]

After a lapse of seven years, the National Negro Convention reconvened in Buffalo in 1843. Fifty-eight delegates were present, thirty-six of whom were from New York state; ten states, including Virginia, North Carolina, and Georgia were represented. Amos Gerry Beman, a New Haven clergyman, was elected president, and Douglass served as one of the vice-presidents. But the outstanding figure at the convention was Henry Highland Garnet, pastor of the Liberty Street Negro Presbyterian Church. In the most savage indictment of slavery delivered by a Negro since David Walker's *Appeal,* Garnet stirred the assembly:

"Brethren, arise, arise! Strike for your lives and liberties. Now is the day and the hour. Let every slave throughout the land do this, and the days of slavery are numbered. You can not be more oppressed than you have been —you cannot suffer greater cruelties than you have already. Rather die freemen than live to be slaves. Remember that you are four millions."

Still under the influence of the Garrisonian principles of non-resistance and moral suasion, Frederick Douglass took issue with Garnet. He observed that there was "too much physical force both in the address and remarks of Garnet; that the address, could it reach the slaves, and the advice . . . be followed, while it might not lead the slaves to rise in insurrection, for liberty, would nevertheless, and necessarily be the occasion for insurrection. . . ." And that, Douglass concluded, was what he wished "in no way to have any agency in hurrying about and what we were called upon to avoid."

For several days, the convention debated Garnet's proposal, and finally, by the narrow majority of one vote, 18 in favor of Garnet's measure and 19 against it, Douglass' position was sustained.

Later in the convention, Douglass proposed a plan of moral suasion to induce the slave-owners to release their slaves from bondage. Garnet objected bitterly to reliance on such tactics, and asked that the plan be rejected. Douglass resumed the floor in defense of his report, and won a majority vote at the final count.[6]

The proceedings revealed that important sections of the Negro population were definitely breaking away from Garrison's moral suasion doctrine. By still adhering to this doctrine, Douglass, at this stage, was not as advanced as the most militant section of the Negro people. But, as we shall shortly see, Douglass soon recognized the futility of relying on moral suasion as a chief weapon to end slavery.

Although they rejected Garnet's proposal, the delegates were so aroused by his address that they attacked the problems confronting the Negro people with renewed determination. They voted to send capable Negro speakers into northern communities to inform whites and Negroes about "the claims, disabilities, sentiments, and wishes of the colored people," to impress the free Negroes with the importance of education, of improvement in science and literature, and of applying themselves to the mechanical arts. The convention also went on record as favoring the circulation of petitions to Congress for the abolition of slavery in the territories and opposing the annexation of Texas.[7]

Meeting in Troy, New York, in 1847, the National Colored Convention was attended by sixty-eight delegates from nine states, forty-six of whom were from New York and fourteen from Massachusetts. Nathan Johnson of New Bedford, who had befriended Douglass a decade previously, was elected president. Vice-presidents included Rev. J. W. C. Pennington and Dr. James McCune Smith.

Douglass took a prominent part in the debates, creating "some excitement" among the delegates by urging the Negro people "to come out from their pro-slavery churches; exclaiming that his right arm should wither before he would worship at their blood-stained altars; they were not the places for colored men." As chairman of the committee to draft a report on the best means of abolishing slavery and destroying caste in the United States, Douglass revealed that he was still under the influence of the Garrisonian wing of anti-slavery thought. The committee condemned "any attempt to lead our people to confide in brute force as a reformatory instrumentality," and endorsed moral suasion—"a faithful, earnest, and persevering enforcement of the great principles of justice and morality, religion and humanity"—as the "only invincible and infallible means within our reach to overthrow this foul system of blood and ruin."[8]

The convention laid plans for a national press with committees in six states appointed to gather pertinent information and opinion. In the meantime, *The Ram's Horn, The National Watchman, The North Star,* and *The Mystery* were considered papers worthy of support. Among other business, Gerrit Smith presented the delegates with 120,000 acres of New York state farming and timber land to which about three thousand Negro people of that state could lay claim if they wished to settle upon the property and put small farms into operation.[9]

Douglass' stand on the question of establishing a national Negro press disappointed many of the delegates. Garnet introduced the resolution calling for a press "solely under the control of the people of color." The suggestion was submitted to a special committee, headed by Dr. James McCune Smith, which endorsed the proposal.

"Of the means for the advancement of a people placed as we are," went the report, "none are more available than a press. . . . Among ourselves we need a press that shall keep us steadily alive to our responsibilities, which shall constantly point out the principles which should guide our conduct and our labors, which shall cheer us from one end of the land to the other, by recording our acts, our sufferings, our temporary defeats, and our steadily approaching triumph, or rather the triumph of the glorious truth 'Human Equality,' whose servants and soldiers we are."

The report paid tribute to the services rendered by newspapers edited and published by Negroes, then pointed out that because of the poverty of their owners their influence was limited. No one man, it declared, among five hundred thousand free Negro people was "yet set apart with a competence for the purpose of advocating our cause and the cause of our brethren in chains." Hence the committee called for setting up:

"In these United States, a printing press, a copious supply of type, a full and complete establishment, wholly controlled by colored men; let the thinking, writing man, the compositors, pressmen, printers' help—all, all, be men of color; then let there come from said establishment a weekly periodical and a quarterly periodical, edited as well as printed by colored men; let this establishment be so well endowed as to be beyond the chances of temporary patronage; and then there will be a fixed fact, a rallying point, towards which the strong and the weak amongst us would look with confidence and hope. . . ."[10]

To the surprise of the delegates, Douglass led the opposition to the report. He favored Negro newspapers, he told the convention, but believed that a national Negro press at that time was a visionary scheme since it could not be successfully sustained. More important, "a paper started as a national organ, would soon dwindle down to be the organ of a clique," and in the end would mean the control of the editor by the group. He was in favor of sustaining the present newspapers instead of killing them off by a national press which was doomed to a brief existence.[11]

The delegates were not impressed by Douglass' reasoning and voted 27 to 9 for the national Negro press. Strangely enough, Douglass published the entire text of the report on the press in his paper, and, at the same time, called on the Negro people to support *The North Star* and make it a real national Negro paper.[12] Evidently his opposition to a national Negro press stemmed basically from his reluctance to relinquish control of his own paper. He was convinced that a paper sponsored by the National Convention and edited by a group of people would prove cumbersome in operation and would create constant dissensions.

While nothing came of the plan to establish a national Negro press, a number of Negro leaders were critical of Douglass for his stand on this issue. They accused him of permitting his own interests to interfere with a program which promised to achieve advances for his people. Douglass' decision in 1851 to call his journal *Frederick Douglass' Paper* also evoked criticism for the same reason. While none of the leaders questioned the outstanding qualities of the paper, they believed it was somewhat inconsistent for the editor to urge the Negro people to support it as their own journal while he insisted on conducting it as his personal organ. These critics overlooked the fact that they were living in an era of personal journalism, and that one of the chief reasons for the attention accorded Douglass' paper was precisely because it was the paper of a man who was recognized as the outstanding American Negro. Moreover, Douglass always insisted in editorials and speeches that the paper was not his personal organ but rather the tribune of the Negro people, both the enslaved and the free.

In September, 1848, between sixty and seventy delegates met in Cleveland and chose Douglass as president of the National Negro Convention. Douglass was delighted to discover in examining the delegates' credentials that they represented a cross-section of the free Negro people—printers, carpenters, blacksmiths, shoemakers, engineers, dentists, gunsmiths, editors, tailors, merchants, wheelwrights, painters, farmers, physicians, plasterers, masons, clergymen, barbers, hairdressers, coopers, livery stable keepers, bath-house keepers, and grocers.

Reversing the position adopted a year before on the national Negro press, the convention anounced that *The North Star* answered the needs and purposes of such a press and urged its support by all Negro people. The delegates also endorsed the Free Soil Party, but declared that they were "determined to maintain the higher stand and more liberal views which heretofore characterized us as *abolitionists."* This meeting recommended "a change in the conduct of colored barbers who refused to treat colored men on a basis of equality with the whites." Committees were appointed in different states to organize vigilante groups, "so as to enable them to measure arms with assailants without and invaders within."[13]

Douglass' voice was heard throughout the proceedings. He opposed the preamble to the seventeenth resolution "inasmuch as it intimated that slavery could not be abolished by moral means alone." He moved to amend the thirty-third resolution, declaring that the word "persons" used in the resolution designating delegates be understood "to include *women."* The motion was seconded, and carried "with three cheers for woman's rights."[14]

Douglass' role at the Cleveland Convention won him nationwide attention. The proceedings were printed in the press, and special comments on the presiding officer appeared in the editorial columns. The pro-southern papers exhausted their vocabulary in slandering Douglass, but other journals were extravagant in their praise. Answering an attack by the *Plain Dealer* of its city, the Cleveland *Daily True Democrat* declared: "Frederick Douglass is a man, who if divided into fifty parts would make fifty better men than the editor of the *Plain Dealer."* Gerrit Smith was so delighted with Douglass' conduct at the convention that he ventured the opinion that "he has the talents and dignity that would adorn the Presidency of the nation."[15]

But there were serious weaknesses in the movement which Douglass was convinced had to be eliminated if the cause was to progress. Basic differences among those adhering to moral suasion and those who believed strongly in political action, differences between various religious sects, and numerous petty jealousies and feuds prevented the adoption of a co-ordinated program that would present the viewpoint of the Negro people to the nation. Furthermore, the absence of a truly functioning organization between conventions resulted in a failure of the delegates to implement the work during the intervening period. Nor was there in existence a national body with sufficient authority to call meetings of the Negro people to take action on the vital issues of the day. Even the conventions themselves were brought into being by groups of individuals acting solely on their own initiative. Consequently, the movement lacked continuity and authority.

To create harmony and unity among the Negro people and to give the National Convention movement a permanent organizational structure, Douglass projected the idea of a National League of Colored People. In *The North Star* of August 10, 1849, he placed the motto, "The Union of the oppressed for the Sake of Freedom," at the head of the editorial column, and published an outline of a constitution for the "National League." The preamble went:

"Whereas, the voice of reason, and the admonitions of experience, in all ages alike, impress us with the wisdom and necessity of combination; and that union and concert of action are highly essential to the speedy success of any good cause; that as in division there is weakness, so in union there is strength; and whereas, we have long deplored the distracted and divided state of the oppressed, and the manifold evils resulting therefrom, and desiring as we do to see an union formed which shall enable us the better to grapple with the various systems of injustice and wrong by which we are environed, and to regain our plundered rights, we solemnly agree to unite in accordance with the following."

The object of the League was the abolition of slavery, and the elevation and improvement of the free Negro people of the United States. It would seek to achieve these goals by means of lectures and the press, "and all other means within their power, consistent with christian morality." The League would have a president, secretary, treasurer, and a council of nine.

For several weeks after this initial announcement, Douglass' paper featured the constitution of the proposed league and the call for a convention which was scheduled to meet in Philadelphia on September 21. The editor waited anxiously for the reaction of his "colored brethren in different parts of the country on the subject of *union*."[16]

The response was disappointing. Among white Abolitionists, the *Anti-Slavery Bugle* hailed the project, and wished it well, observing that it "has long been a source of grief to Abolitionists that the Free Colored People of this country are so widely separated from each other by sectarian and party lines as to impair their efficiency in the work of their own elevation and in breaking the chains of the enslaved."[17] But the Negro leaders themselves displayed little interest in the proposed organization, and the Negro press did little to publicize it. One Negro correspond-

ent voiced his regret to Douglass that there was "so much apathy manifested on the part of our leading men to your noble and philanthropic
scheme," and attributed it to personal jealousy and to the opposition of
colored clergymen to a plan sponsored by one who had "attacked the pro-
slavery character of the church, and told them that they should not let
slaveholders and their abettors preach in their pulpit."[18] The bitter attack
against Douglass launched by Rev. Henry Highland Garnet at the time
the National League was projected would bear out this conjecture. Garnet
accused Douglass of having spoken lightly and contemptuously of the religious convictions of the Negro people, and of having denied "the inspiration of the Bible." Although Douglass denied the charges and the *Anti-
Slavery Bugle* denounced Garnet for echoing the cries of the "pro-slavery
church," the attack was influential in turning Negro clergymen against
Douglass' League.[19]

Despite the indifference of the Negro leaders and press, Douglass
was determined to proceed with the organization of the National League.
If only thirty persons could be found who were willing to form the League,
he was convinced that "from this small beginning, an institution may be
erected, fraught with untold good to ourselves and to posterity." Unfortunately, the organization meeting at Philadelphia was so poorly attended
that even Douglass was forced to admit that his proposal had been pre-
mature. Criticizing Negro leaders sharply for their refusal to join in the
founding of a national organization for improving the condition of their
people, he abandoned the project. Yet even as he dropped the plan,
Douglass expressed confidence that eventually the Negro would create an
organization such as he envisaged:

"It is impossible to keep a people asunder for any long time, who are so
strongly and peculiarly identified together, when there is a vigorous effort
made to unite them. We shall never despair of our people—an union shall
yet be effected—our ranks cannot always be divided. The injuries which we
mutually suffer—the contempt in which we are held—the wrongs which we endure, together with a sense of our own dignity as men, *must* eventually lead
us to combine."[20]

For five years after the Cleveland convention, the National Conven-
tion movement lay dormant. Following the passage of the Fugitive Slave
Act in 1850, many Negroes were too terrified to attend public gatherings.
Any Negro who was unable to produce proof of his freedom satisfac-
tory to a southern deputy was in danger of being returned to slavery.
Hundreds of Negro families from Ohio, Pennsylvania, and New York

fled to Canada, abandoning their homes and work. Professor Fred Landon estimates that approximately twenty thousand Negroes, the greater percentage of whom were probably former slaves, fled to Canada during the decade 1850-1860.[21]

The very intensity of the drive against the Negro population in the North compelled the revival of the National Convention. In July, 1853, a hundred and forty delegates from nine states gathered in Rochester, New York, in what was the most important of all conventions. The call for the gathering indicated some of the major problems which made the reconvening of the National Convention necessary:

"The Fugitive Slave Act, . . . the proscriptive legislation of several States with a view to drive our people from their borders—the exclusion of our children from schools supported by our money—the prohibition of the exercise of the franchise—the exclusion of colored citizens from the jury box—the social barriers erected against our learning trades—the wiley and vigorous efforts of the American Colonization Society to employ the arm of the government to expel us from our native land—and withal the propitious awakening to the fact of our condition at home and abroad, which has followed the publication of 'Uncle Tom's Cabin'—calls trumpet-tongued for our union, cooperation, and action. . . ."

Reverend J. W. C. Pennington was elected president of the Rochester Convention and the vice-presidents included Douglass, William C. Nell. and John B. Vashon.

Douglass was also chairman of the committee on Declaration of Sentiments and drew up the "Address of the Colored Convention to the People of the United States." This remarkable "Address" set forth the basic demands of the Negro people for justice and equality. Today, one hundred years afterward, it may still be read, not only for the clarity and grace of its prose but also for its significance.

The "Address" demanded that "the doors of the school-house, the work-shop, the church, the college, shall be thrown open as freely to our children as to the children of other members of the community"; that "the white and black may stand upon an equal footing before the laws of the land"; that "colored men shall not be either by custom or enactment excluded from the jury-box"; that "the complete and unrestricted right of suffrage, which is essential to the dignity even of the white man, be extended to the Free Colored Man also," and that laws "flagrantly unjust to the man of color . . . ought to be repealed." These demands were justified on the simple principle that the Negro people were American citizens "asserting their rights on their own native soil."

Realizing that this claim of citizenship was denied by the national government, Douglass presented a masterly historical analysis to buttress his argument, quoting extensively from state Constitutional Conventions, from congressional debates, and from Andrew Jackson's proclamation to the free colored inhabitants of Louisiana during the Battle of New Orleans.

"The case is made out," Douglass concluded. "We and you stand upon the same broad national basis. Whether at home or abroad, we and you owe equal allegiance to the same government—have a right to look for protection on the same ground. We have been born and reared on the same soil; we have been animated by, and have displayed the same patriotic impulses; we have acknowledged and performed the same duty; we have fought and bled in the same battles; we have gained and gloried in the same victories; and we are equally entitled to the blessings resulting therefrom."[22]

"No nobler paper was ever put forth by any body of men," commented the reporter for the *New York Tribune*.[23]

One of the most important and controversial issues before the Rochester Convention was the question of founding a manual labor college for colored youth. As in the case of almost every problem discussed by the delegates, it was by no means a new idea. Samuel Cornish had outlined a plan for a Negro Manual Labor College in *Freedom's Journal* as early as 1827. Four years later, at the National Negro Convention in Philadelphia, the idea, proposed by Garrison and his colleagues, won the support of the delegates. Cornish was elected the agent to collect the necessary funds for the institution, and auxiliary committees to assist him were set up in the important centers of free Negroes.

New Haven was chosen for the site, and plans for the college, with a board of trustees consisting of a majority of Negroes, were drawn up. Arthur Tappan purchased several acres of land in the southern part of New Haven with the intention of presenting it to the Negro Convention for the school campus, but so much opposition arose from the townspeople that, on September 8, 1831, the mayor issued an order prohibiting the proposed school within the city limits. On September 10, the "best citizens" of New Haven, led by the mayor and a number of Yale professors and students, staged riots before the homes of supporters of the college. Many Negroes wished to proceed in the face of this hostility, but some timid white Abolitionists withdrew their support, and the college was abandoned.

Still the idea persisted. The New England Anti-Slavery Society, at its first annual meeting in January, 1833, announced that it was making "strenuous exertions for the establishment of a manual labor school for colored youth, and will probably soon attain its object." The Society appointed Garrison its agent to collect funds for the school, and the Abolitionist leader decided to visit England for the purpose of raising money.[24] England at this time was in the midst of a campaign to abolish slavery in the British West Indies, and the people would extend a hearty welcome to any mission from the United States seeking financial aid against slavery in this country.

Negroes in the United States not only endorsed Garrison's mission to Europe, but provided a large part of the funds for his trip. At the National Negro Convention in June, 1833, the delegates approved Garrison's mission, and, on the basis of the hopes aroused by this new venture, abandoned their efforts to colonize extensively in Canada.[25]

In the *Liberator* of July 5, 1834, Garrison announced that more than fifteen hundred dollars had been subscribed for the manual labor school, and pledged himself to carry on a consistent campaign until the institution was established. But nothing came of the movement, and gradually Garrison lost interest in the project. Negroes themselves, moreover, began to be divided on the issue. Douglass, for example, was at first opposed to a Negro college, contending that it was based upon the principle of segregation and tended to perpetuate prejudice against color.

Events themselves compelled Douglass to change his viewpoint. Negroes were increasingly being shut out from all lucrative employment and compelled to do only the most menial work. Even in firms owned by white Abolitionists a colored man found it impossible to get a job higher than a porter, no matter what his capabilities.[26] What was equally if not more alarming was the influx of immigrants from Ireland who in the 'forties and 'fifties threatened the Negro's position even in the lowliest employments. Negro workers were being displaced as porters, barbers, cab-drivers, wood-sawyers, stevedores, and common laborers. Unable to secure employment as skilled craftsmen and finding themselves pushed out of menial jobs, the Negro workers faced a serious crisis.

As he traveled about the country visiting Negro communities, Douglass became familiar with the economic problems of his people. "Learn Trades or Starve," he wrote in 1853. "We must find new methods of obtaining a livelihood, for the old ones are failing us very fast." He appealed to white anti-slavery men and women to employ Negro boys and girls as apprentices "and teach them trades, by which they can obtain an honorable living." Funds raised to send Negro students to

European colleges were all very well, but it was more important for the Negroes to learn how to make a good living than to learn Latin and Greek. Anti-slavery men who called themselves friends of the Negro people but refused to hire Negro workers for anything but the most menial jobs were hypocrites.[27]

In March, 1853, Douglass visited Harriet Beecher Stowe at her home in Andover, Ohio, to consult with the author of *Uncle Tom's Cabin* "as to some method which should contribute successfully, and permanently, to the improvement and elevation of the free colored people in the United States. . . ." Mrs. Stowe asked Douglass to propose the best plan to achieve that goal. He replied:

"What can be done to improve the condition of the free people of color in the United States? The plan which I humbly submit in answer to this inquiry—and in the hope it may find favor with you, and with many friends of humanity who honor, love and co-operate with you—is the establishment in Rochester, N. Y., or in some other part of the United States equally favorable to such an enterprise, of an *industrial college* in which shall be taught several branches of the mechanical arts. This college is to be opened to colored youth. . . ."[28]

Anxious to secure approval of his plan, Douglass read his reply to Mrs. Stowe to the Rochester National Negro Convention. A number of delegates, Charles L. Remond and George T. Downing among them, were hostile to the proposal. They argued that the college would be too costly; that the Negro people would not be interested in the institution. The old contention that a Negro college was a capitulation to prejudice against color was also raised.

Douglass, Dr. James McCune Smith and James W. C. Pennington led the battle for the industrial college. They pointed out that there were few Negro apprentices since there were not many Negro craftsmen and most white craftsmen were opposed to taking a Negro into service. An industrial college would produce skilled workers, and the presence of an "industrious, enterprising, upright, thrifty and intelligent free black population would be a killing refutation of slavery." Since the college would be open to all students regardless of color, it could hardly be considered a segregated institution.

The majority of the delegates concurred with the arguments in favor of the industrial college, and voted to sponsor the institution.

To implement its program and provide for its operation before the next national meeting, the Rochester Convention organized a National

Council of the Colored People consisting of two members from each of ten northern states. Aided by state councils, the popularly elected members of which were to have direct control of local affairs, the National Council set up four committees: the Committee on a Manual Training School which was to procure funds, select the location and establish the school complete with dormitories and a farm; the Committee on Business Relationships which was to establish a large-scale employment office; the Committee on Publication which was to compile records, statistics, and the history of every phase of Negro life, a collection which was to be made available to the public; and the Committee of Protective Union which was to establish a kind of co-operative at which Negroes could buy and sell staples.[29]

Thoroughly satisfied with their work, the delegates left Rochester imbued with a determination to translate their deliberations into action. They had reason for feeling elated. The Convention had received favorable comments from a large section of the press. A citizen of Rochester, who had never before attended an anti-slavery meeting, wrote a glowing letter to the *New York Tribune* describing his reactions to the sessions:

"Throughout, it has been conducted by colored men, and their debates as well as proceedings generally have been equal to any of the white men who have heretofore espoused their cause as abolitionists or philanthropists of any kind. . . . I have never heard more chaste and refined dictum from any class of men, neither have I seen better oratorical powers displayed. . . . I have never seen delegates come in cleaner apparel, and more dignified manner than have the colored men."[30]

The letter was typical. Douglass informed Gerrit Smith that the deliberations had improved "the current of feeling toward the colored people" in Rochester. The *Rochester Democrat* pointed out that the impressions left upon the minds of many "Anglo Saxon spectators" was "highly favorable." It added:

"What is equally important, it has convinced the colored people themselves, that they have many able and practicable minds among them, and they are resolutely engaged in devising schemes for their own moral, mental and physical improvement. . . . Had *Wm. Lloyd Garrison, Gerrit Smith,* and other able champions of their cause, been present and prominent in their proceedings, they, and not the *Remonds, Douglasses* and others would have received the praise for all that was wisely done, while the colored people would have shared the odium of all that might have been wrong. There can be no doubt that these people have the ability to devise and carry out measures for their own social advancement, and for the general improvement of their condition. . . . Let them have the sympathy and pecuniary aid of others, but let their plans be devised and executed by themselves. . . ."[31]

Inspired by the great success of the Rochester Convention, dozens of local and regional Negro people's conventions were held throughout the North during the closing months of 1853. Numerous mass meetings were held in churches and schools to endorse the proceedings at Rochester, and many leaders of the National Convention visited Negro leaders to help them establish local groups. On October 6, 1853, the Illinois State Negro Convention met in Chicago, heard Douglass discuss the Rochester Convention, voted to support the movement, and adopted the slogans of the 1853 convention in mobilizing the fight against the black laws.[32] As in the case of the Rochester Convention, the sessions made a deep impression upon the community. A letter in the *Chicago Tribune* of October 11, 1853, describes the reaction of a spectator at the sessions:

"During the recent meeting of the convention of colored men in this city, I have several times looked in, to witness their proceedings—and I must be allowed to say, that if the colored men there assembled are to be taken as an example of that race, they have been hitherto very much underrated and abused.

" . . . I have been very much in the habit of mingling with political bodies of men, and taking part in public meetings of a political character, and I do not hesitate to say, that for courtesy, urbanity and kindness towards each other I never saw the members of this colored convention outdone.

"And I have seen many white conventions that would much improve by emulating the conduct of the members of this convention of wronged, despised, abused, and down trodden people. . . .

"To say the speech of Frederick Douglass on Friday evening was good would be too tame an expression to convey to the reader an idea of its real merits. . . .

"As a whole, the colored convention just held must greatly tend to elevate the colored people in the estimation of [the] community generally, and to satisfy many that the estimate usually made of the colored man is much too low; that this branch of the universal brotherhood are capable of high elevation in the moral and intellectual scale; that as men they are entitled to protection, and not oppression by our laws as to equal privileges under those laws."

Unfortunately, most of the plans laid down at Rochester and ratified at local conventions never went beyond the paper stage. At the first meeting of the National Council in January, 1854, not enough delegates were present to constitute a quorum. The second, the last meeting, at Cleveland was disrupted by factional disputes shortly after it got under way.

A combination of factors was responsible for the failure to carry out the program of the 1853 convention. Although defeated at Rochester, the colonizationists increased their efforts to convince the Negro people that emigration was the only solution to their problems. Shortly after the Rochester Convention, a call was issued for a convention in Cleveland on August 24, 1854, to discuss the emigration question. Douglass criticized the move as a deliberate attempt to sabotage the program set up in Rochester for ameliorating the condition of the Negro people. He appealed to the colonizationists to abandon their schemes, and to put all their efforts behind the program of the National Convention.[33]

Douglass' criticism of the call for a colonization convention in Cleveland was justified. A dismal failure, the endless debates and factional disputes preceding and following the convention created confusion among Negro leaders and diverted their attention from the pressing problem of implementing the program of the National Convention.[34]

Little progress was made in the campaign to establish a manual labor college. As chairman of the committee to establish the school, Douglass drew up a detailed plan for the institution, which was to be known as the "American Industrial School." It was to be located within one hundred miles of Erie, Pennsylvania, on a site of at least two hundred acres of land, one hundred and fifty of which would be used as a farm for agricultural instruction. Teachers would be selected and students admitted to the school "without reference to sex or complexion," and special efforts would be made "to aid in providing for the female sex, methods and means of enjoying an independent and honorable livelihood." For every course in literature, there would be a course in handicraft. Each student would occupy half his time while at school working at some handicraft or on the farm, and all handicrafts produced would be sold at a market within easy access of the school.

It was an ambitious program, one which anticipated the curriculum and organization of most of the manual labor schools established since the Civil War. But its fulfillment hinged upon the raising of a fund sufficient to launch the institution. The committee proposed a foundation fund of thirty thousand dollars, two-thirds of which was to be raised through the sale of two thousand shares of stock, at ten dollars a share, and one-third in outright contributions from friends of the cause. As soon as three thousand dollars came into the fund, the site would be selected; when ten thousand dollars was received, construction of the school building and work-shop would start; with fifteen thousand dollars, the school would open its doors.

Designated as agent to raise the foundation fund, Douglass entered upon his duties with his customary enthusiasm, lecturing and writing appeals for funds. But the appeals went unheeded. The Negro people themselves were too poor to contribute. A good deal had been expected from Harriet Beecher Stowe, but she reconsidered her offer and, for reasons not divulged, decided against the project.[35] The Garrisonians not only did not aid the project but Garrison himself criticized the proposal for an industrial school and accused the Negro advocates of laboring under a *"morbid state of mind."*

By June, 1855, two years after the Rochester Convention, Douglass had collected only a pitiful amount of money and the project had to be abandoned. But his conviction that the institution was essential for his people was as strong as ever. On March 21, 1856, Douglass wrote:

"I am yet of the opinion that nothing can be done for the free colored people—remaining in their present employment. These employments—such as waiting at hotels, on steamboats, barbering in large cities, and the like—contribute to no solid character. They require servility, beget dependence, destroy self-reliance, and furnish leisure and temptation to every possible view—from smoking cigars to drinking whiskey. What we want is steady employment at respectable trades, or on the land. To this end if I had money I would establish an industrial school to begin with, where the education of the hands and heart should be the main feature."[36]

The collapse of the program for the elevation of the Negro people outlined at the Rochester Convention practically spelled the end of the ante-bellum Negro convention movement. On October 16, 1855, one hundred and twenty-four delegates representing six states and Canada met in Philadelphia and conferred for three days. The most spirited discussion centered about the manual labor college question. A committee, dominated by the Philadelphia delegates, denounced the college as "a complexional institution" designed to further separate the Negro youth from the population. It declared that there were a number of institutions already in existence which could be utilized by the Negroes, and which could give them proper training. Furthermore, the Negro people could not provide a school which would furnish adequate training; nor would the masses of the Negro people avail themselves of the opportunity to use such a school, even if it were established. A substitute plan was offered whereby a central bureau would be established to collect funds and promote the mechanical arts among Negro youth.

Dr. James McCune Smith led the opposition to the report against the industrial college, and, with Douglass' aid, influenced the convention to have the report amended to include his own recommendations which called for the establishment of industrial associations in communities with large Negro populations. The associations were to correspond and cooperate with one other, and hold a national convention in October, 1857. Douglass warmly endorsed Smith's proposal.[37]

Despite the spirited discussion, the delegates had few illusions concerning the possibility of continuing the National Convention. When they left Franklin Hall on October 18, the majority knew that they had participated in the last National Convention for years to come.

Factional disputes, personal jealousies, fears of disclosure, lack of finances, the exodus of Negroes to Canada and Europe after the passage of the Fugitive Slave Act were among the major reasons for the failure of the Negro Convention movement to maintain a stable existence and to convert large parts of its program into reality. Yet the movement was one of great significance for the Negro people. The auxiliary conventions directed by officers of the National Convention were able to improve the conditions of Negro people living in northern rural sections and remote villages. Throughout all the northern cities, the local Negro meetings organized benevolent societies to provide essentials for needy persons, to create mutual insurance funds for their members, to provide teachers and social workers for the communities, to extend loans, and to furnish jobs and markets for goods. Sponsoring itinerant speakers, the National Convention emphasized the importance of rudimentary education and advanced study in arts and sciences even where public education facilities were restricted. Particularly did the convention address itself to the courage, the self-reliance of the Negro people to counteract the propaganda of white newspapers and speakers. It urged the Negro to apply himself to trades and to respectable daily tasks. At the same time, the convention exposed merchants and industrialists, including white Abolitionist employers, who refused to hire Negro help or insisted on placing them only as porters. The convention's opposition to emigration was influential in dooming the colonization movement to failure. The efforts and accomplishments of the convention stimulated the frank praise of incredulous whites, and did more than any agent to refute the widespread theory of Negro inferiority.

The National Convention and its state and local auxiliary societies created among the Negro people a feeling of confidence and self-respect. It was to these groups that the free Negro turned to voice his opinion. For these bodies were his own organizations; he spoke, wrote, and petitioned not as an individual but as a member of the convention of American Negroes. The convention brought northern Negroes together as no other body did and provided them with an opportunity to arrive at a common perspective of problems and solutions. It developed local and national leaders of the Negro people and prepared the ground for those men who were to play a prominent role during the Civil War and later would go into the old slave areas and co-operate with the freedmen in the struggle to achieve a new life.

Although he entered the movement long after it had been launched, Douglass' contributions to the convention were of major significance. True, he was criticized by other Negro leaders for failing sufficiently to integrate his ideas with the movement. But his position as the outstanding spokesman of and for the Negro people was recognized by the delegates. His newspaper was adopted as the official organ of the National Convention. Twice (1843 and 1853) he was elected a vice president and once (1848), its president. He was the author of the most important document issued by the movement, the "Address of the Colored Convention to the People of the United States." He served on numerous committees and freely contributed his time and energy toward the full implementation of its program. His work in the movement won him nationwide recognition as the leading champion of freedom and equality for the Negro people.

Anti-Slavery Activity in Rochester

"I have now been at home about one week," Douglass wrote from Rochester on March 21, 1856, "and am resting a little from my winters labors. I have travelled this winter between four and five thousand miles, visited communities as far east as Bangor, and as far west as Cincinnati, delivered about seventy lectures, been in snow drifts oft, but have reached this season, always very trying [to] my health with nothing more serious than a soar [sic] throat which is now on the mend."[1]

The letter described a fairly typical aspect of Douglass' life during the 'fifties when he spent about six months of the year on the road. He would return from his tours exhausted, but within a week would fling himself into the local anti-slavery activities.

Under the sponsorship of the Rochester anti-slavery group, Douglass spoke frequently in Corinthian Hall, the city's most popular auditorium. Here, during the winter of 1850-51, he taught a course on slavery. The aim of the course, which consisted of seven lectures, was to counteract the influence of the local press and the pulpit in creating among the people of Rochester "an indifference and coldness" toward the enslavement of their fellowmen "which might be looked for only in men hardened by the most atrocious and villainous crimes."[2] The lectures were well attended and they contributed to the growth of anti-slavery sentiment in the community; several were reported in full in the local press and reprinted in pamphlet form.

It was in the Corinthian Hall, too, that Douglass delivered his famous address on July 5, 1852, commemorating the anniversary of the signing of the Declaration of Independence. In bitter, eloquent prose, he told his audience that had he the ability and could he reach the nation's ear he would "pour out a fiery stream of biting ridicule, blasting reproach, withering sarcasm, and stern rebuke"; for it was not light that was needed but fire. He asked his listeners if they had meant to mock him when they invited him to speak on such an occasion; to him the fourth of July was not a day for rejoicing, but for mourning. Then followed what is probably the most moving passage in all of Douglass' speeches:

"What, to the American slave, is your 4th of July? I answer; a day that reveals to him, more than all other days in the year, the gross injustice and cruelty to which he is the constant victim. To him, your celebration is a sham; your boasted liberty, an unholy license; your national greatness, swelling vanity; your sounds of rejoicing are empty and heartless; your denunciation of tyrants brass fronted impudence; your shouts of liberty and equality, hollow mockery; your prayers and hymns, your sermons and thanksgivings, with all your religious parade and solemnity, are to him, mere bombast, fraud, deception, impiety, and hypocrisy—a thin veil to cover up crimes which would disgrace a nation of savages. There is not a nation on the earth guilty of practices more shocking and bloody than are the people of the United States, at this very hour."[3]

An important phase of the anti-slavery activity in Rochester was the struggle for the abolition of segregated schools for Negro children.

Douglass, the leader of the movement, felt a personal interest in the outcome. The Rochester Board of Education refused to allow his children to enter Public School 15 near his home, and insisted that they travel to the other side of the city to attend the school for Negro children.

Refusing to accept the system of segregated schools, Douglass, in August, 1848, arranged for his daughter, Rosetta, to attend Seward Seminary, a fashionable school for girls in Rochester. He was overjoyed to learn that the principal was an Abolitionist, and left for a visit to Cleveland happy in the thought that his child "was about to enjoy advantages for improving her mind, and fitting her for a useful and honorable life." What was his rage to discover on his return that Rosetta had been isolated in a room by herself and was being taught separately. He promptly protested to the principal "against the cruelty and injustice of treating [my] child as a criminal on account of her color." The principal weakly replied that the trustees of the school had objected to the admission of a Negro girl, and to overcome their prejudices by gradual stages she had hit upon the idea of having the child taught separately until such time as she could be admitted to the regular classes.

Upon Douglass' protest, the principal of the school submitted the question of Rosetta's status to the pupils and then to their parents. "How many of you are willing to have this colored child be with you?" the principal asked. All of the children held up their hands. "The children's hearts were right," Douglass told Mark Twain several years later.

Only one parent objected, but Rosetta was asked to leave the school. Douglass had already decided to withdraw his daughter from the seminary, but he did not permit the incident to pass over quietly. In a scathing letter to H. G. Warner, the single parent who objected to Rosetta's presence, he promised that he would use all his powers to proclaim this "infamy" to the nation. Scores of papers reprinted the letter with its blistering conclusion:

"We are both worms of the dust, and our children are like us. We differ in color, it is true (and not much in that respect), but who is to decide which color is most pleasing to God, or most honorable among men? But I do not wish to waste words or argument on one whom I take to be as destitute of honorable feeling, as he has shown himself full of pride and prejudice."[4]

Publicly announcing that *"in no emergency"* would he send any child of his to a segregated school, Douglass dispatched Rosetta to a private institution in Albany for two or three years; in 1851, he secured the services of a governess for her and the other children. Meanwhile, he worked unceasingly with Samuel D. Porter and other citizens of Rochester to abolish the separate school system which he called "the question of questions for the colored people of this place."[5]

For eight years Douglass pressed the issue of separate schools in Rochester. In 1857 the campaign bore fruit; the separate schools were abolished and Negro children were permitted to attend the public schools.

It was in the capacity of superintendent of the Underground Railroad in Rochester that Douglass made some of his most important contributions to the anti-slavery cause. He took more pride in his work for the Underground than in most of his other activities.

Although the Underground Railroad originated in the seventeenth century, it did not achieve full importance until after 1831 when restrictions upon the slaves were increased. The Underground was a network of routes, stretching northward from the border states and the Appalachian country into Canada. In nearly every important town and city throughout the North, organizations existed, known as Vigilance Committees, ostensibly organized for the purpose of preventing the arrest of a fugitive or of furnishing aid in the case of an apprehension. But in addition to these activities, the members of the committees were nearly always agents of the Underground. Among them Negroes played a distinguished part. The New York Vigilance Committee included David Ruggles, Rev. Theodore S. Wright, and Rev. Samuel Cornish; in Philadelphia, Robert Purvis, William Still, and Charles L. Reason served on the committee. Many of the agents along the 450 to 1,000 mile route, from isolated mountain districts in the South to the great terminals in the North, were unknown to one another, each intent upon his particular job in the chain and depending upon the "grapevine" to keep informed of events in the Underground.

Beginning in the upland country of North Carolina, Tennessee, Virginia, or Kentucky, an escaped Negro found refuge in remote farmhouses or pasture sheds. He was hidden in a cellar or in lofts and cared for until it was time to move on, disguised, or concealed under a load of hay or grain, to another farmhouse where, perhaps, several more fugitives had been smuggled. Divided into pairs, the fugitives traveled northward, always under cover, usually at night. They went from agent to agent, from one remote house and crossroad to others, along infrequently traveled byways. Along all large rivers, ferrymen were stationed to transport the fleeing pairs or small bands. Reaching the North, the first and most dan-

gerous lap of the journey was completed. But now another danger
loomed. Throughout the border counties were scattered southern agents
whose duty it was to capture the slave, present an affidavit before a justice, and transport the fugitive back to slavery. While great numbers
of northern whites hated these officers who enforced the unpopular Fugitive Slave Law, there were others who were opposed to the sudden influx
of unskilled fugitives, or were anxious to prove to the slaveowners
that they were reliable friends and worthy of their trade and patronage,
and would turn the fleeing Negroes over to the authorities. So the journey
through the free states had to be marked with caution until the fugitive
reached the area along the Great Lakes or until he arrived in southern
Ontario or Quebec.[6]

Rochester was the last main stop on the Underground. To this city
came the fugitive slaves by railroad, by wagon, or on foot, exhausted from
the harrowing weeks en route to freedom. They needed money, food,
clothing, rest, and encouragement. By word-of-mouth direction, they
found their way to the homes of the Posts, the Blosses, the Porters, and
other "forwarders" in the community. In the winter of 1847, Douglass'
house on Alexander Street became an important station. By 1850 Douglass was the leader of the Railroad in Rochester, superintending all the
activities and having contact with agents in the rest of the country.

The very first issue of *The North Star* carried the news that its editor
was already involved in the operations of the Underground:

"A SISTER RESCUED FROM SLAVERY

"There has just left our office, an amiable, kind, and intelligent looking
young woman, about eighteen years of age, on her way from slavery."[7]

Horace McGuire, one of Douglass's newspaper employees, recalled
that it was not an unusual thing for him to find fugitives sitting on the
office stairs in the early morning. As soon as Douglass arrived, he went
into action, and the fugitives were escorted either to the Post's cellar, Edward C. Williams' sail loft, Lindley Moore's barn, William Bloss's wood-
shed, or to Douglass' own attic. Throughout the day Douglass visited
trusted sympathizers, passing the word that funds were needed to "ship
a bale of Southern goods," and collecting money, food, and clothing.
When night fell, the escaped slaves were usually sent on to Oswego or
Lewiston. Some, too exhausted to travel, remained during the night, and
were put aboard the morning train to Canada. "They usually tarry with
us only during the night," Douglass wrote, "and are forwarded to Canada

by the morning train. We give them supper, lodging, and breakfast; pay their expenses, and give them a half dollar over."[8]

In 1850 the underground was confronted with new problems. The newly strengthened Fugitive Slave Act provided for the appointment of special federal commissioners to aid in slave catching, and compelled all United States marshals and deputies whom they might designate to aid in the search. Furthermore, all citizens were subject to call to aid in the prosecution of the statute. The decision of the commissioner as to the Negro's identity was final. His fee was five dollars if he discharged the victim, and ten dollars if he decided he was a fugitive slave! Only a white person's testimony was acceptable in determining the status of the Negro.[9]

During the months when the Fugitive Slave Bill was under discussion, Douglass let it be known that he had no intention of abiding by any act of Congress which would facilitate the restoration of fugitives to slavery. He was a member of the committee which drafted the resolution for a mass meeting held at Corinthian Hall on April 5, 1850:

"Resolved, compromise or no compromise, constitution or no constitution . . . no testimony short of a bill of sale from Almighty God can establish the title of the master to his slave, or induce us to lift a finger to aid in his return to the house of bondage."[10]

On August 21, 1850, four weeks before the Fugitive Slave bill became law, Douglass presided at a convention at Cazenovia, New York, known as the "Fugitive Slave Convention." Over 2,000 people attended the meeting among whom were thirty fugitives. An "Address of Fugitive Slaves to Brethren in the South" was drawn up urging the slaves to escape to freedom. The convention pledged itself to raise funds for the defense of William Chaplin, who had been imprisoned in Maryland for assisting in the escape of the slaves of Robert Toombs and Alexander H. Stephens. A week later at an "Anti-Fugitive Slave Bill Meeting" at Syracuse, Douglass and J. C. Hathaway raised three hundred and fifty dollars for Chaplin's defense.[11]

When the news of the passage of the infamous measure reached Rochester, Douglass was again at Corinthian Hall "hurling out anathema" against the Act. A few weeks later, on October 14, he delivered one of the main addresses at a gigantic meeting at Faneuil Hall in Boston. Describing the terror the new law had struck in the hearts of thousands of escaped slaves in the North, he declared that it was the universal feeling of his Negro brethren "to die rather than be returned into slavery."[12]

Douglass became increasingly militant as he saw many of the Negro inhabitants of Rochester fleeing to Canada because they feared capture by slave-hunters.[13] In 1852 he told a Pittsburgh audience: "The only way to make the Fugitive Slave Law a dead letter is to make a half a dozen or more dead kidnappers. . . . The man who takes the office of a blood-hound ought to be treated as a bloodhound. . . ." In his journal he expounded this theme. Raising the question, "Is it Right and Wise to kill a kidnapper?" Douglass presented a long analysis to prove that any person who assisted in restoring fugitives to slavery "labelled himself the common enemy of mankind," and that his slaughter would be "as innocent, in the sight of God, as would be the slaughter of a ravenous wolf in the act of throttling an infant." He urged the Negro people to arm themselves and prepare to fight back. "Every colored man in the country," he cried, "should sleep with his revolver under his head, loaded and ready for use. Fugitives should, on their arrival in any Northern city, be immediately provided with arms, and taught at once that it is no harm to shoot any man who would rob them of this liberty." Such defiance was not only justified but necessary for the vindication of the Negro people against the charge that they were "an inferior race."

"This reproach must be wiped out, and nothing short of resistance on the part of colored men, can wipe it out. Every slave-hunter who meets a bloody death in his infernal business, is an argument in favor of the manhood of our race. Resistance is, therefore, wise as well as just."[14]

In September, 1851, Douglass came to the assistance of three fugitive Negroes who had fought back against the slave-catchers. The leader of the group, William Parker, a free Negro in Sadsbury, Pennsylvania, had sheltered a fugitive slave. The slaveowner, one Gorsuch, together with United States marshals, arrived in Sadsbury to claim the fugitive. Warned by the Philadelphia Vigilance Committee the people of Sadsbury were prepared.

When Gorsuch demanded the fugitive, he was refused. His home attacked, Parker sounded a horn and up sprang a large body of Negroes armed with clubs, axes, and guns. A battle ensued, the slave catchers were routed, several were wounded, and Gorsuch himself was killed.

Parker and two fugitives fled, and, after an exciting journey on the Underground, arrived in Rochester. Douglass, aware that the authorities were hot on their trail, took them into his home and gave them shelter.[15] While the men remained in hiding, Julia Griffiths drove to the boat landing on the Genesee River and made arrangements for their shipment to Canada. When the fugitives boarded the boat, Parker handed Douglass the gun with which he had killed Gorsuch.[16]

"I could not look upon them as murderers," Douglass wrote years later, "to me they were heroic defenders of the just rights of men against men-stealers and murderers."[17]

Douglass did not participate in the exciting Jerry Rescue at Syracuse on October 1, 1851, in which Gerrit Smith and other Abolitionists had forcibly rescued the fugitive, Jerry McHenry, who had been seized and imprisoned by a deputy United States marshal. But at the 1854 celebration of this event, Douglass read a series of resolutions to the gathering which asserted that the rescue had demonstrated "the wisdom and entire rightfulness of forcible resistance to the Fugitive Slave Bill," and declared:

"That the peculiar glory of this day, is not that one man has escaped from slavery, for there have been many such escaped—not that freedom has gained a victory through the blunders of lawyers, or through the faulty network of the law:—but that it consists in the fact, on this day three years ago, the people of Syracuse, and of Western New York, were wrought up to the point of open resistance to what they deemed a cruel, monstrous and inhuman enactment of Congress."[18]

Douglass continually raised money to aid escaped slaves. Frequently his fees from lectures would augment the fund which was used to "help such of our unfortunate countrymen who deem it no longer safe to remain in the United States," to aid fugitives to move on to Canada, and to assist slaves to ransom themselves from slavery. Contributions to the fund came from England and Ireland. In this country, the Negro people themselves, in spite of their limited resources, were the most frequent contributors. "The colored citizens," wrote William C. Nell from Rochester in February, 1852, "have systematically aided their hunted brethren, and have just held a donation festival, exclusively for the benefit of the fugitive." Three months later, Douglass observed: "The colored people of this city have acted well in this matter. They have contributed, heretofore, liberally, but the last meetings held for raising funds among them, show that their resources are nearly exhausted. . . ."[19]

Contributions were regularly listed in Douglass' journal and subscribers were urged to forward their mite. "Gerrit Smith, with his characteristic benevolence," went a notice in The North Star of January 9, 1849, "has kindly sent us his check for ten dollars, to aid John White, the fugitive slave of whom we spoke in last week's *North Star*. This leaves the sum of thirty dollars remaining to be paid to complete the ransom of this brother bondman. We will gladly be the medium of other sums for this truly deserving man.—F.D." During the next two weeks the thirty dollars came in to the paper, John White's freedom was purchased, and the Negro people of Rochester met to celebrate the rescue of another brother from bondage.

The secrecy of the Underground Railroad makes it impossible to determine the number of slaves Douglass aided. But it was a figure which easily ran into the hundreds.[20] "Fugitives are constantly passing through here," William C. Nell wrote from Rochester in 1852, "giving no rest to their feet nor slumber to their eyelids, until the protecting aegis of Queen Victoria makes them welcome freemen on Canada's shore. A party of fifteen thus rid themselves of republican slavery on Thanksgiving day!!!"[21] In 1854 Douglass stated that in two weeks he had aided over thirty fugitives on their way to Canada. In June, 1857, he informed his subscribers that four fugitives "passed through our hands to the Queen's dominions." On January 8, 1858, he wrote to the Ladies' Irish Anti-Slavery Association: ". . . you will be glad to know that the number escaping from Slavery has latterly been unusually large. We have passed over our section of the underground railroad about forty within the last sixty days." The *Rochester Express* of October 25, 1859, reported that in one day "not less than fifteen thousand dollars worth of 'property' passed through this city, on the 'underground,' " in the shape of "a dozen smart, intelligent, young and middle-aged men and women." In May, 1860, ten fugitives found "food and shelter, counsel and comfort," under Douglass' roof, and during the following month he sped ten more on the road to Canada and freedom.[22]

Rochester had only one case of a fugitive being returned to his master. This was in 1827.[23]

Douglass' services as an agent and "forwarder" of the Underground Railroad were of great importance to the anti-slavery movement, but he was the first to recognize the superior contribution made by Harriet Tubman, the heroic woman who fearlessly "carried the war into Africa." In his letter to the Ladies' Irish Anti-Slavery Association, Douglass referred to "one coloured woman, who escaped from Slavery eight years ago, has made several returns at great risk, and has brought out, since obtaining her freedom, fifty others from the house of bondage. She has been spending a short time with us since the holidays. She possesses great courage and shrewdness, and may yet render even more important service to the Cause."[24] Many years later, Douglass wrote to the "Moses of her people":

"Most that I have done has been in public, and I have received much encouragement. . . . You on the other hand have labored in a private way. . . . I have had the applause of the crowd. . . . While the most that you have done has been witnessed by a few trembling, scared and footsore bondmen. . . . The midnight sky and the silent stars have been the witnesses of your devotion to freedom and of your heroism."[25]

Douglass realized that the activities of the Underground Railroad could no more free all the slaves than "a teaspoon could bail out the ocean," but the freedom of one slave was worth any risk, and the increasing number of runaways created a strong repugnance in the North to the entire slave system and so strengthened the anti-slavery cause.

In every phase of his work in Rochester, Douglass had the valuable assistance of his close friend, "Dear Julia." Miss Griffiths arranged the series of lectures in Corinthian Hall, read and corrected Douglass' speeches, collected the funds for their publication in pamphlet form, assisted in the campaign to abolish separate schools for colored children, and was a constant companion in the work of the Underground.

Much as they valued her ability in organizational work and understood her contributions to Douglass' full development as a writer and thinker, Abolitionists in Rochester were concerned over the effect upon public opinion of the unusual relationship between the Negro leader and this white woman. People had recovered from their first shock of seeing Douglass walk down the street with Miss Griffiths on his arm, but they never quite accepted the fact that a white woman should live in the same household with a colored man and his wife. The long hours Douglass and Miss Griffiths spent together in the newspaper office caused the rumor to spread that their friendship went beyond the bounds of intellectual companionship. By 1849 the rumors were so persistent that Douglass, without referring to Miss Griffith, editorially denounced those "who maliciously (and without even the shadow of provocation), artfully and deliberately manufacture lies and insidiously circulate them with no other motive than to blast the fair name of another."[26]

The article had no effect on the scandalmongers. In January, 1852, Samuel D. Porter, Douglass' close associate in the anti-slavery movement, advised his friend that Rochester was "full of scandalous reports" implicating him and Miss Griffiths. Douglass' spirited reply is the only statement we have from him on the subject of the relationship between himself, his family and Miss Griffiths.[27] "I am a husband and a father," he reminded Porter, "and withal a citizen,—honorably, and to the best of my ability, endeavouring to discharge the duties of this three fold relation. When the city, which you allege to be full of scandalous reports implicating Miss G and me, shall put those *'reports'* in a definite shape, and present a responsible person to back them, it will be time enough for me to attempt to refute them." Miss Griffiths, he went on, had decided to leave his household two months before and was living with another family. "When she was in my family, I was necessarily much in her society. Our walking and riding together was natural. Now we are separate and only meet at my office at business hours and for business purposes, where we are open to the observation of my printers and the public, from ten o'clock or earlier in the morning until four o'clock in the afternoon." How long she intended to remain in Rochester he did not know, but the decision was entirely hers. And, under no circumstance, would he permit rumors to blind him to the fact that she had "a just claim upon my gratitude, respect and friendship."[28]

It is unfortunate that this letter was not made public for the matter did not die in 1852. The following year the question of Douglass' relations with Miss Griffiths became an important issue in the conflict between the Negro leader and the Garrisonians.

The Split with the Garrisonians

Douglass' relations with the Massachusetts Abolitionists after he left Lynn in the fall of 1847 to establish his residence in Rochester remained cordial. The Massachusetts Anti-Slavery Society expressed regret that he would be working in a region so far from New England, but assured him that he would be "followed to his new home and new sphere of usefulness by the most good wishes of his many friends in this his first home of freedom."[1] Douglass maintained close contact with the Garrisonians during the next three years, and at the annual meetings of the American Anti-Slavery Society, he spent much time in the company of his old friends. With Garrison, however, he was not entirely at ease. He knew that the Abolitionist leader had neither forgotten what he regarded as

Douglass' lack of solicitude during his illness in Cleveland, nor forgiven him for the decision to publish his paper. The two men shared the same platform at the annual meetings, but their courteous references to each other lacked the old warmth.[2]

Within a few years this strained relationship turned into bitter antagonism, and the anti-slavery press, much to the dismay of its subscribers and to the delight of its enemies, was treated to a unique spectacle as charges and counter-charges were hurled against each other by the participants in the conflict. Personal antagonisms, often of the most petty character, were so deeply intertwined with ideological issues that it became almost impossible to separate the two. Yet fundamentally the conflict emerged out of a sharp difference of opinion over questions of vital importance to the anti-slavery movement.

During the first ten years of his work as an Abolitionist, Douglass had accepted all of the doctrines of the Garrisonian school. In his speeches, letters, and early editorials in *The North Star,* he reiterated his belief that the Constitution was wholly a pro-slavery document, called for the destruction of the American Union, reaffirmed his opposition to the use of the ballot against slavery and again asserted his conviction that moral suasion was the major instrumentality for ending slavery. "I am willing at all times to be known as a Garrisonian Abolitionist," he wrote on September 4, 1849.[3]

But as he moved outside the orbit of the Massachusetts Abolitionists and came into contact with anti-slavery men who differed with the Garrisonian school, Douglass began for the first time to examine his beliefs critically. After considerable study and extensive reading in law, political philosophy, and American government, he concluded that there were serious flaws in the Garrisonian doctrines. Gradually he formulated a new anti-slavery creed.

The weakening of Douglass' faith in the Garrisonian principle of non-resistance came first. It was John Brown who led Douglass to doubt the value of relying mainly on "moral suasion." Late in 1847, while on a lecture tour in New England, Douglass met Brown, then a merchant in Springfield, Massachusetts. In his editorial correspondence to *The North Star,* he wrote of having a "private interview" with Brown who "though a white gentleman, is in sympathy a black man, and as deeply interested in our cause, as though his own soul had been pierced with the iron of slavery." Douglass did not reveal the nature of the interview, merely reporting Brown's joy at the appearance of men "possessing the energy of head and heart to demand freedom for their whole people," the result of which "must be the downfall of slavery."[4] Years later he filled in the details. After dinner at Brown's simple home, his host expounded his views on slavery. Brown not only condemned the institution, but added that the slaveholders "had forfeited their right to live, that the slaves had the right to gain their liberty in any way they could." "Moral suasion" could never liberate the slaves nor political action abolish the system. Brown outlined a plan to establish five bands of armed men in the Allegheny Mountains who would run off slaves in large numbers.[5]

Douglass thought that Brown's plan had "much to commend it," but was still convinced that "moral suasion" would succeed in converting the entire nation, including the slaveholders, to the anti-slavery position. None the less, Brown's belief that slavery was actually a state of war profoundly impressed him. "My utterances," Douglass wrote later, "became more tinged by the color of this man's strong impressions." A year after his visit he was echoing Brown's language, writing editorially that slaveholders had "no rights more than any other thief or pirate. They have forfeited even the right to live, and if the slave should put every one of them to the sword to-morrow, who dare pronounce the penalty disproportionate to the crime, or say that the criminals deserved less than death at the hands of their long-abused chattels?" In June, 1849, he astonished a Boston anti-slavery audience in Faneuil Hall with the announcement:

"I should welcome the intelligence tomorrow, should it come, that the slaves had risen in the South, and that the sable arms which had been engaged in beautifying and adorning the South, were engaged in spreading death and devastation."

Noticing the alarm his remark had caused, Douglass swept on with lashing irony and bitter criticism:

"Why, you welcomed the intelligence from France, that Louis Phillipe had been barricaded in Paris—you threw up your caps in honor of the victory achieved by Republicanism over Royalty—you shouted aloud—'Long live the republic!'—and joined heartily in the watchword of 'Liberty, Equality, Fraternity'—and should you not hail with equal pleasure the tidings from the South that the slaves had risen, and achieved for themselves, against the iron-hearted slaveholder, what the republicans of France achieved against the royalists of France?"[6]

The fury of his language did not mean that Douglass had entirely abandoned his faith "in the operation of moral force." But more and more he began to justify the right of the slaves to revolt "on the ground that it is consistent with the conduct of the revolutionary patriots." Step by step he abandoned his belief in the efficacy of moral instrumentalities, and by the late 'fifties was one of the leading exponents of "militant abolitionism." In 1856 he wrote that while it was still necessary to use "persuasion and argument" and every means that promised "peacefully" to destroy slavery, he was convinced "that its peaceful annihilation is almost hopeless. . . ." Four years later he no longer had any doubts.

"I have little hope of the freedom of the slave by peaceful means," he wrote on June 29, 1860. "A long course of peaceful slaveholding has placed the slaveholders beyond the reach of moral and humane considerations. They have neither ears nor hearts for the appeals of justice and humanity. While the slave will tamely submit his neck to the yoke, his back to the lash, and his ankle to the fetter and chain, the Bible will be quoted, and learning invoked to justify slavery. The only penetrable point of a tyrant is the *fear of death.*"[7]

As Douglass abandoned sole reliance on moral power for the overthrow of slavery, he was forced to re-examine his attitude toward political action. During 1841-1848 he had placed his hopes in the non-political activities of the anti-slavery societies. In a speech at the Higham Anti-Slavery Convention in November, 1841, he ridiculed political action, exclaiming that the slaveholders "care nothing about your political action, they don't dread the political movement; it is the *moral* movement, the appeal to men's sense of right, which makes them and all our opponents tremble."[8]

The belief in non-political action Douglass maintained consistently during the next few years. Like all Abolitionists under the influence of the Garrisonian wing of anti-slavery thought, he would have nothing to do with a government and a constitution framed and administered by men who "were and have been until now, little better than a band of pirates." Until the government and the Constitution were replaced by institutions which would "better answer the ends of justice," no true friend of liberty in the United States could vote or hold office.[9]

The key to Douglass' anti-political views was his interpretation of the Constitution "as a most foul and bloody conspiracy against the rights of three millions of enslaved and imbruted men." As a Negro, he knew at first hand the farce that history had made of the Declaration of Independence; his personal suffering made him only too ready to accept the Garrisonian doctrine that the Constitution was "a Covenant with death and an agreement with hell." If slaveholders appealed to the Constitution, he would appeal to a higher law, to divine morality. The founders of the American Union, he told an audience in England, while proclaiming liberty throughout the land, were themselves trafficking in their fellow men, and since then American government and society had been dedicated to defending the great lie of slavery. Slavery, he claimed, was not a southern but an American institution, a system that derived its support as much from the non-slaveholding states as from those where slavery was accepted. By swearing to uphold the American Constitution and the American Union, the people of the North had sworn before high heaven that the slave would be kept a slave. As long as they accepted the Constitution and its compromises in favor of the slaveholders, they were responsible for the existence of slavery in the United States and must share the guilt for that great crime.[10]

It required two years of study and discussion for Douglass to change his attitude toward the Constitution. The first indication he gives that he was beginning to re-examine his thinking is the brief comment in *The North Star* of February 9, 1849: "On a close examination of the Constitution, I am satisfied that if strictly 'construed according to its reading,' it is not a pro-slavery instrument. . . ." Six weeks later he wrote that if he could be convinced that the Constitution was essentially anti-slavery in its origins and purposes, he would be quick to use the ballot box against slavery, and to urge others to do likewise. He doubted, however, that he could be easily persuaded that such were the origins and purposes of the document.

Operating in central New York among men who adhered to an anti-slavery constitutional interpretation, Douglass was constantly being called upon to justify his view that the Constitution was a pro-slavery instrument. The more he discussed this question with Gerrit Smith and William Goodell and the more he studied their writings the more difficult it became for him to uphold his theory. Through these discussions and readings, Douglass became convinced that the preamble to the Constitution—that the national government had been formed to establish a more perfect union, promote the general welfare and secure the blessings of liberty—governed the meaning of the document in all its parts and details. The Constitution was thus, by its avowed purpose, anti-slavery.

Slavery was not, nor could it become legalized, and it was the duty of the federal government to eradicate it. Political action to secure that end was both warranted and necessary.

As Douglass saw it, national necessity compelled him to accept an interpretation of the Constitution which might not be evident in the document itself. Realizing the importance of having the Constitution fight for him, he interpreted it in a way most convenient for the anti-slavery crusade. The Garrisonians, by their insistence on an interpretation which the slaveholders shared, no matter how apparently correct that interpretation might be, not only played directly into the hands of their enemies, but created enmity for themselves. Whatever the average Northerner felt about slavery, he did not believe that his country was built upon falsehood and iniquities. While the Garrisonians announced their determination to destroy the Constitution and the Union to end slavery, Douglass decided to use both in the struggle against "a system of lawless violence; that never was lawful and never can be made so."

Step by step Douglass arrived at the conclusion that there was no need to dissolve the Union. He saw clearly that disunion would isolate the slaves and leave them at the mercy of their masters. For the North to secede, as the Garrisonians advocated, would relieve it of its share of responsibility for slavery and deny the slaves their most important allies. For the Garrisonian slogan, "No union with slaveholders," Douglass substituted "a more sensible motto, namely, 'No union with slaveholding.' "[11]

The change in Douglass' anti-slavery creed had been developing for a number of years but it did not become public until 1851.[12] At the eighteenth annual meeting of the American Anti-Slavery Society held in Syracuse in May, 1851, a resolution was submitted by Edmund Quincy proposing that the *Anti-Slavery Standard,* the *Pennsylvania Freeman,* the *Anti-Slavery Bugle,* and *The North Star* receive the recommendation of the society. When Samuel J. May suggested that the *Liberty Party Paper* be added to the list, Garrison opposed this motion on the ground that this journal did not stand for the dissolution of the Union and believed that the Constitution was an anti-slavery document. This in turn led to a resolution that no paper should be endorsed which did not assume the Constitution to be a pro-slavery document. Douglass thereupon announced that he could not consider his paper eligible for endorsement since he had "arrived at the firm conviction that the Constitution, construed in the light of well-established rules of legal interpretation, might be made consistent in its details with the noble purposes in its preamble," and that in the future he would insist that the Constitution "be wielded in behalf of emancipation." His changed attitude had not been suddenly or impulsively arrived at, and he attributed it to "a careful study" of the writings of Lysander Spooner, Gerrit Smith, and William Goodell. His opinions had "recently changed materially in relation to political action," and he now believed that it was "the first duty of every American citizen, whose conscience permits him so to do, to use his political as well as his moral power for its [slavery's] overthrow."

These words created a stir. Enraged, Garrison cried out: "There is roguery somewhere." He moved that *The North Star* be stricken from the list and this was promptly voted by the convention.[13]

Douglass never forgot Garrison's "insulting remark," though in his paper he wrote that he could "easily forgive" the man for whom he still cherished "a veneration only inferior in degree to that we owe to our conscience and to our God." What really concerned him was that his former associates greeted the union of *The North Star* and the *Liberty Party Paper* in June, 1851, with the cry that he had sold out his principles to gain financial support from Gerrit Smith and other political Abolitionists.[14]

Douglass hotly denied that this change had been sudden and unheralded or that he had been primarily influenced by his financial dependence upon Smith. He offered proof that he had gradually altered his attitude toward political action and had reached the conclusion that the Constitution was an anti-slavery document long before the question of uniting his paper with the *Liberty Party Paper* was broached. But neither his protests nor his evidence convinced his former associates. Samuel J. May voiced the sentiments of the Garrisonians when he wrote: "It would be a strange thing, indeed, if a mind so acute as that of Mr. D. could not find plausible reasons for the change he has made."[15]

For almost a year after the 1851 convention, the conflict between Douglass and the Garrisonians lay dormant. To be sure, the *Liberator*, early in 1852, carried a critical article charging that party spirit had "made some havoc of the character of Frederick Douglass," but adding that "his genius had placed him at the head of the colored race, and that his magnificent oratory and powerful writings have demonstrated the natural intellectual equality of his race with that of the Caucasian tyrants by whom even he is trampled upon and degraded in the United States."

Douglass continued publishing speeches of the leading Garrisonians in his weekly, and praised the American Society for "doing a great and good work."[16]

But this was only the calm before the storm. At the next annual meeting of the American Society, held in Rochester, May 11-13, 1852, the feud between Garrison and Douglass flared up again. Garrison again called for the dissolution of the Union and charged that "never had any political constitution in this country taken the colored race as equal to the white." Douglass proceeded to defend his position on the Union as opposed to that of Garrison. At once, he was regarded "as an enemy." Taking the bull by the horns, he asked why he was "treated as an alien." To which Phillips, Remond, Foster, and Robert Purvis listed more than ten reasons. These boiled down to four basic charges: that Douglass had changed his opinion about the Constitution; that he had aided in forming an anti-slavery society in central New York not affiliated with the American Society and had become friendly with its *deadliest* enemies"; that his journal was "a political and not an anti-slavery paper," and that he had attacked George Thompson. Douglass answered the charges. Evidently he was sufficiently impressive for he was later in the session elected to the Board of Managers of the American Society. But the rupture had been seriously widened by the barrage of accusations let loose at the convention. In December, 1852, Phillips informed Elizabeth Pease that "Douglass is completely estranged from us."[17]

But the worst was still to come. The differences led to personal attacks and by the fall of 1853 the conflict reached a stage of vituperation unparalleled in the entire history of the anti-slavery movement. In reporting the 1853 convention of the American Anti-Slavery Society, Douglass threw out the remark that Pillsbury, Wright, and Foster "had been induced to absent themselves on this occasion because their presence might give new force to the charge of infidelity, which is brought against the Anti-Slavery Society." The remark went unanswered for two months. Then at the celebration of West India Emancipation at Framingham, Massachusetts, Wendell Phillips publicly lashed Douglass for daring to attend the ceremonies after his diatribe, and demanded that Douglass justify his slur "upon the integrity of the American Anti-Slavery Society." Unprepared for the severity of the attack, Douglass, who had arrived in Framingham during a storm and was "shivering with cold, wet to the skin, tired and hungry," offered a feeble defense. He denied that he had said that the three men had been subjected to pressure to prevent them from attending the annual meeting, asserted his right to criticize in his paper "the character of any anti-slavery effort or any anti-Slavery Society in existence," and protested that it was improper to turn a celebration of the first of August into a discussion of relations between himself and the Massachusetts Abolitionists.[18]

Aware that his rejoinder had not been too convincing, Douglass wrote a long editorial on the Framingham incident which he entitled, "Something Personal." It closed with a quotation from the Apostles: "If it is possible, as much as lieth in you, live peaceably with all men." But Douglass must have been under no illusions as to the effects of the article. He refused to retract the charge of "infidelity" he had leveled against the three Garrisonians, maintaining that they gloried in their disbelief in the Bible. He denied that his charge was the invention of the pro-slavery church and its allies; he said that it arose from their statements ridiculing the recognition of any book as of divine authority. Furthermore, he contended that "Messrs. Foster, Pillsbury and Wright might have been induced to remain away to screen the Society from the odium of their infidel opinions."[19]

Douglass moved next to a denunciation of the Negro Garrisonians, referring to Remond, Nell, and Purvis as *practical* enemies of the colored people." Nell was also a "contemptible tool," and Purvis' inherited wealth was described as "blood-stained riches."[20]

The Garrisonians were stunned momentarily by the vituperative nature of Douglass' offensive, but they were too well versed in the give-and-take of such battles to remain silent for long. Soon after the appearance of Douglass' "Something Personal" editorial, the entire Garrisonian press hit back. Douglass had torn off the mask and revealed himself as an ally of "the whole pro-slavery press and pulpit in the United States," went the general refrain in column after column of denunciation. He had become so clearly the victim of "the curse of worldly ambition" that he could only be regarded as a deadly foe of the entire anti-slavery cause.[21]

Heretofore Garrison himself had refrained from engaging in the controversy with his former co-worker. But convinced that "with Douglass the die seems to be cast," he now joined in the attack. Not satisfied with using his bitter pen to demolish the Negro leader, he published extracts from Douglass' articles in his "Refuge of Oppression" column in the *Liberator,* a place usually reserved for material from pro-slavery papers.[22]

This was a notification to his fellowers that their leader regarded Douglass as among the worst enemies of the slave.

Nor did Garrison halt here. One of his followers had reacted critically to the attacks on Douglass. He had just heard the Negro orator deliver several addresses in Chicago, and was convinced that he was completely sincere in advocating political action and an anti-slavery interpretation of the Constitution. Douglass was "faithful to the cause of the slave and to the highest convictions of his soul," and was still "bestowing upon that cause all the energies of his mind, his pen, his God-given genius, and his powerful eloquence." Hence he asked Garrison:

"Why is he ostracized from the sympathies of yourself and of the Society which acknowledges you as its exponent and head? Why do you characterise his course as wayward and hostile? Why do you place his articles in the 'Refuge of Oppression,' side by side with the vilest pro-slavery venom from the vilest sheets in the land? Is it on account of his change of opinion on the constitutional question? Shall it be said with truth that you and your particular coadjutors cannot tolerate an honest difference of opinion?"[23]

Garrison made short shrift of his critic. He denied that the conflict with Douglass was the result of differing opinions on anti-slavery issues, blaming it entirely on the latter's selfish spirit. Douglass had not been expelled; he had "ostracized" himself. "He has lost much of moral power, and will finally lose what yet remains, if he persists in defaming those whose infidelity to the anti-slavery cause has never been impeached." Having attacked Douglass' integrity and his motives, Garrison plunged on to attack even his family life:

"For several years past, he has had one of the worst advisers in his printing-office, whose influence over him has not only caused much unhappiness in his own household, but perniciously biased his own judgment; who, active, futile, mischievous, has never had any sympathy with the American Anti-Slavery Society, but would doubtless rejoice to see it become extinct; and whose sectarianism is manifestly paramount to any regard for the integrity of the anti-slavery movement."[24]

The reference, of course, was to Julia Griffiths, Douglass' able assistant in his newspaper office. This was by no means the first attack on Miss Griffiths during the controversy (the *Anti-Slavery Standard* had already referred to her as "a Jezebel whose capacity for making mischief between friends would be difficult to match")[25], but no one heretofore had publicly raised the question of domestic discord in the Douglass household.[26]

Mrs. Douglass immediately sent a short note to Garrison stating: "It is not true, that the presence of a certain person in the office of Frederick Douglass causes unhappiness in his family. . . ." Garrison printed the letter, but commented that it was "evasive in its language, as our charge had reference to the past and not to the present." A bit later he denied that he had intended to imply anything immoral in his charge and expressed regret that he had ever raised the question of relations between Douglass and his wife.[27] But by that time the damage had already been done.

So many charges had been leveled against him in the Garrisonian press that Douglass decided to devote almost the entire issue of his weekly to a final answer. On December 9, 1853, *Frederick Douglass' Paper* carried six columns of denunciatory articles from the *Liberator,* the *Anti-Slavery Standard,* and the *Pennsylvania Freeman*.[28] The next twelve columns were devoted to Douglass' rejoinder. He calmly defended his position and injected a minimum of personal charges or bitterness in his reply. He was under attack only because he dared differ from the American Anti-Slavery Society and its leaders as to how he should exercise his powers "for the promotion of the anti-slavery cause, and the elevation of the Free People of color in the United States." For four months, since the celebration at Framingham, he had been systematically "pursued, misrepresented, traduced and vilified, with a bitterness ever increasing and a steadiness and violence only characteristic of malice, deep, broad, lasting, and in its worst form." He had been silent through all this, but he could remain silent no longer.

Douglass was especially furious at Garrison for the personal character of his attacks. "He has seen fit to invade my household," he wrote bitterly, "despite the sacredness of my home, break through the just limits of public controversy, and has sought to blast me in the name of my family." He refused to discuss his family relations in the press, arguing that it involved "considerations wholly foreign to the present controversy," and that "a man's wife and children should be spared the mortification involved in a public discussion of matters entirely private. . . ." But he did get back at Garrison, charging him with harboring contempt for the contributions of the Negroes in the struggle against slavery. Quoting Garrison's observation that "the Anti-Slavery cause, both religiously and politically, has transcended the ability of the sufferers from American Slavery and prejudice, *as a class,* to keep pace with it, or to perceive what are its demands, or to understand the philosophy of its operations," Douglass commented caustically:

"The colored people ought to feel profoundly grateful for this magnificent compliment (which does not emanate from a Colonizationist) to their high, moral worth, and breadth of comprehension so generously bestowed by William Lloyd Garrison!—Who will doubt, hereafter, the natural inferiority of the *Negro,* when the great champion of the Negroes' rights, thus broadly concedes all that is claimed respecting the Negro's inferiority by the bitterest despisers of the Negro race."

Douglass' reply to the charge that he was more concerned about his own interests than about those of the anti-slavery cause was both moving and effective:

"Was it *selfish,* when in England, surrounded by kind friends, and strongly invited by them, to make my home among them, with every provision made for my comfort and security in a land where my *color* was no crime—I say, was it selfish in me to *quit* the shores of that country, and return to this, to endure insult, abuse, and proscription, with the rest of my oppressed people? Was it selfish in me, when my English friends gave me more than two thousand dollars, leaving the disposal of the Testimonial to my own option, whether to appropriate it to my own personal wants, or to devote it to the establishment of a paper to advocate the cause of my enslaved fellow countrymen and to promote the elevation of the free colored people—I say, was it *selfish* in me to prefer the latter to the former? Was it selfish in me to refuse a donation of five hundred dollars, raised in Finsbury Chapel, London, at one meeting; simply because that sum had been raised with a view of taking my family over to England, and not having been devoted to that object, I refused to receive it for my *personal benefit?*"

Douglass' defense made little impression upon Garrison and his associates. Oliver Johnson, who had specifically accused Douglass of selfishness, called the reply "an exhibition of moral perversity, blindness and malice." He was thankful that Douglass was now "an avowed enemy instead of a secret, stealthy foe," but was apprehensive that "of all the seceders and apostates from our ranks, he will prove the most malignant in spirit, the most efficient and sleepless in his hostility."[29]

To attempt, almost a century later, to evaluate the relative merits of the contentions of all parties in a controversy which raked the anti-slavery movement during the closing months of 1853 is scarcely a pleasant task. The men involved were all sincere people who honestly believed that their critics were inspired by unworthy motives and that they were the ones sinned against. All lamented the schism, but regarded it as unavoidable, believing that their opponents were the aggressors. As tempers flared, judgment suffered and with it the entire cause.

Unquestionably the Garrisonians had good reason to resent Douglass' charge of infidelity against many anti-slavery men who had made great sacrifices for the movement. Douglass may have been perfectly correct as to the facts, but he must have been aware from personal experience of the use to which the pro-slavery forces could put his charge.

There is, however, a broader issue involved in this controversy between Douglass and the Garrisonians that cannot be ignored. During his early years as an Abolitionist, Douglass had been unsparing in his criticism of the American churches. He had charged that slavery had been "made part of the religion of the land," and that he would have nothing to do with any church which remained indifferent to the existence of slavery or actually supported the slaveholders. "I . . . proclaim myself an infidel to the slaveholding religion of America," Douglass had declared.[30]

The Garrisonians had good cause for their hostility to the church. Many ministers defended slavery, more gave their support to political candidates of the slavocracy, and a great majority assailed the anti-slavery men as "dangerous radicals," not even excluding fellow ministers who opposed slavery. Nevertheless, the Garrisonian attitude toward organized religion was basically unwise, for it ignored the strong anti-slavery sentiment within the churches which was growing in influence and authority. In the 'forties, a series of events occurred that changed the entire picture of American religion. The South had been completely victorious in keeping any discussion of slavery out of national conventions of religious groups, and, from 1826 to 1836, even succeeded in excluding Abolitionists from the Methodist conventions. Elon Galusha was dismissed from the Board of Managers of the Baptist convention in 1841 for his anti-slavery sentiments and was replaced by a man sympathetic to the slaveowners. But gradually, the northern anti-slavery men gained strength, and succeeded in defeating their southern opponents on the crucial issue of whether or not religious leaders, from preacher to bishop, could own slaves—in other words, whether or not slavery was *morally* acceptable. In 1845, after this defeat, southern Baptists formed their own independent society, while, about the same time, southern Methodists formed the Methodist Episcopal Church, South. These breaches became wider as the Civil War approached, and were not healed untill well into the present century. The Old School Presbyterian Church alone remained firm in its defense of slavery, for the church was entirely in the control of the southern leaders.[31]

The schism between northern and southern churches showed clearly that the former were not as reprobate and willing to serve the southern slaveholders as the Garrisonians had charged. New tactics consequently had to be devised to gain the support of these churches. But the Garrisonians continued to battle the churches as if nothing had happened, alienating many people who should have been their allies, and earning for themselves the epithet, "infidel." Douglass understood the weakness of the Garrisonian approach to the churches, and as the importance of the separation between northern and southern churches became clear to him, he began to reconsider his views on the issue. When he refused to defend the agnostics centered about Garrison (men such as Wright, Foster, and Pillsbury) from the charge of infidelity so insistently leveled against them, it was not because he opposed their right to their opinions, but because he was determined to dispel all doubts in the minds of anti-slavery religious leaders that he adhered to these views. While criticizing every manifestation of pro-slavery and anti-Negro tendencies in the churches, he also let it be known that he was prepared to co-operate with the anti-slavery groups in the northern churches. Thus the charge of the Garrisonians that he had been motivated by pure malice toward Wright, Foster, and Pillsbury is ill-conceived. To gain support for the cause, it was necessary for Douglass as a Negro leader to disassociate himself from the dogmatic and narrow attitude of many of the Garrisonians toward the church.

Douglass' attack upon Garrison for his slur on the Negro people in the anti-slavery struggle was, in the opinion of one contemporary observer, "highly discreditable to him in every respect."[32] Yet it is significant that large sections of the Negro population supported Douglass' position. At a mass meeting of the Negro people in Chicago on December 26, 1853, a report was unanimously adopted denouncing Garrison's remarks as "an insult to the intelligence of the colored people," and condemning the "vile crusade" conducted by the Garrisonians to destroy Frederick Douglass, "the voice of the colored people." A similar stand was adopted at the Rhode Island Convention of the

People of Color late in 1853, where Douglass was hailed as "our acknowledged leader."[33]

Douglass' most violent blasts against Garrison came only after the
anti-slavery leader had dragged Douglass' domestic relations into the
controversy and had continued harping on them even after Anna Douglass' letter of denial. Granted that there were reports that the letter
"was concocted by Frederic & Julia"[34] (to which the knowledge that
Anna was illiterate gave credence), the fact remains that it was un-
principled for Garrison to resort to such tactics. Mrs. Jane Swisshelm,
a western female reformer, was thoroughly justified in asking: "How
can any man, professing to know anything of the common courtesies
of life, dare drag a woman before the public as the enemy of her own
husband, and persist in holding her in such a position, despite her
protest?" James B. Vashon, a Negro leader in Pittsburgh, denounced
Garrison for his "savage attack" upon Julia Griffiths, "an innocent
female, whose humanity caused her to leave her native country," and
who had consistently proved to be a "true fighter against oppression."[35]

The side issues and personal recriminations disposed of, the basic
fact remains that however much the Garrisonians protested that their
hostility did not stem from Douglass' conversion to new anti-slavery
principles, their words revealed how bitterly they resented his independent thinking as to what constituted the best policies for the movement. The efforts made to prove that Douglass was simply the puppet
of Gerrit Smith and other political Abolitionists and that he echoed
the opinions of Julia Griffiths, were simply manifestations of this resentment. Certainly the fact that his paper was located in Rochester
where the Liberty Party had its largest support influenced Douglass'
views; certainly he was influenced by Gerrit Smith; certainly he was
indebted to Julia Griffiths for clarification of his views. But fundamentally Douglass' differences with the Garrisonians came after careful
study of every facet of the anti-slavery movement. On the basis of this
study, having decided that the approach of his colleagues was unrealistic,
narrow, and detrimental to an effective struggle against slavery, Douglass
showed great courage in upholding his principles in the face of terrific
opposition.

If Douglass had been mainly concerned with advancing his own
selfish interests, he could, as he pointed out, have taken advantage of
many opportunities to do so. It would have been much easier for him
to have remained with the Garrisonians as an anti-slavery lecturer than

to move to a new community, start a new career and become involved in the heart-breaking struggle to publish a newspaper. But Douglass believed that the most important contribution he could make to the struggle was to demonstrate that the Negro people were active participants in the battle, had their own spokesmen and were not simply passive bystanders watching the white humanitarians relieve them of their burdens. It was Gerrit Smith's sympathy and understanding of this that drew the Negro close to his benefactor; it was Douglass' knowledge that Julia Griffiths shared his belief that played such an important part in their successful collaboration.

For all their sincerity and good-will, it was this emphasis on the important contribution that the Negro himself should make through his own independent efforts that Garrison and his closest associates resented most, and explains why they were a good deal kinder in their treatment of others who had left their ranks than they were of Douglass.[36]

What was certainly the shrewdest comment on the chain of events during the summer and fall of 1853 was offered by Harriet Beecher Stowe in a letter to Garrison. Despite its length, it merits quotation in full:

"Cabin, Dec. 19 [1853]

"Mr. Garrison
"Dear Sir:

"After seeing you, I enjoyed the pleasure of a personal interview with Mr. Douglass & I feel bound in justice to say that the impression was far more satisfactory, than I had anticipated.

"There does not appear to be any deep underlying stratum of bitterness—he did not seem to me malignant or revengeful. I think that it was only a temporary excitement & one which he will outgrow.

"I was much gratified with the growth & development both of his mind & heart. I am satisfied that his change of sentiments was not a mere political one but a genuine growth of his own conviction. A vigorous reflective mind like his cast among those holding new sentiments is naturally led to modified views.

"At all events, he holds no opinion which he cannot defend, with a variety & richness of thought & expression & an aptness of illustration which shows it to be a growth from the soil of his own mind with a living root & not a twig broken off other men's thoughts & stuck down to subserve a temporary purpose.

"His plans for the elevation of his own race, are manly, sensible, comprehensive, he has evidently observed carefully & thought deeply & will I trust act efficiently.

"You speak of him as an apostate—I cannot but regard this language as unjustly severe—Why is he any more to be called an apostate for having spoken ill tempered things of former friends than they for having spoken severely & cruelly as they have of him?—Where is this work of excommunication to end—Is there but one true anti-slavery church & all others infidels? —Who shall declare which it is.

"I feel bound to remonstrate with this—for the same reason that I do with slavery—because I think it, an injustice. I must say still further, that if the first allusion to his family concerns was unfortunate this last one is more unjustifiable still—I am utterly surprised at it—as a friend to you, & to him I view it with the deepest concern & regret.

"What Douglass *is* really, time will show—I trust that he will make no further additions to the already unfortunate controversial literature of the cause. *Silence* in this case will be eminently—*golden*.

"I must indulge the hope you will reason at some future time to alter your opinion & that what you now cast aside as worthless shall yet appear to be a treasure.

"There is abundant room in the antislavery field for him to perform a work without crossing the track or impeding the movement of his old friends & perhaps in some future time meeting each other from opposite quarters of a victorious field you may yet shake hands together.

"I write this letter because in the conversation I had with you, & also with Miss Weston I admitted so much that was unfavorable to Mr. Douglass that I felt bound in justice to state the more favorable views which had arisen to my mind.

"Very sincerely your friend,

"H. B. Stowe"[87]

Mrs. Stowe, a friend of both, was earnestly trying to arrange a reconciliation between Garrison and Douglass. But her words were wasted on the leader of the American Anti-Slavery Society. Garrison met Douglass at various anti-slavery functions but refused to speak to him, still regarding him as one of the "malignant enemies of mine" and as being "utterly unscrupulous in carrying out his own designs." Characteristic of Garrison's attitude was his rejection of an invitation to attend a celebration in Syracuse in October, 1860. After indicating that he was in poor health and had been advised by his doctor not to travel, he wrote:

"But, were I 'in speaking order,' the fact that Frederick Douglass is to be present at the celebration, and to participate therein, would powerfully repel me from attending. I regard him as thoroughly base and selfish, and I know that his hostility to the American Anti-Slavery Society and its leading advocates is unmitigated and unceasing. . . . In fact, he reveals himself more and more to me as destitute of every principle of honor, ungrateful to the last degree, and malevolent in spirit. He is not worthy of respect, confidence, or countenance."[38]

This, at the very same time that the Negro leader was telling his audiences:

"No difference of opinion, no personal assaults, shall ever lead me to forget that some who, in America, have often made me the subject of personal abuse, are, at the same time, in their own way, earnestly working for the abolition of slavery."[39]

Even during the Civil War, when all groups of Abolitionists joined forces in their struggle to achieve emancipation, Garrison and Douglass remained apart. In principle, however, the war brought them closer and Douglass had the satisfaction of seeing the Garrisonians adopt several of the doctrines whose espousal had led to his condemnation. A month after Fort Sumter he announced that he felt "a personal, if not a little malicious pleasure" in learning that Garrison and his associates had abandoned their slogans condemning the American Union and, instead, were calling for the preservation of the Union against rebels and traitors. Ten years before, he reminded his readers, he had concluded that "the battle of freedom should be fought within the Union, and not out of it; that instead of leaving the Union on account of slavery, we should stand by the Union, and drive out slavery." The avowal of these beliefs had led to his being branded an "apostate" and to his expulsion "from the fellowship of those whom he had long loved and venerated as the chosen champions of the cause of the slave."

"We spoke ten years too soon," he concluded, "or rather the slaveholding rebellion came just ten years too late, else today we might have been a member, in good and regular standing, in the Garrisonian anti-slavery church, instead of being, as now, a worker for the slave as a single individual."[40]

In later years, as the anti-slavery struggle faded into the background, Douglass repeatedly praised the contributions of the Garrisonians. "It was they," he said, speaking of Garrison and Phillips, "who made Abraham Lincoln and the Republican party possible. What abolished slavery was the moral sentiment which had been created, not by the pulpit, but by the Garrisonian platform."[41] Looking back on the bitter controversy between himself and the Garrisonians, Douglass observed in 1885, in a letter to Oliver Johnson:

". . . I sincerely do assure you, that, while I cannot pretend to forget some differences which arose between us years ago, I have still no other than feelings of respect, gratitude, and love to you and the noble band of abolitionists led by William Lloyd Garrison, and with whom from first to last you faithfully cooperated.

"Like yourself, I grow less a partizan as I grow older and find it easy to make little of mere personal differences as to methods and even as to estimates of character growing out of such differences. These were but the dust and smoke of the fierce battle with slavery, and now that the enemy is vanquished, I joyfully recognize every instrumentality by which this grand result was attained."[42]

The break with the Garrisonians marked the end of one phase of Douglass' career and the beginning of another. After 1853, when the break was complete, Douglass fully emerged as an Abolitionist leader in his own right. From that year until the end of the Civil War he occupied a place in the anti-slavery movement second to none.

Anti-Slavery Political Action

The first gun fired at Fort Sumter was the climax of the inevitable conflict between two antagonistic systems in the United States—one in the North based upon free farming and free labor, the other in the South, based upon chattel slavery. During the seven years preceding the shot at Fort Sumter this conflict had been reaching the point of explosion. Harbingers of the gathering storm were the passage of the Kansas-Nebraska Bill which repealed the Missouri Compromise and opened northern territory to slavery, the battle between the pioneer farmers and the slaveholders for the possession of Kansas, the Dred Scott decision with its pronouncements that the black man had no rights that the white man was bound to respect, and that Congress had no power to abolish or prevent slavery in any of the territories, the hanging of John Brown from the gallows in a Virginia prison yard, the birth of the Republican Party, and the election of Abraham Lincoln on a program calling for the restriction of slavery to its then existing boundaries. Each of these events, as Frederick Douglass so aptly put it, was "one necessary link in the chain of events preparatory to the complete overthrow of the whole slave system."

By the time the Kansas-Nebraska Bill was passed by Congress, Douglass had already become an influential figure in the American political scene. As a political tactician he ranked far above many of his famous contemporaries.

During most of his political career before the Civil War Douglass was allied to the Liberty Party. The vast majority of American historians have underestimated the Liberty Party since it never carried a state, or even came close to carrying it, in any election. Yet the significance of this party cannot be estimated from the number of votes cast for its candidates at any given time. Its newspapers and propaganda went into the homes of Whigs and Democrats alike; its lecturers spoke to hundreds of people whose sense of party loyalty prevented them from voting the Liberty Party ticket. The Liberty Party men helped to shape the principles, forge the arguments, and train the leaders who in 1854 formed the Republican Party.

The Liberty Party was organized in April, 1840, by an anti-slavery convention representing six states. The chief driving force behind its organization was Myron Holley, the noted Abolitionist from Rochester, New York. The platform of the party, adopted three years later at a convention at Buffalo, added to its denunciation of slavery an announcement of the purpose of the Abolitionists "whether as private citizens or as public functionaries sworn to support the Constitution of the United States, to regard and to treat the third clause of the fourth article of that instrument [relating to the return of fugitive slaves], whenever applied to the case of a fugitive slave, as utterly null and void, and consequently as forming no part of the Constitution of the United States, whenever we are called upon or sworn to support it."

Negroes were active in the Liberty Party from its very inception in April, 1840.[1] Samuel Ringgold Ward allied himself with the Liberty Party as soon as it was formed; Henry Highland Garnet proudly proclaimed himself "a Liberty Party man," and J. W. Loguen and William Wells Brown took the stump for the party. The Buffalo Convention of Colored Citizens in August, 1843, passed a resolution endorsing the principles of the Liberty Party. Two dissenting votes were cast, one by Douglass and the other by Charles L. Remond, both Garrisonians. At the National Convention of the Liberty Party in Buffalo in 1843, Negroes, for the first time in American history, were active participants in a national political gathering. Ward led the convention in prayer; Garnet was appointed on the nominations committee, and Charles B. Ray was elected one of the convention secretaries.[2]

By the time Douglass joined its ranks, the Liberty Party had passed its peak. In the election of 1844 the party, headed as in 1840 by James G. Birney, increased its vote from less than 7,000 in 1840 to 63,324. This was the high mark. After 1844 it rapidly lost strength as the majority of political Abolitionists left the organization, and, merging with practical politicians, labored to build a political mass movement directed against slavery. Dissension among those who remained further weakened the organization. The advocates of the "one idea" policy insisted that the only program to be presented to the voters was a call for the overthrow of slavery "within the limits of national jurisdiction." Another group, aware that the voters wanted to know the party's stand on the tariff, the bank, the distribution of the public lands, called for a broad platform.

The division over issues in the Liberty Party inevitably led to a split. Early in June, 1847, about forty prominent Liberty Party men, all calling for a fuller program, met at Macedon Locke, Wayne County, New York, and, under the leadership of Gerrit Smith, adopted a program of nineteen articles. Separating itself from the Liberty Party, the Macedon Convention nominated Smith and Elihu Burritt, "the Learned Blacksmith," for President and Vice President of the United States.[3]

In October, 1847, the Liberty Party held its national convention in Buffalo. Ignoring the platform and candidates of the seceders, the delegates reaffirmed the "one idea" policy, and chose John P. Hale of New Hampshire and Leicester King of Ohio as their candidates. Not so easily downed, Gerrit Smith issued a call for another convention to be held in Buffalo on June 14, 1848.

The Buffalo Convention of the National Liberty Party, the name assumed by the group to distinguish it from the "one idea" Liberty Party, was the first official political gathering Douglass ever attended. He was impressed by the proceedings, and listened intently as Gerrit Smith read "An Address to the Colored People of the Northern States" urging them "to prove their superiority to the whites in industry, economy, temperance and education, in order to disprove the frequently repeated charge that Negroes were only fit for slavery," and advising them to withdraw "from pro-slavery political parties and churches." Douglass was pleased that the convention went on record for free public lands to actual settlers, for woman's political rights, for the ten-hour system of labor, and the right of workers to organize into trade unions. Suffering from a severe attack of "tonsil inflammation," Douglass was finally prevailed upon to speak and supported vigorously the Garrisonian position on the Constitution and the Union. Despite sharp rebuttal by several delegates, Douglass held his ground, arguing that the Constitution was designed to protect the interests of the slaveholders.[4]

His initial contact with a political convention made no dent in Douglass' confidence in the Garrisonian creed.

"Our attendance at this Convention," he informed his readers, "while it has done much to remove prejudices from our mind respecting some of the prominent men engaged in it, has also deepened our conviction that the only true ground for an American Abolitionist is, *No Union with Slaveholders.*"

But he was irritated by the objections raised by some Garrisonians to his attendance at the Buffalo Convention on the ground that it indicated a willingness "to give his influence" to further the objects of the National Liberty Party. He reminded his critics that he was still a Garrisonian and could well do without a "diplomatic reproof."[5]

But national events were compelling Douglass to revise his thinking regarding political action. In the summer of 1846, when the war with Mexico was only a few months old, President Polk asked Congress for two million dollars to be used in the acquisition of new territory. Thereupon Judge David Wilmot of Pennsylvania offered his famous amendment which became known as the Wilmot Proviso. The essential language of the Proviso was that neither slavery nor involuntary servitude ever exist in any territory acquired from the republic of Mexico. The House of Representatives passed the bill twice, but it failed each time in the Senate.

The idea embodied in the Proviso, however, did not die. Out of the furor aroused over the Wilmot Proviso rose the Free Soil Party.

On May 22, 1848, the Democratic National Convention nominated Lewis Cass of Michigan for President upon a platform framed to suit the South. Cries of anger and disappointment came from the free states. "Had a bombshell fallen into our quiet city yesterday," commented the *Chicago Journal,* "it could not have created more consternation."

On June 10, the Whig National Convention nominated Zachary Taylor, a Louisiana slaveholder, for President, and howled down the Wilmot Proviso. Immediately anti-slavery Whigs, especially in the Western Reserve, rose as one man to repudiate him.

"As we anticipated," declared the Cleveland *True Democrat,* "the Whigs have nominated Zachary Taylor for president. And this is the cup offered by slaveholders for us to drink. We loathed the sight. We will neither touch, taste, nor handle the unclean thing."[6]

Awakened by the controversy engendered by the Wilmot Proviso, Douglass began to see that, valuable as moral suasion was, a basic struggle for the freedom of the slave would take place in Congress, where the attention of the entire people could be focused. Hailing the "Great Uprising of the North," he wrote in his paper: "We look upon the Wilmot Proviso and its supporters as indications of the presence of a great principle in the national heart, which by patient cultivation will one day abolish forever our system of human bondage." Although the true radical principle for him was not opposition to the extension of slavery, but complete extirpation of every vestige of human bondage throughout the entire nation, nevertheless Douglass fully understood how important was the struggle for the Wilmot Proviso.

"It serves to keep the subject before the people—to deepen their hatred of the system—and to break up the harmony between the Northern white people and the Southern slaveholders, which has so long been the safeguard against an uprising of slaves against their cruel masters. . . . To limit slavery where it now is," argued Douglass, "if it does not abolish it, will at least fix upon it the nation's reprobation. Should the North gain in this contest, it will be the first victory gained since the formation of the Government."[7]

Thus while he still considered himself a Garrisonian, Douglass showed an un-Garrisonian delight and enthusiasm for the new political movement which was arising in the summer of 1848 pledged to support the Wilmot Proviso.

Douglass was present at the historic convention held in Buffalo on August 29, 1848, in which discontented members of the Whig and Democratic parties as well as Liberty Party men, not overly rigid in their approach to anti-slavery political action, united to form the Free Soil Party on a platform of opposition to the extension of slavery in the territories. The Democrats were represented by the Barnburners of New York who favored the Wilmot Proviso, had refused to accept Lewis Cass, and had already nominated Martin Van Buren as their standard-bearer. Among the Conscience Whigs were men like Charles Francis Adams and Charles Sumner who could not stomach their party's candidate. These anti-slavery men from all parties were united by their determination to secure the adoption of the Wilmot Proviso.

Eighteen states were represented and there were 465 delegates. As many as ten thousand persons attended some of the large mass meetings. Martin Van Buren, already nominated by the best organized group in the convention, was chosen to head the ticket and Charles Francis Adams was nominated for the second highest office. The platform proposed no interference with slavery in the states, but demanded that Congress halt its advance into the territories—"No more slave States, no more slave territory, no more compromises with slavery; and freedom for Oregon, California and New Mexico." The slogan of the new party was: "Free Soil, Free Speech, Free Labor and Free Men."[8]

Douglass was seated in the convention hall, when a Mr. Husbands of Rochester, addressing the delegates, announced that he saw "Frederick Douglass here." The delegates responded with three cheers. The next day there were loud calls for Douglass to speak. He took the stand and stated that he was grateful for the opportunity to address the delegates, but deeply regretted his inability to speak since he had only recently had an operation on his throat. "One thing, however, I want to say, God speed your noble undertaking." The official reporter added: "The audience appeared to feel a great disappointment when they learned that Mr. Douglass could not address them."[9]

In his first editorial discussions, Douglass placed his stamp of approval on the Free Soil discussions, and argued that as the Free Soilers were the only openly anti-slavery party, it was the duty of the Abolitionists to support Van Buren. The Constitution might be pro-slavery, but the tactical exigencies of the struggle made it necessary that every possible weapon be utilized. The adherents of slavery were gathering around Taylor and Cass, while the forces of freedom were hesitant and disunited. What should the friends of the slave do in this crisis? Douglass' answer reveals his profound grasp of the correct strategy to be used by the Abolitionists:

". . . We may stand off and act the part of fault finders—pick flaws in the Free Soil platform, expose the weakness of some persons connected with it—suspect and criticize their leaders, and in this way play into the hands of our enemies, affording the sticks to break our own heads. Or we may consign ourselves to oblivion . . . remain silent as if we were speechless, and let things take their own course, and thus morally to commit suicide. In neither of these ways can we go. We feel it our duty to pursue the course which will make us in some degree a terror to evil doers, and a praise to all that do well . . . to be a worker on the anvil now before us—that whatever influence we may possess, it shall be given in the right direction."[10]

Douglass' endorsement of the Free Soil Party came in conflict with his Garrisonian beliefs, and he gradually withdrew from the advanced position he had set forth in his first editorials. A month after the Free Soil Party was organized, he announced editorially that "it would be a violation of anti-slavery principles for us to vote." At the Colored Convention in Cleveland, on September 6, 1848, he opposed the adoption of a resolution which hailed "with delight this great movement as the dawn of a bright and more auspicious day." The resolution was defeated.[11]

Despite his reluctance to abandon his faith in the Garrisonian doctrines, Douglass could not refrain from endorsing the new party. He realized that the Free Soil Party had brought the struggle against slavery to the attention of hundreds of thousands whom the Abolitionists had been unable to reach. True, the new party was not to be regarded as "the real anti-slavery movement of the country," but it decidedly was "a noble step in the right direction." It was still necessary for the anti-slavery movement to be kept "mainly a moral one"; the slogan "No Union with Slaveholders in Church or State" must still be inscribed on the banners of those concerned with the wrongs of the slave. But the Free Soilers had already done some good and could do more in the future. On September 10, 1848, *The North Star* editorially recommended the Free Soil candidates, Van Buren and Adams.

It is interesting to note that even before Douglass had left the Garrisonians, he was already ahead of Gerrit Smith in his understanding of the fundamental issues involved in the political campaign. For while Douglass wished the Free Soilers every possible success even though he was not prepared to abandon his Garrisonian principles, Smith declared the new party to be entirely inadequate and refused to support Van Buren. Smith understood the necessity for political action but lacked Douglass' insight into the methods necessary for obtaining the largest popular support for each measure to restrict slavery. Douglass understood that this was the beginning of a great movement which would finally split the Democrats, destroy the Whig Party, and create a new political anti-slavery movement with a mass following.[12]

Douglass was excited by the colorful campaign. Free Soilers sang themselves hoarse up to election day:

The North is ripe for the Proviso
Hurrah! Hurrah! Hurrah!
She'll back the names from Buffalo
Hurrah! Hurrah! Hurrah!

Whigs, Democrats, we'll all unite
And Liberty boys—for our cause is right,
Hurrah! Hurrah! Hurrah![13]

Although Van Buren did not carry a single state, the Free Soil Party received 291,678 votes out of the 2,882,120 which were cast, and elected five men to Congress. The *Liberator* sought to interpret this large vote for the new party as an evidence of the influence of Garrisonian principles:

"The Slave Power is beginning to falter—fresh adherents are daily rallying around the standard of Liberty, and the cry of 'No Union with Slaveholders' is causing the knees of the oppressor to tremble."[14]

While Douglass was bitter over Taylor's election, he was encouraged by the vote cast for the Free Soil candidates. He was convinced that it was the duty of all anti-slavery men to promulgate their principles among the Free Soilers so that gradually "a true Free Soil Party" could be established. "We must go on and lead the Free Soilers," he told the audience at the Thirteenth Annual Meeting of the Rhode Island Anti-Slavery Society a month after the election.[15]

Had the Free Soil Party continued to fulfill his bright hopes, Douglass might have allied himself with the movement. But he was disappointed by the failure of the party's leaders to maintain an active organization after the national elections, and by their formation of coalitions with various conservative political groups, thus abandoning independent political action.[16] On March 23, 1849, he inquired editorially, "What Good has the Free Soil Movement Done?" and answered that it had "promised much and has performed little." It had proved to be "a dull and indolent concern, gone to sleep and refusing to wake, until roused by the thunders of another political campaign." Instead of moving closer to Abolitionism and winning the approval of anti-slavery men, it had sought alliances "with the enemies of that holy cause." It had "swallowed up the Liberty Party press . . . and weakened its once powerful testimony against slavery." It had increased the burdens of the Abolitionists by creating the impression in the public mind that it was unnecessary to deal with slavery in the South as long as it could be kept out of the territories. "No abolitionist," cried Douglass, "who is truly such, will be gratified with, or encourage any measure or doctrine that does not contemplate slavery everywhere as marked out for destruction." Disillusionment bit deeply.

Even the belief expressed by the *Providence Transcript* that he would be nominated by the Free Soil Party in 1852 as its Vice-Presidential candidate did not change Douglass' attitude toward the movement. Instead, as he began "wielding the Federal Constitution for the abolition of American Slavery," and decided to use both moral and political power, he turned in another direction and allied himself with the Liberty Party, associating himself with the Gerrit Smith wing of the organization. On May 15, 1851, he wrote that he knew "of no one principle of that party that I should oppose." The following autumn he attended the convention of the Liberty Party in Buffalo and was appointed to the National Committee and to the Committee on Nominations. And in the fall elections he assured anti-slavery voters that there was "no way in which the cause of the slave can be better promoted than by voting the Liberty Party ticket."[17]

In the meantime, the Free Soilers had not given up hope of winning Douglass to their cause. At the Whig Convention in Rochester in October, 1851, the Free Soil delegates proposed Douglass as representative for the Second Assembly District in the State Legislature and secured twenty-two votes on the first ballot for their candidate. The convention finally nominated another candidate, but the press generally admitted that if the "Free Soilers had been in a majority," Douglass would have secured the nomination.[18]

Douglass, however, rebuffed all overtures from the Free Soilers. Even when a number of Liberty Party members prepared early in 1852 to enter the Presidential campaign under the Free Soil banner, he continued his support of an independent Liberty Party. "I think we ought to stand by and maintain the Liberty Party with all its great principles and purposes," he wrote to Smith on February 19, 1852. Early in April he carried an editorial in his paper, headlined "Stand by the Liberty Party." He reminded the political Abolitionists who were flirting with the Free Soilers that the aim of the Free Soil Party was "to denationalize and sectionalize and not to abolish slavery," whereas the Liberty Party, whether followed "by many or by few," would continue to call for the eradication of slavery everywhere. As for himself he could not see "how a not less comprehensive or a less elevated platform can be occupied by those who would radically oppose slavery at the ballot box."[19]

But in spite of all this, not many months later Douglass was in the ranks of the Free Soil Party. As he marked the busy preparations of the Free Soilers for the national campaign and noted the enthusiasm evoked by this growing mass movement, he realized the futility of the isolationist policy he had been advocating. Recalling his original position that it was the duty of the Abolitionists to lead the Free Soilers, he wrote to Smith on July 15, 1852, that it was their political responsibility to attend the approaching Pittsburgh convention of the Free Soil Party. The gathering could be "made to occupy such a position as the 'Liberty Party' may properly vote for its candidates." The masses who would be present in Pittsburgh were far ahead of their leaders, and were quite prepared to support a program in advance of "mere *Free Soil*." It remained for men like Smith to bring up the issues around which the delegates would rally.[20]

On August 11, 1852, two thousand persons crowded into the Masonic Hall in Pittsburgh to attend the second national convention of the Free Soil Party. Douglass and Smith sat in the New York section. Soon after convening, Douglass was nominated as a secretary of the convention by Lewis Tappan, was elected by acclamation, and took his seat "amid loud applause." Barely had the next speaker started to address the delegates, when loud calls for Douglass drowned out his voice. Amid cheers Douglass moved to the platform. Taken by surprise, he had no prepared address. But he launched immediately into what reporters described as "an aggressive speech."[21]

"The object of this Convention is to organize a party, not merely for the present, but a party identified with eternal principles and therefore permanent," he began. He had come to Pittsburgh "not so much of a Free Soiler as others." He stood, of course, with the delegates "for circumscribing and damaging slavery in every way." But his motto was for exterminating slavery everywhere, not only in California but in New Orleans. He assured them that in making their party platform nothing could be gained by "a timid feeling." The Constitution was directed against slavery since "human government is for the protection of rights." Even if the framers of the document had asserted the right to enslave human beings, it would not have the binding authority of reasonableness.

"Suppose you and I had made a deed to give away two or three acres of blue sky; would the sky fall—and would anybody be able to plough it? You will say that this is an absurdity, and so it is. The binding quality of law, is its reasonableness. I am safe, therefore, in saying, that slavery cannot be legalized at all. I hope, therefore, that you will take the ground that this slavery is a system, not only of wrong, but is of a lawless character, and cannot be christianized or legalized."

The audience applauded Douglass throughout and cheered as he concluded with the advice that "numbers should not be looked to as much as right." As the afternoon session drew to a close, the delegates again called on Douglass to speak, but he declined with the brief statement that his throat was sore from his previous exertion.[22]

The reception of Douglass at the Free Soil Convention aroused comment in Europe as well as in this country. In London *The Anti-Slavery Reporter* viewed it as one of the brightest signs of the time.

"The appointment of Frederick Douglass as one of the secretaries of the convention," it observed, "is a cheering indication of the advance of anti-slavery sentiment in the United States. That a colored man should be called upon to act as an officer in a large political meeting is a sign of progress in that country, where to belong to the enslaved race has been to be proscribed and neglected."[23]

Douglass informed his readers that he had been favorably impressed by the "spirit" displayed at the Free Soil Convention "no less than with its principles" and candidates. John P. Hale of New Hampshire was "a large-hearted philanthropist . . . a dreaded foe to slavery," and George W. Julian of Indiana was "one of the truest and most disinterested friends of freedom whom we have ever met." He urged the Liberty Party convention about to assemble at Canastota, New York, to endorse the Free Soil nominations.

Early in September the Liberty Party convened. The movement to support Hale and Julian ran into opposition when a number of delegates called for the selection of Presidential candidates from the Liberty Party. Outvoted, the faction opposing the endorsement of the Free Soil nominations withdrew and selected William Goodell and Charles C. Foote as their candidates for President and Vice-President.

Douglass was critical of the seceders. He was convinced that it would be unwise for the Liberty Party to "array itself against Free Soilery." Nor did he believe that he was sacrificing a basic principle in supporting Hale and Julian. What was "morally right" was "not, at all times, politically possible." "Our rule of political action is this: the voter ought to see to it that his vote shall secure the highest good possible, at the same time that it does no harm."[24]

The masthead of Douglass' journal carried the names of Hale and

Julian inscribed on an American flag. But the editor's main concern in the autumn of 1852 was in the campaign for representative from the twenty-second Congressional district of New York. His friend and mentor, Gerrit Smith, had been nominated for the office by the Liberty or Free Democrat's Party. Douglass campaigned through the state even though he doubted that Smith, being "too far in advance of the people and of the age," could possibly be elected. He could not believe his ears when people said they were "going to vote for Gerrit Smith" and expressed confidence in Smith's election.

"This however, I deem unreasonable," he wrote to Smith from Chittenango Falls on October 21. "How could such a thing be? Oh! if it could only be so, the cup of my joy would be full. It is too good to be true. Yet *I* am the only man whom I have heard speak disparagingly in private about the matter."[25]

The Free Soil vote of 1852 was about one-half of what it had been in 1848, but Douglass' disappointment was speedily forgotten with the announcement of the election of Gerrit Smith to Congress by an overwhelming majority. The "grand event," which even Garrison admitted was "among the most extraordinary political events of this most extraordinary age," completely filled his "cup of joy." "The election of *Gerrit Smith*— what an era!" he exulted. He was especially overjoyed by the fact that Smith went to Congress "a *free man*," and "not by the grace of a party caucus, bestowed as a reward for party services; not by concealment, bargain or compromise. . . ." As his excitement mounted, he predicted that "with men and money," the Liberty Party could carry New York state "for freedom" in 1856.[26]

Douglass placed great hope in Smith's congressional career. On August 18, 1853, four months before the session convened, he wrote to his co-reformer advising him to master the parliamentary rules of Congress so as "to defy all the mantraps which they will surely set for your feet." Unfortunately Smith did not remain in Washington long enough to put this sound advice to much use. After joining in the attack on the Kansas-Nebraska Bill, introduced into Congress early in 1854, and leading the movement to strike out the word "white" from the bill granting land to actual settlers in New Mexico, he decided he had had enough of life in the nation's capital and returned to Peterboro. On August 7, 1854, Smith resigned his seat in Congress. The only explanation he gave was the "pressure of my far too extensive business."[27]

Many Abolitionists felt let down by Smith's return to private life after an eight months congressional career. They believed that he had accepted a sacred trust when he entered Congress, and that he had no right to permit personal considerations to interfere with his work for the cause. Douglass probably shared the disappointment of his anti-slavery colleagues, but he criticized those who viewed Smith's resignation as evidence of "treachery and meanness." It required courage, he reasoned, for a man to give up "place and power at a point when that place was every hour becoming more honorable, and when that power was becoming more and more widely felt."[28] By the same token, of course, it made Smith's resignation all the more difficult for the anti-slavery men to swallow. Unquestionably Douglass' friendship for Smith caused him to overlook the demoralizing effect the resignation had upon those voters who, like himself, had expected great things of the Liberty Party congressman.

For a few weeks there was some discussion in the press over the possibility of Douglass succeeding Smith in Congress. The *New York Tribune* started the ball rolling with an editorial making the proposal, and several papers immediately took it up. The *Massachusetts Spy* was convinced that "Frederick Douglass would make an admirable member of Congress," and expressed the wish that "we could have the privilege of voting for him." The *Cincinnati Commercial* not only agreed, but ventured the opinion that the Negro would do better in Congress than the white Douglas who was Senator from Illinois.[29]

The discussion caused a terrific outcry in the press friendly to the South, and shrieks arose that the "plot" to place Douglass in Congress proved the real design of the Abolitionists.

"It is time for the people of the North," the *Philadelphia Argus* cried, "to look at the acts and purposes of these abolition traitors who . . . agree to elect, if possible, a Negro to the House of Representatives—are they willing that a Negro should be sent to Congress for an army of avant couriers to shield them in their designs upon the Union."[30]

The furor died as quickly as it was born. No political group took up the *Tribune's* suggestion, nor did Douglass indicate any political ambitions. He did, however, write a prophetic editorial discussing the significance of the proposal:

"The possibility of electing a Negro to the American Congress, is a modern suggestion. The idea is a new one, as little hoped for by the despised colored people, as dreamed of by their white friends. We accept it simply as an indication of a slighly altered state of mind in the country, but without the slightest belief that the idea will ever be realized in our person, tho' we do hope and expect to see it realized in some competent colored man before we shall have done with the journey of life. The thing is in itself reasonable, and, therefore, probable. It is consistent with all the elementary principles of the American government, though it is in conflict with our national prejudices and practices. It is evident of some progress that the subject has called forth an expression so general and so decided at this time—and this is the only importance we feel at liberty to allow it. We certainly do not believe in the existence of any serious intention to offer us or to accept us, as a candidate for Congress, or for any other office in this government, State or National."[31]

The passage of the Kansas-Nebraska Act produced a general re-alignment in American political life. Democrats who refused to stay in their party now that it was dominated by slave owners, Whigs who were fed up with their party's straddling on the slavery question, were looking for a new political organization. Together with Abolitionists, Free Soilers, German-American Communists and other reformers, they organized in the summer and fall of 1854 a political movement dedicated to fight the further extension of slavery. The name of the newly formed coalition was the Republican Party.

The Republican Party attracted the support of all but a small group of diehard political Abolitionists. Some three hundred Liberty Party members remained outside the new coalition, contending that "the signs of the times forbid the dissolution" of their organization. They were the only party, they argued, willing to fight the battle of freedom on the ground that "slavery cannot be legalized" anywhere on the earth; the only party calling for "the utter annihilation of slavery." In September, 1854, thirty Liberty Party men met in Syracuse and nominated William Goodell for Governor on a platform calling upon the federal government to abolish slavery. Douglass attended the convention as a delegate and took the stump for Goodell.[32]

Douglass was not blind to the significance of the rapidly growing Republican movement. "We rejoice in this demonstration," he wrote in July, 1855. "It evinces the fact of a growing determination on the part of the North, to redeem itself from bondage, to bury party affinities, and predilections, and also the political leaders who have hitherto controlled them; to unite in one grand phalanx, and go forth, and whip the enemy."

But he could not abandon the Liberty Party and ally himself with the Republican movement. The Republican Party did not go far enough; it gave aid and comfort to the slaveholders by its willingness "to let Slavery where it is." Yet this was precisely where slavery should be attacked. There was need for a party which calls for "a clean sweep of slavery everywhere," and which "by its position and doctrines, and by its antecedents, is pledged to continue the struggle while a bondman in his chains remains to weep." Such was the Liberty Party, and on its platform "must the great battle of freedom be fought out. . . ." While it could not boast of mass support, the Liberty Party could fulfill an important function by keeping alive the demand for the abolition of slavery throughout the nation until such time as events themselves compelled other political parties with greater numerical support to incorporate this program in their platforms. Douglass was confident that this would come to pass; he was convinced that the Republican Party "as it grows in numbers, will also grow *in the knowledge of the Truth.*"[33] Meanwhile, until this happy event was realized he believed that he could best make his contribution to the political battle against slavery by galvanizing the Liberty Party into life.

With this in mind, Douglass, in March, 1855, urged Gerrit Smith to go forward with plans for a National Liberty Party Convention. A month later, he joined with Lewis Tappan, William Goodell, Gerrit Smith, and James McCune Smith in issuing a call for a convention of the party supporters to be held in Syracuse in June. The call opened: "We are few—but we are not, therefore, to cease from our work. Work for a good cause, be that cause popular or unpopular, must be work to the end." The purpose of the new political movement was toward the removal of slavery from the territories and the states "by means of our national political power." The existing parties were incapable of achieving this goal, the call asserted, the Whig, Democratic, and Know-Nothing parties being dominated by their slaveholding members while the Free Soil Party, although "an anti-slavery party," denied the right of the national government "to touch slavery in the States."[34]

After a three-months preparation, the convention met on June 26-28, 1855. James McCune Smith was elected chairman and Douglass was designated to serve on the Business Committee. A "Declaration of Sentiments," an "Exposition of the Constitutional Duty of the Federal Government to Abolish Slavery," and an "Address to the Public" were drawn up and adopted. The body also endorsed a program calling for the use of the political power of the nation "to overthrow every part and parcel of American Slavery."[35] Following the issuance of a call for a national convention to assemble in October, the meeting adjourned.

Douglass left the convention optimistic. On August 15 he departed on a four-week lecture tour in up-state New York during which he planned "to uphold the great principles of freedom as laid down . . . at the radical abolition convention." At the end of the trip he attended the Liberty Party Convention at Ithaca. Douglass was nominated for the office of Secretary of State of New York, the first time such an honor was bestowed upon an American Negro. But the Liberty Party failed to designate a slate for national offices, as it was awaiting the action of the Radical Abolitionists which, of course, was simply the Liberty Party by another name.[36]

Late in October Douglass traveled to Boston to attend the convention of the Radical Abolitionists. Smith, Beriah Green, and Abram Pyne, a Negro editor, were also present. A terrific downpour and the simultaneous opening of the National Agricultural Fair accounted for the small attendance. Under these circumstances the body decided to take no definite action. Still Douglass was not discouraged. He was as confident as ever in "the ultimate triumph" of the views of this handful of Liberty Party men and Radical Abolitionists. Sooner or later those interested in the struggle against slavery would come to see that these views were correct. "We shall, therefore, contribute our mite toward effecting this desirable consummation," he wrote editorially in mid-November.[37]

The American political scene during the opening months of 1856 was full of confusion and change. The Whig party had practically disappeared. The American Party (Know-Nothings) was in the throes of dissolution over the slavery issue. The Republican Party, carrying a majority in nearly half the states in its first election, was assuming ever increasing importance.

On February 22, 1856, Republican leaders met at Pittsburgh, planned a national convention for June and drew up an "Address to the People of the United States." The document was a severe disappointment to

the political Abolitionists who still clung to the ideals of the skeleton
Liberty Party. They had expected the Republican leaders to move closer
to the radical Abolitionist position. Instead, these leaders, believing that
even their limited anti-slavery program was unacceptable to many in
the North, had actually retreated. In the entire document, said Douglass,
only the demand of freedom for Kansas reflected the influence of the
anti-slavery forces in the Republican Party. "Nothing said of the
Fugitive Slave Bill—nothing said of Slavery in the District of Columbia
—nothing said of the slave trade between States—nothing said of giving
dignity of the nation to Liberty—nothing said of securing the rights
of citizens from the Northern States, in the constitutional right to enter
and transact business in the slave states." He saw only one argument
that might influence Abolitionists to follow the Republican Party and
that argument was "the grand corrupter of all reforms . . . that the
only thing needful, the thing to precede all else, is a large party; and in
order to do this, we are at liberty to abandon almost everything but
a name." With such a philosophy he would have nothing to do. He
looked toward the convention of the Radical Political Abolitionists to
be held in Syracuse on May 28 rather than toward the Republican
convention scheduled to meet in Philadelphia in June.[38]

On March 21, 1856, Garrison wrote somewhat gleefully:

"I see that Lewis Tappan, Douglass, McCune Smith, Goodell and Gerrit
Smith have called a convention for the purpose of nominating candidates for
the Presidency and Vice Presidency of the United States!! Can anything
more ludicrous than this be found inside or outside of the Utica Insane
Asylum?"[39]

Indifferent to such caustic comments, Douglass addressed the convention on the afternoon of its first day. He admitted that he was tempted
to join the Republican Party, but was dissuaded by the realization that
"they do not give a full recognition to the humanity of the Negro,"
that they sought to limit slavery only in Kansas and Nebraska. "Liberty
must cut the throat of slavery or have its own cut by slavery," he concluded.[40]

The convention nominated Gerrit Smith for President and Samuel
McFarland for Vice President. Douglass had been named for Vice
President but an objection was made because Smith and he came from
the same state. Douglass announced that he soon planned to move
from New York to Ohio and therefore "avoid that objection." Although

McFarland was finally nominated, reports arose that Douglass had been the convention's choice. On June 21, 1856, almost a month late, the *New York Herald* declared that "the Abolitionists pure and simple have designated as their standard bearers for the succession, Gerrit Smith (white man), Frederick Douglass (black man)."[41] At the very same time the names of Gerrit Smith and Samuel McFarland appeared at the head of the leading editorial column of *Frederick Douglass' Paper*.[42]

On August 15, Douglass withdrew these names and informed his readers of his purpose "to support, with whatever influence we possess, little or much, John C. Frémont, and William L. Dayton, the candidates of the Republican Party for the presidency and vice-presidency of the United States, in the present political canvass." Coming after his continuous denunciations of the Republican Party and especially after his characterization of it in June as "a heterogenous mass of political antagonism, gathered from defunct Whiggery, disaffected Democracy, and demented, defeated and disappointed Native Americanism," Douglass knew that his political somersault would arouse consternation among his readers. So he accompanied his announcement with a careful explanation of this new course which apparently seemed so inconsistent with the policies he had hitherto advocated. He was not concerned with consistency as commonly understood, for "anti-slavery consistency" required of the anti-slavery voter only that he deliver the severest blow against slavery at any given moment. Such action was "always consistent, however different may be the forms through which it expressed itself." His support of the Republican candidates, he went on, did not signify that he had abandoned his anti-slavery principles. He would continue to contend for the extinction of slavery in every part of the republic, but he could best do this in the ranks of the Republican Party, using his voice and pen to teach and influence the vast numbers who were flocking to its banner. The fact that the Republican Party did not go as far as he wished on the slavery question was no reason for withholding his support for its candidates.

[A man was not] "justified in refusing to assist his fellow-men to accomplish a good thing, simply because his fellows refuse to accomplish some other good things which they deem impossible. Most assuredly, that theory cannot be a sound one which would prevent us from voting with men for the Abolition of Slavery in Maryland simply because our companions refuse to include Virginia. In such a case the path of duty is plainly this; go with your fellow-citizens for the Abolition of Slavery in Maryland when they are ready to go for that measure, and do all you can, meanwhile, to bring them to whatever work of righteousness may remain and which has become manifest to your clearer vision."[43]

In subsequent editorials Douglass enlarged on reasons for his action and in cogent, well-defined arguments set down the correct role for any vanguard reform group. Instead of isolating itself from a mass movement which was not ready to accept a more advanced program, the duty of the vanguard was to work inside the movement, gradually bringing to its membership the understanding that would result in the adoption of an advanced position. In September, 1856, he expressed his conception of political strategy in an editorial entitled "The Republican Party" which showed the genius of a true political organizer, one who knew how to fight on all fronts, to use all avenues of advance:

"From our political philosophy, we are at liberty to consider the state of the public mind, and to look at immediate results, as well as remote consequences. We are at liberty to inquire how far our vote, at a given time, will forward what we conceive to be the highest interests of society; and having considered this, we are at liberty,—nay it is our indispensable duty to cast our vote in that direction, which, upon a survey of the whole facts in the case, will best promote that great end."

Turning directly to the bitter attacks on him for his endorsement of Frémont, he continued:

"That man is a fool," says Mr. L. D. Campbell, "who expects the Republican party to stop with restricting Slavery"; the enlightened public sentiment will stop its onward progress, only when Slavery is abolished, and not till then.—But we must hold back, say some of his friends, we must not join ourselves to this party until they declare for the Abolition of Slavery; to circumscribe it is not enough. . . . We will not refuse our neighbor's aid in breaking the soil and planting our crops, even though he will not pledge himself to aid us in harvesting. We plant the crop, and when it is ready for harvest, there is no fear but that the laborers will be found. Even so with the Republican party. The rescue of our Government from the hands of slaveholders; curbing the mad career of the slave-power, must precede the establishment of liberty wherever the laws of the Republic extend. He who votes the Republican ticket gives no pledge of peace toward Slavery in the future. It is simply a vote for the non-extension to which the party is pledged. When this much is accomplished, invite the party to a higher ground; if they fail to come up, sound the alarm: 'To your tents, O Israel'; and the Republican leaders will see, that while they were true to liberty, they could carry the masses with them, but when they undertake to impede the advancing hosts of freedom, the power will depart from them."⁴⁴

Buchanan won the election with an electoral vote of 174 and a popular vote of 1,838,169. But the Republicans showed that they had gained enormous strength. Frémont received 114 electoral votes and 1,341,264 popular votes.

Douglass summed up all of the arguments in defense of his support of the Republican candidates in a brief note to Gerrit Smith. "We have turned Whigs and Democrats into Republicans and we can turn Republicans into Abolitionists."⁴⁵ He was soon to see his prediction fulfilled.

Douglass' support of Frémont did not mean that he had become a member of the Republican Party; six weeks after the election he announced that he was still a Radical Abolitionist.⁴⁶ He participated in the demise of the Liberty Party when it met in Syracuse on September 30, 1857, and, as its final official act, nominated James McCune Smith as Secretary of State.⁴⁷ A year later he campaigned for Gerrit Smith for governor of New York, candidate of the "People's State Ticket" and the Radical Abolitionists. The insignificant vote cast for Smith, despite an active campaign,⁴⁸ was an indication of how completely isolated were these diehard political Abolitionists. With the Negro voters throwing their support to the Republican Party, there were very few to whom the Radical Abolitionists could appeal. Little wonder that by the summer of 1859 the party had all but ceased to exist. "Where is its committee? where its paper, its lecturers and patrons?" asked Douglass in July, 1859. "All gone!"⁴⁹

Douglass was determined to make a final effort to revive the Radical Abolition Party. But before he could do much, he became involved in the chain of events surrounding John Brown's historic raid on the arsenal at Harpers Ferry, Virginia.

Douglass and John Brown

On October 17, 1859, Douglass lectured in the National Hall at Philadelphia on "Self-Made Men." A capacity audience listened to his recital of men who had risen to fame "from the depths of poverty" as a result of "patient, enduring, honest, unremitting work, into which the whole heart is put. . . ." One of them was Benjamin Banneker, a Negro slave born in Maryland, who became a learned mathematician, an outstanding surveyor, who assisted in the laying out of the city of Washington, "and compelled honorable recognition from some of the most distinguished scholars and statesmen of that early day of the Republic." Douglass quoted Jefferson's letter to Banneker of August 30, 1790, in which the author of the Declaration of Independence praised the Negro's almanac, describing it as "a document to which your whole colour had a right for their justification against the doubts which have been entertained of them."

"This was the impression," Douglass declared, "made by an intelligent Negro upon the father of American Democracy, in the earlier and better years of the Republic. I wish that it were possible to make a similar impression upon the children of the American Democracy of this generation. Jefferson was not ashamed to call the black man his brother and to address him as a gentleman."[1]

At that very moment, a man who not only regarded the Negro slave as his brother but was willing to sacrifice his life for his brother's freedom, was attempting to capture the federal arsenal at Harpers Ferry. The raid was part of a more ambitious plan conceived by John Brown whose ultimate aim was the emancipation of the slaves throughout the South.

Douglass' relations with John Brown, it will be recalled, began more than ten years before the raid on Harpers Ferry. It was at Brown's home in Springfield that Douglass first learned of the former's plan to aid the slaves, a project which embraced the setting up of an armed force which would function in the very heart of the South. At that time Brown pointed to a large map of the United States. These Allegheny mountains stretching from the borders of New York State into the South, he told Douglass, afforded an excellent "pathway for a grand stampede from the Slave States, a grand exodus into the Free States, and, through the latter, into Canada." The mountains were full of hiding places and once the slaves were brought there and scattered among the glens, deep ravines, and rocks, it would be difficult to find them and even more difficult to overpower them if they were found. "I know these mountains well," said Brown, "and could take a body of men into them and keep them there in spite of all the efforts of Virginia to dislodge me, and drive me out. I would take at first about twenty-five picked men and begin on a small scale, supply them arms and ammunition, post them in squads of fives on a line of twenty-five miles, these squads to busy themselves for a time in gathering recruits from the surrounding farms, seeking and selecting the most restless and daring." Once he had gathered a force of a hundred hardy men and drilled them properly, they would run off slaves in large numbers, keeping the braver ones in the mountains, and sending the others north by the underground railroad. Gradually the operations would be enlarged to cover the entire South, and in due course the movement would seriously weaken slavery in two ways—first, by destroying "the money value of slave property," by making it insecure, and second, by keeping alive anti-slavery agitation and thereby compelling the adoption of measures to abolish the evil altogether.

From eight o'clock in the evening until three in the morning, Douglass and Brown discussed this plan. Douglass pointed to serious flaws in the project. Once the plan went into operation, the slaveowners would sell their slaves further South or would use bloodhounds and armed forces to track down and overpower Brown and his band. Again, it would be almost impossible to keep the group in the mountains provided with supplies. Brown brushed aside these objections. If the slaves were removed to the lower South he would follow them; even to drive them out of one county would be a victory. Regardless of difficulties he would persevere in his attempt, for some startling event was necessary to prevent the agitation over the slavery question from dying out. If he should die in the effort he would be giving his life for the cause closest to his heart.[2]

Despite his original skepticism, Douglass came to think favorably of Brown's plan. The more he examined the project, the more convinced he became that it might contribute to undermining slavery, for "men do not like to buy runaway horses, nor to invest their money in a species of property likely to take legs and walk off with itself."[3] At the very least, the plan would reawaken the slumbering conscience of the nation. His sympathy for Brown's project grew as his confidence in the efficacy of moral suasion waned.

Douglass and Brown discussed the project many times after their first meeting in 1847. On several occasions Brown stopped at Douglass' home in Rochester,[4] and spent the night outlining the project for a chain of hide-outs in the Maryland and Virginia mountains from which men could go down to the plantations and encourage the slaves to escape. What Brown did not tell his friend, however, was that in the meantime in Kansas he had added a significant detail to his original plan. He now believed that it would be possible, given a few sound men, to establish a base in the mountains, to which slaves and free Negroes would come, and where, after beating off all attacking forces, whether state or federal, a free state would be set up.

On February 1, 1858, Brown arrived at Douglass' home. He would not stay long, he assured his host, and insisted upon paying for his accommodations. He remained several weeks, spending most of the time in his own room writing to numerous friends for financial assistance for his venture, the nature of which he did not reveal. At other times Brown would talk at length of his plan for mountain strongholds, even explaining them to Douglass' children and illustrating "each detail with a set of blocks."[5] Before he left Rochester he had secured a recruit in the person of Shields Green, a runaway slave who was staying at Douglass' home. Brown had also drawn up a constitution for his projected free state. Consisting of a preamble and forty-eight articles, the document provided a framework of government, under a military commander-in-chief, which was to go into operation after his forces had gained power.

Brown and Douglass were to meet again in Philadelphia on March 5, 1858, but the latter had to postpone the meeting. Writing from Syracuse on February 27, 1858, Douglass expressed the hope that Brown "would find work enough in and about New York" until his arrival. On March 11, Brown and his son John, Jr., conferred with Douglass, Garnet, and William Still, the latter a leading agent in the Underground Railroad. His funds exhausted, Brown appealed to them for men and money. He did not, however, divulge the wide reach of his new plans. Nor did Brown add to Douglass' knowledge of the project when he and his son spent the night at the Negro leader's home early in April.[6] All Douglass knew was that Brown was still proceeding with his original plan of setting up hide-outs in the mountains.

In April, 1858, Brown wrote to Douglass: "I expect to need all the help I can get by the first of May."[7] As this letter indicates, Brown had intended to strike in 1858 instead of 1859. The year's delay was made necessary by the treachery of Hugh Forbes, an Englishman who had fought with Garibaldi and had joined Brown after they had met in Kansas. Forbes had agreed to drill Brown's men and to recruit army officers. But Forbes was primarily interested in the project in order to line his own pocket. After getting as much money as he could from Brown, he began to mulct his leader's friends. When that source of income dried up, he threatened to expose the conspiracy if further funds were not forthcoming.

Douglass had reluctantly assisted Forbes in November, 1857, with "a little money" and with letters of introduction to friends.[8] But he had reacted unfavorably to the adventurer, was unimpressed by his tale of family woes, and so was not surprised when he learned that Forbes was threatening to disclose Brown's plans. He relayed this information to Brown. At the same time a committee of Brown's backers, Samuel Gridley Howe, Gerrit Smith, Theodore Parker, George L. Stearns, and Thomas Wentworth Higginson, met in secret at the Revere House in Boston and counseled Brown to postpone his operations and leave for Kansas. Assured that he would receive additional funds in the spring, Brown eventually traveled to Kansas.[9]

Douglass met Brown soon after his return from the Kansas region. En route to Peterboro during the second week of April, 1859, Brown stopped off for a few hours in Rochester. Horace McGuire, one of the employees in Douglass' printing office, recalled that "a tall, white man, with shaggy whiskers, rather unkempt, a keen piercing eye, and a restlessness of manner" called at the shop "several months prior to October 16, 1859," and asked for Douglass. The visitor gave the appearance of one whose "interview was by appointment." When Douglass returned, "the greeting between the white man and the former slave was very cordial." The two men "talked freely."[10]

In the early summer of 1859, Brown fixed upon Harpers Ferry as the base of his operations in Virginia and rented a farm about five miles from there to collect his arms and his band of followers. By mid-summer he had recruited a little army of twenty-one men, including several Negroes, and was almost ready to strike. In August, Brown decided to reveal the full details of his plan to Douglass in the hope of enlisting him as a member of the company preparing to attack Harpers Ferry. Douglass received a letter from Brown asking him to be present at Chambersburg, Pennsylvania, and to bring Shields Green along. The meeting took place on the night of August 20, in a stone quarry near Chambersburg. Brown, his lieutenant Kagi, Douglass and Green were present. It was in the old quarry that Douglass for the first time learned of Brown's plan to seize Harpers Ferry, capture the leading citizens and hold them as hostages while his band rounded up the slaves in the surrounding areas.[11] Brown was dismayed by the emphatic disapproval registered in Douglass' reaction to this plan. Douglass assured Brown that he was still prepared to join with him in carrying out the original plan of running slaves through the Alleghenies, but the raid on Harpers Ferry was an attack on the national government and was doomed to failure. But no amount of argument could dissuade Brown. The seizure would dramatize the evils of slavery, he argued, capture the attention of the nation and arouse the people to action.[12]

Brown's eloquence and his burning enthusiasm for the cause moved Douglass tremendously, but he remained adamant to all entreaties to participate in the enterprise. As he was preparing to leave, Brown made a final appeal: "Come with me, Douglass! I will defend you with my life, I want you for a special purpose. When I strike, the bees will begin to swarm and I shall want you to help me hive them." Douglass shook his head sadly, and turning to Shields Green he asked him if he had made up his mind. The former slave indicated his decision with the now famous reply that he would go with the "old man."[13]

Brown did not give up hope of recruiting Douglass. With sufficient pressure, he was convinced, the latter would reconsider his decision. A few weeks later, Douglass received a letter signed by a number of Negro men inviting him to represent them at a convention to be held "right away" in Chambersburg. The signers pledged themselves to see that his family would be "well provided" during his absence "or until your safe return to them." They also offered to "make you a remittance." Douglass suspected that Kagi had instigated the letter, but not without Brown's approval.[14] The appeal went unanswered.

The Chambersburg meeting between Douglass and Brown marked the last time these good friends were to see one another. On the night of October 16, Brown gave the order to march on Harpers Ferry. When the morning dawned, Brown and his men were in possession of the United States armory and the bridges leading to the Ferry. A few slaves had been persuaded to join them. The following night a company of United States marines, under the command of Colonel Robert E. Lee, arrived; at dawn the building was taken by assault. Brown fought with amazing coolness and courage, but was finally overpowered. Amid popular excitement, he was tried for treason and found guilty. On December 2, 1859, Brown was hanged at Charlestown.

Douglass received the startling news of Brown's capture while lecturing in the National Hall at Philadelphia. He was informed that letters had been found in Brown's possession implicating him, among others, of knowledge of the plot.[15] He knew at once that with the mounting hysteria his life was in extreme danger. At the advice of his friends he left Philadelphia and hastened to New York City, pausing at Hoboken to wire to B. F. Blackball, telegraph operator in Rochester: "Tell Lewis to secure all the important papers in my high desk."[16] Later Douglass learned how fortunate he had been in following the advice of friends in Philadelphia. John W. Hurn, a telegraph operator, and an admirer of Douglass, suppressed for three hours the delivery of a message to the sheriff of Philadelphia ordering him to arrest Frederick Douglass.[17]

Douglass' alarm increased as he read the New York papers. The *New York Herald* headlined a report of Brown's alleged confession to Governor Wise of Virginia: *"Gerrit Smith, Joshua Giddings, Fred Douglass and Other Abolitionists and Republicans Implicated."* "Enough it seems has been ascertained to justify a requisition from Governor Wise of Virginia, upon Governor Morgan, of New York, for the delivery over to the hands of justice of Gerrit Smith and Fred. Douglass, as parties implicated in the crime of murder and as accessories before the fact." From Richmond came an announcement that one hundred Southerners were offering rewards for the heads of "Traitors" among whom Douglass' name was prominently featured.

On his arrival in Rochester, several friends warned Douglass that the New York Governor would probably surrender him to the Virginia authorities upon request. As most citizens of Rochester would resist the attempt to return Douglass to the South and bloodshed and rioting would follow, he was advised both for his own safety and for the peace of the community, to cross over the border to Canada.[18] Aware that President Buchanan would employ the full power of the federal government to achieve his arrest, Douglass took the advice of his friends and fled to Canada.

Douglass barely evaded his pursuers. He had already been charged in Virginia with "murder, robbery and inciting to servile insurrection in the State of Virginia." Moreover, Govenor Wise had asked President Buchanan and the Post-Master General of the United States to grant two agents from Virginia authority to serve as detectives for the post-office department for the purpose of delivering Douglass to the Virginia courts.[19] On October 25, 1859, the Rochester *Union and Advertiser* reported:

"It is understood that United States Attorney Ould of Washington, and other federal officers, were here yesterday. It is supposed they came

hither for the purpose of arresting Frederick Douglass for his alleged participation in the organized scheme against the slaveholding states, of which
the Harper's Ferry insurrection was one of the appointed results."[20]

Had Douglass been arrested by federal authorities at that time the
chances are that in the prevailing tense atmosphere he would have followed Brown to the gallows. Despite its facetious tone, the *New York
Herald* knew whereof it spoke when it commented: "The black Douglass having some experience in his early life of the pleasures of Southern
society had no desire to trust himself again even on the borders of the
Potomac."[21] No evidence would have been required to sentence a Negro
Abolitionist to death in Virginia during the weeks following the attack
on Harpers Ferry.

Douglass has been severely criticized for his refusal to join Brown's
expedition and for having fled to Canada after the raid.[22] John E. Cook,
one of the men captured with Brown, even blamed Douglass for the
failure of the expedition, charging that the latter had been assigned to
bring a large body of men to reinforce Brown. In a letter to the editor of
the Rochester *Democrat* from Canada on October 31, Douglass denied
the charge. It was a brilliant document, opening with the caustic observation that Cook was "now in the hands of the thing calling itself the
Government of Virginia, but which in fact is but an organized conspiracy
by one party of the people against the other." Douglass admitted that
"tried by the Harpers Ferry insurrection test," he was "deficient in courage," but denied that he had ever at any time encouraged the taking
of Harpers Ferry or promised to join the expedition. This denial was
motivated more by "a respectful consideration of the opinion of the
slave's friends, than from my fear of being made an accomplice in the
general *conspiracy* against Slavery." He was willing to support any movement against slavery, when there was "a reasonable hope of success," and
he believed that any effort to overthrow the system of human bondage
was basically moral. He had not joined Brown because he did not believe
that this was the way in which he could best work for the abolition of
slavery. "The tools to those who can use them," was the way Douglass
put it. No shame could be attached to him, he added, for keeping out of
the way of the United States marshals. Would a government that recognized the validity of the Dred Scott decision be likely "to have any very
charitable feelings" toward a Negro Abolitionist?[23] The question answered itself.

There is not the slightest evidence that Douglass at any time indicated his intention of joining Brown's expedition. The very fact that he had made plans to leave for Europe in November, 1859, long before the attack on Harpers Ferry, is proof that he had made no commitments to Brown and his band.[24]

Douglass felt justified at his decision not to join Brown's company. The venture, as he had told Brown, was doomed to fail, and he believed that there was more work for him to do than to end his life at this stage of his career on the gallows in Virginia. "It is gallant to go forth single-handed," he later observed, "but is it wise?"[25]

All this did not mean that Douglass failed to grasp the significance of John Brown's raid. Two weeks after Harpers Ferry, Douglass wrote an editorial on John Brown which cut through the hysterical outpourings of the press and predicted the course the nation would soon follow:

"Posterity will owe everlasting thanks to John Brown for lifting up once more to the gaze of a nation grown fat and flabby on the garbage of lust and oppression, a true standard of heroic philanthropy, and each coming generation will pay its installment of the debt. . . .

"He has attacked slavery with the weapons precisely adapted to bring it to the death. Moral considerations have long since been exhausted upon slaveholders. It is in vain to reason with them. . . . Slavery is a system of brute force. It shields itself behind *might,* rather than right. It must be met with its own weapons. Capt. Brown has initiated a new mode of carrying on the crusade of freedom, and his blow has sent dread and terror throughout the entire ranks of the piratical army of slavery. His daring deeds may cost him his life, but priceless as is the value of that life, the blow he has struck, will, in the end, prove to be worth its mighty cost. Like Samson, he has laid his hands upon the pillars of this great national temple of cruelty and blood, and when he falls, that temple will speedily crumble to its final doom, burying its denizens in its ruins."[26]

On November 12, 1859, Douglass, in line with previously laid plans, sailed from Quebec for Liverpool. In his farewell note to his "Readers and Friends" in America, he cautioned them against losing heart because, owing to the frenzy aroused by Brown's raid, slavery seemed "to have gained an advantage" for the moment, and created "a more active resistance to the cause of freedom and its advocates." But this, he assured them, was only "transient." The "moment of passion and revenge" would pass away, and "reason and righteousness" would grow stronger. "Men will soon begin to look away from the plot to the purpose—from the effect to the cause." Then would come the reaction, "and the names now covered with execration will be mentioned with honor, or, as noble martyrs to a righteous cause. . . . The benumbed conscience of the nation will be revived and become susceptible of right impressions." The ultimate victory had been made more certain than ever by the "battle of Harpers Ferry."[27]

On his return to Rochester in May, 1860, Douglass found that sentiment around John Brown and those associated with him had changed. In December, 1859, a Senate Committee, headed by James M. Mason of Virginia, had been appointed to investigate the attack on Harpers Ferry. On June 14, 1860, the committee submitted an innocuous report which stated that while Brown had planned "to commence a servile insurrection" which he hoped to extend "throughout the entire South," he did not appear to have intrusted even his immediate followers with his plans. After much consideration, the committee announced that it was "not prepared to suggest any legislation."[28]

In a letter to a group of Abolitionists assembling at North Elba, in the Adirondacks, on July 4, 1860, to do honor to the memory of John Brown, Douglass wrote:

"To have been acquainted with John Brown, shared his counsels, enjoyed his confidence, and sympathized with the great objects of his life and death, I esteem as among the highest privileges of my life. We do but honor to ourselves in doing honor to him, for it implies the possession of qualities akin to his."[29]

The Eve of the Civil War

The news that Frederick Douglass was on the high seas bound for England aroused considerable excitement in British anti-slavery circles. Here was the one man who could revive the drooping spirits of anti-slavery forces and inspire the English people into vigorous activity for the cause of abolition. His talents and reputation were enough, but the report of his implication in the Harpers Ferry affair and his narrow escape from imprisonment were additional guarantee that he would address capacity audiences. The British *Anti-Slavery Reporter* was confident that Douglass' visit would do much "to stimulate the energy and increase the efficiency of the existing Societies, and to lead to the formation of many new ones."[1]

As in his previous visit thirteen years before, Douglass did much to strengthen the British anti-slavery movement. His lectures, dealing mainly with the significance of John Brown's raid and the anti-slavery interpretation of the Constitution, were not only well-attended but were widely distributed in pamphlet form. "His *powerful* and eloquent appeals," wrote James Walker, secretary of the Leeds Young Men's Anti-Slavery Society, "deepen our detestation of slavery, and have imparted to us a stronger impulse for, and led us more actively and devotedly into anti-slavery work than ever."[2] The impetus Douglass gave the British anti-slavery forces during his five months' visit in 1859-1860 became evident during the Civil War and was in some measure responsible for the tremendous support of the English masses for the Union cause.

Douglass' tour of England was cut short by the tragic news of the death of his youngest daughter, Annie, "the light and life of my house." Very devoted to her father, the ten-year-old child had grieved since his abrupt departure for Canada. She had been a constant companion of John Brown during the weeks he had spent in Rochester, and Douglass was convinced that her death in March, 1860, resulted from her anxiety over her father's safety, and "deep sorrow" for the death of the old man upon whose knee she had so often sat.

Although he was urged to continue his tour into Ireland and the south of England, Douglass decided "to fly to my sorrow-stricken family." He promised to resume his tour in the fall but this was not to be. He did not return to England until long after the Civil War. In the September, 1860, issue of his monthly he announced that he was giving up his plan to return to British soil where he breathed "freer . . . than elsewhere." "Were we to consult our own pleasure," he told his British friends, "our freedom from insult, proscription, social ostracism and oppression on account of color, we should be back to England in the next steamer. But we have something better than personal ease and security to live for, and that is the cause of our enslaved and oppressed people. That cause seems to make it our duty to stay here for the present." A presidential election was confronting the American people, and the public mind was "peculiarly awake. He who speaks now may have an audience. We wish to avail ourselves of the opportunity to strike while the iron is hot."[3]

When Douglass returned to this country, he found that the Presidential campaign was already under way. At their national convention at Charleston in April, the Democrats had split into two separate factions with Stephen A. Douglas heading one and John C. Breckenridge the other. Early the following month, the Constitutional Union Party had selected James A. Bell and Edward Everett as their candidates for President and Vice-President. In mid-May, the Republicans, in high glee over the dissension in the Democracy, assembled at Chicago and nominated Abraham Lincoln to head their national ticket.

The readers of *Douglass' Monthly* for June, 1860, were treated to a masterly analysis of the significance of Lincoln's nomination. Douglass did not share the prevailing opinion among eastern journalists that "the Rail-Splitter candidate" for President was an absolute nonentity whose nomination was the result of pure accident plus vote-swapping, logrolling and wirepulling. "Mr. Lincoln," he wrote, "is a man of unblemished private character; a lawyer, standing near the front rank at the bar of his own State, has a cool well balanced head; great firmness of will; is perseveringly industrious; and one of the most frank, honest men in political life. . . . His political life is thus far to his credit, but it is a political life of fair promise rather than one of rich heritage." Lincoln merited the support of the more radical elements among the Republicans. "In his debates with [Stephen A.] Douglas, he came fully up to the highest mark of Republicanism, and he is a man of will and nerve, and will not back down from his own assertions."

Douglass criticized the Republican Party for its slogan in the campaign "No more Slave States" instead of "Death to Slavery." He conceded, however, that the people were not yet ready for the more advanced slogan, and announced that as between the Democrats and the Republican Party, "incomplete as is its platform of principles," he could not hesitate to choose the latter. "While we should be glad to co-operate with a party fully committed to the doctrine of 'All rights, to all men,' in the absence of all hope of rearing up the standard of such a party for the coming campaign, we can but desire the success of the Republican candidates."[4]

When this was written, the Radical Abolitionist movement was quite dead. But in the excitement engendered by the Presidential campaign the political anti-slavery men felt that they could stage a comeback. On August 29, they met in convention at Syracuse. Douglass attended this meeting and was appointed to the Business Committee which presented the resolutions to the gathering. These resolutions condemned the Democratic Party, but also indicted the Republican Party for its "almost infinitesimal amount of anti-slavery professions" which were "inadequate

. . . to 'quiet the agitation' upon the subject of the slave's right to liberty."[5] Unwilling to go along with the Republicans, the convention nominated Gerrit Smith and Samuel McFarland on a strong anti-slavery platform. Douglass was chosen as one of two presidential electors-at-large, the first time a Negro was nominated for such a position.

Three weeks after the Radical Abolition National Convention, Douglass went to Worcester to attend an adjourned meeting of a Political Anti-Slavery Convention called by Stephen S. Foster and John Pierpont "to consider the propriety of organizing a *Political Party* upon an Anti-Slavery interpretation of the U. S. Constitution, with the avowed purpose of abolishing slavery in the states, as well as the Territories of the Union."[6] For some time he had hesitated to attend the gathering in Worcester as he did not want to be snubbed by the Garrisonians scheduled to be present. But, dissatisfied with the inadequacies of the Republican platform, he was anxious to co-operate with Foster in the endeavor "to re-unite the scattered anti-slavery elements of the country, and produce one solid abolition organization, who will use all the powers of the Federal as well as State Governments of the country for the abolition of slavery."[7] So he attended the convention.

Douglass served on the Executive Committee, and introduced a resolution extending "earnest sympathy and their hearty God-speed for the little band of faithful Abolitionists which has nominated Gerrit Smith as their candidate to be supported for the Presidency in the coming election." Despite the opposition of the Garrisonians who still clung to their non-voting beliefs, the resolution was adopted.[8]

In October, Douglass advised his readers that ten thousand votes for Gerritt Smith would accomplish more for the abolition of slavery than two million for Lincoln, "or any man who stands pledged before the world against the interference with slavery in the slave states and who is not opposed to making free states a hunting ground for men under the Fugitive Slave Law."[9] What part Douglass played in the Presidential campaign during the next few weeks is difficult to decide. In his auto-biography Douglass stated that he worked actively for Lincoln's election during the closing month of the campaign.

"Against both Douglas and Breckenridge," he wrote, "Abraham Lincoln proposed his grand historic doctrine of the power and duty of the National Government to prevent the spread and perpetuity of slavery. Into this contest I threw myself, with firmer faith and more ardent hope than ever before, and what I could do by pen or voice was done with a will."[10]

Knowing how suddenly Douglass had switched to Frémont in 1856, it is not at all unlikely that, as the campaign developed, he decided it was wiser to use whatever influence he could wield to secure a Republican victory rather than waste it on a fruitless effort for Gerrit Smith. It is certain that in October he agreed with Smith that the weaknesses in the Republican Party were such as made it "unworthy the support of all genuine Abolitionists," but at the same time he criticized his fellow-reformers for lumping the Republican Party with the Democrats and indicating indifference as to which party triumphed. Douglass argued that the Republican Party was "now the great embodiment of whatever political opposition to the pretensions and demands of slavery is now in the field," and that "a victory by it in the coming contest must and will be hailed as an anti-slavery triumph."[11]

Actually, most of Douglass' energy in the closing weeks of the campaign was directed toward securing the repeal of the New York state law requiring that Negro citizens own real estate valued at two hundred and fifty dollars as a condition for voting.[12] Some idea of the hysteria whipped up in the press over the proposed measure which would place Negro citizens on an equal footing with others in the exercise of the right of suffrage, can be gleaned from the following appeal in the *Brooklyn Daily Times:*

"Give the Negroes an unlimited suffrage, and the logical and inevitable result is a Negro alderman, a Negro representative on the county ticket, and so forth.

". . . If [the Negro] Alderman officiates in places of civil honor, with his badge and staff of office, can you deny him the entree to your semi-public assemblies—can you keep him from meeting even the ladies of your family, on many semi-public occasions, as a social equal?

". . . It needs no prophetic eye to foresee that ere long, the countless millions of Asiatic barbarians, Chinese and Japanese—will overflow the narrow limits in which these fecund hordes have been confined—and spread through the Pacific states, all over this continent. Gladly will the Negro voters of this State welcome these allies. The unrestricted franchise which we are now asked to extend to Negroes, may be a fearful weapon when turned against us."[13]

In the face of such vicious outpourings, Douglass dedicated himself to the battle for an unrestricted franchise. For almost twelve weeks prior to November 6, he toured the western part of the state, distributing twenty-five thousand tracts on the *Suffrage Question in relation to colored voters* issued by "The New York City and County Suffrage Committee of Colored Citizens."[14] On election day, Douglass remained at the polls in Rochester from dawn to dusk to prevent fraudulent ballots from being cast. The defeat of the equal suffrage measure by a two-to-one majority[15] was a bitter pill to swallow.

What, asked Douglass, had the anti-slavery cause gained by Lincoln's election? His answer was:

"Not much, in itself considered, but very much when viewed in the light of its relations and bearings. For fifty years the country has taken the law from the lips of an exacting, haughty and imperious slave oligarchy. The masters of slaves have been masters of the Republic. Their authority was almost undisputed, and their power irresistible. They were the President makers of the Republic, and no aspirant dared to hope for success against their frown. Lincoln's election has vitiated their authority, and broken their power. It has taught the North its strength, and shown the South its weakness. More important still, it has demonstrated the possibility of electing, if not an Abolitionist, at least an *anti-slavery reputation* to the Presidency of the United States. The years are few since it was thought possible that the Northern people could be wrought up to the exercise of such startling courage. Hitherto the threat of disunion has been as potent over the politicians of the North, as the cat-o'-nine tails is over the backs of the slaves. Mr. Lincoln's election breaks this enchantment, dispels this terrible nightmare, and awakes the nation to the consciousness of new powers, and the possibility of higher destiny than the perpetual bondage to an ignoble fear."[16]

What next? The duty of the Abolitionists was clear. It was to revitalize their activities; organize, lecture, hold meetings, build the spirit manifested in the earlier stages of the anti-slavery movement; make this spirit the watch-dog of the Republican Party, preventing them from yielding to the demands of slavery and pushing them forward toward the total annihilation of the accursed system. For that goal, Douglass announced, he was prepared to work with any group, few or many.

It was no simple task, however, to revive the old spirit of the anti-slavery movement in the weeks following Lincoln's election. As threats of secession of the southern states mounted, northern conservatives tried to convince the slaveholders that they had nothing to fear from remaining in the Union. Personal liberty laws to prevent the return of fugitive slaves were repealed, resolutions condemning the Abolitionists were adopted by Union-Saving gatherings, and paid hoodlums were hired to disrupt anti-slavery meetings. Northern newspapers fanned the flames of hysteria, calling for demonstrations wherever Abolitionists gathered.[17]

Douglass was once again the special target for attack. At a meeting in Boston on December 3, 1860, to commemorate the anniversary of John Brown's execution, ruffians, hired by merchants engaged in the southern trade, invaded the hall, disrupted the proceedings, and singled out Douglass for attack. Fighting "like a trained pugilist," the Negro Abolitionist was thrown "down the staircase to the floor of the hall."[18]

The meeting was adjourned to a church on Joy Street. As the audience poured into the street, Negroes were seized, knocked down, trampled upon, and a number seriously injured. "The mob was howling with rage," Douglass recalled years later. "Boston wanted a victim to appease the wrath of the south already bent upon the destruction of the Union."[19]

A few days later, Douglass spoke in Boston's Music Hall and presented one of the most stirring pleas for free speech in American history. He described at length the attack on the meeting by both respectable gentlemen and rowdies. The right of free speech was basic to all other rights. No other right "was deemed by the fathers of the Government more sacred than the right of speech." "Liberty is meaningless," cried Douglass, "where the right to utter one's thoughts and opinions has ceased to exist." Nor did the right of free speech belong only to the rich and powerful. In words that have never lost their meaning, Douglass concluded:

"There can be no right of speech where any man, however lifted up, or however old, is overawed by force and compelled to suppress his honest sentiments. . . . When a man is allowed to speak because he is rich and powerful, it aggravates the crime of denying the right to the poor and humble. . . .

"A man's right to speak does not depend upon where he was born or upon his color. The simple quality of manhood is the solid basis of the right—and there let it rest forever."[20]

As the secession movement progressed, Douglass saw only one ray of hope for the cause—Lincoln's inauguration. His admiration of Lincoln had increased in the weeks following the election. He observed with satisfaction the President-elect's determination not to capitulate to the demands for a compromise policy that would appease secessionists and "his refusal to have concessions extorted from him under the terror instituted by thievish conspirators and traitors. . . ." The Negro leader shared Lincoln's attitude toward the pro-compromise advocates, pointing out: "All compromises are now but as new wine to old bottles, new cloth to old garments. To attempt them as a means of peace between freedom and slavery, is as to attempt to reverse irreversible law."[21]

Together with the entire nation Douglass looked forward to Lincoln's inaugural address. Late in February, 1861, a convention of slave owners had set up a provisional government at Montgomery, Alabama, with Jefferson Davis as President of the Confederate States of America. How would Lincoln meet this unprecedented crisis?

Douglass was bitterly disappointed by the inaugural address. Lincoln had pledged himself not to interfere directly or indirectly with slavery in the states where it then existed; promised to support the enforcement of the fugitive slave law; and declared he would maintain the Union. Douglass saw little in this message to gladden the hearts of the Negro people.

"Some thought we had in Mr. Lincoln the nerve and decision of an Oliver Cromwell," he wrote bitterly, "but the result shows that we merely have a continuation of the Pierces and Buchanans, and that the Republican President bends the knee to slavery as readily as any of his infamous predecessors."

Further analyzing the address, Douglass admitted that Lincoln's announcement "that the laws of the Union shall be faithfully executed in all the United States," was a significant advance over Buchanan's "shuffling, do-nothing policy." But he doubted whether the President had the courage to carry out his program. "It remains to be seen," he concluded, "whether the Federal Government is really able to do more than hand over some John Brown to be hanged, suppress a slave insurrection, or catch a runaway slave—whether it is powerless for liberty and only powerful for slavery."[22]

Viewing events following Lincoln's election, Douglass, for the first time since he had joined the anti-slavery movement, began to feel some doubt about the ultimate triumph of the cause. For years he had announced his conviction that forces of history were on the side of the Abolitionists, and that while they might suffer setbacks the final victory was theirs.

"In the spirit of the age," he had told an audience in Canandaigua in 1847 at a celebration of West India Emancipation, "in the voice of civilization, in the improvement of steam navigation, in every bar of railroad iron, I read the approach of that happy period, when, instead of being called upon to celebrate the emancipation of eight hundred thousand persons in the West Indies, we shall be summoned to rejoice over the downfall of Slavery in our own land."

Up to now, almost every speech and editorial contained some reference to the inevitability of emancipation. "The hour which shall witness the *final struggle,* is on the wing," he had assured Abolitionists in 1855. "Already we hear the *booming* of the bell which shall yet toll the death knell of human slavery." Anti-slavery men must not allow temporary discouragements to cause them to forget that "the Principles which form the basis of the Abolition movement . . . must triumph. . . ."[23] Precisely because he was convinced that the cause would triumph, he had used his pen and voice against all emigration schemes, believing that the free Negro people must remain in the land where they lived, where their brothers and sisters were held in slavery, and where they could contribute to the liberation of their people.

But events since the election of Lincoln—the repeal of the Personal Liberty Laws by the Republican legislatures and the attacks upon innocent Negro people by northern mobs—made Douglass doubt whether his confidence had been justified. He began to look with some favor on the emigration movement of Haiti.[24]

Early in April, 1861, Douglass made plans to visit Haiti so that he could investigate conditions for himself and report back to the people in the United States. His steamer, chartered by the Haitian Bureau of Emigration at Boston, was scheduled to sail on April 25. Douglass notified his readers that his trip would take about ten weeks.

Following this announcement was a paragraph which revealed that Douglass had fully recovered from his momentary feeling of despair:

"Since this article upon Haiti was put into type, we find ourselves in circumstances which induce us to forego our much desired trip to Haiti, for the present. The last ten days have made a tremendous revolution in all things pertaining to the possible future of the colored people in the United States. We shall stay here and watch the current of events, and serve the cause of freedom and humanity in any way that shall be open to us during the struggle now going on between the slave power and the government. When the Northern people have been made to experience a little more of the savage barbarism of slavery, they may be willing to make war upon it, and in that case we stand ready to lend a hand in any way we can be of service. At any rate, this is no time for us to leave the country."[25]

The events referred to were the firing on Fort Sumter by the Confederates, the call for volunteers by President Lincoln, and the outbreak of the Civil War.

Fort Sumter to the
Emancipation Proclamation

With the outbreak of the Civil War, Frederick Douglass entered upon a new phase of his career as an Abolitionist. Up to this time he had fought the slaveholders as an individual or together with the many thousands of men and women who abhorred slavery and gave freely of their time and money in the struggle against it. Now the full might of an aroused North was to be thrown against the slavocracy. And the forces of circumstance would compel the country to listen attentively to what the Abolitionists had to say. Before the war was many months old, Douglass was to find himself no longer the despised agitator, but the distinguished anti-slavery advocate who had warned that the nation must abolish slavery or be abolished by it. Many Americans, remembering that for years Douglass had insisted that slavery would be drowned in a sea of blood since its "peaceful annihilation" was "almost hopeless," now weighed carefully his observations on the nature and conduct of the war.

These observations related mainly to one aspect of the conflict. Douglass had little time to discuss the problems relating to the tariff, internal improvements, and a national banking system. One issue alone consumed his thoughts night and day—the Negro slave. He viewed the conduct of the war "more as a bondman than as a freeman." His mission in the war, he announced early in the conflict, was "to stand up for the downtrodden, to open my mouth for the dumb, to remember those in bonds as bound with them."[1]

When the news flashed over the North on April 12, 1861, that "Fort Sumter has surrendered," Douglass cried out: "God be praised!" The tension was broken; the war had begun. In that moment the current of popular feeling changed. Gone were the months of appeasement when politicians and business men had vied with each other "to purchase peace and prosperity for the North by granting the most demoralizing concessions to the Slave Power." The cannons booming over Charleston had compelled everyone "to elect between patriotic fidelity and pro-slavery treason." The flag had been fired on, and from the North and West came countless expressions of patriotism and loyalty. "Since they will have it so," declared Governor Andrew of Massachusetts, "in the name of God—amen." To this Douglass added: "Again, we say out of a full heart, and on behalf of our enslaved and bleeding brothers, thank God."[2]

There were different views as to the causes and purposes of the war. Some Abolitionists and politically advanced German-American Communists entered the struggle with a consciousness of the need to abolish Negro slavery as well as to save the Union. But the vast majority of the northern people who took to arms the moment Fort Sumter was attacked joined the Union forces with the sole aim of saving the Union. They shared with Lincoln the belief that the only issue at stake in the war was "whether in a free government the minority have the right to break it up whenever they choose."[3] Some argued that the war was simply a conflict between states' rights and nationalism. Others saw in the war merely a struggle between low and high tariffs.

From the very beginning, Douglass perceived clearly that the war was a struggle to complete the historic task left uncompleted by the first American Revolution which had failed to root out the cancer of slavery fom the body of America, that it would mean the emancipation of the Negro people and the liberation of the North from slaveholding domination.

The fact that in the popular uprising pledging full support to the federal government there were few references to slavery was of little importance to him. Slavery was involved in the war whether or not the people or their government knew it. In attacking Fort Sumter, the slaveholders had not been seeking merely to protect their "peculiar institution," but "to make themselves masters of the Republic." With amazing power of acute observation, Douglass pointed out directly after the bombardment of Fort Sumter: "It is not merely a war for slavery, but it is a war for slavery dominion." So the very men who entered the struggle with the sole objective of defending the flag and saving the Union were unconsciously engaging in antislavery activity. "He who faithfully works to put down a rebellion undertaken and carried on for the extension of slavery," Douglass argued, "performs an anti-slavery work."[4]

Several months later, on November 7, 1861, Karl Marx wrote in the Vienna *Presse*:

"One sees, therefore, that the war of the Confederacy is in the true sense of the word a war of conquest for the extension and perpetuation of slavery."[5]

On the first page of the May, 1861, issue of *Douglass' Monthly* appeared an American eagle and the flag, followed by the stirring slogan—"Freedom for all, or chains for all." The leading article carried the title, "How to End the War." Douglass called upon the administration to proclaim freedom to the slaves, to call the slaves and free people of color into service, and organize them *"into a liberating army,* to march into the South and raise the banner of Emancipation among the slaves." The slaveholders, he reminded the government, did not hesitate to use Negroes in waging their war of aggression. Negroes (both the free and the slaves) were being impressed to serve the Confederacy in the mills, mines, and industries, and were employed as teamsters, cooks, hospital attendants, stretcher bearers in the Confederate Army. The important work of keeping roads, bridges, and railroads open for movement of Confederate troops fell to Negro labor groups under the supervision of mounted troops. And the slaveholders openly boasted that the use of Negro labor in the fields and factories enabled them to send troops to the front without diminishing production behind the lines. Consequently sound policy, not less than humanity, demanded that the government of the United States turn this powerful force to its own use by being "as true to liberty as the rebels, who are attempting to batter it down, are true to slavery." One Negro regiment carrying the Stars and Stripes into the South would do more to educate the slaves "as to the nature of the conflict . . . than . . . a thousand preachers."[6]

Two ideas thus took possession of Douglass from the moment the war started: free the slaves as a war measure and recruit the Negroes into the Union Army. He urged this policy without compromise. In editorials, speeches, letters, and interviews, he stressed again and again the theme—"The Negro is the key of the situation—the pivot upon which the whole rebellion turns." A proclamation of freedom to the slaves would "smite rebellion in the very seat of its life," depriving it of the labor which kept the rebel army supplied with food, clothing, and the sinews of war. It would also unmask the rebels' cry that they were fighting for the right to govern themselves. Abolition of the slaves would immediately unite the world in favor of the government of the United States.

"From the first," Douglass wrote later in his autobiography, "I reproached the North that thay fought the rebels with only one hand, when they might strike effectively with two—that they fought with their soft white hand, while they kept their black iron hand chained and helpless behind them—that they fought the effect, while they protected the cause, and that the Union Cause would never prosper till the war assumed an anti-slavery attitude, and the Negro was enlisted on the loyal side."[7]

Negroes rushed to offer their services to the Union, but they were rejected. Moved by Douglass' call, Philadelphia Negroes offered to go South to organize slave revolts. Everywhere in the North Negroes asked to be received into the Union Army. At a meeting of Boston Negroes late in April, a resolution was passed urging the government to enlist them:

"Our feelings urge us to say to our countrymen that we are ready to stand by and defend our Government as the equals of its white defenders; to do so with 'our lives, our fortunes, and our sacred honor,' for the sake of freedom, and as good citizens; and we ask you to modify your laws, that we may enlist,—that full scope may be given to the patriotic feelings burning in the colored man's breast."[8]

These appeals fell on deaf ears. Determined to mollify the border slave states—Delaware, Maryland, Kentucky, and Missouri—and keep them in the Union, Lincoln was deaf to pleas that the war be turned into a war against slavery and that Negroes be recruited into the Union Army.

Douglass' faith that the war would mean the end of slavery, although often severely shaken, was never completely destroyed. Even when Union soldiers seemed more concerned with hunting fugitives than shooting rebels and when General George B. McClellan assured the slaveowners that his army would not interfere with their chattels and would "on the contrary, with an iron hand, crush any attempt at insurrection on their part," Douglass still believed that "the mission of the war was the liberation of the slave as well as the salvation of the Union." This conviction did not stem from any single event or group of events. Rather it was the result of his fundamental understanding of what he called "the very core and vital element and philosophy of the strife." The American people and their government might for a time refuse to recognize this, but in the end the "inexorable logic of events" would compel the recognition of the truth that it was impossible to separate freedom for the slaves and victory for the Union. Men may be indifferent to moral issues and may have grown weary of the Abolition movement. But necessity was master over all. The end of slavery would be due "less to the virtue of the North than to the villany of the South." The war itself would supply the necessary education. When the Union Army had sustained defeat after defeat and thousands of lives and millions of dollars had been sacrificed to the mistaken policy of expediency, the people and the government would be forced to recognize that the war "is a war for and against slavery; and that it can never be effectually put down till one or the other of these vital forces is destroyed."[9]

"Events themselves drive to the promulgation of the decisive slogan— *the emancipation of the slaves,*" Karl Marx wrote in the Vienna *Presse* of November 7, 1861. The same dialectical approach to the basic issues of the Civil War which was revealed in Douglass' speeches and editorials led Marx to remark in a letter to Frederick Engels, chiding him for his lack of faith in the final victory of the North caused by its vacillating policies and its early defeats:

"In my opinion all this will take another turn. In the end the North will make war seriously, adopt revolutionary methods and throw over the domination of the border slave statesmen. A single Negro regiment would have a remarkable effect on Southern nerves. . . .

"The long and short of the business seems to me to be that a war of this kind must be conducted on revolutionary lines, while the Yankees have so far been trying to conduct it constitutionally."[10]

While Douglass was probably familiar with some of Marx's articles in the *New York Tribune* of 1861-1862, he could not have known of the attitude expressed in the articles in the Vienna *Presse* or in the letters to Engels. Again and again, however, during the Civil War, Douglass' interpretation of the course of events and of the path necessary to follow to insure victory coincided with that of the fathers of scientific socialism.

In 1864, in explaining the Emancipation Proclamation and his decision to recruit Negro soldiers into the Union Army, Lincoln declared: "I claim not to have controlled events, but confess plainly that events have controlled me." Three years earlier Douglass had written of Lincoln's administration: "It has been from the first, and must be to the last, borne along on the broad current of events. Its doctrines, its principles, and its measures are all subject to the modifying power of this great current."[11] This was the basis of his faith, the foundation of his hope. It was up to the people to bring the power of "this great current" to bear on the government. And it was up to the Abolitionists to educate the people to support a program which in bringing freedom to the slaves, would bring victory to the Union.

Douglass was alarmed by the virtual disappearance of the organized Abolition movement directly after the outbreak of the war. Too many anti-slavery men operated on the principle that everything be subordinated to the war effort. They no longer attended Abolitionist meetings, subscribed to anti-slavery papers, or contributed to the national and local anti-slavery organizations. When asked about the lot of the slave, they replied that the complete abolition of slavery was certain, and "that by some means now inscrutable, Providence will bring freedom to the slave out of this Civil War." In short, they became indistinguishable from any other patriotic group engaged in war activities.[12]

As early as June, 1861, Douglass called attention to the dangers inherent in this course of action. Faith in the triumph of Abolition was comforting and necessary, but it was valuable only if it enabled anti-slavery men to work better. The history of the anti-slavery movement had demonstrated that progress came only as a "result of earnest, persevering, long-continued and faithful enforcement of anti-slavery principle, by argument, appeal and warning, and by the stringent application of truth to the heart and conscience of the nation." There never was a time when the labors of the Abolitionists were more needed. Patriotism itself required unflagging activity, for only the Abolitionists could teach the nation the course of action that alone could bring victory. Moreover, the war provided vast opportunities that had never existed for anti-slavery men before. To the moral infamy of slavery was now added treason and rebellion. People hitherto untouched by the moral question of slavery were now ready to listen to the Abolitionists.

"Down with the ten-thousand-times accursed slave system," cried Douglass, "should now thunder from every platform and pulpit in the land. Instead of giving up anti-slavery meetings, we should increase them; instead of calling home our anti-slavery agents, we should send out more; and instead of allowing anti-slavery papers to languish for support, we should earnestly labor to extend their circulation and to increase their influence."[13]

Douglass entered heart and soul into the movement to educate the public and galvanize the government into action. He took to the lecture platform and made a personal canvass of the North. During the summer and fall of 1861 and the winter of 1862, he traveled thousands of miles bringing his message to people in Massachusetts, New York, New Jersey, Ohio, and Illinois.

"I have only one voice," he announced as he started on his lecture tour, "and that is neither loud nor strong. I speak to few, and have little influence; but whatever I am or may be, I may, at such a time as this, in the name of justice, liberty and humanity, and in that of the permanent security and welfare of the whole nation, urge all men, and especially the Government, to the abolition of slavery."

In season and out of season, he urged Congress, the Cabinet, the President to proclaim emancipation—to hurl the bolt that could save the Union.

"Keep pounding on the rock," Douglass urged his fellow-Abolitionists. He called for petitions and delegations to convince the President that the people would support measures to bring the war to a victorious conclusion. If he could but speak to Lincoln, he would tell him the story of Negro people in Rhode Island and Connecticut who had fought valiantly in the War for Independence, and of Negroes who had fought side by side with General Jackson at New Orleans. He would tell him that the North needed what the South had—positive convictions—and the same will to fight for freedom that southerners displayed in battling for slavery. He would urge him to ally with the pro-Union, anti-slavery, popular forces in the Border States rather than relying upon the slaveowners who had never been friends of the Union and were now doing "the work of enemies in the garb of friendship." He would tell him that the very life of the nation required revolutionary methods and that this was not time "to talk of constitutional power."[14]

"We would tell him that this is no time to fight with one hand, when both are needed; that this is no time to fight with your white hand, and allow your black to remain tied."[15]

In the summer of 1863, when Douglass finally did get to see the President, Lincoln had already embraced most of the program the Negro leader had called for from the beginning of the war. But in the summer of 1861, the President had still a long way to go. On August 30, 1861, General John C. Frémont issued a proclamation establishing martial law in Missouri and declared free the slaves of those in arms against the United States. Even critics of Frémont admit that the people of the North hailed his action. "The popular outburst endorsing this order was tremendous and spontaneous," writes T. Harry Williams, one of these critics.[16] But Lincoln was dominated by the fear of alienating the conservative and banking interests and of antagonizing the slaveholders of the border states. And so he revoked Frémont's order.

Douglass' anger flamed when he heard of the revocation of Frémont's proclamation. Many blunders had been committed by the administration since Fort Sumter, he cried, but this was the worst. The administration had been six months in office and what had it done? Had it set forth any principle? Any avowal of purpose? Not a line, not a word. The only step "indicating an anti-slavery tendency on the part of the Govern-

ment" was the somewhat half-hearted approval of General Butler's ruling
that slaves who flocked into Union lines as "contraband of war" should
not be returned to their owners. On the other hand when other Union
officers returned all fugitives and permitted owners of slaves to cross the
Potomac and recover their property, the administration had assented
silently. And only with the greatest reluctance had the President signed
the Confiscation Act of August 6, 1861, which granted freedom to slaves
used by the Rebels in prosecuting the war.

Now at last General Frémont had cleared the atmosphere with his
bold proclamation. The President and his Cabinet should have thanked
him for furnishing "an opportunity to convince the country and the world
of their earnestness, that they have no terms for traitors . . . and that the
rebels must be put down at all hazards, and in the most summary and
exemplary way." The President had taken a stand which could "only
dishearten the friends of the Government and strengthen its enemies."
In Lincoln's letter to Frémont disapproving of his act could be found the
key to "all our misfortunes in connection with the rebellion."[17]

Douglass would not accept the argument of administration supporters
that acceptance of Frémont's proclamation would have driven the slaveholders of the border states into the arms of the rebels. He doubted that
this would happen as the proclamation was directed against only slaveholding rebels. But even if it did, he would consider it a gain for the
Union cause. He was weary of having the Border States argument
hurled at him every time he talked of emancipation. "From the beginning," he declared, "these Border Slave States have been the mill-stone
about the neck of the Government, and their so-called loyalty has been
the very best shield to the treason of the Cotton States."[18]

Precisely at this time, Karl Marx was writing in the Vienna *Presse*:
" . . . in the course of the war up to now, they [the border states] have
constituted the chief weakness of the North. . . . Tender regard for the
interests of these ambiguous allies has smitten the Union government
with incurable weakness since the beginning of the war, driven it to half
measures, forced it to dissemble away the principle of the war and to
spare the foe's most vulnerable spot, the root of evil—*slavery itself.*"[19]

Sick at heart over the vacillating policy adopted by the government,
Douglass wrote to Reverend Samuel J. May, on August 30, 1861, that it
seemed "much like hoping against hope" to believe that "the war would
finally become an abolition war." He was convinced that persuasion

alone would never get the government to adopt the correct policy. "Nothing short of dire necessity will bring it to act wisely."[20]

Public reaction to his lectures revived Douglass' spirits. His attacks on the timid administration—insistent, fiery, denunciatory, often vituperative, enraged some people. But many more were anxious to hear what he had to say and insisted on his right to speak. The Syracuse incident was very encouraging. In November, 1861, Douglass was scheduled to lecture in that city on the "Rebellion, its Cause and Remedy." When he entered Syracuse he noticed that at every corner, side by side with the handbill announcing his lecture was a placard calling upon "Freemen" to rally and "drive him from the city."

But the scheduled demonstration never materialized. Mayor Charles A. Andrews appointed fifty special policemen and ordered out a military company to prevent any interference. The owner of Weiting Hall refused to be intimidated by a delegation who demanded that the lecture be cancelled. Reminded that the lecturer was a Negro, he replied that his principles of freedom "applied to humanity not to color."

When Douglass arrived, soldiers stood at the entrance to the hall, armed and equipped. Inside the auditorium policemen were scattered about, ready to pounce on any trouble-maker. The large audience burst into applause when Reverend May escorted Douglass to the platform and introduced him. No sign of disturbance was evident during the ninety-minute lecture. On the conclusion of Douglass' speech, Gerrit Smith addressed the gathering. Reverend May followed with an announcement that this lecture was only the first in a series. Douglass would be followed by William Lloyd Garrison, Wendell Phillips, Gerrit Smith, and Parker Pillsbury.

On November 16, Reverend May wrote to Garrison joyfully describing the "glorious triumph" in Syracuse. "Honor to your city," Garrison replied.

Douglass' joy at the victory over the mobocrats was deepened by Reverend May's courageous conduct. Since his split with the Garrisonians, Douglass' relations with the distinguished pastor had been cool. But the war had pushed past differences into the background and all groups of Abolitionists were now ready to co-operate for the common cause. Douglass made his position very clear.

"Every man who is ready to work for the overthrow of slavery, whether a voter, or non-voter, a Garrisonian or a Gerrit Smith man, black or white, is both clansman and kinsman of ours. We form a common league against slavery, and whatever political or personal differences, which have in other days divided and distracted us, a common object and a common emergency makes us for the time at least, forget those differences, and strike at the common foe—and to give victory to the common cause."[21]

After Syracuse, Douglass renewed his friendship with other leading Garrisonians. In November, 1861, the Emancipation League was organized in Boston by Wendell Phillips, William Lloyd Garrison, George S. Boutwell, Samuel Gridley Howe, and others with the object "of urging upon the people and the Government emancipation of the Slaves, as a measure of justice, and military necessity." By means of public lectures the League hoped to arouse the nation for the annihilation of slavery.[22] Douglass was selected to deliver the fourth lecture in its course.

He accepted the invitation with joy. Now he could join with his former colleagues in the vital work of educating the people, delighted that they had revived their organizations and activity after the unfortunate lull in the early months of the war. Events since Fort Sumter, he told the Boston audience, had demonstrated "that all efforts to save the country are vain, unless guided by the principles which the Abolitionists know best how to teach." He rejoiced "in the formation of the Emancipation League."[23]

Douglass directed a stinging attack at the "vacillation, doubt, uncertainty and hesitation" whish characterized the administration "in regard to the true methods of dealing with the vital cause of the rebellion." The crowded auditorium agreed as he declared that "our policy seems to be, to have no policy." The nation's duty was to free the Negro and then "accord to him equal justice and a chance to live." Any effort to maintain slavery was an attempt to "outwit Jehovah, and defy the laws of God's universe."[24]

Six days later at Cooper Institute in New York, Douglass repeated the Emancipation League address. Again there was the insistent prodding, again the demands for action, for a summary destruction of the slave system. And again his remarks were greeted with "most hearty and enthusiastic applause." The *Anti-Slavery Standard* reported that "more than one judge expressed the opinion that no more effective discourse had been delivered in the city."[25]

To Douglass the most significant thing about both addresses was the response of the audience. There were no catcalls, no hissing, no disorder as he excoriated the administration. He was well aware that it was national safety and not burning hatred of the slave system which was responsible for the enthusiasm to his call for immediate emancipation. Nevertheless, he rejoiced in the change in public sentiment, for now he was less concerned with the motives which would lead the nation to abolish slavery than in achieving this goal. He directed all of his attention to winning recruits for the abolition of slavery. "Every consideration of expediency and justice," he argued, "may be consistently brought to bear against the sum of all villainies."[26]

During the winter and spring of 1862, Douglass continued to stump the country, using the lecture platform "to swell the trumpet cry for instant and universal Emancipation, as the right of the slave and duty of the nation." The work of the Abolitionists was bearing fruit and the "slow coach at Washington" was beginning to pick up speed in the right direction. Lincoln had refused to mitigate Captain Nathaniel P. Gordon's sentence for commandering an American slave ship. On February 21, 1862, Gordon was hanged. Three weeks later, on March 31, the President signed a bill forbidding the army or the navy to return fugitive slaves. Any officer violating the law would "be discharged from service, and be forever ineligible to any appointment in the military or naval service of the United States."[27]

Meanwhile, Congress was debating a bill calling for the abolition of slavery in the District of Columbia, with compensation to slaveholders. The measure encountered bitter opposition from slaveholders and their sympathizers.

"Senators," cried Senator Saulbury of Delaware, "abandon now, at once and forever, your schemes of wild philanthropy and universal emancipation; proclaim to the people of this whole country everywhere that you mean to preserve the Union as established by the fathers of the Republic, and the rights of the people as secured by the Constitution they helped to frame, and your Union can never be destroyed; but go on with your wild schemes of emancipation, throw doubt and suspicion upon every man simply because he fails to look at your questions of wild philanthropy as you do, and the God of heaven only knows, after wading through scenes before which those of the French revolution 'pale their ineffectual fires,' what ultimately may be the result."[28]

But popular pressure for abolition of slavery in the nation's capital was too strong to be diverted by predictions of a reign of terror. On March 30, 1862, Senator Sumner, who with Henry Wilson, the junior Senator from Massachusetts, was most active in pushing the measure, delivered a notable address urging its speedy adoption. "It is the first instalment," he declared, "of the great debt which we all owe to an enslaved race, and will be recognized as one of the victories of humanity." The effect, he predicted, would soon be felt throughout the South. "What God and nature decree, rebellion cannot arrest," he concluded.[29]

Douglass hastened to send a letter of thanks to Sumner for his magnificent address. "The events taking place seem like a dream." He rejoiced for the slaves in the nation's capital, and he was overjoyed that Sumner had lived "to strike down in Washington, the power which lifted the bludgeon against your own free voice." The Negro people, he assured the Senator, looked to him "as the best embodiment of the Anti-Slavery idea now in the counsels of the Nation."[30]

On April 3, 1862, the bill passed the Senate. Eight days later it received final approval in the House. On the sixteenth day of April, the President signed the bill outlawing slavery in the nation's capital.

For the first time since the outbreak of the war, Douglass' joy was unbounded. The measure, he informed his readers, was "the first great step towards that righteousness which exalts a nation." He called for hosannahs: "Let high swelling anthems (such as tuned the voice and thrilled the heart of ancient Israel, when they shouted to heaven the glad tidings of their deliverance from Egyptian bondage) now roll along the earth and sky. . . . "[31]

But less than a month later the cheers died on Douglass' lips. The administration took another backward step. When on May 9, 1862, General David Hunter, commanding the Department of the South, issued an order proclaiming: "Slavery and martial law in a free country being altogether incompatible, the slaves in Georgia, Florida, and South Carolina are therefore declared free," Lincoln hesitated once more. He learned of Hunter's order through the newspapers a week after the proclamation. Secretary Chase urged him to let the order stand. "No commanding general shall do such a thing upon my responsibility without consulting me," the President replied. On May 19, even before receiving official notice, he issued a message declaring Hunter's order unauthorized and null and void.[32]

In a bitter mood Douglass assailed the administration at a Fourth of July meeting at Himrods Corner, New York. Bluntly and fearlessly he told the audience of two thousand that the President, the Cabinet and "our rebel worshipping Generals in the field" were guilty of treason. Singling out General McClellan, he denounced the Commander of the Army of the Potomac "as either a cold blooded Traitor or . . . an unmitigated military impostor." "His whole course," he declared, "proves that his sympathies are with the rebels, and that his ideas of the crisis make him unfit for the place he holds. . . . He has shown no heart in his conduct, except when doing something in favor of the rebels, such as guarding their persons and property and offering his services to suppress with an iron hand any attempt on the part of the slaves against their rebel masters." Douglass characterized McClellan's conduct as "military insanity." Marx and Engels continually criticized McClellan, charging him with serving the interests of the Confederacy, and observed: "Never yet has a war been waged in such fashion. . . . "

Again Douglass picked up the theme he had been stressing since the first day of the war. Rebellion and slavery were "twin monsters," and "all attempts at upholding one while pulling down the other" would end in disaster for the nation. The only choice left was "abolition or destruction. You must abolish slavery or abandon the Union." He was certain that if only it had the will, the government could speedily abolish slavery. All that was necessary was a proclamation by the President announcing the freedom of the slaves. His reply to the argument that a proclamation of emancipation would only be "a paper order" was simple and direct:

"It would act on the rebel masters, and even more powerfully upon the slaves. It would lead the slaves to run away, and the masters to Emancipate, and thus put an end to slavery. . . . " [33]

Unknown to Douglass, Lincoln was being forced to the same conclusion. The forces that Douglass had predicted would compel the government to pursue a revolutionary course of action were now in full operation. Lincoln was beginning to realize the impossibility of his own program. His pleas to the slave-owners to accept compensated emancipation had fallen on deaf ears. The slaveholders continued to use the labor of their slaves to wage their war, while the Union government continued to deprive itself of the valuable services of the slaves, the natural enemies of the slaveholders. Also, the failure of the Lincoln administration to make the war clearly one for the abolition of slavery was aiding the Confederate agents in Europe who were confusing the common people as to the nature of the war. Only when the war became clearly defined as an issue of slavery—for and against—would the danger of European recognition of the Confederacy end.

"It is my profound conviction," wrote Carl Schurz, American Ambassador to Spain, in his dispatches to Washington, "that as soon as the war becomes distinctly one for and against slavery, public opinion will be so strongly, so overwhelmingly in our favor, that in spite of commercial interests, or secret spies, no European government will dare to place itself by declaration or act, upon the side of a universally condemned institution."[84]

Aware at last of these forces, Lincoln read a draft of an emancipation proclamation to his Cabinet on July 21, 1862. Rebels were to be warned of the penalties of the Confiscation Act, reminded that they could still emancipate their slaves and receive compensation, and on January 1, 1863, all slaves in the possession of rebels were to be declared free. For two days the Cabinet debated the draft of the proclamation. Despite the opposition of most of the Cabinet members, Lincoln decided to go ahead with his plan to issue it. He agreed, however, with Seward that it was not wise to issue the proclamation until the military situation became more favorable.

But all this was known to only a few people. Lincoln's public utterances provided little encouragement for the friends of the slave; on one occasion he told a delegation that the Constitution did not allow the freeing of the slaves, because it could not be enforced in the rebel states. Douglass was filled with deeper despair when he saw how the President was riding the colonization hobby. In August, 1862, Lincoln called a group of prominent free Negroes to the White House and urged them to support colonization. "Your race suffer greatly, many of them, by living among us," he told them, "while ours suffer from your presence. In a word we suffer on each side. If this is admitted, it affords a reason why we should be separated." If not for the institution of slavery, he declared, "and the colored race as a basis, the war could not have an existence." The white people were not willing for the Negroes to remain in the country. New Granada in Central America had indicated that it was prepared to receive them. Lincoln urged the delegation to help him in a colonization plan to send Negroes to that country.[35]

Douglass' anger increased as he read the account of the interview. Overlooking the fact that this was the first time a President of the United States had addressed a Negro audience, he accused Lincoln of revealing "his pride of race and blood, his contempt for Negroes and his canting hypocrisy." He assailed the President's arguments, and pointed to Mexico, Central America, and South America where "many distinct races live peaceably together in the enjoyment of equal rights. . . ." He cut to shreds Lincoln's argument that the presence of the Negro in the country was the basic cause of the war:

"A horse thief pleading that the existence of the horse is the apology for his theft or a highway man contending that the money in the traveler's pocket is the sole first cause of his robbery are about as much entitled to respect as is the President's reasoning at this point," he wrote bitterly. "No, Mr. President, it is not the innocent horse that makes the horse thief, nor the traveler's purse that makes the highway robber, and it is not the presence of the Negro that causes this foul and unnatural war, but the cruel and brutal cupidity of those who wish to possess horses, money and Negroes by means of theft, robbery, and rebellion."[36]

In dejection over Lincoln's plan, Douglass concluded that there was "less ground to hope for anti-slavery at his hands" than at any previous time since the outbreak of the war. To Gerrit Smith he confided the opinion that "the nation was never more completely in the hands of the slave power."[37]

The letter to Smith was written on September 8, 1862. Nine days later, September 17, the cannons roared for fourteen hours at Antietam and thousands went down to death. By the end of the week the Confederate Army was in retreat. On Monday, September 22, Lincoln issued the preliminary Emancipation Proclamation. He mentioned again the possibility of compensated emancipation and said that he would continue to encourage the voluntary colonization of Negroes "upon this continent or elsewhere." But the time had come for direct action. Hence he proclaimed:

"That on the Frst day of January, in the year of our Lord one thousand, eighteen hundred and sixty-three, all persons held as slaves within any State or any designated part of a state, the people whereof shall then be in rebellion against the United States, shall be then, henceforward, and forever free;"[38]

"Forever free"—Douglass could scarcely believe his eyes as he read these words. He rushed into print to give vent to his happiness. "We shout for joy that we live to record this righteous decree," he wrote in his journal. His pen was jubilant:

"Oh! long enslaved millions, whose cries have so vexed the air and sky, suffer on a few days in sorrow, the hour of your deliverance draws nigh.

"Oh! ye millions of free and loyal men who have earnestly sought to free your bleeding country from the dreadful ravages of revolution and anarchy, lift up now your voices with joy and thanksgiving for with freedom to the slave will come peace and safety to your country."[39]

There were distinct limitations to the Proclamation. It did not cover all the slaveholding territory. Then, what if the war should end and there

were no states in rebellion on the first of January, 1863? Some Abolitionists viewed the Proclamation as an empty gesture. Douglass rejected
this outlook. This was the most important document ever signed by a
President of the United States. When Negroes in the South heard of it
they would flock in thousands to the Union Army. It was a "moral
bombshell" to the Confederacy more destructive than a hundred thousand
cannon. The effect of the document on Europe, he predicted, "will be
great and increasing. It changes the character of the war in European
eyes and gives it an important principle as an object, instead of national
pride and interest. It recognizes, and declares the real nature of the
contest, and places the North on the side of justice and civilization, and
the rebels on the side of robbery and barbarism. It will disarm all purpose
on the part of European Government to intervene in favor of the rebels
and thus cast off at a blow one source of rebel power."[40]

Karl Marx summed up the significance of the Proclamation in a
similar vein when he wrote Frederick Engels on October 29, 1862:

"The fury with which the Southerners have received Lincoln's Acts prove
their importance. All Lincoln's Acts appear like the mean pettifogging
conditions which one lawyer puts to his opposing lawyer. But this does not
alter their historic content. . . . "[41]

The real question, as Douglass saw it, was not whether the Proclamation would prove effective but whether northern conservatives would
compel Lincoln to retract his pledge. But he was confident that the
opposition to the Proclamation would not prevail. "Abraham Lincoln
may be slow," he argued, "Abraham Lincoln may desire peace even
at the price of leaving our terrible national sore untouched, to fester on
for generations, but Abraham Lincoln is not the man to reconsider,
retract and contradict words and purposes solemnly proclaimed over
his official signature." The careful, tortured path of deliberation the
President had pursued was itself "a guarantee against retraction." But
even if this were not true, the events which had slowly brought Lincoln
to recognize the need for the proclamation would carry him to the next
step on the first of January. For a recall of the proclamation would "only
increase rebel pride, rebel sense of power and would be hailed as a
direct admission of weakness on the part of the Federal Government,
while it would cause heaviness of heart and depression of national
enthusiasm all over the loyal North and West."

A mass campaign in support of the Proclamation, Douglass maintained, was necessary to counteract the pressure sure to be exerted on Lincoln by conservative elements in the North. "During the interval between now and January next," he appealed, "let every friend of the long enslaved bondman do his utmost in swelling the tide of anti-slavery sentiment, by writing, speaking, money and example." Given this popular support, there would be no doubt where the President would stand on the first of January, 1863:

"No, Abraham Lincoln will take no step backward. His word has gone out over the country and the world, giving joy and gladness to the friends of freedom and progress wherever these words are read, and he will stand by them and carry them out to the letter."[42]

With the issuance of the preliminary Proclamation, Douglass' attitude toward the administration underwent a complete transformation. "From the 22d of September, 1862, in the second year of the rebellion, the American Government entered upon a new career," he informed his readers and friends in Great Britain and Ireland. The war had passed the stage of constitutional quibbling and entered the stage of revolutionary action. The object of the government was to destroy, not to preserve, slavery; to set fugitive slaves at liberty, not to recapture them and return them to their owners; to assist slaves in rising up for freedom, not to prevent slave insurrections. In a direct plea to the English public, "The Slave's Appeal to Great Britain," Douglass urged Englishmen to forget the past mistakes of the Lincoln administration:

"The proclamation of emancipation by President Lincoln will become operative on the first day of January, 1863. The hopes of millions, long trodden down, now rise with every advancing hour. Oh! I pray you, by all your highest and holiest memories, blast not the budding hopes of these millions by lending your countenance and extending your potent and honored hand to the blood-stained fingers of the impious slaveholding Confederate States of America."[43]

As the weeks passed, Douglass' anxiety increased. Perhaps, after all, emancipation would not be proclaimed. Perhaps the victories scored by the Democrats at the November elections, when they carried seven important states including New York, Pennsylvania, Ohio, and Illinois, would cause Lincoln to reconsider. Why had it been necessary for the President to wait three months before making his decree final? If only Lincoln had made his proclamation of freedom "absolute and immediate instead of conditional and prospective. . . ." A week before the first of January, he wrote: "The suspense is painful . . ."

In the closing days of 1862, Douglass traveled to Boston to participate in the celebrations arranged by the Union Progressive Associations to greet the announcement of the Proclamation. Three large meetings, conducted mainly by Negroes, were held at Tremont Temple on the first day of the new year. Douglass spoke at the afternoon session. A report of his address in the *Boston Journal* went in part:

"Frederick Douglass thanked God that to-day he was living to see the end of slavery. He did not feel sure that emancipation would be successful in the immediate future, but in the end he had no doubt, for it was a struggle between the beautiful truth and the ugly wrong. Error cannot safely be tolerated unless truth is left free to combat it, and the only antidote to error is freedom, free speech and a free press. We have had a period of great darkness, but now we are having a period of illumination by the rosy dawning of the new truth of freedom, and we are here to-day to rejoice in it. (Voices of 'Amen,' 'Good,' 'Bless the Lord,' etc.)

" . . . He was glad that the people of the country were finding out that the blacks were Americans, and that the color of a man's skin does not disqualify him from being a citizen of the United States. He concluded by rejoicing that he was here to share in the deliverance of his race from bondage."[44]

At about eight o'clock in the evening of December 31 Douglass entered the packed hall in Tremont Temple to join the audience of three thousand waiting for the word from the White House. He walked to the platform where a seat had been reserved for him and shook hands with William Wells Brown, the Negro historian and orator, J. Sella Martin, the Nego preacher, and Anna M. Dickinson, the young advocate of woman's rights and abolition of slavery.

Reverend Martin and Miss Dickinson addressed the restless audience during the first hour of waiting. By nine o'clock a feeling of despondency descended upon the gathering. Douglass and Brown sought to revive the spirits of the audience by brief, hopeful speeches. But as ten o'clock passed without word from Washington, the gloom deepened. Suddenly a messenger burst into the hall shouting, "It is coming! It is on the wires." The cheers shook the hall. Soon the text of the proclamation was received. The excited audience, unable to restrain its feelings, interrupted reading of each paragraph with shouts of joy. Douglass led the audience in singing: *Blow ye the trumpet, blow!* A Negro preacher burst into the psalm:

> *Sound the Loud Timbrel O'er Egypt's dark sea,*
> *Jehovah hath triumphed, his people are free.*

At midnight Tremont Temple had to be vacated. But the audience was in no mood to go home. A proposal was made that the meeting adjourn to the Twelfth Baptist Church on Phillips Street. Within a half-hour the church was filled. Rev. Leonard A. Grimes, its Negro pastor who had been imprisoned in Virginia for attempting to aid fugitive slaves led in public prayer. The demonstrations of joy continued for several hours. The dawn was breaking when the meeting finally disbanded.[45]

As Douglass walked back to his lodgings his thoughts turned back to the days when the small band of Abolitionists had fought against such tremendous odds for the emancipation of the slaves. How long, how long he had asked himself during those years. He had not expected the legal downfall of slavery would come so soon. Now it had come, and his faith had been justified. Not only was emancipation achieved under the Constitution, as he had long insisted it would be, but it had come about as a result of the war he had said would end slavery.

There were grievous exceptions in Lincoln's final Proclamation. Missouri, Tennessee, Maryland, and Kentucky were left out of the Proclamation as were parts of Virginia and Louisiana. Cynics pointed out that Lincoln had excepted the only areas in the South occupied by the Union armies. But Douglass took the Proclamation "for a little more than it purported; and saw in its spirit, a life and power beyond its letter."[46] He understood that the Proclamation inaugurated the new stage of the war, the revolutionary waging of it, and that because of this the doom of slavery was sealed.

It was, in his own words, "a day for poetry and song, a new song."[47]

From the Emancipation Proclamation to Appomattox

January, 1863, was a month of jubilee celebrations for the Negro people. In the slaveholding Confederacy, Negroes gathered secretly in their cabins to give thanks and whisper: "We are free," "We are free." In the North, the voices of jubilation rang out loud and clear in a grand chorus of liberty as the Negro people met in a round of celebrations. Douglass spoke at the happy gatherings. For a month he traveled over two thousand miles, speaking "almost without intermission" at meetings from Boston to Chicago.[1]

Back in Rochester, Douglass turned his attention to the question of Negro troops. Under the pressure of military necessity, the government's opposition to the utilization of Negro soldiers had slowly changed. In May, 1862, General David Hunter, at Port Royal, South Carolina, sent out a call for Negroes to serve in the army, basing his action on an authorization from the Secretary of War "to employ all loyal persons offering their services in defense of the Union and the suppression of this Rebellion." Within a few months, the "First South Carolina Volunteer Regiment," consisting mainly of slaves deserted by their masters, was organized. Washington, however, objected and Hunter was forced to disband the regiment. But in July, 1862, Congress authorized the President to employ Negro troops. Four months later, the "First South Carolina Volunteers," commanded by Colonel Thomas Wentworth Higginson of Massachusets, was mustered into service.

In September, 1862, General Benjamin F. Butler, commander of the Louisiana sector, began organizing three regiments of Infantry Corps d'Afrique and one regiment of heavy artillery. In December, General Augustus Chetlain took charge of Negro volunteering in Tennessee and rapidly organized several Negro regiments.[2]

As the need for manpower increased, Washington countenanced the policy of local recruiting of Southern Negro troops. But up to December, 1862, a national call for Negro volunteers had not been issued. The final Emancipation Proclamation, however, announced that freed slaves would be received into the armed forces of the United States "to garrison forts, positions, stations, and other places, and to man vessels of all sorts in said service." Early in 1863, a bill was passed in the House of Representatives authorizing the President "to enroll, arm, equip and receive into the land and naval service of the United States such number of volunteers as he may deem useful to suppress the present rebellion." The Senate returned the bill to the House, deeming it unnecessary legislation since the President had such power under previous acts of Congress.[3]

Acting on this interpretation, Governor John A. Andrew of Massachusetts requested permission to raise two regiments of Negro troops to serve for three years. On January 20, 1863, the War Department issued a general order to the Massachusetts executive which contained the clause: "Such volunteers to be enlisted for three years, unless sooner discharged, and may include persons of African descent, organized into separate corps." Immediately upon receipt of the order, Governor Andrew announced the formation of the 54th Massachusetts regiment, the first Negro regiment to be recruited in the North.

But Massachusetts with a comparatively small Negro population could sign up only a hundred volunteers in the first six weeks. Governor Andrew turned to his friend George L. Stearns, a leading New England Republican and formerly a close associate of John Brown, and persuaded him to take full charge of recruiting. An able organizer, Stearns promptly collected five thousand dollars, advertised widely for enlistments, and set up recruiting posts from Boston to St. Louis. To speed up the work, Stearns called on Negro leaders to act as recruiting agents. On February 23, he left for Rochester to enroll Douglass as an agent.[4]

Douglass needed little prodding. He had been urging the recruiting of Negroes into the Union army from the first month of the war. Within three days after Stearns's visit, he issued his famous call, "Men of Color, to Arms." He urged his people to "fly to arms, and smite with death the power that would bury the government and your liberty in the same hopeless grave." To be free they must themselves strike the blow. Now they could prove their manhood, demonstrate their equality with the white man in fighting prowess and in love of country. The gratitude of the country would be given the Negroes, and prejudice against them greatly diminished if they proved by force of arms that they deserved an improved status. "Liberty won only by white men would lose half its lustre," he cried. He told his people to remember Denmark Vesey, Nat Turner, and Shields Green. The call closed with the information that Douglass would forward all applications to Boston if contacted within two weeks.[5]

Originally appearing in Douglass' journal, the stirring message was republished by the leading papers of the North. Printed in pamphlet form, the call was widely circulated and became the most important agent for recruiting Negro soldiers.

In March, Douglass covered numerous towns in western New York to recruit a company of one hundred men for the regiment being organized in Massachusetts. His son Charles was the first to enlist; soon afterward his other son, Lewis, signed up. In Buffalo, Douglass obtained seven recruits. Rochester furnished thirteen. By April 1 he had sent twenty-three Negroes to Boston.[6]

His recruiting tour convinced Douglass that many Negroes did not fully understand why they should join the Union army. To meet this problem, he wrote an article in his journal listing and discussing nine reasons why the Negro should enlist. He should join the Union army because (1) manhood required him to take sides; he was "either for the Government or against the Government," (2) he was a citizen as well as a man, and citizenship brought with it the obligation of serving one's country when it was in peril, (3) every Negro-hater and lover of slavery viewed the arming of Negroes as a calamity, (4) the Negro should learn the use of arms, for "the only way open to any race to make their rights respected is to learn how to defend them," (5) he would demonstrate his courage and disprove the slanders against his people, (6) he would establish his right of citizenship in the country, (7) enlistment would enable the Negro to recover his self-respect, (8) enlistment would be "one of the most certain means of preventing the country from drifting back into the whirlpool of pro-slavery compromise at the end of the war," (9) "the war for the Union, whether men so call it or not, is a war for Emancipation."

"Enlist, therefore, enlist without delay," Douglass appealed, "enlist now, and put an end to the human barter and butchery which have stained the whole South with the warm blood of young people, and loaded its air with their groans. Enlist, and deserve not only well of your country, and win for yourselves, a name and a place among men, but secure to yourself what is infinitely more precious, the fast dropping tears of your kith and kin marked out for destruction, and who are but now ready to perish."[7]

In April and May, 1863, Douglass continued his recruiting tour, visiting Oswego, Syracuse, Ithaca, Troy, Auburn, and other towns in western New York. Late in May he traveled to Boston to witness the departure for South Carolina of the Massachusetts all-Negro Fifty-Fourth.

On the morning of May 28, excitement prevailed in Boston. The *Boston Transcript* observed: "Since Massachusetts first began to send her brave sons into the field, no single regiment has attracted larger crowds into the street than the 54th." As the regiment of one thousand Negroes, under the command of Colonel Robert Gould Shaw, marched through the downtown streets on their way to the Common, the crowd cheered. Douglass was proud that his sons, Charles and Lewis, were in the front ranks, the latter in the uniform of a sergeant-major. The soldiers made an excellent showing. One reporter noted the "general precision attending their evolutions," and their "ease and uniformity in going through the manual."

After the dress parade on the Common, the regiment marched to Battery Wharf, passing en route over ground moistened by the blood of Crispus Attucks, the runaway slave who was one of the five men killed in the Boston Massacre in March, 1770. Shortly after one o'clock, the soldiers boarded the *DeMolay*. A few visitors were permitted on board and Douglass remained on the ship until she was well down the harbor, returning on a tug.[8]

Having bade farewell to his sons, Douglass returned to his job of recruiting. But the unjust treatment of Negro soldiers made his work difficult. Audiences pointed out that wages of Negro soldiers did not equal those of the white soldiers. After July, 1862, the latter received rations, $13 a month, and a $3.50 allowance for clothing. The Negro was paid as a laborer, not as a soldier, receiving rations, $7 a month, and a $3 allowance for clothing.[9]

The Negro soldiers objected vigorously to this discrimination, and many Negroes refused to enlist because of the differential in pay. Recruiting agents found it more and more difficult to secure signatures.

No one understood more clearly than Douglass the strategic importance of the active participation of Negro troops in helping determine the successful outcome of the war. Hence nothing should interfere with participation of the Negro in the Union army. Discrimination against Negro soldiers must be consistently fought, but it must not serve as a barier to the full participation of the Negro in the war. The major issue was to win the war against slavery, and just as necessity and organized protests had forced the administration to emancipate the slaves, they would compel it to place Negro soldiers on an equality with the white soldiers. "Colored men going into the army and navy," Douglass wrote as early as February, 1863, "must expect annoyance. They will be severely criticized and even insulted—but let no man hold back on this account. We shall be fighting a double battle, against slavery in the South and against prejudice and proscription in the North—and the case presents the very best assurances of success."[10]

But many Negroes were not convinced. On June 17, Philadelphia received permission to raise a Negro division. Encountering difficulty in securing enlistments, Stearns, now in charge of recruiting Negro regiments for the Federal government, arranged a mass meeting at National Hall on July 6 with Douglass as the main speaker.

In his speech to the Negro youth of Philadelphia Douglass offered a brilliant analysis of the two forces that were struggling for mastery in the War: the concept that the Negro people were an inferior people and should be enslaved forever as against the principle that all men are naturally and fundamentally equal. True, vacillation and weakness on the slavery question were to be found in high places of government, but Douglass pointed out that progress had been made since the "dark and terrible days" when United States officers "performed the disgusting duty of slave dogs to hunt down slaves for rebel masters." He admonished his people to join the Union army and fight for freedom regardless of wages. If the government offered the Negro a chance to enlist and serve even without salary, it still would be best to enlist. He saw in the Negro soldier the foundation for the Negro citizen.

"Once let the black man get upon his person the brass letters U.S.; let him get an eagle on his button, and a musket on his shoulder, and bullets in his pocket, and there is no power on earth or under the earth which can deny that he has earned the right of citizenship in the United States."[11]

If discrimination in pay had been the only grievance of Negro soldiers Douglass' appeals would have been more effective. Actually, innumerable obstacles faced the Negro soldier in the Union army. White soldiers received enlistment bounties; Negro soldiers received none until after June 15, 1864. No opportunity existed for the commissioning of Negro officers. Many Union commanders regarded trained Negro troops as fit only for fatigue duty and assigned all unhealthy and unpleasant details to Negroes. Weapons provided Negro troops were generally of an inferior quality.

Suffering from poor arms and equipment, inferior training, and incompetent officers, Negro soldiers were often hurried into battle without adequate preparation. Although they fought bravely in every engagement, earning the praise of Union officers, under such circumstances the slaughter was fearful. For example, in mid-July, 1863, the 54th Massachusetts, sick and exhausted from days of fighting and forced marches, was ordered to storm Fort Wagner. A weary regiment led the ill-starred assault and suffered about 42 per cent casualties. Colonel Shaw and many of his soldiers were killed.

The treatment of Negro soldiers who fell into the hands of the enemy was particularly cruel. In December, 1862, Jefferson Davis announced that any Negro soldier who was taken prisoner would be turned over to state authorities and dealt with as an insurrectionist according to the slave codes of the South. As these codes stipulated death sentence for "subversive" activities, many free Negro soldiers died convicted of "conspiring to murder or maim a white person." Under the regulation no exchange of prisoners could be effected where Negroes were concerned. In most cases Negroes captured in battle were brutally murdered by the Confederates. Even the wounded were not spared.[12]

From the South came reports detailing grievances and complaints of Negro soldiers at the very time that Douglass was engaged in securing volunteers for Negro regiments. Infuriated, he published an open letter in which he lashed out at Lincoln for failing to redress the grievances of Negro soldiers. When white soldiers were threatened with assassination, he wrote, the President immediately informed the Confederacy that the Federal government "will retaliate sternly and severely." But when Negro soldiers were murdered, "no word comes from the Capitol." Until Lincoln would use his authority "to prevent these atrocious assassinations of Negro soldiers, the civilized world will hold him equally with Jefferson Davis responsible for them."

Douglass knew his moderate friends would say, "Wait a little longer," but he wondered how long. "If the President is ever to demand justice and humanity for black soldiers, is not this the time to do it?" He demanded that Negro soldiers be adequately trained, be provided with competent officers, and a halt be called to the practice of assigning Negro soldiers to demoralizing, unpleasant, and unhealthy garrison, fatigue, and labor details. Finally, he insisted that Negroes be granted equal pay for equal work and the right to become commissioned officers. "Colored men," he wrote, "have a right not only to ask for equal pay for equal work, but that merit, not color, should be the criterion observed by Government in the distribution of places."[13]

Having set forth these demands, Douglass called a halt to his recruiting work until the government's policies for Negro soldiers were changed. His duty, he felt, was to provide decent conditions for Negroes in the armed forces before asking any more to enlist. "I owe it to my long abused people," he informed Stearns in giving up his recruiting activities, "and especially of them already in the army, to expose their wrongs and plead their cause."[14] With this in mind, Douglass sought an interview with President Lincoln. Senator Pomeroy of New Jersey carried the request to the President and reported to Douglass that it had been granted.

Late in July, 1863, Douglass paid his first visit to Washington. "No man who had not worn the yoke of bondage and been scourged and driven beyond the beneficent range of the brotherhood of man by popular prejudice," he told an audience a quarter of a century later, "can understand the tumult of feeling with which I entered the White House."[15] The stairway to Lincoln's office was crowded with the usual throng of patronage-seekers, and Douglass fully expected to have to wait "at least half a day" before he would be able to see the President. But two minutes after he had sent in his card, he was ushered through the crowd into Lincoln's office.

"When I went in," Douglass recalled, "the President was sitting in his usual position, I was told, with his feet in different parts of the room, taking it easy." Lincoln arose and put his visitor at ease. When Senator Pomeroy started to introduce Douglass, the President stopped him, saying: "Mr. Douglass, I know you; I have read about you, and Mr. Seward has told me about you." He referred to a speech Douglass had made in New York in which the Negro leader had listed "the tardy, hesitating, vacillating policy of the President of the United States" as "the most disheartening feature in our present political and military situation. . . . " Lincoln admitted that he had sometimes been slow, but denied the charge of vacillation. ". . . I think it can not be shown," he told Douglass, "that when I have once taken a position, I have ever retreated from it."[16]

After these introductory remarks, Douglass came directly to the point. As a recruiting agent he wished to present the case of the Negro soldier. If the War Department wished to recruit Negro men, it had to reverse its policies; give the Negro soldiers the same pay white soldiers received; compel the Confederacy to treat Negro soldiers, when taken prisoners, as prisoners of war; promote Negro soldiers who distinguished themselves for bravery in the field just as white men were promoted for similar service, and retaliate in kind when any Negro soldiers were murdered in cold blood.

Lincoln listened attentively and sympathetically to these proposals. The time was not yet ripe, he replied, to give Negro soldiers the same pay as a white man, for opposition to recruiting Negroes in the Union army was still too strong. "I assure you, Mr. Douglass," he continued, "that in the end they shall have the same pay as white soldiers." He admitted the justice of Douglass' request for the promotion of Negroes in the army, and promised "to sign any commission to colored soldiers" which the Secretary of War recommended. He agreed that Negro soldiers should be treated as prisoners of war when captured. But he balked at Douglass' suggestion for retaliation. "Once begun," he declared, "I do not know where such a measure would stop."[17]

Douglass left the White House with the impression that Lincoln was "an honest man." He could not recall ever having met a man "who, on the first blush, impressed me more entirely with his sincerity, with his devotion to his country, and with his determination to save it at all hazards." There were other impressions, too, which later interviews with Lincoln were to confirm. One was the President's "entire freedom from popular prejudice against the colored people. He was the first great man that I talked with in the United States freely, who in no single instance reminded me of the difference between himself and myself, of the difference of color. . . . " Throughout the interview with this great man, "as great as the greatest," Douglass had felt "as though I could go and put my hand on his shoulder. . . . "

These impressions were decisive in Douglass' decision to continue his recruiting work. He was not entirely satisfied with Lincoln's reactions to his requests, but he "was so well satisfied with the man and with the educating tendency of the conflict" that he was convinced the government's treatment of the Negro soldiers would soon radically change for the better.[18]

From the executive mansion Douglass went to the war office where Secretary Stanton granted him an interview. When Douglass expressed a willingness to accept a military commission, Stanton promised him the rank of assistant adjutant on the staff of General Lorenzo Thomas. The latter had been sent to the Mississippi Valley in the spring of 1863 to put machinery into operation for recruiting Negro soldiers in the South.[19]

Douglass was delighted. In great glee he hastened to Rochester to bring out the last issue of his monthly journal. Any day now the commission would arrive from Secretary Stanton.

Douglass' decision to cease publication was not sudden. In the fall of 1862, he had informed his old friend, Julia Griffiths, that on January 1, 1863, when the President issued the Emancipation Proclamation, he would give up his editorial duties and retire to a farm. Julia's keen counsel evidently caused him to postpone his decision. She wrote from England on December 5, 1862:

"Now a word, my dear friend, about your personal matters & *give attention* to what I say. Even if all goes as you wish it on the 1st January 63 *you must not give up your paper*. This is the 15*th* year of its existence in some shape, & tho' the name has varied, the Editor has always been *one* & the *same* man, Now more known than ever. The paper was started from this side the water and the ground of obtaining material aid for your branch of the cause is the paper. Surely, the more free colored people are in the North, the more they will need a paper—to assist in elevating them & educating them. No, my dear friend, do not be led astray, or make a mistake by giving up the paper. You know nothing about farming yourself and would be like a fish out of water without mental *labors* & public work! I wish I could fly over the water & have a consultation with you. I have felt quite uneasy in my mind since this farm business was first mentioned."[20]

On August 16, 1863, Douglass wrote his "Valedictory" to the "Respected Readers" of his monthly. He was not abandoning the journalistic field because his paper was no longer supported, because he was motivated by a love of change or adventure, or because he thought that "speaking and writing against slavery and its twin monster prejudice against the colored race are no longer needful." However, there was no longer a need for a special organ for him to express his views. "Indeed, I may say with gratitude, and without boasting, that humble as I am in origin and despised as is the race to which I belong, I have lived to see the leading presses of the country, willing and ready to publish any argument or appeal in behalf of my race, I am able to make."[21] Then in a single sentence Douglass stated the most important reason for his act:

"I am going South to assist Adjutant General Thomas, in the organization of colored troops, who shall win the millions in bondage the inestimable blessings of liberty and country."[22]

The final sentence of Douglass' "Valedictory," marking the end of sixteen years of continuous publication of his journal, was indeed touching: "With a heart full and warm with gratitude for you for all you have done in furtherance of the cause of these to whom I have devoted my life, I bid you an affectionate farewell."

Douglass made preparations to leave for Vicksburg. The following pass bearing Lincoln's signature would enable him to go safely through Union lines:[23]

Department of Interior
Washington, D. C.   Aug. 10, 1863.

To whom it may concern,

The bearer of this, Frederick Douglass, is known to us as a loyal, free man, and is, hence, entitled to travel, unmolested,—

We trust he will be recognized everywhere, as a free man, and a gentleman.

I concur	Respectfully,
A. Lincoln	J. Pillsher
Aug. 10, 1863	Secy
	S. Pomeroy
	N.J.S.

Pass the Bearer Frederick Douglass who is known to be a free man.

M. Blaiı

A letter from C. W. Foster, Assistant Adjutant General, dated August 13, instructed Douglass to go to Vicksburg and report to General Thomas. Four days later Douglass wrote to the War Department asking "upon what conditions" he was "expected to enter upon the recruiting service in the South West." Foster replied on August 21, made no mention of a commission, but stated that Douglass would be paid by Stearns, the Recruiting Commissioner. "It is of course expected," he added, "that you go to aid General Thomas in any way that your influence with the colored race can be made available to advance the object in view." A week later Stearns informed Douglass that his salary would be a hundred dollars a month, subsistence, and most likely transportation.[24] But again there was no mention of a commission. And without a commission, Douglass refused to report.

The commission never materialized. Douglass did not doubt Stanton's sincerity, but concluded that, in thinking it over, the Secretary of War had decided that "the time had not come for a step so radical and aggressive."[25] The "radical" step involved conferring the rank of assistant adjutant on the outstanding Negro leader in the nation, on a man who, more than anyone else, had been responsible for recruiting Negro regiments in the North. Yet the Lincoln administration feared to take this step. By offering Douglass the post in the first place, Secretary Stanton showed that he was fully aware of what it would mean to the Negro people in the South to have their outstanding protagonist by their side; how it would strengthen the entire campaign to recruit Negro soldiers and thus make an invaluable contribution to the war effort. But expediency, fear of criticism by the Copperhead elements, and anti-Negro prejudice in the administration itself pushed the nation's welfare into the background.

The failure to receive a military commission naturally made Douglass bitter, but there was no time for moroseness. There were too many issues confronting the nation that required clarification. Chief among them, as Douglass saw it, was the pressing problem of the Negro's status as a free man. In the fall of 1863, after a three weeks' vigil at the sick bed of his son Lewis, Douglass returned to the lecture platform. In his speech, "The Mission of the War," which he repeated week after week in different communities, he warned Abolitionists that "there never was a time when Anti-Slavery work was more needed than now," and impressed upon the nation the necessity of securing full freedom for the Negro people. On February 17, 1864, he wrote: "I am, this winter, doing more with my voice than with my pen. I am heard with more than usual attention and hope I am doing some good in my day and generation."[26]

At no time before the issuance of the Emancipation Proclamation had Douglass been under the illusion that legal emancipation alone would provide freedom for the Negro slaves. He had continually reminded the Abolitionists that their work would really begin with the abolition of slavery and the defeat of the rebel states. A new class of men in the South would have to be trained to take the place of the leaders of the rebellion. They would have to be educated to understand that slavery had ever been "their direct calamity and curse," that labor was honorable, not degrading, and that "the liberty of a part is never to be secured by the enslavement or oppression of any." The whole South would become missionary ground. Family relations which had no real existence under slavery would have to be established, schools set up for ex-slaves, and all the benefits of republican institutions introduced. In short, the work that would confront the Abolitionists was "nothing less than radical revolution in all the modes of thought which have flourished under the blighting slave system."

And what of the ex-slave himself? Law and the sword could abolish slavery, but it was too much to expect that those who had "a mountain of gold of twenty hundred millions of dollars" invested in slavery would let such profits slip from their hands. They would squirm and twist in every conceivable way to reinstate some form of slavery in the South. The slaves might be emancipated in form but remain slaves in fact. As early as November, 1862, Douglass asked:

"What shall be their [the slaves'] status in the new condition of things? Shall they exchange the relation of slavery to individuals, only to become slaves of the community at large, having no rights which anybody is required to respect, subject to a code of black laws, denying them school privileges, denying them the right of suffrage, denying the right to keep and bear arms, denying them the right of speech, and the right of petition? Or shall they have secured to them equal rights before the law?"

Douglass' answer in 1862 to the question of what should be done with three or four million slaves, if and when emancipated, was at first rather simple.

"Do nothing with them," he declared, "mind your business and let them mind theirs. If you see him ploughing, let him alone. If you see him on his way to school, spelling-book, geography, and arithmetic in hand, let him alone. Don't shut the door in his face. Don't pass laws to degrade him. If he has a ballot in his hand, let him alone. Deal justly with him. He is a human being. Give him wages for his work, and let hunger pinch him if he don't work." The Negro asked nothing from the American people "but simple justice, and an equal chance to live."

But as Douglass grappled with specific aspects of the problem his answers became more concrete. Should the freedmen be permitted to remain in the United States? Certainly, he answered. Who had a better right than the Negro to remain in the South? Who could show a better title to the land on which they lived than the Negro people of the South?

"They have watered the soil with their tears and enriched it with their blood, and tilled it with their hard hands during two centuries; they have leveled its forests, raked out the obstructions to the plow and hoe, reclaimed the swamps, and produced whatever has made it a goodly land to dwell in, and it would be a shame and a crime little inferior to enormity to Slavery itself if these natural owners of the Southern and Gulf States should be driven away from their country to make room for others—even if others could be obtained to fill their places."[27]

There was one colonization plan that Douglass did endorse— that which proposed to colonize the Negroes on the abandoned lands of the South. In November, 1862, he called upon the government to use the hundreds of thousands of dollars it now spent to deport Negroes to foreign countries for the purpose of colonizing freed slaves on land abandoned by retreating Florida slaveholders. He urged that these freed slaves be equipped with implements to till the soil and arms to defend themselves. They would "organize society there on free labor principles, and thus introduce Northern civilization in the place of Southern barbarism."[28]

For several months after the issuing of the Emancipation Proclamation, Douglass was too busy recruiting Negro troops to devote much attention to the status of the freedmen. But in May, 1863, he returned to the question in a lecture in New York City entitled "The Present and Future of the Colored Race in America." He minced no words in announcing his future course of action:

"I shall advocate for the Negro, his most full and complete adoption into the great national family of America. I shall demand for him the most perfect civil and political equality, and that he shall enjoy all the rights, privileges and immunities enjoyed by any other members of the body politic. I weigh my words and I mean all I say, when I contend as I do contend, that this is the *only solid,* and *final solution* of the problem before us."[29]

Douglass' lectures dwelt with this theme again and again. His speech at the annual meeting of the American Anti-Slavery Society in Philadelphia on December 3, 1863, revealed his concern over the civil status of the Negro. He expressed regret that the other speakers, reminiscing about the founding of the society in Philadelphia thirty years before, had spoken as if the work of the organization was finished. The Anti-Slavery Society, he reminded his colleagues, had been organized for the emancipation of the slave and the elevation of the colored people. The second task would still remain even after slavery was abolished, and he, for one, believed that the work of the Society "will not have been completed until the black men of the South, and the black men of the North, shall have been admitted, fully and completely into the body politic of America." The best way to work for the Negro's elevation was to fight for his enfranchisement. Douglass had only scorn for the argument that the Negro was not qualified to vote. He was as well qualified as many others who participated freely in the political life of the nation. "If he knows enough to take up arms in defense of this Government, and bare his breast to the storm of rebel artillery, he knows enough to vote."

Douglass ended by skillfully knitting together national aspirations and Negro suffrage. Men who talked about saving the Union, he declared, and restoring it as it was before the war were simply deluding themselves. The old Union was dead, slain by the first shot fired at Sumter. "We are fighting for something incomparably better than the old Union." The war was being waged for a new Union in which there would be "no black, no white, but a solidarity of the nation, making every slave free, and every free man a voter."[30]

During the winter and spring of 1864 Douglass became increasingly distrustful of Lincoln's program for the freedmen. He was disturbed by the President's proposal to establish state governments in those southern states with a population loyal to the Union sufficient to cast a vote equal to one-tenth of that cast at the presidential election in 1860. Lincoln was obviously ready to reconstruct the southern states without Negro suffrage. Nor was the President doing anything to remove the disabilities against Negro soldiers. Negro troops had already demonstrated their competence and courage at Port Hudson, Milliken's Bend, and Fort Wagner, and were distinguishing themselves every day on the battlefield. Yet they still received less pay than white soldiers, were unable to secure commissions, and were slaughtered by the Confederate soldiers when captured in battle.[31]

Douglass revealed his disappointment at the President's slow progress in a letter to an English friend late in the spring of 1864, writing:

"The treatment of our poor black soldiers—the refusal to pay them equal compensation, though it was promised them when they enlisted; the refusal to insist upon the exchange of colored prisoners when colored prisoners have been slaughtered in cold blood, although the President has repeatedly promised thus to protect the lives of his colored soldiers—have worn my patience threadbare."

The government considered the Negro good enough to fight, but not quite good enough to vote. If the President had his way the Negro, after peace, would be turned back "to the political power of his master, without a single element of strength to shield himself from the vindictive spirit sure to be roused against the whole colored race."[32]

This was Douglass' frame of mind when he was asked to sign a call issued by a group of Radical Republicans and Abolitionists opposed to the re-election of Lincoln and asking the people to assemble in Cleveland on May 31, 1864, "for consultation and concert of action in respect to the approaching Presidential election."[33] He replied on May 23:

"I mean the complete abolition of every vestige, form and modification of Slavery in every part of the United States, perfect equality for the black man in every State before the law, in the jury box, at the ballot-box and on the battlefield; ample and salutary retaliation for every instance of enslavement or slaughter of prisoners of color. I mean that in the distribution of offices and honors under this Government no discrimination shall be made in favor of or against any class of citizens, whether black or white, of native or foreign birth. And supposing the convention which is to meet at Cleveland means the same thing, I cheerfully give my name as one of the signers of the call."[34]

On May 31, 1864, four hundred delegates, including some outstanding Abolitionists, met in Cosmopolitan Hall in Cleveland and nominated John C. Frémont and John Cochrane, nephew of Gerrit Smith, for President and Vice-President on a most advanced platform. It called for uncompromising prosecution of the war, constitutional prohibition of slavery, for free speech, free press, for a one-term presidency, for reconstruction administered exclusively by Congress, and for the confiscation of rebel lands to be divided among soldiers and actual settlers.[85]

The National Convention of the Republican or "Union" Party was held at Baltimore on June 8, 1864. Lincoln was unanimously nominated to stand for re-election and Andrew Johnson of Tennessee was selected for Vice-President to win the support of the War Democrats. Although not one word was spoken publicly against the President at the convention, Lincoln was aware that there was much silent opposition to his policies. In an address to the National Union League on June 9, he commented:

"I do not allow myself to suppose that either the Convention or the League have concluded to decide that I am either the greatest or the best man in America, but rather they have concluded it is not best to swap horses while crossing the river, and have further concluded that I am not so poor a horse that they might not make a botch of it in trying to swap."[36]

The summer of 1864 was a period of intense gloom throughout the North. The Union reverses, the sluggish character of the war, the open clamor of the Copperheads and even Republicans like Horace Greeley for peace at any price, the dissension in the President's cabinet, the conflict between Congress and the chief executive, all weakened the support of the administration. "Mr. Lincoln is already beaten," cried Greeley. "He cannot be elected." Senator Sherman predicted that if the Democrats should select a candidate who had "any particle of patriotism or sense," they would sweep the Republicans out of office like an avalanche."[37]

Until late in August, Douglass was unsparing in his criticism of Lincoln. Not only did he join Wendell Phillips in denouncing the President's policies, but he called upon his friends in England to expose *"the swindle* by which our Government claims the respect of mankind for abolishing slavery. . . . "[38]

Early in August, Douglass met Reverend John Eaton in Toledo, Ohio. During his discussions with the young army chaplain who had been appointed by General Grant superintendent of freedmen in the department of Tennessee, Douglass expressed his criticism of Lincoln's failure to redress the grievances of Negro soldiers and his readiness to reconstruct the southern states without Negro suffrage. Eaton conveyed Douglass' misgivings to Lincoln when he met the President. Lincoln questioned Eaton further, admitted that he was concerned about Douglass' attitude, and declared "that considering the condition from which he had arisen and the obstacles that he had overcome, and the position to which he had attained that he regarded him one of the most meritorious men, if not the most meritorious man in the United States. . . . " He expressed a desire to see Douglass. Eaton promptly arranged the interview.[39]

About August 25, Douglass met Lincoln for the second time. He found the President in an "alarmed condition," frightened by the repercussions of Lincoln's "To Whom It May Concern" letter, in which he had guaranteed a careful hearing and safe conduct to anyone who brought an authoritative proposition "which embraces the restoration of peace, the integrity of the whole Union, and the abandonment of slavery. . . . "[40] The letter had been written on July 18, 1864, at the request of Horace Greeley, the distinguished editor of the *New York Tribune,* who was about to hold an interview with two Rebel emissaries at Niagara Falls. Greeley had asked Lincoln to grant a safe-conduct to these emissaries, in order that they might come to Washington and discuss terms of peace. In reply, the President sent the "To Whom It May Concern" letter by a special messenger, Colonel John Hay, one of his private secretaries.

Although nothing came of the peace negotiations, since it was soon apparent that the Rebel emissaries had no authority whatever to treat for peace, a howl had arisen from Copperheads and moderate Republicans on the publication of the letter. Lincoln was denounced for having said in so many words that even if the war were ended and the Union saved by a negotiated peace the conflict would go on until slavery was abolished. Pressure was being exerted upon Lincoln by Republicans to force him to modify his conditions for peace.

Lincoln had framed a letter to answer the charges. When Douglass entered, the President read the contents to him, and asked him if he should release it. Lincoln's letter denied the accusation that he stood in the way of peace, first, because no person authorized to speak for the Confederate government had ever submitted a proposition for peace to him, and, second, even if he wanted to commit himself and the country to an abolition war rather than a war for the Union, he would not have been able to do so since the country would not support such a war. Such was the letter. In response to the President's query whether the letter should be released, Douglass replied:

"Certainly not. It would be given a broader meaning than you intend to convey; it would be taken as a complete surrender of your anti-slavery policy, and do you considerable damage. In answer to your Copperhead accusers, your friends can make the argument of your want of power, but you cannot wisely say a word on that point."[41]

Whether or not Douglass' advice was considered, the fact remains that Lincoln did not release the letter. Undoubtedly Douglass felt highly honored that the President had sought his advice on so vital a matter of national policy. He was equally impressed by the fact that at no time during the discussion did Lincoln assert, as he had in the past, that his aim was to save the Union with or without slavery. "What he said on this day," Douglass wrote later, "showed a deeper moral conviction against slavery than I have ever seen before in anything spoken or written by him."[42]

Lincoln told Douglass that the acute feeling of despondency in the North, the growing clamor for peace, and the efforts made by Greeley and others to discuss peace terms with the Confederacy, might force him to conclude the war by a negotiated peace. He, himself, was convinced that no real and lasting peace could be had "short of absolute submission on the part of the rebels," but he might have to yield to the pressure for a speedy end to the conflict. In that event all Negroes who had not come into the Union lines would continue in slavery after the war was over. Hence he wished to set in motion a plan to bring as many slaves as possible within the Union territory. He asked Douglass to organize a band of scouts, composed of Negro men, to move into the rebel states, beyond the lines of the Union Army, spread the news of the Emancipation Proclamation, and conduct squads of runaways into the Union lines.

What a far cry, Douglass must have thought, this plan was from the days when the administration had permitted Union officers to return fugitive slaves to their owners and had even allowed the slave owners to cross the Potomac and recover their property!

Lincoln's proposal reminded Douglass of John Brown's original plan to send trained men into the plantations to lead slaves into mountain hide-outs and conduct them to the North and Canada. He was somewhat concerned that the President believed that his proclamation of freedom would cease to operate once the war was over. But he eagerly undertook the task assigned him, believing that even if the war did not end quickly, the more slaves brought into the Union lines the better. As he informed Lincoln from Rochester on August 29, after consulting "several Trustworthy and Patriotic colored men" about the President's plan:

"All with whom I have thus far spoken on the subject, concur in the wisdom and benevolence of the Idea, and some of them think it practicable. That every Slave who Escapes from the Rebel States is a loss to the Rebellion and a gain to the Loyal cause. I need not stop to argue the proposition is self-evident. The Negro is the stomach of the rebellion."[43]

Douglass submitted a detailed outline to Lincoln. It called for the appointment of a general agent who would employ twenty-five assistants "having the cause at heart," who, operating at various points in the Union Army, would send sub-agents into rebel territory to conduct squads of slaves into the Union lines. But the plan never went into operation. The fall of Atlanta on September 2 and Farragut's victory in Mobile Bay soon after knocked the bottom out of the peace-at-any price maneuvers.

On August 29, the same day that Douglass sent his outline to Lincoln, the Democratic Party met in Chicago. With no difficulty General George B. McClellan was nominated for President. The convention's attitude toward the war was summed up by Congressman Clement L. Vallandigham of Ohio, the dominant figure at the sessions:

"The war for the Union is . . . a most bloody and costly failure. War for the Union was abandoned, war for the Negro openly begun. With what success? Let the dead at Fredericksburg make answer. Ought this war to continue? I answer, 'No, no, no!' Stop fighting. Make an armistice."

The Democratic platform was drawn up by the Copperhead group in the party, and included a plank, written by Vallandigham, which asserted:

"That this Convention does explicitly declare, as the sense of the American people, that after four years of failure to restore the Union by the experiment of war . . . justice, humanity, liberty, and the public welfare demand that immediate efforts be made for a cessation of hostilities, with a view to an ultimate convention of the States or other peaceable means, to the end that at the earliest possible moment peace may be restored on the basis of the Federal Union of the States."[44]

The result of the Chicago convention compelled Abolitionists who had thrown their support to Frémont or refrained from endorsing Lincoln to re-evaluate their position. Douglass did not hesitate; as soon as he learned of the proceedings at Chicago, he decided to support Lincoln. "All dates changed with the nomination of McClellan," he declared. For the election of McClellan and the victory of "the policy avowed in the Chicago platform, would be the heaviest calamity of these years of war and blood, since it would upon the instant sacrifice and wantonly cast away everything valuable purchased so dearly by the precious blood of our brave sons and brothers on the battlefield for the perfect liberty and permanent peace of a common country." Moreover, he felt as did Karl Marx who wrote to Frederick Engels on September 7, 1864: "If Lincoln gets through this time—as is very probable—it will be on a much more radical platform and under wholly changed circumstances."[45]

On September 22, after much pressure had been exerted upon him by Republican leaders, Frémont withdrew his candidacy. His withdrawal, he made it clear, was not because he approved of Lincoln's policies, but as General McClellan had come out for restoration of the Union with slavery, the Democrats must be defeated at all costs.

There were now only two candidates in the field—Lincoln and McClellan. Which candidate would win the support of the Negro people? The answer came quickly. Ten days after Frémont's withdrawal, the National Convention of Colored Men which had not met for almost a decade gathered in Syracuse. One hundred and forty-four delegates from eighteen states, including seven slave states, were present. The Reverend Garnet called the convention to order; John Mercer Langston, an Oberlin graduate, was elected temporary chairman; Douglass was named president. Accepting the presidency, Douglass noted with delight the presence on the platform of young men who "had come up in this time of whirlwind and storm." The convention would deal with the attitude in the country toward the Negro people and "answer the question, as we pass to and from this hall, by the men on the streets of Syracuse, 'Where are the damned n — rs going?' " He sounded a defiant note: "In what is to be done we shall give offense to none but the mean and sordid haters of our race."

After several speakers, including a Negro woman from Syracuse, had addressed the delegates, the convention proceeded to organize the National Equal Rights League. In the declaration announcing its formation, the delegates petitioned Congress to remove "invidious distinctions, based upon color, as to pay, labor, and promotion" among Negro soldiers. They thanked the President and Congress for abolishing slavery in the District of Columbia, for the recognition of the Negro republics, Liberia and Haiti, and for the retaliatory military order invoked because of "barbarous treatment of colored soldiers of the Union army by the rebels." A special resolution expressed the delegates' gratitude to Senator Sumner and General Butler for their activities in behalf of the Negro people.

The "Address of the Colored National Convention to the People of the United States," written by Douglass, made clear in bold and unmistakable language where the Negro people stood in the election of 1864 as well as what they expected in the future. Every point raised by Douglass in the "Address" was, in the words of Carl Sandburg, "a living human issue that had taken on new intensity with every month of the war. . . ." [46]

Douglass approached the problems confronting his people realistically. Vast advances had been achieved in a relatively short time, but powerful forces were at work to "reverse the entire order and tendency of the events of the last three years," and prevent further progress. The Negro people not only had to contend with the bitter opposition of pro-slavery forces but they were confronted with the timidity and confusion in the ranks of anti-slavery men. With the *Anti-Slavery Standard* denying that the American Anti-Slavery Society advocated the ballot for Negro people, and Garrison's *Liberator* apologizing "for excluding colored men of Louisiana from the ballot box," [47] the Negro people realized that they had to suffer with the "injudicious concessions and weaknesses" of their friends as well as the strength of their enemies. Such astonishing remarks by Abolitionist journals "injure us more vitally than all the ribald jests of the whole proslavery press."

The "Address" analyzed the policies of the contending political parties in the campaign. Despite the fact that the Republican Party was composed of "the best men in the country" and had been responsible for the enactment of a number of progressive measures, it was "largely under the influence of the prevailing contempt for the character and rights of the colored race." The Republican Party still was not prepared to make the abolition of slavery a precondition for the re-establishment of the Union. "However antislavery in sentiment the President may be, and however disposed he may be to continue the war till slavery is abolished, it is plain that in this he would not be sustained by his party." A single reverse on the battle-field would arouse strong opposition in the party to the President. Moreover, Secretary Seward, the leading administration spokesman next to the President, had said in a recent speech that when the insurgents "laid down their arms, the war will instantly cease; and all the war measures then existing, including those which affect slavery, will cease also. . . . " Freedom for the Negro people thus hung upon the slender thread of Rebel power, pride, and persistence.

Yet with all its weaknesses and prejudices, the Republican Party was the only party the Negro could support. Compared to its rival it officially proclaimed abolition as its goal. "In the ranks of the Democratic party, all the worst elements of American society fraternize. . . . " From that quarter Negroes "need not expect a single voice for justice, mercy, or even decency." A victory at the polls for the Democratic Party would "comprise the sum of all social woes" for the Negro people.

The main body of the "Address" dealt with the necessity for the complete abolition of slavery and the granting of the ballot to the Negro people. In discussing the first point Douglass issued a warning that was all too soon to prove its validity. "Be not deceived," he told those who argued that slavery had "already received its death-blow." "Slavery is still the vital and animating breath of Southern society. The men who have fought for it on the battle-field will not love it less for having shed their blood in its defence. . . . Let Jefferson Davis and his Confederate associates, either in person or by their representatives, return once more to their seats in the halls of Congress,—and you will then see your dead slavery the most living and powerful thing in the country."

Douglass went into great detail in presenting the claims of the Negro to the ballot. The right to vote was "the keystone of the arch of human liberty." Why did the Negro want to vote? "Because we don't want to be mobbed from our work, or insulted with impunity at every corner. We are men, and want to be as free in our native country as other men."

"We are asked, even by some abolitionists, why we cannot be satisfied, for the present at least, with personal freedom; the right to testify in courts of law; the right to own, buy, and sell real estate; the right to sue and be sued. We answer, Because in a republican country, where general suffrage is the rule, personal liberty and the other foregoing rights become mere privileges, held at the option of others. What gives to the newly arrived emigrants, fresh from lands governed by kingcraft and priestcraft, special consequence in the eyes of the American people? Not their virtue, for they are often depraved; not their knowledge, for they are often ignorant; not their wealth, for they are often very poor; why, then, are they courted by the leaders of all parties? The answer is, that our institutions clothe them with the elective franchise, and they have a voice in making the laws of the country."

But Douglass did not press the demand for Negro suffrage only from the standpoint of the benefits to be derived by his people. With prophetic insight he pointed out that once the rebellion in the South was suppressed "a sullen hatred toward the National Government" would be "transmuted from father to son as sacred animosity." Treason, crushed by the federal armies, would go underground and strive in various ways "to disturb the peaceful operation of the hated Government." The ballot and, "if need be, arms," in the hands of four million Negroes in the South would be the most effective counterpoise against southern treason and hostility.

"You are sure of the enmity of the masters,—make sure of the friendship of the slaves; for, depend upon it, your Government cannot afford the enmity of both."[48]

Despite his criticism of the Republican Party, Douglass was anxious to take the stump for Lincoln. But Republican committees were cool to the offer. A campaign pamphlet issued by the Democrats, entitled *Miscegenation Indorsed by Republican Party*, quoted from Douglass' speech at the meeting of the American Anti-Slavery Society in December, 1863, describing his first visit to Lincoln. The Democrats pointed gleefully to Douglass' statement that "the President of the United States received a black man at the White House just as one gentleman received another." Republican politicians, frightened by the label attached to their candidate, felt that Douglass' campaign speeches would only provide further ammunition to the Democrats, and rejected his offers to assist in the campaign.[49] Already the reactionary wing of the Republican Party was foreshadowing its later betrayal of the Negro people.

After Lincoln's triumphant re-election, Douglass resumed his lecturing activities. The war was near its end. Sherman was marching through the Confederacy to the sea. Lee was being pushed back, stubbornly but vainly contesting each step. As the Confederate armies retreated, Douglass ventured South. His winter tour took him to Virginia and Maryland. He delivered six lectures in Baltimore "without molestation." But as exciting as the fact that he was at last speaking as a free man in the state of his birth and bondage was his meeting with his sister Eliza whom he had not seen for nearly thirty years. "Our meeting," he wrote to a friend in England, "can be better imagined than described." He was proud that his sister had bought herself and her nine children out of slavery "by her own toil."[50]

Douglass went to Washington to witness Lincoln's second inauguration. After the ceremony, he set out to attend the evening reception at the White House, determined to see that his people were represented. He took his place in the long line moving into the White House, but when he reached the door he was seized by two policemen and ordered to stand aside. Negroes were not permitted to attend the reception, he was bluntly told. When Douglass insisted that he knew the President personally, the officers agreed to escort him to the reception hall. Actually they brought him to the passage through which visitors made their exit. Douglass, however, refused to leave, and he finally got word through to the President. A few minutes later he was ushered in to see the President. When Lincoln saw Douglass approaching he turned to the officials about him and said, "Here comes my friend Douglass." Lincoln asked Douglass' opinion of the inaugural address and looked pleased when he heard it described as "a sacred effort."[51]

Early in April Richmond was captured. The official surrender at Appomattox soon followed, and on April 9, 1865, the rebellion collapsed.

A jubilee meeting was held in Faneuil Hall on April 4. Douglass' address sounded the joy of the Negro people at the triumph over the slavocracy, but it also reflected a note of concern. The chairman had referred to Negroes as "fellow-citizens," and Douglass pointed out that Negroes were citizens only in times of national crisis. They were citizens in 1776, in 1812 "when Jackson had a little for them to do at New Orleans," and in 1863 when Massachusetts raised two regiments of Negro soldiers. The "Negro must also be a citizen in time of peace. He must have the right to vote. The American people, in calling upon the black man to take part in this war, have bound themselves to protect the Southern Negro from all consequences that may arise from his allegiance to the Union."[52]

Before the jubilation had ceased, the nation suffered a terrible shock. President Lincoln sitting in his box at Ford's Theatre on the night of April 14, was fired upon by John Wilkes Booth, a fanatical partisan of the slave power. The President lingered unconscious until the next morning when he died.

Douglass was in Rochester when the tragic news of the assassination reached the city. On the evening of the President's death he attended a memorial meeting at the City Hall. He had not been invited to speak, nor to occupy a place on the platform, but as the meeting progressed cries for Douglass resounded through the auditorium. He came forward and addressed the audience. Speaking as if inspired he told what Lincoln had meant to the Negro people. A member of the audience reported:

"I have heard Webster and Clay in their best moments, Channing and Beecher in their highest inspirations; I never heard truer eloquence! I never saw profounder impressions. When he finished, the meeting was done."

Douglass' speech in honor of the martyred President contained a paragraph of advice to the nation which was to gain more and more significance in the critical years that lay ahead. He said:

"Let us not be in too much haste in the work of restoration. Let us not be in a hurry to clasp to our bosom the spirit that gave birth to Booth. . . . When we take to our arms again, as brethren, our Southern foes, let us see to it that we take also our Southern friends. Let us not forget that justice to the Negro is safety to the nation."[53]

When the New York Common Council refused to permit Negro people to participate in the funeral procession when Lincoln's body passed through the city, a committee of Negroes answered with a meeting on the life and death of the martyred president, with Douglass the featured speaker. On May 30, Douglass spoke to a huge audience in Cooper Institute under the sponsorship of this committee. He denounced the action of the Common Council as "the most disgraceful and scandalous proceeding ever exhibited by people calling themselves civilized." The forces responsible for the action, he warned, could be expected to ally themselves with the former slave-owners in an effort to re-establish slavery and keep the Negro people and poor whites in the South in a degraded position. But he predicted that the mass of the people would defeat this conspiracy. He closed on an optimistic note:

"Slavery has been blotted out and abolished forever, and the Negro is to be enfranchised and clothed with all the dignity of the American citizen. The poor whites of the South, who have been looked down upon and oppressed by the slaveholders, are also to be lifted up from their social and political debasement."

Douglass' optimism was based on his conviction that the people had learned a vital lesson from the war. It was now clear that the war was more than a battle over slavery; that, in fact, the war of the Rebels had been "a war of the rich against the poor." The conflict had taught the nation that it could not "outlaw one part of its people without endangering the rights and liberties of all people," and that it could not "put a chain on the ankle of the bondmen without finding the other end of it about their own necks." As long as slavery had existed, all labor had been degraded. Once slavery was abolished; once Negro labor was no longer fettered, chained, flogged, and branded; once Negro workers were paid decent wages, "then we shall see as never before, the laborer, in all sections of this country, rising to respectability and power."[54]

Many struggles, of course, still lay ahead. But the deck was now cleared for further advances. The nation was now unified and controlled by an industrial bourgeoisie based upon free wage-labor. The labor movement had an opportunity to develop unhindered by the obstacle of chattel slavery. Douglass said in 1865 what Karl Marx was to say years later in his great classic, *Capital*:

"In the United States of America," Marx wrote, "every independent movement of the workers was paralysed so long as slavery disfigured a part of the Republic. Labor cannot emancipate itself in the white skin where in the black it is branded."[55]

Reconstruction, 1865-1868

When slavery fell Frederick Douglass was in his forty-eighth year. He was still in the prime of his life, mentally and physically alert, steady, vigorous. The crucial war years had both ripened his faculties and immensely enhanced his prestige. Friends felt that after twenty-five years of struggle in the cause of freedom, he was now entitled to a rest. At first Douglass was inclined to agree. For a time he believed that with the cessation of hostilities his work would be ended, and that he would be able to buy a farm, retire from public life, and enjoy some well-earned leisure. But Douglass dismissed the thought of such a pleasant existence. He soon found "that the Negro still had a cause, and that he needed my voice and pen, with others, to plead for it."[1]

During the early months of the administration of President Andrew Johnson, who succeeded Lincoln after the assassination, the former slaveholders regained political domination of the South. During the Civil War, Johnson had frequently called for the punishment of traitors and had expressed the belief that only loyal men, white and black, should be permitted to participate in the reconstruction of the seceded states.[2] Once President, however, Johnson appointed men who had held office under the Confederacy to the position of Provisional Governor of the southern states. These governors reinstated in public office those who had held such positions prior to the end of the war, conferred suffrage upon loyal citizens who had been voters before secession, but completely ignored the demand of the Negro people for suffrage.[3] At the same time, Johnson was granting pardons to leaders of the Confederacy enabling them to participate in the reconstruction of the southern states.[4]

The state legislatures, dominated as they were by former slaveholders, promptly adopted legislation which all but re-enslaved the Negro masses. Under the "Black Codes"—the name applied to the statutes enacted in eight southern states—a Negro who was not at work was arrested. To pay off the prison charges and fines he was hired out. If a Negro quit work before his contract expired, he was imprisoned for breach of contract and the reward to the person performing the arrest was deducted from his wages. Some of the codes also provided that if a Negro laborer left his employer he would "forfeit all wages to the time of abandonment." Negro children whose parents were considered too poor to support them were bound out as apprentices, girls until 18 years of age and boys until 21. In Mississippi the code provided that if a Negro could not pay taxes to care for the poor, he would be regarded as a vagrant and hired out. The code also asserted that the laws under chattel slavery were to be in full force again "except so far as the mode and manner of trial and punishment have been changed and altered by law."[5]

At the same time, the federal government, following Johnson's orders, drove the Negroes off land they had received during Lincoln's administration, and in every way helped the planters to keep the freedmen in a state of servitude. When the Freedmen's Bureau threatened all laborers without contract or employment with a vagrancy charge, the Negroes were finally forced to return to their former masters. "This device," General Tillson of the Bureau gleefully reported, "worked like a charm."[6]

Landless, without citizenship, without the right to vote and denied civil rights, the Negro masses were finding their new freedom little different from their former bondage. Following a tour through the South after the war, Carl Schurz reported that the former slave owners still regarded and treated the freedmen as their natural property, and that the prevailing attitude among the former masters was that the "Negro exists for the special object of raising cotton, rice and sugar *for the whites,* and that it is illegitimate for him to indulge like other people in the pursuit of his own happiness in his own way."[7]

Small wonder that many freedmen bitterly complained that all that was "needed to restore slavery was the auction block and the driver's lash." Small wonder, too, that Douglass decided to abandon his plans to retire from public life, and again use his voice and pen to bring real meaning to the abolition of chattel slavery.

The events in the South under Johnson's administration did not come as a complete surprise to Douglass. Even during the war he had warned the Abolitionists of the danger of counter-revolution when victory was achieved. Pointing to the overthrow of the Revolutions of 1848 in Europe by the forces of despotism, he declared that it was naïve for anti-slavery men to believe that a similar outcome might not occur in the United States. "Thoughts of this kind," he said in 1864, "tell me that there never was a time when Anti-Slavery work was more needed than right now. The day that shall see the Rebels at our feet, their weapons flung away, will be the day of trial. We have need to prepare for that trial."[8]

Two years before Appomattox Douglass had made it clear that Reconstruction meant not only the return of the rebellious states to the Union; it meant the most profound alteration in the entire manner of the South. The historical tasks of Reconstruction consisted in crushing forever the slave power and creating the conditions for a democratic South. The slavocracy had been routed on the battlefield, but its stranglehold upon southern life had to be broken before the democratic forces could count the victory complete.

But many Abolitionists were ready to call it a day. With the end of the war Garrison held that the work of abolition was ended, and that the American Anti-Slavery Society could now be disbanded. At the annual meeting in May, 1865, he declared:

"We organized expressly for the abolition of slavery; we called our Society an *Anti-Slavery Society*. The other work [Negro suffrage] was incidental. Now, I believe, slavery is abolished in this country, abolished constitutionally, abolished by a decree of this nation, never, never to be reversed, and, therefore, that it is ludicrous for us, a mere handful of people with little means, with no agents in the field, no longer separate, and swallowed up in the great ocean of popular feeling against slavery, to assume that we are of special importance, and that we ought not to dissolve."

Garrison was sure that the North in reconstructing the southern states would insist on "guarantees for the protection of the freedmen," would give them the vote, and protect them by force of arms.[9]

Douglass did not share his faith. The work of the Abolitionists was not finished. Slavery was not ended. Even if the Thirteenth Amendment was ratified, the South "by unfriendly legislation" could make liberty for the freedmen "a delusion, a mockery and a snare." The "Black Codes" ruled the South. The slave oligarchy was coming back into power, and with the Negro deprived of political rights, he could speedily be reduced "to a condition similar to slavery." It would not be called slavery, but it would still be the "old monster" under a different name.

"Where shall the black man look for support, my friends, if the American Anti-Slavery Society fails him? From whence shall we expect a certain sound from the trumpet of freedom, when the old pioneer, when this Society that has survived mobs, and martyrdom, and the combined efforts of priest-craft and state-craft to suppress it, shall all at once subside, on the mere intimation that the Constitution has been amended, so that neither slavery nor involuntary servitude shall hereafter be allowed in this land?"

The majority agreed with Douglas that discontinuance of the American Anti-Slavery Society meant abandoning the Negro and the cause of freedom. Garrison's resolution to disband was rejected by a vote of 118 to 48. A new executive committee, with Wendell Phillips as president, was chosen.[10]

"Slavery is not abolished until the black man has the ballot," Douglass had told the members of the American Anti-Slavery Society during the debate over Garrison's resolution to disband. During the summer and fall of 1865 he struck the same insistent note—"the immediate, complete, and universal enfranchisement of the colored people of the whole country." Every aspect of the freedman's future, he argued, hinged upon the right to vote. On July 30, 1865, he wrote to Lydia M. Child: "I am just now deeply engaged in the advocacy of suffrage for the whole colored people of the South. I see little advantage in emancipation without this. Unfriendly legislation by a state may undo all the friendly legislation by the Federal Government." Two weeks before Frederick Engels had written to Karl Marx expressing a similar opinion. "Without colored suffrage, nothing whatever can be done there. . . .,"[11] he wrote of Reconstruction in the South.

Douglass' motives in demanding Negro suffrage were quite different from those of many leading opponents of Johnson's policies. Among the champions of Negro suffrage were Republican politicians interested in granting the franchise to the freedmen only because they knew their political careers were at stake. They were heartily supported by the manufacturing and financial interests of the North. Enriched by wartime profiteering and speculation, northern industrialists and financiers were determined to consolidate their victory. Johnson's policies threatened to nullify the political and economic results of the war. A union of northern and southern Democrats and groups of discontented farmers of the West might quickly end the political supremacy of the Republican Party, the representatives of the big bourgeoisie of the North. High protective tariffs, the national banking system, lavish mineral and timber land grants, and railroad subsidies might be ended if the ex-slaveholders of the South regained their former dominant position in Congress and were to be aided by northern Democrats and western farmers. By granting suffrage to the freedmen, the supremacy of the Republican Party could be assured and the victories of the Civil War for the bourgeoisie safeguarded. As James S. Allen has so aptly put it: "The struggle of the industrial bourgeoisie for national power was therefore inseparable for a time from the battle for democracy in the South."[12]

All this was of no concern to Douglass. His interest in equal suffrage was solely the result of a burning determination to achieve justice for his people. As he traveled about the North, he kept on stressing the point that the effective uprooting of the old rebel power could only be accomplished if the Negro people were enfranchised. In speech after speech he sought to drive home the idea that "the general welfare of the Negro was best served by the franchise." With the ballot the Negro was bound to elevate himself, for something then would be expected of him. To leave him without the ballot would be "to make him the helpless victim of the resentment provoked by freeing him." To give him the ballot, would provide him "with a right and power which will be ever present, and will form a wall of fire for his protection." Aside from all this, the Negro had earned the ballot by rushing to the aid of the nation in its hour of distress.[13]

It all boiled down to the fundamental point:

"Without the elective franchise the Negro will still be practically a slave. Individual ownership has been abolished; but if we restore the Southern States without this measure, we shall establish an ownership of the blacks by the community among which they live."

And again:

"Without this, his liberty is a mockery; without this, you might as well almost retain the old name of slavery for his condition; for; in fact, he is not the slave of the individual master, he is the slave of society, and holds his liberty as a privilege, not as a right. He is at the mercy of the mob, and has no means of protecting himself."[14]

To the oft-repeated argument that the Negro was not prepared for suffrage, Douglass had a ready answer: "As one learns how to swim by swimming, the Negro must learn how to vote by voting. This will cause him to see his ignorance, and seek the corrective. As slaves, to be intelligent was to be dangerous. As freemen, to be ignorant is to be dangerous." With the ballot the Negro people could secure education for themselves and their children, and establish institutions of learning in which they "can confront ignorance and prejudice with the light and power of positive knowledge, and array against brazen falsehood the rightful influence of accomplished facts."[15]

Douglass' influence on public opinion in the North and West was of incalculable value during the critical years when the people were deciding whether to support Johnson's reactionary policies or a truly democratic program of Reconstruction. No account of the triumph of radical Reconstruction is complete which ignores the contributions of the great Negro leader who went up and down the North instructing, warning, and inspiring the people.

Douglass looked forward anxiously to the Thirty-Ninth Congress which was to meet in December, 1865. On October 8, he wrote to Gerrit Smith: "I wish you could be in Congress this winter, for Congress is now to determine whether all that has been fairly purchased by the patriots' blood of the North, and by the brave Negroes of the South, shall be given back again to the spoilers of the Nation." Two months later he wrote again to Smith: "We must demand Suffrage, but rejoice if we can get the Slave code abolished, and future ones made impossible."[16]

The Radical Republicans in Congress, representing a coalition of spokesmen for the industrial bourgeoisie and the Abolitionist democracy and led by Thaddeus Stevens of Pennsylvania in the House and Charles Sumner of Massachusetts in the Senate, were successful in postponing the admission of the recently elected representatives from the southern states under Johnson's Reconstruction program. A Joint Committee on Reconstruction was appointed by Congress to investigate the entire question. The conflict between Johnson and the Radical Republicans had opened in earnest.

During January and February, 1866, Douglass journeyed thousands of miles warning the people against the Presidential policy of Reconstruction. The country, he emphasized, was threatened by "the crime of crimes . . . nothing less than the base and wanton betrayal by a triumphant nation of their only allies and friends back again into the hands of their common enemies." Everywhere he denounced Johnson as "a traitor to the cause of freedom." The President felt the lash of Douglass' tongue when the latter delivered his blistering lecture, "The Assassination and its Lessons,"[17] on January 29, at the Brooklyn Academy of Music. "Every seat in the Academy was filled," reported the *Brooklyn Daily Eagle*. "The moment the orator of the evening appeared, volley after volley of applause rolled through the building until the roof rang again with the echoes."[18] The enthusiasm was largely the result of victory over prejudice. The directors had refused to permit Douglass to speak at the Academy of Music because it was against their policy to open the hall to men of a "colored complexion." After a furious campaign by progressive Brooklyn citizens, the directors had been forced to capitulate and, by a vote of eleven to five, permitted the lecture to be held. Douglass dwelt on the struggle for the right of a Negro to speak at the Academy of Music in his opening statement:

"I thank you very sincerely for this welcome, and all the more as I take it, or regard it as a telling rebuke to the contemptible feeling which induced parties to object to my appearing here. The spirit that would drive me from this platform, if allowed, would drive me from the face of the earth, and if it had control in any other world than this, and if possible for me to get into any other world than this, it would drive me thence. It's a mean spirit altogether, too mean for so large a city as is Brooklyn; and the day is coming when Brooklyn will be quite ashamed that any such objection could have been made, to a man's appearing before an audience in it for the purpose of vindicating the cause of justice, of humanity and of liberty."[19]

In his two hour address, Douglass devoted much time to a comparison of Lincoln and Johnson. If Lincoln were alive he would be standing with the men "who go foremost for the assertion of equal rights at the south as a condition of their reconstruction." Had Lincoln lived, loyal black men would not have been insulted in Washington as they had been by President Johnson, when he told a delegation of Negro soldiers to go home and work and prove that they were entitled to freedom. Had Lincoln lived, he would have been in favor of the enfranchisement of the colored people, for he was "a progressive man; he never took any step backwards. He did not begin by playing the role of Moses and end by playing that of Pharaoh; he began by playing Pharaoh and ended by playing Moses.[20] His last days were better than his first." Lincoln had told Douglass that he was in favor of the enfranchisement of two classes of southern people: "First, all those who had taken part in suppressing the rebellion; and secondly, all those who read and write. . . ." He was in favor of thus extending the enfranchisement of the colored people of the South. "He told me so, over and over again," Douglass declared.[21]

Douglass had only contempt for a man like Johnson who had promised to punish traitors and had pardoned instead "the guiltiest of traitors"; who had promised that in reconstruction of the southern states "traitors were to take back seats and loyal men front ones," but who, on assuming the Presidency, enunciated a policy in which "traitors and rebel generals were placed in the front seats and made provisional Governors." This policy was "a most wanton and dishonorable abandonment of our allies, our only allies during the war, at the South."

Douglass closed his address with a warning and a prediction. The nation had called in the Negro to help save it, and vengeance would be in store for the country if it were so ungrateful and false as to fail to do justice to the colored people. If the Negro did not obtain equal rights, the agitation for these rights would continue, "for while there was any injustice left, the Black men would not keep silent."[22]

The victory over prejudice and discrimination in Brooklyn was followed a few days later by a similar triumph in Washington. Douglass was scheduled to deliver the same address at the First Presbyterian Church. The proceeds of the lecture were to go to the Colored Orphan Asylum of Washington. Several days before the lecture, two deacons and ten pew-holders issued a public protest "against the church being occupied by a promiscuous gathering of white and colored persons to listen to a lecture from Frederick Douglass on a subject not religious in its character but calculated to destroy the harmony of the church, and to bring it into great disrepute; the lecture although ostensibly to obtain funds for the benefit of colored orphans, being in reality, to enable certain political groups to promulgate their peculiar doctrines in opposition to the views of the President of the United States, and a large majority of the American people. We therefore respectfully request the sexton not to permit the church to be thus desecrated." The protest was overwhelmingly rejected, and Douglass lectured to "one of the largest and finest audiences ever convened in Washington." Chief Justice Chase presided, and introduced Douglass as "one of the first orators, and foremost of American citizens."[23]

While in Washington Douglass attended a convention of colored men called to express the sentiments of the Negro people on the issues of Reconstruction. Delegates from Wisconsin, Alabama, Florida, Pennsylvania, Maryland, New York, the District of Columbia, and the six New England states met in the Fifteenth Street Presbyterian Church and, with Reverend Henry Highland Garnet as presiding officer, discussed for two days the Freedmen's Bureau Bill, the Civil Rights Bill, the proposed Fourteenth Amendment, and other pending legislation. The meeting went on record that while they were "unalterably opposed to foreign colonization and would resist to the utmost any attempt at compulsory emigration or removal to any place, in this country, or out of it not of our own free choice," they were prepared to support any effort of the government "to provide homes for the homeless in any portion of our country." It also urged the government, through congressional legislation, to "guarantee and secure to all loyal citizens, irrespective of race or color, equal rights before the law, including the right of impartial suffrage." Such legislation was deemed "essential to secure liberty to the freedmen and a republican form of government to the States lately in rebellion."[24]

The Convention of Colored Men appointed a delegation consisting of George T. Downing, William Whipper, John Jones, Douglass, and his son, Lewis, to visit President Johnson to get his views on the program set forth in their resolutions. On February 7, the delegation called at the White House.

After being greeted by the President, Downing, the chairman, opened with an expression of respect to "your Excellency." He told the President that the delegation had come "feeling that we are friends meeting a friend." As spokesmen for the colored people, they were here to voice dissatisfaction with the lax enforcement of the Thirteenth Amendment and to express the hope that the Negro "may be fully enfranchised, not only here in this District, but throughout the land."

Douglass followed Downing, and, in a brief statement, reminded Johnson that his "noble and humane predecessor" had called upon the Negroes to assist in saving the nation. He hoped that the President would take the next logical step, and favor the granting of the ballot to colored men "with which to save ourselves." Douglass condensed the right of the Negro to the ballot in a single sentence: "The fact that we are the subjects of the Government and subject to taxation, to volunteer in the service of the country, subject to being drafted, subject to bear the burdens of the State, makes it not improper that we should ask to share in the privileges of this condition."

In his reply Johnson stated he had "periled" everything for the colored race, and that he did not like "to be arraigned by some who can get up handsomely-rounded periods and deal in rhetoric, and talk about abstract ideas of liberty, who never periled life, liberty or property." He was willing to be the Negro's Moses "to lead him from bondage to freedom," but he was unwilling to support a policy which would result "in great injury to the white as well as to the colored man." Approaching

"very near to Mr. Douglass," the President advanced the argument
that the poor whites and the Negro had always been bitter enemies.
If they were "thrown together at the ballot-box with this enmity and
hate existing between them," a race war would begin.

When Johnson inquired if it was right to force the majority to
"receive a state of things they are opposed to," Downing asked if he
would apply this principle to South Carolina "where a majority of the
inhabitants are colored." The President ignored this, and continued
to insist that it was for the people of a state, not Congress, to determine
who should vote. He closed on a mystical note. All that was necessary
was to search for "a great law" controlling the proper relations between
Negro and white. "All the details will then properly adjust themselves
and work out well in the end."

Douglass thanked the President, but indicated a desire to differ with
some of the points that had been advanced. Johnson shrugged this off
with the observation that he believed that all that had been expected of
him was that he set forth his views. But Douglass persisted, and declared
that the enfranchisement of the Negro would prevent the very thing
the President feared—"a conflict of races." To this Johnson gave the
familiar argument that the problems could best be solved by the emigration of the Negroes. Douglass countered with the statement that even
if the Negro wanted to leave the South he could not do so because he
was "absolutely in the hands" of the master class. Johnson seized on
this to advance the argument that the master would also control the
Negro's vote when he was enfranchised. Douglass assured the President
that once given the vote, the Negro and poor whites would unite and
form a new party in the South. "There is this conflict that you speak
of between the wealthy slaveholder and the poor man," he added. Irritated by the effective demolition of his main argument, Johnson charged
that Douglass' statement proved that danger of a conflict existed in the
South. He repeated his suggestion of emigration as the solution.

On departing, Douglass remarked to his fellow-delegates: "The
President sends us to the people, and we go to the people." "Yes, sir,"
said Johnson; "I have great faith in the people. I believe they will do
what is right."[25]

On leaving the White House, the delegates were immediately
interviewed by a group of Radical Congressmen. A correspondent for
the *New York Tribune* who was present reported the delegates as saying
that the President had spoken to them "not without courtesy, but in a

manner which indicated a subdued excitement, or 'repressed anger.' . . ."
They also expressed the conviction that Johnson would oppose the
extension of suffrage to Negroes.[26]

Later in the day Douglass wrote a reply to the President in behalf
of the entire delegation which was published in the *Washington Chronicle*.
Johnson's views, went the open letter, were "unsound and prejudicial"
to the best interests of the Negro people as well as to the country as a
whole. The President's argument that Negro suffrage was unwise because
of the hatred between the poor whites and the slaves failed completely
to take into account the fact that this hostility had been incited by the
planter aristocracy. Now that slavery was abolished, the cause of the
conflict had been removed. Yet even if the hostility still existed, how
could the President reconcile his professed desire to promote the Negro's
welfare with a policy which deprived the Negro of all means of defense
at the same time arming his enemy with political power? "Peace between
races is not to be secured by degrading one race and exalting another,
by giving power to one race and withholding it from another; but by
maintaining a state of equal justice between all classes."

Johnson's colonization theory, if carried into effect, the letter concluded, would seriously deprive the country of the usefulness of the
Negro laborer in time of peace and the Negro soldier in time of war.
"Besides, the worst enemy of the nation could not cast upon its fair
name of greater infamy than to suppose that Negroes could be tolerated
among them in a state of the most degrading slavery and oppression,
and must be cast away, driven into exile, for no other cause than having
been freed from their chains."[27]

The story of the Negro delegation's interview with Johnson received
wide publicity, and was used effectively in mobilizing public support
for the Negro people. Republican Congressmen were quick to point
out that the Negro delegates had "altogether the best of the argument,"
and showed "no inferiority in point of deportment either." The Abolitionists went even further. "Who that reads the speeches of the colored
delegation, and the President's," wrote Elizabeth Cady Stanton, "can
help seeing how much better Douglass understands the philosophy of
social life and republican institutions than the President?" The *Anti-
Slavery Standard* agreed:

"One of the speakers in this dialogue is President of the United States,
representing by his official position what there is best in the civilization of
the Anglo-Saxon race. The other is Frederick Douglass, a Negro, with nothing

to back him but his own manhood and talent. Yet, if we are compelled to accept Andrew Johnson as our representative, we blush for the white race. Dignity, force of speech, modesty, manliness, simple faith in justice, weight of character, are all on the side of the Negro. It would be hard to surpass the brief address of Frederick Douglass, for fitness to the occasion and point. It would be hard to find a worse speech than the diffuse, illogical, clumsy, and coarse reply of the President."[28]

Ten days after the White House interview, Congress passed an act extending the Freedmen's Bureau. Johnson vetoed the bill on February 19, and the veto was sustained. But it was the last Johnson veto that was upheld in Congress. On April 19, the Civil Rights Act was passed over the President's veto. The law declared the freedmen to be citizens and specifically endowed them with civil rights adherent to citizenship, including the right to possess real and personal property. In June, Congress passed the Fourteenth Amendment and, over Johnson's objection, started it on its way through the state legislatures. The Amendment was intended to insure by constitutional change the maintenance of the Civil Rights Act, and while it did not specifically provide for Negro suffrage, it presented the alternatives of the enfranchisement of all male citizens or the reduction of representation in Congress.

Johnson's supporters decided to meet the Radical offensive by rallying the Democrats and conservative Republicans in defense of the President's policies. On June 25, 1866, the Executive Committee of the National Union Club issued a call for a national convention to be held in Philadelphia in mid-August. Among other things, the delegates were required to pledge themselves to "sustain the Administration," to uphold the principle that each state had "the undoubted right to prescribe the qualifications of its own electors," and to acknowledge that the Radical Republican policies were "unjust and revolutionary."[29]

Delegates representing every state in the Union marched into the convention hall at Philadelphia on August 14, led by Governor Orr of South Carolina and General Couch of Massachusetts, the North and South arm in arm. They convened for three days, listening to speeches which praised Johnson and condemned the Radicals, and adopting a series of resolutions which hailed the President as "worthy of the nation and equal to the great crisis upon which his lot is cast." They appealed to the country to elect men to Congress who would follow his leadership.[30]

The Radicals quickly countered with a convention of their own. A call was issued on July 4 to the southern loyal Unionists inviting them to send delegates to a meeting in Independence Hall, Philadelphia, on the first Monday of September. The call denounced the doctrine of state sovereignty, demanded "the restructure of Southern state government . . . on constitutional principles," endorsed the Congressional plan of Reconstruction, and asked: "Shall loyalty or disloyalty have the keeping of the destinies of the nation?"[31]

A few weeks after the call was released, the sponsors of the National Loyalist Convention—loyal Unionists in Tennessee, Texas, Georgia, Missouri, Virginia, and North Carolina—decided to invite northern representatives to be present as honorary delegates. Late in August, the Republican convention of Rochester appointed Douglass as one of its delegates "to meet with the true Southern Unionists about to convene in Philadelphia." Douglass "cheerfully and gratefully" accepted the "unexpected honor." In his letter of acceptance he noted: "If the Convention shall receive me, the event will be somewhat significant progress. . . ."[32]

Douglass had reason to question the reaction of the convention's sponsors to his appointment, for many Radicals were dismayed by the action of the Rochester Republicans. "Our friends," wrote a Radical Republican to Thaddeus Stevens, "are unanimous in the belief that this is unfortunate & I write at the suggestion of several to you to request that you will use your influence with Mr. Douglass to advise him to remain at home or decline the appointment. If he goes it will certainly injure our cause & we may lose some Congressman in the doubtful districts." A committee of these worried Republicans approached Douglass on the train en route to Philadelphia and pleaded with him not to attend the convention. They insisted that his presence would imperil a Republican victory at the polls, especially in Indiana. But Douglass was adamant. He believed that these fears were groundless, and he did not intend to "abdicate his manhood" even if the demand came from Radical Republicans. He told the committee that they might as well ask him "to blow my brains out." The only thing the Republican Party would gain from his staying away would be a reputation "for hypocrisy and cowardice." "But ignoring the question of policy entirely," he concluded, "and looking at it as one of right and wrong, I am bound to go into that convention; not to do so would contradict the principle and practice of my life."[33]

As Douglass continued his trip, his confidence in the correctness of his decision was bolstered by the cheering demands for his appearance at every station en route. He arrived amid cheers in Philadelphia on

September 2, in company with Generals Butler and Burnside. His presence in Philadelphia created "quite a sensation." Conservative newspapers carried shrieking headlines: "Fred Douglass the lion of the city"; "Black and white convention"; "The Quaker City full of miscgens"; "First grand national convention of Negro worshippers, free lovers, spiritualists, fourierites, women's rights men, Negro equality men"; "Negro insurrection to be incited."[34]

The headlines had their effect. When the delegates assembled at Independence Hall the next day to march to National Hall where the convention was to be held, General Butler was the only one to remain near Douglass. Just when it looked as if Douglass would have to walk in the procession without a companion, Theodore Tilton came forward and locked arms with him. Cheer echoed cheer as the Negro leader and the white editor marched down the streets arm in arm and entered the hall.[35]

Tilton's spontaneous act of warm friendship filled Douglass "with admiration and gratitude." But it disturbed many Radicals still further. Even Thaddeus Stevens was annoyed. "A good many people here are disturbed by the practical exhibition of social equality in the arm-in-arm performance of Douglass and Tilton," he wrote angrily from Bedford Springs on September 6. "It does not become radicals like us particularly to object. But it was certainly unfortunate at this time. The old prejudice, now revived will lose us some votes. Why it was done I cannot see except as a foolish bravado."[36]

But the public display of "social equality" was quickly forgotten in the heat of another controversy at the convention—the issue of Negro suffrage. A majority of the southern loyalists (for practical political reasons since most of their constituents were Negroes) favored an endorsement of Negro suffrage. A number of border state and many northern delegates were not prepared to accept this advanced program. Consequently the northern and southern delegations met separately. The New York delegation, under Tilton's leadership, held its own meeting and went on record in favor of Negro suffrage. Fearing the radicalism of the southern delegates and the New York delegation, twelve governors, one lieutenant governor, seven ex-governors, and one ex-lieutenant governor from northern states met in secret and cautioned moderation on the issue of Negro suffrage.[37]

His status as an accredited delegate uncertain, Douglass did not participate in the proceedings of the New York delegation on the first day of the convention.[38] At a public meeting that evening, however, he was invited to speak and "amid deafening applause and cheering," he stepped to the platform. After expressing his surprise at the "unexpected call," and amusing his listeners with several stories about his experiences in Philadelphia as a fugitive slave thirty years before, he proceeded seriously to speak of the claims of the Negro. The war had settled the question as to whether the Negro could fight, he pointed out, and the history of the United States had settled the question as to whether he was "to be a permanent part of the American people." The Negro was here and "no scheme of colonization or no mode of extirpation can be adopted by which he shall be entirely eradicated from the land. . . . For two hundred and fifty years we have been subjected to the exterminating forces of slavery—marriage abolished, organization unknown, if more than five meet together, stripes, education denied, the right to learn to read the name of the God that made us denied, the family broken up—yet under it all, under all the exterminating forces of slavery here we are today." The only question that remained to be settled was whether the Negro's presence in America was to be a blessing or a curse to the nation. The answer was simple:

"It is this, the thorough and complete incorporation of the whole black element into the American body politic. (*Great applause.*) Anything less than this will prove an utter failure in my judgment. You want me to speak my honest sentiments? (*A voice—"yes."*) He should have the right to sue, and be sued, and have the right to the jury box, the witness box and the ballot box. The Negro is a man. A political revolution for manhood suffrage is going on here as well as in Europe. The masses must be respected everywhere. It is dangerous to deny any class of people the right to vote. But the black man deserves the right to vote for what he has done, to aid in suppressing the rebellion, both by fighting and by assisting the Federal soldier wherever he was found. He deserves to vote, because his services may be needed again. . . . " [39]

The next morning a "touching incident" occurred. Douglass met Lucretia Auld, daughter of his former mistress, in the street. He was deeply moved when she told him that she had come to Philadelphia from Baltimore just to see him march in the procession. When he addressed the New York delegation that same morning, Douglass was in a solemn mood. He spoke of the efforts that had been made to induce him not to attend the convention, and remarked that Abraham Lincoln had not been "ashamed to invite him to Washington, and to take tea with him also." If he was considered good enough to have tea with Lincoln at the White House, he was certainly eminently qualified to serve as a delegate to the convention.

During the first three days of the meetings, the delegates had confined themselves mainly to criticizing Johnson and his policies. The early rift between the southern and northern delegates appeared to be healed, and on the evening of the third day a joint meeting was held. It was a joyous occasion. Speeches, torch-light processions, bands, a display of rockets and Roman candles enlivened the proceedings.

The next morning the conflict was out in the open again. Attending the meeting of the Southern loyalists, Douglass noticed that the border state delegates were pressing for an early adjournment in order to prevent an endorsement of Negro suffrage. Leaving the room, he called upon Anna M. Dickinson and Tilton to join him in forestalling the maneuvers to secure a speedy adjournment. When Douglass entered again with Miss Dickinson and Tilton, the speaker "was unable to proceed for some minutes in consequence of the excitement." The border state delegates hurriedly proposed a motion to adjourn *sine die*. But the southern delegates refused to be "gagged," defeated the motion, and called on Miss Dickinson and Douglass to address them.

The presiding officer hurriedly left the chair as Miss Dickinson ascended the platform. This "interesting young woman, threw off her jockey hat, wiped her face with a dainty cambric handkerchief, ran her fingers through her short locks, and prepared to respond to the enthusiastic call." She roundly criticized the delegates from Kentucky and Maryland for trying to stave off a declaration in favor of Negro suffrage. The American people, she firmly announced, would support such a declaration. She concluded with an eloquent appeal to the southern delegates to stand firm.

"My friends," she declared, "this Convention is not closed. The word comes to you. A world stands listening. The millions who love the principles of the cross, stand listening. Ireland, to which you have sent greeting, stands listening. The great loyal mass of the North, the wronged, persecuted and the suffering ones of the South stand listening. The great God stands listening and waiting for your word to go out that the good fight shall go on."

Douglass followed Miss Dickinson. Southerners, he remarked, frequently told him, "Keep still; it will all come in good time; don't pile it on too heavy; don't do that; let us get out of the well and we will attend to you afterwards." Amid laughter and applause, he continued: "You remember the fable of the fox and the goat who were in the well together, the fox said he could get out by mounting the goat's horns, and then he would help the goat out. Reynard forgot the poor goat, and it remains in the well still." He asked for the suffrage for the black man only because it was "his right," and he asked for it *now* because this was the time when the nation was keenly aware of the contributions of the Negroes to the victory achieved in the Civil War. "Surely if the black man can pay taxes, he can vote. If he can use the loyal musket he can vote. . . ."

Miss Dickinson's and Douglass' eloquent appeals had stiffened the determination of the southern delegates to fight the issue through to a victorious conclusion. As a compromise, the unreconstructed states were permitted to submit a report that would express their sentiments on suffrage but would not be binding on the convention as a whole. But when the report was about to be submitted, Speed of Kentucky, the presiding officer at the final session, declared that the work of the convention was finished and withdrew. Immediately Miss Dickinson and Tilton moved that the convention be reorganized by electing James Botts of Virginia, the first vice-president, to the chair. With the majority of the delegates still present, Botts took the gavel and asked for the report of the Committee on the Condition of the Unreconstructed States. The most important part of the report consisted of a resolution calling upon the national government to "confer on every citizen in the states we represent the American birthright of impartial suffrage and equality before the law." The resolution was greeted with thunderous applause, but Botts interrupted to present a series of resolutions denying Congressional authority to legislate on the suffrage. When the delegates refused to permit him to enter his resolutions in the "Journal of Proceedings," Botts angrily withdrew.

Without an official chairman, the rump convention proceeded to adopt the report advocating Negro suffrage. The delegates gave a vote of thanks to Miss Dickinson and Douglass for their moving addresses, and, after a closing prayer, the convention "tumultuously adjourned *sine die*."[40]

Recalling the exciting closing session of the convention, Douglass wrote in 1882: "The occasion was in no sense ordinary. It was in fact a crisis in the movement for equal rights. . . ." Together with Miss Dickinson and Tilton, Douglass was responsible for turning "the tide of political sentiment in favor of enfranchisement" and in saving the convention "from a reactionary and non-progressive influence."[41] The public endorsement of Negro suffrage by the National Loyalist Convention began a series of significant events which culminated four years later in the adoption of the Fifteenth Amendment.

Meanwhile, Johnson's conduct during his "Swing Around the Circle" was undermining his cause with the people. Even Johnson's friends admitted that it was a gross breach of dignity for the President of the United States to engage in wordy brawls and bandying words with heckling toughs. Henry J. Raymond of the *New York Times,* the President's friend, remarked that no matter what the people might think of Johnson's principles, they were "startled and bewildered" by the way in which he advocated them.[42] Others less friendly said that Johnson had sunk the Presidency to the level of a grog house.

The election of 1866 was an overwhelming victory for the Radicals. When the returns were in, they revealed that the House had a two-thirds majority that could override any Presidential veto.

Douglass had taken to the stump for the Radicals during the campaign. As Congress was about to assemble he analyzed the Republican victory in two articles in the *Atlantic Monthly,* December, 1866, and January, 1867. The people, he insisted, had voted for a reconstruction policy that would protect loyal men of both races, in their persons and property. Every vestige of slavery "must be utterly destroyed" by the new Congress, and the tragic error of permitting the southern states to disfranchise the Negro should be "retrieved." Congress' duty was clear. It was "to establish in the South one law, one government, one administration of justice, one condition to the exercise of the elective franchise, for men of all races and colors alike."

"It must enfranchise the Negro, and by means of the loyal Negroes and the loyal white men of the South build up a national party there, and in time bridge the chasm between North and South, so that our country may have a common liberty and a common civilization."[43]

During the first six months of 1867 the Radical Republican plan of Reconstruction was adopted by Congress over Johnson's veto. On January 8, three days after Johnson had returned the bill with his veto, Congress passed a law giving suffrage to the Negroes of the District of Columbia. In February, March, and July, 1867, the first series of Radical Reconstruction Acts were passed, in each case over Johnson's veto. They declared that no legal governments existed in the late Confederacy, and therefore divided these ten southern states into five military districts each under a general officer of the United States Army. These states were to hold constitutional conventions the delegates to which were to be elected "by the male citizens . . . of whatever race, color, or previous condition." The new constitutions, when accepted by the same electorate, were to retain Negro suffrage, whereupon Congress would restore the lately rebellious states to their place in the Union as soon as they had ratified the Fourteenth Amendment guaranteeing equal rights and citizenship to Negroes.

Commenting on the Reconstruction measures passed by the radicals in Congress, Senator Sumner declared:

"I cannot forget . . . that there is no provision by which each freedman can be secured a piece of land, which has always seemed to me important in the work of reconstruction. . . . It is true that suffrage is given to the Colored race, but their masters are left in power to domineer and even to organize. With their experience, craft and determined purpose, there is too much reason to fear that all your safeguards will be overthrown. . . . "

Like Sumner, Douglass sorely regretted the absence of provisions in the radical plan of Reconstruction to enable the freedmen to become landowners. "The Negro must have a right to the land," he declared. Without land, he would be completely dependent upon the old slave owners whose object was "to get as much work for as little pay as possible." It was impossible for the freedmen to obtain land "on any fair terms" from the former slave owners. "These men," Douglass pointed out, "don't want them to have land. They want to keep them poor and dependent."

Douglass did not call for confiscation and division of the landed estates in the South. But he did urge Congress to enact legislation enabling the Negro masses to purchase land on easy terms. It was the duty of the government, he insisted, "to see not only that the Negro has the right to vote, but that he has a fair play in the acquisition of land; that when he offers a fair price for the land of the South, he shall not be deprived of the right to purchase, simply because of his color."

Douglass knew only too well that the vast majority of the freedmen were too poor to offer "a fair price" for land. After much thought, he outlined a plan for the establishment of a National Land and Loan Company which would be chartered by Congress and capitalized at a million dollars. The company would issue stock "to be sold, and the proceeds held as a fund, with which large tracts of land which are to be sold in any state, can be purchased by the 10 20 50 and even 100,000 acres. These lands thus procured can then be sold or leased to the Freedmen and some capital advanced to aid them to commence working the soil, security being taken on their land and labor."

"What is wanted," Douglass wrote in his "rough outline" of the plan, "is capital that can buy and hold those lands until they can be divided up into small farms, and sold to the colored people, who with proper instructions, can then go to work and make themselves homes. They will do it, and do it successfully if they have a fair chance. . . . Unless something of this kind is done thousands, I fear, will continue to live a miserable life and die a wretched death."[44]

But Douglass' plan, like all proposals for distribution of land among the freedmen, was too radical for the bulk of the industrial and financial leaders who dominated the Republican party, and was shelved. Years later, Douglass pointed to the failure to provide for the economic emancipation of the freedmen as the basic flaw in the Reconstruction policies of the Republican Party. By rejecting the Negro's cry for land, the Republican Party had sealed the fate of democracy in the South, and paved the way for the retention of strong remnants of the old slave system based upon the plantation system.

"Could the nation have been induced to listen to those stalwart Republicans, Thaddeus Stevens and Charles Sumner," Douglass declared in 1880, "some of the evils which we now suffer would have been averted. The Negro would not today be on his knees, as he is, supplicating the old master class to give him leave to toil. He would not now be leaving the South as from a doomed city and seeking a home in uncongenial climes, but tilling the soil in comparative independence. He would not now be swindled out of his hard earnings by money orders for wages with no money in them . . . as is now the case because left by our emancipation measures at the mercy of the men who had robbed him all his life and his people for centuries."[45]

The summer of 1867 was an exciting period in Douglass' life. In July he met his brother Perry for the first time in forty years. When Reverend T. W. Conway met Perry in New Orleans and learned that he was Frederick Douglass' brother, he arranged to send him and his family of six to J. J. Spellman in New York City who in turn helped them reach Rochester. Douglass returned from a visit to Virginia to find his brother and his family awaiting him. "The meeting," he wrote Spellman, " . . . is an event altogether too affecting for words to describe." Douglass built a "snug little cottage" on his grounds where his brother and his family could live. "I have been keeping a kind of hotel all summer," he wrote joyfully to Tilton in September.[46]

On the last day in July Douglass received a letter with the words "Executive Mansion, Washington, D. C." embossed on the stationery. It read:

"July 29, 1867

"Mr. Frederick Douglass

"My Dear Sir

"I hope you will not be surprised at this proposition, I make to you—in a *Private* and Confidential manner.

"There are great many Persons that are of the opinion that the Freedman's Bureau, (its *affairs*), are not conducted as they ought to be, and the object of this note is to know if I secure the appointment of you at the head of the Bureau (in the place of Gen'l Howard), now with regard to Genl Howard, he is a good man, yet at the same time he is timid and lacks moral courage.

"And I must confess I know of no man—white or colored would be better adapted to the Place than your Humble Self.

"Hoping this will find you and yours in good Health.

"I am truly

"your friend

"Wm. Slade.

"P.S. Let me hear from you at your earliest convenience. Keep this Private & Confidential."[47]

Behind the letter lay palace politics. In the summer of 1867, Johnson had finally decided to remove Secretary Stanton from office. Stanton had been a thorn in his side because of his radical views. Aware of the indignant outbursts that would arise from the Radical Republicans, the President hit upon the plan of confusing the issue by appointing a Negro as commissioner of the Freedmen's Bureau.[48] With Douglass as head of the Bureau, it would be difficult for the Radicals to accuse Johnson of being the slaveholder's tool.

Johnson sounded out several members of the Cabinet. When O. H. Browning, secretary of the interior, was told that "it would be a good thing" to appoint Douglass, the latter agreed, but advised Johnson to ascertain whether Douglass would accept the post. On July 17 Johnson dispatched Carter Steward, a friend, to Rochester. But Douglass was out of town and the message was never delivered. A week later, the President discussed the subject with Gideon Wells, the Secretary of the Navy. Welles was cool to the idea of appointing Negroes to fill important public positions, but agreed that if for political reasons a colored man had to be appointed to some office, the Commissioner of the Freedmen's Bureau was an appropriate post. Besides, he felt that though General Howard was "a very good sort of man," he was "loose in talking and appropriating public property," and was "so intensely Radical" that he "wished him removed, and an overturn in the management of the Bureau."⁴⁹

William Slade, one of Johnson's personal friends, was assigned the task of approaching Douglass. While his letter to Douglass did not mention the President, it was clear that Slade spoke for Johnson. Douglass thought the matter over carefully for two weeks, and, on August 12, he wrote to Slade declining the offer. He admitted that he was tempted by the offer since the post would "furnish me instrumentalities and opportunities which I doubt not I should have the heart and head to employ to the great advantage of our newly emancipated people." " . . . With my present views of duty," he added, "I could not accept that office if it were tendered to me."

Evidently Slade was not convinced that Douglass meant what he had written, for on August 18, he wrote again expressing regret that his offer had not been accepted and urging Douglass to "give the subject more consideration." But Douglass stuck to his original reply. Undoubtedly he had been sorely tempted to accept. The position was one of major political importance, and as head of the Bureau he would have had over two thousand men—officers, agents and other employees—under him. But he realized that acceptance of this position would immediately rouse a storm of indignation among the Negro people and would completely cut him off from the Radical Republicans. As Carl Schurz pointed out later: " . . . when a Republican accepted office from Andrew Johnson on Andrew Johnson's terms to take the place of an officeholder dismissed for fidelity to his principles, he could not be forgiven. The so-called 'bread-and-butter-brigade' was looked down upon with a contempt that could hardly be expressed in words."⁵⁰

The news of the offer and of Douglass' refusal became public in September when Tilton published the story in *The Independent*. Tilton added his own editorial comment in a sentence which was widely reprinted: "The greatest black man in the nation did not become a tool of the meanest white." Douglass, however, was somewhat annoyed that the story had come out since his letter to Tilton "though not marked private was not intended for publication." Evidently he was also a bit embarrassed by Tilton's fulsome praise, for he wrote to Smith: "Friend Tilton has made a little too much of my declining the Freedmen's Bureau. I told him I had been applied to by parties near the President to know if I would accept the office, and that I said no."[51]

Events soon convinced Douglass that his decision had been a wise one. Every day the Johnson administration became more discredited as the Radicals redoubled their attacks on the President. The removal of Secretary Stanton from office climaxed the discontent. A clamor arose for the President's impeachment. Articles of impeachment were voted by the House and the trial began before the Senate, the Chief Justice of the United States presiding.

Johnson was acquitted, but his power was extensively curtailed. The important question now was: who should succeed Johnson? General Grant was the hero of the day, and nobody was surprised when the Republican convention at Chicago in May, 1868, nominated him for President on a platform calling for "equal suffrage." A month later the Democratic Party nominated Horatio Seymour of New York for President on a platform condemning the whole Republican policy of Reconstruction, including Negro suffrage, as "unconstitutional, revolutionary, and void."[52]

Douglass supported Grant. Some Abolitionists were reluctant to endorse the Republican standard-bearer on the grounds that a civilian, not a soldier, was needed in the White House and that a Presidential candidate should be a man of frank convictions who spoke out boldly on the issues of the day.[53] Douglass brushed all this aside. There was but one choice. In nine Southern states—Alabama, Arkansas, Florida, Louisiana, Georgia, North Carolina, South Carolina, Virginia, and Mississippi—conventions had been held at which Negroes and whites had drawn up the most progressive constitutions in the history of the South. These constitutions granted the franchise to the common people regardless of race or color, provided public education and social legislation to the poor people, and included many other progressive reforms which promised to bring a more democratic way of life to the South. A vote for Seymour meant a vote for the overthrow of these constitutions; it meant Negro disfranchisement; it meant ignorance for the mass of the southern people. Seymour's election would signify that Lee had triumphed at Appomattox. A victory for the Republican Party meant the continuance of the new southern governments; it meant the recognition of Negro suffrage.

Cognizant of the importance of the election, Douglass helped to deliver votes to Grant. "I am not much of a *stumper*," he wrote to Smith, "but I shall do a little in this line during the canvass."[54] His major contribution was the oft-repeated speech, "The Work Before Us," originally published in *The Independent* of August 27, 1868. Douglass reminded his audiences that for several decades the Democratic Party had had but one purpose—"to serve the great privileged class at the South." If victorious it would continue its role by delivering the Negro laborers back to the slaveholding class. The election of 1868 was "but a continuation of the mighty struggle of a great nation to shake off an old and worn-out system of barbarism, with all its natural concomitants of evil. It is a part of our thirty years' effort to place the country in harmony with the age, and to make her what she ought to be—a leader, and not a mere follower, in the pathway of civilization." The duty of progressive Americans was clear—to elect Grant "by a vote so pronounced and overwhelming as to extinguish every ray of hope to the rebel cause."

When Grant rolled up his decisive majorities, Douglass rejoiced. The blood and treasure of the last seven years had not been spent in vain. The opportunity for further advances was now at hand.

The Fifteenth Amendment

Undoubtedly Douglass expected to receive a political appointment for his services in the campaign of 1868. But other than the unimportant appointment to the Legislative Council of the District of Columbia in 1870 which permitted him to use the title Honorable, nothing was forthcoming from the administration. Through an unfortunate misunderstanding, he barely missed the appointment of minister to Haiti.

Early in April, Grant nominated Ebenezer D. Bassett as minister to Haiti. Delighted at the selection of a Negro for the post, Douglass hastened to congratulate his friend.

"Your appointment," he wrote on April 13, "is a grand achievement for yourself and for our whole people. It forms an important point in the History of our progress and upward tendency. I have no doubt you see the importance of your position. As you shall acquit yourself in it—wisely or otherwise, we shall be effected favorably or unfavorably."[1]

Some opposition, however, developed in the Senate to Bassett's confirmation. Several Senators doubted his fitness for the office, and were disappointed that Douglass had not received the appointment. Suddenly a report appeared in the press stating "that Frederick Douglass has written to his friends at Washington, declining to accept the Haytian mission, stating that he could not afford to accept it, and that he had made up his mind to live and die in his native land." Among these friends George T. Downing, Negro leader in Rhode Island, was prominently mentioned.[2]

Infuriated, Douglass wrote to his friend Tilton of *The Independent* urging him to print a denial of the report. Tilton published the following statement from Douglass: "It is quite true that I never sought this office or any other, but it is equally true that I have never declined it, and it is also true that I would have accepted, had it been offered."[3]

When J. Sella Martin, Negro leader in Massachusetts, learned that Douglass had not declined the Haitian mission, he urged Senator Sumner to oppose confirmation of Bassett's appointment. Sumner agreed that Douglass was the logical man for the post, doubted Bassett's fitness, but declared that only Grant could withdraw the nomination. Martin decided to get to the President. "Believing that all intelligent colored men and knowing all the fair-minded men of whatever party among the whites," he wrote Douglass, "preferred you to any colored man in America for the position of Minister to Haiti; I requested a good and true member of Congress to convey to Gen. Grant the information that the Nation had been rushed in regard to you."

Grant was actually approached, but refused to withdraw Bassett's name. He told Martin that, as many of his nominations would be rejected, he felt unwilling to aid his enemies by withdrawing any "except for absolute unfitness."

After Bassett was confirmed by the Senate, Martin tried to persuade Sumner to push for Douglass' nomination as minister to Brazil or Costa Rica on the theory that "a colored man should be sent to a white government." Sumner agreed, but upon inquiry discovered that a man who had proved his "service to the party and fitness for the place" had already been promised the post. When Martin suggested that he urge Grant to appoint Douglass Minister to Equador, Sumner replied:

"If Mr. Douglass will do me the honor of consulting me I would recommend that he take no place abroad so far away as to deprive us of the [*illegible*] influence of his talents and position at home."[4]

Swallowing his disappointment, Douglass turned his attention to launching a movement to protect the Negro vote. Under Radical Republican pressure, Congress had passed and the states had ratified the Fourteenth Amendment. But Douglass was aware that any state could disfranchise the Negro if it wished. It would mean reduced representation in Congress, but if a state was willing to surrender a number of seats in the House, it could bar Negroes from the ballot-box. In a score of northern states, moreover, Negroes were still disfranchised. A constitutional amendment was needed stating unequivocally that a citizen's right to vote should not be denied by any state or by the national government because of race or color.

For many Republican politicians cold facts spoke more effectively than doctrines of freedom and equality. Although Grant had won by an electoral vote of two hundred and fourteen to eighty, his popular vote had been 3,000,000 to Seymour's 2,700,000. Without the four hundred and fifty thousand Negro votes, Grant would have been defeated![5] This gave the Republicans cause for alarm. It lent impetus to the movement for a constitutional amendment that would not only make safe the Negro majorities in the South, but would give the ballot to Negroes in northern states and thus assure for a time at least more than a half million Negro votes for the Republican Party.

On January 11, 1869, a joint resolution from the Committee on the Judiciary was reported in the House of Representatives proposing an amendment which provided that the right to vote of no citizen be abridged by the United States or any state by reason of race, color, or previous condition of servitude. The following day a convention of Negroes met in Washington. The delegates had come from seventeen states to discuss the major problems confronting their people. But uppermost in their minds was the effect the gathering would have on those members of Congress who were hesitating about throwing their support behind the proposed constitutional amendment. "No ordinary motive or occasion," observed the *Washington Chronicle,* "could call together a hundred and fifty men, many of them travelling long distances at heavy cost, and but few of them wealthy. They came under the pressure of a great need, and inspired with a sense of the vital importance of their wishes not merely to themselves, but to all loyal men in the South, and to the peace and welfare of the Republic."[6]

The 1869 Colored Convention was the first truly *national* convention of the Negro people in the United States. In addition to the large percentage of the northern and western states, all the southern and Border States were represented by "colored men, of fine presence and manly bearing, from Virginia, North Carolina, Georgia, Alabama, Florida, Mississippi, Louisiana, Tennessee, Maryland and Delaware, of the old slave States."[7] As one paper noted: "Many of them but yesterday held as property, to-day coming together to ask full and equal rights, defended by law and guaranteed by the Constitution all over the land, and making their just requests with a dignity, eloquence, clearness, and breadth of comprehension that command respect."[8]

Outstanding Negro leaders were present at the Convention—Douglass, Langston, Garnet, Downing, J. Sella Martin, Purvis, William Howard Day, George B. Vashon, Isaiah Wier, and others. The honorary delegates included Radical Republicans, southern white Senators and Representatives in Congress.

Douglass was elected permanent president of the gathering. His opening remarks, greeting the delegates, expressed gratification that many colored men from the South were present. He was especially interested in learning how they felt and what program they believed necessary for the Negro people. The answer came quickly enough as delegate after delegate from the South arose to demand "a guaranteed political equality, and equal education, industrial, and social freedom, irrespective of complexional difference."

The delegates adopted resolutions urging colored people throughout the land to observe January 1 "as a proper time to celebrate the practical carrying out of the great principles enunciated in the Declaration of Independence." One resolution called upon the nation to keep sacred "the memory of the late great Commoner, Thaddeus Stevens," who had died during the previous summer. The resolutions praised the "original Abolitionists," noting that "the present advanced public sentiment" was largely due to their "heroic, self-sacrificing advocacy and defence of the right." They congratulated Congress on its Reconstruction policies, called on it to establish governments in states yet unreconstructed, to pass a pending bill which would throw open the public lands of Mississippi, Georgia, and Alabama to homestead settlers, Negro and white, and to appoint two Negro justices of the peace in the District of

Columbia. They called for continued support of the Republican Party, declaring that "whatever shortcomings may be laid to the Republican party, it is the party through which the rights legally secured to the colored American in his country were secured; that it has our gratitude, and shall receive our support; that no other party need hope to alienate us therefrom unless by outstripping it in consistency and in an honest advocacy of genuine democratic principles."

But the delegates did more than listen to speeches and pass resolutions. A committee visited President Grant to congratulate him on his election, and reported that the President had promised to use his authority to guarantee that "the colored people of the Nation may receive every protection which the law gives to them." Another committee interviewed Congressmen to urge them to support the Fifteenth Amendment, and was happy to report that it had met with a "favorable reception." Still another committee had a session with the Senate Committee on Military Affairs and demanded that Negro soldiers be granted whatever bounties were given to others in the armed forces.

After issuing an address to the people of the United States stressing the need for a guaranteed franchise, and appointing a committee, with headquarters in Washington, to organize a campaign "to secure homes for the homeless of the South," the Colored Convention adjourned. "The assemblage," wrote a reporter who had attended the sessions, "presented a remarkable spectacle, one never to be forgotten by those who were in attendance."[9]

On February 25, 1869, after receiving the necessary two-thirds vote in both houses of Congress, the Fifteenth Amendment was submitted to the State legislatures. Douglass was jubilant, and intensified his agitation. From platforms all over the North he reiterated his message that the nation's interest would best be served by guaranteeing the Negro's right to the ballot. He called on the veterans of the anti-slavery struggle to lend their influence to the campaign for the ratification of the new amendment.

From one quarter Douglass' appeal met with a painful rebuff. Susan B. Anthony, Elizabeth Cady Stanton, and many of their followers accused Douglass of pushing one reform at the expense of another, of advancing Negro suffrage and neglecting woman suffrage.

During the war the country had been so engrossed in the conflict that the woman's movement could make no headway. The women had abandoned their conventions, devoting their energies to the Sanitary Commissions and the Women's Loyal Leagues.

The war over, the women revived their campaign for equality. As in the past, Douglass was ready to champion their cause. When the American Equal Rights Association was founded in May, 1866, with the aim of securing suffrage for Negro men and all women, he was chosen one of the three vice-presidents.[10] Despite an avalanche of ridicule heaped upon the association by the press he continued to co-operate with the organization. The following description in the *New York Herald* of the Albany Convention of the Equal Rights Association in November, 1866, was typical:

"All the isms of the age were personated there. Long-haired men, apostles of some inexplicable emotion or sensation; gaunt and hungry looking men, disciples of bran bread and white turnip dietetic philosophy; advocates of liberty and small beer, professors of free love in the platonic sense, agrarians in property and the domestic virtues; infidels, saints, Negro-worshippers, sinners and short-haired women. . . . Long geared women in homespun, void of any trade mark, and worn to spite the tariff and imposts; women in Bloomer dress to show their ankles and their independence; women who hate their husbands and fathers, and hateful women wanting husbands. . . . altogether the most long-necked, grim-visaged, dyspeptic, Puritanical, nasal-twinged agglomeration of isms ever assembled in this or any other state."[11]

It was at the Albany Convention of the Equal Rights Association that Douglass seriously clashed with the feminist leaders. He was concerned that Miss Anthony and Mrs. Stanton seemed more interested in the woman question than in a solution of the problems of Reconstruction, and that they were beginning to talk of opposing any extension of suffrage to male Negroes if political enfranchisement of their sex was not included. Douglass warned the Equal Rights Association that it was in danger of becoming "*merely* a woman's rights convention," and appealed that the "women must take the Negro by the hand." True, the Association had been organized to secure the suffrage for women as well as for colored men. But the question of the hour was which group should receive priority. To women the ballot was desirable, to the Negro it was a matter of life and death. Pointing to riots against Negroes in a number of cities, Douglass declared: "With us disfranchisement means New Orleans, it means Memphis, it means New York mobs."

Douglass objected to Susan B. Anthony's praise of James Brooks' championship of woman suffrage in Congress, pointing out that it was simply "the trick of the enemy to assail and endanger the right of black men." Brooks, former editor of the *New York Express,* a viciously anti-Negro, pro-slavery paper, was playing up to the leaders of the women's movement in order to secure their support in opposing Negro suffrage. Douglass warned that if the women did not see through these devices of the former slaveowners and their northern allies, "there would be trouble in our family."[12]

Despite his differences with the woman's rights leaders, Douglass still co-operated with them on certain specific issues. He joined Miss Anthony and Mrs. Stanton in petitioning the New York legislature to permit women and colored men to vote for delegates to the state constitutional convention. Along with Henry Ward Beecher and Mrs. Stanton, Douglass was appointed a representative of the Equal Rights Association to the constitutional convention to argue for the elimination of the $250 property qualification for Negro suffrage and the extension of the franchise to women.[13]

But the areas of co-operation rapidly narrowed. The women leaders were incensed at the indifference of the Republican Party to their demands, and in their anger began to echo the arguments of the most backward opponents of Negro suffrage. Women who had been active Abolitionists now argued that before the "ignorant black man" should be given the ballot, intelligent and cultured white women should be enfranchised. Some ardent feminists went as far as to appeal to southerners to support their cause on the ground that the enfranchisement of women would provide a bulwark in the South against Negro rule. Henry B. Blackwell, husband of Lucy Stone, even dispatched an open letter to southern legislatures in which he set out to prove that by granting suffrage to women the combined white vote would be increased sufficiently to defeat the combined Negro vote and thus "the Negro question would be forever removed from the political arena."[14]

Douglass was conscious of the women's bitterness that a golden opportunity was slipping through their fingers. At the second anniversary of the Equal Rights Association in May, 1868, he attempted to assuage their feelings. There had never been an hour, he told them, in which he had denied the right of women to the ballot. He shared their desire for a quick victory, but the realities of the political situation demanded that they hold off for a while. The great danger was that the linking of woman suffrage with Negro suffrage would seriously lessen the chances of securing the ballot for colored men, and to the Negro, he repeated, the ballot was "an urgent necessity." The people were ready to listen to the Negro's claims, but they still remained to be convinced of the necessity of woman suffrage. Why then jeopardize the real possibility of securing Negro suffrage by making it dependent upon the achievement of woman suffrage? In ten years, in five years, perhaps in three, it would be the woman's hour. But Gettysburg and Atlanta had not been fought on the woman question.

The women were not moved by Douglass' arguments, but they re-elected him a vice-president of the Equal Rights Association.[15]

Douglass reiterated his position later in the year at the Boston Woman's Convention, this time stressing the point that the achievement of woman suffrage "depended upon the preliminary success of Negro suffrage." The reporter for *The Independent* noted that Douglass "shone; all the old revolutionary fire broke out" as he advanced this argument. But Lucy Stone was unconvinced, and vigorously disagreed with Douglass.[16]

The real split between Douglass and the feminists occurred during the period of the ratification of the Fifteenth Amendment. As the proposed amendment did not bar discrimination at the ballot-box because of sex, the adherents of Miss Anthony and Mrs. Stanton were indifferent to Douglass' appeal that they support its ratification. A heated controversy broke out at the annual meeting of the Equal Rights Association in New York early in May, 1869. Douglass stressed the special character of the problems confronting his people. "When women," he said, "because they are women, are dragged from their homes and hung upon lamp-posts; when their children are torn from their arms and their brains dashed upon the pavement; when they are objects of insult and outrage at every turn; when they are in danger of having their homes burnt down over their heads; when their children are not allowed to enter schools; then they will have an urgency to obtain the ballot." When a person in the audience shouted, "Is that not all true about black women?" Douglass replied: "Yes, yes, yes, it is true of the black woman, but not because she is a woman but because she is black." Women, he went on, had many ways to redress their grievances; the Negro had only one.

The women applauded, but they were by no means convinced. They revealed their feelings by rejecting a resolution introduced by Douglass stating that the Association "hails the extension of suffrage to any class heretofore disfranchised, as a cheering part of the triumph of our whole idea," and that the delegates "gratefully welcome the pending fifteenth amendment, prohibiting disfranchisement on account of race, and earnestly solicit the State Legislatures to pass it without delay." A majority of the women were not impressed by the fact that Douglass' resolution spoke of the amendment as the "culmination of one-half of our demands," that it called for the redoubling "of our energy to secure the further amendment guaranteeing the same sacred rights without limitation to sex." They retaliated by asserting: "That until the constitution shall know neither black nor white, neither male nor female, but only the equal rights of all classes, we renew our solemn indictment against that instrument as defective, unworthy, and an oppressive charter for the self-government of a free people."[17] The feminists who dominated the convention were quite prepared to see the Fifteenth Amendment go down to defeat rather than support a progressive measure which did not include the enfranchisement of women. Before the meeting adjourned, they dissolved the Equal Rights Association and formed the National Woman's Suffrage Association which was completely divorced from the question of Negro suffrage.

Douglass regretted that he had to part company with many women who were his personal friends and with whom he had worked so closely for almost thirty years. But his spirit was lifted. Victory was in the air. The Fifteenth Amendment was being ratified by state after state. On February 25, 1870, Hiram R. Revels, a free Negro born in North Carolina, came to Washington to fill the seat in the United States Senate previously occupied by Jefferson Davis.

March 30, 1870, was a memorable date: President Grant proclaimed the adoption of the Fifteenth Amendment. In his special message to Congress, Grant declared that the amendment was "a measure of grander importance than any other one act of the kind from the foundation of our free government to the present time."[18]

The Negro people and their friends were jubilant. Celebrations were the order of the day. Amid the rejoicing, Douglass did not forget his pledge to the women of America. He called for the immediate organization of a campaign for a new amendment to the constitution, granting woman suffrage, and he advised colored women to prepare themselves "when the sixteenth amendment becomes law to co-operate in the various schemes which will be presented to their favor."[19]

On April 19, 1870, ten days after the ratification of the Fifteenth

Amendment, the American Anti-Slavery Society met for the last time. Its mission was fulfilled. All that remained was to meet and disband. The streets in the neighborhood of Apollo Hall in New York City were alive with Negroes in joyous procession. The hall was crowded. Wendell Phillips, president of the Society, was in the chair, and the "old guard"—Lucretia Mott, O. B. Frothingham, Robert Purvis, Julia Ward Howe, Abby Kelley Foster, John T. Sargent, Douglass, Garnet, and others—sat on the platform.

Letters were read from a host of co-workers who could not be present. Then came the speeches. Douglass, suffering from hoarseness, made a brief but moving address. He found it difficult to believe that the events of the past few years had actually occurred: "I seem to myself to be living in a new world. The sun does not shine as it used to. . . . Not only the slave emancipated, but a personal liberty bill, a civil rights bill, admitted to give testimony in courts of justice, given the right to vote, eligible not only to Congress, but the Presidential chair—and all for a class stigmatized but a little while ago as worthless goods and chattels. . . ."

Many gave credit to God for this amazing change, but he believed that it was men and women who deserved the thanks. "I like to thank men," he declared. " . . . I want to express my love to God and gratitude to God, by thanking those faithful men and women, who have devoted the great energies of their soul to the welfare of mankind. It is only through such men and such women that I can get a glimpse of God anywhere."

Douglass concluded on a characteristic note. The final meeting of the Anti-Slavery Society did not mean that the work of the movement was done. It had merely changed its form:

"I don't want to part from you at all; and I am glad to know that we are to unite in other works, and that though the form of this association shall be dissolved, the spirit which animates it . . . is to continue its activity through new instrumentalities, for the Indian whose condition to-day is the saddest chapter of our history. . . . And our energies are not only to be devoted to this, but to the interests of suffering humanity everywhere; and of woman, too, for whose cause we can now labor upon a common platform."

Phillips stressed the same theme in closing the evening's proceedings. "And so, friends," were his final words, "we will not say, 'Farewell,' but we will say, 'All hail, welcome to new duties.' We sheathe no sword. We only turn from the front rank of the army upon a new foe."[20]

At the business meeting which followed, the American Anti-Slavery Society adjourned *sine die*.

Douglass devoted the next few weeks to a round of ratification celebrations. Speaking in Tweedle Hall, Albany, he paid tribute to those who were most responsible for the great victory. He assigned the number one position to Wendell Phillips. "None have been more vigilant, clear-sighted, earnest, true and eloquent," he declared. "Without office, without party, only a handful at his back, he has done more to lead and mould public opinion in favor of equal suffrage than any man I know of." After Phillips came Miss Dickinson and Theodore Tilton who had started the ball rolling for equal suffrage by their determined stand at the Loyalist Convention in September, 1866. Then came Charles Sumner—"where shall we find one man to whom the colored citizens of the United States owe a larger debt of gratitude than to Charles Sumner"— Thaddeus Stevens, William D. Kelley, Benjamin F. Butler, and General Grant. The last-named merited special praise, for "though all else had been for us, if he had been against us we could not have met here."

Douglass also read off the names of the honored dead—Owen Lovejoy, Joshua R. Giddings, Henry Winter Davis, and especially Lincoln and John Brown. "This is their day as well as ours," he went on. "The event we celebrate will serve better than marble, brass, iron or granite, to keep their memories fresh in the minds of their countrymen and mankind."

"We are a great nation—not we colored people particularly, but all of us [he concluded]. We are all together now. We are fellow-citizens of a common country. What a country—fortunate in its institutions, in its fifteenth amendment, in its future. We are made up of a variety of nations—Chinese, Jews, Africans, Europeans, and all sorts. These different races give the Government a powerful arm to defend it. They will vie with each other in hardship and peril, and will be united in defending it from all its enemies, whether from within or without."[21]

Modesty had kept Douglass from including himself among those primarily responsible for the achievement of equal suffrage. But letters from Negroes all over the country poured in on Douglass assuring him that his contribution was not forgotten. The following is typical:

"Let me congratulate you & your friends, you have won the victory! How gladdening must it be for your heart to consider the great triumph you have so considerably contributed to win for your race.

"For my part, as a member of that same race, I feel that I owe you in admiration, & gratitude a debt which is in no mortal power to pay on this earth."²²

Mingled with the words of gratitude were some of condemnation. A number of Negroes, especially colored clergymen, were shocked at the failure to list God as primarily responsible for the victory. They were also indignant because of Douglass' remark at the final meeting of the American Anti-Slavery Society. Douglass decided to meet his critics head-on, and, in his speech on April 26 at the great ratification celebration in Horticultural Hall, Philadelphia, he returned to the subject:

"I dwell here in no hackneyed cant about thanking God for this deliverance. . . .

"I object to it largely, because I find that class of men who have done nothing for the abolition of slavery themselves, and would do nothing for the abolition of slavery, but led everything against the abolition of slavery, always holding us back by telling us that God would abolish slavery in his own good time. So they want us to join them in thanking God for the deliverance.

"God has given to man certain great powers, and man, in the exercise of these great powers, is to work out his own salvation—the salvation of society—eternal justice, goodness, mercy, wisdom, knowledge, with these gospels of God to reform mankind, and my thanks to-night are to willing hearts and the willing hands that labored in the beginning, amid loss of reputation, amid insult and martyrdom, and at imminent peril of life and limb. My thanks are to those brave spirits who in an evil hour had the courage and devotion to remember and stand by the cause of liberty, and to demand the emancipation of the bondmen."

Douglass' forthright assertion of his philosophy by no means placated his critics. Neither did other sections of his Philadelphia address. Discussing the duty of the Negro voters now that the Fifteenth Amendment was a reality, he criticized those who cried that "if the black man, in this enlightened age, should vote the Democratic ticket, let him be accursed; let him be denounced."

"Gentlemen," he continued, "I do not share that opinion at all. I am a Republican—a Black Republican dyed in the wool—and I never intend to belong to any other party than the party of freedom and progress. But if any one of my colored fellow-citizens choose to think that his interests, and his rights, and the interests of the country, can be better subserved by giving his vote against the Republican party, I, as an American citizen, and as one desirous to learn the first principles of free government, affirm his undoubted right—to vote as he chooses. . . . I believe in a free conscience, both religiously and politically. . . . I am down upon any one who begins to question a man who is going to vote a ticket different from his own. . . . Nothing! nothing! nothing! will tarnish our liberty in this country so much as doing that. We are to respect each other's rights."

Douglass turned next to the question of religious liberty. Many Negroes, he observed, boasted that in Cincinnati "the first vote given by the colored people was in favor of retaining the Bible in our common schools." He acknowledged that they had "an undoubted right" so to vote, but insisted that his people respect the right of any colored man to vote to remove the whole question of religion from the schools "who, by experience, by reading, by knowledge, honestly believes that it is unjust to the Catholic population of this country to impose upon them the reading of King James' version of the Bible to the exclusion of theirs. . . ." He, for one, would have voted against the measure: ". . . my command to the church, and all denominations of the church whether Catholic or Protestant is, hands off this Government. And my command to the Government is hands off the church."[23]

Douglass' profound and courageous remarks were greeted with cheers. But a number of Negroes of Philadelphia, particularly the colored clergymen, were furious. Not only did they disagree with Douglass, but they were frightened lest his observations be accepted as the sentiments of the Negro people generally. To meet this problem a meeting was held on May 18 in the Bethel Colored Methodist Episcopal Church of Philadelphia. After the usual devotional exercises, Reverend James Williams addressed the audience. With an air of sorrow he gently rebuked Douglass. "We have assembled to-night to give utterance to our views," he declared, "and while we love Frederick Douglass, we love truth more. We admire Frederick Douglass, but we love God more." He was confident that once Douglass was shown the errors of his thinking, he would change his views.

The other speakers were by no means so mild in their criticism. Reverend J. Frisby Cooper expressed amazement that any intelligent man should even dream of not thanking God for the deliverance of the Negro people from bondage or conceive of public schools without the Bible. Once removed from the schools, the Bible would soon be taken from the churches, and finally it would be removed from the courts of law. The result would be that theft, murder, and every crime known to society would be rampant. He had revered Douglass "for the past twenty-five years," but it now appeared that in his quest for "notoriety or popularity," the Negro leader had made "a fatal mistake."

Isaac C. Weir was bursting with indignation as he addressed the audience. He related that he had hurriedly left Horticultural Hall during Douglass' speech, fearing that if he had remained he would be compelled to stand up and publicly rebuke the speaker. The trouble was that Douglass had been pampered for too many years, and "after so much had been said to pamper him, it is not surprising that he has fallen." No man had a right to vote as he pleased, Douglass to the contrary. "A man has only the right to vote as he pleases in so far as he votes right."

Two sets of resolutions were adopted. The first pointed to the need of the Negro people to thank God continuously "for his interposition in the deliverance of our race," referred to the "strong effort being made by the Roman Catholic Church to exclude the Bible . . . from the public schools of this country," and demanded that the Bible be retained in all schools. The resolution concluded: "That we will not acknowledge any man as a leader of our people who will not thank God for the deliverance and enfranchisement of our race, and will not vote to retain the Bible, the book of God, in our public schools."

The second set of resolutions condemned the "reckless political postulate" that any man had the right to vote as he pleased, asserted that this doctrine actually justified the right of the secessionists in breaking up the Union, and declared that in view of the existence of 1,500,000 enemies of the Negro people in the Democratic Party, they could not conceive of separating themselves "from the political love that exists only in the Republican party."[24]

The severity of the attack upon him did not surprise Douglass. As he pointed out in a letter to the *Philadelphia Press* in reply to his critics: "History proves that there is no malice or cruelty so bitter and unrelenting as that malice and cruelty which clothes itself in saintly robes. . . ." Religious malice was the same in 1870 as in medieval times. Only the methods of punishment had changed. Three centuries ago the weapons of religion against heresy were fire and the rack, but owing "to the enlightenment of the age and the growth of rational ideas among men, to differ with the church to-day does not bring torture and physical death." The worst that bigotry could now do was "to assail reputation." But the fear of such punishment would not keep him from telling the

people the truth. If he had been willing to join in the hallelujahs to religious leaders in his speech at Horticultural Hall, he would have escaped
"the dreadful censure" which had since been heaped upon him. Why did
he refuse to do this?

"I will tell you. Because I would not stultify myself. During forty years
of moral effort to overthrow slavery in this country, this system with all its
hell-black horrors and crimes, found no more secure shelter anywhere than
amid the popular religious cant of the day. One honest Abolitionist was a
greatèr terror to slaveholders than whole acres of camp-meeting preachers
shouting glory to God."

Douglass accused Bishop Campbell, the leading colored clergyman
of Philadelphia, of having instigated the "sham trial" in Bethel Church.
He offered the Bishop a bit of sound advice:

"If Bishop Campbell . . . in place of getting up these church meetings to
try distant heretics like myself, would honestly go to work and endeavor to
reform the character, manners, and habits of the festering thousands of
colored people who live in the utmost misery and destitution in the immediate
vicinity of Big Bethel, he would do more to prove his church sound than by
passing any number of worthy resolutions about thanking God. It was always
more common to meet with men who would profess love to God whom they
have not seen than to show love to man whom they have seen."

In concluding his reply, Douglass challenged Bishop Campbell to
meet him in any public hall in Philadelphia for a full and fair discussion
of the issues involved in the controversy. He had no taste for public
dispute, and he was busy enough "in battling for our common rights
against prejudice and proscription without engaging in debate." But
the people were entitled to have the issues fully clarified. He assured the
Bishop that he held no opinions which he was "not ready to abandon
when convinced of their unsoundness."[25]

While the dispute over thanking God for the Fifteenth Amendment
raged in Philadelphia, the ratification celebrations continued elsewhere.
The month of celebration was climaxed with a tremendous demonstration
in Baltimore on May 19. It opened with a parade during which ten
thousand Negroes, representing regiments, drum corps, fraternal clubs,
secret lodges, and trade unions, marched through the streets to Monument Square. Here Isaac Myers, president of the Colored Caulkers' Union
of Baltimore and of the National Colored Labor Union, opened the
formal part of the day's proceedings. Amid cheers, Myers read letters
from Sumner and Garrison expressing regret that they could not attend.

Then John Mercer Langston spoke and was followed by John A. J. Creswell, the Postmaster-General of the United States.[26]

The audience listened patiently, but they were waiting for the main speaker—Frederick Douglass. A selection from one of the bands preceded his address. Then came the introduction and the tumultuous applause punctuated with loud cheers.

Four and a half years before Douglass had addressed a distinguished audience in Baltimore to celebrate the formal opening of the Douglass Institute founded in his honor for "the intellectual advancement of the colored portion of the community."[27] At that time he had delivered a carefully prepared address. But on May 19, 1870, he was in no mood for a formal speech. His thoughts rambled. He recalled his experiences in Baltimore as a slave, and thanked God that he had been spared to be present at a celebration in the same city to express joy at the granting of the elective franchise of his people. To him it was "the day of all days." He reminded the audience of the progress of the colored man:

"The Negro has now got the three belongings of American freedom. First, the cartridge box, for when he got the eagle on his button and the musket on his shoulder he was free. Next came the ballot-box; some of its most earnest advocates now hardly saw it three years ago, but we'll forgive them now. Next we want the jury-box. While the Negro-hating element sits in the jury-box the colored man's welfare is insecure, and we demand that he be represented in the halls of justice. Nobody will be injured by justice."

He urged the colored people to pay special attention to the education of their children. "Educate your sons and daughters, send them to school, and show that besides the cartridge box, the ballot-box and the jury box, you have also the knowledge box." He pledged his life to the further advancement of his people, saying:

"Forty years ago I sat on Kennard's wharf, at the foot of Philpot Street, and saw men and women chained and put on the ship to go to New Orleans. I then resolved that whatever power I had should be devoted to the freeing of my race. For thirty years, in the midst of all opposition I have endeavored to fulfill my pledge. I am here to-day to pledge myself that whatever remains to me of life shall go in the same direction."

As the day-long celebration drew to its close, the secretary read the resolutions. They expressed the Negro's thanks to God, to the Republican Party and to President Grant. The last of the eight resolutions was adopted with "loud acclaim." It was a tribute to the great leader of the Negro people:

"Resolved, That recognizing in Frederick Douglass the foremost man of color in the times in which we live, and proud to claim him as one 'to the manor born,' we do here most respectfully, yet earnestly, request him to return to us, and by the power of his magnificent manhood help us to a higher, broader, and nobler manhood."[28]

Reconstruction, 1870-1872

In the glow of enthusiasm evoked by the adoption of the Fifteenth Amendment, many of Douglass' friends felt that his work was finished. They were convinced that "all distinctions founded upon race or color have been forever abolished in the United States, and that all special efforts recognizing a different state of fact, are uncalled for, out of time, and hurtful." One went as far as to exclaim: "There are no colored people in this country." Others cautioned Douglass against "demanding too much for the colored people." They reminded him that only a decade ago Negroes were slaves without any rights, and that in an amazingly short time, they had been freed and transformed into American citizens and even granted the right to vote. Why not be satisfied with these gifts, they asked, "at least long enough to allow the nation to take a breath?"[1]

But at the very time Douglass was receiving such advice, a new pattern of oppression, replacing the old slave system, was growing up in the South. The plantation owners, shorn of their source of power by emancipation, devised new methods of reducing the freedman to a state of peonage that would keep him bound hand and foot to the plantation. These former masters banded together and secretly swore never to sell a foot of land to a Negro. Furthermore, they made neighborhood agreements which kept wages for Negro farm workers very low.[2]

When freedmen managed to set themselves up as independent farmers, raids were organized against them. Contracts to Negro farm workers were habitually violated and the freedmen systematically defrauded of their meager earnings. As one freedman put it at a colored convention in Columbia, South Carolina, on November 25, 1869:

"Our people cannot buy decent clothing, nor buy medicine, nor send children to school. The planter says, when the crop is gathered, 'Now, I get two-thirds—you get one-third. You owe me so much, and so much, and this comes out of your third.' And then the man has left but two or three dollars. The magistrates do not do justice. The white men swindle and swindle, and the magistrates say the white man is right every time. We cannot get justice."[3]

Terrorist societies such as the Ku Klux Klan, the Pale Faces, and the Knights of the White Camelia swept down upon Negroes who dared to protest the violation of their rights. Any Negro community which sought to defend its civil liberties soon found its churches and schools a smoking shambles. The knout, the rope, the club, the torch, and the gun were used unsparingly to make the constitutional amendments adopted after the Civil War little better than a mockery of freedom.[4]

When Douglass met delegates at Negro conventions who had lived through the horrors of seeing their families massacred, their churches and schools burned to the ground, and their homes left in smoking ruins, he realized the ridiculousness of the contention that his work was over. Constitutional amendments guaranteeing the Negro equality and fair play looked very well in print, he reminded his friends, but "law on the statute book and law in the practice of the nation are two very different things, and sometimes very opposite things." What were the Fourteenth and Fifteenth Amendments worth to the victims of the Klan terror? What did the ballot mean to men reduced to a state of peonage?

"At the South," he argued, "the Negro dependent upon his enemy for his daily bread cannot long vote or act contrary to the will of those to whom he must necessarily look to that food and raiment which he must have. . . .

"It is a grand thing to have rights secured by constitutional provisions and by legal enactments," Douglass concluded, "but without a public opinion and a Government to enforce them, they are a mockery. To be one half freeman and the other half a slave, to be a citizen and yet treated as an alien, to be a man, and yet not be a man among men, may do for a monster but not for genuine manhood. Until the new citizen can step to the ballot box and deposit his vote in every state in this union with the feeling that every bayonet of the Republic is pledged to his protection and that this pledge will be faithfully redeemed, the work of the war is not complete and freedom is not secure."

To those who called for a halt to agitation on the Negro question, Douglass replied:

"We certainly hope that the time will come when the colored man in America shall cease to require special efforts to guard their rights and advance their interests as a class. But that time has not yet come, and is not even at the door. While the doors of nearly every workshop in the land are closed against the colored race, and the highest callings opened to them are of a menial character; while a colored gentleman is compelled to walk the streets of our large cities like New York unable to obtain admission to the public hotels; while state-rooms are refused in our steamboats, and berths are refused in our sleeping-cars, on account of color, and the Negro is a by-word and a hissing at every corner, the Negro is not abolished as a degraded caste, nor need his friends shut up shop and cease to make his advancement in the scale of civilized life a special work."[5]

Douglass was aware that the battle for the full implementation of the Fourteenth and Fifteenth Amendments would not be easy. "A bitter contest, I fear, is before us," he wrote to Sumner on July 6, 1870. Every agency capable of influencing public opinion had to be brought into play. "Press, platform, pulpit should continue to direct their energies to the removal of the hardships and wrongs which continue to be the lot of the colored people of this country because they wear a complexion which two hundred and fifty years of slavery taught the great mass of the American people to hate, and which the fifteenth amendment has not yet taught the American people to love."[6]

Instead of retiring from the field, Douglass undertook the arduous work of editing and publishing a paper which would assist in "the removal of the hardships and wrongs which continue to be the lot of the colored people of this country. . . . " His explanation for the undertaking was simple:

"From the time I learned to read, and learned the value of knowledge, it was among the deepest and sincerest wishes of my soul, to assist in the deliverance of my people, not only from the terrible bondage of slavery, but from the more terrible bondage of ignorance and vice.

"This sentiment has lost nothing of its vigor by years of active service. Those years of labor have only served to increase and intensify the desire to do yet more in the same cause."[7]

The story of Douglass' second newspaper venture begins before the adoption of the Fifteenth Amendment. As far back as the fall of 1866, Chief Justice Chase and Congressman John C. Underwood had urged Douglass "to establish a press on the soil of Virginia in the interests of Equal Rights." Douglass considered the proposal for several weeks and then decided against it. He explained that the proposed project would limit his work for the full freedom of his people:

"For sometime yet to come," he wrote to Congressman Underwood, "the future of the colored race, will depend more upon the sentiments and opinions of the people of the North and West than upon those of the South. The sceptre has passed from Virginia and the law from beneath her feet. The loyal North and West must now and for sometime to come control not only the destinies of the Negro but that of the nation. I now act upon the mind of the country from Maine to the Mississippi, and am probably doing as much to disseminate sound views of human rights in this way as I could were I to place Baltimore between me and the North and West."[8]

Not until the Fifteenth Amendment had been passed by Congress and submitted to the states for ratification did Douglass feel that he could devote time to a newspaper project. In February and March, 1869, Douglass, his son Lewis, George T. Downing, and a number of other Negro leaders sent out circulars asking financial aid for the publication "of a first class weekly journal in the City of Washington, in the interest of the colored people of America; not as a separate class, but as a part of the *Whole People*. . . ." Such a paper would serve as an educator of the colored people, and would guarantee that "the growing political power in the land represented in the colored man . . . will be wielded . . . not for his special benefit alone, but for the benefit of all who with him compose this Nation."[9]

In late March, 1869, the shareholders of the proposed paper planned that Douglass become editor and J. Sella Martin associate editor. Agreeing that Douglass' work as a lecturer was of vital importance, the shareholders thought that he should continue on the platform and that Martin should serve as resident editor in Washington. Lewis Douglass was proposed as chief compositor and manager of the print shop which, it was hoped, would be manned entirely by colored people. Twenty-five hundred dollars had already been pledged by colored people in Washington, and an equal sum would soon be forthcoming from other Negroes and their white friends. The five thousand dollars would guarantee publication of the weekly for six months after which additional support could be expected, especially when it became known that Douglass was the editor-in-chief. By printing the news vitally affecting the welfare of the colored people in the South, the paper would secure a large body of southern subscribers. Given Douglass' vast experience in journalism and his "great ability and willingness" to serve his people, there was every assurance that "a well conducted weekly paper" would be the result.[10]

Douglass expressed gratitude for the honor conferred upon him, but,

in a letter to J. Sella Martin early in April, refused to accept the invitation
to become the editor-in-chief. It was futile, he pointed out, to attempt
"to venture upon this voyage of journalism upon so slender a Bark as
'five thousand dollars' as a basis. . . . " The vast majority of colored
newspapers hitherto published had "died in their infancy and from
starvation." Should the newspaper be discontinued after six months
because of lack of funds, it "would bring more shame and mortification
to our already sadly depressed people, than had not the attempt been
made at all." He strongly favored the founding of a newspaper for the
freedman which would speak out frankly and without fear of antagonizing anyone. But it should be a paper "which will upon first sight, go
straight to his heart, raise his respect for his race, and kindle his enthusiasm.
A small sheet imperfectly printed upon coarse paper—on the penny-wise
principle, will not answer the purpose. Such a paper will depress rather
than elevate the spirits of our people."[11]

Although deeply disappointed by Douglass' decision, the shareholders
decided to proceed with the publication of the paper. Sella Martin,
however, refused to accept the editorship unless Douglass agreed to serve
as corresponding editor. He assured Douglass that like him he believed
the paper should

"reflect the sentiments and wants of the Freedmen. In other words we
as Northern people should use the advantages that belong to our position in
free Society to lay bare mere party machinations and so draw out the best
intelligence of those to whom we speak while at the same time we should
fearlessly express the peculiar grievances of those who might become the
victim of even the Radicals.

"I insist in short upon our organ being the *Radical* of the radicals."[12]

Douglass agreed to serve as corresponding editor and the final plans
to launch the weekly were drawn up. On January 13, 1870, it made its
appearance in Washington as *The New Era*. Two weeks later Douglass'
first article appeared under the heading, "Salutatory of the Corresponding
Editor." His part in the new journal would be a subordinate one, he
informed the readers, but he assured them "that whatever we can do
consistently with our many other duties and occupations to make *The
New Era* a credit to our cause, our color and our country, shall be earnestly and faithfully done." He called upon "every intelligent and patriotic
colored man in the land" to give full support to a grand national organ
"through which our minutest wrongs may be exposed, our equal rights
asserted, our character defended, our efforts for improvement encouraged,

and our whole relation to the body politic, to which we have already been virtually admitted against long continued and determined opposition, triumphantly vindicated."[18]

As Douglass had predicted, the paper encountered difficulties at once. By the summer of 1870 it was heavily in debt. The shareholders had abandoned the project, Martin had resigned as editor, the type and press were in the hands of creditors, and the paper was about to fold up. Convinced "that this was not the time to allow any proper instrumentality which could be wielded for the benefit of his people to perish," Douglass moved swiftly to prevent the journal from going out of existence. Late in August, he moved to Washington, gave up his lecturing engagements, and purchased one-half interest in both *The New Era* and the printing plant in which it was printed. On September 8, 1870, the paper carried the news that Douglass was the editor of the paper which now was to be called the *New National Era* to distinguish it from many newspapers in the country bearing the old name. In his first editorial, Douglass promised the readers that he would exert every ounce of energy to make the journal "an honor and a help to the newly enfranchised millions whose organ it will in some sense be made. . . . " The paper would serve as "an Advocate and an Educator," and would consider "the whole circle of moral, social, political, educational, and material interests of the newly enfranchised citizen." The editor could not promise to please every one; he could only offer the assurance that he would use his talents for the benefit of all mankind, regardless of race, country, or color:

"To the former slave I say, I too am a former slave; to the colored man I say, I too am a colored man; and to the Indian, Mongolian, Caucasian, to the men of every nation, kindred tongue, and people of all latitudes, longitudes, and altitudes, I say, that I too am a man, and would scorn to demand for the men of my race a single right or privilege that I would not freely grant to you."[14]

On December 12, 1870, Douglass purchased the remaining one-half interest in the *New National Era* and its printing plant for $8,000. Three days later he announced that he was now the sole proprietor of the paper. Two sentences were all that Douglass required to set forth "the broad and strong platform" of the *New National Era:* "Free men, free soil, free speech, a free press, everywhere in the land. The ballot for all, education for all, fair wages for all."[15]

To win support for this platform and to bring his paper closer to the Negro masses, Douglass attended the second annual convention of the National Colored Labor Union in the capacity of "a friend of the labor movement." Delegates from Alabama, Missouri, the District of Columbia, Maryland, Virginia, Rhode Island, New York, Texas, Michigan, Massachusetts, and North Carolina were present when Isaac Meyers, the pioneer Negro labor leader, opened the convention in Washington on January 9, 1871.[16]

This was not the first time Douglass had appeared before a meeting of the colored labor movement. In August, 1869, he had been the principal speaker at a meeting held in Baltimore by the State Labor Union Society organized by Negro trade unionists in Maryland. Using as his subject, "The Equal Right of All Men to Labor," Douglass emphasized the necessity for establishing statewide and national organizations to fight for better conditions for urban and rural Negro workers. Stressing the importance of organizing Negro and white workers together, he warned that discrimination by labor unions because of nationality, sex, or color was suicidal, for it arrayed against each other groups which ought to be allied in the closest union. Unfortunately, he remarked, very few white trade unionists understood the necessity of making common cause with Negro labor. He cited the case of his own son, Lewis. Returned home from the Union army "somewhat broken in health, but still able and willing to work at his trade" as a printer, he could not obtain a job because white members of the Rochester Typographical Union refused to work with a Negro:

"Day after day, week after week, and month after month, he sought work, found none, and came home sad and dejected. I had felt the iron of Negro hate before, but the case of this young man gave it a deeper entrance into my soul than ever before. For 16 years I had printed a public journal in Rochester; I had employed white men and white apprentices during all this time, had paid out in various ways to white men in that city little less than $100,000, and yet here was my son, who had learned his trade in my office, a young man of good character, and yet unable to find work at his trade because of his color and race."[17]

His son's experience had led Douglass to favor the efforts of Negro workers to set up separate trade unions such as the National Colored Labor Union. He shared the attitude of many Negro labor leaders that the trade unions of white workers were showing little interest in the problems that were of special importance to the Negro people. Very few white labor leaders of the period had a real understanding of the issues of Reconstruction as the Negro people understood them. Even William H. Sylvis, one of the most progressive labor leaders in American history and a champion of Negro-white unity in the trade unions, did not understand the significance of the Reconstruction policies of the Radical Republicans for the Negro people. Because the Negroes had not been fully emancipated by the Civil War, Sylvis, like many labor leaders of the post-Civil War era, believed that the immediate future of the Negro people lay in an independent labor party. But the labor reform parties that were launched during Reconstruction ignored the special demands of the Negro people: the protection of political and civil rights, land distribution, and equal rights for black and white workmen.[18]

The Negro workers refused to align themselves with a labor party which did not recognize their special problems. Nor would they vote for a labor party when their votes were necessary for a victory for the Republican Party. While to many white workers there was little difference between the Republican and the Democratic parties, to the Negro workers there was a basic difference. To some white workers the Republican Party was the party of industrialists and financiers responsible for their exploitation. To the Negro workers it was the party that was responsible for their liberation and, despite its limitations, represented their major hope for the future. To imperil the victory of the Republican Party at this historical stage by supporting a third party was to guarantee the destruction of the gains already made by the Negro people.

At the convention of the National Colored Labor Union in January, 1871, Douglass was elected president for the coming year. It was a sign that the organization was becoming a political rather than a trade union movement. Delegate after delegate from the South stressed the fact that the immediate task confronting the Negro workers was to compel the federal government to take vigorous action against Ku Klux terrorism, to protect the colored man's right to vote, and to force Congress to enact Sumner's Supplementary Civil Rights bill. This bill, made into law, would have opened inns, juries, schools, public conveyances, etc., to all without distinction of color. Douglass was viewed as the logical man to lead in the struggle for these demands.[19]

Douglass' conviction that the battle for the freedom of his people was by no means ended was strengthened by his participation in this convention of the National Colored Labor Union. After listening to the description of miserable economic conditions facing Negro workers, he declared:

"Though not political in character, the facts presented in the addresses and reports of the condition and needs of the colored workingmen and women of the South are of a most important character, showing conclusively that 'Reconstruction' is far from complete, in assuring independence and actual personal freedom and safety to colored citizens."[20]

Douglass' paper reported the proceedings, and called upon the federal government to heed the demands of the delegates. "This Government will not have done its duty," cried the editor, "until a school-house is placed at every cross-road of the South and a bayonet between every ballot-box." "Shall the Ku-Klux rule the South?" Douglass asked. "Are our citizens in the South to be protected from this murderous band, or are they to be their victims until the advent of another administration?" He demanded that Congress instantly pass laws giving the President power to abolish the conspiracy against the Federal government and to secure life, liberty, and property in the South. And he added: "We ask Congress, in the name of a continually outraged people to give us some law wherewith we can protect ourselves against the malignity of semi-civilized law-makers and juries in most of the States of the Union."[21]

But a rift had developed in the ranks of the Radical Republicans, and conservative forces in the Republican Party were actively opposing the policy Douglass demanded. Spokesmen for business interests were convinced that as long as the common people in the South—Negroes and poor whites—exercised an influence in the state governments, it would not be safe to invest in southern mines, woolen mills, and cotton factories. Former Radical Republicans, Horace Greeley, editor of the *New York Tribune,* among them, now argued that the South offered vast opportunities for the investment of northern capital, but they insisted that only when Radical Reconstruction was ended would it be profitable for northern business men to look southward for economic expansion. Hence they called for a new southern policy. They urged Congress to pass a universal amnesty bill eliminating discrimination against former Confederates. They frowned upon every suggestion advocating the use of force by the federal government to break up the Ku Klux Klan. They viewed Sumner's Supplementary Civil Rights Bill as a continuation of the mistaken policies of the Radicals. It was time to "have done with Reconstruction," they argued, and to call a halt to legislation in favor of the freedmen. Let bygones be bygones, extend the olive branch to the former secessionists, and prove to the nation that the Republican Party favored wiping out the punitive spirit and replacing it with a program of sectional reconciliation.[22]

In vigorous editorials in the *New National Era,* Douglass lashed out at the Conservative Republicans. His fury mounted when the conservatives balked at enacting legislation to protect the freedmen, and, instead, compelled the appointment of a senatorial committee to conduct an inquiry into conditions in the South.

"What do Republican Senators mean by refusing to give to the black people of the United States the same protection as any other class of citizens?" he asked indignantly. "For they do refuse by their actions in appointing committees of inquiry into the Ku-Klux matter, and giving more time to the rebels to be used in killing and intimidating colored voters. Is there one Republican Senator who doubts the existence of the Klan? We apprehend not."

When Conservative Republicans from the South refused to support Sumner's Supplementary Civil Rights Bill, Douglass was furious:

"Do Republican Senators from the Southern States wish their colored constituents to understand that it is a matter of no consequence to them whether colored people are forced to travel in a manner such as no lady in the land would allow her pet dog to travel," he wrote in January, 1871. "It is the duty of Republican representatives in the Senate and House from the Southern States to aid him in the work, and not sit listlessly as they did in the Senate on the 17th instant when Senator Sumner was striving to bring a measure before the Senate remedying the evil of proscription on account of color."

Douglass warned the Republican Party "not to be over-confident," and not to take the Negro vote for granted. "The colored people are loyal and grateful," he argued, "but they are *people,* and are ready to resent any undue disregard of their just expectations." To give strength to this warning, Douglass appealed directly to the freedmen:

"Colored voters of the South, you must not forget those who forget you and your rights. You must teach them that they are mistaken in considering you mere voting machines, ready and willing to vote for any man calling himself a Republican, who comes before you for your suffrages. . . . Do not vote for a member of Congress who does not aid in giving you 'Equality before the law.' "[23]

Douglass' warnings to the Republican Party together with similar warnings by Negro conventions in the South, at which freedmen resolved that they would not "blindly follow the lead of any sham Republicanism,"[24] were not lost upon the Grant administration. At the time President Grant assumed office, he had indicated that he was not entirely hostile to the southern policy of the Conservative Republicans. In a message to Congress on April 7, 1869, he had recommended that the people of Virginia and Mississippi be allowed to ratify their new constitutions in such a way that clauses discriminating against former Confederates be eliminated. Within three days Congress acted, and Grant signed the measure. The Conservative Republicans were overjoyed. Horace Greeley gleefully predicted that the President would soon go the whole way toward sectional reconciliation thereby hastening "industrial progress and material prosperity" in the South.

But as protests poured in from Negro conventions and mass meetings, the Radical Republicans reminded the administration that in the election of 1868 the colored vote had been decisive in determining the Republican victory. If Grant pursued the policy of the Conservative Republicans, ignored the demands of the Negro people for redress of their grievances, and remained passive while the Klan murdered and intimidated Negro voters, Republican ascendancy in the government would be jeopardized.

As the Klan terror mounted, Grant responded to the proddings of the Congressional Radicals. On February 24, 1871, Hamilton Fish, his Secretary of State, noted in his diary:

"The President refers to the condition of affairs in the South, especially in South Carolina. Read the reports of the State Constable of the condition in several counties; murders, whippings, and violence. He expressed a determination to bring a regiment of cavalry and perhaps one of infantry from Texas, where (he says) they are protecting from the Indians a population who annually murder more Union men, than the Indians could kill of them. . . . "[25]

A month later, Grant sent a message to Congress asking for immediate passage of a law authorizing him to put down lawlessness in the South. The Democrats and Conservative Republicans shrieked that the law would be "an encroachment of the national authority upon the legitimate sphere of self government." But Congress heeded the President's demand, and enacted the Enforcement laws. Undeterred by the outcries of the conservative Republicans, Grant moved against the Klan by proclamations, martial law, suspension of the writ of habeas corpus, the use of troops, federal marshals and deputies, and by vigorous federal prosecutions.[26]

Douglass applauded Grant as vigorously as he denounced the Conservative Republicans. He was not deeply concerned with reformers' complaints about Grant's lack of refinement, his adherence to the spoils system, and his tendency to conduct public affairs as if he still were on the battlefield. What mattered to Douglass was that Grant had retreated from his early flirtations with the Conservative Republicans, and had acted promptly to invoke the power of the federal government against the Ku Klux Klan.

"If we stand by President Grant and his administration," he wrote on April 6, 1871, "it is from no spirit of hero worship or blind attachment to mere party, but because in this hour there is no middle ground. [Grant was] for stamping out this murderous *ku-klux* as he stamped out the rebellion. To desert him now, to refuse to sustain him, to seek in any way to weaken his influence, is the surest way to undo the work of the last ten years, and remand the Negro to a condition in some respects worse than that from which the war for the Union delivered him."[27]

In supporting Grant, Douglass came into conflict with a number of his former associates who were disturbed by corruption in the administration, the hearty reception at Washington of manufacturers' and corporation lobbies, government aid to bankers and brokers, the high tariff policy, and large grants of public land to railroads. Douglass tended to minimize these problems as his eyes were riveted on the success of the President's vigorous southern policy in crushing Klan terrorism and in safeguarding the lives and civil rights of the freedmen. What did concern him deeply was that Sumner, the heroic champion of the Negro people in the government of the United States, had joined the opponents of the Grant administration.

Of all Americans in public life, Sumner ranked highest in Douglass' estimation. "During nearly twenty years you have been to a few of us the leading Statesman of the Republic," he wrote to the Massachusetts Senator on April 29, 1869. "You have so linked your name with the cause of my race that we share in all your triumphs. We are brighter for your glory."[28] Only once in the twenty years had Douglass remonstrated with Sumner. In 1855 he had gently rebuked him for having said in a lecture that the anti-slavery movement "does not undertake to change human nature, or to force any individual into relations of life for which he is not morally, intellectually, and socially adapted." Douglass wrote to Sumner: "Considering the obstinate and persecuting character of American prejudice against color, and the readiness with which those who entertain it avail themselves of every implication in its favor, your remark on the point was unfortunate."[29] Sumner took the advice to heart.

For fifteen years after this incident, Douglass had not once differed with Sumner. But now in 1871 the two men came into sharp conflict over their attitude toward the Grant administration. It started with Grant's attempt to annex the Dominican Republic.

An effort to annex the Negro republic of Santo Domingo had been made during Johnson's administration, but, despite the pressure of business men who were deeply interested in exploiting the resources of the island, it had ended in failure. Grant, an advocate of national expansion, sent General Orville E. Babcock, military secretary to the Chief Executive, to Santo Domingo on a warship with definite instructions from Secretary Fish to resume negotiations for annexation. Babcock was connected with American business men who held speculative concessions in Santo Domingo the value of which would be greatly enhanced by annexation. He met with President Buenaventura Baez according to instructions and, on September 4, 1869, signed an agreement providing for a treaty of annexation between the United States and the Dominican Republic. The agreement contained a specific promise that President Grant would "use all his influence, in order that the idea of annexing the Dominican Republic to the United States may acquire such a degree of popularity among members of Congress as will be necessary for its accomplishment; and he offers to make no communications to that body on the subject until he shall be certain that it will be approved by a majority."[30]

On September 6, Babcock left the Dominican Republic. When he arrived in Washington with his plan for a definitive treaty of annexation, Grant immediately set out to line up senatorial support. With this in mind, he visited Sumner, then Chairman of the Senate Committee on Foreign Relations, and returned to the White House fully convinced that Sumner would back the treaty of annexation.

But Sumner began to see the motives of the business interests behind the treaty of annexation and became convinced that the Dominicans did not want to surrender their independence. He insisted that the landslide for annexation in the plebiscite in Santo Domingo proved nothing because he had learned that "overwhelming force" had been exerted to produce the result. He maintained that the independence of Santo Domingo was of vital importance to the Negro people the world over, and he feared that Haiti's independence would be menaced by the annexation of the Dominican Republic.

Since Sumner's views were supported by a large group of Senators, it soon became evident that Grant would encounter difficulty in securing ratification of the treaty. In an effort to overcome this opposition, Grant presented a lengthy document outlining the merits of annexation to the Senate on May 31, 1870. The people in the Dominican Republic "yearned for the protection of our free institutions and laws, our progress and civilization." If they were not allowed to enter the American Union, they would seek refuge with some European power. The United States had much to gain from annexation: an important naval outpost would be secured, and valuable commercial trade connections established. In short, ratification of the treaty would "redound greatly to the glory of the two countries interested, to civilization and to the extirpation of slavery." It would be "a rapid stride toward that greatness which the intelligence, industry and enterprise of the citizens of the United States entitle this country to assume among nations."

Grant believed sincerely in his arguments for annexation, but they made little impression upon the Senate. On June 30, 1870, when the vote was taken in the Senate, it resulted in a tie—twenty-eight to twenty-eight. Since a two-thirds vote is required for ratification, the treaty was defeated.[31]

As a result, Grant was consumed with violent hatred for Sumner. The latter denied that he had pledged to support the treaty, but Grant was convinced that the Chairman of the Senate Committee on Foreign Relations had broken a promise.[32] As he was unable to hit at Sumner directly as yet, he decided upon an indirect course. John Lathrop Motley, minister to England, was one of Sumner's closest associates. For a long time Grant had wanted to dismiss him, but had not done so out of courtesy to Sumner. Now that Sumner had openly flouted him, Grant acted. The very next day after the treaty of annexation went down in defeat, Grant asked Motley to give up his post.

The Senate having rejected the treaty, Grant still refused to acknowledge failure. In his message of December 5, 1870, he again outlined the advantages to the United States from the annexation of the Dominican Republic. He recommended that Congress authorize the President to send a commission to Santo Domingo to investigate conditions in the republic and to examine the charges that had been brought against the administration. Grant hoped in this way to pave the way for annexation by a joint resolution of Congress which would require only a simple majority in each house.[33]

Before December, 1870, Douglass remained silent on annexation. He had supported the Cuban Revolution of 1868 for independence from Spain. "The first gleam of the sword of freedom and independence in Cuba secured my sympathy with the revolutionary cause, and it did seem to me that our government ought to have made haste to accord the insurgents belligerent rights."[34] Perhaps he therefore felt it incongruous to advocate annexation of a Latin American republic.

Actually, Douglass had been veering toward supporting annexation, and had not come out publicly for the treaty because he was still not convinced that the people of Santo Domingo had really endorsed the proposal.

"To all who have spoken to me in respect to the St. Domingo question," he wrote to Sumner on December 12, 1870, "I have said I must learn the views of Senator Sumner before I commit myself entirely to the annexation of that country to ours. I have no hesitation however in assuring you that if that country honestly wishes to come to us, I now see no reason against the policy of receiving her. I say this supposing the conditions upon which she comes in are all right."[35]

Douglass was in an unhappy position. He was reluctant to differ publicly with Sumner whom he still considered to be "higher than the highest, better than the best of all our statesmen." On the other hand, he could not condone the bitterness with which Sumner attacked Grant. Yet he was profoundly impressed by Sumner's fiery address on December 21, 1870 in opposition to the proposal to send a commission to Santo Domingo. He was hurt, however, that Sumner's hostility to the President had become so acrimonious that he associated Grant's name "with the infamous names" of Pierce, Buchanan, and Johnson. "These names," he reminded Sumner, "in the minds of all loyal and liberty loving men stand under the heaviest reproach, and I candidly think you did wrong to place Grant in that infamous category even by implication." He assured Sumner that he was "slave to no man," and that if Grant should prove to be "unworthy," he would be ready to join "the whole Democratic party in denouncing him." But until that time, he was unalterably opposed to creating a breach in the Republican Party which would lead to the Democrats coming to power. In fact, if the controversy over annexation resulted in splitting the Republican Party, he would have no choice but to oppose annexation. "With the Democratic party in power," he argued, "the annexation of San Domingo would be a calamity to us, and a curse to the people of the country."[36]

On January 10, 1871, Congress passed Senator Morton's resolution authorizing the President to appoint three commissioners to make a careful survey of conditions existing in Santo Domingo and ascertain whether the inhabitants were desirous of being annexed to the United States. Congress also added an amendment stating that the measure did not commit the body to the policy of annexing the republic. Douglass editorially praised the action of Congress. The very fact that Sumner opposed annexation, he wrote on January 12, 1871, "is among the best reasons that can be given for caution and searching inquiry. We say, therefore, let the commissioners go to San Domingo, master the whole facts of the case, and give the country an honest report, upon which Congress can proceed in this business intelligently, and with due regard to the interest of all parties."[37]

Two days after this editorial appeared in the *New National Era*, Douglass was surprised to receive a letter from Hamilton Fish, Secretary of State, notifying him that he had been appointed assistant secretary to the commission of inquiry to Santo Domingo,[38] the commission consisting of former Senator Benjamin F. Wade, Andrew D. White, president of Cornell University, and Dr. Samuel Gridley Howe, the noted Boston reformer.

It is not difficult to understand the President's motive in appointing Douglass. If the latter was convinced, after his visit to the Dominican Republic, to throw his full support to annexation, Douglass could do much to offset Sumner's major arguments against the treaty. Especially would this be true if he were joined in a recommendation in favor of annexation by Dr. Howe who was widely known as a former Abolitionist leader, an advocate of equal rights for the Negro people, and one of Sumner's closest friends.

On January 18, 1871, the commission, accompanied by its secretaries and numerous scientific experts and journalists, set sail for Santo Domingo. It arrived at Samana Bay on January 24, and returned to the United States on March 26.

During the voyage to Santo Domingo and the stay in the Dominican Republic, Douglass was treated with "cordial respect and friendship" by practically all the members of the mission. On board the United States naval steam frigate, *Tennessee,* quarters were assigned to him adjoining those of the commissioners and they all ate their meals together in the Admiral's cabin. He participated, on equal terms, in all the investigations conducted in Santo Domingo and in the adjoining republic of Haiti. The

New York Times later reported that Douglass was "placed on a complete equality in the expedition to San Domingo with the most favored persons attached to it." This, said the *Times,* was in keeping with President Grant's explicit order.[39]

Douglass could not conceal his surprise at such treatment, and leaped to the conclusion that his experience proved that "while all the fools are not dead yet, the American people are rapidly outgrowing their slavery-engendered prejudices, and will one day wonder how they could have so long lived under its degrading spell." At any rate, the attitude of some of the members of the expedition towards Negroes was somewhat altered by their five-week contact with Douglass. W. H. Hurlbert, correspondent of the viciously anti-Negro *New York World,* reported to his paper:

"Widely as I differ from Mr. Douglass on almost all public questions, and decided as is my preference for the Caucasian over the African race, in most of my personal relations, it is impossible to see so much of him as I have seen of him without cordially recognizing, not his abilities only, but the estimable, amiable, and manly strain of his whole nature."[40]

Yet at times Douglass was made painfully aware that there were adherents of the doctrine of "skin aristocracy" among members of the expedition. But it was not until the mission was practically over that the first serious instance of discrimination occurred. On the voyage from Charleston to Washington, Douglass was denied admission to the dining room by the captain of the Potomac mail packet. Commissioners White and Howe remonstrated with the officials of the steamer, but they remained adamant. White was so furious at the discrimination against "a man who had dined with the foremost statesmen and scholars of our Northern States and of Europe,—a man who by his dignity, ability, and elegant manners was fit to honor any company,"[41] that he refused to eat, and left the dining room. He was joined by Howe. Both commissioners also turned down the captain's offer to set a special table in a separate room for them and their assistant secretary.

In the report which Grant submitted to Congress in a special message on April 5, 1871, the commissioners emphasized the "productiveness and healthfulness of the republic of San Domingo, of the unanimity of the people for annexation to the United States, and of their peaceable character." Immediately after the report was released, Douglass, in a series of seven articles in the *New National Era,* made public his views on annexation.

The articles revealed that he had returned from his visit to Santo Domingo a warm advocate of annexation. He informed his readers that he had had little enthusiasm for annexation when he had left the United States. "So far from going to Santo Domingo in the interest of the President," he said in answer to the charge that he had been sent on the mission because he had assured Grant that he was in favor of annexation, "I went there with my views and feelings considerably influenced by the great speech made by Mr. Sumner [on December 20], and by conversations with him subsequent to that speech, down to a few days before leaving this country for Santo Domingo." These conversations had all but convinced Douglass that President Baez had instituted "a military despotism," and that annexation "would commit the American people to a dance of blood."

Douglass' conversations with reporters during the voyage to Santo Domingo had strengthened his belief that annexation would be a mistake. The newspapermen minced no words in describing the annexation scheme as "gotten up to serve the purpose of certain land sharks who had large claims, whose value would be greatly enhanced by annexation." "Even the commission on the voyage out seemed to lean toward opposition to annexation," Douglass insisted. "I do not remember a single word indicating a purpose to favor the measure."[42]

Douglass explained his conversion at great length. He found Santo Domingo to be "a country of truly marvelous fertility" occupied by a people, the vast majority of whom lived in "squalor and destitution and misery."[43] "Oh, the Negroes won't work," he was told by the wealthy white inhabitants when he sought an explanation, for the miserable condition of the people. This infuriated him.

". . . Everywhere I went in the West Indies, I found the Negroes about the only people who do work. The white people and half white people of those islands are the shirkers of society; they are the shop keepers and traders, the lawyers and doctors, the politicians and law-makers, the men who live by their cunning and not by physical exertion. The Negroes do not perform any too much labor, but whatever labor is performed is performed by them. They work the fields, they raise the produce, they cut the lignum-vitae, the satin-wood, the mahogany, the dye-wood, and they bring these woods to the markets. They load the ships; they, in a word, do all the hard work that is done in Santo Domingo, and, indeed in the entire West Indies."

After some study, Douglass was led to believe that the miserable status of the people in the Dominican Republic was caused by slavery which had degraded labor and honored idleness, by absenteeism which squandered "the results of labor in foreign lands which ought to be employed at home in the interest of civilization," and by revolution, civil war, and by superstition. Annexation to the United States, he argued, would put an end to the causes of degradation in Santo Domingo. From the United States the "distracted country" would acquire "stable, enlightened, free government," because the immediate result of annexation would be "to put an end to the wars of rival chiefs." He was not surprised when he discovered that the people in Santo Domingo were "earnest and eager for annexation." "Were I a citizen of Santo Domingo," he wrote, "I would hold up both hands from the rising till the going down of the sun, if need be, in favor of the annexation of that country to the United States; for I see no better way to improve the fortunes and promote the highest interests of that country."

But would not annexation prove that self-government in a Negro republic had been a failure? Answering this "from a colored man's point of view," Douglass maintained that as a territory and ultimately as a state in the American union, Santo Domingo could contribute as much to the "world's opinion of the mental and moral possibilities of the colored race" as if she were "to rise to greatness in isolation." The same result would follow if Haiti, "of her own free will," should decide "to join the American Union as a state."

While he agreed that the commercial advantages of annexation were important to the United States, Douglass emphasized that he was not primarily interested in that phase of the question. "The anti-slavery side of annexation," he wrote, "is to me the strongest and most controlling." The tropical products consumed in the United States were made by slave labor. Consequently the American people "help to perpetuate the barbarous and inhuman system of slavery abroad which we poured out millions of treasure and rivers of blood to abolish at home." By annexing Santo Domingo, the people would "strike a blow at slavery wherever it may exist in the tropics." They would insure the speedy abolition of slavery in Cuba and throughout the western world.

"If we are really in favor of freedom and free institutions, if we would be as a nation a grand civilizing force among the nations of the earth, and bless the world as well as ourselves, we want Santo Domingo as one instrument of power in carrying out that beneficent mission."[44]

Douglass genuinely believed that annexation was desirable both from the standpoint of the people of Santo Domingo and the people of the United States. Like Dr. Howe and Andrew C. White he was convinced that president Baez's policies reflected Dominican opinion. Nor was Douglass alone among American Negroes in advocating annexation. The National Conventions of Colored Men in St. Louis, and in Columbia, South Carolina, in September and October 1871, both endorsed annexation even though by that time it was a dead issue.[45]

Nevertheless, many of Douglass' closest associates in the struggle for freedom and equality must have been filled with pain and disquiet when they read some of his arguments for annexation. They must have wondered how a man who could write that "the first gleam of the sword of freedom and independence in Cuba secured my sympathy with the revolutionary cause" could now speak blithely of the acquisition of Cuba by the United States. Then too, Douglass' confidence in the ability of the United States to plant the seeds of liberty and equality all over Latin America must have puzzled a number of his colleagues especially when they remembered what he had written in October, 1870, to a meeting held in Cooper Institute protesting the refusal of New York hotels to accept Negroes as guests:

"It belongs to free, democratic America, a land of Bibles, Sabbath Schools, Churches and missionary societies (perpetually boasting of liberty, manners and morals as compared with other nations) to furnish such examples of inhuman brutishness. . . . Neither in London, Paris, Berlin, St. Petersburgh, Rome, Vienna, nor Constantinople, could two decent persons with money in their pockets and willing to pay, be refused accommodation at any hotel on account of color. But here in the city of New York, the commercial Metropolis of the United States, sustaining relations of commerce with all nations, kindreds, tongues and peoples, men stoop to the narrowness and littleness to peep under a man's hat to find out whether he shall for his money and manhood, be accommodated with food and shelter."[46]

To subject the colored people of Santo Domingo to "such examples of inhuman brutishness" would hardly be lifting them up in the scale of civilization. Nor did the plight of Negro workers in the South, victimized by the landed aristocracy and murdered by the Klan if they dared to protest, hold out too much hope that by annexation the masses in the Dominican Republic would put an end to poverty and misery. The business men who desired Santo Domingo as a market and a new source of raw materials would have much more to say about the economy and government of the territory than would the progressive forces in the United States. These business men would certainly be more interested in exploiting the population than in raising their standard of living.

One cannot escape the conclusion that while Douglass was sincere in his belief that annexation was justified, he was closing his eyes to some very glaring facts because he felt it necessary to uphold Grant and prevent a serious setback for the Republican Party as a result of which the Democrats might emerge victorious. When Sumner revived his attack on Grant in the Senate even before the report of the commission of inquiry was released, Douglass criticized him for "playing into the hands of the Democratic party, and thus serving to strengthen the worst enemies the colored man has." By pursuing a course which tended to "cripple and divide the Republican party . . . and give the victory and power to the Democratic party," Sumner was "practically (not intentionally) the most dangerous and most effective power now arrayed against what we consider the cause of our race." These were harsh words, but Douglass clung to them. He wrote:

"Whatever else may be said of the Republican party and of General Grant, they are now the only visible hope of the colored race in the United States. Outside of these we see no power that is likely to stand between the Negro and murder, which is even now reveling in loyal blood, and rendering the constitutional guarantees which Mr. Sumner did so much to frame null and void. We feel strongly, and speak strongly, but none too strongly. The same principles that have made us devoted to Mr. Sumner and to follow him with unhesitating step in the past, now makes us cry out against his present alarming position."[47]

So firmly did Douglass believe that everything had to be subordinated to insuring the ascendancy of the Republican Party that he even accepted without public protest an act of discrimination directed against him. On March 27, the commission of inquiry reached Washington. Three days later, White, Howe, and Wade were invited to dine at the White House. Douglass' presence in Washington was known to everyone, for on March 29, he had been elected permanent chairman of the Republican convention to nominate a delegate to Congress from the District. Nevertheless, he was not invited to the White House along with the commissioners.

Douglass was deeply hurt not for himself alone but because he felt Grant had muffed an opportunity to administer "a proper rebuke" to the captain of the Potomac steamer. But publicly he said nothing.

Nor did he speak out when he learned that Grant had turned down the request of a delegation of Washington citizens to appoint Douglass secretary of the newly formed Legislative Council for the District of Columbia.[48]

Douglass kept his silence because he believed that there was a bigger issue at stake—the victory of the Republican Party in the Presidential election in 1872. Convinced that if the Democratic Party triumphed "our new-born liberties would be strangled in the cradle," Douglass refused to furnish ammunition to the movement that was splitting wide open the Republican Party. He made his position clear to Cassius M. Clay in July, 1871, in response to a letter urging him to join the ranks of the Liberal-Republican movement:

"The Republican party cannot be broken up at this juncture without, in my judgment, putting in peril not only the Freedmen of the South, but the honor and safety of the country. In my view, I had better put a pistol to my head and blow my brains out, than to lend myself in any wise to the destruction or defeat of the Republican party."[49]

The Liberal-Republican movement had been launched in Missouri in 1870 by a group of Republicans led by Carl Schurz and B. Gratz Brown who believed that it was time to call a halt to Radical Reconstruction and concentrate on issues like civil service reform and reduction in the tariff. Uniting with the Democrats, the "liberals" elected Brown governor of Missouri on a platform calling for general amnesty for the former Confederates. The movement spread outside of Missouri in 1871 and rapidly gained strength. Executive committees were formed in several states, and important newspapers—the *New York Tribune,* the *Chicago Tribune,* the *Springfield Republican,* the *New York Evening Post,* the *Cincinnati Commercial*—rallied public support for its cause. By the summer of 1871, there was a powerful bloc in Congress fighting to achieve the Liberal-Republican program.

Civil service and revenue reforms were key points in this program, but primarily the "liberals" were exponents of the principles of the "new departure." Originally drawn up by Vallandigham and other former Copperheads in the Democratic Party, this program, while it called for an acceptance of "the natural and legitimate results of the war" including the Thirteenth, Fourteenth and Fifteenth Amendments, insisted on leaving everything else connected with the status of the freedmen to the local governments. According to the proponents of the "new departure," the question of Reconstruction had already been settled and should be taken out of the realm of party politics. If the Republican Party did not realize that the time had come to put an end to special legislation in belief of the freedmen and to repeal all laws imposing force upon the southern states, then the "liberals" advocated the formation of a new and separate national party.

To the astonishment of most of his friends, Sumner joined the Liberal-Republican movement. Blinded by his hatred of the Grant administration, he did not see that the "liberals" were advocating policies that would hand over the Negro people in the South to the tender mercies of the former master class. Sumner had personal reasons for his violent antagonism toward Grant. He was being ignored by the party that he had helped to create and inspire. He had been deposed from the chairmanship of the committee of Foreign Relations, and been humiliated in committee assignments. His animosity toward the President had become so great that he announced publicly: "I tremble for my country when I contemplate the possibility of this man being fastened upon us for another four years."[50] It was all-consuming hatred that drove Sumner into the camp of the very elements who had consistently fought his policies for the Negro people.

The leaders of the Liberal-Republican movement were confident that Sumner would take a large section of the Negro people with him into the new political organization. Considerable dissatisfaction with the Republican Party existed among the Negro people. The party's leaders had failed to push for the enactment of Sumner's Supplementary Civil Rights Bill. They showed reluctance in the appointment of Negroes to office. Many of the Republican politicians in the southern states ignored the needs of the freedmen but paid careful attention to the desires of corporations and individual business men. Republican leaders refused to carry through a program of land distribution. All this resulted in widespread indignation among the Negro people. Some Negro leaders openly advocated going over into the Liberal-Republican camp, while others felt that the best strategy for Negroes was to continue their ties with the Republican Party but that it would be good policy also to throw a substantial number of votes to the Democrats. George T. Downing believed that there were sufficient signs of "a change in policy" in the Democratic Party to entitle it "to share with the Republican party the colored vote in the next Presidential election."[51]

More than any other man, Douglass was responsible for preventing a disastrous bolt of Negro voters to the Liberal-Republicans in the presidential election of 1872. He understood why many Negroes were dissatisfied with the Republican Party. The Republicans, he agreed, had not done enough for their most loyal supporters, the Negro people. "Loyalty should not be landless, hungry, ragged, ignorant and despised," he wrote bitterly.

"We admit that there is a good ground of complaint against the Republican party and against the present administration that they have overlooked and disregarded the claims of colored voters in the bestowment of offices and honors; that they have assumed that colored men should be satisfied with the right to vote for white men, and for white men alone in too many instances; and that they have done so in deference to the well-known prejudice against the colored race. We admit this, and, if possible, much more against the Republican party."

Douglass, however, insisted that while it was necessary to battle constantly to engraft "into the whole policy of the Republican party" a clear and unequivocal program to meet their needs, the Negro people had no choice but to support the Republican candidates. He dismissed Downing's suggestion that groups of colored voters should support the Democrats.

"The very thought is repulsive, scandalous, and shocking," he wrote. " . . . If as a class we are slighted by the Republican party, we are as a class murdered by the Democratic party. Whatsoever may be the faults of the Republican party, it has within it the only element of friendship for the colored man's rights, which is found anywhere in this country."

To those Negro leaders who argued that it was time to support a new party, Douglass responded:

"If in the course of time the Republican party should become faithless to its own principles, degenerate as the Democratic party has degenerated within a comparatively short time, outlive itself like the Whigs and Know-Nothings, and another party should spring up that should promise to be a better custodian of the rights and liberty of the people, a party of more progressive tendencies, we shall certainly join it, and urge all others to do so too. For the present there is none, while the Democrats are the inveterate and irreconcilable enemies of all the principles we are struggling for."[52]

Douglass saw no hope for the Negro people in the Liberal-Republican movement. He did not favor a "blind party spirit," and although he had respect for Carl Schurz, Lyman Trumbull, Cassius M. Clay, and other former Abolitionists who were active in the movement for a new party, he could not agree with them that "the proscription course against the South" was evil, that the action taken by the federal government against the Ku Klux Klan was "an iniquity," and that even if many Negroes would suffer, "we must leave the remedy to the legal normal action of the States." Nor could he agree that the issue which had brought the Republican Party into existence was a thing of the past, and that new issues demanded a new party. He would be "ready for the new" when his people were "no longer assailed and menaced by the old."

"We look at this question as a black man," he wrote in the *New National Era* of August 10, 1871, "and as one too, who would be happy to see the Negro outside of all political questions, and no longer assailed on party grounds, nor requiring defense on such grounds. It is among the greatest misfortunes of our race that we are subject to such controversy, and that it is for the interest of any party to employ their skill and power to disparage, degrade, and persecute us. But our deliverance has not yet come, nor will it come while the black man in any State of the Union finds his way to the ballot-box through intimidation, through violence, through murderous assaults by Ku-Klux Klans. Slavery is indeed abolished, but the teachers of colored children are flogged and driven away, school-houses are burned to the ground, and the victims can find no jury to punish the violators of the law. Driven from the statute book, slavery still finds a refuge in Southern sentiment and in the Democratic party, and the ascendancy of that party in 1872 must tend to revive and re-invigorate all the malign feelings and practices of the Southern people towards the newly-enfranchised black citizens of the South."

In editorials and speeches Douglass stressed the same theme, pointing out that "there is no path out of the Republican Party that did not lead directly into the Democratic Party . . . away from our friends and directly to our enemies." That the logic of Douglass' argument had its effect on the Negro people is illustrated in the stand taken by the National Convention of Colored Men which assembled in New Orleans in April, 1872.

Essentially the New Orleans Convention was a gathering of southern Negroes who came together to unite the efforts of the colored people in the South "to the bringing about a full and continued recognition of their rights as guaranteed by several amendments to the Constitution."[53] A number of Negro leaders from the northern states were invited to be present. Douglass, George T. Downing, J. Sella Martin, John M. Langston, and A. M. Green accepted the invitation and arrived on the fourth day of the convention.

As Douglass was escorted into the convention hall by a special delegation, the entire audience rose to its feet and greeted him with cheers. He was conducted to the platform by Lieutenant Governor Pinchback of Louisiana, Lieutenant Governor Ransier of Arkansas, and Isaac Myers. Before his arrival, Douglass had been elected permanent chairman of the convention, and, in turning over the chair to him, the temporary chairman remarked that it was "a fit place in that very hall, where so many colored men had been murdered for opinion's sake, for him who stands head and shoulders above all of his race, for him who has done so much through so many weary years to elevate and ameliorate the condition of his people, to preside over the assembled representatives of those who love and honor him."[54]

On the opening day of the convention, the delegates had listened to the reading of a letter from Charles Sumner. It was a moving appeal for complete equality before the law. "There can be but one liberty and one equality," wrote Sumner, "the same in Boston and New Orleans, the same every where throughout the country." The letter had started a movement to follow Sumner into the Liberal-Republican movement, but Douglass' opening address as permanent chairman, had much to do with ending this sentiment.

Douglass urged the delegates to make full use of their "moral and political power" to strengthen the progressive forces in the Republican Party, but he warned that under no circumstances should they throw their support to those who, despite new disguises, were their deadliest enemies. After announcing, amidst tremendous applause, that he expected to vote for General Grant in the fall, Douglass paid tribute to Senator Sumner whom he described "as steady as the north star." He concluded with a dramatic announcement:

"May my right hand lose its cunning; may my tongue cleave to the roof of my mouth, and may the day I was born grow dark and be cursed when I say one word that reflects on Charles Sumner."

With Douglass in the chair, the delegates proceeded to pay tribute to Sumner as "the Gibraltar of our cause and the north star of our hopes." Then they "sincerely and gratefully endorsed the administration of President U. S. Grant in maintaining our liberties, in protecting our privileges, in punishing our enemies." They pledged their "unwavering devotion" to the nominees of the Republican Party in the forthcoming Presidential election.[55]

Douglass admitted that while the delegates had reaffirmed their confidence in the Grant administration and in the Republican Party, it "was done with less force and effect than could have been the case had the convention been assured that a Supplementary Civil Rights Bill would pass the present Republican Congress." He was convinced that the bill would provide one of the most important means of defeating the conspiracy of the ex-slaveowners against the common people of the South. By outlawing Jim-Crow schools and providing that Negro and white children should be educated together the Bill would strike a blow at the common enemy:

"From our observations during a trip to the South," wrote Douglass, "we are convinced that the interests of the poor whites and the colored people are identical. . . . In that section everything that will bring the poor white man and the colored man close together should be done; they should be taught to make common cause against the rich land-holders of the South who never regarded a poor white man of as much importance as they did slaves. . . . The cunning ex-slave-holder sets those who should be his enemies to fighting each other and thus diverts attention from himself. Educate the colored children and white children together in your day and night schools throughout the South, and they will learn to know each other better, and be better able to co-operate for mutual benefit."[56]

When Douglass left New Orleans he was accompanied to his train by all of the delegates. A military escort of two companies of colored soldiers headed the procession. "The occasion was one that will long be remembered," commented the *New Orleans Louisianan,* "as we believe it the first instance in the history of this country where military honors were paid to a distinguished colored man."[57]

Douglass retained many pleasant memories from his first visit to the deep South. But his greatest joy came from the knowledge that vigorous and able leaders of the Negro people were arising in a region where the great mass of the freedmen lived. He informed the readers of the *New National Era* immediately after his return from New Orleans:

"There was much talent and character exhibited among the members of the New Orleans Convention to confirm our oft-repeated conviction—that the South will produce its own colored leaders. The colored man from the North who goes South expecting to find himself head and shoulders above his Southern brethren, will soon have that conceit taken out of him. He may for the time have the advantage that experience and education at the North has given him, but this advantage will speedily disappear."[58]

A few days after his arrival in Washington, Douglass had the distinction of being nominated for the Vice Presidency of the United States. The Presidential nominee on the ticket was Victoria Claflin Woodhull, an advocate of woman suffrage and "social freedom." Leader of section No. 12 of the American sections of the International Working-men's Association (the First International), and publisher of *Woodhull's and Claflin's Weekly,* Mrs. Woodhull persuaded Elizabeth Cadey Stanton to use the National Woman's Suffrage Association as sponsor of a People's Convention for the organization of a new political party.

On May 11, 1872, 688 delegates met in Apollo Hall in New York City to organize the Equal Rights Party and to nominate candidates for President and Vice President of the United States. "The hall," wrote a reporter for the *New York Times,* "was decorated with a number of peculiarly-worded banners, was nearly filled with ladies, wearing eye-glasses and short hair in general. There were a few men present."

The ladies and the handful of gentlemen adopted a platform calling for a c nplete reconstruction of the government of the United States, and the adoption of a new constitution "to meet the present wants of the people." They demanded that all monopolies be abolished, their charters revoked, and that the government "take charge of all public enterprises which are to be for the public use." The platform called for employment of the unemployed by the government; the abolition of capital punish-ment; the free use of public lands for actual settlers, and the right to vote for every person, male and female.

On this far-reaching platform, Mrs. Woodhull was nominated for President by acclamation. Then Moses Hall of Louisiana nominated Douglass for Vice President, declaring: "We have the oppressed sex represented by Woodhull; we must have the oppressed race represented by Douglass." The delegates agreed, and after considering Robert Dale Owen, Theodore Tilton, Wendell Phillips, and Ben Wade, they selected Douglass as their Vice Presidential candidate. He was "eulogized by half a dozen speakers in succession."

To the tune of "Coming Through the Rye," the delegates sang:

> *"Yes! Victoria we've selected*
> *For our chosen head;*
> *With Fred Douglass on the ticket*
> *We will raise the dead."*

The convention closed, hailing, "The Woman's Negro's and Workingman's Ticket—Victoria Woodhull of New York for President; Frederick Douglass of the District of Columbia for Vice President."[59]

Early in June, Mrs. Woodhull accepted her nomination. But Douglass was too busy with personal affairs even to notify the new party that he could not be its candidate.[60] On June 2, his house in Rochester was burned to the ground. Mrs. Douglass, her daughter and son-in-law Mr. and Mrs. Nathan Sprague, and their three children managed to escape. But the furniture and Douglass' library, including twelve volumes (1848 to 1860) of *The North Star* and *Frederick Douglass' Paper,* were destroyed.

Douglass hastened back to Rochester. He arrived at one o'clock in the morning in a drenching rain. Unaware of just where his family was staying, he decided to put up overnight at a hotel. At the Congress Hall and the Waverly House he was bluntly reminded of his color when the clerks told him that there were no empty rooms. The proprietor of the Waverly House rebuked his clerk when he discovered that Douglass was the visitor who was being turned away, and offered him accommodations. But Douglass refused to stop at a hotel which permitted only a distinguished colored man to use its facilities.

Douglass was fairly certain that the fire was "the work of an incendiary." Rochester was among "the most liberal of Northern cities," he admitted, but it had "its full share of that Ku-Klux spirit which makes anything owned by a colored man a little less respected and secure than when owned by a white citizen." In a letter to his readers, Douglass wrote:

"The spirit which would deny a man shelter in a public house, needs but little change to deny him shelter, even in his own house. It is the spirit of hate, the spirit of murder, the spirit which would burn a family in their beds. I may be wrong, but I fear that the sentiment which repelled me at Congress Hall burnt my house."[61]

All told Douglass' loss as a result of the fire amounted to about five or six thousand dollars, not counting many things to which he could "attach no money value." Rochester friends urged him to rebuild his home in the city but Douglass decided to live in the nation's capital, and moved his wife and Rosetta's family to Washington.[62]

By the time Douglass returned to Washington with his family, the Presidential campaign was in full swing. Three major conventions had been held, and two candidates had been nominated—Grant by the Republicans and Horace Greeley by the Liberal-Republicans and the Democrats.

On May 1, 1872, the Liberal-Republicans had met in Cincinnati to draw up their platform and nominate their Presidential candidates. As was to be expected, the platform advocated civil service reform and emphasized that the new party represented a revolt against privilege and corruption. But the greatest stress was placed upon the principles of the "new departure": acceptance by the nation of "the questions settled by the Thirteenth, Fourteenth and Fifteenth Amendments," universal amnesty, and "state self-government."

Horace Greeley was nominated for President on the seventh ballot. B. Gratz Brown of Missouri was nominated for the Vice Presidency. A month later the Democrats accepted the Liberal-Republican candidates, and nominated Greeley and Brown as Democratic standard-bearers.

The Democrats were not fooled by the verbal respect for the rights of the Negro people expressed in the Liberal-Republican platform. All they had asked for since 1868 was the government removal of federal troops from the South, the repeal of the Enforcements Acts, and the turning over of the issue of civil rights to the states. Consequently, they were quite willing to overlook the fact that Greeley had once called Democrats "traitors," "rebels," "copperheads," "slave-holders," and "slave-whippers." Ex-Senator Doolittle of Wisconsin, the permanent chairman at the Democratic convention, spoke for the vast majority of the delegates when he said that the major objective of the combined Liberal-Democratic ticket was the "overthrow of Negro supremacy."[63]

On July 11, a group of twenty-four Washington Negroes addressed a letter to Sumner, as a friend of the colored people, asking him which of the two candidates—Grant or Greeley—"will, if elected, enforce the requirements of the Constitution and the laws respecting our civil and political rights with the most heart-felt sympathy and the greatest vigor." In his reply, Sumner urged the Negro people to support Greeley. Grant had struck a blow at the independence of the Negro Republic of Haiti; he had been responsible for a wave of corruption in public life unparalleled in American history. "Nor can it be forgotten," he went on, "that . . . Hon. Frederick Douglass, the colored orator, accomplished in manners as in eloquence, was thrust away from the company of the Commissioners [to Santo Domingo] at the common table of the mail-packet on the Potomac, almost within sight of the Executive Mansion, simply on account of his color; but the President, at whose invitation he had joined the commission, never uttered a word in condemnation of this exclusion, and when entertaining the returned Commissioners at dinner carefully omitted Mr. Douglass, who was in Washington at the time, and thus repeated the indignity." For this and other high crimes and misdemeanors, Grant deserved impeachment rather than re-election.

Greeley, Sumner continued, had always been an Abolitionist, and, unlike Grant, had fought for Negro suffrage. He was the colored man's "truest friend," and had "among his immediate supporters, in all parts of the country, devoted and consistent Republicans. . . ." True, he had been nominated by the Democrats, but by supporting Greeley and his platform, the Democrats had turned Republicans. "They may continue Democrats in name, but they are in reality Republicans. . . ."

Many of Sumner's old comrades were amazed by this letter of advice. Garrison in a bitter reply excoriated Greeley, accused Sumner of permitting his personal pique to drive him into the slaveholder's camp, and praised the "illustrious administration of Grant." Wendell Phillips did not go so far in praising Grant, but like Garrison he felt that Greeley was "the worst of all counsellors, the most unsteady of all leaders, the most pliant of all compromisers in time of great public emergency." He urged Negro voters not to heed Sumner's advice:

"My judgment," Phillips wrote in a letter to the colored citizens of Boston, "is the exact opposite of Mr. Sumner's. I think every loyal man, and especially every colored man should vote for General Grant, and that the nation and your race are safe only in the hands of the old, regular republican party."[64]

Douglass agreed wholeheartedly with the stand taken by Garrison and Phillips. A week after Sumner's letter of advice to the Negroes of Washington was released, he published a lengthy defense of the President entitled, "U. S. Grant and the Colored People." Analyzing the President's Civil War career, Douglass maintained that General Grant "was always up with, or in advance of authority furnished from Washington in regard to the treatment of those of our color then slaves." He showed that Grant, while in command of the Thirteenth Army Corps, in the Department of Tennessee, anticipated the Proclamation of Emancipation by an order, dated November 11, 1862, which organized a system for receiving all fugitives from slavery, feeding, clothing, sheltering, and, as far as possible, giving them employment. He traced the wide operation of this system, and indicated the encouragement it gave to Lincoln to carry for-

ward the policy of emancipation. He then demonstrated by General
Grant's letters and orders, his early and firm conviction that no peace could
be permanent, and none was desirable, that did not forever set at rest the
question of slavery. Douglass then turned to Grant's role after the war,
pointing out that he had commended the industry of the freedmen,
rejoiced in the Fifteenth Amendment, and appointed colored men to
places of honor and importance. Douglass then proceeded to ask:

"And what shall I say of his enforcement of the law for the preservation
of life and property in the South, whereby the savage outrages of organizations,
known as Ku-Klux Klans upon an innocent and suffering people have been
so generally suppressed? What a change has come? These outrages, the
burning of school-houses and churches, the whipping and shooting of teachers,
the midnight murder of men and women without cause by masked villains,
were so contrary to the ideas of the country that they hardly seemed possible
in a civilized land. But by the quiet yet firm course of General Grant in
enforcing the law, thousands have openly acknowledged the crimes charged,
the organizations stand confessed to the amazement of all good men North
and South, and peace has come to many places as never before. The scourging
and slaughter of our people have so far ceased."

Having alluded to the fact that Grant in his relations with him was
always gentlemanly and cordial—"after Lincoln and Sumner no man in
his intercourse with me gave evidence of more freedom from vulgar
prejudice. . . . "—Douglass turned to Sumner's charge that the President
had not invited him to dine with the San Domingo commissioners. He
argued that the omission was unintended and unimportant. It could not
have stemmed from prejudice, for Grant "never withheld any social
courtesy" to the Negro Minister Plenipotentiary from the Republic of
Haiti. Moreover, the President had insisted that he be accorded full
equality on the voyage to Santo Domingo. Had he been with the Commissioners at the time they visited the White House, he would undoubtedly have been invited to dinner with the rest. "It is further obvious that
color had nothing to do with the omission, because other gentlemen
accompanying the expedition equally with myself, though white, failed
to receive an invitation to dine at the White House." In any event, his
devotion to General Grant rested "upon high and broad public grounds,
and not upon personal favor." He saw in him "the vigilant, firm, impartial, and wise protector of my race from all the malign, reactionary, social,
and political elements that would whelm them in destruction."[65]

In his loyalty to Grant, and believing that the President's failure to invite him to dinner was being blown up by men who were not sincerely interested in the fight against discrimination, Douglass had convinced himself that the incident was of no real importance. But the issue did not die. Sumner accused Douglass of twisting the facts around to suit himself, and repeated his allegation that the incident revealed Grant's contempt for the Negro people. Douglass was reluctant to discuss the matter further, but, in a speech in Bangor, Maine, on August 20, he made a telling point by alluding to the strange fact that the Democrats were using Sumner's charge to prove that Grant was "not sound on the Negro."

"They are suddenly much concerned about my dignity," he declared ironically. "They are all at once anxious that I should be properly appreciated and that all the little technicalities and circumstances of etiquette should be observed. How long has this been so? I know that when I came down here seventeen years ago it was to denounce a Democratic decision—the Dred Scott decision—which declared that a Negro had no rights that a white man was bound to respect. Have they got over it?"

Although Douglass believed that Grant should have reproved the insult made him on his return to Washington by inviting him to dinner he also believed that the omission was no proof of the President's prejudice against his people. Grant had personally assured him "that had I been present when the three commissioners called upon him, he would have invited me to dine with him and them." "...I am with all my heart laboring to elect U. S. Grant President of the United States for a second term," he wrote to a friend. "I certainly should not so labor if I thought him capable of offering me an insult because of my skin."[66]

Douglass spent the pre-election months in Maine, Massachusetts, and New York stumping for Grant. His speeches stressed one major theme—the effect of the election on the future of the Negro people, and particularly those in the South. He told an audience of colored citizens in Cooper Institute that while taxes, civil service reform, and foreign policy were important, "the chief and all commanding interest which all feel in the contest is found in its bearing upon the great questions of human liberty and equality."

"Here it touches us deeply, and is a matter of supreme concern. To the millions of our color in the South it is vastly more important than to us. It is, in effect, a thing of peace and war, of order and disorder, of life and death, if not of liberty and slavery. It, in fact, involved the maintenance of all the progress made during the last dozen years, and the inauguration of a process of reaction, which may land our race into a condition only a little better than bondage and degradation of ages from which we have just begun to emerge."[67]

The importance of Douglass' speeches in the campaign cannot be over-estimated. On September 26, the *New York Times* devoted a long editorial to this question:

"From the outset of the present contest . . . the speeches of Frederick Douglass have been among the most powerful weapons of the party. They have, in addition to their special force derived from their authorship, possessed a degree of epigrammatic point and terseness which stands unexcelled among the productions of the campaign. Such sharp vigorous sentences as these, for example, are of the kind which at once take hold upon the memory and appeal to the understanding: 'Tell me not of gratitude; talk not to me of deserting an old friend. No man is my friend who betrays the cause of my people.' 'The trouble never was in the Constitution, but in the administration of the Constitution.' 'In front of us today we have the same old enemy, the same old snake in a new skin.' 'The wolf is all the more dangerous because of his white coat.' Connected by close and vigorous argument, and illustrated by appeals to an experience which is absolutely unique of its kind, such sentences as these are so many thrusts which enter the vital parts of the enemy. Fred. Douglass has done and is doing some of the best service of the campaign, and at its triumphant close no man will bear away a larger share of its laurels."

Grant was swept into office. Greeley carried only six states. In New York he lost by more than 50,000 votes, in Massachusetts by 75,000, in Pennsylvania by 137,000. He was the worst beaten candidate ever to seek the Presidency.[68]

Usually Douglass' role in a political campaign ended on election day. But in 1872 it was different. Late in August, the Republican State Committee had assembled to select New York's Presidential electors. The delegates chose Gerrit Smith as one of the two electors-at-large. Then Thurlow Weed, the State Republican leader, arose and announced that "in his judgment the best name to be associated with G. Smith as elector-at-large, was that of Frederick Douglass." Weed's suggestion was received "with great satisfaction and was responded to by acclamation."

Two months after the election, Douglass, as official messenger, conveyed the results of the balloting in the Empire State to the president of the Senate. On the eve of the opening session in December, he issued an appeal to the members of the legislative body under the dramatic title, "Give Us the Freedom Intended for Us." He demanded the immediate passage of appropriate legislation to enforce the Thirteenth, Fourteenth, and Fifteenth Amendments. "Freedom from the auction block and from legal claim of property," he cried, "is of no benefit to the colored man without the means of protecting his rights." On election day in November, he reminded Congress, the vast majority of the American people had signified their understanding of this fact. By triumphantly re-electing President Grant on the Republican platform, they had "reiterated in thunder tones their demand 'that complete liberty and *exact equality* in the enjoyment of all civil, political, and public rights should be established and effectually maintained throughout the Union by efficient and appropriate State and Federal legislation.'" It was now up to the Republican Congress to carry out the will of the people![69]

But Douglass was soon to discover that there was a wide gap between the platform pledges and the Republican Party performance. He was to learn that progress for basic civil rights for all could not be attained by reliance upon generalized exhortation in party platforms and in campaign speeches.

The Closing Years of Reconstruction, 1872-1877

A week after Grant's re-election, the press reported that a serious effort was being made by the militant Republicans to secure a cabinet post for a Negro leader. Douglass' name figured prominently in the speculations that immediately followed.[1] But the rumor died as quickly as it had been born. No political appointment came Douglass' way and he was keenly disappointed. After having "worked hard and long" to secure Grant's election, the President had not deemed it necessary to reward him. However, in March, 1874 Douglass was named president of the Freedmen's Savings and Trust Company, commonly known as the Freedmen's Bank. Created by the federal government in 1865, the bank was a result of the efforts of northern friends to assist the emancipated freedmen in their new adjustment from slavery and to aid them "in securing a stronger economic position in the social order." Lincoln hailed the institution as an important contribution to the Negro's welfare and General O. O. Howard welcomed the bank "as an auxiliary to the Freedmen's Bureau."

Under the impression that the bank was a government institution, the freedmen responded enthusiastically. Before the end of 1865, ten branches had been set up, and during the next year ten more were organized. By 1872 there were 34 branches in existence, 32 of which were in the southern states. By 1874 the deposits in all branches totaled $3,299,201.[2]

But behind the "magnificent brown stone front" of the bank's headquarters in Washington, built at a cost of $260,000, things were happening which rendered meaningless the rapid accumulation of deposits and the increase in the number of branches. Careless bookkeeping and incompetent cashiers were bad enough. But when the honest and capable trustees neglected their duties, and left the bank in the hands of sharpers and speculators, the results were disastrous. The large deposits of the bank caught the eye of financiers, political jobbers, and real estate speculators. Loans were handed out to them indiscriminately. Jay Cooke, the financier, was able to borrow $500,000 at 5 per cent interest although his business was on the verge of collapse. Other loans, secured through fraud and political influence, were made to unknown speculators.

Raids upon the bank seriously reduced its assets. With the panic of 1873, the bank was left holding worthless notes. Alarmed, the depositors made three runs on the bank within eighteen months.

Realizing that the bank was doomed, the speculators who now managed the institution resigned, and left the remaining trustees with a deficit of over $200,000. In an effort to stave off the threatened collapse, a number of trustees proposed Douglass as president to replace John W. Alvord. John M. Langston, one of the trustees, insisted that the bank be closed, that Douglass "would find the presidency . . . difficult, trying and disappointing to him." But the majority were counting on Douglass' prestige among Negroes to hold off another run on the bank, and to gradually restore confidence in the institution. Outvoting Langston, they offered Douglass the presidency.[3]

When he took over, Douglass was assured by both Alvord, the outgoing president, and Stickney, the actuary, that the institution was sound. So although he had "neither taste nor talent for the office," he entered upon his duties with the sincere hope of bringing order out of chaos and promoting "honesty, vigor and efficiency in every part of the Institution." On March 30, 1874, his first day in office, he wrote: "I believe that the Bank and its branches have done good service, and that there is need for their continuance. I have no sympathy with those who are in haste to destroy either the root or the branches, and shall give no encouragement to those who are favoring that policy."[4]

Douglass set out to restore the confidence of the depositors. He sent a "quieting telegram" all over the southern states assuring them that if they were patient a little longer, the bank would be able to pay dollar for dollar. So confident was he in his own prediction, that he loaned the bank $10,000 of his own money.[5]

But Douglass' suspicions were aroused when strenuous efforts were made to keep him ignorant of what was going on. He soon discovered that the bank faced a large deficit, that it was loaded with poor securities, and that its business was practically non-existent. His conviction that the bank was already a failure was strengthened when he learned that many of the very same trustees who had assured him of its soundness had withdrawn their deposits and opened accounts elsewhere.[6]

Once his suspicions were confirmed, Douglass went into action. Over the objections of most of the trustees, he turned to Congress for relief, and called for immediate action by the government. With the aid of the Senate Committee on Finance, Douglass secured the passage of an act, approved June 20, 1874, which placed the bank in liquidation so that it could be reorganized.[7]

Douglass, hopeful that he could still save the bank, issued a circular to the depositors assuring them that the bill had placed the bank "upon a broader and firmer basis." He outlined some of the chief reasons for the bank's difficulties: exorbitant interest rates, non-paying branches in remote places in the South, hostility to the Negro and consequently a "race malignity" toward the bank's "senseless runs," and "the general prostration of business."

Under the reorganization plan, new depositors would be protected from the old debts of the institution, while old depositors would get every dollar owed them by the company. He promised economy and prudence in future management. Wild and visionary schemes of banking would be abandoned; non-paying branches would be closed; salaries would be cut; the number of employees drastically reduced; the constant drain of deposits to Washington from all over the country would cease, and investments be made in the vicinity of the branches:

"With this retrenchment in expenses, with wise and vigorous management, and with the returning confidence of our people, it is believed that the Freedmen's Savings and Trust Company, which has already been a powerful instrument in promoting the moral, social, and intellectual welfare of our people will survive and flourish despite the machinations of its enemies."

But optimistic circulars could not restore life to an institution that was already dead. On June 28, 1874, the trustees voted to close the doors, and nominated commissioners to wind up affairs. Five days later, Douglass wrote to Gerrit Smith:

"Despite my efforts to uphold the Freedmen's Savings and Trust Company it has fallen. It has been the black man's cow, but the white man's milk. Bad loans and bad management have been the death of it. I was ignorant of its real condition till elected as its president."[8]

It was a long time after the bank closed before the depositors received any of their money, and even then they were paid less than fifty cents on the dollar.[9]

Douglass' connection with the Freedmen's Bank opened his eyes somewhat to the widespread corruption in American political life. "The moral atmosphere is more than tainted, it is rotten," he wrote to Smith in September, 1874. "Avarice, duplicity, falsehood, corruption, servility, fawning and trickery of all kinds, confront us at every turn."[10]

Douglass' faith in the bank had cost him a thousand dollars. Soon after he suffered another financial setback. The *New National Era* failed and ceased publication. In April, 1873, he had invested $10,000 in the paper and had turned it over to his sons. By combining it with the *New Citizen* (formerly the *Colored Citizen*), the new publishers hoped to produce a paper "with facilities in the way of pecuniary support such as no other paper devoted to the interests of the colored people has ever enjoyed." Unfortunately, before these hopes could be fulfilled, the panic of 1873 and the five years of severe depression that followed swept the country. By October, 1873, one month after the depression started, the publishers found it impossible to collect from the subscribers and by February, 1874, eighty per cent of the subscribers were in arrears. The publishers announced that they could no longer continue "the publication of a paper that was loading us down with debt and poverty," and so publication was suspended for three weeks while Lewis and Frederick Douglass, Jr. sought frantically to obtain financial assistance. But it was hopeless. "We have met with little or no pecuniary encouragement," Frederick Douglass, Jr. wrote bitterly, "and have been placed under embarrassments for the good of the cause." The paper staggered along until September, 1874, when it finally passed out of existence.[11]

The Negro people did not suffer a great loss with the demise of the *New National Era*. At no time was Douglass able to give the paper the personal attention he had given the *North Star* and its immediate successors. The high literary standard of the earlier papers was absent in the *New National Era*. Moreover, the paper had become a political organ of the Republican Party. As early as January, 1872, Douglass complained that during his frequent absences from Washington "too much space is given to the Tariff" and not enough to the problems which were of real concern to the Negro.[12] After April, 1873, when Douglass severed all connection with the paper, the *New National Era* read like a journal issued by lobbyists for big business. This paper which had once been the official organ of the National Colored Labor Union and had been characterized by Isaac Myers as "the national organ of the colored men of the United States" now became increasingly bitter toward the trade unions. This paper which once had criticized the labor movement for refusing to allow Negroes to join unions or to become apprentices and learn a trade, began to oppose every aspect of trade unionism. On May 7, 1874, it featured an editorial entitled, "The Folly, Tyranny, and Wickedness of Labor Unions." The editorial, incorrectly attributed by many historians to Douglass, set out "to convince workingmen of the absolute injury to their interests of the labor unions of the country, and also their oppressions and tyrannical course toward fellow workmen, as well as their employers."[13]

Douglass failed to understand the real reasons for the paper's failure. He attributed its difficulties to the fact that the Negro was "not yet a reader" and was "unconscious of having an associate existence or common cause." "Our confidence," he went on, "is in the white race. White schools, white character, white Theology, white Legislators, white public journals, secure our highest confidence and support." He did not consider this strange since the white race monopolized so much of "the honor, the wisdom, wealth and the glory. . . . "[14] Years later, however, he admitted that the failure of most Negro papers was due more to weaknesses in the journals themselves than in the Negro people. Negroes did not support these papers, he wrote in 1891, because they "cost more and give their readers less, than papers and publications by white men."[15]

In spite of the losses incured in the burning of his house in Rochester, the failures of the Freedmen's Bank and the *New National Era*, Douglass' finances were soon in good order again. From the close of the war onward, his chief source of income was the lecture platform. No lecture course was considered complete without Douglass, and his dates were filled months in advance.[16] His name was a magnet. "The largest audience ever assembled in the Hall greeted Frederick Douglass on Friday evening," the *Warsaw Western New Yorker* reported in February, 1872. "Fifty per cent more single tickets were sold than at any previous lecture, and every available foot of space was occupied."[17] His lecture fee was a hundred dollars, but sometimes communities would offer $500 for two or three successive lectures. During a three month period, he earned $3,700 from various literary societies before which he lectured.[18]

But life on the road was difficult. The lecture season which began in November and lasted until April took him on long tours through every state of the North. In the winter of 1872-73, he lectured "from Bangor to Omaha, and from St. Louis to St. Paul." Railroads were bad enough, but western rural travel was something formidable. Along the old "corduroy" roads, one had to cling vigilantly to one's seat to keep from being thrown from the wagon into the apparently bottomless mud. Once Clara Barton, founder of the American Red Cross, wrote to Douglass: "My imagination points to you making the final arrangements for that long Western tour, and my very soul sympathizes with you, and yet it is pleasant, with all its weariness."[19]

But thirty years of the hardships of the lecturer's life had removed all of the pleasure and left only the weariness. Douglass' hopes for a more stationary life had been blasted by his financial losses. "But for the burning and destruction of my hard earnings," he wrote to his daughter in November, 1872, "I should be able to spare myself the coming winter from the labors, perils and fatigues of a lecturing campaign."[20]

Douglass' reluctance to continue lecturing arose also from the fact that the cause with which he had been identified for almost half a century was losing its appeal. Audiences were no longer so interested in lectures on the anti-slavery movement, even when the speaker had himself been an active participant in the struggle.[21] Moreover, Douglass discovered that the managers of Lyceum Bureaus shied away from subjects dealing with the Negro and his problems. One manager put it bluntly to Douglass:

"No Sir, you can earn no money that way. There is nothing in instructive lectures, and we don't want to have anything to do with them—never touch them in fact. People don't want to be instructed. What we need is sensation and amusement. If a fellow has killed his wife, he is a good man to lecture. People don't care to hear what he says, but they pay money to look at him. But instructive lectures are never included in Lyceum courses."[22]

To recoup his financial losses and maintain a stable income, Douglass was often compelled to lecture on a wide variety of subjects which had little connection with his work.[23] But such was the magnetism of his manner, the lightning in his words and the thunder in his voice that regardless of the topic, men and women flocked to hear him speak. And, in spite of the advice of the managers, he never spoke merely to amuse. His main purpose was to instruct. Whether the subject was "Folklore of Different Nations," "Hints on Journalism" or "The Age of Pictures," he would manage to tie it up with the cause nearest his heart. Once under his spell, the audience forgot the topic listed for the lecture.

"For ourselves," wrote a journalist in the 'seventies, "we were constantly astonished at the massiveness of mind, the wonderful accuracy and felicitous use of language, the admirable elocution, and the evidence of intellectual strength and culture that characterized this oration of a man who lived until past twenty years old as a slave, and has since then been mainly self-taught. Not Schurz with all the advantages of European universities, official position, and a varied experience of life in many lands, was the superior of Douglass in the evidences and results of culture, while in vigor and weight of mind they fell below him."[24]

One of the finest descriptions of the orator in action was painted by a Negro minister who heard Douglass speak in Boston's Faneuil Hall in the 1870's:

"There he stood, over six feet in height, erect, broad-shouldered, deep-chested, with massive, well-formed head, covered with thick, bushy hair, about half gray. I judged him then to be midway in his fifties. His face, strongly leonine, was clean shaved, except moustache, while those eyes, that even in the seventies could flash fire, lighted up the whole countenance, and made the general effect such as not to be easily forgotten by a young man. There stood the orator and the man, and never since have I seen the two in such exquisite combination. . . .

"As the old orator swept on in his own inimitable style, sprinkling his remarks with genuine, original wit, I forgot everything else around me. His voice, a heavy baritone, or rendered a little heavier than usual by a slight hoarseness contracted in previous speaking, could be distinctly heard in that historic but most wretched of auditoriums. I was particularly struck with his perfect ease and naturalness, a seemingly childlike unconsciousness of his surroundings, while, like a master of his art, as he was, he swayed the feelings of that surging multitude. In the most impassioned portion of his speech, however, it was evident to the thoughtful observer that there was in the man immense reserved force which on momentous occasions might be used with startling effect. At first I had entered the hall to remain but a few minutes, and, consequently, had taken my stand just inside the door. How long I did remain I cannot tell, but it was until the speaker finished, at which time I found myself half way up towards the rostrum in the midst of that thickly standing audience. Such was my first sight and impression of one of the world's great orators, and beyond comparison the greatest man of the race yet produced on this continent."[25]

"People [who attend lectures] want to be amused as well as instructed," Douglass pointed out to James Redpath, the lecture promoter, in July, 1871.

No one who heard Douglass speak failed to comment on his wit and humor. But his was a humor wholesome and dignified. Nothing infuriated Douglass more than the attempts of orators to amuse their audiences by telling "darky stories." Once a speaker who preceded him used this device to evoke laughter. When Douglass was introduced, he simply said: "Those stories were very funny, very funny, but I felt each of them to be a foot pressing upon my mother's grave."[26]

Even when he was not specifically lecturing on the problems of his people, Douglass found ways of bringing them to the attention of the public. At one point or another on his lecture tour, he was bound to meet with discrimination on trains and in hotels. Immediately, he would send an indignant letter to the local press, and soon outcries of protest from aroused citizens would fill the papers. Often the proprietors of local hotels would be forced publicly to apologize to Douglass for their conduct.

Few things endeared Frederick Douglass to the Negro masses as much as did his consistent protest against discrimination wherever he was confronted by it. One Negro wrote in December, 1873:

"The indignities that are offered to our leading men on the cars and in hotels are seldom ever mentioned by them, and many persons suppose that because we have colored legislators and other high functionaries that these barriers of caste were broken down; but the Hon. Frederick Douglass never fails to inform the public that they still exist, and he is constantly meeting with them in his travels. Can it be possible that he is the only leading colored man that meets with such treatment? Or are there others ashamed to let the people know what insults they have to endure?"[27]

Douglass' personal encounters with the advocates of white supremacy were used effectively by Charles Sumner in his battle to secure the passage of a national civil rights bill. On the first day of the new

Congress in December, 1873, Sumner pressed for the immediate enact-
ment of a civil rights bill. But he did not live to see the bill reported.
Sumner was taken ill on March 9, 1874, and died two days later.
Douglass and the Negro leaders George T. Downing and Sumner
Wormeley joined the distinguished officials at Sumner's death-bed. Too
sick to recognize anyone, Sumner kept entreating: "You must take care
of the civil rights bill—my bill, the civil rights bill—don't let it fail."
This was his last public message.

Douglass led the funeral procession of 300 Negroes who followed
the hearse to the railroad depot. That evening at a great memorial
meeting of colored people in Washington, Douglass delivered a eulogy
in honor of the greatest friend of his people. "Earnest, loving, sorrowful,
but hopeful words fell from his lips in such a flow of eloquence," wrote
an observer, "that few who were there will forget them."

"What was the great truth for which Sumner struggled, and made his
name dear to every colored man's heart?" Douglass asked. He answered:
"Simply that each individual man belongs to himself!—and yet for asserting
this but a few years ago our deceased friend was struck down beneath the
dome of yonder capitol, and his warm, red blood made to stain the floor
supposed to be sacred to freedom of speech."

In Douglass' opinion, Sumner's best work for the Negro was done
after the Civil War. "He opposed every step towards reconstruction
without a full, clear, complete recognition of the rights of the colored
man. He chided Massachusetts for her haste, and his voice did more
to reconstruct the union on a true basis than that of any other man
in the United States." The more Sumner obtained for the Negro, the
more he wanted. "Each higher level he brought us to only prepared us
for another still higher." Others wavered, but Sumner stood firm,
"untainted by corruption—pure, spotless, stainless." No man could fully
replace him, but one man still lived who could "tread in his footsteps."
Wendell Phillips was the logical man to fill Sumner's seat in the United
States Senate.

Douglass concluded with the following message of advice to his
people:

"Let us go home and teach our children the name of Charles Sumner;
tell them his utterances, and teach them that they, like him, can make their
lives sublime by clinging to principles."[28]

Douglass headed a committee which set out to raise funds from the Negro people for a monument in Sumner's memory. But the best monument, he believed, would be the passage of the civil rights bill. It seemed at first that Sumner's work would be completed, for the bill passed the Senate on May 23, 1874. But in the House the Democrats defeated the bill with the assistance of twelve Republicans.

Denouncing the timidity and perfidy of the Republican Party, Gerrit Smith asked Douglass: "What can we do?—we who are black men, and we white men who are their friends?" He wished it were possible to quit the Republican Party for a time "and thus punish and improve it." But this was no solution, for the moment the Negro people and their friends deserted the Republicans, the Democrats would come into power. And that party remained "bad, very bad, hopelessly bad." Smith ended on a somewhat hopeful note. "Let us be patient with the Republican Party, a year longer."

Douglass, of course, was hardly in need of such advice. He was disappointed but not discouraged. It would take time, but in the end the cause would triumph. "Time and effort will prevail," he assured Smith.[29]

The families of Negroes murdered in broad daylight by the White League found cold comfort in Douglass' assurances. Organized in July, 1874, in New Orleans, the White League had 40,000 members throughout the South before the end of the year. As it spread, the number of Negroes murdered increased. In Mississippi alone some 200 Negroes were killed and thousands wounded in 1874.

Douglass realized that faith alone would not halt the outrages against his people. In October, 1874, he urged "that some formal and impressive notice should be taken of the murderous warfare going on against the newly emancipated citizens and their friends at the South." He proposed "a National Convention of the friends of equal civil and political rights." If prominent Abolitionists would join hands in the new crusade the counter-revolution in the South might still be halted.[30]

But many former Abolitionists were either too tired or were now concentrating on corruption in government. Douglass' appeal evoked the old response: "We have done enough for the Negro." In general, northern reformers were finished with the Negro, and some of them were openly asserting that Negro enfranchisement had been a great mistake.

Douglass pleaded again for a renewal of the struggle for complete freedom, in April, 1875, at the centennial anniversary of the Pennsylvania

Society for Promoting the Abolition of Slavery. After describing the achievements of the anti-slavery crusade, he implored the friends of the Negro to save "the results obtained by the immense labor and suffering of long years of agitation and of war and bloodshed." Then followed a lengthy and penetrating analysis of the fatal flaw in Radical Reconstruction:

"It is said by some: 'We have done enough for the Negro.' Yes, you have done a great deal for the Negro, and, for one, I am deeply sensible of it, and grateful for it. But after all, what have you done? We were slaves—and you have made us free—and given us the ballot. But the world has never seen any people turned loose to such destitution as were the four million slaves of the South. The old roof was pulled down over their heads before they could make for themselves a shelter. They were free! free to hunger; free to the winds and rains of heaven; free to the pitiless wrath of enraged masters, who, since they could no longer control them, were willing to see them starve. They were free, without roofs to cover them, or bread to eat, or land to cultivate, and as a consequence died in such numbers as to awaken the hope of their enemies that they would soon disappear. We gave them freedom and famine at the same time. The marvel is that they still live. What the Negro wants is, first, protection of the rights already conceded by law, and, secondly, education. Talk of having done enough for these people after two hundred years of enforced ignorance and stripes is absurd, cruel, and heartless."

Those who claimed that enough had been done for the Negro simply did not know what was taking place in the South.

"To-day, in the South, the school-house is burned. To-day in Tennessee, Lucy Haydon is called from an inner room at midnight and shot down because she teaches colored children to read. To-day in New Orleans and in Louisiana, and in parts of Alabama, the black man scarcely dares to deposit the votes which you gave him a right to deposit for fear of his life."

Douglass appealed for new Abby Kellys and Anna Dickinsons "to stir this country anew in behalf of humanity." "We need you, my friends, almost as much as ever,"[31] were his final words.

Douglass' plea stirred the audience. But the industrialists and financiers who controlled the economy and dominated the government did not hear him, or if they did, they did not care. Yet these were the men who controlled the destinies of the Negro people. Failing to understand the class character of the struggle in which he was engaged, Douglass did not see that the growing apathy of the Republican Party and the Grant administration toward the problems of his people was simply a reflection of the fact that the former slave owners were no longer a threat to big business and so it was no longer concerned about the Negro.

Big business was having its troubles in the North, for labor, farmers, and small property holders were in revolt against the oppression of the industrialists and the high-handed financial manipulations of Wall Street brokers. Militant strikes, unemployment demonstrations, and the growth of independent political action heralded the fact that the class struggle was sharpening. Frightened by the popular upheaval, the masters of capital began to look with favor at the prospects of an alliance with reactionary elements in the South. Together they could build a solid front against the people's movements. Assured by the southern conservatives that the status quo of the tariff, the national banks, and the national debt would not be disturbed, northern capitalists no longer hesitated. Once the popular governments in the South were overthrown and control restored to the old oligarchy, they reasoned, the way would be cleared for capitalist expansion below the Mason-Dixon line without the risk of social unrest and continued upheaval. Northern industrialists and financiers were ready to unite with southern propertied interests in the super-exploitation of millions of human beings through the oppression of the Negro people.

The northern capitalists had been interested in the Negro only to maintain political leadership of the national government. If they could make a settlement with the southern oligarchy assuring them that economic legislation favorable to them would not be disturbed and that exploitation of southern resources would be encouraged, there was no further need for the Negro vote.[32] As a result the Negro would practically be restored to slavery. But that did not concern the men who feared and fought democracy, who violently opposed every increase in wages, every decrease in hours, every advance that the workingman sought to achieve.

The new alliance between northern and southern propertied interests was to be forged at the expense of the hard-won rights of the Negro people.

While Douglass appealed for renewed effort to halt the counter-revolution in the South, amnesty was being granted to Confederate leaders, and Union troops were withdrawn from state after state. Hand in hand with this, violence was used to suppress the Negro vote and keep the freedman economically oppressed, and the Negroes were left with no protection to face the armed might of the Ku Klux Klan and the White League.

Embittered by the turn of events, Douglass did not succumb to despair. The firm conviction that the struggle "for the ultimate peace and freedom of my race" would continue in spite of defeats and betrayals kept hope alive. As he told a meeting of the colored citizens of Washington in March, 1876:

"But one thing I know, and that is that there is no middle ground for us. We must either have all the rights of American citizens, or we must be exterminated, for we can never again be slaves; nor can we cease to trouble the American people while any right enjoyed by others is denied or withheld from us."[33]

A month later Douglass had a unique opportunity "to trouble the American people." On April 14, 1876, the anniversary of Lincoln's assassination and of the emancipation of the slaves in the District of Columbia, the freedmen's memorial monument to Abraham Lincoln was to be unveiled in Washington.[34] By a joint resolution Congress had declared the day a holiday. President Grant and his cabinet members, Supreme Court justices, and many Senators and Congressmen were seated on the platform erected for the meeting. Douglass was the "orator of the occasion."

Douglass later admitted that he did not like the statue which showed Lincoln standing erect holding the Emancipation Proclamation in his right hand while his left was poised above a kneeling slave on whose wrists were broken shackles. The statue "showed the Negro on his knees when a more manly attitude would have been indicative of freedom."[35] But the truth was that the Negro people in the South were being beaten to their knees by armed ruffians, and the Republican Party, the party of Lincoln, was doing nothing to prevent it. On the platform with Douglass was the man who had just refused to use his power as chief executive to stamp out the new terror unleashed against the Negro people and who was content simply with appealing to the southerners to stop these crimes.

Douglass' oration was impressive. Senator George S. Boutwell wrote the orator:

"I can not refrain from saying after reading your oration twice, once aloud to my family, that it is the best contribution made to the department of literature in which it takes place, since the time of Mr. Webster."[36]

But in one important respect, this famous oration was disappointing. In his fourth of July oration in Rochester fourteen years before, Douglass had said: "We have to do with the past only as we can make it useful to the present and to the future."[37] Very little in his dignified address now reflected this philosophy. The bulk of the oration dealt with the past, with Lincoln's gradual acceptance of anti-slavery measures after two years of vacillation and procrastination, and his stature in the closing years of the war. But Douglass left unmentioned the fact that everything Lincon had achieved for the Negro was being wiped out in state after state in the South. Other than the remark about "the spirit of barbarism, which still lingers to blight and destroy in some dark and distant parts of the country," there was nothing to remind the American people that Lincoln's mission had not yet been accomplished.

No other Negro had ever had so great an opportunity to reach the American people with his message. As Douglass himself pointed out in the opening passages of his address: ". . .we are here where every pulsation of the national heart can be heard, felt, and reciprocated. A thousand wires, fed with thought and winged with lightning, put us in instantaneous communication with the loyal and true men all over this country."[38] Here was the place to repeat the stirring words uttered at the centennial anniversary of the Pennsylvania Anti-Slavery Society. Here, with the President of the United States and other notables listening, was the place to demand "ample protection" for the Negro people in exercising their "sacred right to vote."

Overwhelmed by the honor bestowed upon him, Douglass remained silent on the crucial issues facing his people. And almost a year later, during the Hayes-Tilden bargain that sealed the doom of the Radical Reconstruction, Douglass was again silent.

The bargain came as the climax of the disputed Presidential election of 1876. Samuel J. Tilden, the Democratic candidate, had received 184 electoral votes; he needed only one more vote to be proclaimed President. Rutherford B. Hayes, the Republican candidate, had 166 undisputed votes, but he claimed the votes of South Carolina, Louisiana, and Florida which were being disputed. These electoral votes would give him the necessary 185 for election. Since both sides claimed victory in the three states, the Presidency hung on the outcome of a decision regarding these votes.

The dispute was finally turned over to an electoral commission which gave Hayes the contested states of Florida, Louisiana, South Carolina, and also that of Oregon. But the commission's decision required the approval of both houses of Congress.

To win over the Southern Democrats who had a large majority in the House of Representatives, Hayes struck a hard bargain. The price was the complete abandonment of the Negro masses to the southern reactionaries (along with Republican support of liberal appropriations for Southern internal improvements and the passage of the Texas Pacific Railroad Bill).

On February 26 and 27, 1877, a series of conferences was held between Hayes' followers and the leaders of the southern Democrats. The outcome of these conferences was a letter, under the signature of Stanley Matthews and Charles Foster, personal friends and political advisers of Hayes, to the southerners with promises as to Hayes' future southern policy. The writers would urge Hayes to "adopt such a policy as will give the people of the States of South Carolina and Louisiana the right to control their own affairs in their own way, subject to the constitution of the United States and the laws made in pursuance thereof. . . ." They added "that from an acquaintance with and knowledge of Governor Hayes and his views, we have the most complete confidence that such will be the policy of his administration."[39]

This was what the southern Democrats had been waiting for. In referring to the people of South Carolina and Louisiana, they knew that Hayes' representatives meant white people. They were not disturbed by the allusion to the "constitution of the United States and the laws made in pursuance thereof" for once the federal troops were removed, they would deal with the constitution as they saw fit.[40]

At 4 A.M. March 4, 1877, came the announcement that Rutherford B. Hayes had been elected President of the United States.

Twelve years later, Douglass vigorously denied the charge that he had been "silent in 1876, when Hayes abandoned the colored people of the South." "Everybody who knows me and knows of my course before and during the administration of Mr. Hayes, knows that I was not silent. I was, from first to last, outspoken, and among those known to be opposed to his Southern policy, and of this no one knew better than President Hayes himself. He knew it before he came to Washington. . . ."[41]

The evidence does not entirely support Douglass. Although he did speak out later against Hayes' southern policy, he remained silent while the President, soon after his inauguration, withdrew federal troops from Columbia, South Carolina, and New Orleans—a step which assured the complete triumph of the counter-revolution in the South. Moreover, the evidence does not sustain Douglass' statement that even before coming to Washington, Hayes knew that the Negro leader opposed his southern policy. The following appears in Hayes' diary for February 18, 1877:

"The indications still are that I am to go to Washington. I talked yesterday with Fred Douglass and Mr. Poindexter, both colored, on the Southern question. I told them my views. They approved. Mr. Douglass gave me many useful hints about the whole subject. My course is a firm assertion and maintenance of the rights of the colored people of the South according to the Thirteenth, Fourteenth, and Fifteenth Amendments, coupled with a readiness to recognize all Southern people, without regard to past political conduct, who will now go with me heartily and in good faith in support of these principles."[42]

The interview took place before the bargain between Hayes and the southern Democrats, and it may be argued that the southern policy outlined above was one that Douglass could in all sincerity endorse. But it was clear by inauguration day that Hayes' agreement to remove the last remaining federal troops from the South had rendered meaningless his pledge to uphold the rights of the colored people. At this crucial moment Douglass voiced no opposition to Hayes' policy.

Douglass' critics charged that "a fat office gagged him,"[43] referring to his appointment as U.S. Marshal of the District of Columbia. By accepting the appointment, said Douglass' critics, he had done a disservice to his people. For now Hayes could pose as a champion of Negro rights while bargaining away the Negro's freedom.

Douglass saw the appointment in a different light. To him it was "an innovation upon long established usage," and would prove "gratifying to a large class of the American people of all colors and races."[44] The nomination, confirmed by the Senate over the bitter opposition of the leading lawyers of the District of Columbia, was enough to convince him that he had made a contribution toward the progress of his people. Shortly after his appointment had been confirmed by a vote of 30 to 12, he wrote to his friend, Samuel D. Porter:

"Only men like yourself, men born in advance of their time, men who saw and comprehended the dignity of human nature, whether under one complexion or another, long before these sunny days, can now fully comprehend the significance of this appointment and confirmation."[45]

The criticism of Douglass was not wholly justified. The political appointment did not gag him. The bright flame of the man's passion for truth and justice blazed forth with its old fire. In May, 1877, he lashed out at Jim-Crow in Washington, declaring the city "a most disgraceful and scandalous contradiction to the march of civilization as compared with many other parts of the country." It had been a great mistake, he argued, to have placed the nation's capital between two of the oldest slave states, "each of which was a nursery and a hot bed of slavery."[46]

As soon as Douglass' remarks were published, Washington was in an uproar. If it were Douglass' express purpose to lay before the world the seamy side of American politics and culture, he could hardly have found a more dramatic way to do so than exhibiting the pattern of segregation and discrimination which prevailed within the capital. Washingtonians had hailed the compromise of 1877, and now Douglass had upset the apple-cart by attacking segregation in their own city. *The New York Times* put it well:

"A man who was not only black, but who was born in bondage, had been appointed Marshal of the District. Worse than this, he had, in a public lecture, said some things about Washington which everybody knew to be true. If these had not been true, perhaps nobody would have cared. They have been said about Washington a great many times before, but never by a man whose skin was dark-colored, and who had been appointed to office in the District. "Unhappily, the basis of agreement of which Mr. Douglass formed a part was already accepted by the 'Conservative' element of Washington. His remarks, therefore, were calculated to 'revive the old war feeling,' and reopen the chasm which had been closed by several citizens going on his bond. The faithlessness of this act will be seen at a glance. When a class of men consent to let bygones be bygones, every consideration should be shown their tender feelings. If they have consented to receive a colored office-holder, after due protest, as a man and a brother, it stands to reason that he ought to walk very softly before them. He is, in a manner, on probation. But the conduct of this dark-skinned official was simply monstrous. If he had been white and free-born, he could not have affected greater independence of manner. He actually said just what he thought, and, what was worse, he admitted that he had said it before he was an accepted compromise. It was clear that he did not realize his position as a national olive branch and a token of reconciliation."[47]

Petitions signed by leading business men of Washington were presented to President Hayes demanding Douglass' removal from office but the President refused to act. Gradually the uproar subsided.

Douglass was grateful to Hayes, but this did not prevent him from publicly criticizing Hayes because he "withdrew our few troops from the South, recognized the Shot-Gun Governments of South Carolina and Louisiana, and thoroughly adopted and carried out a declared policy of pacification." In a speech in Washington on November 7, 1877, Douglass said bluntly: "I do not disguise the fact, that office-holder though I am, that the way this peace has been sought is not my way, nor do I believe that it will or ought to succeed." He favored the establishment of peace in the South. But he wanted peace with justice!

"Yes, let us have peace, but let us have liberty, law and justice first. Let us have the Constitution, with its thirteenth, fourteenth, and fifteenth amendments, fairly interpreted, faithfully executed and cheerfully obeyed in the fullness of their spirit and the completeness of their letter. . . . When the supreme law of the land is practically set at naught, when humanity is insulted and the rights of the weak are trampled in the dust by a lawless power; when society is divided into two classes, as oppressed and oppressor, there is no power and there can be no power, while the instincts of humanity remain as they are, which can provide solid peace."[48]

No, Douglass was not "gagged" by his government position. Early in 1879 he wrote in all sincerity: "When the influence of office, or any other influence, shall soften my hatred of tyranny and violence, do not spare me, let fall upon me the lash of your keenest and most withering censure."[49] To the very end, in and out of public office, he would continue to press the claims of the Negro people. And never once did he preach submission.

The Post-Reconstruction Era

With the ending of the Reconstruction period Douglass' position among the Negro people remained as firm as ever. He was their elder statesman to whom they looked for counsel and guidance. In such high esteem was he held by the Negro people that, in spite of the criticism of his conduct during the closing years of Reconstruction, his leadership remained substantially unimpaired.

Yet much of the criticism was justified. He had failed to use his great influence among his people to force the Republican Party to stop talking about its past achievements for the colored man and to do something for his immediate future. As George T. Downing correctly pointed out:

"Frederick Douglass might have brought home to the republican party the points that should have been made; it would have been more chary of its course had he done so in a bold manner. If a half-dozen colored men I could name had spoken out fearlessly as to the faithlessness of that party they would have been heeded; it has calculated upon falling back on certain colored men."[1]

Douglass himself admitted that he had been used by the Republicans "to stand in the gap and prevent the stampede" of Negro voters to the Democrats.[2] He had been willing to assume this role because he sincerely believed this was in the best interests of the Negro people. His stand was in his people's best interest as long as the Republicans had pressed for the enforcement of the Fourteenth and Fifteenth amendments, but not when the Republican Party lost interest in fighting for the cause, came to terms with the southern Democrats, and abandoned them to the former slaveowners. Yet Douglass continued to talk as if nothing had happened to the Republican Party. As late as the Presidential campaign of 1876 he wrote: "It is the same old conflict: Liberty, union and civilization on the one hand and Slavery, disunion and barbarism on the other."[3] This must have sounded hollow indeed to the Negroes who were fighting desperately against lynchings, beatings, and terrorization while the Republicans—the upholders of "Liberty, union and civilization"—were withdrawing federal troops and capitulating to the forces of "Slavery, disunion and barbarism."

In addition to his lack of understanding of the class forces during the closing years of Reconstruction, Douglass' failing as a leader in this crucial period was mainly because he was completely out of touch with Negro masses. Operating almost exclusively in the North and lecturing in the main to white audiences, he had no way of learning first-hand the real condition of the southern Negro. After 1872, he did not even have the advantage of establishing contact with southern Negroes at colored people's conventions.

His changing economic status in the post-war period was largely responsible for making Douglass a stranger to the problems of his people.

He confesses in his autobiography that he was no longer fit for physical labor after his career as anti-slavery agitator. Instead he became a lecturer at the then fat fee of one hundred dollars a lecture. By 1876 he had enough money to purchase a twenty-room house on a fifteen-acre estate just across the bridge that spanned the Anacostia branch of the Potomac.

Douglass continued to receive great honors. He was always invited to speak at prominent national and local gatherings, and men of the loftiest positions in the government came to hear him. In 1879 the citizens of Rochester placed his bust in the Sibley Hall of the University of Rochester. It would be unfair to say that his head was turned by this special treatment, for he always made it clear to those who invited him that he would "bring the colored man with me."[4] Yet it is certain that he was less able to feel the terrible hardships his people were facing.

It was precisely during the years when Douglass' personal fortune was rising that a new form of slavery was established in the South for the older form which had been outlawed by the Thirteenth Amendment. After the withdrawal of federal troops, conditions for the Negro became intolerable. He was systematically disfranchised and kept from voting by force, economic intimidation and later by a system of election qualification which, by the turn of the century, had nearly excluded the Negro from politics. He was just as systematically defrauded of his meager earnings by the vicious share-cropping system, with its pernicious credit arrangement, involving payment in "scrip" good only at plantation-owned stores at which exorbitant prices were charged. With the police, the courts, and the entire governmental apparatus in the hands of white planters, the widespread and severe exploitation of black labor went unchecked. Mob law, murder, and lynching awaited any Negro who dared to stand up for his rights. Negroes were arrested on the slightest provocation and given long sentences or fines which they were compelled to work out under a vicious peonage system. Sworn public documents reveal that nearly 3,500 persons, most of whom were Negroes, were killed between 1866 and 1879, and their murderers were never brought to trial or even arrested.[5]

Denied all rights of citizenship, without even the minimum standards of existence, and terrorized by physical violence, the Negro was receptive to any plan which would help him escape the new regime in the South. After 1876 emigration movements arose in many southern states, and in 1878, a colonization council, organized by Henry Adams of Shreveport, Louisiana, had recruited ninety-eight thousand Negroes from Louisiana, Mississippi, Alabama and Texas, all of whom were ready to leave the South even if they "had to run away and go into the woods." By 1879 thousands of Negroes had joined in a great trek to Kansas, Missouri, and Indiana. "Pap" Singleton, a Negro undertaker from Tennessee, styled himself the father of the movement, and distributed circulars and pamphlets all over the South urging Negroes to come to "sunny Kansas" where they would enjoy "the advantage of living in a Free State."[6]

Negro leaders were in wide disagreement over whether or not Negroes should leave the South. Richard T. Greener, Harvard's first Negro graduate and dean of Howard law school, advocated emigration as the only way to put an end to the exploitation of the Negro. The exodus, he argued, would not only bring better economic and political opportunities to Negroes who migrated, but would even benefit those who remained.[7]

Douglass vigorously disagreed. In letters to the newspapers and in a debate with Greener, he voiced opposition to this migration to Kansas. He reminded the "exodusters" that "the way of an oppressed people from bondage to freedom is never smooth." The Negro possessed a mighty power in the South which would in time win for him greater freedom and equality. Negro labor, he explained, was essential to the South because the black man was able to work in that climate and under those conditions. This labor belonged now to a free man, who could give it or withhold it, or move wherever he desired with it. The Negro should use this weapon to secure for himself a free, comfortable, and independent life. His labor was more to him, said Douglass, "than fire, swords, ballot boxes or bayonets." And now, when the freedman had proved that he could work better as a free man than as a slave and he was working his way up—(his conditions were far worse at the close of the Civil War said Douglass)—he was now leaving his old home. The rights of the Negro may have suffered a setback in the South, but this was temporary. For the American Constitution was pledged to secure the rights of the Negro, and the American people would get behind the Constitution unless the Negroes themselves, by mass migration, confessed that "on the soil of the South, the United States Constitution cannot be enforced, and that the National Government is either unwilling or powerless to protect the lives and liberties of loyal citizens."

"If the people of this country," Douglass continued, "cannot be protected in every State of the Union, the government of the United States is shorn of its rightful dignity and power, the late rebellion has triumphed, the sovereignty of the nation is an empty name, and the power and authority in the individual States is greater than the power and authority of the United States."[8]

These arguments aroused the anger of the advocates of emigration. Hisses and yells greeted Douglass' name at emigration meetings. Critics openly accused the one-time runaway slave of denying freedom for others. In opposing the exodus, they charged, Douglass had openly allied himself with the planter class of the South.[9]

Douglass' opposition to migration was sincere. He felt that this was an attempt at a solution of the problem by flight when it should be solved by the intervention of the national government. As he put it forcefully on August 22, 1879: "A government that cannot, or does not protect the humblest citizen in his right to life, liberty and the pursuit of happiness, should be reformed or overthrown without delay."[10]

Nevertheless, many of the arguments Douglass advanced against "a general stampede of the colored people from the South to the North" proved how little he knew about the life and the conditions of his people. That Negro labor was essential to the South was correct but the southern ruling class and their northern big-business allies had no intention of allowing the Negro to use that labor to improve himself. When he spoke of the Negro's ability to withhold his labor, he ignored the fact that the black laborer had either to work or starve. When he said that the Negro could leave his job and move away he revealed an ignorance of the existence of vagrancy and labor contract laws which practically tied the black worker to the soil. Nor did he understand the operation of the various systems of peonage by which Negroes were hired out by the county to pay the fine for a crime or to pay a debt.

Douglass displayed a weakness for legalistic methods when he relied on the Constitution to settle the problems of the Negro. The Republicans were doing nothing to uphold the constitutional rights of the Negro people, and for the southern Bourbons the Fourteenth and Fifteenth amendments did not seem to exist. Moreover, the Supreme Court very readily wiped out most of the progressive legislation on which Douglass' hopes were based. In the cases of United States *vs.* Reese and United States *vs.* Cruikshank, the Supreme Court declared unconstitutional the laws designed to enforce the Fourteenth and Fifteenth amendments and rendered them innocuous so far as the Negro was concerned.

The exodus proved a failure. The emigrants were attacked and denied transportation by white mobs who realized their importance to the southern labor market. Those who were able to reach the northern states arrived penniless and without prospect of immediate employment, and many faced a Kansas winter destitute, unhoused, and ill-clad. Once out of the South, they found that the poison of Jim Crow still prevailed. Houses prepared for the "exodusters" were burned, crowds gathered at railroad stations to warn them they could not stop and must go elsewhere, and in St. Louis the mayor issued a proclamation advising them to steer clear of the city.[11]

With the aid of northern relief agencies and by their own remarkable sturdiness, some Negroes established a new life in Kansas where they enjoyed some security and peace. But the majority of the weary migrants returned to the South and to the miseries imposed upon them by the old slave owners.

Douglass never wavered in his belief that fundamentally the battle for Negro freedom could not be solved by running away from the South. But in time he began to modify many of the arguments he had raised during the controversy over the exodus. In 1883 when the Supreme Court declared unconstitutional the Civil Rights Act of 1875 which had granted equal rights to all citizens on public conveyances on land or sea, at hotels, inns, theaters, and other places of public amusement, the decision was to weaken one of the major arguments Douglass had raised against the exodus.

Speaking at a mass indignation meeting at Lincoln Hall in Washington, Douglass denounced the decision as "a further illustration of the reactionary tendencies of public opinion against the black man." He looked upon it "as one more shocking development of the moral weakness in high places which has attended the conflict between the spirit of liberty and the spirit of slavery from the beginning. . . . " It had "inflicted a heavy calamity upon seven millions of the people of this country, and left them naked and defenceless against the action of a malignant, vulgar and pitiless prejudice." And it had presented "the United States before the world as a Nation utterly destitute of power to protect the right of its own citizens upon its own soil."[12]

Douglass' forthright address frightened some of his former associates in the anti-slavery movement.

"If the colored leaders take to denouncing the Supreme Court," wrote Albert H. Walker, "they will alienate the sympathies of their best friends in the North. . . . If the colored leaders counsel a dignified submission to the inevitable, it will raise their reputation both in the North and in the South. It will show that they are above being bothered by trifles."[13]

Douglass had only scorn for such timid advice. And his indignation and scorn increased when in 1888 he visited South Carolina and Georgia and realized how little he had known about the true conditions of his people in the South. On April 10, soon after his return, he wrote to one of the leaders of a movement for encouraging the emigration of southern Negroes to the northwest:

"I had hoped that the relations subsisting between the former slaves and the old master class would gradually improve; but while I believed this, and still have some such weak faith, I have of late seen enough, heard enough, and learned enough of the condition of these people in South Carolina and Georgia, to make me welcome any movement which will take them out of the wretched condition in which I now know them to be. While I shall continue to labor for increased justice to those who stay in the South, I give you my hearty 'God-speed' in your emigration scheme. I believe you are doing a good work."[14]

A few days later, he spoke in Washington at the celebration of the twenty-sixth anniversary of emancipation in the District of Columbia. His address revealed how deeply he had been moved by his southern tour. His voice quivered with rage as he described how the Negro was "nominally free" but actually a slave. In earnest tones, he told the nation: "I here and now denounce his so-called emancipation as a stupendous fraud—a fraud upon him, a fraud upon the world." He drew a terrifying picture of the exploitation of the southern Negro:

"Do you ask me why the Negro of the plantation has made so little progress, why his cupboard is empty, why he flutters in rags, why his children run naked, and why his wife hides herself behind the hut when a stranger is passing? I will tell you. It is because he is systematically and universally cheated out of his hard earnings. The same class that once extorted his labor under the lash now gets his labor by a mean, sneaking, and fraudulent device. That device is a trucking system which never permits him to see or save a dollar of his hard earnings. He struggles and struggles, but, like a man in a morass, the more he struggles the deeper he sinks. The highest wages paid him is $8 a month, and this he receives only in orders on the store, which, in many cases, is owned by his employer. . . . The only security the wretched Negro has under this arrangement is the conscience of the store-keeper—a conscience educated in the school of slavery, where the idea prevailed in theory and practice that the Negro had no rights which the white men were bound to respect, an arrangement in which everything in the way of food or clothing, whether tainted meat or damaged cloth, is deemed good enough for the Negro. For these he is often made to pay a double price."

But Douglass did not give only his own observations. He quoted the text of landlord and tenant laws in the South to show "how completely and rigidly the rights of the landlord are guarded and how entirely the tenant is in the clutches of the landlord." These laws were "a disgrace and a scandal to American civilization." They sounded like "the grating hinges of a slave prison," and held the Negro "firmly bound in a strong, remorseless, and deadly grasp, a grasp from which only death can free him."

After summarizing all he had seen in the South, Douglass cried:

"I ask, in view of it all, how, in the name of human reason, could the Negro be expected to rise higher in the scale of morals, manners, religion, and civilization than he has during the twenty years of his freedom. Shame, eternal shame, on those writers and speakers who taunt, denounce, and disparage the Negro because he is to-day found in poverty, rags, and wretchedness."

But Douglass did not confine his blasts to the southern plantation owners alone. He denounced the national government for having abandoned the Negro, ignored his rights as an American citizen, and left him "a deserted, a defrauded, a swindled, and an outcast man—in law, free; in fact, a slave." Toward the Negro, "every attribute of a just government is contradicted. For him, it is not a government of the people, by the people, and for the people. Toward him, it abandons the beneficent character of a government, and all that gives a government the right to exist." The government professed "to give him citizenship and silently permits him to be divested of every attribute of citizenship. It demands allegiance, but denies protection. It taxes him as a citizen in peace, and compels him to bear arms and meet bullets in war. It imposes upon him all the burdens of citizenship and withholds from him all its benefits."[15]

Here was the old Douglass, the forceful anti-slavery orator who had moved audiences on two continents, the man who could bring home more vividly than any other speaker the evils of slavery and the necessity to overthrow it. Here was the tribune of the Negro people presenting the most powerful indictment of the new slavery in the new South.

Douglass' speech created a sensation. Hamilton J. Smith, who described himself as "a humble Negro citizen of Massachusetts," hastened to thank Douglass "for the noble and manly words spoken . . . in behalf of my race." Senator George B. Edmonds called it "the greatest political speech that I have read or heard in perhaps twenty years," and believed that "it will revive fires of devotion to freedom and justice that in our boasts for past achievements had nearly died out. Your speech should be printed broadcast through our land, and similar speeches should be made in every school district in this country." Congressman J. B. White wrote: "You spoke sorrowful facts—and such things must be stopped if this free Nation is to live." Charles N. Hunter, Negro editor of *The Progressive Educator,* official organ of the North Carolina State Teachers' Association, reported the reaction of southern Negroes to Douglass' speech.

"The colored people here," he wrote from Durham, "are eagerly seeking papers containing the speech and are reading it with an interest and enthusiasm which I have not witnessed since the early days of emancipation. You should have the assurance of our people in all parts of the country that you have comprehended our situation clearly and that the noble sentiments so eloquently enunciated in your address meet a warm response from the Negro of the South. I have been longing and waiting and waiting and longing for some one of our great men to rise to the height of the occasion. I need not conceal the discouragement which your grand effort has lifted. A ray of hope pierces the gloom and I can now look hopefully forward. And is there not inspiration for us all when Douglass buckles on his armor and his gleaming cementer [*sic*] glistens in the glare of battle?"[16]

As financial success came to Douglass it seemed at times that this militant champion of freedom was becoming a cautious conservative. But these were surface manifestations. Douglass understood that the future of the Negro workers was linked with the struggles of the trade unions for better conditions and with those of radical movements that advanced far-reaching changes in the economic system. Douglass repeatedly urged the rising labor movement of the 1880's to lower the barriers against Negro workers and make use of the mighty power of colored labor in its battle for the eight-hour day, higher wages, and better working conditions. Speaking at a Convention of Colored Men at Louisville, Kentucky in September, 1883, he appealed directly to the trade unions to welcome Negro workers into their ranks:

"Their cause is one with the labor class all over the world. The labor unions of the country should not throw away this colored element of strength. . . . It is a great mistake for any class of laborers to isolate itself and thus weaken the bond of brotherhood between those on whom the burden and hardships of labor fall. The fortunate ones of the earth, who are abundant in land and money and know nothing of the anxious care and pinching poverty of the laboring classes, may afford to be indifferent to the appeal for justice at this point, but the laboring classes cannot afford to be indifferent. . . . Experience demonstrates that there may be a slavery of wages only a little less galling and crushing in its effects than chattel slavery, and that this slavery of wages must go down with the other."[17]

There were times during the post-Reconstruction period when Douglass seemed discouraged. Yet never did he weary of the fight. As in the days of the anti-slavery crusade, he constantly preached the need for agitation. There was no "room for complacency" in his philosophy. "We can expose fraud, we can denounce violence, we can kindle the moral indignation of the country against meanness and crime," he told those who were ready to admit to defeat, and creep, brooding, into their tents. He was the sworn foe of all who cautioned the Negro to conform and accept the domination of white officials, white police, and the laws and ordinances made by white men. In simple but image-creating words he would reply:

"We are making war against those who say we cannot have our rights. When you drop the seed of injustice there will invariably spring up contention, strife, and blood. England cannot have peace while her heel is on the heart of Ireland; nor Russia while she places spies at every hearthstone and sends her children into exile; nor Turkey while it will not tolerate Christians; nor the South while it stamps upon the Constitution, and denies the colored people the rights guaranteed by the Constitution."[18]

This was the Douglass the Negroes revered. Because he was fearless in fighting the forces of reaction, they forgave him his shortcomings: "Of course I do not agree with all your views, but the fight for the race is there and that satisfies me," wrote one Negro in 1886.[19] From the deep South came a letter written by a Negro which expressed love and devotion:

"I am one of those way down here in Mississippi born and bread [sic] here being a subscriber to the Washington National Republican, I read your speech and can say that it is one of the best that I ever read from you. Go on with your good & glorious work in defense of the Negroes of this country—and I will in my feeble prayers ask God to aid & assist you in the struggle. May God add a blessing to you & prosper you to the end of life and at last save you in heaven."[20]

Douglass himself offered the best reason for his hold on the Negro people. Speaking extemporaneously at a surprise birthday party held by the Bethel Literary Society on the occasion of his seventy-first birthday, he said:

"I think I can understand what you mean by this demonstration. It is not for any ability or attainments of which I can personally boast. You notice me on the only ground upon which I have any claim on your consideration—and that is that during nearly fifty years of my life I have been an unflinching, unflagging and uncompromising advocate and defender of the oppressed. When the slave was a slave I demanded his emancipation, and when he was free, I demanded his perfect freedom—all the safeguards of freedom. In whatever else I may have failed, in this I have not failed.

"And I can now only say in conclusion, that with the help of God, in the future as in the past, while life shall endure, you shall find me faithful in the support of every movement and measure looking to the enlightenment and improvement of our yet much oppressed, abused and slandered people."[21]

Some Personal Notes

After his appointment as Marshal of the United States for the District of Columbia, Douglass knew the meaning of leisure for the first time. He did not abandon the lecture platform, but he was no longer required to devote six months of each year traveling. His duties as a government official were hardly fatiguing, for the Marshal no longer even had the function of introducing guests at the White House on state occasions as had been the practice under Presidents Grant and Lincoln.[1]

His newly acquired leisure gave Douglass the opportunity to do those things he had long wanted to do. When his life had been "mainly spent upon the platform and upon Railroads during winter and spring," he had had little time for social life in his home community. Now he visited a great deal, read with the Uniontown Shakespeare club, and frequently attended the theatre.[2] Now he was able to maintain his huge correspondence in some order, and did not have to apologize for the lateness of his replies. Most important of all, he could spend time with his family. At his spacious home in Anacostia which he named "Cedar Hill," Douglass felt like a patriarch. His children and grandchildren visited him throughout the year, and stayed on for weeks. Two of his granddaughters lived at "Cedar Hill" for several years. Douglass was proud of their accomplishments.

"Annie has considerable taste and skill in music," he wrote. "Hattie sings—and is blest with a joyous disposition."[3]

Douglass remained in public office almost a decade after Hayes' election, although he did not hold the marshalship for more than four years. In December, 1880, he learned that "an earnest effort" was being made to prevent his reappointment by President-elect Garfield. "In respect to this movement," he wrote to Garfield asking for a reappointment, "I want to say whatever may be the ostensible reasons given for it, the real ground of opposition to me is that I am a colored man, and that my sympathies are with my recently enslaved people." His reappointment thus was more than a personal issue. It was tied up with the whole campaign to deprive the Negro people of their rightful place in American life.

Among those who urged Garfield to reappoint Douglass was the great American humorist and novelist, Mark Twain. On January 12, 1881, he wrote to the President-elect:

"Several times since your election persons wanting office have asked me 'to use my influence' with you in their behalf.

"To word it in that way was such a pleasant compliment to me that I never complied. I *could* not without exposing the fact that I hadn't any influence with you and that was a thing I had no mind to do.

"It seems to me that it is better to have a good man's flattering estimate of my influence—and to keep it—than to fool it away with trying to get him an office. But when my brother—on my wife's side—Mr. Charles J. Langdon —late of the Chicago Convention—desires me to speak a word for Mr. Fred Douglass, I am not asked 'to use my influence' consequently I am not risking anything. So I am writing this as a simple citizen. I am not drawing on my fund of influence at all. A simple citizen may express a desire with all propriety, in the matter of a recommendation to office, and so I beg permission to hope that you will retain Mr. Douglass in his present office of Marshall of the District of Columbia, if such a course will not clash with your own preferences or with the expediencies and interest of your administration. I offer this petition with peculiar pleasure and strong desire, because I so honor this man's high and blemishless character and so admire his brave, long crusade for the liberties and elevation of his race.

"He is a personal friend of mine, but that is nothing to the point, his history would move me to say these things without that, and I feel them too."[4]

When Garfield told Douglass that he wished to appoint a close friend to the office of Marshal, Douglass withdrew his application. His feelings, however, were assuaged when Garfield assured him that he would be appointed Recorder of Deeds for the District of Columbia.[5] The appointment came through shortly after Garfield's inauguration. After Garfield's assassination, Douglass remained in office during President Arthur's administration.

As Recorder of Deeds Douglass had even less work. His health, none too good since his return from Santo Domingo in 1871, improved rapidly. "Of myself I can say," he wrote in 1882, "I have not felt in better health at any time during the last five years. I now walk every morning from 'Cedar Hill' to the City Hall and am less fatigued than when I adopted the practice. . . . " A five mile walk every morning was no mean accomplishment for a man well over sixty. Douglass attributed his endurance to his personal habits. In 1884, four years after he gave up cigars, he wrote: "I neither drink, smoke, chew nor take snuff."[6]

In August, 1882, Anna Douglass died. She had been suffering from rheumatism for several years and was almost completely paralysed during the last month. Despite "faithful constant care and nursing" she passed away.

"Mother was the post in the center of my house and held us together," wrote Douglass shortly after her death. He had been sincerely devoted to his wife and appreciated her amazing capacity to manage her increasing family and household duties. He had often regretted that her illness had kept her confined indoors. In 1877 Douglass, writing of his joy in reading from *The Merchant of Venice* at the Uniontown Shakespeare club, added: "I find it very pleasant and entertaining but I have no one at my house to go with me, and I often fancy I am losing one-half of the happiness of such occasions because in such matters I am alone."[7]

In January, 1884, eighteen months after Anna Douglass' death, Douglass married Helen Pitts, a college-trained white woman of forty-six who had been his secretary in the recorder's office. Her relatives opposed the marriage, but Helen was not persuaded by their arguments. "Love came to me," she said later, "and I was not afraid to marry the man I loved because of his color."[8]

Two hours after the wedding, the news of the marriage became public. Immediately a storm descended upon the happy couple. The overwhelming majority of the Negroes were bitter and felt betrayed by their leader. Some charged that Douglass had shown "contempt for the women of his own race," while others denounced him for having "married a common, poor white woman."[9]

White people responded too. The *Gazette* of Franklin, Virginia, called Douglass "a lecherous old African Solomon." A correspondent from Atlanta wrote Reverend Francis J. Grimké who had performed the marriage ceremony that he "ought to be damned out of Society." A "Little Tar and Fetters [sic] would be good for you," he added.[10]

But there were letters of congratulations also both from Negroes and whites. H. W. Gilbert, an old friend, expressed "great joy that you have taken for a wife a lady [of] so firm accomplishment and one who will make happy your remaining years." Elizabeth Cady Stanton denounced "the clamor" raised against the marriage. Julia Griffiths Crofts hastened to send congratulations from England and "to express the hope that the step you have now taken may tend to promote your true happiness in the evening of your days." One correspondent was convinced that though the marriage had "startled the public . . . it has set it to thinking, and a happy result of your union will do more to harmonize the 'races,' than all constitutional amendments, civil rights laws and judicial decisions."[11]

Douglass had a ready answer to the criticisms of his second marriage. He would laughingly remark that it proved that he was quite impartial—his first wife "was the color of my mother, and the second, the color of my father." In a more serious vein, he pointed out that his marriage was in keeping with his entire philosophy of life. He had always insisted that the question of color was an artificial issue raised to justify and continue the degradation of the Negro people, that men and women "no matter of what race or complexion" should "be allowed to enjoy the rights of a common nature" which included the right to obey the conviction of their own minds and hearts in marriage. He had always viewed with scorn the clamor raised against amalgamation of the races. "For 200 years and more in slavery and outside of marriage," he wrote in the 'eighties, "amalgamation went on under the fostering care of church, pulpit, press, and American statesmanship with only here and there a voice, and that a hated and despised voice, raised against it. But now that the Negro is free, and has been invested with political and civil rights, sounds of alarm reach us from all quarters." The existence of quadroons and mulattoes all over the South was sufficient proof to Douglass that the outcry against the intermarriage of Negroes and whites was pure hypocrisy.[12]

In a broader sense, it must be remembered that while he spoke and acted all his life as a Negro, Douglass always insisted that his devotion to freedom and justice had no relation to color and race. Two months after his second marriage he wrote:

"I have held all my life and shall hold to the day of my death, that the fundamental and everlasting objection to slavery, is not that it sinks a Negro to the condition of a brute, but that it sinks a *man* to that condition. I base no man's right upon his color and plead no man's rights because of his color. My interest in any man is objectively in his manhood and subjectively in my own manhood."

And again:

"My sympathies are not limited by my relation to any race. I can take no part in oppressing and persecuting any variety of the human family. Whether in Russia, Germany or California, my sympathy is with the oppressed, be he Chinaman or Hebrew."[13]

Douglass felt that had he yielded to the fear of public disapproval of his marriage his whole life would have been a sham and mockery. "I could never have been at peace with my own soul or held up my head among men had I allowed the fear of popular clamor to deter me from following my convictions as to this marriage," he wrote to Elizabeth Cady Stanton. "I should have gone to my grave a self accused and a self convicted moral coward."[14]

The marriage brought Douglass great happiness. He and Helen had common interests. For example, both were active in the woman suffrage movement. In reply to an invitation to attend a suffrage convention in 1884, Douglass wrote: "Of course, if I come, as I now think I shall, I will bring Helen with me, for she is not less a woman suffragist than myself."[15]

"Sometimes," writes Mrs. Mary Church Terrell, the great Negro woman fighter for civil rights, who was a "frequent visitor to Cedar Hill," "Douglass took out his fiddle, sang Scottish songs of which he was very fond, and played a few tunes. Then he and my husband would usually get up and dance a few steps, entertaining us immensely."[16]

Visitors to "Cedar Hill" would often come upon Douglass playing the violin to Helen's piano accompaniment. After one such visit, a correspondent concluded that "it is not strange that Douglass should have wished to marry this woman somewhat his equal intellectually." "Mrs. Douglass," he added, "is very much in love with her husband. That she admires and is proud of him is plain to see."[17]

Not all of the visitors to "Cedar Hill" were of the "distinguished" variety. Students from Howard University were welcome and were often invited either for Sunday tea or for a game of croquet at which sport Douglass was very skillful. Many young Negroes came to "Cedar Hill" from all parts of the country to discuss their problems with Douglass. For they knew of his work in encouraging and aiding promising and talented Negroes. He had done much, for example, to publicize the work of Paul Laurence Dunbar, the poet, and to assist him in his bitter struggle for recognition.

"I first heard of Dunbar from Douglass," Mrs. Mary Church Terrell recalls. "One day by appointment I went to see Douglass in his Anacostia home. After we had finished our business, Douglass, who was widely known as 'the Sage of Anacostia,' asked me, 'Have you ever heard of Paul Dunbar?' I told him I had not. Then Douglass told me Dunbar's story.

" 'He is very young,' he said, 'but there is no doubt that he is a poet. He is working under the most discouraging circumstances in his home in Dayton, Ohio. He is an elevator boy and on his meager wage of four dollars a week he is trying to support his mother and himself. Let me read you one of his poems.' Douglass left the room and returned with a newspaper clipping from which he began to read Dunbar's *The Drowsy Day*. When he had read several stanzas his voice faltered and his eyes grew moist. He was deeply moved. 'What a tragedy it is,' he said, 'that a young man with such talent should be so terribly handicapped by poverty and color.' I shall never forget Douglass' reading of that poem."[18]

Douglass was the commissioner in charge of the exhibit from Haiti at the World's Fair held in Chicago in 1893, to celebrate the 400th anniversary of the discovery of America by Columbus. He employed Paul Laurence Dunbar to assist him.

In April, 1886, "Gath," the famous Washington correspondent for the *Cincinnati Enquirer,* paid a visit to "Cedar Hill." His description of the Douglass household went in part:

"When I entered the house with Mr. Gorham, he introduced us carefully to the different persons there—quite a little party. We had gone to see him without invitation, and therefore broke in upon his ordinary Sunday family circle. There were three white ladies present, one of whom was Mrs. Douglass. The other ladies heard the conversation, smiled affably, but made few or no remarks. Mrs. Douglass is a lady of tall form; well-made, but neither stout nor thin. Her complexion is a little reddish. She gives you the idea somewhat of a woman who had been the matron or superintendent of some philanthropic institution in which charity plays the principal part. She dresses herself plainly and modestly, and in the intercourse of the family shows the subordination of a younger person to her husband. She speaks of him as 'Mr. Douglass,' watches and hears what he says with careful respect, and we had been talking to him, perhaps, fifteen minutes before she made any remark, when, in some matter of the reminiscence of his slave life, she called his attention to an interesting matter he had omitted. . . .

"Over the mantelpiece in this well-ordered house, which looked like the abode of a literary man of fair means, was a picture of 'Othello' relating his experiences to 'Brabantio' and 'Desdemona.' It was the most suggestive thing in the room. . . . In another place in the room was Mr. Douglass' portrait when he was a young man about twenty-five years old. One could see looking at it the observant lines in the face, eyes wide apart and the individual resisting nature. A picture of Wendell Phillips was in the same room on an easel. In different parts of the house were other pictures of Mr. Douglass, one a crayon, taken in recent years. . . .

"His library would be quite a creditable one for the editor of a newspaper or ordinary literary man. All over the house are the indications of gratitude to the white men who supported the cause of the African race—Garrison and Lundy and Thaddeus Stevens and Sumner and others occupy places on the wall. . . ."[19]

At the time of "Gath's" visit, Douglass was ex-Recorder as well as ex-Marshal. He had remained in office during the first year of Cleveland's administration, and both he and his wife had attended the President's grand receptions.[20] Since Douglass had done all he "could to defeat the election of Mr. Cleveland," the action of the Democratic president aroused considerable comment. On January 5, 1886, at Cleveland's request, Douglass handed in his resignation to take effect on March 1. He expressed "grateful appreciation of your kind consideration in allowing me to choose both the time and the manner of my retirement from the office I have so long held subject to your pleasure."[21]

When Douglass' resignation was made public, Republicans in the Senate tried to make an issue of the case, charging Cleveland with violating his pledge to end the spoils system and with discriminating against an outstanding American Negro. Senator Hoar asked Douglass whether his resignation "was requested by the President or purely voluntary."

Douglass refused to join the anti-Cleveland forces even though he would probably have liked to remain in office. On the contrary, he praised the President for his invitation to state dinners and other public functions at the White House, something neither Garfield nor Arthur had had the courage to do.

"I am a Republican," Douglass wrote on April 6, 1886, "and if living I shall do all I can to elect a Republican in 1888; but I know manliness wherever I find it; and I have found it in President Cleveland, and I should despise myself if I should let any one think otherwise. Whatever else he may be, he is not a snob; and he is not a coward."[22]

Now that he was no longer an office-holder Douglass had an opportunity to satisfy a long-felt desire. After Anna Douglass' death, his first impulse had been "to break up my home and possibly go to Europe."[23] He pushed aside this desire, but he did not give up his "long intended purpose to visit Europe." On September 15, 1886, he and Helen sailed for Liverpool on the *City of Rome*.

The Douglasses Abroad

Almost thirty years had passed since Douglass made his last trip to Europe. At that time he had fled to England for refuge, an outlaw hunted by the government because of his connections with John Brown. Now he went as a man who had known presidents, senators, and congressmen. His letters of introduction to prominent Europeans likened him to "Abraham Lincoln, Garfield, Charles Sumner and Wendell Phillips." "Few men can tell more of American history for the last-half century than Mr. Douglass can, and no one has been able to see it from the same point of view," went one letter of introduction.[1]

After a week's sailing, the couple arrived in Liverpool. Douglass found "everything about the Docks the same as forty years ago except forty years older and by reason of smoke darker." The people were "full of life and activity."[2]

During the week's stay in Liverpool, the Douglasses visited art galleries, the Free Library, and the exhibition of new paintings. They also spent a day on the *Great Eastern,* "that wonder of Naval architecture . . . now used as a show and a low class of Theatricals."[3]

On October 1, the couple left for St. Neots "to spend a few days there before going to London." Here they were met by Julia Griffiths Crofts "with open arms." Twenty-six years had passed since Julia and Douglass had seen one another, and the five day stay at St. Neots was filled with reminiscences. Julia's husband had died ten years before and she now supported herself by running a school for girls. Douglass addressed the children at Julia's request.[4]

After two weeks in London, the Douglasses left for Paris. With Theodore Stanton, son of Elizabeth Cady Stanton, and Theodore Tilton as their guides, the couple visited the interesting places in Paris.

Deeply impressed by a visit to the Bastille, Douglass wrote to his son Lewis, urging him to "read of the manner in which it was taken in your cyclopedia." He added:

"I find the people here singularly conscious of their liberty, independence and their power. They show it in their whole carriage and in the very lines of their faces, and no wonder, for they, more than any other people in Europe, have asserted all three in the face of organized oppression and power. But in no act have they done this more than in their taking the Bastille."[5]

Douglass was moved by the culture and art about him, with one exception: the statue of Alexander Dumas left him cold. On meeting eighty-two-year-old Victor Schoelcher, the senator who had drawn up the law emancipating the slaves in the French colonies, Douglass had spoken to him of the elder Dumas. He had learned that the famous writer had "never said one word for his race."

"So we have nothing to thank Dumas for," Douglass wrote to friends in America. "Victor Hugo the white man could speak for us, but this brilliant colored man who could have let down sheets of fire upon the heads of tyrants and carried freedom to his enslaved people, had no word in behalf [of] Liberty or the enslaved. I have not yet seen his statue here in Paris. I shall go to see it, as it is an acknowledgement of the genius of a colored man, but not because I honor the character of the man himself."

In Paris a few weeks, Douglass began to see himself as the unofficial ambassador of the American Negro. He felt that his presence "even in silence, has a good influence in respect of the colored race before the world." The mass of the people in England and France were "sound in their convictions and feelings concerning the colored race." But "the lepros distilment of the American prejudice against the Negro" was having its effect in Europe. In part, it was caused by "Ethiopian singers [from America] who disfigure and distort the features of the Negro and bur-lesque his language and manners in a way to make him appear to thousands as more akin to apes than to men"—a "mode of warfare . . . . purely American." In addition to "these Ethiopian Buffoons and serenaders who presume to represent us abroad," prejudice against the Negro was stirred by "malicious American writers who take pleasure in assailing us, as an inferior and good for nothing race of which it is impossible to make anything."

In private conversations both in England and France, Douglass sought to counteract these vicious influences. He planned to deliver a number of speeches in England "in vindication of the cause and the character of the colored race in America, in which I hope to do justice to their progress and make known some of the difficulties with which as a people they have to contend."[6]

The Douglasses left Paris early in January, 1887, for a trip to Rome, stopping at Dejun, Lyons, Avignon, and Marseilles. At Avignon, "one of the oldest, quaintest, crookedest and queerest places" he had ever seen, Douglass visited the ancient Palaces of the Popes. When he peered into the dungeons "where people were tortured and doomed to death for rejecting the Roman faith," Douglass' critical attitude toward organized religion asserted itself. "I almost hated the name of church," he confided to his diary. "What a horrible lie that Romish church has palmed of[f] upon the people of this and other country pretending that its Pope is the Vice regent of God, the creator of the Universe, and how strange it is that millions of sane men have believed this stupendous and most arrogant lie."

The diary Douglass kept during his stay in Rome contained much of his resentment over the contradictions between the theory and practice of Christianity. The splendor of the dome of St. Peters, the largest cathedral in the world, evoked his admiration, but he noted "its utter contradiction to the life and lessons of Jesus. He was meek and lowly, but here was little else than pride and pomp." Through the intervention of Mrs. E. J. Putnam who was a friend of "an eminent priest," the Douglasses were able to see some of the "interior treasures" of St. Peters. Douglass' anger mounted as he examined the "costly vestments" decorated with gold and silver, rich laces "and all manner of precious stones worn by Popes, Cardinals, Bishops," the gold and silver crosses, and "other brilliant things with which [the] papacy well knows how to dazzle the eyes of the credulous and superstitious."

"The sight of these things only increased my sense of the hollowness of the vast structure of the Romish church and my conviction that Science must in the end do for that church what time has done for the vast structures of kingly pride and power which is broken and mouldering all over Rome."

The Douglasses were also shown many sacred relics, among them two of the thorns which pierced the brow of Jesus on the day of his crucifixion, a casket containing the head of St. Luke, the shin bones of Lazarus, a lock of hair of the Virgin mother, and a piece of the cross upon which Jesus was crucified. Douglass noted dryly that the "gowned priest" who was their guide "seemed to believe what he said." At the Vatican they saw another example of the attempt of the church to tax "the credulity of the faithful"—a picture proclaiming the "new dogma" of the immaculate conception of the Virgin mother. Some of the cardinals, Douglass commented, "seemed to be a little doubtful and had been brought to consent to the new dogma under external pressure rather than internal conviction."

The couple walked on the Appian way, strolled on Pincian Hill, and viewed the ruins of the Coliseum and the Forum. Leaving Rome late in January, they were delighted by the trip to Naples, especially the view of the snow clad Appenines "with their changing forms and lofty heights." Before arriving in Naples, they were entranced by the "wondrous spectacle" of Mt. Vesuvius. The sight, Douglass wrote, "almost paid us for our voyage across the sea," and "held us in almost breathless interest, and became more imposing and impressive the longer we beheld it."[7]

They spent three days in Naples, visiting the Bourbon Palace and its beautiful grounds and dining on the shore of the river Styx. They saw the landing place of Paul, the tomb of Virgil, and the home of Cicero.

"It was a day long to be remembered," Douglass noted. "That which interested me most was the fact that I was looking upon the country seen eighteen hundred years ago by the Prisoner Apostle on his way to Rome to answer for his religion. It somehow gave me a more vivid impression of the heroism of the man as I looked upon the grand ruins of the religion against which Paul dared to preach. These heathen Temples represent a religion as sincerely believed in as men now believe in the Christian religion, and Paul was an infidel to this heathen religion as much as Robert Ingersol[1] is now to the Christian religion."

After a day of rest, the couple viewed the ruins of Pompeii. It was "almost worth the voyage across the Atlantic to see the part of Pompeii already unearthed and to think of the two thirds of it still underground."

Douglass was quick to note that the Pompeians had been "wealthy and powerful slaveholders."

On Sunday, February 6, Douglass listened to a sermon in Italian at the Methodist church. Called upon to say a few words, which were interpreted by Reverend Jones, Douglass congratulated the congregation for having acquired "the Liberty to worship outside the Romish church and said a few words of human brotherhood."

A visit to Amalfi gave Douglass "the greatest treat of all"—a ride upon a donkey to the Capuchin convent. After viewing the celebrated Temple of Neptune built 7000 years before the birth of Christ, the couple returned to Naples. Here on February 11, they decided to extend their tour to Egypt and Greece. "The thought of this trip to Egypt and Greece will probably keep me awake tonight," Douglass wrote excitedly. "This tour is entirely outside of my calculation when leaving home, but it will be something to contemplate when it is done. It is no small thing to see the land of Joseph and his brethren, and from which Moses led the children of Abraham out of the home of bondage." He remembered how often this story had stirred him when he was a slave, how often it had lifted his spirits when he thought he was doomed to live forever in bondage.[8]

On February 13, the couple boarded the ship for Port Said. Douglass could not refrain from reflecting "that born as I was a slave marked for a life under the lash in the cornfield that [I] was abroad and free and privileged to see these distant lands so full of historic interest and which those of the most highly favored by fortune are permitted to visit." The February 14 item in his diary opened: "If right in my estimate of the length of time I have been in the world, I am now 70 years old."

Two days later, they arrived at Port Said, "the queerest of queer places." As the Arab laborers carried baskets of coal on board the ship, Douglass was astonished by the "strength, cheerfulness and endurance of these sable children of the desert." He was quick to notice "several genuine Negroes among them," and commented that "they seemed not a whit behind their fellow workmen either in poise or physical ability."

The voyage down the Suez Canal to Ismalia was through barren and desolate country. At Ismalia Douglass saw a Greek patriarch in a flowing robe, and his objection to outward manifestations of religious beliefs came to the surface immediately. "I find it hard to look with patience upon people who thus parade their religion in their clothes, and who evidently wish to exact homage on account of such pretention," he wrote.

From Ismalia they traveled through the "Bible famous Land of Goshen" where everything reminded Douglass of "the days of Moses." The great mass of the people, he noted, would in America "be classed with mulattoes." But he quickly added that "this would not be a scientific description, but an American description." He saw now why the Mohammedan religion appealed to these people, " for it does not make color the criterion of fellowship as some of our so called Christian nations do."

In Cairo Douglass was depressed by the "squalor, disease and deformity—all manner of unfortunate beggary." But even "more pitiful" than the sight of a people "thus groveling in filth and utter wretchedness" was the daily encounter with "hooded and veiled women." He remarked: "It is sad to think of that one-half of the human family should be thus cramped, kept in ignorance and degraded, having no existence except that of minister[ing] to the pride and lusts of the men who own them as slaves are owned. . . . "

Douglass was also distressed by the sight of the Howling Dervishes at worship. The frenzy and the shouting saddened him. He could not understand how rational beings "could be made to believe that such physical contortions could be pleasing to God or secure his favour." This led him to reflect on the "form of worship adopted by many other denominations." He marveled that "man should imagine to secure Divine favor by telling God how good and great he is—and how much they love and adore him."[9]

But there were more pleasant experiences in Egypt: the twelve-mile trip to the site of ancient Memphis; the visit to Gizeh and the 470-foot climb to the top of Cheops, the highest pyramid in the Valley of the Nile. It was a difficult and dangerous undertaking, and only with the aid of four Arabs was Douglass able to reach the top. It took him two weeks to recover, and he vowed that he would not undertake it again "for any consideration." But the view of the Sphinx, the Nile and the desert, compensated him for his aches and pains.[10]

Early in March, the couple left Cairo and took a five-day trip up the Nile to Alexandria. Douglass left the boat with a clear understanding of the importance of the river to the Egyptians. It was to them, he now saw, "the source of life and whatever of health and prosperity they enjoyed."

From Alexandria they moved on to Athens. Douglass felt excited as he paced the deck of the Egyptian steamer. "The thought of soon treading the classic shores of Greece is very exhilarating," he exclaimed. For twelve days the exhilaration mounted as the Douglasses visited the Acropolis, the Parthenon, the theatre of Dionysus, the Temple of Jupiter, and ascended by a zigzag path to the top of Lycabettis, 919 feet above sea level. As he looked down, Douglass saw "a scene never to be forgotten."

"The Plains of Attica were spread out at our feet. Over the mountain we could almost see the fields of Marathon, off towards the sea we could see clearly the Mountains of Sparta. In the city of Athens, solemn and grand with its many pillars—stood out the form of the Temple of Theseus one of the most perfect and striking of all the fallen architectural ruins left to tell us the wealth pride ambition and power of the ancient people of this famous city."

Leaving Athens, the couple spent two weeks at Naples and then returned to Rome. Here they witnessed the colorful Easter services at St. Peters which Douglass described as "abounding in excellent music, much kneeling, changing of vestments, much posturing, making signs of the cross, and which seemed to my eyes mere pantomime but which to the worshippers I must try to believe was full of devotion."[11] The glaring contrasts between wealth and poverty in Rome deepened Douglass' belief that that religion was best which best served the interests of the mass of the people on earth. Here in Rome, he pointed out, one found a "city of divinity and dirt, of Religion and rags, of grandeur and squalor, piety and poverty, of church bells and beggars, of lofty domes, towers and turrets pointing to heaven, and of dark cavernous rooms never reached by pure air or sunshine, crowded with the poor and diseased." Douglass favored less religion and fewer rags, less piety and fewer poor, fewer churches and more pure air and sunshine for the poverty-stricken. Thus he had often said to philanthropists who sought to build churches in the Negro communities of the South:

"It is something to give the Negro religion. It is more to give him justice. It is something to give him the Bible, it is more to give him the ballot. It is something to tell him that there is a place for him in the Christian's heaven, it is more to let him have a place in this Christian country to live upon in peace."[12]

After a month at Rome, the Douglasses arrived in Florence. Their "first excursion" was a visit to the grave of Theodore Parker in the Protestant Cemetery. As he stood by the brown headstone above the mound that covered the remains of the Unitarian clergyman, Douglass recalled "the many services rendered the cause of human freedom by him, freedom not only from physical chains but the chains of superstition, those which not only galled the limbs and tore the flesh, but those which marred and wounded the human soul." A few feet away from the grave of the one clergyman who "had a voice for the slave when nearly all the pulpits of the land were dumb," was the tombstone of Richard Hildreth, the famous American historian. Douglass recalled the great contribution his book *Despotism in America* had made to the anti-slavery struggle. In the Protestant Cemetery Douglass also came upon the grave of Elizabeth Barrett Browning, whose soul, like Parker's and Hildreth's, was "devoted to liberty."

During the five days of sightseeing, the couple visited the Uffizi Palace, the Church of San Marco, the grand mausoleum of the Medici, and the tombs built by Michelangelo. They left for Venice feeling that their stay in Florence had been "all too brief."

Venice where "climate, sea, and sky" were beautiful surpassed "all the ideas" Douglass had formed of it. It was in many respects "the most beautiful" of all the cities they had visited. At the "Bibliotec" Douglass saw the original manuscripts of letters from John Adams, Thomas Jefferson, and Benjamin Franklin. On the great canal, he saw the house where Desdemona lived when wooed by Othello.

After Venice came Milan which "aside from its splendid Cathedral" was "not remarkable," Lucerne with its "beautiful lake," and then Paris again. Arriving on May 25, they remained only five days. Before he left Douglass called again on Senator Schoelcher. "In parting with [the] venerable Senator he kissed me on both cheeks," Douglass confided to his diary.[13]

Early in June, Helen left for America to be with her mother who was seriously ill. Douglass remained in the British Isles for two more months, visiting old friends, giving an occasional lecture, and seeing some of the sights he had missed during previous visits. He returned to the United States in August, 1887.

It had been a memorable trip. His reaction to many of the things he had seen was fairly typical of the average tourist. But as a Negro in the old world he also saw things which were ignored by most travelers. His observations on the attitude of the common people toward men and women of color were significant. He himself had been happy to get away from the color line, to "walk the world unquestioned, a man among men."[14] But he was especially stimulated by the knowledge that his people had missed him and welcomed his safe return. As one young Negro wrote in his letter of welcome:

"The loss of your presence and the opportunity to consult you in important

matters that concerned our welfare were keenly felt by your many friends and
the colored people generally:—by your absence we were made more fully to
appreciate our great advantage in having you to speak for us and protect our
interests."[15]

Minister to Haiti

Two months before the Republican National Convention met in
June, 1888, to draft a platform and nominate a candidate for President,
Douglass warned the party that "it can no longer repose on the history
of its grand and magnificent achievements." If the platform would reveal
the party's determination to "make the path of the black citizen to the
ballot box as safe and smooth as that of the white citizen," he would
lend his aid to assure a Republican victory in November. But if the party
vacillated, if it refused to enforce the constitutional rights of every citizen,
he would pray for its defeat and "welcome the bolt which shall scatter it
into a thousand fragments."[1]

Although not a delegate, Douglass was present at the Republican
National Convention in Chicago, in June. In response to a call from
the convention, he delivered a brief address on the opening day. As in
his pre-convention speeches, he pressed for a platform which would guarantee protection for "the black citizen" and make his way to the ballot
box "as smooth and as safe as any other citizen of the republic." He told the
10,000 Republicans at the convention:

"We have a right to demand of the Republican party that we shall have
emblazoned on the platform of the party itself, that there shall be no more
fooling, no more hazing, no more humbug, no more keeping the promise to
the ear and breaking it to the heart."[2]

Three days later, the convention adopted a platform which expressed
indignation at the suppression of suffrage among the Negroes in the
South, and advocated fuller control of Congressional elections by the
Federal government so that the Negro should be assured of, and guaranteed, a free exercise of his rights. Benjamin Harrison, the Republican
candidate for President, announced that he subscribed fully to the policy
set forth in the platform.[3]

Happy over the pledge of the Republican platform and candidate,

Douglass was eager to stump the country for the ticket, and readily accepted when asked by the Republican National Committee "to make as many speeches as you will find it within your ability to do, especially in the doubtful states." He was assigned to cover Connecticut, New York, New Jersey, and Michigan, but he also ventured into Indiana and Iowa, delivering speeches "indoors and out-of-doors, in skating rinks and public halls, day and night."[4]

As in previous campaigns, Douglass' electioneering speeches touched only briefly on general economic and political issues of the day. The paramount issue of the campaign was still the treatment of the Negro.

"What to me are questions of gold and silver, of tariffs and currency, while my people are torn from their little cabins, snatched from jails by furious mobs with no chance to prove their innocence of the crime imputed to them, shot down, hanged and burned to death?" he exclaimed. "The National obligation to protect, defend and maintain the liberties of the people, and fulfill the guaranties of the Constitution transcends all merely economic considerations. What shall it profit a nation if it gain the whole world and lose its own soul?"[5]

Yet economic issues could not be ignored, and Douglass set out to convince his northern audiences that they could not afford to tolerate the absence of democracy in the South. By means of the suppression of the Negro vote, the southern white ruling class had secured "an unfair advantage" over the rest of the country. Before the war, in time of slavery, the South's representation in Congress and in the Electoral College was based on three-fifths of its colored population. But now that slavery was abolished, the whole Negro population was included in the basis of representation. With the suppression of the Negro vote, Douglass pointed out, the southerners had "an advantage now two-fifths greater than in the time of slavery." Thus Mississippi sent seven representatives to Congress with 44,557 votes, Georgia with 27,575 votes while New Jersey sent a similar number of representatives with 239,344 votes, Ohio with 126,152 votes, and Kansas with 251,971 votes. The Third District in Ohio sent one representative with 36,597 votes—9,222 more votes than the whole state of Georgia gave her 10 representatives!

"Hence you will see," Douglass argued, "that outside of the great wrong inflicted upon the Negro outside of the flagrant nullification of the Constitution of the United States, you have a direct and indispensable duty to correct this stupendous and impudent violation of justice, and of the inequality of the States. You are not asked merely to protect the Negro. You are asked to protect yourselves, to protect your constitution, to protect the industry and enterprise of your section of the Republic."[6]

Once the election returns were in, Douglass hastened to congratulate Harrison, and to remind the President-elect of the Republican pledge "to defend the right of every man to vote and to guarantee equal rights to all, regardless of race or color." "I shall expect Mr. Harrison to enforce this view," he declared in a public interview late in November. One month after Harrison's inauguration, in a speech before the Bethel Literary and Historical Society of Washington, Douglass again returned to this theme. "Not only the Negro, but all honest men, north and south, must hold the Republican party in contempt if it fails to do its whole duty at this point," he declared. "The Republican party has made the colored man free and the Republican party must make him secure in his freedom, or abandon its pretensions. . . . If the Republican party shall fail to carry out this purpose, God will raise up another party which will be faithful."[7]

During the first two years of Harrison's administration, Douglass was too far removed from the American scene to check on the degree to which the Republicans fulfilled their pledge. On July 1, 1889, President Harrison announced Douglass' appointment as Minister-Resident and Consul-General to the Republic of Haiti. Late in September, Harrison added the post of Chargé d'Affaires for Santo Domingo.

Many of Douglass' friends urged him not to accept the Haitian mission. For one thing, they felt that the office was not "big enough," and hardly commensurate with his "ability and position." For another, they feared he would be running too much of a risk moving to a tropical climate at his advanced age. Then again, they argued that it was his duty to remain in the United States and continue to lead the battle against "the spirit of slavery." Some even felt that the appointment was a Republican maneuver to remove a troublesome thorn in their side. Thus Julia Griffiths Crofts wrote from England:

"I feel certain that your last able & searching address has alarmed the government of the U.S. and they are politely sending you away, to a far country and leaving the poor coloured people of the U.S. *deprived* of their greatest & *truest* friend. I like none of it & seem to see plainly through it all. . . . Oh! I do so fear & feel that you are leaving one important sphere of labor for another less important & *far more dangerous.*"[8]

Douglass ignored the advice of his well-wishers. The nomination

had come unexpectedly. He had hoped for an appointment as recorder
of deeds, but President Harrison, he wrote, "has done more and better
for me than I asked—and has done it without my asking." He brushed
aside the claim that the position was not good enough for the foremost
Negro in the United States. Rather he agreed with the Boston *Advertiser*
when it said: "Frederick Douglass has an opportunity before him to win
fame such as no American diplomat has achieved since the Civil War.
He will be in a position to do immense good at a critical period in the
history of the people to whom he is accredited." Whatever he could
accomplish in this direction, Douglass believed, would be only a partial
payment for the great contribution Haiti had made to the Negro people.
Finally, the fact that many American businessmen, particularly New
York City merchants, opposed the appointment of a Negro minister
convinced Douglass that he should accept the nomination. For the business men feared that a Negro minister would not be inclined to ignore
Haiti's interests for the sake of their profits.[9]

In September, Douglass prepared to leave Washington for Port-au-
Prince. He soon discovered that he could not get first-class accommodations on a steamboat or train going South. When he refused to travel
second-class, the federal government ordered the naval steamer, the *Dispatch,* to carry the Douglasses to Norfolk and the *Ossippee* to transport
them to Haiti. Captain Kellogg of the *Ossippee* refused to eat at the same
table with a Negro, but Douglass informed him that he did not intend "to
be treated in any other way upon a United States vessel than would a white
diplomat." Without the captain's presence, the Douglasses used the chief
officer's dining room.[10] Although the federal government was made
aware of the incident, it did nothing.

Douglass arrived in Haiti during the closing stage of a conflict
between the forces led by François Denys Légitime and by Louis
Modestin Florvil Hyppolite. Légitime had been proclaimed provisional
president of the republic on October 16, 1888, by thirty-three of eighty-four
elected delegates to the constituent assembly in Port-au-Prince. The
opposition group denied the validity of these proceedings, formed a
provisional government of their own at Cap Haitien, and chose Hyppolite
as their leader.

Légitime received the prompt recognition of France, Great Britain,
Italy, and Portugal. The United States, however, threw its support behind
Hyppolite and refused to recognize Légitime's government. In the
spring of 1889, Hyppolite began an offensive against the "constitutional

president," and by August had advanced to the gates of Port-au-Prince. On August 22, Légitime resigned and on September 9 the full membership of the constituent assembly unanimously elected Hyppolite president of Haiti.[11]

Douglass' arrival at Port-au-Prince coincided with the inauguration of President Hyppolite. He was impressed by the tranquility in Haiti, and the "popularity and stability of the Government." He informed Secretary of State Blaine that everyone with whom he talked expressed the conviction "that Haiti has had enough of war and is willing now to acquiesce in a condition of peace."[12]

In mid-November Douglass was officially presented to President Hyppolite whom he described as "a man of about the medium height, of dark brown complexion and gray hair . . . [with] a clear, steady eye, calm temper and high intelligence." In a brief but moving address, Douglass presented his credentials to the President. He spoke of the great honor bestowed upon him by the government of the United States in appointing him Minister Resident and Consul General to the Republic of Haiti. In his reply President Hyppolite paid tribute to the new minister's eminence as a leader of the Negro people, and declared that the United States could have offered no better evidence of their esteem for Haiti than that of Douglass' appointment. Douglass was deeply moved at the words: "As to you, Mr. Minister, your reputation is known in the two hemispheres. You are the incarnation of the idea which Haiti is following—the moral and intellectual development of the African race by personal effort and mental culture."[13]

Everywhere in Haiti Douglass received similar tributes. His rise from slavery to a position of world renown and his long battle for the freedom of the Negro had endeared him to the Haitian people. In his first annual message, President Hyppolite paid tribute to Douglass as "the illustrious champion of all men sprung from the African race, himself one of the most remarkable products of that race which we represent with pride on the American continent."[14]

Douglass was keenly aware of the dignity of the Haitians, and noted with joy that they walked erect "as if conscious of their freedom and independence." His dispatches to the State Department are replete with evidence of his concern for Haiti's well being and development as a great Negro republic. He expressed the hope that European countries would send ministers instead of consuls to Haiti "and perhaps secure men of larger sympathies than the consuls usually commissioned to this country possess." He pointed to the signs of economic progress evidenced "in the manifold projects for improving streets, roads and wharves, and in the increasing number of private dwellings in process of erection both within and without the limits of Port-au-Prince. The sound of the hammer and the trowel is heard late and early. Soon an electric cable from Port-au-Prince will connect the cable at the Môle St. Nicolas and thus bring Port-au-Prince *en rapport* with the outside world."[15]

Ironically enough, Douglass' mission was lending strength to the very forces in Haiti that were bent upon ending the era of peace and tranquility ushered in by the Hyppolite administration. Hyppolite's opponents had been defeated on the battlefield, but they were gaining new adherents as a result of an effective propaganda campaign against the new government. Charging that the President owed his success solely to aid rendered him by the United States, they pointed to the American naval vessels which had anchored in Haitian waters during the final stage of the war. Most important of all, they maintained that in return for American aid, Hyppolite had promised to cede the Môle St. Nicolas to the United States.[16]

Actually, the desire of the Harrison administration to get the Môle St. Nicolas as a naval base and a coaling station had had much to do with Douglass' appointment as Minister. With the control of this port in northwest Haiti, an important obstacle to American business penetration and naval expansion in the Carribbean would be removed. With Douglass conducting the negotiations, Haiti's fear of domination by American interests might easily be allayed. Certainly Haiti could trust the outstanding American Negro to safeguard its interests?

Douglass did not oppose the extension of American influence in Haiti. Just as on the controversy over Grant's project for the annexation of the Dominican Republic, the removal of slavery in the United States had removed Douglass' chief objection to American expansion into the Caribbean. But Douglass was aware of the nationalistic feeling in Haiti, and he knew that an American attempt to gain possession of Haitian territory by fair means or foul would seriously endanger the nation's peace.

"A safe and convenient mode just now of assaulting the Government," he reminded Blaine, "is to accuse it of dangerous friendship for the United States. Under the guise of patriotic concern for the integrity and independence of Haiti, some adopt a course which tends to weaken their Government, and which, if successful, would open another chapter of blood in the annals of Haiti, and bring upon her greater perils than any they profess to be anxious to avert."[17]

Douglass was critical of the failure of the American government to understand the Haitians' feelings about their national integrity. As early as December, 1889, in his complaint that the U.S.S. *Yantic* had been making an unauthorized survey of the harbor of Môle St. Nicolas, he wrote Secretary of State Blaine, that it lent weight to the widespread feeling in Haiti "that already the preliminary steps have been taken 'to sell the country to the Americans.' "[18]

Douglass had clashed with representatives of American business even before the Môle affair. Soon after his arrival in Haiti, an agent of the steamship company, William P. Clyde and Co., had informed the American minister that he was trying to obtain a half-million dollar subsidy so that his firm could establish a steamboat service between New York and seven Haitian ports. Douglass gave the Clyde concession his support, but he refused to resort to unscrupulous methods in favor of the American corporation. Antenor Firmin, the Haitian Minister of Foreign Affairs, objected to granting the Clyde concession on the ground that his government had to recognize the private claims of many American citizens. The Clyde agent coolly proposed to Douglass that he go to Firmin and assure him that if he would grant the Clyde concession, the American minister "would withhold and refrain from pressing the claims of other American citizens."

Douglass was "shocked" by the proposal. Although he believed that it would be a good thing for Haiti to have the line of steamers, he was definitely of the opinion that the government of Haiti and not an American business firm should decide that question. He refused to do anything underhanded to persuade the Haitian government to adopt a course of action which it felt was against its interests. The fact that the agent was a South Carolinian who openly showed his contempt both for the Haitians and the American minister did not help the Clyde interests.

In July, 1890, Douglass was granted a three months' leave of absence. As he was about to call upon President Hyppolite before departing for the United States, the Clyde agent again asked him to take advantage of the interview "to press anew the Clyde contract upon the attention of the President." Douglass declined to use the visit as a means of advancing the interests of an American corporation.[19]

Douglass' insistence upon honest dealings with the Haitians did not endear him to American business men. Were it not for his reluctance to antagonize the Negro voters, Blaine would have probably yielded to the demand of American business men that he send another representative to Haiti. As it was, Douglass' return to Port-au-Prince was delayed two months while Blaine considered the matter.[20]

Douglass finally sailed for Haiti in December, but even before he arrived at Port-au-Prince, negotiations for the lease of the Môle St. Nicolas had been taken out of his hands. Blaine decided that the Minister could not be relied upon to drive a hard bargain, and had empowered Admiral Bancroft Gherardi, commander of the North Atlantic fleet, to manage the affair. On January 1, 1891, instructions were transmitted to Douglass asking him to "cooperate to the best of your ability in bringing about the end to which the Admiral will give all his energies." The Admiral had already demonstrated during his previous visit to Haiti that his "energies" included a fleet of warships in full sight of the Haitian government.

On January 25, on Admiral Gherardi's arrival at Port-au-Prince, he sent an officer to the United States legation to invite Douglass to his flagship, the *Philadelphia*. In "strict politeness" Gherardi should have called on him but Douglass swallowed his pride and went to meet the Admiral. During the conversation Douglass learned that he had been virtually superseded. Gherardi had been appointed a United States special commissioner to obtain the lease, and it was the wish of President Harrison and the State Department that Douglass "should earnestly cooperate with him in accomplishing this object."[21]

Douglass' first impulse was to resign, but, on second thought, he decided to serve in the capacity assigned to him. He knew that many businessmen in the United States were only waiting for him to leave Haiti, and he "did not propose to be pushed out of office in this way." He knew in advance, however, that the task would prove "a thankless one, since if they succeeded, Gherardi would get the credit, and if they failed, Douglass would get the blame."

Three days after the interview, Gherardi and Douglass called on Hyppolite and Firmin. The Admiral reminded the President "of services rendered, . . . and of certain promises made by the Haitian Provisional Government which now it was the desire of the Government at Washington to have fulfilled." He argued that the Hyppolite government owed its very existence to the assistance of the United States, and warned that his government would take all steps necessary to secure fulfillment of the moral obligation.[22]

Douglass said little, referring only to the importance of cementing closer relations between the two countries and the part the granting of the lease could play in this connection. He was disturbed by Gherardi's belligerent attitude and by his emphasis on the use of all necessary means to secure the lease. He knew that the presence of Gherardi's warships at Port-au-Prince was already creating considerable apprehension among the people of Haiti.[23]

As the three-hour conference drew to a close, Firmin repeated again and again that the lease of the Môle would provoke a revolution. But Hyppolite agreed to submit the question to his cabinet.

Formal written application for leasing the Môle was filed with the Haitian government on February 2, 1891. Only Gherardi signed the application; Douglass' signature does not appear. Firmin, determined to hold off a decision, asked to see Gherardi's full powers for the negotiation of the treaty. It was a shrewd move, as Gherardi had not considered it necessary to bring credentials. Evidently he believed that the United States warships at Port-au-Prince were sufficient evidence of his "full powers." The Admiral was all for refusing the Minister's request, but Douglass persuaded him to comply, arguing that it would strengthen the United States' position. A cablegram was dispatched to Washington for a letter of credence.

It took three weeks before the credentials arrived giving full powers of negotiation to Gherardi and Douglass jointly. Another six weeks went by before Gherardi presented them and demanded a categoric answer. One reason for the delay was a dispute between Douglass and the Admiral over the terms of the negotiations. Gherardi's request to Hyppolite had included the stipulation that Haiti agree not to sell or lease territory to any nation other than the United States. But the official dispatch containing the credentials mentioned no such condition and referred only to the lease of the Môle. Douglass urged that the request for the lease make no mention of any limitation on Haiti's right to sell or lease territory. Gherardi, however, insisted on the original demand.

Another cause for the rift between Gherardi and Douglass was the Admiral's action in ordering every available warship to Port-au-Prince. As the naval vessels arrived, Douglass hastened to express his violent disapproval to Blaine:

". . . I think it clearly my duty to state to you that the presence in this harbor, at the same time, of five of our war vessels and the knowledge that others are soon to join them, coupled with a general vague information that negotiations are pending between the two Governments, concerning some matter in regard to which the Haitian people are unduly and perhaps unreasonably, sensitive, has created a feeling of apprehension, anxiety and even of alarm, beyond anything of the kind that I have ever before personally known to exist here.   '

"This feeling of apprehension and anxiety is not confined to the uninformed classes merely, but extends to the intelligent classes as well.

"Fear is expressed that if on the one hand the Môle Saint Nicolas be ceded or leased to us, the Government that makes the concession will fall under the crash of popular condemnation; that, if, on the other hand, the cession or lease be not granted, the Môle may be seized by our naval forces now here, and that in either case internal disorders, violence and revolutionary uprisings will follow."[24]

On April 22, 1891, one day after Douglass sent this dispatch, Haiti formally refused the request of the United States for the lease of the Môle St. Nicholas. In justifying this decision, Firmin placed special emphasis on the presence of seven American men-of-war in the port. It had, he said, "made a most unfortunate impression on the entire country. . . . Haiti could not enter negotiations without appearing to yield to foreign pressure and to compromise, *de facto* [her] existence as an independent people. . . ."

The two American plenipotentiaries expressed their regret at Haiti's decision. Douglass inquired whether the negotiations might be reopened after the withdrawal of the ships, but he received a negative reply. No other answer could have been expected. In fact, even though Firmin had resolutely opposed the lease, he was so bitterly attacked for having even negotiated with American representatives, that he was compelled to resign.[25]

On May 31, Douglass applied for a sixty-day leave of absence stating that he desired "to spend the month of August and September in the United States." The tropical climate did not agree with him, and he felt that he had "aged more during the two years in Haiti . . . than . . . in five years in the states." He was also anxious to get back to Washington to defend himself against the hysterical attacks in the American press charging him with the failure to obtain the lease. Editorial comment in the newspapers accused him of permitting his identity with the Negro people of Haiti to interfere with his duty as American minister. A number of newspapers, particularly those below the Mason-Dixon line, claimed that Douglass' experience in Haiti proved that a Negro was unfit for the diplomatic service.[26]

While he was at Port au Prince, Douglass had refrained from taking issue with the press. "My position here," he wrote to Magnus L. Robinson in April, 1890, "does not permit me to write anything for the press . . . . I see lots of erroneous statements concerning me in the papers which I must leave it to time to correct. . . ."[27]

Anxious to tell his side of the story, on July 30, 1891, Douglass resigned as Minister giving "personal considerations" as his reason. The State Department accepted his resignation on August 11. Douglass then hastened to release his side of the story in newspaper interviews and magazine articles. His articles proved that he had served the interests of the United States by refusing to ignore the interests of a million or two Haitians. Although he was condemned for revealing diplomatic secrets to the public, he emerged spotless from what a historian has correctly described as "one of the more unsavory episodes in the history of American diplomacy."[28]

The popular resentment in Haiti over the Môle incident did not include the American Minister. Letters poured in expressing regret that Douglass would not return to their country. One letter signed by twenty-three members of the Haitian college called Douglass a symbol for the people of Haiti. To them he represented "one of the greatest champions of liberty, justice and equality."[29]

The clearest indication of the high esteem with which Douglass was held in Haiti was his appointment as Haitian Commissioner at the World's Columbian Exposition at Chicago in 1893. With Charles A. Preston, formerly secretary of the Haitian legation at Washington, as co-commissioner, Douglass supervised the erection of the Haitian Pavilion at the first world's fair. Main speaker at the building's formal dedication on January 2, 1893, Douglass paid great tribute to Haiti:

"She has grandly served the cause of universal liberty. We should not forget that the freedom you and I enjoyed to-day; that the freedom that eight hundred thousand colored people enjoy in the British West Indies; the freedom that has come to the colored race the world over, is largely due to the brave stand taken by the black sons of Haiti ninety years ago. When they struck for freedom, they builded better than they knew. Their swords were not drawn and could not be drawn simply for themselves alone. They were linked and interlinked with their race, and striking for their freedom, they struck for the freedom of every black man in the world. . . ."[30]

Long after the recriminations in the American press had ceased and the Môle affair had been forgotten, Douglass was remembered by the Haitian people as their warm and devoted friend. "The Haitian people . . . admire you beyond expression," wrote a correspondent from Port-au-Prince in May, 1894. "They are very anxious to keep up with your utterances on the race question."[31] Such sincere and moving tributes would remain as evidence that Douglass had succeeded in his mission.

The Last Years

"We miss you very much indeed," a southern Negro wrote to Douglass while he was in Haiti. ". . . In whatever direction I look the tide seems to be setting in strongly against us and there is not a single man in the country able to stem it or turn it or break its force. You are needed here."[1]

Of all the sufferings and hardships of the Negro people during the 'nineties, the alarming increase in the bestial practice of lynching disturbed Douglass most deeply. Every month reports from the South told of new hangings and burnings at the stake, of Negroes taken from jails and brutally killed by white mobs, of Negroes tortured and burned to death in the sight of thousands of persons, of the savagery, brutishness, and the blood lust of white southerners. And for every Negro lynched a hundred others were in peril of their lives.

Some Negro leaders and many white friends of the Negro counseled silence. Rape, the crime of which the lynch mobs accused their victims, was too horrible to be defended. Also, by publicizing the lynchings, the position of the northern Negro would be jeopardized. The wisest thing was to say nothing.

But Douglass did not remain silent. His voice and pen were never more active. In these last years of his life he threw himself into a campaign to arouse the nation against this savage attack on his people.

"In the opinion of some of us," he declared. "it were well to say nothing about it, that the least said about it the better. They would have us suffer quietly under the odium in silence. Taking this charge in its broad and comprehensive sense, the sense in which it is presented and is now stated, it strikes at the whole colored race, and, therefore as a colored man, I am bound to meet it. . . . I hold that a people too spiritless to defend themselves against unjust imputations, are not worth defending, and are not worthy to defend anything else."[2]

Accompanied by Mrs. Mary Church Terrell, Douglass went to urge President Harrison to speak out boldly against lynching in his annual message to Congress. Mrs. Terrell "listened spellbound while he [Douglass] eloquently pleaded the case for anti-lynching legislation. He implored President Harrison to act immediately against the lynching evil." Mrs. Terrell recalls that while President Harrison listened attentively, he took no action against lynching. "But Frederick Douglass," she adds, "never ceased to fight vigorously against lynching and all the wrongs of which his race was the victim."[3]

All the fire of his early years returned as Douglass struck out hard against the defenders of lynching. Writing in the *North American Review* of June, 1894, he exposed the claim that only the "ignorant mob" in the South was responsible for the crime. "The men who break open jails and with bloody hands destroy human life are not alone responsible," he cried. "These are not the men who make public sentiment. They are simply the hangmen, not the court, judge or jury. They simply obey the public sentiment of the South, the sentiment created by wealth and respectability, by the press and the pulpit." It was the men of "wealth and respectability" who, by raising the cry of "an outrage of a Negro upon some white woman," offered the excuse for the lynchers. Yet for two hundred years or more, these very men had "committed this offence against black women, and the fact has excited little attention. . . ."

Douglass' attack upon the wealthy classes of the South aroused a storm of protest. D. H. Chamberlin, former governor of South Carolina, publicly attacked Douglass for failing to use his influence to "stamp out the infamous crime" for which Negroes were lynched. Frances Willard, founder of the Women's Christian Temperance Union, appealed to Douglass to join in pitying the southerners. "The problem in their hands is immeasurable," she fairly wept. "The colored race multiplies like the locusts of Egypt. The safety of women, of childhood, of the home, is menaced in a thousand localities at this moment, so that men dare not go beyond the sight of their own roof tree."[4]

Infuriated by these indictments of his people, Douglass answered his

critics in a brilliant lecture, "The Lesson of the Hour." Beginning with
the stinging sentence, "Not a breeze comes to us from the late rebellious
states that is not tainted and freighted with Negro blood," it analyzed
and demolished every excuse offered by the defenders of lynching and exposed the real reasons for the brutal murder of Negroes in the South. As
if aware that this was the last blow he would strike for his people, Douglass poured into the address not only a most powerful indictment of
lynching but a condemnation of the entire system by which the Negro
people in the United States were oppressed.

Douglass minced no words. "We claim to be a highly civilized and
Christian country," he began. "I will not stop to deny this claim, yet I
fearlessly affirm that there is nothing in the history of savages to surpass
the blood-chilling horrors and fiendish excuses perpetrated against the
colored people of this country, by the so-called enlightened people of
the South." Again, he directed his main attack against "the upper class
of the South" which he charged with being the real power behind "the
mob and its deeds." Their cry about "assaults upon white women" was
only a new excuse to justify their continued persecution of the Negro, a
new device to keep him in chains. It had never been used before because
the southern ruling class had no need for it. In the days of slavery, they
had used the fear of Negro insurrection to justify their persecution. In
the period of Reconstruction and immediately afterward, they had raised
the danger of Negro domination to justify the terroristic activities of the
Klan.

"And now that Negro insurrection and Negro domination are no longer
defensible as an excuse for Negro persecution, there has come in due course
another suited to the occasion, and that is the heart-rending cry of the white
women and little white children. . . . "

With brilliant logic, Douglass demonstrated that the charge was part
of a conspiracy "to degrade the Negro" and "to pave the way for his entire disfranchisement as an American citizen." The ruling class knew that
"if they can once divest the Negro of the elective franchise and nullify
his citizenship, the partition wall between him and slavery will no longer
exist. . . ." Knowing only too well that even a friend of the Negro would
hesitate to defend him against such a heinous crime, they had invented
the myth of attacks on white womanhood. Douglass pointed out that this
attack against the Negro had been made because he had merely demanded
that a man accused of a crime should, through proper counsel, "be al-

lowed to question his accusers in open court and in open daylight, so that his guilt or his innocence may be duly proved and established."

"If this is to make me liable to the charge of apologizing for crime, I am not ashamed to be so charged. I dare to contend for the colored people of the United States that they are a law-abiding people, and I dare to insist upon it that they and any other people, black or white, accused of crime, shall have a fair trial before they are punished."

But a fair trial, he continued, would expose the falsehood of the charge against the Negro; hence the necessity for lynchings. This brutality would also serve as an object lesson to other Negroes who were chafing under the burden of the vicious tenant system in the South and who were determined to do something to redress their grievances.

The shocking increase in lynchings, Douglass said, brought forth a flood of proposals for the solution of the so-called "Negro problem." Douglass analyzed and exposed the weaknesses of some of the leading suggestions. There was, for example, the claim that the "problem" stemmed from the fact that the Negro still retained the right to vote and that he had even voted in some states during the Presidential campaign of 1892. Hence the proposal to solve the problem by limiting suffrage, by imposing an educational qualification on the right to vote. Douglass called this a cunning device "to make this entirely a white man's government." The very people who shouted the loudest about the illiteracy of the Negro were the most vicious opponents of every move to increase educational facilities in the South. Without the ballot, the Negro would be truly doomed to ignorance, for he would be deprived of the "means and motives that made for education." Aside from all this, Douglass opposed the entire principle of making suffrage more exclusive.

"I would not have it embrace only the elite, but I would have it include the lowly. I would not only include the men, but would include the women, and make our government in reality, as in name, a government by the people, of the people, and for the whole people."

In like manner, Douglass rejected the proposal to solve the "problem" by colonization in Africa. Aware that the increased persecution of the Negro had revived the colonization movement, he insisted, nevertheless, that none of the earlier objections to colonization had lost their validity. The native land of the American Negro was still the United States, and he objected to any attempt to take him away from a country which he and his ancestors had done so much to build. The Negro people in Africa needed aid, but the need of the Negro in the United States was even more urgent. The American Negro could best aid his African brother by continuing the battle for freedom in his native land, for "a blow struck successfully for the Negro in America, is a blow struck for the Negro in Africa." In short, colonization was an "evasion" and not a solution. It diverted the attention of the Negro from the immediate task of fighting for his rights in the country of his birth.

What then was the "problem"? It was not, as Douglass saw it, a "Negro problem." In fact, the very name was itself a clever device of the old master class to confuse the American people and make them believe that the Negro was responsible for whatever trouble existed in the South. It was a "national problem," for it involved the question as to whether the American nation had the power to protect its citizens against fraud and violence and whether it could compel obedience to the Constitution. This was the problem and no amount of word-juggling could confuse it.

If the men who were dreaming up these countless solutions would only meet the question squarely it could be solved without too much difficulty. Instead of worrying about colonizing the Negro in Africa, let them turn their attention to abolishing the tenant system which kept the southern Negro "poor, degraded, ignorant and half-starved, and support the Negroes' desires and struggles for land." Instead of devising plans for restricting the suffrage, let them demand that the Constitution be enforced and that the civil and political rights of the Negro guaranteed by the basic law be made to mean something more than high-sounding phrases. "If this were done," Douglass concluded, "there would be no Negro problem or national problem to vex the South or to vex the nation."

Excerpts from Douglass' last great address filled the columns of newspapers and magazines both in the United States and in England. And as Negroes read the burning sentences they felt a great weight being lifted from their shoulders. "As a race we can rest our cause on your argument and plea," a Negro wrote from the deep South.[5]

It is on this note that the career of Frederick Douglass draws to its close.

On the afternoon of February 20, 1895, Douglass left his home at Cedar Hill to attend a meeting of the National Council of Women in

Washington. Returning shortly after five o'clock for his dinner, he planned to deliver a lecture in the evening at the Hillsdale African Church near his home.

After dinner, as he sat talking to Helen about the events of the day at the Women's Council, he suddenly fell to his knees. Helen thought at first that he was merely mimicking one of the speakers. But as he sank down to the floor she rushed for aid. But it was too late. His heart had failed and the greatest of Negro leaders passed away quickly without regaining consciousness.

The news reached the delegates of the National Council of Women as they were opening their evening session. Mary Wright Sewall, the presiding officer, adjourned the meeting, but before the hall was darkened she told the hushed women:

"Surely it will be regarded as an historic coincidence that the man who, in his own person, embodied the history of almost a century, in the struggle between freedom and oppression, should spend his last day as a witness of the united efforts of those who have come from so many different places and along such various avenues, to formulate some plan upon which they may unite to demand a new expression of freedom in the relation of woman to the world, to society, and to the state; and in the application of woman's brain and conscience to the great questions pending at this hour."[6]

Douglass would have appreciated this comment. He himself had once said that "in some respects this woman suffrage movement is but a continuance of the old anti-slavery movement." It was fitting that the end should have found him in the ranks of those who were carrying on this tradition.

In every home the death of Frederick Douglass was discussed, and in every newspaper there were detailed accounts of his life and lengthy editorials evaluating his contributions to mankind.

"From first to last," editorialized the London *Daily News,* "his was a noble life. His own people have lost a father and a friend, and all good men have lost a comrade in the fight for the legal emancipation of one race and the spiritual emancipation of all."[7]

In North Carolina the legislature voted to adjourn for the day.[8] The legislatures of Indiana, Illinois, Massachusetts, and New York adopted resolutions of regret. "His death," the New York Assembly declared, "removes one of the foremost citizens and most striking figures of the

Republic, as well as the most distinguished member of his race of modern times."[9]

Expressions of condolence poured into the stricken family from all over the world. "In his removal humanity has sustained a great loss," cabled the Central Council of the International Society for the Recognition of the Brotherhood of Man from England. "He was the Toussaint L'Ouverture of the nineteenth century," wrote a group of citizens of Haiti. The Pennsylvania Society for Promoting the Abolition of Slavery expressed its "appreciation of a life that has made grander the history, not only of our country and our lives, but of the world."

Most touching were the messages received from Negroes north and south. The Negroes of Washington wrote:

"We present Frederick Douglass to the world today as what is possible to the Negro when placed under favorable conditions. . . . We challenge here and now, those in this fair land of ours who detract from us, who ostracise us and demean us, to produce from their kind his equal or one near thereto. We safely affirm that mankind has never furnished his equal along all the lines that he so faithfully pursued.

"We not only extend our condolence to his widow and his family, but to civilization, for Frederick Douglass belonged to the world."

Meeting in solemn assembly, the Negro citizens of Americus, Sumter County, Georgia, voted to contribute "out of our poverty and still-existing oppression" to a fund to erect a monument in Douglass' honor. "No people who can produce a Douglass need despair," they assured their fellow-countrymen. In two resolutions, they summed up the sentiments of the entire Negro population of the United States:

"Resolved, That his withering philippics, spoken and wielded by his mighty pen against human slavery, Ku-Kluxism, the rape of the ballot box, the indifference and supineness of the North, and the injustice heaped upon the people of his race by their American enemies, are not surpassed in true eloquence and power by those of any agitator, leader or martyr of any people in the history of the world; while the purity and beauty of his productions are worthy to rank as classics in the English language.

"Resolved, That the recent great and masterly exposition of the cause of the lynching of his people in the South, and his inestimable ability in defending them against the charge of being a race of rapists and general criminals, entitle him to the unanimous and individual love of the Negro racce the world over, and to the esteem of all persons who love honor, truth, justice, and fair play, especially when they are wielded in behalf of the weak, innocent and oppressed."[10]

The family services at Cedar Hill on Monday morning, February 25, 1895 were most simple—a scripture reading and a brief prayer. The remains of Frederick Douglass were then carried to the Metropolitan African Methodist Episcopal Church in Washington. Here the body lay in state for four hours. Thousands upon thousands of people passed in double file to view the body, whose guard of honor was composed of members of a colored division of the Sons of Veterans. Delegations from the Negro societies of New York, Annapolis, Baltimore, Wilmington, and Philadelphia joined in the line, eager for a last look at their champion. Fathers and mothers lifted little children to see the face of the great Douglass.

Finally, the church doors were closed and the services began. After the many speeches, John W. Hutchinson repeated the words his brother Jesse had dedicated to Douglass more than fifty years before:

> *I'll be free, I'll be free, and none shall confine*
> *with fetters and chains this spirit of mine;*
> *From my youth I have vowed in God to rely,*
> *And, despite the oppressor, gain freedom or die.*

Then he sang:

> *As man may, he fought his fight,*
> *Proved his truth by his endeavor,*
> *Let his name in golden light*
> *Live for ever and for ever!*
> *Lay him low, lay him low*
> *Under the clover or under the snow;*
> *How we loved him none can know;*
> *Lay him low.*

Two hours later, the casket was placed on a train for Rochester. It was met at the depot the next morning by Mayor Lewis, the members of the Common Council, the Douglass League of Rochester, the honorary pall bearers, and a cordon of police. Throngs followed the procession to the City Hall where the body lay in state for three hours. After the funeral services in Rochester's Central Presbyterian Church, the hearse passed through endless lines of uncovered and silent spectators to the Mount Hope Cemetery. Here Frederick Douglass was laid to rest.

Conclusion

The story of Frederick Douglass, as brought out in this study of the man and his times, is one of the truly great epics of America. It is a story of a slave who insisted on being a man and who in this struggle became the leader, the voice, and the symbol of a vast oppressed section of the American people.

Perhaps no one in our history with so little official position ever achieved so much. He lived to see most of the demands he had raised before, during, and immediately after the Civil War to establish and guarantee freedom for the Negro people become the law of the land. Unfortunately, he also lived to see many of these laws, particularly the Fourteenth and Fifteenth Amendments, become dead-letters after the betrayal of the Negro people in the "peace agreement" of 1876 and in the resulting victory of the former Southern ruling class.

But Douglass did not retreat to his study to reminisce over the battles and victories of the past. Once again he took to the lecture platform to explain the issues and to raise the demand that the nation enforce the democratic rights guaranteed to the Negro people and now being denied to them. He had no patience with the doctrine of gradualism. To those who insisted: "Be patient! We must move slowly. Remember, your people have made wonderful progress in your own lifetime; don't upset the apple cart"—he invariably replied: "We demand full equality now!" While he recognized that all the barriers against the Negro people could not be leveled overnight by executive fiat, court decisions, or legislative action, he was convinced that the battle for the achievement of full rights for the Negro American must be waged persistently and consistently.

We have spoken of certain shortcomings of Douglass' leadership in his declining years. Douglass did not wage a sufficiently effective struggle for the economic guarantees of Negro freedom; he did not ally himself sufficiently with the emerging labor movement; he did not do enough to mobilize opposition to the Republican Party's betrayal of the Negro freedmen and of democracy. At a time when Douglass was still clinging to the Republican Party, significant sections of the Negro population, disillusioned with that party because of its failure to live up to its promises, were allying themselves with independent labor and farmer parties as a means of winning full political rights and bettering their economic conditions. But Douglass, still tied to the Republican Party, remained aloof from the alliance between sections of the Negro population and the independent political movements of workers and farmers.

In truth, Douglass failed to understand that the big-business interests which dominated the Republican Party had long since receded from their advanced position during the early stages of Reconstruction when they had championed Negro civil and political rights in order to consolidate the triumph of Northern capitalism over the former slavemasters. He did not understand that when the bourgeois power had been consolidated and the conditions established for the rapid evolution of trusts and monopolies, the big-business interests which dominated the Republican Party would, in alliance with the Bourbon elements in the South, become the chief obstacle in the path of Negro liberation.

All this, while true, cannot obscure the fact that at all times, Douglass stood squarely and uncompromisingly for the full freedom of the Negro people. Nor can it obscure the fact that at a time when some Negro leaders were advocating conciliation and compromise, not to say surrender, Douglass uncompromisingly adhered to his principles of unflinching opposition to the entire pattern of segregation.

In his phenomenal rise above some of the restrictions of the American caste system, Douglass consistently fought for those who were trapped in its tentacles. He bitterly denounced the unjust and brutal treatment of the mass of his people. Never fearing whom it might offend, he unflinchingly raised the cry for equality.

In the very year in which Douglass died, a Negro first came to national attention who espoused a sharply different philosophy. In September, 1895, in a speech at the Cotton States and International Exposition at Atlanta, Georgia, Booker T. Washington, head of Tuskegee Institute in Alabama, recommended "acquiescence or at least no open agitation," for civil and political rights. The Negro could be happy in the South as long as he was subservient!

Ruling out agitational methods for the franchise on the ground that it might inflame public opinion, Washington placed stress on thrift, patience, and industrial education for the Negro masses. It was the duty of the Negro "to deport himself modestly in regard to political claims, depending upon the slow but sure influences that proceed from the possession of property, intelligence, and high character for the full recognition of his political rights." There were "peculiar conditions that justify the protection of the ballot in many of the states, for a while at least, either by an educational test, a property test, or by both combined. . . ." The Negro could depend upon his white friends in the South to correct matters in due time. In any event, the South must not be "forced by 'foreigners' or 'aliens,' to do something which it does not want to do."

Douglass' career had no contemporary significance to Washington. In the preface to his biography of Douglass, written in 1906, Washington observed:

"Frederick Douglass' career falls almost wholly within the period of revolution and liberation. That period is closed. We are at present in the period of construction and readjustment. . . . This book will have failed of its purpose just so far as anything here said shall serve to revive or keep alive the bitterness of those controversies of which it gives the history."[1]

Such an observation is not surprising, coming as it did from a man who condoned the cruelties of the Ku Klux Klan in the Reconstruction days as acts committed "simply for the purpose of calling attention to the great change that has taken place. . . . Today [1906] there are no such organizations in the South, and the fact that such ever existed is almost forgotten by both races."

Kelly Miller, a Negro spokesman who knew both Douglass and Washington, summed up the two men as follows:

"Douglass was like a lion, bold and fearless; Washington is lamblike, meek and submissive. Douglass escaped from personal bondage which his soul abhorred; but for Lincoln's proclamation, Washington would have arisen to esteem and favor in the eyes of his master as a good and faithful servant. Douglass insisted upon his rights; Washington insists upon duty. Douglass held up to public scorn the sins of the white man; Washington portrays the faults of his own race. Douglass spoke what he thought the world should hear; Washington speaks only what he feels it is disposed to listen to. Douglass' conduct was actuated by principle; Washington's by prudence. . . ."[2]

In the early days of 1895, a young Negro student living in New England journeyed to Providence, Rhode Island, to seek the advice of the aged Frederick Douglass who was visiting that city. As their interview drew to a close the youth said, " 'Mr. Douglass, you have lived in both the old and the new dispensations. What have you to say to a young Negro just starting out? What should he do?' The patriarch lifted his head and replied, 'Agitate! Agitate! Agitate!' "

In 1899 the same youth posed the identical question to Booker T. Washington who answered, " 'Work! Work! Work! Be patient and win by superior service.' "[3]

This story is an accurate reflection of the gulf that divided Douglass' and Washington's thoughts on the Negro question. Douglass urged a militant, relentless struggle for the retention of civil, political and economic rights gained during the Civil War and Reconstruction, and a ceaseless fight for the extension of these rights. Washington counselled moderation, retreat, and accommodation to the philosophy of the dominant ruling class of the South.

"He [Washington]," Professor Oliver C. Cox points out, "was not a leader of the masses . . .; his function was rather that of controlling the masses. He deflated and abandoned their common cause. He demanded less for the Negro people than that which the ruling class had already conceded. . . .

"Leaders of Washington's type are exceedingly serviceable to the southern ruling class. They are vastly more effective than white spokesmen in controverting the movement for democracy among Negroes."[4]

Interest in Douglass' principles declined among the followers of Booker T. Washington's school of thought. Douglass' name still commanded their respect, but rather as a legend than a living force. His ideas, his experience, the warp and woof of his militancy were not necessary to a leadership which preached that in the South "the relations between the two races are pleasant."

But the spirit of fearless challenge which characterized the pioneer leader in the battle for Negro liberation did not perish. Negro men like Lewis H. Douglass, the departed leader's son, who fought against American imperialism, and Negro women like the remarkable Ida B. Wells, who fought the crime of lynching despite every attempt to silence her, and like Mrs. Mary Church Terrell and Mrs. Josephine S. Yates, who helped to form the National Association of Colored Women in 1896, continued to uphold the principles of Frederick Douglass by their militant resistance to oppression.

Less than a decade after Douglass' death, Dr. W. E. B. Du Bois took up the fight, challenging the leadership and philosophy of Booker T. Washington. Born in Massachusetts, educated at Fisk, Harvard, and the University of Berlin, a keen thinker, a brilliant writer, a forceful speaker, Du Bois was eminently fitted to lead the movement to recapture the militancy epitomized in Douglass' career. In 1903 appeared his powerful epic, *The Souls of Black Folk,* in which Du Bois spoke out against Washington's policy of apologizing "for injustice North and South," and announced in a passionate voice: "By every civilized and peaceful method we must strive for the rights which the world accords to men."[5] Two years later, in 1905, Du Bois led the historic Niagara movement, heralding the rise of a new leadership in Negro life. This group then declared:

"We shall not be satisfied with less than our full manhood rights. We claim for ourselves every right that belongs to a free-born American, civil and social, and until we get these rights we shall never cease to protest and assail the ears of America with the stories of its shameful deeds toward us. We want our manhood suffrage and we want it now."[6]

Through the medium of the magazine, *The Crisis,* and the organization of the National Association for the Advancement of Colored People, which he helped to found in 1910, Dr. Du Bois continued his struggle for the full freedom of his people. And while American scholarship paraded racist prejudice and bias as historical fact, Dr. Du Bois' scholarly works, which began to appear in the dawn of the twentieth century, educated a whole generation of teachers, writers, and young scholars to take their place in the Negro liberation movement.

But the major trend persisting among Negro leaders was either to divert the Negro liberation movement into a "Back to Africa" utopian gesture or to cherish a "gentle and gradual" solution of the Negro question and to shy away from "radical" proposals. In March, 1926, Francis J. Grimké, a distinguished Negro minister in Washington, wrote:

"The disposition to stand up for our rights, to stand where Frederick Douglass stood for fifty years, insisting upon just treatment for his race, is rather at a discount today in these degenerate times,—at a discount with certain of our white friends, and also with a certain class of Negroes. We hear a great deal of the evils of agitation, about the little good that it does, and the great amount of harm that comes of it. . . . The attempt is to discourage all agitation, and to undervalue the services of the men who are keeping up the agitation for our civil and political rights. And yet was it not through agitation that the great revolution in public sentiment was effected before which slavery went down; was it not because of such men as Douglass and Phillips and Garrison and Sumner and others of the noble band of Anti-Slavery leaders who went everywhere through the free states and inaugurated a campaign of education? Fortunately for us there were men like Douglass, gifted orators and writers, who were willing to speak out in behalf of the oppressed millions of bondmen in this land. We must not fall into the silly, foolish notion that it does no good to agitate, to speak out, and to speak out boldly and strongly. It is our duty to do all that we can to hasten the coming of a better day.

"Mr. Douglass pointed the way—the way of persistent efforts to improve ourselves, and of manly resistance to all efforts to curtail our opportunities, to abridge our rights. Let us see to it that we keep the way, and continue to walk in it, to the end."[7]

Today Frederick Douglass still points the way. His struggle against all forms of discrimination, his exposure of the peonage system in the South, his campaign against lynching, and his demand that the Constitution be enforced, are as timely and significant today as they were in Douglass' lifetime. For Douglass' militant principles, carried out logically and translated into terms of today's problems, lead to the immediate outlawry of Jim-Crowism and all other manifestations of bigotry, to the passage and enforcement of anti-lynching legislation, to the removal of all barriers on the full exercise of the right of suffrage, and greater Negro representation in both elective and appointive offices, to the abolition of inequalities in education, to the elimination of the ghetto and restrictive covenants, to the abolition of discrimination in employment and the extirpation of every vestige of peonage, to common action between white and Negro Americans for an end to Negro oppression and for the removal of the stumbling blocks which stand in the way of full economic, political and social equality for the Negro people and progress and freedom for the entire nation.

During the half-century since Douglass' death, the country has witnessed the steady advance of the Negro liberation movement. In 1896, a year after Douglass died, the Supreme Court in Plessy v. Ferguson officially accepted the doctrine of "separate but equal accommodations" which, among other things, fully sanctioned segregation in public schools and colleges, with educational facilities for Negroes being "separate" but anything but "equal." Justice John M. Harlan, who had dissented in the Civil Rights Case, again wrote a scorching dissent. "Our Constitution is blind," he insisted in declaring unconstitutional all laws requiring segregation, "and neither knows nor tolerates classes among citizens. . . . The law regards man as man, and takes no regard of his surroundings or his color when his civil rights as guaranteed by the supreme law of the land are invoked."[8]

In May, 1954, after over a half-century of persistent struggle by the Negro people and their progressive white allies to end segregation in education, the Supreme Court reversed Plessy v. Ferguson, unanimously deciding that segregation in public schools and colleges must be abolished.

"Power concedes nothing without a demand," Frederick Douglass had warned. The demand is being raised by the Negro people and their white allies that the Supreme Court decision be fully enforced, and that, despite efforts of the Southern ruling class to ignore or evade it, the historic decision become the law in every state in the Union.

Behind this and many other demands stands today a powerful movement, much of which did not exist when Douglass died. Today there are nearly two million Negro workers in the organized labor movement as compared to less than fifty thousand fifty years ago. Various types of mass organizations, religious, fraternal and professional, have been built up among the Negro people in the past half-century, with the most powerful, the N.A.A.C.P., having passed the quarter of a million mark in membership. Today the readers of the Negro press, whose history extends over more than a century, number several millions.

Today this extensive network of Negro organizations, local and national, have dedicated themselves to achieve effective F.E.P.C.—federal, state and city; an end to discrimination and Jim Crow in education, and in every other phase of American life; an end to lynching, legal as well as extra-legal; abolition of the poll tax; the right of Negroes to vote and the election and appointment of Negroes throughout the nation to all levels of political life—executive, legislative, and judicial. Similarly, a struggle is taking place for jobs in industry and the upgrading of Negro workers, and the election of Negroes to trade union leadership on all levels.

Today the Negro people, with the working class, women and youth playing an ever more important and leading role, are uniting, as never before, to win the causes for which Frederick Douglass fought during his lifetime. In the spirit of Frederick Douglass, they are telling the nation: "We want to be free and we want to be free now!"

Montgomery, Birmingham, Danville, Plaquemine, Washington, D.C., Philadelphia, Chicago, New York and hundreds of other communities, North and South, have heard this cry in the last few years, and they will continue to hear it until the objectives of the Negro Protest Movement are achieved.

But to achieve these goals constant, unremitting struggle will be necessary all the way. As Douglass himself put it:

"If there is no struggle there is no progress. Those who profess to favor freedom, and yet depreciate agitation, are men who want crops without plowing up the ground. . . . This struggle may be a moral one; or it may be a physical one; or it may be both moral and physical; *but it must be a struggle. . . .* Power concedes nothing without a demand. It never did and it never will."

Not only a great Negro and passionate fighter against every injustice heaped upon his people, but a far-sighted statesman enlisted in the "cause of humanity the world over," and one who saw his people's liberation movement as part of the democratic advance of all Americans, Frederick Douglass has grown in stature and significance since his death. "It is 58 years since Frederick Douglass, that most illustrious Negro and to my mind the greatest of all Americans died . . .," wrote Mrs. Mary Church Terrell in the September, 1953, issue of *Ebony* Magazine. "The passing of the years, far from diminishing his importance, has made Douglass an even greater figure in his country's history." His memory and his heritage will not die, for he takes his deserved place with Jefferson and Lincoln in the democratic tradition of our country.

The distinguished Negro poet, Robert E. Hayden, writing in the *Atlantic Monthly* of February, 1947, expressed the yearnings of the Negro people for full freedom and the place that Frederick Douglass occupies in this struggle:

> *When it is finally ours, this freedom, this liberty, this beautiful*
> *and terrible thing, needful to man as air,*
> *usable as the earth; when it belongs at last to our children,*
> *when it is truly instinct, brain-matter, diastole, systole,*
> *reflex action; when it is finally won; when it is more*
> *than the gaudy mumbo-jumbo of politicians:*
> *this man, this Douglass, this former slave, this Negro*
> *beaten to his knees, exiled, visioning a world*
> *where none is lonely, none hunted, alien,*
> *this man, superb in love and logic, this man*
> *shall be remembered—oh, not with statues' rhetoric,*
> *not with legends and poems and wreaths of bronze alone,*
> *but with the lives grown out of his life, the lives*
> *fleshing his dream of the needful, beautiful thing.*

REFERENCE NOTES

Reference Notes

PART ONE   EARLY YEARS

FROM SLAVERY TO FREEDOM

1. *Frederick Douglass' Paper,* April 29, 1853. "It has always been a source of dissatisfaction to the writer," Douglass wrote in 1870, "that he neither knows when nor exactly where he was born." As late as 1894, a year before his death, he was still trying to fill in gaps in his early life. On March 16, 1894, he called upon Dr. Thomas Edward Sears, a grandson of his former owners, Thomas and Lucretia Auld, and discovered that he had been sent to live with Hugh Auld in Baltimore in 1825. "I know," he wrote in his diary, "that it must have been in that year that I went to live in Baltimore because the spring lambs were big enough to be sent to market, and I helped to drive a flock of them from Smiths Dock to Fells Point on the day I landed in Baltimore." (*Frederick Douglass Diary,* Mar. 17, 1894, entry, Douglass Papers, Frederick Douglass Memorial Home, Anacostia, D. C.)

2. In his first autobiography, *Narrative of the Life of Frederick Douglass,* published in Boston, 1845, Douglass stated positively: "My father was a white man. He was admitted to be such by all I ever heard speak of my parentage" (p. 2). On several occasions Douglass intimated that his master might have been his father. In May, 1850, he introduced himself to a New York audience with the remark: "The son of a slaveholder stands before you, by a colored mother." (*National Anti-Slavery Standard,* May 23, 1850.)

3. Harriet Bailey was the mother of an older son, Perry, and of four daughters, two of whom were named Sarah and Eliza. "While I am addressing you," said Douglass in 1848, "four of my own dear sisters and one brother are enduring the frightful horrors of American slavery." (*The North Star,* Aug. 4, 1848.)

4. Frederick Douglass, *My Bondage and My Freedom,* New York, 1855, pp. 56-57.

5. Douglass to Theodore Tilton [September, 1867], *The Independent,* Sept. 12, 1867.

6. *New York Herald,* Sept. 6, 1866.

7. Ethan Allen Andrews, *Slavery and the Slave Trade in the United States,* Boston, 1836, p. 42; John L. Carey, *Slavery in Maryland Briefly Considered,* Baltimore, 1845, pp. 25-27; *Narrative of the Life of Frederick Douglass,* Boston, 1845, p. 31. Hereafter cited as *Narrative.*

8. "The education of free Negroes and slaves was not forbidden by law in Maryland, but the black was indebted for what he got to the interest of individuals or of such societies as the Society of Friends." (Jeffrey R. Brackett, *The Negro in Maryland,* Baltimore, 1889, p. 196.)

9. Speech of Frederick Douglass in Belfast, *Anti-Slavery Standard,* Feb. 26, 1846; *Narrative,* pp. 38-39.

10. In January, 1856, *The Columbian Orator* was listed as one of the Abolition books found in southern schools. (See *De Bow's Review,* vol. XX, p. 69.) The copy of *The Columbian Orator* purchased by Douglass is still preserved in the Frederick Douglass Memorial Home in Anacostia.

11. *My Bondage and My Freedom*, p. 99; Douglass to Mrs. Livermore, Apr. 4, 1885, Douglass *Mss.*, Frederick Douglass Memorial Home, Anacostia, D. C.

12. *Narrative*, pp. 35-36; *Baltimore Gazette*, May 19, 1870.

13. *Narrative*, p. 73; *Reception Speech at Finsbury Chapel, Moorfelds, England, May 12, 1846.*

14. In *My Bondage and My Freedom*, Douglass prefaced his account of his experiences at Gardiner's shipyards with a brilliant analysis of the effects of slavery upon the southern white workers. He was confident that the "competition and its injurious consequences, will, one day, array the non-slaveholding white people of the slave states, against the slave system, and make them the most effective workers against this great evil" (pp. 309-10). For a discussion of relations between white and Negro workers in the South, see Philip S. Foner, *History of the Labor Movement in the United States*, New York, 1947, pp. 258-65.

15. In addition to these benevolent societies, both male and female, each with from thirty-five to fifty members, the free Negro population of Baltimore had ten churches. ". . . Also, among us," went a report of the free Negroes, "there are various mechanics and others, who have by industry and frugality purchased houses and lots of grounds, horses, drays,' carts and carriages. . . ." ("A Reply to a Note from 'A White Citizen,'" signed by John Fortie, Nathaniel Peck, William Levington, *Niles' Register*, vol. XLIX, Oct. 3, 1835, p. 72.)

16. *My Bondage and My Freedom*, p. 330.

17. Douglass did not publicly divulge the method of his escape until March 10, 1873, when, in a speech at the Academy of Music in Philadelphia, he broke his long silence. Even in July, 1865, he was reluctant to permit the story to be made public. "Use the story of my life in any way you see fit," he wrote to Lydia M. Child. ". . . I do not think it well to make known the manner of my escape from slavery. No good end could be served by such publication and some evil might possibly come of it." (Douglass to Lydia M. Child, July 12, 1865, Douglass *Mss.*) Douglass kept the story secret for fear that the conductor who had passed him from Baltimore to Philadelphia would be responsible to Hugh Auld for the loss (from $500 to $650) he had sustained in his slave's escape. Also, he did not want to expose his friends Stanley and Rhodes and did not wish to reveal to slave owners a method employed by fugitive slaves. In his *Narrative*, Douglass sharply criticized some of the Abolitionists in the Underground Railroad for publicizing their activities. Such procedures stimulated the master "to greater watchfulness, and enhance his power to capture his slaves. We owe something to the slaves south of the line as well as to those north of it; and in aiding the latter on their way to freedom, we should be careful to do nothing which would be likely to hinder the former from escaping from slavery. I would keep the merciless slaveholder profoundly ignorant of the means of flight adopted by the slave." (*Narrative*, pp. 100-01.)

18. Quoted by Philip S. Foner, *Business and Slavery*, Chapel Hill, N. C., 1941, p. 1.

19. The New York Vigilance Committee was founded in November, 1835, by a group of white and Negro "Friends of Human Rights" to assist any colored person who might be arrested under pretense of being an escaped slave. But much of its work was to feed and clothe runaways and send them on to some points of safety outside of New York with money and letters of introduction to friends. Ruggles, who had been a traveling agent for *The Emancipator*, a New York anti-slavery newspaper, was, at the time Douglass came to him for aid, publishing *The Mirror for Liberty*, the first magazine edited by a Negro. (For a study of Ruggles, see Dorothy B. Parker, "David B. Ruggles,

An Apostle for Human Freedom," *Journal of Negro History,* vol. XXVIII, Jan., 1943, pp. 23-50.) Ruggles estimated that during the five years he was secretary of the Vigilance Committee, he aided over six hundred slaves to escape. (*The North Star,* Apr. 14, 1848.)

20. *Life and Times of Frederick Douglass,* Hartford, Conn., 1881, p. 183.

21. *Anti-Slavery Standard,* Dec. 23, 1841. Reverend Thomas James relates in his autobiography that while he was preaching in New Bedford in 1841 he heard Douglass speak and licensed him to preach. (*Wonderful Eventful Life of Thomas James, By Himself,* Rochester, 1887, p. 6.) This may actually have happened, but there is no mention of Douglass in the official list of ministers and preachers of the African Methodist Church in 1842. (See *African Methodist Episcopal Church Magazine,* vol. I, Dec., 1842, p. 89.)

22. *Narrative,* p. 117.

23. *Anti-Slavery Standard,* Aug. 26, 1841; *Liberator,* July 9, 1841.

24. Frederick Douglass, "Reminiscences," *The Cosmopolitan,* vol. VII, Aug., 1889, p. 378; *Liberator,* Aug. 20, Sept. 3, 1841.

25. *Boston Evening Transcript,* Aug. 11, 1841; *Anti-Slavery Standard,* Aug. 26, 1841.

26. *Anti-Slavery Standard,* Aug. 26, 1841. No authentic account of Douglass' speech is available. The Nantucket papers did not even mention it and none of the Abolition journals carried a verbatim report. Parker Pillsbury, who was present, recalls that in the course of his remarks, Douglass "gave a most side-splitting specimen of a slave-holding minister's sermon, 'servants obey your masters.' . . ." (*The Acts of the Anti-Slavery Apostles,* Boston, 1884, p. 326.) None of the other accounts mention this and it is doubtful whether Douglass would have used this material on this occasion.

27. In later years different Abolitionists claimed credit for having been the first to induce Douglass to become an anti-slavery lecturer. Garrison's children wrote that it was their father who had advised this step. (W. F. Garrison and F. J. Garrison, *Life of William Lloyd Garrison* [4 vols., New York, 1885-1889], vol. III, p. 292.) However, Edmund Quincy wrote in 1845, "I believe I was the first person who suggested to him becoming an Anti-Slavery speaker." (Quincy to Richard D. Webb, Dec. 13, 1845, Anti-Slavery Letters to William Lloyd Garrison and others, Boston Public Library.) Forty years later still another Abolitionist, James Buffum, insisted that he, too, was responsible for bringing Douglass into the movement as a lecturer. "Mr. Garrison and myself thought it would be a good thing if a man who had endured some of the penalties of slavery could go out and tell his story. And so he was engaged." (James N. Buffum, *Commemoration of the Fiftieth Anniversary of the American Anti-Slavery Society,* Philadelphia, 1884, p. 42.)

THE GARRISONIANS

1. See Gilbert H. Barnes, *The Anti-Slavery Impulse,* New York, 1933; Dwight L. Dumond, *Anti-Slavery Origins of the Civil War,* Ann Arbor, Michigan, 1939, pp. 99-100; Gilbert H. Barnes and Dwight L. Dumond, editors, *Letters of Theodore Dwight Weld, Angelina Grimké Weld and Sarah Grimké,* New York 1934, pp. v-xxvii. (Hereafter cited as *Weld-Grimké Letters.*) Barnes and Dumond are guilty of overemphasizing Weld's influence and underestimating Garrison's. For a summary of their views, see Dwight L. Dumond, "Race Prejudice and Abolition," *Michigan Alumni Quarterly Review,* vol. XLI, Apr., 1935, pp. 377-85.

2. Mary Stoughton Locke, *Anti-Slavery in America, 1619-1808*, Boston, 1901, pp. 15-32; Philip S. Foner, editor, *The Complete Writings of Thomas Paine*, New York, 1945, vol. II, pp. 15-18; Philip S. Foner, editor, *Basic Writings of Thomas Jefferson*, New York, 1944, pp. 14-28, Herbert Aptheker, *To Be Free*, New York, 1948, p. 43; Herbert Aptheker, *The Negro in the American Revolution*, New York, 1940, pp. 7-13.

3. The organization was known, after 1818, as the American Convention for Promoting the Abolition of Slavery and Improving the Condition of the African Race.

4. Quoted by Alice Dana Adams, The *Neglected Period of Anti-Slavery in America, 1808-31*, Boston, 1908, p. 178.

5. L. R. Mehlinger, "The Attitude of the Free Negro toward African Colonization," *Journal of Negro History*, vol. I, July, 1916, pp. 276-301.

6. See *Liberator*, June 18, 1831; *Minutes and Proceedings of the Second National Negro Convention, held in Philadelphia, June 6-11, 1831*.

7. Aptheker, *To Be Free*, p. 50.

8. Arthur M. Schlesinger, *New Viewpoints in American History*, New York, 1932, pp. 201-20; Avery Craven, *The Coming of the Civil War*, New York, 1942, pp. 128-34; Vernon L. Parrington, *Main Currents in American Thought*, New York, 1926, vol. II, pp. 339-78; Albert Bushnell Hart, *Slavery and Abolition*, New York, 1906, pp. 170-74.

9. Garrison was brought to the anti-slavery movement by Benjamin Lundy, a New Jersey Quaker who had learned to hate slavery while working at the saddler's trade in Virginia. Garrison became Lundy's assistant in Baltimore, and edited the weekly *Genius of Universal Emancipation* which Lundy had founded at Mount Pleasant, Tennessee, in 1821. When Garrison began calling the known slave-traffickers by name, his audacity was rewarded with seven weeks in a Baltimore jail.

    Garrison moved rapidly ahead of his mentor after his return to Boston. Lundy had never been won over to the radical idea of immediate emancipation and remained a staunch colonizationist. At first Garrison shared his teacher's views, but, moved by the arguments of the Negro people against the Colonization Society, he investigated for himself. Soon he became an outstanding enemy of the African Colonization Society and the champion of immediate emancipation. (See William Lloyd Garrison, *Address to the Colored People*, 1831, and *Thoughts on African Colonization*, 1832.)

10. *Liberator*, Dec. 14, 1833. The following Negroes were among the delegates to the founding convention of the American Society: James G. Barbadoes, of Massachusetts; James McCrummell, Robert Purvis, James Forten, John B. Vashon and Abraham D. Shadd of Pennsylvania; and Peter Williams of New York. The Negroes who signed the Declaration of Sentiments were: James G. Barbadoes, Robert Purvis, and James McCrummell.

11. See G. M. Stroud, *A Sketch of the Laws Relating to Slavery*, New York, 1858, pp. 33-34.

12. Quoted by Dwight L. Dumond, "Race Prejudice and Abolition," *Michigan Alumni Quarterly Review*, vol. XLI, Apr., 1935, p. 378.

13. Quoted by Henry Wilson, *History of the Rise and Fall of the Slave Power in America*, Boston and New York, 1872, vol. I, p. 257.

14. Printed in *The Liberty Bell*, 1842, pp. 64-66.

15. *Fourteenth Annual Report of the Massachusetts Anti-Slavery Society,* 1846, p. 48; Elizur Wright to James G. Birney, July 16, 1836, Dwight L. Dumond, ed., *Letters of James Gillespie Birney,* New York, 1938, vol. I, p. 334. Theodore Weld, an outstanding worker for the cause, received an annual salary of $416 from the American Anti-Slavery Society (Wright to Weld, Dec. 31, 1833, Barnes and Dumond, editors, *Weld-Grimké Letters,* vol. I, p. 122). Many agents did not even receive the meager salary allotted to them. In 1840 Henry B. Stanton's salary was two years in arrears. (Weld to Tappan, Apr. 10, 1840, *Weld-Grimké Letters,* vol. II, p. 828.) For a detailed study of Abolitionist finances, see Benjamin Quarles, "Sources of Abolitionist Income," *Mississippi Valley Historical Review,* vol. XXXII, June, 1945, pp. 63-76.

16. Weld, son of a New York State Presbyterian minister, had been influenced by Charles G. Finney in the Great Revival, and became chief assistant to the revivalist. Later he went to Oneida Institute to prepare for the ministry. In the winter of 1833-1834 he organized a great anti-slavery revival among the students of Lane Seminary at which they discussed the question of immediate emancipation. When the trustees objected to the discussion, Weld and his followers left Lane Seminary and went to Oberlin which was founded as an Abolitionist institution with Finney as its president. Twelve of the Lane rebels became agents of the American Anti-Slavery Society, and, under Weld's leadership, abolitionized Ohio. All American Society agents were trained by Weld. At the Agents' Convention in New York City, Weld met the Grimké sisters, daughters of a Charleston slaveholder, who had become Abolitionists and come north. Weld married Angelina Grimké.

When Weld turned his talents to writing and editing, the cause gained a remarkable force whose achievements are miracles even by today's standards. Determined to publish a factual, first-hand proof that emancipation of slaves would work, James A. Thomas and Joseph A. Kimball were sent off to the West Indies to gather facts on the results of emancipation. After the enormous work of cutting and editing, Weld published their *Emancipation in the West Indies* and ran it through several editions of which one alone totaled one hundred thousand copies. When bought in quantity, the book sold for twelve cents a copy.

Together with his wife, Angelina Grimké Weld, he wrote the greatest of all anti-slavery pamphlets, *Slavery as it is; the testimony of a thousand witnesses.* Assiduously assembling facts on the conditions of the slaves in the South from southern newspapers and from statements of fugitive slaves, Weld and his wife arranged them in a pamphlet of 224 pages which became one of the most powerful weapons in the struggle against slavery.

In 1842, Weld went to Washington, where he took the leading part in organizing the anti-slavery Congressmen into an effective group.

17. Charlotte Morse to Elizur Wright, Oct. 28, 1845, Elizur Wright Papers, Library of Congress.

18. *National Anti-Slavery Standard,* Nov. 11, 1841; *Liberator,* Jan. 1, 1841; Quarles, *op. cit.,* pp. 75-76; Hart, *op. cit.,* pp. 170-87; *Quarterly Anti-Slavery Magazine,* vol. I, Oct., 1835, p. 104; vol. II, Apr., 1836, p. 310; vol. III, July, 1837, p. 340.

19. Barnes, *op. cit.,* pp. 121-27.

20. Quoted by Philip S. Foner, *History of the Labor Movement in the United States,* p. 267.

21. Wilson, *op. cit.,* vol. I, p. 405; Oliver Johnson, *William Lloyd Garrison,* Boston, 1881, p. 314; *Fourth Annual Report of the American Anti-Slavery Society,* Boston,

1839, p. 23; Wendell Phillips to the *Liberator*, Dec. 2, 1841, in *Liberator*, Dec. 31, 1841.

22. William Lloyd Garrison, *An Address to the Abolitionists of Massachusetts on the subject of Political Action*, pp. 7, 15.

23. *Liberator*, Dec. 15, 1837; Massachusetts Abolition Society, *The True History of the Late Division in the Anti-Slavery Societies*, Boston, 1841; Wendell Phillips Stafford, *Wendell Phillips*, New York, 1911, p. 18; Parker Pillsbury, *The Anti-Slavery Advocate*, Dec., 1844, pp. 218-19; Eliza Wigham, *The Anti-Slavery Cause in America and its Martyrs*, London, 1863, pp. 67-71.

24. Elaine Brooks, "The Massachusetts Anti-Slavery Society," *Journal of Negro History*, vol. XXX, July, 1945, pp. 311-31.

25. W. P. and F. J. Garrison, *Life of William Lloyd Garrison*, vol. II, p. 347; *Liberator*, Apr. 24, 1840; Wilson, *op. cit.*, vol. I, pp. 415-20.

26. Barnes and Dumond, editors, *Weld-Grimké Letters*, vol. II, p. 849.

27. Hart, *op. cit.*, p. 201; *Tenth Annual Report of the Massachusetts Anti-Slavery Society*, Boston, 1842, Appendix, p. 8.

28. Garrison to Henry C. Wright, Oct. 1, 1844, Garrison *Mss.*, Boston Public Library. On Mar. 21, 1856, Garrison wrote to Samuel J. May: "The dissolution of the Union must first precede the abolition of slavery." (Garrison *Mss.*, Boston Public Library.)

ANTI-SLAVERY AGENT

1. One writer branded the whole galaxy of Abolitionists as "a group of fanatics or zealots who never saw a slave in slavery." (J. B. Robinson, *Pictures of Slavery and Anti-Slavery*, Philadelphia, 1853, pp. 74-75.

2. "A South Carolinian," *An Appeal to the People of the Northern and Eastern States*, New York, 1834, pp. 14, 18; A. E. Miller, *A Refutation*, Charleston, 1822, pp. 53-54; H. Manly, *The South Vindicated*, Philadelphia, 1836, *passim*. See also Wilfred Carsel, "The Slaveholders' Indictment of Northern Wage Slavery," *Journal of Southern History*, vol. VI, Nov., 1940, pp. 514-20.

3. Anonymous, *Twofold Slavery*, Baltimore, 1838, p. 122. See also J. L. Carey, *Slavery in Maryland*, Philadelphia, 1836, p. 13.

4. G. Barnes and D. L. Dumond, editors, *Weld-Grimké Correspondence*, vol. II, p. 717.

5. John A. Collins to Garrison, Jan. 18, 1842, *Liberator*, Jan. 21, 1842. See also Vernon Loggens, *The Negro Author*, New York, 1931; pp. 131-32.

6. See *Liberator*, Sept. 17, 24, Oct. 15, 29, Nov. 12, 19, Dec. 3, 14, 1841; Jan. 14, 1842; *Herald of Freedom*, (Concord), Dec. 10, 1841.

7. Abby Kelley to *Herald of Freedom*, (Concord), Nov. 12, 1841; See also *Providence Journal*, Jan. 1, 1842; *Anti-Slavery Standard*, Dec. 23, 1841.

8. See *Liberator*, Nov. 12, 26, Dec. 3, 1841; *Anti-Slavery Standard*, Dec. 23, 1841.

9. Quoted by Parker Pillsbury, *Acts of the Anti-Slavery Apostles*, p. 31; Frederic May Holland, *Frederick Douglass*, New York, 1891, pp. 68-69.
    There is no complete copy of Douglass' famous "Slaveholders' Sermon." The text used here is from reports of the meeting at Faneuil Hall on Jan. 8, 1842, and before the Plymouth County Anti-Slavery Society in December, 1841. See *Tenth Annual Report of the Board of Managers of the Massachusetts Anti-Slavery Society*, Appendix, p. 19, and *Anti-Slavery Standard*, Dec. 23, 1841. For another version of the "Sermon," see *Anti-Slavery Standard*, Oct. 25, 1847.

10. *Tenth Annual Report of the Board of Managers of the Massachusetts Anti-Slavery Society*, Boston, 1842, pp. 105-06.

11. Douglass was paid $170.34 by the Society for his three months' service. (*Ibid.*, p. 106.)

12. *Herald of Freedom* (Concord), June 3, 1842; A.W.P. in *Liberator*, June 17, 1842. See also *Nantucket Islander* in *Ibid.*, July 8, 1842.

13. *Liberator*, Oct. 1, 8, 15, 1841; Aug. 26, Sept. 2, 1842; *Herald of Freedom* (Concord), Aug. 19, 1842.

14. *Eleventh Annual Report of the Board of Managers of the Massachusetts Anti-Slavery Society*, Boston, 1843, pp. 45-46.

15. *Liberator*, Nov. 18, 1842.

16. *The Latimer Journal and North Star*, Nov. 26, 1842. After Latimer's purchase, the Abolitionists presented a petition to the State Legislature praying that fugitive slaves should never again be arrested by town or city officials, nor held as prisoners in the jails of Massachusetts, and that the State Constitution should be "so amended as shall forever separate the people of Massachusetts from all connection with slavery." The petition, signed by 60,000 persons headed by George Latimer himself, was presented on February 17, 1843, to the Massachusetts House of Representatives. It resulted in the passage of a law, with very few dissenting votes, making it a penal offense for any magistrate or executive officer of the state to assist in the arrest or delivery of any person claimed as a fugitive slave and prohibiting those having charge of the jails and other places of confinement to use them for his detention. (See *The Latimer Journal and North Star*, Nov. 23, 1842; *Twelfth Annual Report of the Massachusetts Anti-Slavery Society*, Boston, 1844, p. 45.)

17. *Salem Register* reprinted in *Liberator*, Dec. 9, 1842.

18. *Twelfth Annual Report of the Massachusetts Anti-Slavery Society*, Boston, 1844, pp. 34-35.
   Early in the year the Rhode Island Anti-Slavery Society employed Douglass to lecture and collect funds. He worked for three months for the Society, meanwhile continuing his lectures in Massachusetts.

19. Frederic May Holland, *op. cit.*, pp. 86-87.

20. Douglass to Maria W. Chapman, Sept. 10, 1843, *Anti-Slavery Letters to Garrison*, Boston Public Library.
   Douglass was dismayed by Mrs. Chapman's reaction to his letter. "Strange to say," he reveals in his autobiography, "my course in this matter did not meet the approval of Mrs. M. W. Chapman, an influential member of the board of managers of the Massachusetts Anti-Slavery Society, and called out a sharp reprimand from her, for insubordination to my superiors. This was a strange and distressing revelation to me, and one of which I was not soon relieved." (*Life and Times of Frederick Douglass*, p. 255.) Douglass' role in this incident foreshadowed his later controversy with the Garrisonians.
   After his resignation, Collins deserted the anti-slavery movement and devoted his entire energies to an experiment in community living in Skaneateles, New York. In 1869 he wrote to Douglass recalling their conflict in Syracuse. (John A. Collins to Douglass, Apr. 12, 1869, Douglass Papers, Frederick Douglass Memorial Home, Anacostia, D. C.)

21. William A. White to Garrison, Sept. 22, 1843, *Liberator*, Oct. 13, 1843; Douglass to William A. White, July 30, 1846, Douglass *Mss.*, Frederick Douglass Memorial Home, Anacostia, D. C.

22. George Bradburn to John A. Collins, Nov. 21, 1843, Anti-Slavery Letters to Garrison, Boston Public Library; F. M. Holland, *op. cit.*, p. 97; *Twelfth Annual Report of the Massachusetts Anti-Slavery Society*, Boston, 1844, pp. 34-35; *Liberator*, Mar. 15, 1844.

23. *Herald of Freedom* (Concord), Feb. 16, 23, 1844.

24. *Life and Times of Frederick Douglass*, p. 242.

25. *The North Star*, Jan. 8, 1848; Frederika Bremer, *The Homes of the New World*, translated by Mary Howitt, New York, 1853, pp. 583-85.

26. *Lynn Pioneer* in *Liberator*, May 30, 1845; *The North Star*, Mar. 12, 1848.

27. As early as Feb. 24, 1845, Wendell Phillips wrote to Elizabeth Pease: "Douglass who is now writing out his story thinks of relaxing by a voyage whether with the Hutchinsons or alone I don't know." (Anti-Slavery Letters to Garrison, Boston Public Library.) According to a statement made by Douglass in 1886, it was Phillips who first suggested that he go abroad. (See Douglass' speech before the Wendell Phillips Club of Boston, *Boston Journal*, Sept. 13, 1886.)

28. James N. Buffum to Gerrit Smith, June 21, 1845, Gerrit Smith Papers, Syracuse University. Buffum urged Smith to raise funds for Douglass' voyage, adding: "Frederick feels a natural delicacy in soliciting funds for this purpose."

29. Frederick, junior, was born in New Bedford early in 1842. Charles Remond was born Oct. 21, 1844, in Lynn.

30. For 1842 Douglass received $300.36 from the Massachusetts Society. For 1843 there was no listing of any payment to Douglass, but it is likely that Collins paid him out of the funds allotted to the general agent. At any rate, Douglass felt keenly the need of money during this year. "I have received a few lines from my wife," he wrote to Maria W. Chapman on Sept. 10, 1843, "asking for means to carry on household affairs. I have none to send her. Will you please see that she is provided with $25 or $30." (Anti-Slavery Letters to Garrison, Boston Public Library.)
    For 1844 Douglass received $142 from the Massachusetts Society. (See *Thirteenth Annual Report of the Massachusetts Anti-Slavery Society*, Appendix, p. 6.)

31. Wendell Phillips to R. D. Webb, July, 1845; Wendell Phillips to James Haughton, Richard Allen and R. D. Webb, Aug. 13, 1845; Maria W. Chapman to R. D. Webb, Aug. 16, 1845, Anti-Slavery Letters to Garrison, Boston Public Library; *Herald of Freedom* (Concord), July 11, 1845. Douglass insisted that only $60 had been raised to help him pay for the passage. (See Douglass to Maria W. Chapman, Mar. 29, 1846, Anti-Slavery Letters to Garrison, Boston Public Library.)

32. Wendell Phillips to Elizabeth Pease, Feb. 24, 1845, Anti-Slavery Letters to Garrison, Boston Public Library. "Language, taste, fancy—eloquence—vigor of thoughts—good sound common sense—manliness are all his," Phillips added. "His imitation is so large that they say he lays in all under contribution & grows fat on the spoils of all the other speakers he hears—but he does not want originality. He never thinks of his color & we never do. He is one of our ablest men."

33. *Philadelphia Elevator* reprinted in *The British and Foreign Anti-Slavery Reporter*, vol. VI, no. 25, Dec. 10, 1845.

A CHATTEL BECOMES A MAN

1. *British and Foreign Anti-Slavery Reporter*, vol. I, new series, Nov. 12, 1845, p. 212; John Wallace Hutchinson, *Story of the Hutchinsons*, Boston, 1896, vol. I, p. 145; Douglass to Thurlow Weed, Dec. 1, 1845, *Liberator*, Jan. 16, 1845; Douglass to Garrison, Sept. 1, 1845, *Liberator*, Sept. 26, 1845.

2. Richard D. Webb to Elizabeth Pease, Sept. 25, 1845, Anti-Slavery Letters to Garrison, Boston Public Library. Webb supplied Douglass with paper and binding for the edition "at cut prices," and estimated that when all of the volumes were sold the author would gain a profit of £180.

3. Douglass to Garrison, Sept. 16, 1845, *Liberator*, Oct. 10, 1845; Douglass to Richard D. Webb, Nov. 10, 1845, Anti-Slavery Letters to Garrison, Boston Public Library; Douglass to Garrison, Feb. 26, 1846, *Liberator*, Mar. 27, 1846.

4. James N. Buffum to Henry Clapp, Jr., Sept. 1, 1845; *Lynn Pioneer*, Sept. 25, 1845; Douglass to Garrison, Sept. 29, 1845, *Liberator*, Oct. 24, 1845; Dublin *Evening Post* reprinted in *Liberator*, Oct. 24, 1845.

5. Cork *Examiner* reprinted in *Liberator*, Nov. 28, 1845; Douglass to Garrison, Oct. 28, 1845, *Liberator*, Nov. 28, 1845.

6. Douglass to Garrison, Jan. 1, 1846, *Liberator*, Jan. 20, 1846.

7. *Free Church Alliance with Manstealers*, Glasgow, 1846, p. 11; *Letter from the Executive Committee of the American and Foreign Anti-Slavery Society to the Commissioners of the Free Church of Scotland, April 2, 1844*, Edinburgh, 1844; Douglass to Richard D. Webb, Feb. 10, 1846; Douglass to Francis Jackson, Jan. 29, 1846; Anti-Slavery Letters to Garrison, Boston Public Library.

8. Douglass to Anonymous, Apr. 23, 1846, *Albany Evening Journal* reprinted in *New York Tribune*, July 8, 1846. In reprinting the letter, the *Tribune* remarked: "The writer, be it remembered, is a 'Runaway Slave,' who, during his eight years of stolen Freedom, in defiance of all the disadvantages under which his class labors, has qualified himself to think and write thus."

9. Douglass to Richard D. Webb, Mar. 29, 1846; Douglass to Maria W. Chapman, Mar. 29, 1849, Anti-Slavery Letters to Garrison, Boston Public Library. Years later, Douglass wrote that Mrs. Chapman's suspicions "stuck in my crop. I could not get it 'down' no how." (Douglass to Richard D. Webb, Sept. 12, 1850, Anti-Slavery Letters to Garrison, Boston Public Library.)

10. Douglass to Richard D. Webb, Apr. 16[?], 1846, Anti-Slavery Letters to Garrison.
    Webb was somewhat critical of Douglass. He wrote to Maria W. Chapman as early as Aug. 30, 1845, that he found Douglass "touchy, huffish, haughty, and I think selfish," and "ever ready to sacrifice his friends to his joke." He admitted, however, that the Negro had "many of the characteristics of the man of genius," and was "a much greater and more powerful man than Remond." "As an advocate and orator—as a company man—as a remarkable example of the triumph over difficulties he is a wonder indeed," he added. "He is exceedingly pleasant and amusing when he pleases." (Anti-Slavery Letters to Garrison, Boston Public Library.)
    Douglass must have heard of this criticism, for in an undated letter to Webb he wrote: "If Mr. Garrison or Phillips have given you any reason to expect perfection in me, they did both you and me a serious wrong." (Anti-Slavery Letters to Garrison, Boston Public Library.)

11. Douglass to Maria W. Chapman, Aug. 18, 1846, Anti-Slavery Letters to Garrison, Boston Public Library.

12. George Thompson to Henry C. Wright, May 23, 1846, Anti-Slavery Letters to Garrison, Boston Public Library.

13. *Report of a public meeting held at Finsbury Chapel, Moorefields, to receive Frederick Douglass, the American slave, on Friday, May 22, 1846*, London, 1846.

14. George Thompson to Henry C. Wright, May 23, 1846, Anti-Slavery Letters to Garrison, Boston Public Library.
    Douglass told Thompson that he could not remain away from his family much longer and would be forced to return home in August unless he should decide to bring his family to England. The conversation led to the raising of a fund for this purpose. "This result was entirely unexpected to me," wrote Douglass to Garrison on May 23, 1846. (*Liberator*, June 26, 1846.)

15. W. P. Garrison and F. J. Garrison, *Life of William Lloyd Garrison*, vol. III, p. 157. (Letter dated London, Aug. 4, 1846); Douglass to Samuel Hanson Cox, D.D., Oct. 30, 1846, *Liberator*, Nov. 27, 1846.

16. *Oswego Daily Advertiser*, reprinted in *Anti-Slavery Standard*, Oct. 29, 1846.

17. Douglass to Horace Greeley, Apr. 15, 1846, *Liberator*, June 26, 1846.

18. Garrison to his wife, Aug. 18, 1846, Garrison *Mss.*, Boston Public Library.

19. Garrison to Henry Clapp, Jr., Aug. 27, 1846, Garrison *Mss.*, Boston Public Library; Garrison to Henry C. Wright, W. P. Garrison and F. J. Garrison, *op. cit.*, vol. III, p. 170.

20. Garrison to his wife, Sept. 17, 1846, W. P. Garrison and F. J. Garrison, *op. cit.*, vol. III, p. 167; *Dunham Herald*, reprinted in *Liberator*, Nov. 13, 1846; *Liberator*, Dec. 25, 1846.

21. Douglass to William A. White, July 30, 1846, Douglass *Mss.*, Frederick Douglass Memorial Home, Anacostia, D. C.; *Farewell Speech of Mr. Frederick Douglass Previously to Embarking on Board the Cambria upon his Return to America, Delivered at the Valedictory Soiree Given to Him at the London Tavern, on March 30, 1847*, London, 1847.

22. Douglass to William A. White, July 30, 1846; Douglass to Isabel Jennings, Sept. 22, 1846; Douglass *Mss.*, Frederick Douglass Memorial Home, Anacostia, D. C.; Garrison to Elizabeth Pease, April 1, 1847, Garrison *Mss.*, Boston Public Library.

23. The manumission document read: "To all whom it may concern: Be it known, that I, Hugh Auld, of the city of Baltimore, in Baltimore county, in the State of Maryland, for divers good causes and considerations, me thereunto moving, have released from slavery, liberated, manumitted, and set free, and by these presents do hereby release from slavery, liberate, manumit, and set free, *My Negro Man*, named *Frederick Bailey*, otherwise called *Douglass*, being of the age of twenty-eight years, or thereabouts, and able to work and gain a sufficient livelihood and maintainence; and him the said Negro man, named *Frederick Bailey*, otherwise called *Frederick Douglass*, I do declare to be henceforth free, manumitted and discharged from all manner of servitude to me, my executors, and administrators forever.
    "In witness whereof, I the said Hugh Auld, have hereunto set my hand and seal, the fifth of December, in the year one thousand eight hundred and forty-six.
    "*Hugh Auld.*"
    To this document was annexed the bill of sale.
    Douglass published these documents in *The North Star*, December 3, 1847. He added these words as a preface: "We give our readers the evidence of our right to be free in this democratic and Christian country—not so much however

to establish our right to ourself as to expose the cold-blooded Methodist man-stealer, who claimed us as his property, and the hypocritical nation that has sanctioned his infamous claim. We shall send him a copy of this paper."

24. Lucretia Mott to Richard D. Webb, Feb. 21, 1847, Anti-Slavery Letters to Garrison, Boston Public Library; Philadelphia Female Anti-Slavery Society in *Liberator,* Mar. 19, 1847; Increase S. Smith in *Ibid.,* Jan. 15, 1847; Garrison to Elizabeth Pease, Apr. 1, 1847, Garrison *Mss.,* Boston Public Library; *Liberator,* Mar. 19, 1847.

25. Douglass to Henry C. Wright, Dec. 22, 1846, *Liberator,* Jan 29, 1847.

26. *Liberator,* Apr. 30, 1847; *London Morning Advertiser,* reprinted in *Liberator,* Apr. 30, 1847; *Farewell Speech of Mr. Frederick Douglass . . . March 30, 1847,* London, 1847.

27. Douglass to the London *Times,* Apr. 6, 1847; Douglass to Garrison, Apr. 21, 1847, *Liberator,* Apr. 30, 1847; *Liberator,* May 14, 1847; *Howitt's Journal,* vol. I, 1847, p. 225.

28. Ralph Varian to *British and Foreign Anti-Slavery Reporter,* vol. VI, Dec. 10, 1845. See also the poems "Farewell to Frederick Douglass who sailed from England for America, April 4th, 1847, Easter Sunday," *Howitt's Journal,* vol. I, 1847, pp. 222-23; *Poem on the Embarkation at Liverpool of Mr. Frederick Douglass upon his return to America, by F. N. D.,* Manchester, July 8, 1847 (pamphlet in Schomburg Collection, New York Public Library, 135th Street Branch); Garrison to Elizabeth Pease, Apr. 1, 1847, Garrison *Mss.,* Boston Public Library; Douglass to Julia Griffiths, Oct. 13, 1847, *Howitt's Journal,* vol. II, 1848, p. 319.

29. *Liberator,* June 8, 1849.

FOUNDING *THE NORTH STAR*

1. *Lynn Pioneer and Herald of Freedom,* Apr. 25, 1847; *Anti-Slavery Standard,* May 6, 1847; *Liberator,* May 21, June 4, 1847; *Sixteenth Annual Report of the Massachusetts Anti-Slavery Society,* Boston, 1848, p. 41.

2. *Abolition Fanaticism in New York: Speech of a Runaway Slave from Baltimore at an Abolition meeting in New York Held May 11, 1847.*
   The introduction to the pamphlet went: "The following report will show to Marylanders, how a runaway slave talks, when he reaches the Abolition regions of the country. This presumptive Negro was even present at the London World's Temperance Convention last year; and in spite of all the efforts of the American Delegates to prevent it, he palmed off his Abolition bombast upon an audience of 7000 persons! Of this high-handed measure he now makes his boast in New-York, one of the hot-beds of Abolitionism. The Report is given exactly as published in The New York Tribune. The reader will make his own comments."

3. *The National Era,* June 3, 1847.

4. *Howitt's Journal,* vol. I, 1847, p. 239; Douglass to the *Boston Daily Whig* reprinted in *Liberator,* July 9, 1847; *The North Star,* Dec. 22, 1848.

5. Douglass to Mary Howitt, May 10 [1848], *Howitt's Journal,* vol. I, 1847, p. 352.

6. I. G. Penn, the *Afro-American Press and its Editors,* Springfield, Mass., pp. 25-57.
   There is also record of the *Albany Sentinel* issued by a Negro in 1832. I am indebted to Dr. Herbert Aptheker for this information.

7. *New York Tribune* and *Albany Evening Journal,* reprinted in *Liberator,* Feb. 13, 1846.

8. Wendell Phillips to Elizabeth Pease, Aug. 29, 1847, Anti-Slavery Letters to Garrison, Boston Public Library. Phillips suggested that the money raised for the launching of a paper should be invested "in stock yielding 7 or 8 percent—say $240 per year—which will relieve him for staying at home, more than his press would. Even at 6 per cent it would do well. He is gathering golden opinion—rolling up popularity—all wonder at his talents, so much improved by travel."

9. *Liberator*, July 23, 1847.

10. London *People's Journal*, July 24, 1847, reprinted in *Anti-Slavery Standard*, Aug. 26, 1847.

    The journals referred to were *The Mystery*, published in Pittsburgh and edited by Martin R. Delaney; *The Genius of Freedom*, published and edited in New York City by David Ruggles; *The Ram's Horn* also published in New York City and edited by Willis Hodges and Thomas Van Rensselaer.

    The Ram's Horn announced that it had offered to suspend publication if Douglass decided to publish his paper, "that there might be no strife between us. . . ." (Reprinted in *Liberator*, July 23, 1847.)

    For some months after abandoning his project, Douglass served as an assistant editor for *The Ram's Horn* and as a regular contributor for the *Anti-Slavery Standard*. The *Standard* proudly announced its accession of "a writer of no common power." (Reprinted in *Liberator*, Aug. 20, 1847.)

11. Quoted by Goldwin Smith, *William Lloyd Garrison*, New York and London, 1892, p. 150; *Liberator*, Sept. 3, 10, 1847.

12. Douglass to Sidney B. Gay, Aug. 7, 1847, *Anti-Slavery Standard*, Aug. 19, 1847; *Liberator*, July 23, Aug. 20, 1847; Frederic May Holland, *Frederick Douglass*, pp. 155-57; Garrison to his wife, Aug. 12, 13, 1847, W. P. Garrison and F. J. Garrison, *Life of William Lloyd Garrison*, vol. III, p. 193.

13. *Cleveland Plaindealer*, reprinted in *Anti-Slavery Standard*, Sept. 9, 1847; Garrison to his wife, Aug. 25, 1847, *Liberator*, Sept. 10, 1847.

14. Minute Book of the Western Anti-Slavery Society, Library of Congress, Manuscript Division.

15. Garrison to his wife, Aug. 20, 28, 1847, W. P. Garrison and F. J. Garrison, *op. cit.*, vol. III, pp. 203-04; *Liberator*, Sept. 10, 1847.

16. *Anti-Slavery Bugle*, Sept. 10, 1847; *Cleveland True-Democrat*, reprinted in *Anti-Slavery Standard*, Sept. 23, 1847.

17. Samuel J. May to Garrison, Oct. 8, 1847, Anti-Slavery Letters to Garrison, Boston Public Library.

18. Garrison to his wife, Oct. 20, 1847, Anti-Slavery Letters to Garrison, Boston Public Library.

19. Douglass to J. D. Carr, Nov. 1, 1847, *British Friend*, reprinted in *Anti-Slavery Standard*, Jan. 27, 1848; *Life and Times of Frederick Douglass*, p. 317.

20. Garrison to his wife, Oct. 20, 1847, Samuel J. May to Mary Carpenter, Mar. 4, 1848, W. P. Garrison and F. J. Garrison, *op. cit.*, vol. III, p. 209.

21. Douglass to J. D. Carr, Nov. 1, 1847, *British Friend*, reprinted in *Anti-Slavery Standard*, Jan. 27, 1848; *Anti-Slavery Bugle*, reprinted in *Anti-Slavery Standard*, Sept. 30, 1847. In his letter to his wife from Cleveland, Oct. 30, 1847, Douglass referred to his intention "for establishing a paper here, to be called 'The North Star'. . . . " (W. P. Garrison and F. J. Garrison, *op. cit.*, vol. III, p. 209.)

22. In explaining the choice of the title for his journal, Douglass wrote in its first issue: "Of all the stars in this 'brave old, overhanging sky,' *The North Star* is

our choice. To thousands now free in the British dominions it has been the *Star of Freedom*. To millions, now in our boasted land of liberty, it is the *Star of Hope.* . . ."

A newspaper issued during the Latimer case was called the *Latimer Journal and North Star,* and a paper published in Danville, Vermont, was called *The North Star.*

It is well known, that one of the most celebrated of the songs of fugitive slaves referred to the north star:

I kept my eye on the bright north star,
And thought of liberty.

23. William Peck, *History of Rochester and Monroe County,* Rochester, 1892, vol. I, p. 77; Orlo J. Price, "The Significance of the Early Religious History of Rochester," *Publications of the Rochester Historical Society,* Rochester, N. Y., vol. III, 1924, pp. 180-81; Adelaide Elizabeth Dorn, "A History of the Anti-Slavery Movement in Rochester and Vicinity," unpublished M.A. Thesis, University of Buffalo, pp. 49-51.

24. Douglass to J. D. Carr, Nov. 1, 1847, *British Friend,* reprinted in *Anti-Slavery Standard,* Jan. 27, 1948.

THE EDITOR AND PUBLISHER

1. Douglass to Gerrit Smith, May 1, 1851, Gerrit Smith Papers, Syracuse University; Horace McGuire, "Two Episodes of Anti-Slavery Days," *Publications of the Rochester Historical Society,* Rochester, N. Y., vol. IV. 1925, p. 219. Douglass laid the blame for frequent errors and inaccuracies in *The North Star* on the fact that the paper was printed outside of his shop.

2. *The North Star,* Jan. 8, 1848; *Liberator,* Jan. 28, 1848; *Anti-Slavery Standard,* Jan. 27, 1848; Frederick G. Detweiler, *The Negro Press in the United States,* Chicago, 1922, p. 42; *Howitt's Journal,* vol. III, 1848, p. 288.

3. *Sunday Dispatch* reprinted in *The North Star,* Jan. 21, 1848; *Rochester Daily Advertiser,* Dec. 18, 1847; William C. Nell to Garrison, Jan. 23, 1848, *Liberator,* Feb. 11, 1848.

4. Douglass to Martin R. Delany, Jan. 12, 1848, Douglass *Mss.,* Frederick Douglass Memorial Home, Anacostia, D. C.

The mortgage deed was for $500. The deed itself is in the Douglass Papers in the Frederick Douglass Memorial Home at Anacostia, D. C.

5. Douglass to Julia Griffiths, Apr. 28, 1848, Douglass *Mss.,* Frederick Douglass Memorial Home, Anacostia, D. C.

6. *The North Star,* Apr. 27, 1849.

7. *Ibid.,* Nov. 17, 1848.

"I have been on a little lecturing tour to Geneva," Douglass wrote on Feb. 21, 1848, "and had to ride all night in order to meet my engagements here. This riding all night is killing me, and I am resolved to stop it." (Douglass to Abigail and Lydia Mott, Feb. 21, 1848, Frederick Douglass *Mss.,* Henry E. Huntington Library. See also *The North Star,* Jan. 8, 1848.)

It is of some interest in this connection to consider a remark made by one of Garrison's sons in 1891 who wrote that "selfishly considered his [Douglass'] journalistic step was advantageous in giving him a more settled life than that of an itinerant lecturer." (*The Nation,* vol. LII, May 7, 1891, p. 388.)

8. Douglass to Gerrit Smith, Mar. 1, 1849, Gerrit Smith Papers, Syracuse Uni-

versity; *The North Star*, Dec. 22, 1848, Jan. 19, 1849; *Anti-Slavery Standard*, July 12, 1849.

9. Douglass to Julia Griffiths, Oct. 13, 1847, Douglass *Mss.*, Frederick Douglass Memorial Home, Anacostia, D. C.; *Life and Times of Frederick Douglass*, p. 242; Douglass to Gerrit Smith, May 1, 1851, Gerrit Smith Papers, Syracuse University.

10. Douglass to Gerrit Smith, May 1, 1851, Gerrit Smith Papers, Syracuse University; *The North Star*, Mar. 15, Apr. 12, May 30, Oct. 31, Dec. 5, 1850. *Frederick Douglass' Paper* of Jan. 15, 1858, printed documents showing that the mortgage was paid off in 1853. (See *The Anti-Slavery Reporter*, Apr. 1, 1858, p. 96.)

11. John Thomas to Gerrit Smith, Jan. 27, Feb. 4, May 6, June 14, Dec. 30, 1850, Gerrit Smith Papers, Syracuse University; Douglass to Gerrit Smith, May 1, 28, June 4, 18, 1851, Gerrit Smith Papers, Syracuse University.
    Thomas wanted to receive eight dollars a week as assistant editor while Douglass thought he could only afford to pay six dollars. Furthermore, Thomas wished the paper to be published in Syracuse while Douglass insisted on Rochester. Douglass won out on both points. (See John Thomas to Gerrit Smith, June 14, 1851; Douglass to Gerrit Smith, May 28, 29, June 4, 1851, Gerrit Smith Papers, Syracuse University.)

12. *Frederick Douglass' Paper*, June 26, 1851.
    In 1852 Smith contributed $1200 to the paper. (See *Frederick Douglass' Paper*, Dec. 17, 1852.) On Jan. 14, 1853, Douglass wrote to Smith: "Paper getting along well." (Gerrit Smith Papers, Syracuse University.)

13. *Frederick Douglass' Paper*, June 26, 1851.

14. *Frederick Douglass' Paper*, Jan. 9, 1854.

15. *Frederick Douglass' Paper*, Feb. 24, 1854.

16. *British Banner*, reprinted in *Frederick Douglass' Paper*, Apr. 8, 1853; *Autographs for Freedom*, Rochester, 1854, pp. 44-60, 70-76.

17. "The Anti-Slavery Appeal to Christian Public of Glasgow and Edinburgh," *The Anti-Slavery Reporter*, Apr. 1, 1857, pp. 80-82; May 1, 1857, pp. 118-19; Sept. 1, 1857, p. 215.

18. *The Anti-Slavery Reporter*, Nov. 1, 1855, p. 263.

19. *Ibid.*, Apr. 1, 1857, pp. 80-82, May 1, 1857, pp. 119-20, May 2, 1859, p. 120; Douglass to Mrs. Maxwell, Treasurer of the Clogher Anti-Slavery Society, Oct. 10, 1857, *The Anti-Slavery Reporter*, Dec. 1, 1857, p. 279, Oct. 1, 1858, p. 238.

20. Douglass to Gerrit Smith, July 2, 1860, Gerrit Smith Papers, Syracuse University. A copy of the weekly for July 8, 1859, is in the Wisconsin State Historical Society at Madison. Very few copies of *Frederick Douglass' Paper* for the period 1856-1860 are in existence.

21. Douglass to Elizabeth Pease, Nov. 8, 1849, Anti-Slavery Letters to Garrison, Boston Public Library; Jane Marsh Parker, "Reminiscences of Frederick Douglass," *The Outlook*, vol. LI, Apr. 6, 1895, p. 552. "Think what editing a paper was to me before Miss Griffiths came," Douglass once wrote.

22. Not infrequently the subscribers would read: "We have been so much on the wing of late as to have little time to devote to our editorial duties. . . ." (*Frederick Douglass' Paper*, Sept. 10, 1852.) In the Dec. 18, 1851, issue Douglass wrote: "I have during the last month, been for the most part, too much disabled by illness to attend to the Editorial department of this paper—or to do anything towards its publication."

23. One of the books serialized was Charles Dickens' *Bleak House*. The book reviews were usually written by Julia Griffiths, but occasionally Douglass would review an important book on the editorial page.
24. *Frederick Douglass' Paper*, May 26, 1854.
25. Douglass to Gerrit Smith, Apr. 24, 1868, Gerrit Smith Papers, Syracuse University.
26. *New York Tribune*, Sept. 18, 1857; Francis Julius Lemoyne to Gerrit Smith, July 28, 1851, Gerrit Smith Papers, Syracuse University; Quoted in A. H. Payne, "The Negro in New York Prior to 1860," *The Howard Review*, vol. I, June, 1923, p. 24.
27. Lindsly M. Moore to Gerrit Smith, Nov. 10, 1852, Gerrit Smith Papers, Syracuse University; *Life and Times of Frederick Douglass*, p. 323.
28. Dr. James McCune Smith to Gerrit Smith, July 28, 1848, Gerrit Smith Papers, Syracuse University.
29. *The North Star*, Jan. 7, 1848; *Anti-Slavery Bugle*, Aug. 24, 1850.
30. *The North Star*, July 14, 21, 1848; *Frederick Douglass' Paper*, Apr. 3, 1855.
31. *Anti-Slavery Bugle*, Aug. 10, 1850; *The North Star*, Jan. 7, 1848.
32. *Frederick Douglass' Paper*, Apr. 8, 1855. "She should be called no longer the *Black Swan*, but the White Raven," wrote Douglass. (*Ibid.*, Feb. 26, 1852.)
33. *The North Star*, May 30, 1850.
34. *Frederick Douglass' Paper* reprinted in *Autographs for Freedom*, edited by Julia Griffiths, Rochester, 1853, pp. 158-60.
35. *The North Star*, Jan. 26, Mar. 23, 1849; *Frederick Douglass' Paper*, Feb. 26, 1852; *Douglass' Monthly*, Feb., 1859. *The African Repository* (vol. XXVI, Oct., 1850, pp. 289-94) contains several excerpts from Douglass' editorials dealing with colonization as well as the answer of the emigrationists.
36. Annual Report of the American and Foreign Anti-Slavery Society for 1853, New York, 1854.
37. *The North Star*, Feb. 18, 1848; *Frederick Douglass' Paper*, Jan. 22, 1852. Douglass made it quite clear that he did not oppose missionary work in Africa. In a letter to Benjamin Coates he wrote: "My heart can never be indifferent to any legitimate movement for spreading the blessings of Christianity and civilization in that country. But the effort must not be to get the Negroes out of this country but to get Christianity into that." (Douglass to Benjamin Coates, Apr. 17, 1856, William M. Coates Papers, Historical Society of Pennsylvania.)
38. *Frederick Douglass' Paper*, Jan. 12, 1855.

Reference Notes

PART TWO   THE PRE-CIVIL WAR DECADE

THE UNIVERSAL REFORMER

1. *The North Star*, July 14, 1848.
2. *Ibid.*, Mar. 10, 1848. Douglass attended the Woman's State Temperance Convention in 1852 at Rochester and joined in the discussion. (See *The Lily*, May, 1852, especially p. 42.) In May, 1853, he was present at the organizational meeting of the New York State Woman's Temperance Society, and "closed the affair in the happiest manner." (*The Una*, June 1, 1853, p. 75.)
3. *The North Star*, July 14, 1848; Jan. 26, 1849.
4. *The North Star*, Nov. 9, 1849; *Frederick Douglass' Paper*, Aug. 15, 1856.
5. *The North Star*, Apr. 7, 1849.
6. *Liberator*, Oct. 22, 1858; Rochester *Daily American*, Oct. 5-6, 1858.
7. Lucy N. Colman in *Liberator*, Oct. 22, 1858.
    Douglass declared that capital punishment "instead of repressing and preventing the horrid crime of murder . . . really serves by shocking and blunting the finer and better feelings of human nature, to undermine respect for human life, and leads directly to the perpetuation of the crime which it would extinguish." It was necessary, went the resolutions, to develop the criminal's "higher nature," hence Douglass called for "a thorough reform in our criminal laws—basing them on the truly Christian principle of love and good will towards man—and to reject forever the cold blooded and barbarous principle of retaliation." (*Liberator*, Oct. 22, 1858.)
8. *The North Star*, Mar. 9, 1849.
9. Elizabeth Cady Stanton, Susan B. Anthony, Mathilda Joslyn Gage, editors, *History of Woman Suffrage*, New York, 1881, vol. I, pp. 70-71.
10. *The Woman's Journal*, Apr. 14, 1888, p. 116; Stanton, Anthony, Gage, *op. cit.*, vol. I, p. 73.
    Years later a tablet was erected commemorating the occasion. It read:
    > On this spot stood the Wesleyan Chapel
    > Where the first Woman's Rights Convention
    > in the World's History was held
    > July 19 and 20, 1848
    > Elizabeth Cady Stanton
    > moved this resolution
    > which was seconded by Frederick Douglass
    > That it was the duty of the women
    > of this country to secure to themselves
    > their sacred right
    > to the elective franchise.
11. *The Woman's Journal*, Apr. 14, 1888.

12. Stanton, Anthony, Gage, *op. cit.*, vol. I, p. 86; *The North Star*, Aug. 11, 1848. Mrs. Stanton and Lucretia Mott had proposed Douglass as the chairman of the meeting, but the women of Rochester had opposed the suggestion and elected Abigail Bush, a local resident, to the office.

13. Harriet Jane Robinson, *Massachusetts in the Woman Suffrage Movement*, Boston, 1881, p. 25. The Rochester *Daily American* of Dec. 16, 1850, referred to the "She-Socialists" who had been prominent in the convention.

14. Susan B. Anthony to Gerrit Smith, Dec. 25, 1855, Gerrit Smith Papers, Syracuse University; *Frederick Douglass' Paper*, Oct. 30, 1851; Douglass to Gerrit Smith, June 14, 1853, Gerrit Smith Papers, Syracuse University.

15. Lucretia Mott to Elizabeth Cady Stanton, Oct. 3, 1848, Elizabeth Cady Stanton Papers, Library of Congress.

16. Douglass to Gerrit Smith, July 15, 1853, Gerrit Smith Papers, Syracuse University.

17. *Douglass' Monthly*, Nov., 1860; S. S. Foster to Gerrit Smith, Aug. 25, 1860.

DOUGLASS AND THE NEGRO CONVENTION MOVEMENT

1. "Public Warning to Cincinnati Negroes and commentary on their reaction," *Journal of Negro History*, vol. VIII, July, 1923, pp. 331-32.

2. Eighteen delegates were from Pennsylvania, four from New York, one from Connecticut, two from Rhode Island, seven from Maryland, three from Delaware, three from Virginia, and one each from New Jersey and Ohio.

3. Sixteen delegates met in Philadelphia in June, 1831; 29 delegates met again in Philadelphia in June, 1832; 56 delegates convened in Philadelphia in June, 1833; 40 delegates from seven states met in New York City in June, 1834; the 1835 convention met in June in Philadelphia, and the next national convention met in June, 1836, in New York City.

4. Bella Gross, *Clarion Call: The History and Development of the Negro Convention Movement in the United States from 1817 to 1840*, New York, 1947, pp. 40-41.

5. *Journal of Negro History*, vol. I, July, 1916, pp. 323-38.

6. *Minutes of the National Convention of Colored Citizens, Buffalo, New York, August, 1843*, pp. 8, 10, 13-15; W. M. Brewer, "Henry Highland Garnet," *Journal of Negro History*, vol. XIII, Jan., 1928, pp. 44-46.

7. *Minutes of the National Convention of Colored Citizens, Buffalo, New York, August, 1843*, pp. 24, 37-39; *Herald of Freedom*, (Concord) Sept. 1, 1943.

8. *Proceedings of the National Convention of Colored People, And their Friends held in Troy, N. Y. . . . October, 1847*, pp. 31-32. Other members of the committee on Abolition who signed the report were Alexander Crummel, John Lyle, and Thomas Van Rensselaer.

9. Zita Dyson, "Gerrit Smith's Efforts in behalf of the Negroes in New York," *Journal of Negro History*, vol. III, Oct., 1918, pp. 354-59.

10. *The North Star*, Jan. 14, 1848. The Committee on a National Press consisted of J. McCune Smith, G. B. Wilson, and Wm. H. Topp.

11. *Proceedings of the National Convention of Colored People, And their Friends held in Troy, N. Y. . . . October, 1847*, pp. 7-8.

12. *The North Star*, Jan. 14, 1848.

13. *The North Star*, Sept. 19, 1848; *Liberator*, Oct. 20, 1848.

14. *Report of Proceedings of Colored National Convention, Held at Cleveland, Ohio, on Wednesday, September 6, 1848,* Rochester, 1848, pp. 8, 12.

15. Cleveland *True Democrat,* Sept. 11, 1848; Gerrit Smith to Chas. B. Ray, Nov. 11, 1848, *Model Worker,* Dec. 29, 1848, reprinted in leaflet form, the Gerrit Smith Papers, Syracuse University.

16. *The North Star,* Aug. 17, 1849.

17. *Anti-Slavery Bugle,* Aug. 18, 1849. For a British reaction to the plan, see *London Inquirer,* reprinted in *The North Star,* Nov. 23, 1849.

18. W.R.G. to Douglass, Nov. 4, 1849, in *The North Star,* Nov. 16, 1849.
    Douglass wrote bitterly in *The North Star* of Oct. 26, 1849: "*The Impartial Citizen,* edited by a colored man, did not even notice it. *The Ram's Horn,* has been dumb over it. Very few of our public men have, as yet, given to the idea the slightest encouragement."

19. "Many of the colored people, unfortunately, are bitter sectarians," commented the *Anti-Slavery Bugle* on Aug. 18, 1849, "and Mr. Garnet has done his worst to array this class in hostility to the eloquent Fugitive."
    Garnet also attacked Douglass for having told the Negro people that "we have no country." Douglass replied: "In making the declaration, we meant only to exhibit forcibly the glaring fact that the colored man is denied the rights and privileges of an American citizen, by the American government; and that, in this respect, he is an outlaw in the land. . . . If any colored man wants to know whether he has a country, let him go to Charleston, South Carolina, under the protection of the American Constitution, and his country will be limited to a prison. That the colored people have a right to a country here, we have ever affirmed; and Mr. Garnet will never succeed in trying to make the colored people, nor any other enlightened people, believe the contrary." (*The North Star,* Aug. 17, 1849.)

20. *The North Star,* Oct. 26, Nov. 19, 1849.

21. Fred Landon, "The Negro Migration to Canada after 1850," *Journal of Negro History,* vol. V, Jan., 1920, p. 22.

22. *Proceedings of the Colored National Convention Held in Rochester, July, 1853.* Although written by Douglass, the "Address" was also signed by J. M. Whitfield, H. O. Wagoner, Rev. A. N. Freeman, and George B. Vashon.

23. *New York Tribune,* July 9, 1853.

24. *Minutes and Proceedings of the First Annual Convention of the People of Colour,* . . . Philadelphia, 1831, pp. 6-9; *Liberator,* Aug. 20, Nov. 26, Dec. 3, 1831, Jan. 12, July 6, 1833.

25. *Liberator,* May 11, June 15, 1833.

26. See Charles L. Reason, "The Colored People's Industrial College: What Some of the Builders have Thought," *Autographs for Freedom,* Rochester, 1854, pp. 13-15.

27. *Frederick Douglass' Paper,* Mar. 4, 1853.

28. Douglass to Harriet Beecher Stowe, Mar. 8, 1853, *Proceedings of the Colored National Convention Held in Rochester, July 6th, 7th and 8th, 1853,* Rochester, 1853, pp. 33-38.
    In July, 1851, after she had published five installments of *Uncle Tom's Cabin* in the *National Era,* Harriet Beecher Stowe wrote to Douglass asking him to assist her in gathering information about life on a cotton plantation which she could use in her novel. The main part of her letter was devoted to a long

defense of the church against the charge of many Abolitionists, Douglass among them, that it was pro-slavery. We do not know if Douglass answered the letter. (See Charles Edward Stowe, *The Life of Harriet Beecher Stowe*, Boston and New York, 1890, pp. 149-53.)

29. *Proceedings of the Colored National Convention Held in Rochester, July, 1853*, pp. 17-22.

30. *New York Tribune*, July 12, 1853.

31. Douglass to Gerrit Smith, July 15, 1853, Gerrit Smith Papers, Syracuse University; *Rochester Democrat*, reprinted in *Liberator*, July 22, 1853.

32. *Frederick Douglass' Paper*, Aug. 19, 1853, Oct. 2, 9, 16, 1853; *Chicago Tribune*, Oct. 5, 14, 1853.

33. *Frederick Douglass' Paper*, Aug. 19, 26, 1853. See also *Arguments, Pro and Con on the Call for a National Emigration Convention, to be held in Cleveland, Ohio, August, 1854, by Frederick Douglass, W. J. Watkins, and J. M. Whitfield*.

34. Louis R. Mehlinger, "The Attitude of the Free Negro Toward African Colonization," *Journal of Negro History*, vol. I, 1916, pp. 299-30.

   There were three groups at the emigration convention: one led by Martin R. Delaney favored going to the Niger Valley in Africa; another under J. M. Whitfield favored Central America, and James Theodore Holly of Canada sponsored the movement to Haiti. The leaders of the groups were commissioned to go to these countries to see what they could accomplish in carrying out their plans. Little of concrete value emerged from the enterprises.

35. *Frederick Douglass' Paper*, Jan. 2, 1854, carried the following announcement from the editor: "It is, however, but justice to say that our eminent and philanthropic friend, Mrs. Stowe, for reasons which she deems quite satisfactory, does not, at present, see fit to stand forth as the patron of the proposed institution. It is equally our duty to state that Mrs. Stowe desires the work to go forward in the hands of the National Convention."

36. "Communipaw" in *Frederick Douglass' Paper*, Jan. 9, 1854. The article was written by Dr. James McCune Smith; Douglass to Mrs. Tappan, Mar. 21, 1856, Douglass *Mss.*, Henry P. Slaughter Collection.

37. *Proceedings of the Colored Convention Held in Franklin Hall, Sixth Street, Below Arch, Philadelphia, October 16th, 17th and 18th, 1855*, Salem, New Jersey, 1856.

ANTI-SLAVERY ACTIVITY IN ROCHESTER

1. Douglass to Mrs. Tappan, Mar. 21, 1856, Douglass *Mss.*, Henry P. Slaughter Collection.

2. "Lecture No. 1 Delivered in Corinthian Hall, Rochester, N. Y., on Sunday Evening, Dec. 1st, 1850," *The North Star*, Dec. 5, 1850.

3. *Oration, . . . Delivered in Corinthian Hall, Rochester, July 5, 1852*, Rochester, 1852, p. 19.

4. Douglass to H. C. Warner, Esq., *The North Star*, Mar. 30, 1849. "No one," observed the *Liberator* in reprinting the letter, "who begins to read the following admirable and manly letter of Mr. Douglass, will fail to finish it." (*Liberator*, Oct. 6, 1848.)

   See also Dixon Wecter, editor, *The Love Letters of Mark Twain*, New York, 1949, p. 127.

5. *The North Star*, Nov. 9, 1849.

6. See E. O. Preston, Jr., "The Genesis of the Underground Railroad," *Journal of Negro History*, vol. XVIII, Apr., 1933, pp. 144-70; William Siebert, *The Underground Railroad*, New York, 1898.

7. *The North Star*, Dec. 3, 1847.

8. Horace McQuire, "Two Episodes of Anti-Slavery Days," *Publications of the Rochester Historical Society*, Rochester, N. Y., vol. IV, 1925, p. 219; Jane Marsh Parker, *Rochester*, Rochester, N. Y., 1884, pp. 257-58; Dorn, *op cit.*, p. 79; Amy Post, "The Underground Railroad," in William Peck, editor, *Semicentennial History of Rochester*, Rochester, 1924, p. 458; Douglass to Anna H. Richardson, July 2, 1860, in William Still, *The Underground Railroad*, Philadelphia, 1872, p. 598.

9. *United States Statutes at Large*, vol. IX, p. 462; Marion Gleason McDouglass, *Fugitive Slaves*, Boston, 1891, pp. 87-90.

10. *The North Star*, Apr. 12, 1850.

11. *New York Tribune*, Aug. 23, 1850; *Anti-Slavery Standard*, Aug. 29, Sept. 5, 1850; *Syracuse Daily Standard*, Aug. 29, 1850.

12. Jane Marsh Parker, *Rochester*, p. 257; *Boston Atlas*, Oct. 15, 1850.

13. A. E. Dorn, in her study of the anti-slavery movement in Rochester, writes of the effects of the Fugitive Slave Act on the Negro population: "The character of the Negro population of Rochester changed considerably due to the passage of the new Fugitive Slave Law of 1850. Before 1850 there had been 114 members of the colored Baptist Church but after the law came into effect 112 of this number were forced to leave the town on account of this law. The fact that so many from this one group had to leave indicates that there must have been a large number of fugitives, who realized that they had to leave or be captured, and a great number who were simply afraid that they would be taken for fugitives because the law was so severe." ("A History of the Anti-Slavery Movement in Rochester and Vicinity," M.A. thesis, University of Buffalo, p. 77.)

14. *New York Herald*, Aug. 12, 1852; *Frederick Douglass' Paper*, June 9, 1854.

15. About thirty Negroes and two white men were arrested and charged with treason and with levying war against the government of the United States. The defense was conducted so brilliantly by John M. Read and Thaddeus Stevens that all the defendants were acquitted. (*The History of the Trial of Castner Hanway for Treason, by a Member of the Philadelphia Bar*, Philadelphia, 1852.)

16. The following hastily scribbled note sent by Douglass to Samuel D. Porter in Sept., 1851, probably refers to the three fugitives who had been involved in the Sadsbury affair: "There are three men now at my house who are in great peril. I am unwell, I need your advice. Please come at once." The note was signed "D.F." (Samuel D. Porter Papers, University of Rochester.)

17. Amy Hamner Croughton, "Anti-Slavery Days in Rochester," *Publications of the Rochester Historical Society*, Rochester, N. Y. vol. XV, 1936, pp. 133-34.

18. *Frederick Douglass' Paper*, Nov. 24, 1854. Douglass usually served as vice-president of the annual celebrations, with Smith as president.

19. *Ibid.*, May 27, 1852; *The Anti-Slavery Reporter*, July 1, 1858, pp. 167-68; *Douglass' Monthly*, May, 1859, Dec., 1861; William C. Nell to Garrison, Feb. 19, 1852, *Liberator*, Mar. 5, 1852.

20. Benjamin Quarles estimates that in ten years "Douglass personally helped approximately four hundred fugitives gain their freedom." ("The Public Life of Frederick Douglass," unpublished Ph.D. thesis, University of Wisconsin, 1938, p. 118.)

21. William C. Nell to Garrison, Feb. 19, 1852, *Liberator*, Mar. 5, 1852.

22. *Frederick Douglass' Paper*, May 19, 1854, June 19, 1857; *The Anti-Slavery Reporter*, July 1, 1858, p. 168; *Annual Report of the American Anti-Slavery Society, for the year Ending May 1, 1860*, New York, 1861, p. 49; *Douglass' Monthly*, June, 1860; Douglass to Anna H. Richardson, July 2, 1860, Still, *op cit.*, p. 598.

23. Dorn, *op. cit.*, p. 78.

24. *The Anti-Slavery Reporter*, July 1, 1858, p. 168.

25. Sarah H. Bradford, *Scenes in the Life of Harriet Tubman*, Auburn, New York, 1869, p. 233.
    In December, 1851, Harriet Tubman brought a party of eleven, including her brother and his wife, to Canada. Douglass may have met her on this occasion, for he wrote in his autobiography: "On one occasion, I had eleven fugitives at the same time under my roof." (*Life and Times of Frederick Douglass*, pp. 329-30; Earl Conrad, *Harriet Tubman*, Washington, 1943, pp. 45-46.)

26. *The North Star*, Oct. 26, 1849.

27. Douglass to S. D. Porter, Jan. 12, 1852, Samuel D. Porter Papers, University of Rochester.

THE SPLIT WITH THE GARRISONIANS

1. *Sixteenth Annual Report of the Massachusetts Anti-Slavery Society*, Boston, 1848, p. 42.

2. See *The North Star*, June 16, 1848, report of the New England Anti-Slavery Convention. In June, 1848 Douglass was elected vice-president of the New England Anti-Slavery Society.

3. Douglass to Oliver Johnson, *Anti-Slavery Bugle*, Oct. 6, 1849; *Liberator*, Nov. 26, 1841.

4. *The North Star*, Feb. 11, 1848. Douglass met Brown again late in 1848. He visited Springfield in October and November, 1848, and, after his return to Rochester "alluded prominently to his recent interview with Mr. John Brown of Springfield," in a speech to a group of Negro people. (*The North Star*, Nov. 17, 24, Dec. 8, 1848.)

5. *Life and Times of Frederick Douglass*, pp. 338-39. In this account Douglass states that the interview took place in 1847.

6. *Ibid.*, pp. 340-41; *The North Star*, Feb. 9, 1849; *Liberator*, June 8, 1849.

7. *The North Star*, Aug. 10, 1849; *Frederick Douglass' Paper*, Nov. 28, 1856; *Liberator*, July 27, 1860. *See also* William Chambers, *American Slavery and Colour*, New York, 1857, p. 174. For an analysis of militant abolitionism, see Herbert Aptheker, "Militant Abolitionism," *Journal of Negro History*, vol. XXVI, Oct., 1941, pp. 413-84.

8. *Liberator*, Nov. 26, Dec. 3, 1841; *Anti-Slavery Standard*, Feb. 24, 1842.

9. *The North Star*, Mar. 30, 1849.

10. *Report of a Public Meeting at Finsbury Chapel, Moorefields, to Receive Frederick Douglass . . .*, 1846, p. 6.

11. For a detailed analysis of Douglass' position on the Constitution and the Union, see his speeches, *The Constitution of the United States: Is it Pro-Slavery or Anti-Slavery*, Halifax, 1860, and *The Anti-Slavery Movement*, Rochester, 1855.

12. Douglass privately informed Stephen S. Foster and Samuel J. May of his new beliefs early in the spring of 1851. (Douglass to Gerrit Smith, May 21, 1851, Gerrit Smith Papers, Syracuse University.) In his letter to the *Liberator* of May 16, 1851, May wrote that Douglass' announcement of his changed sentiments was "not unexpected."

13. *The North Star*, May 15, 1851, reprinted in *Liberator*, May 23, 1851, and in *Frederick Douglass' Paper*, Dec. 9, 1853.

14. Douglass to Frederick May Holland, reprinted in *Open Court*, vol. IX, Mar. 7, 1895, p. 415; *The North Star*, May 15, 1851, reprinted in *Liberator*, May 23, 1851, and *Frederick Douglass' Paper*, Dec. 9, 1853.

15. Douglass to Gerrit Smith, May 21, 1851, Gerrit Smith Papers, Syracuse University; *Liberator*, July 4, 1851.

16. N. Farmer in *Liberator*, Jan. 2, 1852; *Frederick Douglass' Paper*, Feb. 5, 26, 1852.

17. Douglass to Gerrit Smith, May 15, 1852, Gerrit Smith Papers, Syracuse University; *Frederick Douglass' Paper*, May 20, 1852; Wendell Phillips to Elizabeth Pease, Dec. 4, 1852, *Anti-Slavery Letters*, Boston Public Library.

18. *Frederick Douglass' Paper*, Aug. 12, 1853.

19. *Ibid.*, Aug. 19, 1853. This issue contained a reprint of the original article which had appeared in the weekly three months before.

20. Robert Purvis to Garrison, Sept. 12, 1853, Anti-Slavery Letters to Garrison, Boston Public Library; William C. Nell to Garrison, Aug. 19, 1853, *Liberator*, Sept. 2, 1853. Nell claimed that Douglass refused to print one of his letters.

21. *Anti-Slavery Standard*, Sept. 3-24, 1853; *Liberator*, Sept. 2-16, Nov. 18, 1853.

22. Garrison to S. J. May, Sept. 23, 1853, Garrison *Mss.*, Boston Public Library. Douglass copied the idea for his paper, calling the column "Den of Villainy." In March, 1853, when he inaugurated the feature, he wrote: "The idea of such a department in our paper, is borrowed from one to whom we gladly acknowledge ourselves debtors for many others equally good, and that is to William Lloyd Garrison." (*Frederick Douglass' Paper*, Mar. 11, 1853.) Ironically enough, in a few months Douglass was to find himself quoted in Garrison's unique department.

23. J.T.C. in *Liberator*, Nov. 18, 1853.

24. *Liberator*, Nov. 18, 1853.

25. *Anti-Slavery Standard*, Sept. 24, 1853.

26. The question, however, had been privately discussed. In Jan., 1852, Samuel D. Porter had warned Douglass that Rochester was "full of scandalous reports" concerning his relations with Miss Griffiths. Douglass had emphatically denied that there was anything in these relations that should cause him to feel ashamed, and expressed resentment that his close friend had given even slight credence to the rumors. (Douglass to Samuel D. Porter, Jan. 12, 1852, Samuel D. Porter Papers, University of Rochester.)

27. *Liberator*, Dec. 2, 15, 1853. Garrison maintained that he "could bring a score of unimpeachable witnesses in Rochester" to prove his charge. *Liberator*, Dec. 17, 1853.

28. In reprinting these articles, Douglass wrote: "If I have not published, hereto-fore, the articles from the *Freeman, Standard* and *Liberator*, it was from the laudable wish to avoid a controversy which seemed to be pregnant only of mis-chief, and unwholly uncalled for.—From the beginning, however, I have de-signed to give my adversaries a fair hearing before my readers, whenever I should feel it worth while to reply to their lucubrations.—This intention is now fulfilled to the letter."

29. Oliver Johnson to Garrison, Dec. 10, 1853, Anti-Slavery Letters to Garrison, Boston Public Library.

30. *Report of a Public Meeting at Finsbury Chapel, Moorefields, to Receive Frederick Douglass . . .*, 1846, p. 14.

31. For a detailed picture of the split in the churches over slavery, see W. H. Sweet, *The American Churches and Slavery*.

32. William G. Allen to Gerrit Smith, London, Jan. 24, 1854, Gerrit Smith Papers, Syracuse University.

33. *Chicago Daily Tribune*, reprinted in *Frederick Douglass' Paper*, Jan. 13, 1854; *Frederick Douglass' Paper*, Dec. 30, 1853. See also James B. Vashon's letter to Douglass, Dec. 17, 1853, *Ibid.*, Jan. 13, 1854.

34. Susan B. Anthony to Garrison, Dec. 13, 1853, Anti-Slavery Letters to Garrison, Boston Public Library. The entire section of Miss Anthony's letter dealing with this question went: "We were all surprised & shocked at the appearance of Anna Douglass' letter in the Liberator. *Anna did* not to my certain knowledge, intend that letter to cover all the *essentials* of the Liberator's charge—for she declared to Amy Post, who happened to call there about the time it was con-cocted by Frederic & Julia; that she would *never* sign a paper that said, Julia had not *made her trouble.* Said she, *Garrison is right*—it is Julia *that has made* Frederic hate all his old friends—Said she, I don't care anything about her being in the *office*—but I won't have her in my house."

35. *Saturday Visitor*, reprinted in *Liberator*, Jan. 13, 1854; James B. Vashon to Douglass, Dec. 17, 1853, *Frederick Douglass' Paper*, Jan. 13, 1854

36. *Saturday Visitor*, reprinted in *Liberator*, Jan. 13, 1854.

37. Anti-Slavery Letters to Garrison, Boston Public Library.

38. Garrison to Samuel J. May, Mar. 21, Sept. 28, 1860; Garrison to his wife, Feb. 17, 1857; Garrison to Samuel J. May, Sept. [?], 1857, Garrison *Mss.*, Boston Public Library. Garrison was especially infuriated by Julia Griffiths' efforts to raise funds in England for Douglass' paper on the ground that he was "the Christian champion who is nobly battling our 'infidel' abolitionism." (Garrison to Samuel J. May, Mar. 21, 1856, Garrison *Mss.*, Boston Public Library.) For evidence on which Garrison's charge was based, see *The Anti-Slavery Reporter*, Apr. 1, 1857, pp. 80-82.

39. *The Constitution of the United States: Is it Pro-Slavery or Anti-Slavery*, Halifax, 1860, p. 3.

40. *Douglass' Monthly*, June, 1861.

41. *The Nation*, vol. LII, p. 391. Garrison's son was not nearly so generous to Douglass. In the same issue of *The Nation* (p. 388), he recalled the controversy between his father and the Negro leader and spoke of "Mr. Douglass' animus toward those to whom he owed everything but his native talent for oratory. . . ." It was precisely this attitude on the part of Garrison and a number of his

associates during the 'forties and 'fifties that had so much to do with provoking the controversy.

42. Douglass to Oliver Johnson, 1885, Douglass Papers, Frederick Douglass Memorial Home, Anacostia, D. C.

ANTI-SLAVERY POLITICAL ACTION

1. Negroes could vote in Maine, New Hampshire, Vermont, Massachusetts and Rhode Island, since there was nothing in the constitutions of these states which forbade colored people from exercising the suffrage. In New York, under the constitution adopted in 1821, a Negro had to own real estate worth two hundred and fifty dollars and had to be a citizen of the state for three years.

2. Charles H. Wesley, "The Participation of Negroes in Anti-Slavery Political Parties," *Journal of Negro History*, vol. XLII, 1945, pp. 39-45.

3. William Goodell, *Slavery and Anti-Slavery*, New York, 1853, p. 475.

4. Henry Wilson, *History of the Rise and Fall of the Slave Power in America*, vol. II, pp. 109-11; Wesley, *op cit.*, p. 51; *The North Star*, June 23, Aug. 4, 1848.

5. *The North Star*, July 7, 1848.

6. Quoted by T. C. Smith, *The Liberty and Free Soil Parties in the Northwest*, New York, 1897, pp. 126-28.

7. *The North Star*, June 16, July 21, 1848.

8. Wilson, *op. cit.*, vol. II, pp. 114-49. Douglass referred later to the convention as one of the most important events which led directly to emancipation. (*Life and Times of Frederick Douglass*, pp. 282-83.)

9. Oliver Dyer, *Phonographic Report of the Proceedings of the National Free Soil Convention at Buffalo, New York, August 9th and 10th, 1848*, New York, 1848, p. 21. Among those present at the convention were other Negro leaders such as Samuel R. Ward, Henry Highland Garnet, Charles L. Remond, and Henry Bibb. Douglass said there were "other colored gentlemen" also present. (*The North Star*, Aug. 11, 1848.)

10. *The North Star*, Aug. 18, 1848.

11. *The North Star*, Sept. 1, 29, 1848.

12. *Ibid.*, Aug. 18, Nov. 10, 1848.

13. "Campaign of 1848," *Free Soil Songs for the People*, Boston, 1848, front cover.

14. *Liberator*, Jan. 19, 1849.

15. Wesley, *op cit.*, p. 44.

16. T. C. Smith, *op. cit.*, pp. 160-61. Free Soil papers in the West cried: "Fight on! Work on and keep working."

17. Douglass to Gerrit Smith, May 15, 1851, Gerrit Smith Papers, Syracuse University.

18. Buffalo *Commercial Advertiser*, reprinted in *Frederick Douglass' Paper*, Oct. 30, 1851. See also Douglass to F. Gorton, B. E. Hecock, N. H. Gardner, etc. Oct., 1851), *Ibid.* In an appeal to the workingmen of the United States from the working classes of Glasgow there appeared the remark: "As a matter of self-interest, we conceive that any community within the Union who are unable to discern the representative powers of Frederick Douglass, are wholly at fault. In all earnestness our opinion of him is, that he would do honor to the most gifted legislative assembly in the world, and from such statement you may pos-

sibly draw your own conclusions as to what interests we would confide to his care, were it in our power to honor such an one with our suffrages either in matters municipal or parliamentary." (*The North Star*, Jan. 16, 1851.)

19. Douglass to Gerrit Smith, Feb. 19, 1852, Gerrit Smith Papers, Syracuse University; *Frederick Douglass' Paper*, Apr. 8, 1852.

20. Gerrit Smith Papers, Syracuse University.

21. *Frederick Douglass' Paper*, Aug. 20, 1852; Frederic May Holland, *Frederick Douglass*, pp. 210-12.

22. *New York Herald*, Aug. 12, 1852; *Frederick Douglass' Paper*, Aug. 20, 1852.

23. *The Anti-Slavery Reporter*, Oct., 1852, No. 1, p. 6.

24. *Frederick Douglass' Paper*, Aug. 20, Sept. 10, 1852.

25. Douglass to Gerrit Smith, Oct. 21, 1852, Gerrit Smith Papers, Syracuse University.
Actually the candidates of the Liberty Party were William Goodell and S. M. Bell of Virginia. A committee of Liberty Party men had been appointed to ask Hale and Julian certain questions with the understanding that the party's support hinged on their answers. They asked whether a political party should regard itself as organized for the purpose of securing equal rights to all, and "whether you believe that slavery, so far as capable of legislation is a naked piracy, around which there can be no legal covering." Hale and Julian ignored the questions, so the Liberty Party met again in Syracuse on September 30 and made the nominations referred to above. Douglass was one of the vice-presidents of the convention, but he did not remove the names of Hale and Julian from the masthead of his paper.

26. *Liberator*, reprinted in *Frederick Douglass' Paper*, Nov. 19, 1852; Douglass to Samuel J. May[?], Nov. 10, 1852, Frederick Douglass *Mss.*, New York Historical Society; Douglass to Gerrit Smith, Nov. 6, 1852, Gerrit Smith Papers, Syracuse University.

27. Douglass to Gerrit Smith, Aug. 18, 1853, Gerrit Smith Papers, Syracuse University; *New York Tribune*, Aug. 19, 1854.

28. Douglass to Gerrit Smith, Aug. 22, 1854, Gerrit Smith Papers.

29. *New York Tribune, Massachusetts Spy, Cincinnati Commercial*, reprinted in *Frederick Douglass' Paper*, Aug. 4, 1854; *Syracuse Standard*, reprinted in *Liberator*, Aug. 25, 1854. See also *Liberator*, July 14, 1854.

30. *Philadelphia Argus* reprinted in *Frederick Douglass' Paper*, Aug. 4, 1854. The *Norfolk Daily News* commented: "The n——r statesmen of the North, we learn, are to be brought forward for Congress . . . if the presence of the Honorable Frederick Douglass in Washington will purge that noxious atmosphere of its poisons, chloride of lime will no longer be needed in the purlieu. . . ."

31. *Frederick Douglass' Paper*, Aug. 4, 1854.

32. *Ibid.*, Sept. 15, 1854; Frederic May Holland, *op. cit.*, pp. 233-37.

33. *Frederick Douglass' Paper*, July 27, 1855; Frederick Douglass, *The Anti-Slavery Movement*, Rochester, 1855, p. 35.

34. Douglass to Gerrit Smith, Mar. 27, 1855, Gerrit Smith Papers, Syracuse University; *The American Jubilee*, Apr., 1855; *Anti-Slavery Bugle*, reprinted in *The Anti-Slavery Advocate*, June, 1855, No. 33, p. 269.

35. *Proceedings of the Convention of Radical Political Abolitionists Held at Syracuse, N. Y., June 26, 27, and 28, 1855*, New York, 1855. Copy in Library of Congress.

36. Douglass to Gerrit Smith, Aug. 14, 1855, Gerrit Smith Papers, Syracuse University; *New York Herald*, Sept. 13, 17, 27, 1855; *D.A.S. Alexander, A Political History of the State of New York*, New York, 1906, vol. II, p. 216.

37. *Radical Abolitionist*, Dec., 1855 (copy in library of Cornell University); *Frederick Douglass' Paper*, Nov. 16, 1855.
    Gerrit Smith was the chief sponsor of the Radical Abolitionist Party as he was of the Liberty Party. He financed its organs, *The American Jubilee* which was published in March and April, 1855, and *The Radical Abolitionist* which replaced it and appeared from August, 1855, to December, 1859.

38. *Frederick Douglass' Paper*, Apr. 25, 1856; *Radical Abolitionist*, Apr., 1856.

39. Garrison to Samuel J. May, Mar. 21, 1856, Garrison *Mss.*, Boston Public Library. Garrison expressed pity for Smith. "It is really sad to see so good a man as Gerrit Smith befooled in this manner," he added in his letter to May.

40. *Radical Abolitionist*, July, 1856. While in Syracuse Douglass also addressed the Republican State Convention and made the same point. "You are called Black Republicans," he declared. "What right have you to that name. Among all the candidates you have selected, or talked of, I haven't seen or heard a single black one." *Syracuse Daily Standard*, May 29, 1856.

41. Wesley, *op. cit.*, pp. 70-71; *New York Morning Express*, May 30, 1856. James A. Woodburn, in his *Political Parties and Party Problems in the United States*, states that the Radical Abolitionists "nominated Gerrit Smith for president and Frederick Douglass for vice-president." (New York, 1924, p. 249.) James Ford Rhodes also makes this statement. (*History of the United States*, New York, 1900, vol. II, p. 186n.) Both base it on the report in the *New York Herald*.

42. The Liberty Party and the Radical Abolition Party were scheduled to meet together in Syracuse on September 17. Douglass looked forward to the meeting hoping they would definitely fuse. On August 8 he wrote in his paper that he was glad to see that "the radical friends of the slave 'still live'; that they are determined to carry their convictions of the utter unlawfulness and sinfulness of Slavery to the ballot-box." "The issue presented by the Republicans, for the restriction of the evil is too narrow," he added. (*Frederick Douglass' Paper*, Aug. 8, 1856, reprinted in *Liberator*, Sept. 5, 1856.)

43. *Frederick Douglass' Paper*, June 20, 1856, reprinted in *Liberator*, Sept. 5, 1856; *Frederick Douglass' Paper*, Aug. 15, 1856.

44. See the editorials "The Republican Party," "A Brief Response To Our Assailants," "Can An Abolitionist vote for Fremont," "To Colored Voters," "The Present Hour and Our Duty," *Frederick Douglass' Paper*, Aug. 29, Sept. 12, Oct. 3, 24, 1856.

45. Douglass to Gerrit Smith, Apr. 30, 1847, Gerrit Smith Papers, Syracuse University.

46. "No, my Dear Sir," he wrote to Smith on Dec. 16, 1856, "I am not a member of the Republican Party. I am still a radical Abolitionist." (Gerrit Smith Papers, Syracuse University.)

47. *Radical Abolitionist*, Oct., 1857.

48. A report in the *Gerrit Smith Banner*, a publication issued during the campaign, reveals some of the enthusiasm of the radical Abolitionists: "Already the 'Gerrit Smith movement' is producing a great commotion among the class who make politics a trade. Their craft is in danger." (*Gerrit Smith Banner*, Oct. 18, 1858.)

49. Henry Highland Garnet to Gerrit Smith, Sept. 10, 1858, Gerrit Smith Papers, Syracuse University; *Frederick Douglass' Paper*, July 8, 1859. (Copy in Wisconsin State Historical Society.)

DOUGLASS AND JOHN BROWN

1. Douglass delivered the lecture, "Self-Made Men," many times after 1859. The text quoted here is from a copy of the speech in the Rochester Public Library.

2. *John Brown—An Address by Frederick Douglass at the Fourteenth Anniversary of Storer College, Harper's Ferry, West Virginia*, May 30, 1881; *Life and Times of Frederick Douglass*, pp. 339-41.
   There is no discussion of Brown's relations with Douglass in the recent study by James C. Malin, *John Brown and the Legend of Fifty-Six*, published by the American Philosophical Society. In a letter to the writer, Feb. 6, 1947, Professor Malin writes: "You ask about Frederick Douglass. I did not find anything that struck me as particularly important which relates him to my field of investigation."

3. *Life and Times of Frederick Douglass*, p. 341.

4. On Nov. 15, 1856, Elizabeth Cady Stanton wrote that in December she expected to see Brown at Rochester where he would be "on a visit to Frederick Douglass." (T. Stanton and H. S. Blatch, *Elizabeth Cady Stanton*, New York, 1901, vol. II, p. 69.)

5. J. M. Parker, "Reminiscences of Frederick Douglass," *Outlook*, vol. LI, Apr. 6, 1895, p. 553; F. B. Sanborn, *The Life and Letters of John Brown*, Boston, 1885, p. 434. Brown probably stayed a little more than two weeks at Douglass' home. There are, however, conflicting reports on this question. Richard J. Hinton says he was at Douglass' home "for three weeks," and Douglass says he "remained for about a month." (Richard J. Hinton, *John Brown and His Men*, New York, 1899, p. 165; *Life and Times of Frederick Douglass*, p. 385.)

6. Douglass to John Brown, Feb. 27, 1858, Sanborn, *op. cit.*, pp. 443, 451-52.

7. John Brown's diary, Apr. 14, 1858, Ralph Volney Harlow, *Gerrit Smith*, New York, 1939, p. 339.

8. *New York Herald*, Oct. 27, 1859; Anonymous, "John Brown and His Friends," *Atlantic Monthly*, vol. XXX, July, 1872, pp. 50-61; *Life and Times of Frederick Douglass*, p. 387.

9. Franklin B. Sanborn, *Recollections of Seventy Years*, Boston, 1909, p. 138; *Atlantic Monthly*, vol. XXX, July, 1872, pp. 55ff. Douglass' daughter wrote to her father on Feb. 2, 1859, concerning Brown's exploits in running off slaves from Missouri: "Old Brown will have to keep out of sight for a little while. The Governor of Missouri has a reward of $3,000 for his capture." (Douglass *Mss.*, Frederick Douglass Memorial Home, Anacostia, D. C.)

10. Horace McQuire, "Two Episodes of Anti-Slavery Days," *Publications of the Rochester Historical Society*, Rochester, N. Y., vol. IV, 1925, pp. 219-20.

11. On Aug. 9, 1867, Douglass wrote to Gerrit Smith: "I wish to say distinctly that John Brown never declared nor intimated to me that he was about to embark in a grand or unqualified insurrection; that the only insurrection he proposed was the escaping of slaves and their standing for their lives against any who should pursue them. For years before, Captain Brown's long entertained plan was to go to the mountains in the Slave States and invite the Slaves to flee there. . . . Three or four weeks previous to his invasion of Harper's Ferry Captain

Brown requested me to have an interview with him at Chambersburg, Pa. I did it and in this interview he had determined upon that invasion instead of carrying out his old plan of going into the mountains. . . . I do not suppose that any of his friends at the North knew of it." (Frederick Douglass *Mss.*, Frederick Douglass Memorial Home, Anacostia, D. C.) The last sentence would seem to indicate that Douglass was the first person outside of his band to whom Brown told his plan for attacking Harper's Ferry.

12. Sanborn, *Life and Letters of John Brown*, pp. 536-38; *Life and Times of Frederick Douglass*, p. 387. Douglass brought with him a letter to Brown containing twenty-five dollars from Mrs. J. N. Gloucester, a prosperous Negro woman in Brooklyn. (Sanborn, *Life and Letters of John Brown*, p. 538.)

13. *Life and Times of Frederick Douglass*, p. 390. Douglass'·meeting with Brown lasted for three days. (Douglass to F. B. Sanborn, Apr. 15, 1885, Sanborn, *Life and Letters of John Brown*, p. 538.)

14. Sanborn, *Life and Letters of John Brown*, p. 541n. A copy of the letter to Douglass was found among the papers of John Brown captured at the farm Brown had rented early in the summer.

15. Sanborn, *Recollections of Seventy Years*, p. 153. Only a brief, unimportant letter from Brown to Douglass was found by Brown's captors. No other material involving Douglass was discovered among his papers at the farm.

16. Amy Hamner-Croughton, "Anti-Slavery Days in Rochester," *Publications of the Rochester Historical Society*, Rochester, N. Y., vol. XV, 1936, p. 143. Letters from Brown and a copy of the "Provisional Constitution" Brown had drawn up while at Douglass' home were in the desk. After the message was received they were removed.

17. Washington *Evening Star*, Feb. 21, 1895.

18. *New York Herald*, Oct. 20, 1859; *Liberator*, Dec. 23, 1859; Hamner-Croughton, *op. cit.*, p. 144.

19. *Life and Times of Frederick Douglass*, p. 379; *New York Herald*, Oct. 22, 1859.

20. See also Rochester *Democrat*, Oct. 26, 1859, and Rochester *Union*, Oct. 25, 1859, reprinted in *New York Herald*, Oct. 28, 1859.

21. *New York Herald*, Nov. 4, 1859.

22. As late as 1919 several of the surviving members of Brown's family, Henry Thompson, Salmon Brown, Annie Brown Adams, and Sarah Brown, told Oswald Garrison Villard that they had always believed that Douglass had failed "to live up to his obligations." (Oswald Garrison Villard, *John Brown*, New York, 1943, pp. 323, 627.)

23. Douglass to Rochester *Democrat*, reprinted in *New York Herald*, Nov. 4, 1859.

24. ". . . It is only truth to state," Douglass wrote in the Nov., 1859, issue of his monthly, "that for more than a year past I have been making arrangements not to go to Harper's Ferry, but to England."

25. Douglass to John C. Underwood, Nov. 14, 1866, John C. Underwood Collection, Library of Congress, Manuscript Division. Douglass to Elizabeth Keckly, Oct. 29, 1867, Elizabeth Keckley, *"Behind the Scenes or Thirty Years a Slave and Four Years in the White House,"* New York, 1886, p. 319.

26. *Douglass' Monthly*, Nov., 1859.

27. *Douglass' Monthly*, Dec., 1859.

28. Henry Wilson, *History of the Rise and Fall of the Slave Power in America*, vol. II, p. 606.

29. Douglass to James Redpath, June 29, 1860, *Liberator*, July 27, 1860.

THE EVE OF THE CIVIL WAR

1. *The Anti-Slavery Reporter*, Dec. 1, 1859, p. 276.

2. *The Anti-Slavery Advocate*, vol. II, No. 42, June 1, 1860, pp. 393-94.
   Douglass entered into a heated debate with George Thompson over the interpretation of the Constitution of the United States as it related to the anti-slavery movement. See *Lecture on the Constitution of the United States by Mr. Thompson Delivered in the City Hall, Glasgow, February 27th, 1860, London Emancipation Committees Tracts, No. 5*, London, 1860; *Lecture by Mr. Douglass in Reply to Mr. Thompson, Delivered in the Queen's Rooms*, Glasgow, Mar. 26, 1860, and *Mr. Thompson's Rejoinder, A Lecture Delivered in the City Hall, Glasgow, April 3rd, 1860*. All the speeches were published in the Tract No. 5 issued by the London Emancipation Committee. A copy of the pamphlet is in the Boston Public Library.

3. Rosetta Douglass to Gerrit Smith, Apr. 11, 1860, Gerrit Smith Papers, Syracuse University; *Douglass' Monthly*, June, 1860, "To My British Anti-Slavery Friends." Douglass also had planned to visit France. After the American minister, Dallas, refused his application for a passport on the ground that he was not a citizen of the United States, the French minister at London granted Douglass a permit. Before he could cross the channel, the news arrived of his daughter's death. (See *Douglass' Monthly*, Sept., 1860; F. M. Holland, *Frederick Douglass*, p. 277.)

4. *Douglass Monthly*, June, 1860.

5. Another resolution adopted by the convention read: "*Resolved*, That for the Abolitionists to vote for a candidate like Abraham Lincoln, who stands ready to execute the accursed Fugitive Slave Law, to suppress insurrections among slaves, to admit new slave States, and to support the ostracism, socially and politically, of the black man of the North is to give the lie to their professions; to expose their hypocrisy to the world; and to do what they can, to put far off, the day of the slave's deliverance." (*The Principia*, Sept. 15, 1860; *Douglass' Monthly*, October, 1860.)

6. The initial meeting was held in Boston on May 29, 1860. Douglass was present and agreed to the calling of the second meeting. (*The Principia*, Sept. 15, 1860.)

7. Douglass to Elizabeth Cady Stanton, Aug. 25, 1860, Elizabeth Cady Stanton Papers, Library of Congress. Two weeks later, however, he wrote to Smith: "The more I think of the Worcester Convention the more [I] feel the importance of your attending it." (Douglass to Gerrit Smith, Sept. 7, 1860, Gerrit Smith Papers, Syracuse University.
   Douglass' fears that a conflict would arise between himself and the Garrisonians were justified. George Howland, a Garrisonian, criticized Douglass in his report of the convention published in the *Liberator*. Douglass replied with a letter to the *Liberator* referring to Howland's "ill-mannered charge." He added an editorial to the discussion which closed: "The ranks of genuine Abolitionists—men who really desire to effect the abolition of slavery—are quite too *few* and *thin* to court strife or division among themselves. . . ." (*Douglass' Monthly*, Nov., 1860.)

8. *Douglass' Monthly*, Nov., 1860. The convention also adopted a resolution recommending the organization of "a Political Association, to be known as the Union

Democratic Party of the United States" which would have as its program the principle that "the Constitution, rightly interpreted, is entirely and unequivocally on the side of freedom." A "National Political Education Committee" was appointed to carry the resolution into effect. Douglass was chosen a member of the committee.

9. *Douglass' Monthly*, Oct., 1860. Douglass was probably referring to the fact that on Jan. 10, 1849, Lincoln had introduced a bill in Congress requiring the municipal authorities of Washington and Georgetown "to arrest and deliver up to their owners, all fugitive slaves escaping into said District." It had been introduced as a concession in the scheme of ridding the District of both the slave trade and slavery.

10. *Life and Times of Frederick Douglass*, p. 265.

11. *Douglass' Monthly*, Nov., 1860. According to a letter of Hamilton Fish of Sept. 21, 1860, "the Gerrit Smith element of opposition to the Republicans" was negotiating with the anti-Republican fusion groups in New York State and demanding that "Fred Douglass must be one of the names" of the electors on the fusion ticket. While there is little evidence that such negotiations were under way, the letter would seem to indicate that as late as September 21, Douglass was not campaigning for the Republicans. Hamilton Fish was a leading Republican in New York and would have known of Douglass' activities for his party if he had been campaigning for Lincoln. (Hamilton Fish to Sidney Laurence, Sept. 21, 1860, *Hamilton Fish Letterbooks*, pp. 26-27. Library of Congress, Manuscript Division.)

12. In 1837 the Negroes of New York City sent petitions to the State Legislature appealing for "an alteration of the constitution, so as to extend the right of voting to all male citizens of the state, on the same term, without distinction of color." Nine years later the question was submitted to the voters, but was rejected by a three to one majority. In 1860 the legislature again submitted the question of equal suffrage to the voters to decide upon it at the time of the presidential election. (See Emil Olbrich, *The Development of Negro Suffrage to 1860*, Madison, Wisconsin, 1901, pp. 30 ff., 126-28.)

13. *Brooklyn Daily Times*, reprinted in *The Principia*, Oct. 20, 1860.

14. James McCune Smith to Gerrit Smith, Sept. 29, 1860, Gerrit Smith Papers, Syracuse University. The tract was signed by James McCune Smith, James P. Miller, and John J. Zuille. (See *The Principia*, Oct. 20, 1860.)

15. The vote was 337,984 against ratification to 197,503 for. The vote for equal suffrage was greater by 112,097 over that cast in 1846 while the negative vote was greater by 113,648. In 1846 the majority against equal suffrage was 138,930 and in 1860 it was 140,481. (*The Principia*, Feb. 16, 1861.)

Douglass was bitter at the Republicans for failing to take a strong stand in favor of equal suffrage. "The black baby of Negro Suffrage was thought too ugly to exhibit on so grand an occasion," he wrote. ". . . We were told by some of our Republican friends to keep still—make no noise—they would do the work. Now, the fox is out of the well, and the goat is in it." (*Douglass' Monthly*, Dec., 1860.)

16. *Douglass' Monthly*, Dec., 1860.

17. For an analysis of conditions following Lincoln's election, See Philip S. Foner, *Business and Slavery*, pp. 224-84.

18. *Boston Evening Transcript*, Dec. 3, 1860; *New York Tribune*, Dec. 6, 1860; *Liberator*, Dec. 7, 1860. "The mob," wrote James Redpath, "was incited, and

chiefly composed of merchants, traders with the South—nearly all of whom have uncollected debts there, and many of them mortgages on slaves."

19. *Douglass' Monthly*, Jan., 1861; Douglass to Mrs. Livermore, Apr. 19, 1886, Douglass *Mss.*, Frederick Douglass Memorial Home, Anacostia, D. C.

20. *Liberator*, Dec. 4, 1860.

21. *Douglass' Monthly*, Feb., Mar., 1861.

22. *Douglass' Monthly*, Apr., 1861.

23. *Anti-Slavery Standard*, Aug. 19, 1847; *Frederick Douglass' Paper*, Nov. 16, 1855.

24. *Douglass' Monthly*, Jan., 1861. James Redpath, a former associate of John Brown and general agent of the Haitian Bureau of Emigration, claimed that he had been responsible for converting Douglass from "an energetic opponent of emigration . . . into a friend of Hayti." (James Redpath to Hon. M. Plesance, Secretary of State, Republic of Haiti, June 8, 1861, "Letters and Reports of James Redpath, General Agent of Emigration to Hayti," pp. 91-3. Library of Congress, Manuscript Division.)

25. *Douglass' Monthly*, May, 1861.

Reference Notes

PART THREE   THE CIVIL WAR

FORT SUMTER TO THE EMANCIPATION PROCLAMATION

1. *Douglass' Monthly*, Mar., 1862.
2. *Ibid.*, May, 1861; Henry G. Pearson, *The Life of John A. Andrew*, Boston, 1904, Vol. I, p. 176.
3. Carl Sandburg, *Storm over the Land: A Profile of the Civil War*, New York, 1942, p. 43.
4. *Douglass' Monthly*, May, 1861.
5. Karl Marx and Frederick Engels, *The Civil War in the United States*, New York, 1937, p. 79.
6. *Douglass' Monthly*, May, 1861.
7. *Douglass' Monthly*, Sept., 1861; *Life and Times of Frederick Douglass*, p. 421.
8. *Boston Courier*, Apr. 24, 1861.
9. T. Harry Williams, *Lincoln and the Radicals*, Madison, Wisconsin, 1941, p. 25; *Douglass' Monthly*, May, June, 1861, Feb. 1862; F. Holland, *Frederick Douglass*, p. 285.
10. Marx and Engels, *op. cit.*, p. 253.
11. John G. Nicolay and John Hay, *Complete Works of Abraham Lincoln*, New York, 1905, vol. X, pp. 65-69; *Douglass' Monthly*, Aug., 1861.
12. *Douglass' Monthly*, June, Aug., Oct., 1861.
    Wendell Phillips was a notable exception for he continued actively in the battle for emancipation from the moment the war started.   "Grandly Phillips comes up to the work," Douglass wrote to Smith on Aug. 12, 1861. (Gerrit Smith Papers, Syracuse University.)
    For an illustration of the paralysis that descended upon many of the Abolitionists after the outbreak of the war, see *Executive Committee of the American Anti-Slavery Society, Printed notice, dated Oct. 30, 1861*, Anti-Slavery Letters to Garrison, Boston Public Library. The letter was signed by L. Maria Child, Helen E. Garrison, and Mary May.
13. *Douglass' Monthly*, June, July, 1861; Mar., 1862.
14. *Ibid.*, Aug., 1861.
15. *Ibid.*, Sept., 1861.
16. Williams, *op. cit.*, p. 41.
17. *Douglass' Monthly*, Sept., Oct., Nov., Dec., 1861, Feb., 1862.
18. *Ibid.*, Oct., 1861.
19. Marx and Engels, *op. cit.*, pp. 81-82.
20. Douglass to Rev. Samuel J. May, Aug. 30, 1861, Frederick Douglass Mss., Arthur H. Spingarn Collection.
21. *Douglass' Monthly*, Dec., 1861, March, 1862; Samuel J. May to Garrison, Nov. 16, 1861, Anti-Slavery Letters to Garrison, Boston Public Library.

22. *Boston Courier*, Dec. 11, 16, 17, 1861.

23. *Douglass' Monthly*, Mar., 1862; *Boston Journal*, Feb. 6, 1862.
"We owe to the truth of anti-slavery history," Douglass wrote in his journal, "to note . . . that no class of men are doing more according to their numbers, to conduct this great war to the Emancipation of the slaves than Mr. Garrison and the American Anti-Slavery Society." (*Douglass' Monthly*, Mar., 1862.)

24. *Douglass' Monthly*, Mar., 1862.

25. *Ibid.*, *Anti-Slavery Reporter*, Feb. 22, 1862.

26. *Douglass' Monthly*, Mar., 1862.

27. *Ibid.*, Carl Sandburg, *Abraham Lincoln: The War Years*, New York, 1939, vol. I, pp. 384-86, vol. II, p. 32; Henry Wilson, *History of the Rise and Fall of the Slave Power in America*, Boston and New York, 1877, vol. III, pp. 291 *ff.*

28. Wilson, *op. cit.*, vol. III, p. 276.

29. *Ibid.*, p. 274.

30. Douglass to Charles Sumner, Apr. 8, 1862, Charles Sumner Papers, Harvard University.

31. *Douglass' Monthly*, May, 1862.

32. Wilson, *op. cit.*, vol. III, p. 383; John G. Nicolay, *A Short Life of Abraham Lincoln*, New York, 1906, p. 327.

33. *Douglass' Monthly*, Aug., 1862; Marx and Engels, *The Civil War in the United States*, p. 243.

34. Carl Schurz, *The Reminiscences of Carl Schurz*, New York, 1909, vol. II, pp. 285-86. For a discussion of the role of the English working class during the Civil War, see Philip S. Foner, *History of the Labor Movement in the United States*, pp. 312-17.

35. Philip Van Doren Stern, ed., *The Life and Writings of Abraham Lincoln*, New York, 1940, pp. 715-23.
In September, Lincoln submitted to his cabinet "the question of the propriety of seeking to make treaties with Latin America or European countries with colonies of tropics" for the purpose of providing a "refuge for colored people." Seward addressed a circular letter to the governments of England, France, Holland and Denmark, informing them of Lincoln's colonization plans and asking their cooperation. (See Edward Bates' diary, Sept. 25, 1862, Howard K. Beale, ed., *Diary of Edward Bates*, Washington, 1933, p. 262.)

36. *Douglass' Monthly*, Sept., 1862.

37. Douglass to Gerrit Smith, Sept., 8, 1862, Gerrit Smith Papers, Syracuse University.

38. Stern, *op. cit.*, pp. 718-19.

39. *Douglass' Monthly*, Oct., 1862.

40. *Ibid.*

41. Marx and Engels, *op. cit.*, p. 258.

42. *Douglass' Monthly*, Oct., 1862.

43. *The Independent*, Nov. 20, 1862. The "Appeal" was also published in the London *Daily News* and widely reprinted in England, Scotland, and Ireland. On Dec. 4, 1862, Henry Richardson, who had inserted the "Appeal" in the London *Daily News*, wrote to Douglass: "I quite think there is a turn of the tide observable, and that the Northern States are beginning to be looked upon with some favour. Your appeal has doubtless helped in this change." (Frederick

Douglass Papers, Frederick Douglass Memorial Home, Anacostia, D. C. See also Alexander Innes to Douglass, Dec. 23, 1862, *Ibid.*)

44. *Douglass' Monthly*, Nov. 1862, Jan., 1863; *Boston Journal*, Jan. 2, 1863.
45. *Boston Transcript*, Jan. 2, 1863; *Life and Times of Frederick Douglass*, pp. 429-31.
46. *Life and Times of Frederick Douglass*, pp. 462.
47. *Douglass' Monthly*, Jan., 1863.

THE EMANCIPATION PROCLAMATION TO APPOMATTOX

1. *Douglass' Monthly*, Feb., 1863.
2. F. A. Shannon, "The Federal Government and the Negro Soldier, 1861-1865," *Journal of Negro History*, vol. XI, Oct., 1926, pp. 569-74; B. I. Wiley states that, contrary to the Union policy of placing white commissioned officers over all units of colored troops, the Corps d'Afrique were officered almost entirely by Negroes. (See B. I. Wiley, *Southern Negroes, 1861-1865*, New Haven.)
3. Shannon, *op. cit.*, p. 572.
4. Luis F. Emilio, *History of the Fifty-Fourth Regiment of Massachusetts of the Massachusetts Volunteer Infantry, 1863-1865*, Boston, 1894, pp. 11-12.
5. *Douglass' Monthly*, Mar., 1863.
6. Emilio, *op. cit.*, p. 13; *Douglass' Monthly*, Apr., 1863; Douglass to Gerrit Smith, Mar. 6, 1863, Gerrit Smith Papers, Syracuse University.
7. *Douglass' Monthly*, Apr., 1863.
8. *Boston Transcript*, May 28, 1863; Emilio, *op. cit.*, pp. 32-34.
9. Herbert Aptheker, *Essays in the History of the American Negro*, New York, 1945, p. 195.
10. *Douglass' Monthly*, Feb., 1863.
11. *Address by Frederick Douglass at National Hall, Philadelphia, July 5, 1863*, Philadelphia, 1863. The address was reprinted under the title *Negroes and the National War Effort*, with a foreword by James W. Ford, New York, 1942.
12. Herbert Aptheker, *To be Free: Studies in American Negro History*, New York, 1948, pp. 83-92, 94-98; Brainerd Dyer, "The Treatment of Colored Union Troops by the Confederates," *Journal of Negro History*, vol. XX, July, 1935, pp. 273-86.
13. *Douglass' Monthly*, Aug., 1863.
14. *Ibid.*
15. *Washington Post*, Feb. 13, 1888.
It is difficult to determine the exact date of the interview, but very likely it took place between July 18 when the Fort Wagner disaster occurred and July 30 when Lincoln issued an order decreeing retaliation for every soldier enslaved or killed in violation of the laws of war.
16. *Liberator*, Jan. 29, 1864; *Prooceedings of the Thirteenth Anniversary Meeting of the American Anti-Slavery Society*, 1864, New York, pp. 116-18.
17. Allen Thordike Rice, ed., *Reminiscences of Abraham Lincoln by Distinguished Men of his Time*, New York, 1866, pp. 185-88.
Lincoln's prediction that discrimination in pay would be abolished was to come true a year after his interview with Douglass. On July 14, 1864, Congress passed a bill granting Negro soldiers the same pay as white soldiers, retroactive to Jan. 1, 1864.

18. *Liberator,* Jan. 29, 1864; *Proceedings of the Thirteenth Anniversary Meeting of the American Anti-Slavery Society,* p. 118; Rice, *op. cit.,* pp. 185-88.

19. *Life and Times of Frederick Douglass,* pp. 372-74.

20. Julia G. Crofts to Douglass, Leeds, Dec. 5, 1862, Douglass Papers, Frederick Douglass Memorial Home, Anacostia, D.C.

21. Douglass specifically mentioned the New York *Independent,* the *New York Tribune* and the Negro journal, the *Anglo-African,* as papers open to him. On April 30, 1862, Theodore Tilton, editor of *The Independent,* informed Douglass that he had added his name as a contributor to the journal. "I would be happy to publish, with your name, (as before,) an occasional article which you may feel moved to write, and to pay you the unworthy sum of Ten Dollars for it. . . . I believe that if you were to come occasionally before the 65,000 subscribers of the Independent, with a thoughtful, careful, striking, eloquent article (such as would make part of a good lecture or oration)—something to quicken the pulse & the heart of the nation—something of Slavery such as only a man once a slave himself can know & tell, you would add to the number of men who respect you, and would lend a helping hand to the Good Cause. Don't say no, but do it for the sake of your friend, Theodore Tilton." (Frederick Douglass Papers, Douglass Memorial Home, Anacostia, D. C.)

22. *Douglass' Monthly,* Aug., 1863.

23. The original is in the Frederick Douglass Papers, Douglass Memorial Home, Anacostia, D. C. There is also one in the Henry P. Slaughter Collection.

24. C. W. Foster to Douglass, Aug. 13, 21, 1863, Frederick Douglass Papers, Douglass Memorial Home, Anacostia, D. C.; Douglass to Thomas Webster, Esqr., Aug. 19, 1863, Frederick Douglass *Mss.,* Historical Society of Pennsylvania; George L. Stearns to Douglass, Aug. 29, 1863, Douglass Papers, Frederick Douglass Memorial Home, Anacostia, D. C.

25. *Life and Times of Frederick Douglass,* p. 380.

26. *New York Tribune,* Jan. 14, 1864; Douglass to Anonymous, Feb. 17, 1864, Henry P. Slaughter Collection. See also Douglass to Gerrit Smith, Oct. 10, 1863, Gerrit Smith Papers, Syracuse University; Charles R. Douglass to Frederick Douglass, Sept. 8, 1863, Douglass Papers, Frederick Douglass Memorial Home, Anacostia, D. C.

27. *Douglass' Monthly,* Jan., Mar., Nov., 1862.

28. *Ibid.,* Nov., 1862.

29. *Ibid.,* June, 1863.

30. *Proceedings of the Thirteenth Anniversary Meeting of the American Anti-Slavery Society,* 1864, p. 118.

31. Wendell Phillips was the outstanding Abolitionist critic of Lincoln's policies during the winter and spring of 1864. Garrison, however, regarded support of Lincoln as a moral obligation upon Abolitionists. A split between these two close friends occurred at a meeting of the Massachusetts Anti-Slavery Society early in 1864. When Phillips proposed a resolution declaring "that the government is ready to sacrifice the honor and interest of the North to secure a sham peace and have the freedmen under the control of the late slaveholders," Garrison took exception and offered the amendment that "the government was only in danger of doing so.". (*Liberator,* Feb. 5, 1864; W. J. and F. P. Garrison, *op. cit.,* vol. IV, pp. 95-97.) Phillips' resolution was upheld by a small majority.

32. Douglass to an English Correspondent, *Liberator,* Sept. 16, 1864. Douglass was

angered by Lincoln's seeming approval of the system introduced in the South by General Nathaniel P. Banks. On Jan. 29, 1863, General Banks issued Order No. 12 from New Orleans which set up a system of sharecropping for the freedmen on a contract basis. The Order assured employers that "all the conditions of continuous and faithful service, respectful deportment, correct discipline and perfect subordination" would be "enforced on the part of the Negroes by the officers of the Government."

33. Three separate calls were issued by Radical Republicans opposed to the reelection of Lincoln. One came from a committee of Radical Republicans, headed by B. Gratz Brown of Missouri; the second from New York and was headed by Lucius Robinson, and the third was issued by a number of Abolitionists.

34. *New York Times,* May 27, 1864.

35. The *Cleveland Herald* declared that the convention was made up of "sly politicians from New York, impetuous hare-brained Germans from St. Louis, abolitionists, and personal friends and parasites of Frémont." (Ruhly J. Bartlett, *John C. Frémont and the Republican Party,* Columbus, Ohio, 1930, pp. 104-05.)

36. Philip Van Doren Stern, *op. cit.,* pp. 815-16.

37. Bartlett, *op. cit.,* p. 118.

38. *Liberator,* Sept. 16, 1864.

39. *In Memoriam Frederick Douglass,* Philadelphia, 1897, pp. 70-71.

40. John G. Nicolay and John Hay, eds., *The Complete Works of Abraham Lincoln,* New York, 1905, vol. X, p. 161.

41. Douglass to Theodore Tilton, Oct. 15, 1864, Frederick Douglass *Mss.,* Buffalo Public Library. So far as this writer has been able to ascertain, this is the only account of the discussion between Lincoln and Douglass over the "To Whom it May Concern" letter. Douglass does not mention this aspect of the interview in his autobiography.

42. *Life and Times of Frederick Douglass,* p. 427.

43. Douglass to Abraham Lincoln, Aug. 29, 1864, Robert Todd Lincoln Collection, Library of Congress. See also *Independent,* Apr. 5, 1866.

44. Christopher Hollis, *The American Heresy,* London, 1927, p. 203.

45. Douglass to Theodore Tilton, Oct. 15, 1864, Frederick Douglass *Mss.,* Buffalo Public Library; Marx and Engels, *The Civil War in America,* p. 272.

46. Carl Sandburg, *Abraham Lincoln: The War Years,* vol. III, p. 266.

47. The reference is to Garrison's defense of Lincoln's reconstruction policy in Louisiana. Discussing the question of Negro suffrage in relation to reconstruction, Garrison wrote: "Chattels personal may be instantly translated from the auction-block into freemen, but when were they ever taken at the same time to the ballot-box, and invested with all political rights and immunities? According to the laws of development and progress it is not practicable. . . . Besides, I doubt whether he [the President] has the Constitutional right to decide this matter. Ever since the Government was organized, the right of suffrage has been determined by each State in the Union for itself, so that there is no uniformity in regard to it. . . ." (*Liberator,* Oct. 14, 1864.)

48. *Proceedings of the National Convention of Colored Men Held in Syracuse, New York, October 4-7, 1864,* New York, 1864, pp. 44-62.

49. *Liberator,* Jan. 29, 1864; *Proceedings of the Thirteenth Anniversary meeting of the American Anti-Slavery Society,* p. 117; Douglass to Theodore Tilton, Oct. 15, 1864, Frederick Douglass *Mss.,* Buffalo Public Library.

50. Douglass to an English friend, *Independent,* Mar. 2, 1865.
51. *Life and Times of Frederick Douglass,* p. 462; F. A. Holland, *Frederick Douglass,* p. 310.
52. *Independent,* Apr. 20, 1865.
53. Holland, *op. cit.,* p. 311; Amy Hammer-Croughton, "Anti-Slavery Days in Rochester," *Publications of the Rochester Historical Association,* vol. XIV, 1936, pp. 151-52.
    Douglass' proudest possession was a cane given to him by Mrs. Lincoln. The following report in the *Rochester Express* appeared more than a year after Lincoln's death: "Mr. Lincoln desired to present Mr. Douglass with some token of his regard, and had spoken of his wish to his wife. After his death, Mrs. Lincoln, in carrying out what she knew was the desire of her honored husband; sent the cane to Mr. Douglass with a letter explaining those circumstances. The cane is a very ordinary one, but is, of course, highly prized by its owner, as a relic of the great and good man who was his friend." (Reprinted in *Anti-Slavery Standard,* July 14, 1866.)
54. Hammer-Croughton, *op. cit.,* p. 152. *New York Times,* May 3, June 1, 1865; See also *Douglass' Monthly,* Apr., 1863.
55. Karl Marx, *Capital:* Vol. I, New York, 1939, p. 287.

Reference Notes

PART FOUR   RECONSTRUCTION AND AFTER

RECONSTRUCTION, 1865-1870

1. *Life and Times of Frederick Douglass*, p. 468.

2. On October 24, 1864, Andrew Johnson addressing the Negro population of Nashville, denounced slavery and the "damnable aristocracy" which had profited from human bondage, and expressed the belief that only loyal men, white and Negro, should have a voice in the reconstruction of the seceded states. He ventured the hope that, "as in the days of old," a Moses might arise "to lead them safely to their Promised Land of freedom and happiness." The audience thereupon cried, "You are our Moses!" Johnson responded: "Humble and unworthy as I am, if no better shall be found, I will indeed be your Moses, and lead you through the Red Sea of war and bondage to a fairer future of liberty and peace." (Frank Moore, ed., *Speeches of Andrew Johnson*, Boston, 1865, p. XXXVI.)

3. On July 3, 1865, before he was appointed Provisional Governor of Georgia, Benjamin F. Perry declared that "there is not now in the Southern States anyone who feels more deeply the humiliation and degradation of going back in the Union, than I do."

4. At first President Johnson demonstrated his deadly hatred of the southern oligarchy by exempting from amnesty persons who had supported the Confederacy and whose taxable property was assessed at $20,000 or more. But soon he began to grant pardons to many of the leaders of the Confederacy. The following report in the *Baltimore American and Commercial Advertiser* of October 13, 1865, is typical: "The President to-day granted two hundred and forty pardons under the amnesty proclamation to parties in the various States late in Rebellion. The pardon warrant of the Rebel General Humphreys, of Mississippi, heretofore reported as having been pardoned, was signed by the President to-day, and sent to the State Department."

5. Paul Lewinson, *Race, Class and Party*, New York, 1932, pp. 32-38; Vernon L. Wharton, "The Negro in Mississippi, 1865-1890," Unpublished Ph.D. Thesis, University of North Carolina, 1939, pp. 145-50.

6. Quoted by Manuel Gottlieb, "The Land Question in Georgia during Reconstruction," *Science and Society*, vol. III, summer, 1939, p. 364.

7. A. D. McCoy, *Thoughts on Labor in the South, Past, Present and Future*, New Orleans, 1865, p. 22; 39th Congress, 1st Sess., *Senate Executive Doc.*, pp. 13, 21, 32, 35, 43, 44.

8. *New York Tribune*, Jan. 14, 1864.

9. W. P. and F. J. Garrison, *op. cit.*, vol. IV, pp. 158-61.

10. *Liberator*, May 26, 1865. At a meeting of the colored people of New York City early in May, a resolution was adopted urging the American Anti-Slavery Society not to dissolve. The Society, it declared, had not accomplished its full objects particulary that of "removing public prejudice," and "could not, in good faith, without a violation of assumed honorable trust, at present dissolve." (*New York Times*, May 3, 1865.)

11. Douglass to Messrs. William Syphan and John E. Cook, July 1, 1865; *Celebration by the Colored People's Educational Monument Association in Memory of Abraham Lincoln on the Fourth of July, 1865, in the Presidential Grounds, Washington, D. C.*, Washington, 1865, p. 5. Copy in Library Company of Philadelphia; Frederick Douglass *Mss.*, Arthur M. Springarn Collection; K. Marx and F. Engels, *The Civil War in America,* p. 277.

12. *Cf.*, Howard K. Beale, "The Tariff and Reconstruction," *American Historical Review*, vol. XXXV, Jan. 1930, pp. 276-94; *The Nation*, Jan. 11, 1866; *Anti-Slavery Standard*, Oct. 19, 1867; *Congressional Globe*, 39th Congress, 1st Session, Appendix, p. 284. James S. Allen, *Reconstruction: The Battle for Democracy, 1865-1876*, New York, 1937, pp. 81-82.

13. *New York Tribune*, Jan. 30, Mar. 12, 1886; *Washington Daily Intelligencer*, Mar 12, 1866; *Atlantic Monthly*, Dec., 1866, p. 762; Jan. 1867, p. 117.

14. *New York Tribune*, Mar. 12, 1866; *The Equality of all Men before the Law Claimed and Defended in speeches by Hon. William D. Kelley, Wendell Phillips, and Frederick Douglass*, Boston, 1865, pp. 36-39.

15. *New York Times*, July 17, 1867; *Liberator*, Oct. 13, 1865.

16. Gerrit Smith Papers, Syracuse University. The second letter is dated Dec., 1865.

17. *New York Tribune*, Jan. 30, 1866; *New York Times*, Feb. 4, 1866.

18. *Brooklyn Daily Eagle*, Jan. 30, 1866.

19. "We understand," wrote Theodore Tilton, "that the names of the five dissenting directors are to be written on shells and deposited in the Brooklyn Historical Society's collection of Long Island fossils." (*The Independent*, Feb. 8, 1866.)

20. See note 2 above for the background for this remark.

21. There is no other source for this statement. As far as can be ascertained, the only time Lincoln expressed his views on the question of Negro suffrage in relation to reconstruction, was in a letter he wrote on Mar. 13, 1864, to Governor Hahn of Louisiana: " . . . I barely suggest for your private consideration whether some of the colored people may not be let in—as for instance, the very intelligent, and especially those who have fought gallantly in our ranks. They would probably help, in some trying time to come, to keep the jewel of liberty within the family of freedom. . . . " (Charles H. McCarthy, *Lincoln's Plan of Reconstruction*, New York, 1901, p. 73.)

22. *Brooklyn Daily Eagle*, Jan. 30, 1866.

23. *Anti-Slavery Standard*, Feb. 17, 1866.

24. Washington *National Republican*, Jan. 31, 1866; George T. Downing to Douglass, Jan. 18, 1866, Frederick Douglass Papers, Frederick Douglass Memorial Home, Anacostia, D. C.

25. See Edward McPherson, *The Political History of the United States During the Period of Reconstruction*, Washington, 1887, pp. 52-55.

26. "Observer" in *New York Tribune*, Feb. 12, 1866.

27. McPherson, *op. cit.*, pp. 55-56.

28. *Anti-Slavery Standard*, Feb. 17, 1866; "Observer" in *New York Tribune*, Feb. 12, 1866.

29. McPherson, *op. cit.*, pp. 118-19.

30. Lloyd Paul Stryker, *Andrew Johnson*, New York, 1930, pp. 320-30.

31. McPherson, *op. cit.*, p. 124.

32. *New York Tribune,* Aug. 31, 1866.

33. Samuel Shock to Thaddeus Stevens, Aug. 27, 1866, Thaddeus Stevens Papers, Library of Congress; Frederick May Holland, *Frederick Douglass,* pp. 317-18; Theodore Stanton, "Frederick Douglass in Paris," *The Open Court,* vol. I, Apr. 28, 1887, pp. 151-52.

34. *New York Herald,* Sept. 3, 4, 7, 1866; *New York Times,* Sept. 5, 1866.

35. Stanton, *op. cit.,* p. 151.

36. *New National Era,* May 5, 1870; Thaddeus Stevens to William D. Kelley, Sept. 5, 1866, Thaddeus Stevens *Mss.,* Library of Congress.

37. *New York Herald,* Sept. 5, 1866.

38. In describing the meeting of the New York delegation, the reporter for the *New York Herald* wrote: "Some one asked about admitting Fred Douglass, when the Chairman stated that he was a regular delegate and was to be admitted. It appeared, however, that until then the question as to his admittance was not settled, for Douglass did not appear at this meeting, probably from fear of being mobbed." (Sept. 5, 1866.)

39. *New York Herald,* Sept. 5, 1866. "As soon as it was learned that Fred Douglass was in the room the audience of delegates grew clamorous to hear him, and in spite of the efforts of the Chairman to obtain a hearing for other speakers, the universal desire was vociferously enforced, and amid deafening applause and cheering the dusky orator stepped on the rostrum. . . . "

40. *New York Herald,* Sept. 6, 7, 8, 1866.

41. Douglass to Elizabeth Cady Stanton, Feb. 6, 1882, Frederick Douglass *Mss.,* Frederick Douglass Memorial Home, Anacostia, D. C.

42. *New York Times,* Sept. 7, 1866.

43. Frederick Douglass, "Reconstruction," *Atlantic Monthly,* vol. XVIII, Dec., 1866; "An Appeal to Congress for Impartial Suffrage," *Atlantic Monthly,* vol. XIX, Jan. 1867.

44. *Anti-Slavery Standard,* May 29, 1869; "Plan to Buy Land to be sold to Freedmen," Frederick Douglass Papers, Frederick Douglass Memorial Home, Anacostia, D. C.

45. Speech in Elmira, New York, Aug. 1, 1880, copy in Frederick Douglass Papers, Frederick Douglass Memorial Home, Anacostia, D. C.

46. Douglass to J. J. Spelman, July 11, 1867, *The Independent,* July 25, 1867; Douglass to Theodore Tilton, (Sept., 1867), *The Independent,* Sept. 12, 1867.

47. Wm. Slade to Douglass, July 29, 1867, Frederick Douglass Papers, Frederick Douglass Memorial Home, Anacostia, D. C.

48. The Bureau of Refugees, Freedmen. and Abandoned Lands was created as a Federal agency under the War Department by an act of Congress, passed Mar. 3, 1865. Its existence as a separate branch of the national government was extended by various acts of Congress until June 30, 1872. It was administered by a commissioner in Washington, assistant commissioners in charge of districts in the South, and agents on the assistant commissioners' staffs. General Oliver O. Howard served as commissioner throughout the life of the bureau.

The duties of the Freedmen's Bureau, as it was popularly called, were to administer abandoned and confiscated plantations, to provide clothing, shelter, medicine, and rations to Negroes and to destitute whites, and to adjust labor relations in the South.

49. James G. Randall, ed., *The Diary of Orville Hickman Browning*, Springfield, Illinois, 1925-33, vol. II, p. 151; Charles R. Douglass to Frederick Douglass, July 18, 1867, Frederick Douglass Papers, Frederick Douglass Memorial Home, Anacostia, D. C.; *Diary of Gideon Welles*, Boston, 1911, vol. III, pp. 142-43; July 26, 1867.

50. Douglass to William Slade, July 29, 1867, Frederick Douglass *Mss.*, Douglass Memorial Home, Anacostia, D. C.; Slade to Douglass, Aug. 1867, Frederick Douglass Papers, Douglass Memorial Home, Anacostia, D. C.; *The Reminiscences of Carl Schurz*, New York, 1908, vol. III, p. 239.

51. *The Independent*, Sept. 12, 1867. See also *Anti-Slavery Standard*, Sept. 21, 1867; Douglass to Gerrit Smith, Sept. 19, 1867, Gerrit Smith Papers, Syracuse University.

52. Ellis Paxson Oberholtzer, *A History of the United States Since the Civil War*, New York, 1928, vol. II, chapter XI.

53. *Anti-Slavery Standard*, Aug. 29, Sept. 26, 1868.
Gerrit Smith supported S. P. Chase whom he praised for his "profound wisdom," and called him "strikingly supplied . . . with all the elements of character for a chief magistrate." (*The Independent*, Mar. 12, 1868.) Chase was a candidate for the Democratic nomination. Douglass refused to go along with Smith. Chase, he charged, had abandoned Negro suffrage to secure the Democratic nomination. (Douglass to Gerrit Smith, Aug. 24, 1868, Gerrit Smith Papers, Syracuse University.)

54. Douglass to Gerrit Smith, Sept. 1, 1868, Gerrit Smith Papers, Syracuse University.

THE FIFTEENTH AMENDMENT

1. Douglass to E. D. Bassett, Apr. 13, 1869, Frederick Douglass *Mss.*, Douglass Memorial Home, Anacostia, D. C.

2. On Apr. 26, 1869, Douglass wrote to Downing explaining his anger over the report in the press. The statement was unauthorized. It not only placed him "in a false position, but in a very ridiculous one" since he was "not so foolish as to decline any office which has not been publicly and officially tendered me." It made him liable to the charge "of acting in such matters under no higher motives than those which grow out of a love of money," and at the same time gave the public "an exaggerated idea of the money value of my vocation." It represented him as "under the control of a sort of sentimental delirium of patriotism; as absurdly and weakly refusing to leave the country for any purpose however limited." Its "natural effect" was not only to prevent his receiving the nomination to the Haitian mission, but "to prevent the offer of any other mission abroad. . . . " (Frederick Douglass *Mss.*, New York Public Library, Manuscripts Division.)
Two days later Downing replied denying responsibility for any announcement in the press that Douglass would decline to accept the Haitian mission. (George T. Downing to Douglass. Apr. 28, 1869, Frederick Douglass Papers, Douglass Memorial Home, Anacostia, D. C.)

3. *The Independent*, Apr. 21, 1869. See also Theodore Tilton, April 20, 1869, Frederick Douglass Papers, Douglass Memorial Home, Anacostia, D. C.

4. J. Sella Martin to Douglass, Apr. 24, 1869, Frederick Douglass Papers, Douglass Memorial Home, Anacostia, D. C.
It is difficult to determine whether J. Sella Martin was acting on his own or

at Douglass' insistence. He assured Douglass that he had "acted in my own name and in no respect compromised you as an office seeker and taken pains to say I was not even in communication with you. . . . " (*Ibid.*)

5. In his study of the election of 1868, Charles H. Coleman concludes "that the Republican popular majority was dependent upon Negro suffrage. . . . " (*The Election of 1868*, New York, 1933, pp. 369-70.)

6. Reprinted in *Anti-Slavery Standard*, Jan. 30, 1869.

7. *Ibid.*, Jan. 23, 30, 1869.

8. *Washington Chronicle* reprinted in *Anti-Slavery Standard*, Jan. 30, 1869.

9. *Anti-Slavery Standard*, Jan. 23, 30, 1869.

10. *New York Tribune*, May 12, 1866. See also Benjamin Quarles, "Frederick Douglass and Woman's Rights," *Journal of Negro History*, vol. XXV, Jan. pp. 39ff.

11. *New York Herald*, Nov. 21, 1866.

12. *New York Tribune*, Nov. 21, 1866.

13. Susan B. Anthony to Douglass, Dec. 15, 1866; Elizabeth Cady Stanton to Douglass, Jan. 8, [1867], Frederick Douglass Papers, Douglass Memorial Home, Anacostia, D. C.; *Anti-Slavery Standard*, June 1, 1867.

14. Henry B. Blackwell, *What the South Can Do*. New York, Jan., 1867, copy in Gerrit Smith Papers, Syracuse University.

15. *The Revolution*, May 21, 1868.

16. *The Independent*, Nov. 26, 1868.

17. *The Revolution*, May 20-27, 1869.

18. McPherson, *The Political History of the United States during the Period of Reconstruction*, p. 545.

19. *New Era*, May 12, 1870.

20. *Anti-Slavery Standard*, May 29, 1869.

21. *New Era*, May 5, 1870. Douglass paid tribute to Garrison for his magnificent struggle against slavery, but pointed out that he had not been active in the battle for equal suffrage.

22. A. Lake to Douglass, Apr. 1, 1870, Frederick Douglass Papers, Douglass Memorial Home, Anacostia, D. C. *See also* A. Post to Douglass, Feb. 28, 1870, *Ibid.*

23. *Philadelphia Press*, Apr. 27, 1870.

24. *Philadelphia Press*, May 19, 1870.

25. *Philadelphia Press*, May 30, 1870. See also *The Independent*, July 7, 1870, and O. O. Howard to Douglass, July 10, 1870, Frederick Douglass Papers, Douglass Memorial Home, Anacostia, D. C.
On Nov. 17, 1870, Douglass wrote to a Philadelphian expressing his astonishment that the Academy of Music in Philadelphia would not admit colored people. In a pointed reference to the religious leaders of Philadelphia, he wrote: "I believe that the 'City of Brotherly love' with its hundreds of Altars to the 'Lamb of God' stands almost alone in the intensity of its wolfish hate and snobbish pride of race. It clings longer to proscription on its cars and other modes of travel than any other city of the North." (Douglass to T. B. Pugh, Nov. 17, 1870, printed in Henkels Catalogue No. 1328, copy in Wisconsin State Historical Society, Madison, Wisconsin.)

26. *Baltimore Gazette,* May 20, 1870; *New Era,* May 26, 1870.

27. In the spring of 1865 an association was formed by thirty or forty colored men of Baltimore, which purchased the building on Lexington Street, near Davis, formerly occupied as the Newton University, for the sum of $16,000, and organized the Douglass Institute. On Oct. 7, 1865, the institute building was formally opened by Douglass. For the full text of the lecture, see *Liberator,* Oct. 13, 1865. See also Douglass to Gerrit Smith, Oct. 8, 1865, Gerrit Smith Papers, Syracuse University.

28. *Baltimore Gazette,* May 20, 1870; *New Era,* May 26, 1870.

RECONSTRUCTION, 1870-1872

1. *New National Era,* Oct. 6, 1870; *National Standard,* Oct. 15, 1870.

2. V. L. Wharton, "The Negro in Mississippi, 1865-1890" (unpublished doctorate, University of North Carolina, 1939), p. 112; Herbert Aptheker, *To be Free,* p. 243.

3. Charleston *Daily Republican,* Nov. 26, 1869; Philip S. Foner, *History of the Labor Movement in the United States,* pp. 402-03.

4. See the volumes of documentary material on Ku Klux Klan violence in Report No. 22, House of Representatives, 42nd Congress, 2nd session.

5. *National Standard,* Jan. 21, 1871; *New National Era,* Oct. 6, 1870; Jan. 12, 1871; *National Standard,* Jan. 14, 1871; unpublished speech, "The Abolitionists," Frederick Douglass Papers, Frederick Douglass Memorial Home, Anacostia, D. C.

6. Charles Sumner Papers, Harvard University Library; *New National Era,* Oct. 6, 1870.

7. *New National Era,* Sept. 8, 1870.

8. Douglass to John C. Underwood, Nov. 14, 1866, John C. Underwood Collection, Library of Congress, manuscripts division.

9. Circulars in Gerrit Smith Papers, Syracuse University. The circular also stated that the journal "will *especially advocate the policy and measures of the Republican Party,* as the most efficient, *if not the only reliable political organization,* through whose efforts Justice can be established and maintained."

10. J. Sella Martin to Douglass, Mar. 29, 1869, Frederick Douglass Papers, Douglass Memorial Home, Anacostia, D. C.

11. Douglass to Rev. J. Sella Martin, Apr. 5, 1869, Frederick Douglass *Mss.* Douglass Memorial Home, Anacostia, D. C.

12. J. Sella Martin, Aug. 24, 1869, Frederick Douglass Papers, Douglass Memorial Home, Anacostia, D. C.

13. *New Era,* Jan. 27, 1870. Douglass was "on the wing" and thus was unable to write anything for the first issue. (*New Era,* Jan. 13, 1870.)

14. *Ibid.,* Sept. 1, 8, 1870.

15. *Ibid.,* Dec. 15, 1870. J. H. Davis sold his interest in the paper to Douglass.

16. *Ibid.,* Jan. 26, 1871. Charles H. Wesley, *Negro Labor in the United States, 1850-1925,* New York, 1927, p. 182.
The National Colored Labor Union was organized at a convention held in Washington on Dec. 5, 1869. For the forces that led to the formation of the organization and its subsequent career, see Philip S. Foner, *History of the Labor Movement in the United States,* pp. 402-08.

17. *Baltimore Sun,* August 23, 1869; *The Revolution,* Aug. 19, 1869. Lewis H. Douglass was later prevented from working in the Government Printing Office when the Columbia Typographical Union refused to permit him to join the organization. The application of Frederick Douglass, Jr., for membership in the union was also turned down. Douglass bitterly denounced the union for its "cowardly prejudice," and called upon colored printers to shun all organizations which treated them "with contempt and scorn." (*New National Era,* Jan. 26, Feb. 2, Nov. 16, 1870.)

18. For a discussion of the attitude of the labor movement towards the issues of Reconstruction, see Philip S. Foner, *History of the Labor Movement in the United States,* pp. 389-95.

19. Wesley, *op. cit.,* pp. 182-83. On taking the chair, Douglass urged the delegates to "go home to work up and form local societies." (*New National Era,* Jan. 12, 1871.)

20. *National Standard,* Jan. 14, 1871. "We have never attended a colored convention," wrote Douglass, "whose proceedings reflected greater credit upon our people, or one likely to be productive of greater good." (*New National Era,* Jan. 12, 1871.)

21. *New National Era,* Jan. 12, Feb. 16, 1871. See also *New Era,* July 21, 1870.

22. *New York Tribune,* Jan. 19, 28, Sept. 21, Oct. 30, Nov. 27, Dec. 16, 20, 1869; Apr. 18, 1870. See also William B. Hesseltine, "Economic Factors in the Abandonment of Reconstruction," *Mississippi Valley Historical Review,* vol. XXII, Sept., 1935, pp. 199-200.

23. *New National Era,* Nov. 24, 1870, March 23, 1871.

24. *Proceedings of the State Convention of the Colored Citizens of Tennessee, Held in Nashville, Feb. 22d, 23d, 24th, &25th, 1871.*

25. Allan Nevins, *Hamilton Fish: The Inner History of the Grant Administration,* New York, 1936, pp. 289-90, 601-02; *New York Tribune,* May 8, 1869.

26. J. D. Richardson, ed., *Messages and Papers of the Presidents,* Washington, 1898, vol. VII, p. 153;

28. Charles Sumner Papers, Harvard University Library.

27. *New National Era,* Apr. 6, 1871.

29. *The Anti-Slavery Enterprise. .... An Address before the people of New York, at the Metropolitan Theatre, May 9, 1855. By Charles Sumner.* Boston, 1855; Douglass to Charles Sumner, Apr. 24, 1855, Charles Sumner Papers, Harvard University Library. See also *Frederick Douglass' Paper,* June 1, 1855.

30. Charles C. Tansill, *The United States and Santo Domingo, 1798-1873,* Baltimore, 1938, pp. 343-50, 362-64; Nevins, *op. cit.,* pp. 254ff., 275ff. Two agreements were drawn up. The first provided for the lease of the bay and peninsula of Samana at an annual rental of $150,000 or the purchase of the region of $2,000,000. The second called for the annexation of the whole republic, and stipulated that the United States would advance the sum of $1,500,000 in order to liquidate the Dominican public debt.

31. Tansill, *op. cit.,* pp. 383-89, 405-06, 421-22; J. D. Richardson, *Messages and Papers of the President,* vol. VII, pp. 61-63.

32. Witnesses to the informal conversation on which this belief was based, supported Sumner's assertion that all he had pledged was "careful consideration" of the treaty.

33. Nevins, *op. cit.*, pp. 372-74; Tansill, *op. cit.*, p. 428.

34. Douglass to S. R. Scottern, March 29th, 1873, Frederick Douglass Mss., Douglass Memorial Home, Anacostia, D.C.

35. Charles Sumner Papers, Harvard University Library.

36. Douglass to Sumner, Jan. 6, 1871, Charles Sumner Papers, Harvard University Library; *New National Era*, Jan. 8, 1871.

37. Tansill, *op. cit.*, p. 436; *New National Era*, Jan. 12, 1871.

38. Douglass' duties were not clear. However, he was asked by the Commissioners "to examine and report . . . regarding the condition of the English speaking immigrants residing in the town of Samana and the country adjacent, with special reference to a schedule of questions to be furnished by the commission." (Allan A. Burton to Douglass, Jan. 26, 1871, Douglass Papers, Frederick Douglass, Memorial Home, Anacostia, D. C.)
Douglass was criticized by James Wormeley, the Negro owner of Wormeley's hotel in Washington, for having accepted the unimportant position of assistant secretary to the commission. (See *Journal of Negro History*, vol. XXI, Jan., 1936, pp. 58-60.)

39. *New York Times*, Aug. 6, 1872.

40. *New National Era*, Apr. 6, 1871.

41. *Autobiography of Andrew Dickson White*, New York, 1905, vol. I, p. 504.

42. *Senate Executive Document*, No. 9, 42 Congress, 1st. sess., pp. 1-34; *New National Era*, Apr. 6, 1871.

43. *Ibid.*, Apr. 6, 13, 1871. According to Andrew D. White, Douglass remarked during his stay in Santo Domingo: "If this is the outcome of self-government by my race, Heaven help us." (*Autobiography*, vol. I, p. 501.) It is doubtful, however, in view of Douglass' comments in his articles in his paper that he made such a statement.

44. *New National Era*, Apr. 13, 27, May 4, 11, 18, 1871.

45. Tansill, *op. cit.*, p. 439. Ludwell Lee Montague, *Haiti and the United States, 1714-1938*, Durham, North Carolina, 1940, pp. 104-05; *New National Era*, Oct. 26, 1871. See also Peter H. Clark to Douglass, Apr. 9, 1871, *Ibid.*, Apr. 13, 1871, and H. O. Wagoner to Douglass, Apr. 29, 1873, Douglass Papers, Frederick Douglass Memorial Home, Anacostia, D. C.

46. Douglass to S. R. Scottern, Mar. 29, 1873, Douglass *Mss.*, Frederick Douglass Memorial Home, Anacostia, D. C.; *National Standard*, Oct. 15, 1870.

47. *New National Era*, Mar. 30, 1871.

48. *The Writings of Charles Sumner*, vol. XV, pp. 205-08; Washington *National Republican*, Mar. 30, 1871; *New York Times*, Apr. 18, 1871.

49. *New National Era*, Jan. 12, 1871; Douglass to Cassius M. Clay, July 26, 1871, Douglass *Mss.*, Frederick Douglass Memorial Home, Anacostia, D. C.

50. E. D. Ross, *The Liberal Republican Movement*, N. Y., 1919, pp. 7-8, 38-39.

51. *New National Era*, June 8, 22, 1871.

52. *Ibid.*, Mar. 23, June 8, 22, 1871; Cassius M. Clay to Douglass, July 15, 1871, Douglass Papers, Frederick Douglass Memorial Home, Anacostia, D. C.

53. *New National Era*, July 15, 1871. The New Orleans Convention resulted from a decision at the "Southern States Convention of Colored Men" at Columbia, South Carolina, Oct., 1871, to hold a national convention the following April.

54. *New National Era,* May 2, 1872.

55. *Works of Charles Sumner,* vol. XX, pp. 68-69; Ross, *op. cit.,* p. 164; *New National Era,* May 2, 9, 1872. See also *New Orleans Republican,* April 11-13, 1872; *Harper's Weekly,* May 11, 1872.

56. *New National Era,* May 2, 9, 1872.

57. Reprinted in *New National Era,* May 9, 1872.

58. *Ibid.,* May 2, 1872.

59. *Woodhull and Claflin's Weekly,* May 18, June 1, 1872; *New York Tribune,* May 11, 1872.
For a discussion of Mrs. Woodhull's work in the labor and radical movements, see Philip S. Foner, *History of the Labor Movement in the United States,* pp. 415-16.

60. On May 12, 1872 Oliver Johnson wrote to Garrison: "Mrs. Woodhull's convention looked and acted like a body of lunatics. A small collection of nobodie's without sense or reason, they talked as if the whole people were at their back and ready to ratify their platforms and candidates. Of course Frederick Douglass will take the earliest opportunity to disclaim all connection with such a body, the proceedings of which were utterly beneath contempt." (*Anti-Slavery Letters to William Lloyd Garrison and Others,* Boston Public Library.) Actually, however, Douglass had once praised Mrs. Woodhull for asserting that the Fourteenth and Fifteenth Amendments already gave women the suffrage. (*New National Era,* Sept. 21, 1871.)

61. *New National Era,* June 13, 1872; Hammer-Croughton, *op. cit.,* pp. 153-54.

62. Douglass to Gerrit Smith, July 1, 1872, Gerrit Smith Papers, Syracuse University. Douglass declared that he moved to Washington because his wife would feel more at home with her own people in the nation's capital.

63. See *New York Tribune,* May 1, 1861, Dec. 10, 1867, Jan. 7, 1868, May 2-4, 1872.

64. *National Standard,* Sept., 1872. Phillips, who was becoming increasingly concerned with the problems of the labor movement, raised an interesting argument in his letter. "The anti-slavery cause," he wrote, "was only a portion of the great struggle between capital and labor. Capital undertook to own labor. We have broken that up. If Grant is elected, that dispute and all questions connected with it sink out of sight. All the issues of the war are put beyond debate, and a clear field is left for the discussion of the labor movement. . . . " Douglass shared Phillips' confidence that Grant's election would settle the questions arising out of the war, but he was by no means as advanced as the Massachusetts reformer in his approach to the labor movement.

65. Frederick Douglass, *U. S. Grant and the Colored People,* Washington, 1872. See also "An Appeal to Colored Voters," *New York Times,* Aug. 12, 1872. The "Appeal" was Douglass' direct answer to Sumner's letter to the colored voters of Washington. "With Grant our security is unquestionable; our happiness will be made lasting. With Greeley, we would enter upon a sea of trouble—an unknown and anxious future. Unscrupulous advisers would be his friends. Our old foes would surround him, as they even do now."

66. *The Works of Charles Sumner,* vol. XV, p. 192, pp. 205-08; *New York Times,* Aug. 22, 1872; Douglass to Gerrit Smith, Sept. 11, 1872, Gerrit Smith Papers, Syracuse University; undated letter of Douglass to George T. Downing, Frederick Douglass Papers, Frederick Douglass Memorial Home, Anacostia, D. C.

67. Douglass received $500 from the Republican National Committee for cam-

paigning for Grant, "a sum," he announced, "a little more than equal to my traveling expenses." (*New National Era*, Nov. 7, 1872.)

68. His defeat followed by the death of his wife plunged Greeley into despair. His mind gave way, and he died on Nov. 29, 1872. For Douglass' editorial on Greeley's death, see *New National Era*, Dec. 5, 1872.

69. *New National Era*, Dec. 5, 1872. See also, "Shall the Colored People of the United States Know Full Liberty?" *Ibid.*, Nov. 14, 1872.

THE CLOSING YEARS OF RECONSTRUCTION

1. *Springfield Republican*, Nov. 15, 1872.

2. Walter L. Fleming, *The Freedmen's Savings Bank*, Chapel Hill, N. Car., 1927, pp. 19, 24-25; *New National Era*, Sept. 8, 1870.

3. *Life and Times of Frederick Douglass*, p. 488; Fleming, *The Freedmen's Savings Bank*, pp. 32-33; John Mercer Langston, *From the Plantation to the Capitol*, Hartford, Conn., 1894, p. 343.

4. *House Report No. 502*, 44 Cong., 1st. session, p. 31; Douglass to Senator Frelinghuysen, May 23, 1874, Frederick Douglass *Mss.*, Frederick Douglass Memorial Home, Anacostia, D. C.; Douglass to Anonymous, Mar. 30, 1874; Douglass to S. L. Harris, Mar. 30, 1874, Alfred William Anthony Collection, New York Public Library. There is a draft of the letter in the Frederick Douglass *Mss.*, Frederick Douglass Memorial Home, Anacostia, D. C.

5. Douglass to *New York Herald*, Apr. 29, 1874, reprinted in *New National Era*, May 7, 1874; *Senate Report No. 440*, 46 Cong., 2nd session, p. 44; *Life and Times of Frederick Douglass*, pp. 489-91.

6. Fleming, *Freedmen's Savings Bank*, pp. 87-88.

7. Douglass told a Senate Committee in 1876: "I began to discredit the bank in the eyes of the Banking Committee of the Senate. . . . I spent my time mostly in doing that sort of business." (Fleming, *Freedmen's Savings Bank*, p. 112.)

8. *New National Era*, June 25, 1874; Douglass to Gerrit Smith, July 3, 1874, Gerrit Smith Papers, Syracuse University.

9. William Wells Brown, *My Southern Home*, Boston, 1880, p. 211. As late as 1890 Douglass was still trying to secure payments to those who held claims against the Freedmen's Bank. (See M. R. Mann to Douglass, Nov. 24, 1890, Frederick Douglass Papers, Frederick Douglass Memorial Home, Anacostia, D. C.

10. Douglass to Gerrit Smith, Sept. 24, 1874, Gerrit Smith Papers, Syracuse University.

11. *New National Era*, June 12, Oct. 30, 1873, Feb. 26, 1874; Circular issued by Frederick Douglass, Jr., Mar. 1874, in Gerrit Smith Papers, Syracuse University.

12. Joseph Warren to Douglass, Jan. 9, 1872, Frederick Douglass Papers, Frederick Douglass Memorial Home, Anacostia, D. C.

13. *New National Era*, Apr. 21, 1870. At Douglass' insistence, the *New National Era* carried the following notice on July 9, 1874: "As many of our exchanges when making extracts from our editorial columns are in the habit of crediting our thoughts and ideas to Frederick Douglass, we take the occasion to say that such crediting is unwarranted by the facts in the matter. Hon. Frederick Douglass is not, nor has he been, editor of the *New National Era* for more than a year."

14. Douglass to Gerrit Smith, Sept. 26, 1873, Gerrit Smith Papers, Syracuse University.

15. Irvine Garland Penn, *The Afro-American Press, and its Editors,* Springfield, Mass., pp. 448-49.

16. Boston Lyceum Bureau to Douglass, Dec. 20, 1872, Frederick Douglass Papers, Frederick Douglass Memorial Home, Anacostia, D. C.

17. Reprinted in the *New National Era,* Feb. 29, 1872.

18. H. O. Wagoner to Douglass, Mar. 12, 1873; U. L. C. Beard to Douglass, Apr. 10, 1873, Frederick Douglass Papers, Frederick Douglass Memorial Home, Anacostia, D. C.; Douglass to *New York Tribune,* Oct. 31, 1872, reprinted in *New National Era,* Nov. 7, 1872.

19. Douglass to John Greenleaf Whittier, Mar. 15, 1873, Frederick Douglass *Mss.,* New York Historical Society; Clara Barton to Douglass, Jan. 26, 1879, Frederick Douglass Memorial Home, Anacostia, D. C.

20. Douglass to Anna Douglass, Nov. 4, 1872, Frederick Douglass *Mss.,* University of Rochester.

21. "I have taken the old subject of Slavery and Anti-Slavery," Douglass wrote to Anna Douglass in Nov., 1872. "But this subject is old, and has been handled by so many able men and has been presented in so many aspects, that I am puzzled to know how I can invest it with a new interest and make it agreeable to lecture going people this winter." *(Ibid.)*

22. L. R. Kohler to Douglass, Mar. 8, 1882, Frederick Douglass Papers, Frederick Douglass Memorial Home, Anacostia, D. C.

23. Some of the topics of Douglass' lectures, as taken from the collection of speeches in his papers at the Frederick Douglass Memorial Home, are: "American Civilization," "The Beginning of Civilization," "Speech on Hita and Hittites," "The Oldest Civilization in Africa," "Self-Made Men," "It Moves—Speech on Galileo," "Enfranchisement of Women," "Regarding the Drum and the Trumpet of Ancient Times," "The Horrors of War," "Human Rights," "Industrial Progress," "Intemperance," "William the Silent," "Aryan Civilization," "Scandinavian History and Icelandic Sagas," "Philip II and William the Silent in the Reformation," "Thoughts and Recollections of the Anti-Slavery Conflict," "The Abolitionists."

24. *Warsaw Western New Yorker,* reprinted in *New National Era,* Feb. 29, 1872. The topics of Douglass' lectures listed above throw light on the comment.

25. William Henry Crogman, *Talks for the Times,* South Atlanta, Ga., 1896, pp. 13-14.

26. Douglass to James Redpath, July 29th, 1871, Alfred William Anthony Collection, New York Public Library; Lloyd Lewis in *New York Times,* Oct. 16, 1946.

27. "Sphynx" in *New National Era,* Nov. 6, 1873. See also *The Revolution,* May 20, 1869.

28. *New National Era,* Mar. 16, 1874; Washington *National Republican,* Mar. 17, 1874.

29. Printed letter of Gerrit Smith to Frederick Douglass, June 27, 1874, Gerrit Smith Papers, Syracuse University; Douglass to Gerrit Smith, July 3, 1874, Gerrit Smith Papers, Syracuse University.

30. W. E. B. DuBois, *Black Reconstruction in America, 1860-1880,* New York, 1935, pp. 684-85; Douglass to Gerrit Smith, Oct. 7, 8, 1874, Gerrit Smith Papers, Syracuse University.

31. *Centennial Anniversary of the Pennsylvania Society for Promoting the Abolition of Slavery, April 14, 1875,* Philadelphia, 1876, pp. 25-26.

32. DuBois, *op. cit.,* pp. 684-86.

33. Speech of Mar. 14, 1876, at Morton and Pinchback meeting in Frederick Douglass *Mss.,* Frederick Douglass Memorial Home, Anacostia, D. C.

34. The idea of the monument originated with Charlotte Scott, an ex-slave, on the day following Lincoln's assassination. Negroes welcomed the project, and contributed $16,242 toward its completion.
    The decline in interest in the anti-slavery period was also reflected in the sales of Douglass' autobiography published in 1881. On July 19, 1882, the Park Publishing Company of Hartford, Douglass' publishers, wrote: "Your book does not sell quite as well as we expected, for the simple reason that the interest in the old days of slavery is not as great as expected." (Frederick Douglass Papers, Frederick Douglass Memorial Home, Anacostia, D. C.)

35. Freeman H. M. Murray, *Emancipation and the Freed in American Sculpture,* Washington, 1916, p. 199.

36. George S. Boutwell to Douglass, Apr. 15, 1876, Frederick Douglass Papers, Frederick Douglass Memorial Home, Anacostia, D. C.

37. *Oration, Delivered in Corinthian Hall, July 5, 1852,* Rochester, 1852, p. 4.

38. *Inauguration Ceremonies of the Freedmen's Memorial Monument to Abraham Lincoln, Washington City, April 14, 1876,* St. Louis, 1876.

39. Charles R. Williams, *Life of Rutherford B. Hayes,* New York, 1914, vol. I, p. 533. For a significant and exciting study of the role that railroad lobbyists played in the great betrayal of 1877, see C. Van Woodward, *Reunion and Reaction: The Compromise of 1877 and the End of Reconstruction,* Boston, 1951.

40. The Supreme Court's decision in the slaughter house cases late in 1872 justified this confidence. The court ruled that a state could not abridge rights arising from national citizenship, but nothing in the Constitution prevented a state from abridging the rights that came from state citizenship. As Douglass remarked, the decision practically annihilated citizenship for the Negro since "dual citizenship means no citizenship." (Douglass to Gerrit Smith, July 3, 1874, Gerrit Smith Papers, Syracuse University.)

41. *New York Age,* Jan. 12, 1889. Copy in Frederick Douglass Papers, Frederick Douglass Memorial Home, Anacostia, D. C.

42. C. R. Williams, ed., *Diary and Letters of Rutherford B. Hayes,* Columbus, 1924, vol. III, p. 417.
    Douglass had campaigned for Hayes in 1876. On Aug. 11, 1876, he received a letter from Zachariah Chandler, chairman of the Republican campaign, urging him to speak in Maine "for two weeks, beginning August 28th." Douglass replied eight days later informing Chandler that he was "quite out of health," and added: "Nevertheless if I find myself stronger in time for the canvass in Maine I shall report to you for service: It is the same old conflict: Liberty, union and civilization on the one hand and Slavery disunion and barbarism on the other." (Zachariah Chandler Papers, Library of Congress.)

43. *New York Age,* Jan. 12, 1889. Copy in Frederick Douglass Papers, Frederick Douglass Memorial Home, Anacostia, D. C.

44. Douglass to John Sherman, Mar. 13, 1877, Rutherford B. Hayes Papers, Hayes Memorial Library, Fremont, Ohio.

45. Williams, ed., *Diary and Letters of Rutherford B. Hayes,* vol. III, p. 427; *New*

York Times, Mar. 16, 1877; Douglass to S. D. Porter, Mar. 21, 1877, Frederick Douglass *Mss.,* University of Rochester.

46. Manuscript copy of speech, "The National Capital," in Frederick Douglass *Mss.,* Frederick Douglass Memorial Home, Anacostia, D. C.

47. *New York Times,* June 1, 1877.

48. *New York Times,* Nov. 9, 1877; Speech in Madison Square Garden, Decoration Day, 1878, Manuscript copy in Frederick Douglass *Mss.,* Frederick Douglass Memorial Home, Anacostia, D. C.

49. *New York Times,* Jan. 19, 1879.

THE POST-RECONSTRUCTION ERA

1. George T. Downing to Douglass, May 10, 1883, Frederick Douglass Papers, Frederick Douglass Memorial Home, Anacostia, D. C.

2. *New National Era,* Nov. 10, 1870.

3. Douglass to Zachariah Chandler, Aug. 19, 1876, Zachariah Chandler Papers, Library of Congress.

4. Douglass to William G. Frost, Apr. 3, 1883, Frederick Douglass *Mss.,* Oberlin College Library.

5. *Report of Senate Committee on Education and Labor,* 1885, vol. IV, pp. 49-51, 70-71, 122.

6. *Senate Report,* 46th Cong., 2nd sess., No. 693, pt. 1; *Journal of Negro History,* vol. IV, Jan., 1919, pp. 57-92.

7. R. T. Greener, "Emigration of colored citizens from the Southern States," *American Journal of Social Sciences,* vol. XI, May, 1880, pp. 22-36.

8. *New York Times,* May 5, 1879; *Journal of Negro History,* vol. IV, Jan., 1919, pp. 56-57; Frederick Douglass, "Negro Exodus from the Gulf States," *American Journal of Social Science,* vol. XI, May, 1880, pp. 1-22. *See also* Douglass to Frank B. Sanborn, Sept. 4, 9, 1879, Alfred William Anthony Collection, New York Public Library.

9. *Appleton's Annual Cyclopedia for 1879,* New York, 1880, p. 572; *American Journal of Social Science,* vol. XI, May, 1880, pp. 26-27.

10. Frederick Douglass *Mss.,* Henry P. Slaughter Collection.

11. Ellis P. Oberholtzer, *History of the United States Since the Civil War,* New York, 1931, vol. V, pp. 530-35; *Appleton's Annual Cyclopedia for 1879,* pp. 358, 537.

12. *Speech at the Civil Rights Mass-Meeting Held at Lincoln Hall, Oct. 22, 1883,* Washington, 1883. Douglass warmly praised Justice John M. Harlan for his dissenting opinion.

13. Albert H. Walker to Douglass, Oct. 19, 1883, Frederick Douglass Papers, Frederick Douglass Memorial Home, Anacostia, D. C.

14. Holland, *Frederick Douglass,* p. 368.
    In 1892 a group of southern Negroes called on Douglass to obtain his advice relative to an exodus of Negro people from Arkansas to Africa. Douglass suggested that they go west instead of Africa. The group formed the Washington Co-operative Improvement Society and settled in Spokane, Washington. On Jan. 9, 1893, Chas. E. Hall, secretary of the society, wrote to Douglass: "Acting upon your suggestion and believing that America is our home and that if unable to

care for ourselves here, it is almost useless to seek other climes, six of us young men have organized the above society whose purpose is clearly indicated. We propose to state facts regarding the resources of Washington, Oregon, Idaho, Montana, particularly those of Washington." The society was organized "to promote the general welfare and assist materially the condition of our fellow Afro-Americans in the pursuit of Independence and Prosperity." (Frederick Douglass Papers, Frederick Douglass Memorial Home, Anacostia, D. C.)

15. Washington *National Republican,* Apr. 17, 1888.

16. Hamilton J. Smith to Douglass, Apr. 17, 1888; Geo. B. Edmonds to Douglass, Apr. 17, 1888; J. B. White to Douglass, Apr. 17, 1888; John W. Curtis to Douglass, Apr. 18, 1888; Charles N. Hunter to Douglass, Apr. 23, 1888, Frederick Douglass Papers, Frederick Douglass Memorial Home, Anacostia, D. C.

17. *Address to the People of the United States, Delivered at a Convention of Colored Men, Louisville, Kentucky, September 24, 1883,* pp. 12-13.

18. *New York Times,* Jan. 19, 1879, Dec. 27, 1880.

19. Thomas Fortune to Douglass, Apr. 20, 1886, Frederick Douglass Papers, Frederick Douglass Memorial Home, Anacostia, D. C.

20. J. H. Conway to Douglass, Apr. 22, 1886, Frederick Douglass Papers, Frederick Douglass Memorial Home, Anacostia, D. C.

21. Undated *Ms.,* Frederick Douglass *Mss.,* Frederick Douglass Memorial Home, Anacostia, D. C.

SOME PERSONAL NOTES

1. When several Negro leaders criticized him for having accepted office "with its honors curtailed," Douglass justified himself with the observation that the duty of attending the President's receptions and introducing his guests at the Executive Mansion were "services not included in the law creating the office of the U.S. Marshal of the D. C." The custom had been introduced by Lincoln because he had appointed his intimate friend and law partner as marshal, and it had been continued for the same reason by Grant. Since he was neither a law partner nor a close relative of President Hayes, he felt that he had "not just ground of complaint" because he had not been selected to perform the duties of his predecessors. "Justice to President Hayes as well as to myself," wrote Douglass, "makes it my duty to say that I was ever a welcome visitor to the Executive Mansion during his administration, that I was spent at his grand receptions, and that I was never humiliated by him or by any of his household." (Douglass to the editor of *The Freeman,* undated letter in Frederick Douglass *Mss.,* Frederick Douglass Memorial Home, Anacostia, D. C.)

2. Douglass to John A. McCallister, June 21, 1864, Frederick Douglass *Mss.,* Library Company of Philadelphia; Douglass to "My Dear Friend," Dec. 21, 1877, Frederick Douglass *Mss.,* Frederick Douglass Memorial Home, Anacostia, D. C.

3. Douglass to Grace Greenwood, Oct. 9, 1882, Frederick Douglass *Mss.,* University of Rochester.
    While Douglass frequently complained that his children depended too much on him and did not do enough for themselves, his chief grievance was caused by Rosetta's husband, Nathan Sprague. He disliked his son-in-law intensely and with good cause. Sprague was constantly getting into trouble and Douglass was always compelled to come to his rescue. Douglass secured Sprague a clerkship in the Rochester post office. He had not been in that position more than a year when he "disgraced and scandalized" Douglass by "breaking open and stealing

the contents of letters." He was caught in the act, arrested and imprisoned. Through Douglass' intercession his sentence was reduced from five years to one. While Sprague was in prison, Douglass supported his children. Later Douglass helped set him up in business in Washington, but Sprague failed. He failed in two other enterprises Douglass helped him start. Rosetta, who was the main support of her six children, was given an appointment in Douglass' office while he was Marshal and Recorder. (See Douglass to Nathan Sprague, undated letter, Frederick Douglass Mss., Frederick Douglass Memorial Home, Anacostia, D. C.)

4. S. L. Clemens to President-elect James A. Garfield, January 12, 1881, James A. Garfield Papers, Library of Congress.

5. Douglass to James A. Garfield, Dec: 18, 1880, Apr. 2, 1881, James A. Garfield Papers, Library of Congress.

6. Douglass to S. M. Fraser, Oct. 27, 1882, Frederick Douglass Mss., Howard University; New York Tribune, Sept. 3, 1884. When Douglass gave up smoking, he gave as his reason that it was "not so much the smoking as the bondage of it."

7. Douglass to Doctress S. M. Logune, Aug. 12, 1882; Douglass to anonymous, Dec. 21, 1877, Frederick Douglass Mss., Frederick Douglass Memorial Home, Anacostia, D. C.

8. Washington Post, May 30, 1897. The Detroit Free Press of May 4, 1886, carried the following report from its Washington correspondent: "Mrs. Douglass' father has never been reconciled to her marriage, but her mother and sister who were deeply grieved at the time have recently visited her. Her uncle's family who have resided here for years have not forgiven her and hold no intercourse with her in any way."

9. Francis J. Grimké, "The Second Marriage of Frederick Douglass," Journal of Negro History, vol. XIX, July, 1934, p. 325.

10. Franklin Virginia, Gazette, Feb. 1, 1884, scrapbook in Frederick Douglass Papers, Frederick Douglass Memorial Home, Anacostia, D. C.; Carter G. Woodson, ed., The Works of Francis J. Grimké, 4 vols., Washington, 1942, vol. IV, p. 1.

11. H. W. Gilbert to Douglass, June 25, 1884; Julia G. Crofts to Douglass, Feb. 11, 1884; Samuel Yorke Atlee to Douglass, Jan. 26, 1884, Frederick Douglass Papers, Frederick Douglass Memorial Home, Anacostia, D. C.
See also Cornelia D. Adams, Jan. 25; S. E. and Helen Shevitch, Jan. 25; George L. Ruffin, Jan. 26; H. B. Nordstrom, Jan. 26; John W. Ewing, Jan. 29; Elizabeth P. Peabody, Feb. 1; Mrs. W. H. Williams, Mar. 18, 1884, Ibid.

12. Undated letter to anonymous, Frederick Douglass Mss., Frederick Douglass Memorial Home, Anacostia, D. C.; Douglass' Monthly, September, 1862.

13. Douglass to the editor of the Hub, Mar. 3, 1884; Speech on "Patriotism," Frederick Douglass Mss., Frederick Douglass Memorial Home, Anacostia, D. C.

14. Douglass to Elizabeth Cady Stanton, May 30, 1884, Elizabeth Cady Stanton Papers, Library of Congress.

15. Lillie B. Chace and Arthur Crawford Wyman, Elizabeth Buffum Chace and Her Environment, 2 vols., Boston, 1911, vol. II, p. 189.

16. Mary Church Terrell, "I Remember Frederick Douglass," Ebony, Sept. 12, 1953.

17. Detroit Free Press, May 4, 1886.

18. Cincinnati Enquirer, April 26, 1886.

19. Mary Church Terrell, "I Remember Frederick Douglass," *op. cit.*

20. On Feb. 11, 1886, Douglass received the following letter from Samuel Harrison, Cleveland's private secretary: "No cards of invitation have been issued to the President's reception in honor of the Diplomatic Corps on Friday evening next from 9 to 11 o'clock, but I am directed by him to say that the Recorder of Deeds is among the officials whose presence, with the ladies of their families, is expected on that occasion." (Frederick Douglass Papers, Frederick Douglass Memorial Home, Anacostia, D. C.)

21. Douglass to Hon. F. W. Bird, Apr. 6, 1886, Holland, *Frederick Douglass,* pp. 356-57; Grover Cleveland to Douglass, Jan. 4, 1886, Grover Cleveland Letter Book No. I, pp. 35-36, Library of Congress; Douglass to Grover Cleveland, Jan. 5, 1886, Grover Cleveland Papers, Library of Congress.

22. Geo. F. Hoar to Douglass, Mar. 11, '86, Frederick Douglass Papers, Frederick Douglass Memorial Home, Anacostia, D. C.; Washington *National Republican,* Mar. 18, 1886; Douglass to Hon. F. W. Bird, Apr. 6, 1886; Holland, *op. cit.,* pp. 356-57.

23. Douglass to Grace Greenwood, Oct. 9, 1882, Frederick Douglass *Mss.,* University of Rochester.

THE DOUGLASSES ABOARD

1. Celso Caesar Moreno to E. L. Moneta, Sept. 12, 1886, original in Italian; unsigned letter dated Sept. 8, 1886, Frederick Douglass Papers, Frederick Douglass Memorial Home, Anacostia, D. C.

2. "Douglass' Diary," Sept. 20, 21, 1886, Frederick Douglass *Mss.,* Frederick Douglass Memorial Home, Anacostia, D. C.

3. *Ibid.,* Sept. 23, 1886.

4. *Ibid.,* Oct. 1, 1886.
   Most writers have stated that Douglass' meeting with Julia Crofts was the first in thirty-two years. But a letter from Douglass to Mrs. Joseph Cash, in December 1860, indicates that he had met Mrs. Crofts during his brief tour of England and Scotland made soon after John Brown's raid on Harper's Ferry. (*See* letter of Douglass to Mrs. Cash in the Alfred William Anthony Collection, New York Public Library.)

5. Douglass to Lewis H. Douglass, November 7, 1886, Alfred William Anthony Collection, New York Public Library.

6. Douglass to Hayden and Watson, Nov. 19, 1886, Frederick Douglass *Mss.,* Fisk University Library; Theodore Stanton, "Frederick Douglass in Paris," *Open Court,* vol. I, Apr. 28, 1887, p. 151.

7. "Douglass' Diary," Jan. 10, 20, Monday [Jan.] 24, 1887.

8. *Ibid.,* Feb. 2, 4, 6, 11, 1887.

9. *Ibid.,* Feb. 14, 17, 19, 25, 1887.

10. *Ibid.,* Feb. 22, 1887; *Life and Times of Frederick Douglass,* p. 611.

11. "Douglass' Diary," Mar. 11, 19, Apr. 15, 1887.

12. Douglass to Amelia Douglass, Apr. 29, 1887, Frederick Douglass *Mss.,* New York Public Library; Douglass to W. H. Thomas, July 16, 1886, Frederick Douglass *Mss.,* Frederick Douglass Memorial Home, Anacostia, D. C.

13. "Douglass' Diary," May 10, 15, 21, 29, 1887.

14. *Life and Times of Frederick Douglass,* p. 617.

15. John A. Brook to Douglass, Aug. 30, 1887, Frederick Douglass Papers, Frederick Douglass Memorial Home, Anacostia, D. C.

THE MINISTER TO HAITI

1. Washington *National Republican,* Apr. 17, 1888.

2. New York *Sun,* June 23, 1888.

3. Richardson, *Messages and Papers of the President,* vol. IX, pp. 32-58.

4. *Life and Times of Frederick Douglass,* p. 621; J. S. Clarkson to Douglass, Aug. 21, 1888; Charles Beardsley to Douglass, Sept. 28, 1888, Frederick Douglass Papers, Frederick Douglass Memorial Home, Anacostia, D. C.

5. Undated campaign speech for Benjamin Harrison, Frederick Douglass *Mss.,* Frederick Douglass Memorial Home, Anacostia, D. C.

6. Undated campaign speech for Benjamin Harrison, Frederick Douglass *Mss.,* Frederick Douglass Memorial Home, Anacostia, D. C.

7. *Cincinnati Gazette,* Nov. 22, 1888; *The Nation's Problem—A Speech Delivered by Hon. Frederick Douglass, before the Bethel Literary and Historical Society in Washington, D.C.,* Apr. 16, 1889, pp. 18-19, 24. (Copy in Harvard University Library.)

8. C. B. Purvis to Douglass, July 3, 1889; Robert Harlan to Douglass, July 1, 1889; Ellen Richardson to Douglass, July 30, 1889; Julia G. Crofts to Douglass, Aug. 3, 1889, Frederick Douglass Papers, Frederick Douglass Memorial Home, Anacostia, D. C.

9. Douglass to anonymous, July 20, 1889, Frederick Douglass *Mss.,* Schomburg Collection, New York Public Library; undated clipping in Frederick Douglass Papers, Frederick Douglass Memorial Home, Anacostia, D. C.; Ebenezer Basset to Douglass, July 11, Sept. 2, 1889; B. K. Bruce to Douglass, July 2, 1889, Frederick Douglass Memorial Home, Anacostia, D. C.

10. Report of trip to Port-au-Prince, in Frederick Douglass Papers, Frederick Douglass Memorial Home, Anacostia, D. C.

11. Ludwell Lee Montague, *Haiti and the United States, 1714-1938,* N. C., 1940, Ch. VIII.

12. Douglass to James G. Blaine, Oct. 26, 1889, Diplomatic Despatches, Haiti, Records of the Department of State, National Archives.

13. Douglass to Blaine, Nov. 18, 1889, Diplomatic Despatches, Haiti, Records of the Department of State, National Archives.

14. Douglass to Blaine, July 9, 1890, Diplomatic Despatches, Haiti, Records of the Department of State, National Archives; Louis Martin Sears, "Frederick Douglass and the Mission to Haiti," *Hispanic American Historical Review,* vol. XXI, May, 1941, p. 231.

15. Douglass, *Lecture on Haiti,* Chicago, 1893, p. 13; Douglass to Blaine, Jan. 16, June 27, 1890, Diplomatic Despatches, Haiti, Records of the Department of State, National Archives.

16. Ludwell Lee Montague (*op. cit.,* pp. 142-43) denies that American aid had much to do with Hyppolite's victory. The American naval vessels, he contends, did not "exert any appreciable influence upon the outcome of the war."

17. Douglass to Blaine, June 27, 1890, Diplomatic Despatches, Haiti, Records of the Department of State, National Archives.

18. Douglass to Blaine, Dec. 9, 1889, Diplomatic Despatches, Haiti, Records of the Department of State, National Archives.

19. Frederick Douglass, "Haiti and the United States," *North American Review*, vol. CLIII, 1891, pp. 455-56.

20. Montague, *op. cit.*, pp. 158-59; James G. Blaine to Douglass, Oct. 3, 1890, Frederick Douglass Papers, Frederick Douglass Memorial Home, Anacostia, D. C.

21. Blaine to Douglass, Jan. 1, 1891, Haiti, Instructions, Records of the State Department, National Archives; Douglass, "Haiti and the United States," *op. cit.*, pp. 453-54; Admiral Gherardi to Blaine, Jan. 31, 1891, Diplomatic Despatches, Haiti, Records of the Department of State, National Archives.

22. Montague, *op. cit.*, p. 148; Douglass to Blaine, Jan. 29, 1891; Gherardi to Blaine, Jan. 31, 1891, Diplomatic Despatches, Haiti, Records of the Department of State, National Archives.

23. Douglass to Blaine, Feb. 9, 1891, Diplomatic Despatches, Haiti, Records of the Department of State, National Archives.

24. Douglass, "Haiti and the United States," *op. cit.*, pp. 454-55; Douglass to Blaine, Apr. 21, 1891, Diplomatic Despatches, Haiti, Records of the Department of State, National Archives.

25. Firmin to Douglass and Gherardi, Apr. 22, 1891, included in Douglass to Blaine, Apr. 23, 1891, Diplomatic Despatches, Haiti, Records of the Department of State, National Archives; Douglass to Blaine, May 7, 1891, Diplomatic Despatches, Haiti, Records of the Department of State, National Archives.

26. Douglass to William F. Wharton, Acting Secretary of State, July 30, 1891, Diplomatic Despatches, Haiti, Records of the Department of State, National Archives; Baltimore *Sun*, Sept. 7, 1891; Sears, *op. cit.*, p. 237; *New York Herald*, July 14, 1891.

27. Douglass to Magnus L. Robinson, April, 1890, Alfred William Anthony Collection, New York Public Library. Robinson was the editor of the Washington (D. C.) *National Leader*, and president of the Frederick Douglass Library Association of Alexandria, Virginia.

28. Montague, *op. cit.*, p. 162.

29. Faculty of the Haitian College to Douglass, Dec. 12, 1891, Frederick Douglass Papers, Frederick Douglass Memorial Home, Anacostia, D. C.

30. Frederick Douglass, *Lecture on Haiti*, Chicago, 1893.

31. J. Christopher to Douglass, May 7, 1894, Frederick Douglass Papers, Frederick Douglass Memorial Home, Anacostia, D. C.

THE LAST YEARS

1. Wm. H. H. Hart to Douglass, Feb. 14, 1890, Frederick Douglass Papers, Frederick Douglass Memorial Home, Anacostia, D. C.

2. Frederick Douglass, *The Lesson of the Hour*, Washington, 1894, p. 12.

3. Mary Church Terrell, "I Remember Frederick Douglass," *op. cit.*

4. Quoted in *The Lesson of the Hour*, pp. 13-14.

5. William V. Tunnell to Douglass, Dec. 22, 1893; H. D. Wagoner to Douglass, Mar. 15, 1894, Frederick Douglass Papers, Frederick Douglass Memorial Home, Anacostia, D. C.

6. *Woman's Journal*, Mar., 1895, p. 35.

7. Reprinted in *New York Times,* Feb. 22, 1895. The *Times* itself struck a vicious editorial note, declaring on Feb. 27: "Amid the universal commendation of Frederick Douglass as a colored man, who, against the greatest difficulties and in the most unfavorable circumstances, achieved well-deserved distinction, it might not be unreasonable, perhaps, to intimate that his white blood may have had something to do with the remarkable energy he displayed and the superior intelligence he manifested. Indeed, it might not be altogether unreasonable to ask whether with more white blood, he would not have been an even better and greater man than he was, and whether the fact that he had any black blood at all may not have cost the world a genius, and be, in consequence, a cause for lamentation instead of a source of lyrical enthusiasm over African possibilities. . . ."

8. The action was taken by the Fusion legislators (Republicans and Populists, many of whom were Negroes) over the opposition of the Democratic members of the legislature, and was denounced by the *Raleigh News and Observer* as an "endorsement of the miscegenation leader." The New Orleans *States* attacked the North Carolina legislature for "the tribute of respect which they have paid to a Negro, whose life was spent in attacking and vilifying the white people of the South." (Reprinted in *New York Times,* Feb. 22, 1895, and *In Memoriam: Frederick Douglass, Philadelphia,* 1897, p. 20.)
The storm of protest from the Southern white press was also caused by the fact that the legislature had refused to adjourn out of respect to Robert E. Lee. This caused the *North American* to observe: "Frederick Douglass did more for the South, for the country, a hundred times over than did Robert E. Lee." (Quoted in Rayford W. Logan, *The Negro in American Life and Thought, The Nadir, 1877-1901,* New York, 1954, p. 232. For a discussion of the action taken by the North Carolina legislature, *see* Helen G. Edmonds, *The Negro and Fusion Politics in North Carolina,* Chapel Hill, 1951, pp. 42-43.)

9. *New York Times,* Feb. 22, 1895.

10. *In Memoriam, Frederick Douglass,* pp. 78-79, 80-81, 91, 127-28, 144-45.

CONCLUSION

1. Booker T. Washington, *Frederick Douglass,* Philadelphia, 1907, preface.

2. Kelly Miller, *Race Adjustment,* New York, 1910, pp. 19-21.

3. Joseph Winthrop Holley, *You Can't Build a Chimney From the Top,* New York, 1948, p. 41.

4. Oliver C. Cox, "The Leadership of Booker T. Washington," *Social Forces,* vol. XXX, October, 1951, pp. 95-96.

5. W. E. B. Du Bois, *The Soul of Black Folk,* New York, 1903, p. 89.

6. Herbert Aptheker, editor, *A Documentary History of the Negro People in the United States,* New York, 1951, pp. 897-915.

7. Carter G. Woodson, editor, *The Works of Francis J. Grimké,* Washington, 1942, vol. III, pp. 104-06.

8. Plessy *v.* Ferguson, 163 U.S., 537 (1896).

INDEX

INDEX

Reconstruction, attitude of organized labor towards, 281; class forces in, 238-39, 283-84, 369-70; counter-revolution against, 321-22; failure to distribute land to Negroes during, 253; Johnson's plan of, 235-36; land distribution during, 235-36; presidential plan of, 235-36; Radical plan of, 252-53

Redpath, James, 315

Remond, Charles B., 107, 114, 120, 155

Remond, Charles Lenox, 52, 54, 55

Republican Party, 153, 154, 167-68, 184-86, 187-88, 238-39, 282-83

Revolution of 1848, 138

Rhode Island, suffrage in, 48

Rhodes, Isaac, 22

Rochester, anti-slavery movement in, 53-54, 83

Rogers, N. P., 47

Ruggles, David B., 23, 26, 77, 424-25

Santo Domingo, effort by Grant to annex to the United States, 286-94

Schoelcher, Victor, 343

Schurz, Carl, 203-04, 236, 256, 295, 297

Secession movement, 99-100

Sewall, Mary Wright, 366

Seward, William H., 89, 90, 204, 216

Seymour, Horace, 257

Shadd, Abraham, 33

Shaw, Robert Gould, 212, 214

Slavery, 29, 33-34, 45-46

Smith, Gerritt, 33, 37, 44, 89, 90, 91, 93, 106, 114, 140, 142, 150, 156, 165-66, 168, 169, 170, 173, 177, 179, 185, 199, 205, 224, 257, 307, 311, 404, 405, 419

Smith, James McCune, 77, 90, 92, 94, 100, 111, 120, 168, 170

South, exodus of Negroes from, 327-28, 428-29; lynching of Negroes in, 361-65

Spooner, Lysander, 142

Stanton, Edwin M., 217, 255

Stanton, Elizabeth Cady, 83, 104-05,

107, 246, 262, 263, 264, 301, 338, 343

Stanton, Theodore, 343

Stearns, George L., 211

Stein, Frederick, 22

Stephens, Alexander H., 137

Stevens, Thaddeus, 240, 247, 261, 268, 341, 398

Still, William, 135, 176

Stone, Lucy, 264, 265

Stowe, Harriet Beecher, 90, 151-52, 180, 182, 396-98

Stuart, Charles, 34

Sumner, Charles, 89, 90, 158, 201-02, 240, 253, 259-60, 268, 276, 281, 285-94, 296, 298, 299, 303, 304, 316-17, 341, 348

Supplementary Civil Rights Bill, 281, 282-83, 296, 300, 316

Swisshelm, Jane, 90

Sylvis, William H., 281

Tappan, Arthur, 33, 89, 118

Tappan, Lewis, 33, 89, 90, 168

Taylor, Zachariah, 157, 158

Temperance movement, 101

Terrell, Mary Church, 339, 340, 362, 372, 376

Thirteenth Amendment, 237

Thomas, Lorenzo, 217

Thompson, George, 33, 66

Tilton, Theodore, 248, 250, 251, 252, 256-57, 259, 269, 301, 343, 417

Toombs, Robert, 137

Trade unions, 39

Trumbull, Lyman, 297

Truth, Sojourner, 83, 106

Tubman, Harriet, 134-35, 399

Turner, Nat, 19, 31, 211

Twain, Mark, 128, 336

Uncle Tom's Cabin, 117, 120

Underground Railroad, 129-35, 398-99

Utopian socialism, 56

Vallindigham, Clement L., 227

Vashon, George B., 261

Vashon, John B., 33, 110
Vesey, Denmark, 211

Wade, Benjamin F., 289, 294, 301
Walker, David, 110
Ward, Samuel Ringgold, 92, 96, 155
Washington, Booker T., 370-72
Washington, Madison, 90
Webb, Richard D., 65
Weed, Thurlow, 78, 307
Weir, Isaac C., 261, 271
Weld, Theodore D., 33, 35, 36, 44, 46, 383
Welles, Gideon, 256
Wells, Ida B., 372
West India Emancipation, 35, 55, 99, 143, 187
Whipper, William, 243, 366
White, Andrew D., 289, 293, 294, 423
White, William A., 55-56

White chauvinism, 99-100
White Leagues, 317, 320
Whittier, John Greenleaf, 33, 54, 76, 157, 158
Willard, Francis, 362
Williams, Peter, 33
Wilson, Henry, 21
Wise, Henry A., 246
Women, role of, in Abolitionist movement, 37-38, 42-43, 103-04
Women's Rights movement, 103-07, 262-66, 394-95
Women's suffrage, 262-66
Woodhull, Victoria C., 301-02
Wright, Elizur, 35
Wright, Frances, 39
Wright, Henry C., 44, 70, 72-73
Wright, Theodore S., 109, 129

Yates, Josephine S., 372

CARMELITE MONASTERY
H*ll

448